NORTH NOTTS COLLEGE

NOR⁣ ⁣LEGE

020581

WITHDRAWN FROM

This book is to be returned on or
the last date stamped b

# FInLanD

**APA PUBLICATIONS**

Part of the Langenscheidt Publishing Group

# ABOUT THIS BOOK

**INSIGHT GUIDE**
**Finland**

### Editorial
*Project Editor*
**Zoë Ross**
*Managing Editor*
**Huw Hennessy**
*Editorial Director*
**Brian Bell**

### Distribution
*UK & Ireland*
**GeoCenter International Ltd**
The Viables Centre, Harrow Way
Basingstoke, Hants RG22 4BJ
Fax: (44) 1256 817988

*United States*
**Langenscheidt Publishers, Inc.**
46–35 54th Road, Maspeth, NY 11378
Fax: 1 (718) 784 0640

*Canada*
**Thomas Allen & Son Ltd**
390 Steelcase Road East
Markham, Ontario L3R 1G2
Fax: (1) 905 475 6747

*Australia*
**Universal Press**
1 Waterloo Road
Macquarie Park, NSW 2113
Fax: (61) 2 9888 9074

*New Zealand*
**Hema Maps New Zealand Ltd (HNZ)**
Unit D, 24 Ra ORA Drive
East Tamaki, Auckland
Fax: (64) 9 273 6479

*Worldwide*
**Apa Publications GmbH & Co.
Verlag KG (Singapore branch)**
38 Joo Koon Road, Singapore 628990
Tel: (65) 6865 1600. Fax: (65) 6861 6438

### Printing
**Insight Print Services (Pte) Ltd**
38 Joo Koon Road, Singapore 628990
Tel: (65) 6865 1600. Fax: (65) 6861 6438

©2003 Apa Publications GmbH & Co.
Verlag KG (Singapore branch)
*All Rights Reserved*
*First Edition 1992*
*Third Edition 2000; updated 2003*

**CONTACTING THE EDITORS**
We would appreciate it if readers
would alert us to errors or out-
dated information by writing to:
**Insight Guides, P.O. Box 7910,
London SE1 1WE, England.
Fax: (44) 20 7403 0290.
insight@apaguide.co.uk**

NO part of this book may be reproduced,
stored in a retrieval system or transmitted
in any form or means electronic, mechanical, photocopying, recording or otherwise, without prior written permission of
*Apa Publications.* Brief text quotations
with use of photographs are exempted
for book review purposes only. Information has been obtained from sources
believed to be reliable, but its accuracy
and completeness, and the opinions
based thereon, are not guaranteed.

**www.insightguides.com**

This guidebook combines the interests and enthusiasms of two of the world's best known information providers: Insight Guides, whose titles have set the standard for visual travel guides since 1970, and Discovery Channel, the world's premier source of nonfiction television programming.

The editors of Insight Guides provide both practical advice and general understanding about a destination's history, culture, institutions and people. Discovery Channel and its website, www.discovery.com, help millions of viewers explore their world from the comfort of their own home and also encourage them to explore it first-hand.

This fully updated new edition of *Insight: Finland* is carefully structured to convey an understanding of Finland and its culture as well as to guide readers through its sights and activities:

◆ The **Features** section, indicated by a yellow bar at the top of each page, covers the history and culture of the country in a series of informative essays.

◆ The main **Places** section, indicated by a blue bar, is a complete guide to all the sights and areas worth visiting. Places of particular interest are coordinated by number with the maps.

◆ The **Travel Tips** listings section, with an orange bar at the top of each page, provides a handy point of reference for information on travel within Finland, hotels, shops, restaurants and more.

NORTH NOTTS. COLLEGE

914·897

EXPLORE YOUR WORLD

## The contributors

This edition of *Insight: Finland* was revised by **Zoë Ross**, a London-based editor, and supervised by managing editor **Huw Hennessy** at Insight Guides. The book has been completely updated with the invaluable help of a number of specialists.

The Places section and the Features essays on Finnish culture, as well as the Travel Tips were all updated by **Markus Lehtipuu**, an experienced, Helsinki-based writer who has contributed to a number of travel guides on Finland and many other countries around the world, both in English and in his native Finnish. **Timothy Bird** is a British writer living in Helsinki and a specialist on all things Finnish: he updated the history chapters for this guide, as well as the essays on architecture and design, and music and film.

The current edition builds on the excellent foundations created by the editors and writers of previous editions of the book, most notably **Doreen Taylor-Wilkie**, editor of the original *Insight: Finland* and its companion guides to Norway, Sweden and Denmark. **Kristina Woolnough**, who contributed to the original guide, acted as consultant on this current edition, using her vast knowledge of the country gained through 25 years of visiting the home of her Finnish-speaking Peruvian husband. She also wrote the Defence of Greenness chapter.

**James Lewis** wrote about Finland's history. **Anne Roston** wrote the original piece on Helsinki, and **Sylvie Nickels** wrote on the Great Lakes region, Lapland, and the traditions of the Laplanders, the Sami people. The West Coast chapter was written by **Robert Spark**.

Like all Insight Guides, this book owes much to the superb quality of its photographs, which aim not just to illustrate the text but also to convey the essence of everyday life as it is lived in Finland. Many of the images were taken by **Lyle Lawson**, an American who lives in England and is an inverterate world traveller.

Other major contributors of new pictures added to the book were **Robert Fried**, **Jim Holmes**, **Michael Jenner** and **Layne Kennedy**. Picture research was undertaken by **Hilary Genin** and **Britta Jaschinski**.

This version was updated by **Dr. Andrew Newby**, a historian at the University of Helsinki's Renvall Institute. He has lived in Finland for four years, travelling extensively throughout the country, and is a regular commentator on Finnish politics. The index was written by **Isobel McLean**.

## Map Legend

| | |
|---|---|
| —-- | International Boundary |
| — — — | County Boundary |
| ⊖ | Border Crossing |
| —•—•— | National Park/Reserve |
| — — — | Ferry Route |
| ● | Metro |
| ✈ ✈ | Airport: International/Regional |
| 🚌 | Bus Station |
| ■ | Parking |
| ❶ | Tourist Information |
| ✉ | Post Office |
| ✝ † ✝ | Church/Ruins |
| † | Monastery |
| ☪ | Mosque |
| ✡ | Synagogue |
| 🏰 🏰 | Castle/Ruins |
| ∴ | Archaeological Site |
| ∩ | Cave |
| 1 | Statue/Monument |
| ★ | Place of Interest |

The main places of interest in the Places section are coordinated by number with a full-colour map (e.g. ❶), and a symbol at the top of every right-hand page tells you where to find the map.

# INSIGHT GUIDE
# FinLanD

# CONTENTS

## Maps

Finland **148**

Inside front cover:
Finland
Inside back cover:
Helsinki

## Introduction

## History

## Features

**Calm reflection in
Finnish Lakeland**

## Insight on ...

## Information panels

## Travel Tips

## Places

# A PLACE IN EUROPE

*The Finns are among Europe's least understood but most dynamic people, revelling in their new status within Europe*

From the moment your plane lands at Helsinki Airport you are confronted with a characteristic of modern Finland, as the scramble for mobile phones begins. It is no exaggeration to say that this device, pioneered and developed by Finns and owned by well over half of them – an unequalled national per capita ratio – is at the heart of Finnish life at the start of the new millennium.

But the prevalent addiction to the phone and its attendant technology is just one aspect of life that, superficially at least, makes nonsense of the conventional wisdom about Finns. Reserved and reticent? You'd never guess it from the constant telephone prattle. The population's proficiency in languages other than its own obscure and difficult tongue also means that Finns, especially the younger ones, are ever happier to converse in English too. The stereotype of the hesitant, sullen Finn was always questionable, but now Finns are really starting to open up.

Since the 1980s Finland's capital Helsinki has swollen, draining the enormous, sparsely populated rural areas, maturing into a distinctive and vibrant metropolis with its own identity. Its restaurants have multiplied and improved; startling new buildings, such as the weird and wonderful Museum of Contemporary Art and the gleaming National Opera, have transformed the city's silhouette.

Celebrating its 450th birthday and the status of European City of Culture in 2000, Helsinki and its residents have found their place in the European scheme of things. Technological innovations, from the ubiquitous mobile phones to state-of-the-art medical equipment and progressive Internet services, have begun to catch up on, and even overtake, Finland's still substantial pulp and paper industry in terms of economic prestige and significance. In spite of the global downturn in the IT market, confidence remains high.

Yet still, the local character is shaped by climatic extremes, of long nightless summer days and bitter winter nights, and its moods swing accordingly. From the rocky archipelago of the southwestern coast to the majestic sweep of the lakeland labyrinth stretching to the border with Russia and the sweeping fells of Lapland that traverse the Arctic Circle in the north, Finland's natural environment is one of Europe's wildest. And modern Finns, mobile phones and all, still claim a special affinity with this landscape, retiring to their lakeside cabins and saunas in the magical summer, gliding on skis through the snow-smothered woods in winter. The urban scene may have been the stage for the most visible recent changes, but the vast serenity of Finland's endless lakes and forests remains uniquely timeless. ❑

**PRECEDING PAGES:** Sami life as captured by the Sami artist Alariesto; shopfront for eager anglers; boathouses of the Åland Islands; at the heart of Finland's forests.
**LEFT:** traditional dress at the Helsinki Midsummer Festival.

# Decisive Dates

## EARLY HISTORY: 8000 BC–AD 400

**8000 BC** Tribes from eastern Europe (ancestors of present-day Sami) settle the Finnish Arctic coast. They hunt bear and reindeer.

**1800–1600 BC** The Central European "Boat Axe" culture arrives from the east. Trade with Sweden begins from Bronze Age settlements along the Finnish west coast.

**C. AD 100** The historian Tacitus describes the Fenni in his *Germania*, probably referring to the Sami.

**C. AD 400** The "Baltic Finns" or Suomalaiset, cross the

Baltic and settle in Finland, gradually absorbing the Sami population. Sweden's influence over its "eastern province" begins, although the migrants live in clans cut off from mainstream European developments.

## SWEDISH RULE: 1155–1807

**1155** Impatient with the danger posed by pagan Finnish clans raiding the Christians of southern Sweden, King Erik of Sweden launches a crusade into Finland; further Swedish invasions take place in 1239 and 1293, subjugating large areas of the country.

**1323** The Treaty of Pähkinäsaari establishes the official border between Sweden and Russia, between today's St Petersburg northwest through the lake region to the Gulf of Bothnia.

**1362** Finland becomes a province of Sweden.

**1523** Gustav Vasa (1523–60) ascends the Swedish throne. The Reformation passes through Finland without any bloodshed. The Lutheran faith is introduced from Germany by Mikael Agricola (1510–57), a bishop of Turku, whose translation of the Bible forms the basis of the Finnish literary language.

**1595** The 25-year war with Russia is concluded by the Treaty of Täyssinä; the eastern border now extends as far as the Arctic coast, allowing Finns to live in the far north.

**1617** The Peace of Stolbovo. Russia cedes Ingermanland and part of Karelia to the kingdom of Sweden-Finland.

**1640** Finland's first university is established in Turku.

**1696** One third of the Finnish population dies of famine Sweden offers no assistance.

**1714–21** The "Great Wrath". Russia attacks Sweden and occupies Finland. Under the Treaty of Uusikaupunki in 1721, the Tsar returns much of Finland but keeps Eastern Karelia.

**1741** The "Lesser Wrath". Following Sweden's declaration of war Russia reoccupies Finland until the Treaty of Turku in 1743. The Russians cede a section of Finland back to Sweden, but move their border westwards.

**1773** Finnish attempts to gain independence fail. A peasant uprising results in several reforms.

## THE RUSSIAN YEARS: 1807–1917

**1807** Tsar Alexander I attacks and occupies Finland in an attempt to force Sweden to join Napoleon's economic blockade. The Treaty of Hamina, signed in September, legally cedes all of the country to Russia.

**1809** The Tsar guarantees Finland beneficial terms at the Porvoo Diet. Finland becomes an autonomous Russian Grand Duchy.

**1812** Because of Turku's proximity to Sweden, Tsar Alexander shifts Finland's capital to Helsinki.

**1863** Differences of opinion between the Swedish-speaking ruling class and the Finnish nationalists are resolved, giving Finnish speakers equal status.

**1899** Tsar Nicholas II draws up the "February Manifesto" as part of the Russification process. Jean Sibelius composes *Finlandia* but is forced to publish it as "Opus 26, No 7". Russian suppression lasts until 1905, fuelling Finnish resistance.

**1905** Russia is defeated by Japan and the general strike in Moscow spreads to Finland. Finland regains a measure of autonomy.

**1906** Finnish women become the first women in Europe to be given the vote.

**1908–14** Tsar Nicholas II reinstates the Russification programme and removes the new parliament's powers; any laws passed in Finland still have to be ratified by the Tsar.

**1915** Finnish volunteers join the Tsar's army.

## EARLY INDEPENDENCE: 1917–1939

**1917** The October Revolution in Russia. Finland declares its independence from the new Soviet Union. The Finnish senate elects PE Svinhufvud as its first president. The new state is officially recognised by Germany, France and the rest of Scandinavia.

**1918** A radical wing of the Social Democratic Party tries to introduce a Russian-style revolution, plunging Finland into Civil War. The "White Guard", right-wing government troops with German military support under the leadership of General Mannerheim, finally defeat the "Red Guard".

**1918–19** Friedrich Karl, Prince of Hessen, is offered the Finnish throne but declines the invitation. On 17 July 1919 the Republic of Finland comes into being, under its first president, KJ Ståhlberg (1919–25).

**1922** The Åland Islands are ceded to Finland and granted autonomy.

## FINLAND AT WAR: 1939–1947

**1939–40** Soviet territorial demands spark off the "Winter War" between Finland and the Soviet Union. Finland successfully defends itself at first, but soon Stalin is victorious. Under the 1940 Treaty of Moscow Finland is forced to surrender 11 per cent of its territory to the Soviet Union.

**1941** Finland clings to its neutrality, but in fear of Soviet invasion is drawn closer to Germany. Hitler begins his Russian campaign. The "Continuation War" breaks out between Finland and the Soviet Union. Britain, allied with Russia, declares war on Finland.

**1943** The Germans are defeated at Stalingrad.

**1944** A peace treaty is signed between Finland and the Soviet Union. Finland is forced to give up the Petsamo region, and the border is restored to its 1940 position. War reparations are severe, and Finland is also compelled to drive the remaining Germans from its territory. The retreating German army destroys many towns in Lapland.

**1947** The final peace treaty is signed in Paris on 10 February, reiterating the conditions of the armistice.

## FINLAND IN EUROPE: 1948–2003

**1948** The Treaty of Friendship, Cooperation and Mutual Assistance (FCMA) is signed, laying the foundations for neighbourly relations with the Soviet Union.

**1952** Finland joins in the formation of the Nordic Council. Helsinki hosts the Olympic Summer Games.

**1955** Finland is admitted to the United Nations.

**1972** The Strategic Arms Limitation Talks (SALT) are held in Helsinki.

**1975** The Helsinki Accords are signed at the Conference on Security and Cooperation in Europe (CSCE).

**1982** President Kekkonen (1956–81) steps down. Social Democrat Mauno Koivisto is elected.

**1990** Finnish government declares several sections of the Paris Treaty of 1947 no longer applicable.

**1991** The FCMA is replaced by a treaty emphasising good neighbourliness and cooperation.

**1994** Social Democrat Martti Ahtissari elected.

**1995** Finland joins the European Union.

**1997** US President Bill Clinton meets his Russian counterpart, Boris Yeltsin, at the Helsinki Summit.

**1999** Finland serves as President of the EU, hosting two Head of State summits.

**2000** Helsinki celebrates its 450th anniversary and is one of nine European Cities of Culture. Tarja Halonen becomes first female, and first Helsinki native, to be elected president of Finland.

**2002** Finland begins using euro coins and notes.

**2003** New government takes contral, led by the Centre Party and supported by the Social Democrats and Swedish People's Party. As a result, Anneli Jäätteenmäki becomes Finland's first female Prime Minister. ❏

---

**PRECEDING PAGES:** the Battle of Poltava ends Swedish domination. **LEFT:** King Gustav Vasa of Sweden. **RIGHT:** athlete Paavo Nurmi, the original Flying Finn.

E igitur clemétissime pa
ter per ihesum xpm filiú
tuú diim nostrú supplices
rogamus ac petimus vti
accepta habeas ⁊ benedicas ✠ Hec
dona ✠ Hec munera ✠ Hec sacra
sacrificia illibata · In primis que tibi
offerimus pro ecclesia tua sancta ca
tholica quã pacificare · custodire · adu
nare et regere digneris toto orbe ter
raꝝ vna cũ famulo tuo papa nĩo · A ·
et antistite nostro · A · et rege nostro ·
et omnibȝ orthodoꝭis · atꝗ catholice
et apostolice fidei cultoꝛibus ·

Memento dñe famuloꝝ famula
rûꝗ tuarû · A · Memoria viuoꝛum
et omniũ circũstantiũ quoꝝ tibi fide
cognita est ⁊ nota deuotio pro quib

# THE FINNS ARRIVE

*The life of the early Finns is one of the most mysterious of all European cultures, but by the 12th century Sweden had dominated its eastern neighbour*

Race study was an infant science in 1844 when M.A. Castrén pronounced: "I have decided to prove to the people of Finland that we are not a… nation isolated from the world and world history, but that we are related to at least one-seventh of the people of the globe." Castrén had persuaded himself that language equalled race and had concluded that the Finns were kith and kin with every single tribe which had originated in the Altai mountains of Siberia and Outer Mongolia.

## A race apart

That the Finnish tongue is a branch of the Finno-Ugric language tree is undeniable and, to those who maintain, like Castrén, that language kinship equals racial relationships, the matter ends there. "The Finns speak a Mongoloid tongue. Ipso facto they are a Mongoloid people." To a scientist-patriot such as Castrén, his Siberian-Outer Mongolian theory had the added attraction of establishing a relationship between his own people and a large part of the global population.

Castrén's and similar fanciful conjectures came about because of the exceptional isolation of Finnish as a language. Hungarian was, and is, often mentioned as a language akin to Finnish, but the connection is remote. Finnish and Hungarian are about as similar to one another as English and Persian, and only Estonian is close enough to perceive some common linguistic base with Finnish.

Castrén's followers, and millions who may never have heard his name, swallowed his theory. This led to the long-held belief that the Finns were a race apart from the mainstream of Europe, their language firmly classifying them as being of Asiatic extraction. No other evidence was ever adduced and even their own scholars and nationalists did not attempt to dispute the issue.

**LEFT:** a page from Finland's first Bible, now on display at Turku Castle.
**RIGHT:** M.A. Castrén, creator of race theories.

## Theory rejected

This rather neat little slot in the huge and ever complex question of the origins of peoples and nations is still accepted by the world at large. The Finns themselves, however, at least those that think and those that research, have for some time totally rejected the theory. As one

leading scholar in the field of philology has written: "No valid reasons for this classification have yet been produced."

Research carried out in this century, based on archaeology, points to a Baltic people moving gradually into Finland from around 1500 BC to about AD 400. There are no signs of a migration from further east. All cultural contacts point to Western Europe and Scandinavia, even from the earliest times.

The anthropological verdict now accepted by all but Castrénite primitives is that the Finns and their racial forebears are "purely European". In common with Swedes, Norwegians, Danes and Germans, Finns are tall and blond, although there are slight height differences and there is a variant type known as the East Baltic. A survey in 2002 deduced that, although natural blondes were becoming more and more rare, the last place to find them would be Finland.

The migrants from the Baltic who took up residence in the land of lakes and forests to the north were destined to live an age-long existence isolated from the mainstream of Europe. A virile and questing people driven to sea and sea-borne exploits by an inhospitable climate and country

> **DIFFERENT FAITHS**
>
> While Western Finns adopted Catholicism from Sweden, the Karelians followed the Orthodox faith, influenced by Russia across the eastern border.

would appear to be a tailor-mad fate for early Finland. But the Finns made no such moves. The longships left from the lands just over the Gulf of Bothnia or the other side of the Danish sounds and the trading, raiding and general sea roving of the Vikings seem to have lacked any Finnish participation. Instead, the Finns were hunters and gatherers, surviving largely on the abundance of fish in the country's lakes.

## Secret past

Cut off in their sub-Arctic homeland from these early days, little light has been shed on the life and times of the early Finns. No single chronicler emerges from the forest mists to give later generations a glimpse of primeval life. There may well have been an oral tradition of poetry, song and story, a collection of folk memories passed down from generation to generation. The *Kalevala*, Finland's national epic, points in this direction, but the *Kalevala* was compiled and published in the 18th and 19th centuries and cannot itself therefore claim immemorial antiquity.

When Finland finally emerged into the history books through the flickering candles of Roman Catholic crusading, around the year 1157, we find the Finns living in clans. They had apparently never developed statehood; the clans were descendants of common ancestors, often warring with one another and submitting to priests who led them in the worship of nature and natural forces.

## Taming pagan warriors

Just as Finnish scholars had established a theory of race and language, a parallel movement in academic circles was growing up on the subject of the arrival of Christianity. According to prevailing wisdom, the Finns were raiding the Christian people of southern Sweden and had become a nuisance and a danger. Furthermore, they were pagans. In 1157, King Erik of Sweden lost patience and set off on a "crusade" to Finland. Taming the Finns was a vital key to trading routes to the east, particularly Russia. Sweden was to control Finland for almost the next 700 years.

Once subdued, the Finns were submitted to baptism by an English-born bishop, Henry of Uppsala. Swedish secular dominance and, in tandem with it, Roman Catholicism, were thereby introduced into Finland.

Yet once again this theory, like the language theory, has all but gone out of the window. Rome has no record of these events and church documents make no reference to Erik or Henry. And again, the archaeologists have come to the aid of Finnish integrity with an assertion that the Finns practised primitive Christianity years before 1157. The Swedes brought Romanism to Finland, but not a new faith. ❏

**LEFT:** an illustration from the epic poem, *Kalevala*, which details ancient folk stories.
**RIGHT:** Orthodox religion came to Finland from Russia.

ANNO 1615.

# BIRTH OF A NATION

*Finland's relationship with Sweden was peaceful in the early days, but by the 16th century Russia wanted control of its western neighbour*

The Finns were part and parcel of Sweden for seven centuries (*circa* 1200–1800), but there was never a Swedish "conquest" of Finland. Instead, a race had developed between Sweden and Russia – in those days known as Novgorod – to fill the power vacuum in the land of the Finns. Sweden won the race – and did so without resorting to conquest or dynastic union or treaty. Remarkably, the future relationship between Sweden and Finland was free for the most part of the stresses and strains that normally accompany such take-overs, and completely free of the vicissitudes of war.

## A happy union

Although there is no official documentation, it is quite likely that Swedes had hunted, traded and settled in Finnish lands for centuries. On both sides of the Gulf of Bothnia the land had sparse resources and gave little cause for friction. In effect, Sweden and Finland merged as constituent parts of a larger whole. No distinctions in law or property were made, and the history of these two people under one crown has been described as "a seamless garment".

Finns took part in the election of the king, although they were not involved in the choice of candidates. In areas of mixed population language was the only real difference. Castles functioned as administrative centres, not as garrisons to subdue the people. The influences of the one people on the other were neutral largely because the cultures were identical. In one respect only did Sweden bring a dominating influence, and that was in the sphere of religion.

## Spreading the faith

Various monastic orders began a slow but steady penetration of Finland during the 14th and 15th centuries. Dominicans, Franciscans and the Order of St Bridget took their place alongside the clergy and greatly strengthened the power and influence of the Roman Catholic Church. This activity gave impetus to church building and church adornment. Life became more settled in the relatively densely populated areas of Western Finland. Further east, it was more mobile, less settled, and depended on

**LEFT:** stained-glass window in Turku Cathedral shows Gustav II Adolf of Sweden.
**RIGHT:** Bishop Henrik in Hollola Church.

## DANISH AMBITION

At the end of the 14th century there was an attempt to unite Denmark, Norway, Sweden and, by implication, Finland as a result of the ill-starred Kalmar Union of 1397. All the devices which had not been employed between Sweden and Finland were invoked in this fated union, the dream of the Danish Queen, Margrethe I.

In 1509 Finland, which had little say in the matter, became violently involved when the Danes burnt and sacked Turku (Åbo), the "capital" of the country. It was just one incident in more than 100 years of conflict over the treaty, which was finally broken in 1523 in a rebellion by Gustav Vasa, who became King of Sweden.

hunting across the sub-Arctic tundra, a region rich in animals and game birds, but not suitable for cultivation.

The most important centres from which the new influences spread were Turku (Åbo in Swedish, *see page 203*), with a bishop's seat and cathedral, and Vyborg (Viipuri in Finnish). Both towns had close links with Tallinn (Estonia), Danzig (now Gdansk, in Poland) and Lübeck (Germany) as well as with Stockholm. In these Finnish towns artisans and professions flourished alongside the clergy and an urban culture came into being, in contrast to the ruder ways of life further east.

## Stirrings of nationhood

Sweden was now powerful and independent. The Middle Ages were over; the Reformation challenged Rome. Here was a cocktail of influences, almost modern in their impact. Sweden and Finland were both slipping away from the old moorings. Slowly, the relationship was changing. The first stirrings of nationhood date from this time, although they were small and they originally arose from the translation of religious text into the vernacular.

Many more Swedes and Finns fell under the influence of Martin Luther in Wittenberg. The Reformation also attracted Gustav Vasa,

### LINGUISTIC REFORMS

"You are instructing your charges in a manner that is both nasty and lazy," wrote the Bishop of Turku, Mikael Agricola, to his clergy in 1548.

Agricola (1510–57) sent out this admonition with a translation of the New Testament in Finnish, a work he had undertaken to make sure, as he put it, "that not a single preacher or teacher could cover up his laziness by claiming that he did not know Latin or Swedish." Agricola created the first Finnish alphabet and Finnish writings, on a religious theme. The whole Bible was published in 1642, and in doing so, it created the first official document of the Finnish language in print, thus formalising the language.

because the Swedish crown needed more revenue and the church could provide it. In fact, the Reformation was so irresistible that Sweden was the first state in western Christendom to break with Rome.

The split took place in May 1527. All over Sweden and Finland the church suddenly lost property, authority, ceremonies and rites. Holy water, customary baptism and extreme unction were banned, so were colourful processions and the worship of relics. But transforming Finns from a Catholic to a Protestant people was not painless. The early Lutheran pastors were a motley rabble – "violaters of the laws of man and God." Yet Finns took a leading part in the transformation and Pietari Särkilahti, Mikael Agricola and Paavali Juusten aided their Swedish brethren in severing links with Rome.

## Peasant soldiers

During the three centuries before 1809, when Finland finally broke with Sweden, the Swedish crown was at war for more than 80 years. Involvement in the Thirty Years' War and wars with both Poland and Russia raised taxes and took Finnish men away from the land – the burden of providing levies always fell

> ### CALL TO ARMS
>
> Military service was compulsory except for the cavalry, in which volunteers enlisted eagerly in order to escape the harder life of an infantryman.

## The Dutch influence

In Turku, Helsinki, Porvoo and Viipuri, as well as in the other Baltic trading cities, many of the leading merchants, who controlled much of the foreign trade, were of German or Dutch descent. "The general area of our economic history during the 17th century and part of the 18th centuries bears a marked Dutch stamp," remarks V. Voionmaa, a prominent Finnish historian. The Dutch were well established, and foreign goods and ways of doing business gained ground in

heavily on the farmers. Finns were a vital part of the Swedish army, comprising a third of the foot soldiers and cavalry. In the wars with Russia, Finland bore the brunt of the suffering. City development became sluggish and, in any case, Finnish cities frequently went up in smoke. Turku (Åbo) suffered 15 major fires between 1524 and 1624; the worst reduced the city to ashes. Pori and Viipuri also suffered a similar fate several times, though fires were not the only dangers that beset the cities.

**LEFT:** Mikael Agricola's 16th-century Bible translated into Finnish (Turku Cathedral).
**ABOVE:** building Häme Castle.

Finland. Foreign as well as Finnish capital fuelled industry and trade.

Sweden no longer dominated the land and conflicts with the Russians kept recurring. The wars were destructive to Finland and read like a litany: 1554–7; a 25-year war (interrupted by truces) which started in 1570; two wars in the 17th century (as well as a devastating famine from 1696–7) and the great Northern War from 1700–21; war again 20 years later; and yet again from 1788–90. In the mid-18th century Sweden regained partial confidence and began to improve Finnish defences with the construction of fortresses such as Suomenlinna *(see page 177)*, but when Peter the Great founded St

Petersburg, just across the border with eastern Finland, Russian power was again in full force.

## Carrot and stick

The Swedish crown demonstrated an inability to hold Finland against Russian assault. It lost Finland on two occasions (1721 and 1743). In 1808, Great Britain became a Swedish ally. The Russians now saw a dire threat to St Petersburg and to Russian naval access to the Baltic. Yet again Russia and Sweden fought. This time Russia held on to Finland and offered the country generous terms as part of a strategy of "carrot and stick" – offering Finns a large say in

constitutional monarch in the newly acquired territory. It was an experiment in kingship, a new departure for an absolute ruler. The experiment was an unqualified success for 60 years.

The Grand Duchy was declared before the end of the 1808-9 war with Sweden at the Diet of Porvoo. As a Grand Duchy, Finland benefited from Russia's precedent of allowing the countries annexed into its empire to retain their legislative and other social systems. The Baltic states, and later Poland, were granted the same rights. The enlightened policies of Alexander I, which included the granting of a degree of freedom for Finnish peasants, could be seen as a

the running of their land, but retaining Russian overall rule. The Swedish centuries had finally come to an end.

## A nation is born

Sweden formally ceded Finland to Russia by the Treaty of Hamina on 17 September 1807. Along with Finland went the Åland Islands, between Sweden and Finland, which had long been an administrative part of the Finnish half of the kingdom. Finland became a separate state whose head, the Tsar-Grand Duke, was an absolute ruler; Tsar of all the Russias. Yet in Finland he agreed to rule in partnership with the Finnish Diet. This made the Tsar a

step towards wider, progressive changes planned in other parts of the empire.

For most ordinary Finns, very little changed. No pressure was put on the people to switch from the Lutheran Church to the Orthodox, and Swedish continued to be the language of government. Yet the setting up of a Finnish Diet, as well as an administrative Senate-led body allowed the gradual rise in influence of the Finnish language and, slowly but surely, the general spread of the idea of Finnish nationalism and independence. ❑

**ABOVE:** the house of Johan Ludvig Runeberg (1804–77), Finland's patriotic poet (see page 95).

# A Winter Journey

At the end of the 18th century, Joseph Acerbi embarked on what was then the only practical way of crossing from Sweden to Finland in winter, by sledge across the frozen Gulf of Bothnia. The distance was 70 km (43 miles) but, using the Åland Islands as stepping stones, that left 50 km (30 miles) "which you travel on the ice without touching on land".

Acerbi was advised that his party of three, plus two servants, would have to double their number of horses and hire no fewer than eight sledges for the crossing. He suspected that he was being swindled by the Swedish peasants but, as things turned out, it was a sensible precaution.

Acerbi published the details of the difficult and at times terrifying journey in his work *Travels Through Sweden, Finland and Lapland to the North Cape. 1802*, as follows:

"I expected to travel 43 miles without sight of land over a vast and uniform plain, and that every successive mile would be in exact unison and monotonous correspondence with those I had already travelled; but my astonishment was greatly increased in proportion as we advanced from our starting-post. At length we met with masses of ice heaped one upon the other, and some of them seeming as if they were suspended in the air, while others were raised in the form of pyramids. On the whole they exhibited a picture of the wildest and most savage confusion... It was an immense chaos of icy ruins, presented to view under every possible form, and embellished by superb stalactites of a blue-green colour.

"Amidst this chaos, it was not without difficulty and trouble that our horses and sledges were able to find and pursue their way. It was necessary to make frequent windings, and sometimes to return in a contrary direction, following that of a frozen wave, in order to avoid a collection of icy mountains that lay before us.

"The inconvenience and the danger of our journey were still farther encreased (*sic*) by the following circumstance. Our horses were made wild and furious, both by the sight and the smell of our great pelices, manufactured of the skins of Russian wolves or bears. When any of the sledges was overturned, the horses belonging to it, or to that next to

it, frighted at the sight of what they supposed to be a wolf or bear rolling on the ice, would set off at full gallop, to the terror of both passengers and driver. The peasant, apprehensive of losing his horse in the midst of this desert, kept firm hold of the bridle, and suffered the horse to drag his body through masses of ice, of which some sharp points threatened to cut him in pieces. The animal... continually opposed to his flight, would stop; then we were enabled to get again into our sledges, but not till the driver had blindfolded the animal's eyes: but one time, one of the wildest and most spirited of all the horses in our train, having taken fright, completely made his escape..."

"During the whole of this journey we did not meet with, on the ice, so much as one man, beast, bird, or any living creature. Those vast solitudes present a desert abandoned as it were by nature. The dead silence that reigns is interrupted only by the whistling of the winds against the prominent points of ice, and sometimes by the loud crackings occasioned by their being irresistibly torn from this frozen expanse; pieces thus forcibly broken off are frequently blown to a considerable distance.

"Through the rents produced by these ruptures, you may see below the watery abyss; and it is sometimes necessary to lay planks across them, by way of bridges, for the sledges to pass over." ❑

**RIGHT:** Count Per Brahe, Turku governor at the time of Acerbi's journey.

# LIVING WITH RUSSIA

*Finland's relationship with Russia was at first peaceful but, with Russia's own*
*political struggles, the union dissolved into revolt and war*

Annexation by Russia defied all gloomy prophecies, at least at the outset. Tsar Alexander I seemed open to suggestions from the Finnish camp, and a group of leading Finns suggested that Finland should hold elections. Alexander agreed and the first Finnish Diet met at Porvoo in 1809. The Tsar had styled himself "the Emperor and Autocrat of all the Russias and the Grand Duke of Finland." Invested with this new title, the proto-type of future constitutional monarchs, Tsar Alexander formally opened the Diet. In return, he promised to respect and maintain the laws, religion and constitution of Finland.

## A diplomatic success

The constitution's main pillar was a unique device in the statecraft of those days. Finland was to be in personal union with the Tsar. This meant that the Finns dealt direct with their head of state, bypassing the Russian government. Ultimately it became the cause of much jealousy, but the arrangement lasted for 90 years and was the basis of the relationship between Russia and Finland. When Nicholas I succeeded Alexander in 1825 a strong bond of mutual trust had developed. The change of overlord had brought advantages: the fear of attack from the east had gone; Finns could con-duct their internal affairs but, if they felt cramped, opportunities existed in the armed forces and civil service of Russia. The Finnish army was disbanded, though its officers received generous pensions. Russian troops garrisoned Finland but never in large numbers. Taxation was raised for domestic needs only.

Behind all this liberality lay firm policy: to pacify Finland and woo it away from Sweden. To keep Sweden sweet, Alexander concluded an agreement, in 1812, in support of moves to unite Norway with Sweden. This was the new Swedish ambition.

---

**PRECEDING PAGES:** Tsar Alexander I leads the Finnish Diet at Porvoo in 1809. **LEFT:** Russia's Imperial throne in Finland. **RIGHT:** Tsar Nicholas II.

## The new capital

The Grand Duchy needed a capital and it was a small, rocky fishing port that was chosen. Helsinki became a city of major importance within two generations. A visitor in 1830 remarked that the Finns were "converting a heap of rocks into a beautiful city". The urban

centre was conceived and planned on an impe-rial scale, with Neo-classical buildings designed by German architect C.L. Engel. The university of Turku moved to Helsinki's in 1828, the year after Turku suffered yet another disastrous fire, making its eclipse inevitable.

The university became a tug of war between languages. There was no discrimination against Finns as a separate linguistic group within the Russian Empire, and the idea of introducing Russian in schools was canvassed, but not much was done. Finns wishing to serve the Tsar abroad had to learn Russian, but to serve the Grand Duke of Finland the requirement, until 1870, was to speak and write Swedish.

## Peasant power

The all-important vernacular being promoted by nationalist Henrik Porthan already resided in the countryside, on the farms and in the forests. But the farmers and peasants of the country were slow to awaken to the power they possessed. In part, the peasants distrusted notions of independence. The rural poor, workers, smallholders and the landless were on the periphery of political life and thought. In contrast to the élite, they were indifferent to ideas of liberty and national independence, which were not hot topics among the masses. There was even some class-based hostility to such notions. When autonomy was in jeopardy under a changed Russian attitude at the end of the 19th century, some pamphleteers got to work to raise national consciousness. Grumpy peasants tossed back at them remarks such as "Now the gentry are in a sweat" and "These new laws don't concern us peasants, they're only taking the power off the gentry."

Yet, all the time, opportunities in higher education were increasing among such people. Into secondary education, university and the new polytechnics they brought their language, which was vernacular Finnish. Russian was still not an issue, but Swedish was, and Swedish

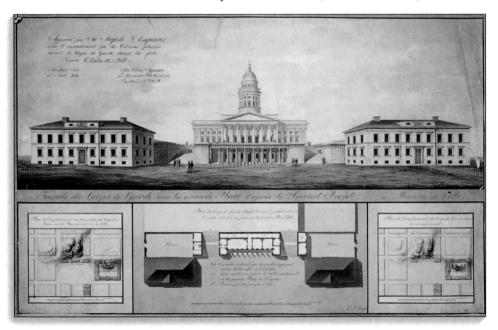

### THE FATHER OF FINNISH HISTORY

Bold ideas of Finnish independence had been nurtured by educated Finns ever since the days when Sweden had started to lose its grip. Henrik Porthan (1739–1804), known as the "father of Finnish history," awakened intellectual leaders. "We must pray," he said "that Russia will succeed in situating its capital in Constantinople… But now that its capital city (St Petersburg) is located so near, I am afraid that Finland will … fall under the power of Russia."

Nevertheless, the Finnish people, he advocated, should use this as an opportunity, and not be despondent. They must think of themselves above all as Finns. History, language and folklore (according to Porthan) all pointed to a Finland that was ultimately free. But Russia – barbarous, Byzantine, eastern Russia – and not western, democratic Sweden, was the stepping stone to this end.

Porthan was ahead of his time, but his long-term, pragmatic philosophy took hold and became the prevailing wisdom of his own and succeeding generations of Finnish nationalists. Their patience was finally rewarded when, within living memory, the goal of nationhood was achieved. His disciples realised very quickly that if the Finnish language would be able to replace Swedish, the battle for independence, at least in the hearts and minds of Finns themselves, was three-quarters won.

was gradually being supplanted. In spite of harvest failures and famine in 1862 and 1868, the peasants were generally growing richer. The demand for timber increased and the price rose. Freehold peasant farmers with timber land grew rich. Their wives could now afford tables, sideboards and chairs in place of rustic benches and chests. Life for some was becoming genteel and not rough-hewn. Since 1864 peasants had been able to buy land on the open market. Now their sons were taking advantage of higher education, more Finnish language fodder.

> **STUDENT SKIERS**
>
> Many of the signatures on the petitions to Tsar Alexander were collected by nationalistic students who skied from remote farm to distant cottage across the country.

## Ruthless governor

Tsar Alexander III, who freed the Russian serfs, knew his Grand Duchy. His son, the ill-starred Nicholas II (1894–1917) did not. The conception of a docile and contented satellite country acting as a buffer on Russia's northwest flank, the cornerstone of policy for 90 years, was cast aside. A new Governor, General Bobrikov, fresh from a ruthless administration in the Baltics, was installed in Helsinki.

Finland lost its autonomy. Laws, soldiering and taxation, those pivotal issues which previous grand dukes had treated so delicately, were henceforth to be Russian concerns. "While leaving in operation the existing regulations for legislation on matters of local interest which bear only on the needs of Finland, we have considered it necessary to reserve to ourselves the final determination of matters of legislation which concern the whole Empire," ran a manifesto promoted by Bobrikov. It was too much for the Finns: 522,931 signatures on a petition were collected in just two weeks,

Abroad, another petition was launched in support of the Finns, signed by many eminent people. They addressed Tsar Nicholas: "Having read and being deeply moved by the petition of the 5th March of over half a million Finnish men and women in which they made a solemn appeal to your Majesty in support of the maintenance of their full Rights and Privileges first confirmed by... Alexander I in 1809... and subsequently re-affirmed in the most solemn manner by all his illustrious successors, we venture to express our hope that your Imperial Majesty will take into due consideration the prayer of the said Petition of your Majesty's Finnish subjects. It would be a matter of great regret if recent events in the Grand Duchy of Finland should retard the cause of amity among the nations of the civilised world which has in your Majesty so Illustrious an Advocate."

The "Illustrious Advocate" was unmoved. *The Times* of London thundered a declaration that

"the Finnish Diet can, legally, only be modified or restricted with its own consent." This too fell on deaf Russian ears. They imposed strict censorship on the Finnish press. Conscription into the Russian army was the final straw.

## The Finns revolt

Resistance started to stiffen and pamphleteers got to work. Half the conscripts ordered to report for military service in the spring of 1902 did not turn up. In 1904 the Governor General was assassinated by a patriotic student, Eugen Schauman, who then committed suicide by turning his gun on himself. Schauman became a national hero and is buried at Porvoo.

**LEFT:** C. L. Engel's original drawing for the design of Senate Square in Helsinki.
**ABOVE:** statue of Alexander II at Helsinki Cathedral.

The Russian Revolution of 1905 and the Russo-Japanese war brought a respite. The Finns took the opportunity to put forward a bold measure. The franchise was by now outmoded. Industrial workers had no representation; women no vote. This was par for the times in Europe, although New Zealand had just granted women the vote. Finland proposed no less than a universal franchise and a unicameral parliament. The Tsar, doubtless distracted by the stirrings of revolt in Russia – a chain of events that would eventually bring

> ### NATIONAL IDENTITY
>
> "We are no longer Swedes, we will not become Russians, so let us be Finns," had been the cry for some decades by nationalists.

The cause, in short, was the overspilling of the Russian October Revolution into Finland, where there remained contingents of Russian soldiers who sided with the Soviets. Thus Finland had a Red Army in its midst. Luckily, the Soviet government did not participate officially in the civil war in Finland, but Russian aid played a significant part in the Red revolt. Finnish Red Guards were supplied with arms by the Russians. Russian officers and NCOs provided leadership; in the case of the artillery, they provided the entire command.

him down – agreed to the changes. The Finns got their modern parliament. The electoral role was increased tenfold. The Social Democrats won the subsequent election.

### Civil war

Now the country was united as never before in a determination to be free Finnish. The moment came during World War I, when the Russian army collapsed and Lenin seized power. Finland was allowed to go free, compliments of the Bolsheviks. Independence had come at last, but the event was to be marred by a bitter civil war which broke out between the "Whites" and the "Reds".

The civil war's major contributory cause was labour unrest. After the Bolsheviks seized power in Russia, radical Finnish socialists became determined to overcome their minority position in parliament by extra-parliamentary activity. A strike was the first step, accompanied by widespread lawlessness on a considerable scale. After a week the strike was called off, but events escalated and a Central Revolutionary Council formed the Red Guards. They struck at the end of January 1918, in the hope that Russian aid would be enough to secure a quick victory. The Civil War saw atrocities by both sides, with Mannerheim, for example, being condemned by the international left as a war criminal. The psychological wounds of this period of Finnish history are only recently being brought out into the open.

## Military genius

The government lacked adequate forces to meet this situation. It did, however, appoint a commander-in-chief to a non-existent army. General Carl Gustaf Emil Mannerheim was an inspired military leader on a par with Turkey's Kemal Ataturk and the British General Montgomery. Mannerheim had been persuaded by Premier Svinhufvud to organise a government force to uphold law and order. On 18 January, Mannerheim disarmed Russian garrisons in central and northern Finland, and then turned them into bases from which government forces waged war against the enemy in the south. Tampere, Helsinki and Viipuri were retaken by the spring. After a last stand on the Karelian Isthmus, the Reds capitulated on 15 May. On 16 May Mannerheim's "people's army" held a victory parade in Helsinki.

After a brief flirtation with the idea of a monarch, during which time both Svinhufvud and Mannerheim acted as regent, the Finns elected K. J. Ståhlberg, author of the Form of Government, as its first president.

he went to Vaasa on the west coast of Finland, to plan for and organise a "White" army. Vaasa became the seat of government when war broke out. Four cabinet members escaped there from Helsinki hours before the Reds seized control of the capital on 28 January.

## Red defeat

The Reds, without full Russian support and up against the strategic ability of General Mannerheim, found their hopes short-lived.

**LEFT:** Eugen Schauman assassinates General Bobrikov in 1904.
**ABOVE:** White and Red troops at war in 1918.

### PREMIER LEADERSHIP

Although different in character from Mannerheim, the civilian leader, Pehr Evind Svinhufvud, was very much his equal. He was an experienced political leader and had been a member of the Turku Court of Appeal which was dismissed early in the 20th century for indicting the Russian governor of Helsinki for his brutal suppression of a peaceful demonstration. In 1917, Svinhufvud travelled to St Petersburg to gain the recognition of the Council of People's Commissars for Finland's independence. When the Red Army seized Helsinki, Svinhufvud was still in the capital and was forced to hide, but eventually escaped to Vaasa, via wartime Germany and many adventures.

## An insecure start

In 1920 the conflicts between Finland and the Soviet Union were dealt with by the Treaty of Tartu, which recognised Finland as an independent republic and ceded to it the Arctic port of Petsamo. Some small adjustments were made to the border and Finland neutralised its islands close to Leningrad. However, the Soviets seemed unable to forgive the Finns for their bourgeois defeat of revolution; in turn, there arose an almost fanatical distrust of the Soviet Union in Finland. Fear of

### EQUAL RIGHTS

Finland was the first European country to give women the vote and an equal political voice when it became independent in 1906.

had been the upsurge of Red rebellion, which was ably put down but which caused a severe shock to the body politic. The second problem was emigration.

## Land hunger

Once Russian overlordship had taken a nasty turn, the resulting insecurity had already started a trend towards emigration. But there were other causes, and land hunger was the foremost. "No land, no fatherland" was the cry. There was a landless proletariat of 200,000 in the 19th century, plus a host of peasants with

Russia, civil war, and the political polarisation that had caused it ran deep and affected the national psyche. Sandwiched between Communist Russia and neutral Sweden, and with a militaristic Germany to the south, independent Finland was born, one historian has noted: "not with a silver spoon, but with a dagger in its mouth". Finland survived because it learned the trick of "sword swallowing".

One matter that needed no adjustment in the constitution of independence was the Parliament Act of 1906, far ahead of its time in granting votes to both men and women. But social and economic disparities were not mitigated by legalities. Two symptoms were manifest. One

meagre plots. These people looked to the New World for opportunities.

Before and after the civil war there had been times of famine in the countryside. "Nature seems to cry out to our people 'Emigrate or die'," one university lecturer told his students in 1867. By the 1920s, 380,000 Finns had left for other lands, the majority to the USA. The Great Depression hit Finland in 1929, and by 1930 the figure for emigration had reached 400,000.

## Divided politics

In the 1920s the two branches of the labour movement (the bulk of the "Reds") grew further apart. For public and election purposes, the outlawed Communist Party metamorphosed into the Socialist Workers' and Small Holders' Election Organisation, while the Social Democrats began to co-operate with the bourgeois parties, culminating in a Social Democrat government in 1926, led by their moderate leader, Väinö Tanner.

Anti-Communist feeling continued, nevertheless, and led to the Lapua movement which resorted to violent methods, such as capturing and driving suspected Communist leaders over the Soviet border. Even the respected former president

### IN SEARCH OF FOOD

"The heart pleaded no, but the stomach commanded yes," ran a line in the novel *Amerikkaan*, referring to Finland's emigration.

period of co-operation between the Agrarian Party and the Social Democrats, the aptly named "red-green" coalition.

## Cultural advances

Though the infant nation's priority had to be to survive and to strengthen its democracy, life was not all gloom. In the 1920s, sport, travel and the cinema all came into their own, with a profound effect on social habits. It was a time of strong cultural expression, particularly in architecture and design. Up until 1939, a degree of cultural and

Ståhlberg did not escape one attempt and was driven close to the border. In 1930, the Lapua movement inspired a great peasants' march to Helsinki, and led to armed rebellion in 1932.

The formidable duo of the Liberation period, Svinhufvud and Mannerheim returned and, after anti-Communist laws were passed, it was left to Svinhufvud to persuade the rebels to disband peacefully. Despite these strains, Finland grew closer to the Scandinavian countries, where democracy was advancing, with a long

commercial harmony had existed between Russians and Finns. Communism kept a low profile, while Fascists failed to gather significant support. By the time of the war, Finland's agriculture had developed and the forest industry took the lead, supporting progress in other industries; forest product exports to other European countries boosted national earnings. Optimism was rife, to the extent that, despite the growing threats in Europe (particularly from Germany) and Mannerheim's warnings, little was done to build up the country's armaments. When parliament eventually approved 3,000 million marks for military procurement in 1938, it was already too late. ❑

**LEFT:** crowds riot in Turku in 1905 in support of Russian uprisings.
**ABOVE:** civil war bomb damage in Tampere, 1918.

# THE TWO WARS

*The bravery and prowess of Finland's soldiers on their treacherous, ice-bound terrain became legendary during the Winter and Continuation wars*

**B**y the spring of 1938 Moscow was making demands on the Finnish Government to give guarantees that, in the event of hostile acts by Germany, Finland would accept Soviet military aid. The railway line between Leningrad and Murmansk was vital to Soviet security: hence Moscow's fear of German invasion through the Gulf of Finland.

## Perilous times

The Finnish Government was reluctant to enter into discussions, fearing that to do so would be to compromise neutrality. The Munich Agreement of September 1938 prompted Finland to build up its defences and Mannerheim advised the government to carry out partial mobilisation. The Soviet Union again made representations to Finland, this time suggesting that the Finns lease the islands of the Gulf of Finland to them for 30 years. Soviet pleas to Britain and France for collective security had fallen on deaf ears and Leningrad was vulnerable from the sea.

Finland was still suspicious of Soviet ambitions. By April 1939, Hitler had managed to drive a wedge through Finland's policy of joint Nordic security. Estonia, Latvia and Denmark accepted a German plan of non-aggression, while Sweden, Norway and Finland refused.

After Sweden withdrew, and Germany and the Soviet Union had signed a non-aggression pact (which included a secret protocol on spheres of influence), Finland, placed within Moscow's sphere, was in a very dangerous position. After the German invasion of Poland, the Soviet Union began to press the small countries within its sphere to make pacts of "mutual assistance". Delegates from Helsinki travelled to Moscow for discussions. Mannerheim now pressed for full mobilisation of Finnish forces, and the Soviet Union moved swiftly on to a war footing.

**PRECEDING PAGES:** Finnish soldiers in the Winter War. **LEFT:** Field Marshal Mannerheim. **RIGHT:** Lotta Svärd, leader of the Women's Group in World War II.

## Winter warriors

The first Soviet demand was that troops be moved from the Karelian Isthmus. When Mannerheim refused, the Kremlin broke off diplomatic relations and launched an attack on Finland on 30 November 1939. What became known as the Winter War had begun.

Soviet forces had almost overwhelming superiority but they were untrained and ill-equipped to fight a war in severe winter conditions. Though short of heavy armaments, by contrast Finnish soldiers had already been training for just this sort of warfare. They were used to moving in dense forests through snow and ice, and the Finnish army's tactical mobility was on a high level. The Finns were also accustomed to the climate and dressed sensibly when winter set in and the temperature dropped several degrees below zero. Soldiers were issued with white "overalls" – now standard for winter warfare – to cover their uniforms so that they blended invisibly with the snow.

By copying the methods used by farmers and lumberjacks to haul logs from the forest, the Finnish army solved a second key problem: how to operate in the forests flanking the roads. They would open a trail in the woods using skis, avoiding gorges, cliffs and steep rises. When a few horses and sleighs had moved over this trail, a winter road would form along which a horse could pull up to a one-tonne load.

## War preparations

Anticipating what might happen, the army had already perfected these techniques in its pre-war winter manoeuvres and, when war started in 1939, Finland had about half a million horses in the country. The army used around 20 per cent of them and, as half the reservists called up to fight were farmers or lumberjacks, there were plenty of skilled horsemen. During the summer of 1939, the Finns had also built dams in the small rivers on the Karelian Isthmus and elsewhere which raised the water level to form an obstruction against the enemy advance. When the Finnish army opened the gates in the Saimaa canal in March 1940, the Russians found operations in the flooded areas difficult.

Attempts to raise the water level were less successful during the coldest winter period; but

### SURVIVING THE LANDSCAPE

One of the most difficult problems for winter warfare had already been solved by Finland in the 1930s: how to camp and make shelter in a winter wilderness. Finland had developed a tent for the use of half a platoon (20 men), which could be folded into a small and easily handled bundle. A portable boxstove was enough to keep the tent warm even if the temperature fell to –40°C. It was also relatively easy to prepare coffee and other basic warm food on top of the stove. The Finns also had the valuable know-how to operate for several weeks in uninhabited regions without tents by building shelters out of snow and evergreens.

equally, as the ice covered the uneven features of the terrain, the enemy had less shelter and was not concealed from air reconnaissance. Later, the Finns opened lanes by blowing up the ice and developed special ice mines which detonated when the Soviets approached.

## Surprise tactics

Finns and Russians fought the Winter War during the darkest period of the year. In the area of Viipuri, daylight lasted from 8am to 5pm. On the level of Kajaani the day was a couple of hours shorter while, at the turn of the year, Petsamo in the north enjoyed hardly any hours of daylight at all. Finnish soldiers made use of the darkness for the loading and unloading of trains, transports and supply traffic. This prevented the enemy (with its command of the air) from noticing and disturbing operations. The troops carried out all their tactical movements in the forests, which offered even better protection.

As the Soviet Army moved west, the Finns had insufficient forces and equipment for classic air, tank, artillery and similar operations, and their aim had to be to force the enemy to attack under the worst possible conditions. But

### BOTTLES VERSUS TANKS

To compensate for the lack of anti-tank guns, the Finns used gasoline-filled bottles and TNT-charges and destroyed a large number of tanks in this way.

pulled them along on sledges, which they also used to evacuate the wounded, often along the specially prepared winter roads through the wilderness. At night, for longer distances, they ploughed a road over the ice to bring troops and equipment. In any attack, surprise was the essence. Strike force commanders and their troops, all on skis, moved stealthily forward to block the road so that the sappers had time to destroy the bridges and lay mines to catch the tanks before any counter-attack.

the Finns, bred on the land, knew the terrain. The Soviet divisions, in contrast, had no choice but to stick to the roads, advancing in a tight column, strung out over some 100 km (60 miles). On either side lay a strip around 110–220 km (70–140 miles) wide of uninhabited, forest-covered wilderness, with numerous lakes and marshes, where the Finnish troops had all the advantages of surprise and manoeuvrability.

For these attacks, the Finns either carried their ammunition, mines and explosives or

**LEFT:** Karelians are forced to evacuate their homeland during World War II.

**ABOVE:** Finnish soldiers with a captured Russian tank.

The Finns fought against great odds during this Winter War (and partly during the Continuation War that followed). Their number of anti-tank guns was so limited that the troops could use them only against an armoured attack on an open road, and gasoline bottles and TNT-charges were more likely to destroy an enemy tank. Despite that, the advantages were not always on the side of the invading army. The ill-informed and often ill-clad Soviet troops could not move from or manoeuvre outside the roads and they, too, often lacked supplies when insufficient air drops left them short of ammunition and food. Throughout the war's skirmishes and more formal encounters, the "ski troops" inflicted hard blows on this badly deployed Red Army. (It was partly this poor performance that persuaded Hitler later to launch an attack on Russia.)

## Honourable peace

Though the resourcefulness of Marshal Mannerheim's white-clad troops had grasped every advantage of territory and climate to achieve several victories, Finland could not last long against an enemy of much greater power. The Finnish army was forced to surrender at Viipuri, and

### HIGH PRAISE

British leader Winston Churchill was unstinting in his praise of Finnish Resistance during the Winter War. He wrote: "Finland – shows what free men can do."

Winter War was mitigated for the Finns by the maintenance of national sovereignty.

The Winter War lasted exactly 100 days. But the European powers were still fighting and the inevitable result for Finland was to be swept up in yet another conflict. On 22 June 1941, Operation Barbarossa went ahead. Hitler attacked the Soviet Union, achieving complete surprise. Russian commanders signalled to Stalin: "We are being fired on – what shall we do?" Stalin replied that they were talking nonsense, and anyway why weren't their

the Soviet Union set up and then abandoned a puppet government on the Karelian Isthmus. But the long front held out to the end. This guaranteed pre-conditions for an honourable peace and, in 1940, the two sides concluded an armistice. The Soviet Union's original aim – a base in Hanko, in the southwest, and the moving of the border further from Leningrad – were its only gains.

Neverthless Finland had to surrender around a tenth of its territory, with a proportionate shift of population and, in this respect, suffered a heavy defeat. On the other hand it was obvious that Stalin's real intention had been to annex the whole of Finland, and their defeat in the

messages coded? There had been some collusion between the German and Finnish military authorities and the Finns had had to allow the west of Finland to be used for transit traffic. Partial Finnish mobilisation was ordered, and 60,000 civilians moved from front-line areas.

## Alongside Germany

On the day preceding Barbarossa, Hitler had announced that "Finnish and German troops stand side by side on the Arctic coast for the defence of Finnish soil." Marshal Mannerheim was convinced that his statement was intended as an announcement of a *fait accompli*. "This will lead to a Russian attack," he said, "though, on the other hand, I am convinced that in any case such an attack would have occurred." The Russian High Command retaliated against the Finns. Russian bombs fell on Finland even before any were dropped on German targets.

The Finnish army was larger, war-hardened and better equipped than at the start of the Winter War. Eleven divisions stood on the frontiers, another faced the Russian base at Hanko, and the Commander-in-Chief had a reserve of four divisions, which he controlled from his old headquarters at Mikkeli.

## PREPARED FOR BATTLE

During the Winter War, some units had been short of potatoes. Veterans reported for duty this time carrying their kit as well as a sack or two of potatoes.

Mannerheim but now he informed the Finnish government that "under no circumstances will I lead an offensive against the great city on the Neva." He feared that the Russians, faced with an advance on Leningrad, might raise irresistible forces and inflict a heavy defeat on the Finnish army.

The campaign aimed to reconquer Ladoga-Karelia, followed by the Isthmus, and finally penetrate Karelia. All these objectives were achieved. Mannerheim had some German units placed at his disposal, but he kept them at arm's

Even so, Marshal Voroshilov, who was in charge of the Russian Northwest Army Group, had formidable numbers under his command: 13 rifle divisions, two armoured divisions, a division of frontier troops, and specialist detachments. The Hanko garrison was estimated to consist of 35,000 men, and there were many fortress units.

Many in Finland expected the army to make an advance towards Leningrad. The idea of capturing this city had at one time attracted

**Left:** World War II gas masks in Hanko Museum.
**Above:** like many Finnish towns, Rovaniemi was largely re-built after World War II.

length. The Finns were co-belligerents, not allies of the Germans. When the Finns had regained all of their old frontiers, Mannerheim commented: "Here we could have stood as neutral neighbours instead of as bitter enemies."

## Admiring Allies

The fact that Great Britain and Russia were allies led to a tricky diplomatic situation between Mannerheim and Churchill, as is illustrated in the following exchange of letters. At this point, the outcome of the war was far from clear.

Winston Churchill wrote to Mannerheim on 29 November 1941: "I am deeply grieved at what I see coming, namely, that we shall be forced within a few days, out of loyalty to our ally Russia, to declare war upon Finland. If we do this, we shall make war also as opportunity serves. Surely your troops have advanced far enough for security during the war and could now halt and give leave? It is not necessary to make any public declaration, but simply leave off fighting and cease military operations for which the severe weather affords every reason, and make a de facto exit from the war.

"I wish I could convince Your Excellency that we are going to defeat the Nazis. I feel far

more confident of that than in 1917 or 1918. It would be most painful to the many friends of your country in England if Finland found herself in the dock with the guilty and defeated Nazis. My recollections of our pleasant talks… about the last war lead me to send you this purely personal and private message for your consideration before it is too late."

Field Marshal Mannerheim replied to Prime Minister Churchill: "Yesterday I had the honour to receive through the American Minister in Helsinki your letter of 29 November 1941, and I thank you for your kindness in sending me this private message. I am sure you will realise it is impossible for me to halt the mil-

itary operations at present being carried out before the troops have reached the positions which in my opinion will provide us with necessary security.

"It would be deplorable if these measures, undertaken for the security of Finland, should bring my country into conflict with England, and it would deeply sadden me if England felt herself forced to declare war on Finland. It was very good of you to send me a… message in these critical days, and I appreciate it fully." Nevertheless, a few days later, in order to satisfy his ally Josef Stalin, Churchill did declare war on the Finns.

## Payment in full

The 1941–44 war is known in Finland as the "Continuation War" because it was understood as an extension of the Winter War and as an attempt to compensate for losses suffered in that war. In the Continuation War Finland's number of dead was 65,000 and wounded 158,000. Homes had to be found for more than 423,000 Karelians. After 1945 the Soviets insisted on staging show trials in Finland of the politicians who had given the orders to fight. These men received prison sentences, but served less than a full term and, in some cases, returned to public life with little or no damage to their reputation.

Finland also had to pay reparations to the Soviet Union, mostly in the form of metal products. The Soviets insisted on calculating their value according to the exchange rates of 1938, thus Finland paid almost exactly twice the price stated in the agreement.The reparations to the Soviet Union were paid in full. This was a point of honour to the Finns.

The years of struggle and of suffering were over at long last, and a war-weary Finland set about the difficult business of national reconstruction. More poignantly, the dead soldiers, who had been removed from the battlefields to their home parishes, were buried with full honours in cemeteries alongside memorials attesting to their courage and sacrifice. Unassuming, dignified and patriotic, the spirit of these graveyards and memorials is a fitting tribute to the memory of a people who had persevered and conquered. ❏

**LEFT:** Vammala war cemetery commemorates Finland's World War II dead.

# The Great General

Carl Gustaf Emil Mannerheim was born at his family's country house at Louhisaari on 4 June 1867. The Mannerheim estate was in Swedish Villnäs, in the Turku district. The family was Swedish-speaking and of Dutch origin.

Furthermore, this great son of Finland to whom the modern nation state probably owes its very existence, was a Russian officer for 28 years before he ever served Finland's cause. Yet Gustaf (he used his second Christian name) was not following any family tradition when he enlisted as a cavalry officer cadet in 1882. He was even expelled from the Cadet School, and considered becoming a sailor. Fortunately for Finland he was given a second chance and went to St Petersburg for cavalry training; in 1889 he was commissioned into the Tsarist army, passing out in the top six, out of a total of 100.

While waiting for a Guard's commission he was posted to Poland as a subaltern in the 15th Alexandriski Dragoons. The Poles were far more restive under Russian rule than the Finns and had nothing like the same freedoms as the Grand Duchy. But Mannerheim later recalled: "The better I got to know the Poles, the more I liked them and felt at home with them." Transferred to the Chevalier Guards, he returned to St Petersburg to train recruits, and in 1892 married Anastasia Arapov, a relation of Pushkin. They had two daughters, and a son who died at birth. The marriage lasted seven years, although they did not divorce until 1919.

Mannerheim served as a colonel in the Russo-Japanese War, journeyed for two years through China and Japan, and then came back to Poland to command a cavalry regiment in 1909. In World War I, he served in the Eastern European theatre, fighting against Germans and Austrians. By 1917 he was a Lieutenant-General.

The Russian Revolution cut short his career in the Emperor's Army, and when the Tsar was murdered Mannerheim considered himself released from his Oath of Allegiance. Russia was seething with revolutionary activity, and the boiling pot overflowed into Finland.

His country had seized the moment and declared itself independent. The Senate named

Mannerheim Commander-in-Chief of the armed forces in Finland. Quickly, he had to raise and mobilise an army against the Red Guards and Russian troops. When the war was over and won, the Senate appointed Mannerheim Regent of Finland but he lost the Presidential election. During the inter-war years he worked for the Red Cross and for the Mannerheim League for Children.

His finest military hour came with the onset of the Winter War in 1940, when Finland fought against Soviet Russia for three-and-a-half months under ferocious winter conditions. It came through the war with its independence intact, due largely to the deployment of mobile "ski troops".

Mannerheim was briefly President of Finland after the war, but retired due to ill health in March 1946. His final years were spent quietly, mainly in Switzerland, where he died in 1951, aged 83. His wartime ADC, Colonel Bäckman, recalls Mannerheim as kind, frugal, disciplined and fond of riding. His home in Helsinki is now a museum, presided over by Bäckman, and holds trophies and mementoes from the five wars in which he fought. On the library wall is a painting of military personnel on skis and in white overalls. Urgency in the human figures contrasts with the peace of the Finnish forest. Curiously, the painting is dated 1890 – an omen? Or rather an idea, which delivered Finland in its hour of desperate need. ❏

**RIGHT:** Field Marshal Mannerheim's statue stands proud in Helsinki.

# A SHIFT IN BALANCE

*In breaking free from Russia and moving towards a higher profile in Europe,*
*Finland has endured economic hardship. But its efforts are beginning to bear fruit*

In 1980, Finnish statesman Max Jacobson wrote that outsiders persist in viewing Finland according to the state of western relations with the Soviet Union: "In 1939–40, Finns were idolised for their resistance against the Red Army; in 1941–44, ostracised for continuing to fight the Russians; at the end of World War II, castigated for their failure to heed western advice to trust Moscow; in 1948, written off as lost for signing a treaty with the Soviet Union; and finally, until the disintegration of the USSR they were subjected to a kind of character assassination through use of the term 'Finlandisation' to denote supine submission to Soviet domination."

The fact that this term, hated by the Finns themselves, has been almost forgotten is a sign of how this country has changed since the beginning of the 1990s. Finland has discarded its dual identity in which it was seen on the one hand as an enlightened, peace-loving Nordic nation, clean and unspoiled and heroic and healthy, and on the other hand as dictated by its position – physical and political – in relation to Russia. By committing itself in the long term to active membership of the European Union, which it joined on 1 January 1995, and by participating in the euro single currency system, Finland has sent a series of unequivocal signals of its wish to move away from the Russian sphere of influence.

## Baltic attitudes

Yet as recently as 1991, President Mauno Koivisto was referring to the crisis in the Baltic republics as "an internal Soviet affair", causing dismay to some western and Baltic leaders. Most betrayed of all, perhaps, were the Finns themselves, among whom pro-independence sentiment for the Baltics, especially Finland's ethnic cousin Estonia, ran high. One newspaper

editorial remarked: "Public opinion is finding it difficult to accept the realism of this country's foreign policy leadership and its appeal to Finland's own national interest."

Defenders of the government line explained their belief that interference from the outside would only increase tensions. (A week after the Koivisto statement, Russian Interior Ministry troops attacked the Lithuanian TV station and more than a dozen ended up dead.) Some also reasoned that other countries could take stronger stances because they did not share a border with the Russians, and that this border has always made things different for Finland.

As well, Finnish Communists played a big role in organising the labour force that powered early postwar industry. At one stage they held 50 out of 200 seats in the *Eduskunta* (Parliament or National Assembly). The Russians used them as a vessel through which to channel influence. This method was most effective when the Communists were most powerful. Twice, the Rus-

---

**PRECEDING PAGES:** President Urho Kekkonen meets Soviet leader Nikita Khrushchev in 1960.
**LEFT:** Workers' Statue in Helsinki.
**RIGHT:** hydrofoil to Estonia.

sians were able to wield enough influence to lead the government to resign.

There was a flip side. Until 1947, Finland was observed by the Allied Control Commission, which included many Russian officers. (The Commission among other tasks observed war crimes trials; the longest sentence given was 10 years, served on ex-president Risto Ryti for his dealings with the Germans.) The officers' presence was repulsive and frightening to anti-Communist Finns. The fear that Finland would go the way of Czechoslovakia in 1948 so rattled even the brave Marshal Mannerheim (who was president briefly after the war) that he made per-

by a centre-right alliance that was the most politically conservative in the republic's history.

The move right kept step with the economic growth of Finland, a phenomenon of rapid change. Divested in 1917 of the lucrative 19th-century trade links it had enjoyed as a trading post of Imperial Russia, Finland had to start-from scratch. Until World War II, Finland had a stagnant subsistence agricultural economy. Postwar industrialisation pulled it out of this quagmire, and Finland became, eventually, rich, even if some of the richest individual Finns were often forced to live abroad in order to avoid the massive bills imposed on them by

sonal provisions to flee the country, just in case.

The Communist left eventually lost its grip. The Social Democrats (SDP), eventually became the dominant political party in Finland and held that position until 1991. The SDP found itself in a so-called "red-blue" coalition with the leading rightist party, the conservative Kokoomus.

## Moving right

The Social Democrats' gradual move towards the centre was emblematic of the political picture as a whole. Since the war, the sympathies of the majority have moved steadily towards more traditional, "bourgeois" European values. After the 1991 parliamentary vote, Finland was ruled

their government's taxation policies. This accomplishment was of crucial importance to Finns, and also somewhat calmed western worries that the country was too close to the USSR.

But long before the economic miracle, Finland had to carve out its political place in the postwar world, a world that rapidly began to militarise along east–west lines. Finland chose neutrality. Fathered by J.K. Paasikivi, as prime minister (1944–46) then president (1946–56) of the Finnish republic, and Urho Kekkonen, president from 1956–83, the doctrine of neutrality was one that shunned commitment in favour of "peace-oriented policy". Non-alignment remains the official government foreign policy line, and was confirmed as such in a security and defence report in March 1997.

But Finnish newspapers no longer temper their criticisms of their eastern neighbour, as was the case under Kekkonen's code of "self-censorship". Finland also allows itself the option of participation in United Nations or NATO crisis management, a policy that saw Finnish peacekeeping forces in Lebanon and Kosovo.

Neutrality has meant many different things in many different situations. In postwar

**INTERNATIONAL VOICE**

In 1955 Finland was admitted into the United Nations; in 1994 it became a member of the NATO Partnership for Peace programme.

Finland, which was not even three decades independent by the war's end, resolved that it wanted "out" of the conflict, and bargained for postwar agreements along this line. The Soviet Union pushed hard for certain concessions, and depleted Finland had little to bargain with. Compromises were inevitable.

## Soviet lease

The most controversial compromise was in the 1944 peace treaty with Moscow. In it, the Finns agreed to lease the Porkkala Peninsula (near

Finland, the neutral Paasikivi-Kekkonen line seemed to reassure Finns that their country would not become a battleground for the Soviet Union and its considerable enemies. To gain such reassurance, Finland had to play a tough political game and walk a narrow line. The tense mistrust that ruled east–west relations during the Cold War caused a foreign policy challenge that would have been formidable even to a nation far older and more powerful than this one.

**LEFT:** the Finnish Parliament *(Eduskunta)* in Helsinki.
**ABOVE:** Finnish Parliament, with one of the world's highest quota of women, in session.

Helsinki) to the Soviets for 50 years for use as a military base *(see page 187)*. The situation was defused in 1955 when the two parties agreed to the lease's cancellation. Porkkala's return seemed to signal good things to the west, as Finland joined the United Nations; in the 1950s, the country also joined the International Monetary Fund.

When Paasikivi began formulating his foreign policy line he stressed "correct and irreproachable neighbourly relations" with the Soviet Union. The phrase may have sounded ingratiating to western ears but made sense to the majority of Finns, who needed to believe that the Soviet Union could be bent into the shape of a benign neighbour.

In 1948, Finland and the Soviet Union signed the Treaty of Friendship, Co-operation, and Mutual Assistance (FCMA), which was originally to have expired in 2003. This complex agreement was not a military alliance *per se*. Drawn up in clear reference to the Germans' having used Finland to attack the Russians, it demanded mutual protection; both pledged to prevent outside forces from using their territory to attack the other; and Finland promised to join no alliances hostile to the Soviet Union.

This last measure was perceived by the Finns to be in line with the neutral policy they had already decided on. Other western nations, however, beginning to labour under sharp Cold War polarities, felt that if Finland was not for them, it could easily be against them. In this way began the declamations that Finland was teetering on the edge of becoming part of the Eastern Bloc.

## The NATO question

Every other nation liberated by the western Allies in World War II eventually became NATO members. It was only Finland, the one country with a border with the Soviet Union to emerge outside the Eastern Bloc after World War II, and Yugoslavia who did not become Allies of either east or west.

When Finland joined in the formation of the Nordic Council in 1952, the Soviet editorials became hysterical: "Surely this means Finland will be joining NATO?" The fact that the Summer Olympics were set to be held in Helsinki also in 1952 added fuel to the fire. The Soviets interpreted preparations for the event, such as the building of a south coast highway, as proof of more plans to include Finland in a general military threat – perhaps even war – against the USSR.

Whatever else is true of the immediate postwar period, the fact that Finland did not decide to enter into the western fold but chose to go it alone did not endear it to the non-Communist world. A lone wolf is always suspect; Finland even refused to join the Marshall Plan.

## Economic progress

Nonetheless, economic progress began in earnest. The Finnish-Soviet 1944 peace agreement had included demands for war reparations of over $600 million. Ironically, this demand for money helped build the new economy. Post-

### SUPPORT FOR THE UNITED NATIONS

In addition to economic success, another Finnish accomplishment has been its deep commitment to the United Nations since it joined in 1955. Marjatta Rasi, the UN ambassador during the 1990–91 Gulf Crisis (Finland was a 1990 non-permanent member of the Security Council) says Finland "joined the UN after the difficulties of the immediate postwar period were safely behind and the main lines of our policy of neutrality had been laid down."

Finland strongly supports UN peacekeeping functions, in which thousands (nearly 30,000 by 1990) of Finns have participated. It has also contributed a high number of UN military observers and specialists. Involvement began during the Suez Canal crisis in 1956. There has since been a strong Finnish presence in peacekeeping operations in Lebanon, Golan, Gaza and the Sinai. But the most outstanding efforts were made on behalf of Namibia. On a Finnish initiative, in 1970 the UN set up a Namibia Fund, and Finland also pursued the 1971 International Court of Justice ruling that South Africa's presence in Namibia was illegal. When Namibia gained independence in 1990, it was Martti Ahtisaari who directed the transition.

Finland contributes generously to refugee aid programmes; the total Nordic contribution equals 25 per cent of the UN High Committtee on Refugees fund.

war Finland was low on cash but met payments by negotiating the payment of some of its debt in manufactured engineering products such as farming and forestry machinery, and ships.

These items became staple sources of export income in Finland's postwar years as a growth economy. Before that economy got off the ground, however, most Finns lived in poverty. To this day, older Finns enthusiastically buy chocolate when they travel abroad because of postwar memories of chocolate being impossible to obtain.

Finland had to stretch its meagre resources yet further to deal with one of the largest resettlements of a civilian population in the world. Nearly 400,000 dispossessed Karelians (and a handful of Skolt Sami) were given free land and donations of whatever the others could afford to give, which was little. Most Karelians, already poor in their homeland, arrived only with what they and their horses could carry.

In 1950, a barter trade agreement was signed between the Finns and the Soviets. It was in force until 1990, when the Soviets abruptly announced they would not sign the next five-year extension. The reason given was that continuing it would hinder Soviet pursuit of survival on a free market economy basis. The true Soviet aim was to sell its oil for hard cash. While in force, the barter agreement was worth a fortune. It provided Finland with a completely protected market for tonnes of consumer goods each year. The heavy equipment and cheap clothes and shoes sent over were traded for Soviet oil, enough to cover 90 per cent of Finnish needs.

The Finnish trade balance suffered for the treaty's cancellation by a disputed but significant amount as the USSR was Finland's fifth-largest trading partner. Soviet-orientated Finnish producers foundered or went bankrupt. The Finns had to pay cash for oil and wait for the Soviets to pay them a $2 million debt.

## Continuing crisis

While Finland was quickly able to shine in the United Nations arena, crises at home went on. In 1961, the USSR sent Finland a note suggesting "military consultations" regarding the 1948

FCMA. That note was probably sent because of Soviet fear of escalating (west) German militarism in the Baltic. The harm the note caused to Finland derived from the term "military consultations". Both sides had maintained the Treaty of Friendship, Co-operation and Mutual Assistance was not a military alliance, but an emblem of co-operation between two neighbours who were not allied.

Nikita Khruschev and Urho Kekkonen conferred privately and the consultations were announced "deferred". What the Soviets had been worried about, though, was clear: that Finland was not equipped to stop the west from

using it as an attack flank. The Kekkonen-Khruschev exchange was never made wholly public, but after the "Note Crisis", Finland began shoring up its military forces. Finland sought, and got, from the British a reinterpretation of the Paris Peace Treaty of 1947 allowing it to purchase missiles, forbidden by the original treaty.

The Soviets throughout the 1970s were to try to make life difficult for the Finns several more times. One Soviet ambassador decided to meddle in an internal wrangle of the Finnish Communist Party – President Kekkonen demanded his recall to the USSR. The fibre of Finnish society was now more firmly

**LEFT:** floating logs down lakes and rivers to Finland's busy wood and paper factories.

**RIGHT:** Finland's first female president, Tarja Halonen.

established and the left-wing elements were mere ragged ends.

A more prosperous Finland was more difficult to "strong-arm"; by now West Germany, Sweden and the United Kingdom were Finland's major trading partners, not the USSR. Trees had become its "green gold", and it looked as though the pulp and paper industry's economic success would mean no looking back.

## High living

In the 1970s and 1980s, Finland enjoyed one of the highest gross national products in the world and pulled up its standard of living and social services to be in line with Sweden's. In 1989–90, a survey showed Finland to be the most expensive country in the world, outstripping Japan. Fantastically high agricultural subsidies, and industrial cartels which set artificially high prices, were the main culprits and brought difficult consequences.

A lot of Finns, though, made a lot of money, and spent it with abandon. But it wasn't so easy to cover up the fact that they'd been poor cousins for so long. It is hard to believe when one explores Helsinki's well-stocked, stylish shops today, but even as late as the early 1980s one could look in shoe-shop windows and gasp

### DISCUSSION ARENA

In 1975, the Final Act of the Conference on Security and Co-operation in Europe (CSCE) was concluded in Helsinki. It was a public relations victory, an event that could help Finland be seen as a place of diplomacy and neutrality. Helsinki established itself as a "Vienna of the north", full of diplomats and police barricades. The CSCE resumed in Helsinki in 1992. Presidents Bush and Gorbachev met here in 1990 as the US sought to clear the way for action against Iraq in the Gulf War, and in 1997 presidents Yeltsin and Clinton held a Helsinki summit. The capital also held talks between US and Russian leaders on the deployment of peacekeeping forces in Kosovo in 1999.

at the ugly, out-of-fashion footwear on display; these were the designs that had been dumped on the Soviets for the past 30 years. One could buy Gucci shoes, but at costs that made Parisian boutique prices look like flea-market deals. There was little to choose from between the two extremes. By the end of the 1980s, the gap was closing, but prices were still wildly high, especially on imports. It was not until EU membership in the latter half of the 1990s that prices levelled and began to bear some resemblance to those in other western European countries. Although it was once the world's most expensive city, 2003 figures show that Helsinki is now cheaper than European rivals such as Oslo, London and Geneva. It also has the honour of being in the top five cities in the world in terms of lifestyle.

## Economic agony

Starting in the late 1980s, Finland went into economic recession. At the same time, the challenges of the "new" Europe were growing. When the rest of Europe was drawing together like a large mutual aid society, Finland seemed to repel the trend. The official word was that it had no interest in joining the European Community, but was firmly committed to continue as a European Free Trade Association

14 per cent of its gross domestic product and unemployment soared from 3 per cent to just under 20 per cent. Pragmatists saw the need to shift from a commodity-based economy looking towards Russia to a manufacturing and service economy looking towards the west. Nokia, the country's leading electronics company, showed the way as its sales of mobile phones doubled its profits, and by the end of the 1990s the company had established itself as the world leader in its field. The changed circumstances also convinced many people that it would be worth seeking shelter within the European Union, and 57 per cent of the country's 4 mil-

member that endorsed a strong European Economic Space. Under such circumstances, however, the Finnish economy was less likely to improve quickly.

Those attitudes changed rapidly in the 1990s. The collapse of the former Soviet Union, which had accounted for a fifth of Finland's trade, combined with the world slide into recession to produce the worst slump suffered by any European state since the 1930s.

Between 1991 and 1993, the economy lost

lion voters opted in a consultative referendum in October 1994 to become part of the EU from January 1995.

## Reluctant members

Objections to EU membership were still vociferous. Many still argued that joining the European Union wouldn't change things for the better since the EU's agricultural policy was not one of its glories. However, in the first year of membership, food prices fell by 8 per cent, and the feeling of being part of a massive trading group created a sense of security that promised well for the future. The five-party "rainbow coalition" that came to power in

**LEFT:** the modern Helsinki lifestyle allows time for an evening of rollerblading on the waterfront.
**RIGHT:** Nokia mobile phones infiltrate Finnish life.

1995 promised little except austerity, but the new mood of realism enabled them to peg pay rises to 1.7 per cent and 2 per cent over two years, helping to keep inflation very low at around 1.5 per cent.

Deeply rooted agrarian loyalties were also hard to shake in Finland, even if full-time farmers were a dying breed. Finally, Finns had an instinctive wish to keep foreigners from buying a slice of their wealth-producing forests. For individuals, the idea of for-

## GO-BETWEEN COUNTRY

"It may take a generation before commercial order returns to Russia, but for sure it will do so," said one industrialist. "And when it does Finland will still be the natural gateway for western trade and investment."

den was keen to join (which it did, also in 1995). Not only was Sweden one of Finland's most important trade partners, it was also a beacon of political and socio-economic policy for Finland.

Ten years previously, the country couldn't have contemplated a move such as joining the EU without first seeking permission from Russia, but now Finns began to enjoy the heady freedom of making their own decisions. They realised, though, that eventually

eigners buying forest brought fears of loss of privacy, something sacred to the national character. The forest industrialists had more pragmatic fears: namely, that introduction of foreign buyers would mean the break-up of the cartel-style domestic price-fixing mechanisms which helped shield the industry from real competition. Prices in this and other industries were thus artificially high, and in some sectors competition was virtually impossible.

The objection to EU membership had always been the risk of compromising Finnish neutrality, although neutral countries like Ireland had flourished in the EU and neutral Swe-

Russia was bound to regain its economic strength and that they could offer to the rest of Europe their own invaluable experience of negotiating with the Russians. There was some immediate benefit, too: because of poor facilities at Russian ports, western exporters began shipping bulk goods to Finnish harbours and transporting them on by road to Russia.

## Pruning back the Welfare State

Until the recession that hit Finland in the early 1990s, the welfare state was one of the great sacrosanct untouchables of Finnish life. Using the model provided by its neighbour

Sweden, Finland launched a programme to extend its state welfare facilities in the years following World War II.

Before the war these facilities had been relatively modest, with the first measure affecting the whole (still largely rural) population taking the form of a Pensions Act in 1937. A Child Allowance Act followed in 1948, giving state recognition to the need for child protection, and the Pensions Act was brought up to date in the late 1950s, along with the introduction of the private pensions option. The 1960s and 1970s also saw the establishment of laws that made provision for sickness insurance

unprecedented postwar peaks of about 20 per cent, and Finnish banks found themselves in a crisis which had to be solved with the backing of state funds. Pressure mounted on the availability of funds for welfare state provision, and the agreements between business, government and then influential trade unions no longer seemed written in stone. Charges for health care increased and taxation on pensions was introduced, at the same time as workers were encouraged by tax breaks to contribute to private pension schemes to supplement their less generous state pensions.

Finland's social structure has withstood con-

and health care – and the whole time state spending on welfare measures mushroomed.

For decades, Finns were prepared to endure massive income tax rates in return for generous and comprehensive welfare benefits. Unemployment was in any case insignificant in European terms, and poverty, which had been deep at the end of the war, was all but eradicated. Then came the economic turmoil of the early 1990s: suddenly, unemployment was soaring into double figures and reaching

**LEFT:** Helsinki was named one of the European Cities of Culture for the year 2000.
**ABOVE:** prominent female politician, Suvi-Anne Siimes.

siderable pressure from the increased poverty and unemployment that followed the recession. There is probably a bigger gap than ever before between the haves and the have-nots. For all that, the welfare state has held firm and still provides a sound, basic safety net. Finns have been prepared to see it trimmed and pruned, but they would still balk at the idea of removing it completely.

## Electing a new future

The last decade has seen an element of stability in Finnish political life, with successive Social Democrat-led coalition governments under Paavo Lipponen ruling from 1995-2003, and

Social Democrat presidents gaining victory in 1994 (Ahtisaari) and 2000 (Halonen).

Recently, however, Finns voted for change, and in the March 2003 election the Centre Party was returned as the largest group in parliament. The former Rainbow Coalition has been replaced by a Rainbow Opposition – the Convervatives lost heavily in 2003, the Left Alliance had their participation in Government vetoed by the Centre Party. The Greens, in spite of making substantial gains, had their return to power blocked by Paavo Lipponen, piqued at their withdrawal from his government over the issue of nuclear power.

The most notable change has been the election of Finland's first female Prime Minister – Anneli Jäätteenmäki, although it remains to be seen if this improves the position of women in general. Lipponen, it is thought, will retain a major role, either at home or within the EU.

## Scandal and success

Modern Finland is quite a different country from the one that started the 1990s in a daze of uncertainty about its future. Its brushes with corruption – or rather the exposure of its extent in public and commercial life – have brought it closer, paradoxically, to a "real world" from which it had always felt protected by the cocoon of its neutrality. The share scandal surrounding the resignation of the Minister of Transport and Communications, Matti Aura, in 1999 proved that accountability had become a valid word in the Finnish political vocabulary. Aura left his post when the president of the Sonera telecoms company, Pekka Vellamo, was dismissed for alleged share-holding irregularities at the time of the state-owned company's first share issue. Sonera – for a while a byword for the IT boom – has also been implicated in scandals involving the bugging of employees' phones and the waste of huge amounts of money on buying almost useless UMTS licences, leading to investigations of many of its leading directors.

In the unrelated but equally political sphere of the Olympic organisation, the Finnish IOC member Pirjo Häggman resigned from her committee position when she was implicated in investigations into the Salt Lake City Games bid.

## The European dimension

At the same time, Finland has evolved into a more outward-looking and cosmopolitan country. Finns, especially the younger, urbanised generations, have looked to Europe as their centre of political reference.

Finland had its chance to prove this in the second half of 1999 when it served as EU President country, hosting over 70 special European meetings, including two major summits. Helsinki's European City of Culture role, shared with eight other European cities in 2000, and the celebration in the same year of the capital's 450th anniversary gave the whole country a confident platform upon which to enter the new millennium.

Helsinki has developed to such a point that it is now a city where many languages – English, Russian, German, Swedish, French and Italian, among others – are heard daily and on a routine basis *(see page 103)*, yet where the local language remains as strong as ever. It is the capital of a country that is newly certain of its place in the world and which is learning to relish that self-confidence. ❑

**LEFT:** a ship unloads its cargo at Helsinki's busy harbour, an economic success story for Finland.

# Ladies First

Finnish women seem to many to have some of the strongest advantages of their gender in Europe. They certainly claim a pioneering pedigree in equal rights, since in 1906 their country was the third in the world, after Australia and New Zealand – and therefore the first country in Europe – to enshrine in its law eligibility to vote and all other full political rights for women. It has been progressive in most areas of gender equality too, making it possible for Finnish women to join the clergy of the country's biggest church, the Evangelical Lutheran, in 1988, and passing an amendment to its Equality Act in 1995 committing national and local government committees to take a 40 percent quota of women.

Having narrowly missed out on electing its first female president, when Martti Ahtisaari pipped Elisabeth Rehn in 1994, Finns made up for lost time in 2000, when the Social Democrat Tarja Halonen beat the Centre Party's Esko Aho. Halonen had a long past in radical and social politics, and in spite of the reduced powers of the President, has enjoyed high approval ratings in the first three years of her encumbency.

Finnish woman-power has spread through all levels of government too, with Eva-Riitta Siitanen, Helsinki's mayor at the end of the 1990s, a conspicuous example. Sirkka Hämäläinen was the first woman governor of the Bank of Finland in the early 1990s, and even before her election as president in 2000, Tarja Halonen had excelled as foreign minister.

Most recently, Finland finally got its first female Prime Minister, with Anneli Jäätteenmäki of the Centre Party leading the new coalition Government from April 2003. Indeed, women enjoy remarkable influence in government compared to other nations. The male–female ratio of parliament members in 1999 was 126 to 74, one of the highest in the world for women, and eight of the 17 Council of State or government ministers were women.

Although on the surface these figures appear enlightened, and although women lawyers, editors-in-chief, doctors and other professionals abound throughout Finland, it takes only a glance through the annual reports of the country's largest

**RIGHT:** Prime Minister Anneli Jäätteenmäki is just one of many high profile women in Finland.

companies to confirm that, despite this, Finnish women have yet to make a significant breakthrough into the higher echelons of business. Sari Baldauf, the Nokia Telecommunications President, born in 1955, is a rare exception to this boardroom gender rule.

"According to the official and theoretical version of things, we are very equal with men," says Anu Ek, a 42-year-old Finnish magazine editor. "But in private business, we still earn only about 80 percent of what men are getting paid. Promotion is by no means automatic for women: men are usually first in line. And this is the case even though Finnish women are very highly educated.

More than 50 percent of university students, for example, are female."

But legislative support for women at work is very strong and very effective. The Finnish woman who does not work full-time has become a rarity and time off to raise a family is not a hindrance. Since 1996, all children up to the age of seven are guaranteed a day-care place. Parents – father or mother – are entitled to child-care leave until their child turns three, during which time their jobs are secured and an allowance is granted. Standard parental leave of 158 days after the birth of a child, usually taken by the mother, is subsidised by an allowance equivalent to two-thirds of the parent's normal income. ❏

# THE FINNISH CHARACTER

*Blond, reserved, rustic – some of these stereotypes remain true, but Finns are moving with the times, embracing a more international approach to modern living*

**A**re Finns manic-depressive by nature? What else can one be when the climate changes so abruptly from freezing winter (with almost total darkness 24 hours a day) to really hot summer with no darkness at all?

Change is so deep-rooted in the Finnish soul that the nation accepts almost any new innovation with little resistance, be it the new currency, the euro, or technological features in mobile phones. "The only constant is change," Finns will tell anyone who asks, but despite this, traditions are never completely forgotten.

Change is most visible in nature – no new day is similar to yesterday. After the springtime thaw, everything grows rapidly until its time arrives for a slow death before winter. Only for a few weeks around the winter solstice, the nature stops, deep frozen, for a pause – but then Finns prepare for the busy Christmas time and their New Year's resolutions. The big wheel keeps on turning, another year means new opportunities for change, and daylight hours start getting longer again.

## Pacifist nation

Finns have reached the beginning of the 21st century with both style and class. Finland has helped broker peace deals in the Balkans and Northern Ireland, and their enthusiasm for UN humanitarianism contrasts with a scepticism about NATO operations.

What a difference to the way the century began. A hundred years earlier, this small nation struggled to defend its language against the Russian Czarist regime. Being dominated by both Swedes and Russians, today Finns resent both nations, and small details such as success in sports or international trade are scrutinised carefully. Finnish Nokia mobile phones, for example, sell more than their Swedish competitors, and, in ice-hockey, Finns often defeat both Swedish and Russian teams. These things

**PRECEDING PAGES:** Tampere's funfair; reindeer races in Lapland. **LEFT:** typical Karelian dress. **RIGHT:** international designers now grace the ski slopes.

matter to Finns. Yet, although they may not forget, they are willing to forgive: across the eastern border, Finnish trucks carry emergency assistance to the struggling Russians now living in great poverty – only a decade after the traumatic period when Moscow dictated many internal issues within Finland.

By nature, Finns are peacemakers. At war, they always lose – there are few national war heroes of any note – but at peace, Finns certainly seem to be winning.

## Ghosts from the past

To what extent can a land be judged by its ancient heroes? In the case of many countries, only an enemy would wish to invoke the memory of certain inglorious characters. With Finland, however, the idea is quite appealing. The main characters in the Finnish epic the *Kalevala* are patriotic, and the heroes are noble warriors (*see page 95*). Yet these strong men are troubled hair-tearers in private, and have great difficulty in waxing poetic when they set out to woo and win the girl. The women, in contrast, are strongheaded, matriarchal, and very family-orientated.

The land itself is full of nature and wood-spirits. No one in the *Kalevala* would deny that the woods have sanctity, and that the lakes and rivers are their little piece of heaven on earth. When one of the female heroes wants to escape her fate, for example, she simply turns into a nimble, stream-swimming fish.

> ### LIVING WITH SPACE
>
> Finns are greatly moulded by their numbers. Europe's fifth largest country in size has a population of just over five million, which is also largely homogeneous.

who's never happier than when he's showing off his possessions and singing his own praises.

Yet some stereotypes are universally recognised as true. "We are forest people," said Jarl Kohler, managing director of the Finnish Forest Industries Federation. "The forests are our security and our livelihood." And the security isn't just theoretical or a romantic notion of rural idylls: more than 400,000 Finns own a plot of forest and everyone has the right of access to the land *(see pages 128–9)*.

One can only take the analogy so far, of course, but it's far better to start with a nation's self-made heroes, with at least some roots in reality, than the stereotypical characters others have created for them.

There are so many paradoxes in the Finnish character that it would be hard to convince the sceptical foreigner that there isn't more than a dash of schizophrenia in the national psyche. For every ranting drunk, there's a raving tee-totaller. For every patriotic Finn who is as attached to Finland as to his own soul, there's one who leaves as soon as he can afford the fare, never to return. For every shrinking violet, there's an arrogant, cigar-smoking bombast

### Nordic links

The "typical Finn" is the result of a genetic combination that is 75 per cent identical to that of Swedes or other Scandinavians, but 25 per cent derived from tribes that wandered to Finland from east of the Ural Mountains, though some experts now dispute this *(see page 21)*. This more Oriental strain accounts for certain physical traits that set Finns apart from their Nordic neighbours – finely pronounced cheekbones and quite small eyes, which are slatey-grey or blue.

Karelians (Finns from the very east of the country) are stockier and also have more sallow complexions than other Finns. They are slightly smaller in stature than people from the west coast, whose ancestors merged with the gargantuan Vikings. Until the end of World War II, the Karelians' diet was extremely poor and they had one of the highest incidences of heart disease in the west, which may in part account for their slightly less healthy looks.

The rest of the Finns are taller, usually fair-haired (though, overall, Finns are the "darkest" of the Nords) and, much like any other nationality, vary greatly in most other ways.

Some of the most famous Finns are sportsmen and women, taking advantage of their generally strong and healthy physiques. As a norm. And the infamous reserve applies as much to other Nords as it does to Finns.

## City versus country

The ideas of those who would totally subjugate Finnish culture are no more appealing than those of the super-patriot who would have nothing change. Finns are on a pendulum swinging out towards the rest of the world, but they are far better equipped than they think they are to meet the challenges with equanimity.

For a traditionally rural country, Finland is becoming more urbanised. Some 80 per cent of Finns live on 2 percent of the land. Domestic

nation, Finns are great lovers of the outdoors and of sport, and some young Finns seem to live for little else but their athletic activities (*see page 111*).

The Finnish personality is harder to pin down but, if you go to Finland with preconceived stereotypes at the ready, you will no doubt be able to satisfy any or all of them. You can't help but notice the drunks, for instance, but if that is what you are expecting to see, you will no doubt see disproportionately more than is the

**LEFT:** out of the sauna and into the ice pool is a healthy winter tradition.
**ABOVE:** in summer, al fresco dining is fashionable.

### A RESERVED NATION

It is characteristic of Finns to speak quietly, even in stage whispers, when a couple are conversing in a public place. If you converse loudly, you will draw stares. (Perhaps many who drink heavily do so in order to gain licence to shout.) Finns put great value on privacy. The summer cabin *(kesämökki)* also tells you something of Finnish privacy. These are usually set back from the lakeshore among the trees, and as far from other dwellings as possible. The idea of time spent here is to revel in your own plot. However, young women are becoming more demonstrative – in Helsinki they greet each other with hugs, kisses and big smiles.

emigration is accelerating – Finns are moving from small towns to Greater Helsinki, Tampere, Turku and Oulu. The much publicised *"etätyö"* (distance working via the Internet) has attracted quite a few, but most people still try to escape to cities. This is often a result of unemployment and decreasing services as post offices, shops and bus services close in villages.

But rural life has its attractions. People tend to live in large houses surrounded by gardens. Farmers are fewer but get enough subsidies to continue a comfortable lifestyle. Farm holidays are common, although some wonder whether rural Finland is turning into a tourist reserve.

### GYPSY ROOTS

One of the oldest groups in Finland who are not ethnic Finns are the Romany gypsies, whose womenfolk are instantly recognisable by their elaborate embroidered lace blouses and voluminous skirts. Although today most speak only Finnish, few have intermarried, so their dark good looks stand out against fairer Finns.

Although most gypsies are no longer nomadic and live instead in houses and flats, some families still tend to wander, especially in autumn, from one harvest festival to another. Little horse-trading is done these days, however, and the gypsies' appearance at these fairs is little more than a vestige of nostalgia.

## Society and culture

Although Finns fought a bloody class war in 1918, modern Finland is less class conscious than it has ever been. Distinction between town and country is more relevant as the "rainbow government" *(see page 61)* includes both left- and right-wing parties, and the "rural" Keskusta party is outside the government.

But the traditional welfare society is losing its grip. The rich are getting richer, the poor remain poor. Unemployment was cut from over 20 percent to around 10 percent during the second half of the 1990s, but poverty still haunts certain suburbs in Helsinki and entire regions in the northern half of Finland.

Popular culture has grown, along with commercial media (there are now four national TV channels, two financed commercially, and many local TV stations) embracing young and old. Even the Swedish-speaking minority is persuaded to consume the mainstream culture, especially in big towns. Many younger Finns, shedding their parents' unease, have gone on to study, work and travel abroad, as well as welcoming all things foreign to Finland. While some older Finns still have not abandoned the dreary, grey outfits that used to dominate the clothing racks, their grandchildren sport fluorescent clothing and embrace fads from Britain and the US with near-fanatical fervour.

Honesty is another Finnish stereotype, but one which is borne out by the annual survey of the world's most honest business practices, which usually has Finland and New Zealand vying for top spot. In spite of high taxes, evasion is no higher than in any other European country. Most Finns, especially those who have returned from low-tax, low-service countries abroad, accept the tax burden as a means of maintaining top-class social services.

The home is still highly venerated and Finns spend a considerable amount of time and money on their properties. As a contrast to many southern countries where people dress well and live poorly, Finns live like royalty but dress crudely. One female minister recently raised eyebrows in an international meeting by wearing a violet jeans jacket. Despite their move towards international lifestyles, sartorial style remains low on the Finnish agenda.  ❏

**LEFT:** Finns are brought up with a deep appreciation of their countryside.

# Finnish Youth

**B**e it rollerskating or bungy jumping (one Finnish company claims to have the tallest bungy-jumping crane in the world), young Finns keenly jump on each new band-wagon and let loose until the next craze comes along. Even Finland itself creates new trends, which transfer to the youth of other nations. Mobile phones and pagers are more common here than anywhere else in the world (Nokia is Finland's largest company); every minute a beep announces a new message in buses, public libraries or restaurants. Young kids get given mobile phones from worried parents – a sort of an electronic nanny which announces meal times. Many parents pay the equivalent of hundreds of pounds each month for their children's phone bills – a heavy price for mere gossiping.

The Internet is another daily tool among Finnish youth. Domestic chatting channels, such as Kiss Chat or City Chat, attract thousands of teenagers daily, to gossip or to talk dirty. Internet is available at most schools and public libraries for free, and home usage is increasing fast. IRC attracts an equally large amount of Finnish "nerds".

Subcultures are strong, from religious networks within the Lutheran or other churches to Devil worshippers who occasionally feature in national headlines through their attacks on graveyards. Indeed, Finland is no longer a land of innocents – if it ever was: almost any phenomenon can be found, from punk hairdos to drunken teenage girls.

Finns watch a Scandinavian version of MTV, but equally enthusiastically a Canadian-created youth programme by the name Jyrki ("George"). Jyrki has a studio in the Lasipalatsi media centre in Helsinki, and the daily live programme attracts large crowds who want to spot their favourite rock stars in the flesh. In 1999, one of Jyrki's hosts, Joonas Hytönen, started his own talk show at the tender age of 24, which has not only been immensely popular, but is the most credible Finnish version of the popular American audience-led chat shows, which is something the older generation never managed to create in Finland.

More commercial attractions are available: vast multiplex-style cinemas have arrived in Helsinki, Tampere and elsewhere – Finnish film production has been booming since 1998. Local radio stations have mushroomed, including Kiss FM and the French-owned NRJ, and popular music keeps getting heavier.

Young rock bands may be homegrown, but success has to be sought internationally. Hybrid Children, a heavy rock band that has been playing since 1991, sells well in Japan, but in Finland, although it attracts an audience of 13 to 25-year-olds, sells only a few thousand records domestically. "It's not a way to get rich – we earn about the same as being on the dole," says one band member. However, numerous summer festivals mean both bands and fans can party and dance almost every warm weekend away.

Many of the youthful IT-millionaires of the late 1990s lost their money as quickly as they had made it, but Finnish youth culture continued to make an impact, with Bomfunk MCs and Darude recording hits throughout the world. Drug use is lower than in much of the rest of Europe, but it is on the increase, along with under-age sex and drinking, causing parents to worry about where the new generation is headed.

Some people think that the recession in the early 1990s was to blame: parents were unemployed and the youth culture boomed, with unpredictable results. Others argue that it would have happened anyway, and that it is merely one aspect of the new, liberal Finland. ❑

**RIGHT:** Summer festivals are the most likely events to see Finnish youth getting together.

# ART, ARCHITECTURE AND DESIGN

*Finland's struggle for national identity has led to an artistic heritage*
*that swings between ancient rural traditions and sparkling Modernism*

When Diaghilev, founder of the Russian Ballet, divided the Finnish painters of the 1890s into two camps – "those with a nationalistic outlook and those who follow the west" – he described a tension which has been present in Finnish art ever since.

Association with the art world of western Europe and the artistic expression of Finnish nationalism have been persistently seen as opposing forces. Taken to extremes, artists either belonged to Europe or to Finland. Paradoxically, those who have achieved world renown were able, by creating something essentially Finnish and therefore unique, to leap over national boundaries. Today, Finnish design and architecture are among Finland's best-known products, partly because they combine a universal modernism and a Finnish quality.

Because Finland is still relatively young as an independent country, much of the art produced during the past 100 years has been concerned with creating a national cultural identity. Until the 1880s, the nascent Finnish cultural scene was influenced by the country's political masters – first Sweden, then Czarist Russia. The few practising Finnish artists who were able to make a living from their work either trained or lived in Stockholm or St Petersburg.

## Searching for identity

The seeds of a specifically Finnish culture were sown when organised art training began in Turku in 1830. In 1845, Finland held its first art exhibition. The Finnish Art Society was founded in 1846. But it wasn't until the 1880s and 1890s that a truly Finnish artistic idiom began to emerge and Finnish artists were at last afforded some recognition at home and, by the end of the 19th century, internationally.

European artistic influences were strong as painters such as Albert Edelfelt (1854–1905) utilised the style of French naturalism. Yet,

while his style was initially imported from abroad, the subject of Edelfelt's paintings became increasingly Finnish in character.

In the 1880s, a motley group of painters took up the struggle for cultural identity, which paralleled the growth of Finnish nationalism and the desire for independence. Among those

artists were Akseli Gallén-Kallela (1865–1931), Pekka Halonen (1865–1933), Eero Järnefelt (1862–1937), Juho Rissanen (1873–1950) and Helena Schjerfbeck (1862–1946). They looked to the Finnish landscape and to ordinary Finns for subjects which were quintessentially Finnish. Within that framework, artistic styles varied from powerful realism to mythology, and sentimental bourgeois or fey naturalism.

## National Romanticism

While some painters, like Hugo Simberg (1873–1917), followed idiosyncratic, transcendental and Europe-based symbolist paths, a body of artists came to represent what was to be

---

**PRECEDING PAGES:** Karelian women, painted by Albert Edelfelt in 1887. **LEFT:** Rovaniemi Art Museum.
**RIGHT:** Akseli Gallén-Kallela, Finland's "national" artist.

called Finnish National Romanticism. Their focus on Finnishness – a subject dear to the heart of every Finn – meant that these artists enjoyed, and continue to enjoy, considerable popular appeal in Finland. Several artists chose deliberately to move among people whose mother-tongue was Finnish (at that time many urban intellectuals spoke Swedish) and whose traditional folk culture and rural living had, the artists believed, remained largely uncorrupted by either Swedish or Russian influences. They maintained that the Finnish peasant was the true Finn, and that a rural landscape was the only credible Finnish landscape – the country's cities

had been planned and designed under the sway of foreign rulers.

## Nationalist hangover

In a general sense, the legacy of National Romanticism is large, and has often been something of an incubus which restricted later artists who wished to look at urban Finland, to follow European movements, or to pursue abstract styles. Finnish popular taste in art continues to be dominated by both a nationalistic and a naturalistic preference. This conservatism has frustrated many an artist who wished to forge ahead in new directions.

### KARELIAN INFLUENCE

Still in hot pursuit of the essence of Finnishness, several painters began to go on forays to Karelia. Gallén-Kallela, often acclaimed as one of the most original talents in Nordic art, went to Karelia in 1890 and started the "Karelia" movement which sent 19th-century artists and writers to the area in droves, and continued the earlier travels of the author Elias Lönnrot *(see page 95).* Aino, The Defence of the Sampo *(Sammon puolustus)* and Joukahainen's Revenge *(Joukahaisen kosto)* show his use of a stylised, allegorical idiom. A seminal figure in Finnish culture, Gallen-Kallela's enormous contribution laid the foundations for contemporary Finnish design.

Groups like the October Group, whose motto was "in defence of Modernism, against isolationist nationalism", pushed hard against what is sometimes forbiddingly described as the "Golden Age" of Finnish art. Sculptor Sakari Tohka (1911–58) was a founding member of the October Group. Overthrowing the classicism of his Finnish forebears, he cast his sculptures in cement.

The October Group was not alone. Townscapes and urban Finland were the chosen subjects of another artistic backlash group, the "Torch Bearers", which consisted of Väinö Kunnas (1896–1929), Sulho Sipilä (1895–1949) and Ragnar Ekelund (1892–1960).

Today, contemporary art in Finland is well supported by state and private grants, and the work on show in the permanent and temporary exhibitions at Kiasma, the new Museum of Contemporary Art in Helsinki, would hardly be recognised as art by the National Romantics. "There are more opportunities to be experimental in Finland because of the support for the arts," says Minna Heikinaho. Her three-screen video installation *"Mun koti on katu ja se on näytelma"* ("My home is the street and it's a performance") was one of Kiasma's early shows, and her work epitomises the bolder attitude of Finnish artists born in the early 1960s.

Square and the Cathedral, the architectural leaders of National Romanticism – the partnership of Herman Gesellius (1874–1916), Armas Lindgren (1874–1929) and Eliel Saarinen (1873–1950) – used peasant timber and granite architecture as their sources.

Another leading exponent of the movement was Lars Sonck (1870–1956). Decidedly Gothic in outline, and uneasy on the eye because of the clash of smooth timber or symmetrical roof tiles with rough-hewn granite, National Romantic buildings like Helsinki's National Museum (designed 1901) and Tampere's Cathedral (designed 1899) have a gawky

"Artists are finding different contexts for what they do, making links between theatre, space and performance."

## National architecture

The pattern of Finnish fine art – swinging from nationalism to modernism – is mimicked in other art forms: crafts, architecture and design. Turning their backs on the Neo-classical designs of their predecessor C.L. Engel (1778–1840), whose buildings include Helsinki's Senate

**LEFT:** the Modernist Kiasma, Museum of Contemporary Art in Helsinki.
**ABOVE:** Alvar Aalto Museum in Jyväskylä.

ugliness. The partnership trio of architects did, however, begin to draw on more soothing, elongated Art Nouveau influences too. The plans for Helsinki Railway Station, originally designed by all three, were amended by Saarinen. The building as it now stands is far more Art Nouveau than National Romantic.

After independence in 1917, the driving need for a national identity diminished in the face of the need to rebuild the country. Beyond the capital, there are abundant instances of original and well-considered municipal architecture: the public library in Tampere, for instance, completed in 1986 is named *"Metso"*, Finnish for capercaillie, the forest bird whose shape its plan resembles. The forest reference is deliberate, but the attractive combination of copper and granite, both indigenous Finnish raw materials, transcends the gimmick. The library's design, like many public Finnish buildings, was the result of an architectural competition and was the work of the husband-and-wife team of Reima and Rauli Pietilä.

## Struggling with Modernism

Finland, a relatively new nation whose cities were also deeply scarred in World War II, has bravely embraced Modernism and tried to make a virtue of it. Not all its efforts have been successful, however. The Merihaka estate of apartment blocks near Helsinki's Hakaniemi Square is bleak and heartless, while individual buildings in the Sörnäinen district make one wonder quite how Finland earned its reputation for fine architecture.

Neither is there a universal consensus about the virtues of various showpieces which shot up in central Helsinki at the end of the 1990s. Kiasma, the extraordinary Museum of Contemporary Art designed by American Stephen Holl and opened in 1998 *(see page 173)*, sprawls in metallic asymmetrical splendour behind the statue of the national hero Field

### ALVAR AALTO

One designer who became a household name in Finnish architecture was Alvar Aalto (1898-1976), who managed to fuse something Finnish with Modernism and revolutionised 20th-century architecture in the process. Aalto was the prime mover in Finland in the struggle to get the principles of modern architecture, and Modernism as a whole, accepted there. Once that was achieved, he then turned his attention to the rest of the world, via his two Finnish pavilions at the Paris exhibition of 1937 and the New York world fair of 1939. This was primarily to prove that Finland could contribute internationally to the world of architecture and design.

Aalto practised "organic" architecture, designing buildings to suit their environment as well as their purpose. Some of his buildings (the Enso Gutzeit building in Helsinki) appear to be of the archetypal, scorned "concrete block" variety – but, aesthetics aside, they are respected because they were the first to employ nakedly modern materials. Far more highly-regarded is Aalto's Finlandia Hall, the capital's concert and congress complex which gained in stature when it served as the main venue for the CSCE summit in 1975. Its crisp white profile seems to complement the contours of the park overlooking Töölö Bay, and it's hard to imagine the Helsinki profile without it.

Marshal Mannerheim, and it was this bold contrast that was condemned by older Finns, who also lamented the fact that a national architect was not chosen for the job. In fact it provides an ingenious counterpoint to the stolid, humourless Parliament House situated across the road.

The adjacent glass cube of the Sanoma-WSOY media group head office is regarded as cold and transparent by some, while the stately new Finnish National Opera House (Karhunen-Hyvämäki-Parkkinen, 1993), another landmark near Töölö Bay, is condemned by some as a characterless block *(see page 170)*.

It's an environment that has given rise to the creative spirit of the spiky inventions of internal and industrial designer Stefan Lindfors (born 1962) on the one hand, and the gentle paper jewellery of Janna Syvänoja (born 1960) on the other. Finland's giant names in plastics (Neste), ceramics (Arabia), textiles (Finlayson, Marimekko), jewellery (Kalevala Koru, Lapponia) and glass (Iittala, Nuutajärvi) industries periodically introduce pieces by new designers as well as those with established reputations such as that of Yrjö Kukkapuro, whose contemporary furniture is now in New York's Museum of Modern Art.

## Superb designs

There is boldness in the field of design too. Whatever the object – a tap, a telephone, a bowl, a chair – if its lines are smooth, if it employs modern materials like chrome or plastic with confidence or reinvents glass or wood, and if it fits its purpose perfectly, it is likely to be Finnish. Encouraged, like architecture, by the financial and prestigious carrot of open competitions, everyday items are ceaselessly redesigned.

**LEFT:** Marimekko textiles on sale in Helsinki.
**ABOVE:** the Pentik factory, producers of fine glassware and ceramics.

A legacy of Alvar Aalto is the Artek design and furniture company set up with his wife Aino, critic Nils-Gustav Hahl, and arts patron Maire Gullichsen in the 1930s and which still has a showroom in central Helsinki. The company's designers, working with bold colours and geometric shapes, have created products which are as identifiably Finnish as the handicrafts – woodcarving, rag-rug weaving and tapestry-making – which pertain to traditional culture. The distinctive and popular Fiskar scissors (Fiskars being a small village in southern Finland and a once thriving foundry) is one more example of how Finnish design has invaded international consciousness.

## A talent for invention

Just to the west of Helsinki, in the neighbouring city of Espoo close to the Helsinki University of Technology, is the Innopoli Building, housing the Foundation for Finnish Inventions. Started in 1971 with backing from the Finnish Ministry of Trade and Industry, the Foundation epitomises Finland's encouragement of the inventive spirit. But this is not a case of inventiveness for its own sake. The Foundation states its function as serving "as a link between inventors, innovators, consumers, businesses and industry in Finland or other parts of the world". The Foundation's activities are also a sign of

how Finns have recognised the need to diversify their industry. The staples of pulp and paper and related metals and engineering remain strong, but there has been a need to look in new directions.

Finland's most conspicuous and commercially successful inventions are those being placed on to the market with dizzying regularity by Nokia. The company, often mistakenly believed to be of Japanese origin, takes its name from the small and uneventful town in central Finland where it was founded. It has stayed ahead of the field in mobile phone technology by virtue of the slim and stylish designs of its basic cellphone models, but also because it has

recognised the need to continuously refresh its product selection with innovative gadgetry. The latest models feature integrated FM radios, multiparty calling, WAP facilities such as banking or receiving sports results, as well as camcorders, calorie counters, e-mailing and video streaming. As Swedish rivals Ericsson have floundered, Nokia has managed to keep ahead in this cut-throat business.

Nokia has given Finnish information technology a powerful boost: evidence of this is provided by the work, for example, of Risto Linturi, one of whose missions as head researcher with the Helsinki Telephone Corporation was to supervise the Helsinki Arena 2000 project, placing every aspect of Helsinki daily life and services on to its own Internet "mini-web". Elsewhere, California-based Finn Linus Torvalds was the inspiration behind the Linuxcomputer operating system, a set-up which had Bill Gates and his mighty Microsoft glancing over their shoulders with concern in the late 1990s.

## A better margarine

But Finnish innovation is not confined to communications technology. It spreads to Benecol, for instance, a margarine which not only contains no cholesterol but which has been proved to decrease blood cholesterol levels by as much as 14 percent, an effect of the ingredient stanol ester, a birch pulp extract. The only problem for the manufacturing company, Raisio, is how to bring the price of this product, a headline-grabber in the fanatically health-conscious USA, down to a level close to that of other margarines. Birch is also the source of the sweetener xylitol, pioneered in Finland in the late 1970s, used to flavour chewing gum and confectionery, and clinically proven to prevent tooth decay.

Finns have exploited their maritime heritage to good effect as well: shipbuilding innovations include the Azipod propulsion unit, a module that can be adopted by different vessels. The Azipod was developed and installed in vessels made at the Kvaerner-Masa ship-builders, whose yards in Helsinki and Turku have turned out the most advanced icebreakers and the biggest passenger ships in the world.  ❏

**LEFT:** Finnish linens incorporate ancient traditions of textiles production.

# Glass and Wood

In view of the prominence of its modern glass design, it is surprising that Finland's glass-making industry dates back only to the late 17th century, when the first glass factory, at Uusikaupunki on the west coast, enjoyed a brief life. Just the same, it is not only one of oldest industries in Finland but the first design industry to make attempts at breaking away from copies of standard European prototype designs, although this only happened in the 1920s. A turning point was a competition staged by the Riihimäki glass company (named after the southern Finnish town of the same name, today the home of the Finnish Glass Museum) for the design of cocktail glasses. Individual glass designers began to make names for themselves, not least Aino Aalto, who was upstaged by her designer/architect husband Alvar in 1936 when he contributed the celebrated Savoy vase to the Milan Triennale *(see page 80)*.

Gunnel Nyman became well known in the following decade for his designs for Iittala, Riihimäki and Nuutajärvi, setting standards which were then equalled and later surpassed by designers such as Tapio Wirkkala (thanks to him the frosty surface of the Finlandia vodka bottle), Kaj Franck and Timo Sarpaneva. Eero Aarnio and Yrjö Kukkapuro were other notable design innovators of the period.

Their traditions of style and a distinctively Finnish grace have been maintained more recently by the likes of Brita Flander, Vesa Varrela and the 1998 winner of the Kaj Franck Design Prize, Heikki Orvola, all of them making sure that Finnish glass is still some of the most beautiful in the world. Items of Iittala and Nuutajärvi's frequently updated glassware ranges include some of Finland's most popular and desirable gift items and souvenirs and a prime export industry. Pentik is another popular glass company.

Finland has also been exceptionally good at taking its natural resources and utilising them for design purposes. Finland's forests have always been (and "touch wood", always will be) the country's most plentiful and ubiquitous natural resource, and Finns know as well as any race on earth their potential as a raw and essentially functional material.

The traditions of woodcraft were crucial to every aspect of Finnish agrarian life right into the early 20th century, providing shelter, tools and even clothing. Old wooden quarters of the earliest urban milieus were vulnerable to, and were frequently ravaged by, fire but the old parts of Porvoo, 50 km (30 miles) to the east of Helsinki *(see page 196)* and Rauma on the west coast, preserved since the 17th century *(see page 237)* contain charming remnants of wooden house-building skills.

These basic timber patterns used in rural buildings around the country are today preserved in the structure of the log cabins and saunas that pepper the shorelines of Finland's thousands of

lakes and which remain the summer retreats for much of the population *(see page 250)*.

On a more intimate scale, the use of wood has been adapted with characteristic Finnish innovation to everyday functions. Alvar Aalto paved the way for furniture design, pioneering the "bentwood" technique in the 1930s, skilfully moulding birch into laminated fluid curls and curves.

The wooden ornaments, everyday utensils and bowls, and jewellery on sale at the Aarikka gift shops are still testament to the continued Finnish versatility and sensitivity when it comes to their most precious and plentiful raw material.  ❑

● *For information on the best places to buy glass and wooden Finnish souvenirs, see page 313.*

**RIGHT:** glassblowing in action at the Iittala factory near Helsinki.

# MUSIC AND FILM

*Finland's musical heritage has long been associated with Sibelius, but modern classical musicians, rock bands and film directors are keeping the country's arts alive*

When people think of Finnish music, they still think of Jean Sibelius. The great Finnish composer, after all, sprang from a little-known country to become one of the most famous composers of all time – and Finland's most famous export. But there is much more to modern Finnish music than simply Sibelius, and audiences everywhere now recognise this. A startling number of Finnish musicians and orchestras have won both domestic and international acclaim.

## Classical music

The Association of Finnish Composers today numbers over 100 members. All have had works performed professionally, and many possess distinguished discographies. Playing their works in Finland are 13 professional orchestras, 18 semi-professional or chamber orchestras and numerous ensembles. Helsinki is home to two symphony orchestras: the Finnish Radio Symphony and the Helsinki Philharmonic.

For a country of only 5 million people, this is nothing short of remarkable, but the seemingly disproportionate number of musicians is not coincidental. Finland takes its music seriously and has proved it through a generous policy of funding for musicians and musical institutes. Close to 130 such institutes, with a student body of 50,000, offer free primary instruction and talented graduates can audition for one of the seven free conservatories or the celebrated Sibelius Academy in Helsinki.

Professional opportunities for musicians are also wide. As well as holding regular concert seasons, Finland sponsors a number of annual music festivals *(see page 92)* attracting both native and foreign artists. Two recording companies concentrate on Finnish musicians.

Finnish instrumentalists have also been winning global attention. Cellists, of whom Finland has an especially strong tradition, have

done particularly well. Arto Noras, second prize winner at the 1966 Tchaikovsky Competition, and Erkki Rautio are renowned *virtuosi*. Now garnering laurels are Anssi Karttunen and Martti Roussi, both born in 1960. Cellists aren't the only ones. As a classical guitarist, Timo Korhonen (born 1965) is less known, but he

looks set to fill the shoes of André Segovia. Pianist Ralf Gothoni commands a confirmed place in Europe and further afield, as does pianist and composer Olli Mustonen (born 1967) – "Finland's Mozart" – who performed his own concerto with the Radio Symphony Orchestra at the age of 12. Esa-Pekka Salonen is the most notable achiever, a principal conductor with an international reputation second only to Sibelius.

After Sibelius and Salonen, however, it is Finland's singers who have gained the most fame. Foreign audiences adore Finnish basses: Matti Lehtinen in the 1950s, Martti Talvela before his premature death in 1989, and now

**PRECEDING PAGES:** the Sibelius Monument in Helsinki.
**LEFT:** conductor Esa-Pekka Salonen.
**RIGHT:** Karita Mattila, Finnish soprano opera singer.

Matti Salminen and Jaakko Ryhänen. Baritones Jorma Hynninen, Tom Krause, Walton Grönroos and tenor Peter Lindroos grace houses like the New York Met, London's Covent Garden and Berlin's Deutsche Opera. Nor have sopranos missed out; Ritva Auvinen, Anita Välkki, Taru Valjakka and Karita Mattila have attained stardom, and Soile Isokoski, winner of the Elly Ameling contest, is joining their ranks.

Although its sopranos have sought fame overseas, the Finnish National Opera, now happily settled in its new showpiece National Opera House in Helsinki, doesn't seem to suffer too much. It made, for example, operatic

history in 1983 as the first foreign company to be invited to perform at New York's Met.

Vocal works have always been the backbone of the Finnish musical tradition, which may, perhaps, explain why about three new Finnish operas are published every year. Among recent ones to have been performed in leading houses outside Finland are Aulis Sallinen's *Ratsumies (The Horseman)*, *Punainen Viiva (The Red Line)*, and *Kullervo*, and Joonas Kokkonen's *Viimeiset Kiusaukset (The Last Temptations)*.

These operas offer additional proof that Finnish composition, too, lives on beyond Sibelius. Joonas Kokkonen might be called the

### WANDERING MAESTROS

Talented Finns are often lured abroad, thereby spreading the musical word. Finnish conductors are particularly in demand. Every Nordic capital has had a symphony orchestra with a Finn as principal conductor. The country has many world-class maestros, including Paavo Berglund, Okko Kamu and Salonen. Prolonging the fine tradition are the likes of Sakari Oramo, who became conductor-in-chief of the City of Birmingham Symphony Orchestra in 1998. The well-loved Leif Segerstam has been extremely active and prolific; both as a conductor in Finland and around the world, and as composer of about 20 symphonies, as well as many songs and concertos.

country's pre-eminent living composer but excellence is also to be found in the works of Erik Bergman and Einojuhani Rautavaara, two other acclaimed senior composers. Among younger composers, Magnus Lindberg (born 1958) and Kaija Saariaho (born 1952) are of special note. Lindberg's KRAFT (1985) won the Nordic Council's music award and the Koussevitzky disc award. *Le Monde de la Musique* has called him "one of the best composers in the world of his age." His most recent orchestral work, *Fresco*, made its world première with the LA Philharmonic, conducted by Esa-Pekka Salonen. Saariaho, an electro-acoustic innovator, has also received much acclaim.

## Popular music

One of the refreshing aspects of Finnish art generally is its lack of élitism. Still, the lines are as well drawn between classical and rock music here as in most places. Finnish rock thrives but on its own terms. The best-known Finnish band was probably Hanoi Rocks, now disbanded and remembered for their kitsch image as much as for their music. While Finland has not been able to compete with Sweden's pop success, from Abba to The Cardigans, Finns

heels in especially deep). But their style is still sufficiently Finnish to restrict them largely to an exclusively Finnish audience.

The language, of course, is what sets many Finnish bands apart. If you don't understand Finnish, you have no hope of grasping the essence of Juice Leskinen's dismal whine, for instance. Yet the pop and rock music scene is proudly eclectic, embracing the techno experiments of Jimi Tenor as well as the sophisticated, harmonic folk-pop of Värttinä, a group

### OPERA FESTIVAL

Even the most recalcitrant sopranos come home for the annual Savonlinna Opera Festival. Held in a 500-year-old castle, it is one of the most delightful summer opera festivals in the world.

have recently felt quiet pride at the international success of Darude and the Bomfunk MCs.

Certainly, there is nothing inferior about Finnish rock music. The best-loved bands, such as the veteran Eppu Normaali outfit, the bluesy J.J. Karjalainen and his various line-ups, and the raucous Don Huonot, can all play as well as any rock group in Europe, and are affected by the same fashions (especially punk and heavy metal bands, which seem to have dug their

of girl singers who have adapted the traditional motifs of ancient styles to a modern, radio-friendly swing, and whose albums have risen to the top of the World Music charts

One other aspect of the Finnish music scene which is a true regional phenomenon is the passion for the tango. It may sound unlikely, but Argentine melodrama converts convincingly to the melancholy of the Finnish crooner. The Tango Festival at Seinäjoki is Finland's best-attended summer gathering: the dancing continues through the night, in the streets, in the bars and restaurants, and a Tango King and Queen are elected. Seinäjoki is also the host for the annual Provinssirock festival *(see page 93)*.

**LEFT:** Finnish composer Magnus Lindberg.
**ABOVE:** Seppo Kimanen (left), cellist and cultural director of Kuhno Chamber Music Festival; and Ralf Gothoni (right), pianist.

Generally, the further north you travel, the louder the music gets – and, some say, the more interesting. Windy and cold Oulu in northern Finland has the most intense core of rock fans, as well as the only male choir in the world that doesn't even try to sing: *Huutajat* (literally "the Shouters"). Dozens of long-haired men in black suits and gum ties shout their hearts out in perfect order – Arctic hysteria at its best.

## Finns on film

It is the Kaurismäki brothers, Aki and Mika, who are largely to thank for wrenching the Finnish cinema industry to worldwide attention

with their rough-edged individuality and prolific output. Contemporary Finnish cinema received little exposure until the advent of the brothers. Refracting a range of influences, they have created a body of work that has been seen in 65 countries, won prizes at international festivals and brought Aki the accolade of being the youngest director ever to receive a retrospective at the Museum of Modern Art in New York

Born in Helsinki in 1957, Aki toiled as a postman and film critic before working as a scriptwriter, assistant and actor on his elder brother's 1980 film *Valehtelija (The Liar)*. The following year, the two men formed a production company. They also own a distribution company, a cinema in downtown Helsinki and were among the founders of the Midnight Sun Festival held each June in Sodankylä, Lapland.

Aki, the better known of the siblings, worked with Mika on the 1983 rock documentary *Saimaa-Ilmiä (The Saimaa Gesture)* before striking out with a freewheeling adaptation of *Crime and Punishment* (1983). A lugubrious figure of laconic manner and dismissive attitudes to his work, Aki has a self-proclaimed reputation as "the biggest drinker in the world". His films revel in the deadpan humour of morose outsiders desperate to escape the confines of a gloom-ridden country. Frequently shot in monochrome, eschewing dialogue whenever possible and rarely running to more than 80 minutes, his films range from *Calamari Union* (1985), an unscripted comedy in which the 17 characters are all called Frank, to *Hamlet Liikemaailmassa (Hamlet Goes Business)* (1987), a modern-day version of Shakespeare set in a rubber duck factory, and *Ariel* (1988), which begins with a suicide and offers tribute to the Finnish tango. Aki then moved his settings away from his native land with the Ealing-style comedy *I Hired a Contract Killer* (1990), filmed in London and, more recently, *Hold On to Your Scarf, Drifting Clouds* and *The Man Without A Past*. In 2002, Aki courted controversy by boycotting an award ceremony in New York in protest at US foreign policy.

Mika, two years older, studied film in Munich and has worked in a variety of genres from the road movie *Helsinki Napoli* (1987) to the comedy *Cha Cha Cha* (1988) and *Amazon* (1990), set in the Amazonian jungle.

Flying the Finnish flag in quite a different way is Hollywood action specialist, Renny Harlin, director of special-effects blockbusters like *Cliffhanger* and *Deep Blue Sea*, whose latest project is a biopic of Mannerheim. Closer to home is *Helsinki is Made at Night* (1999) by Ilkka Järvi-Laituri, with Hollywood star Bill Pullman. Finns have rediscovered their own environment as a setting. In 1999, Finnish films attracted half the cinema audiences, entertained by Raimo Niemi's *Poika ja Ilves (Tommy and the Wildcat)*, Aleksi Mäkelä's *Häjyt* and Markku Pölönen's *Kuningasjätkä (King of the Lumberjacks)*, all set in Finland. ❏

**LEFT:** the film maker Aki Kaurismäki at work on one of his many films.

# Jean Sibelius

I t cannot be easy for a man to find himself a figurehead in his country's search for an identity, yet it was this label rather than the simple genius of his music that many Finns tied on to their most famous composer, Jean Sibelius (1865–1957), during the years before Finnish independence. His tone poem *Finlandia* in particular became an emblem of everything Finnish, and this aura of reverence must have sometimes irked the composer.

Yet Sibelius did embody many things Finnish; even his ancestry took in areas of Finland as far apart as the coastal town of Loviisa, near the Russian border, the Swedish influence of Turku, the northwest Gulf of Bothnia and, nearer at hand, Häme province where he was born. The family already had a daughter but Jean was the first son of Hämeenlinna doctor, Christian Gustaf Sibelius, and his wife Maria. Later, another son, Christian, followed.

Though his father's family in Loviisa was wealthy, Dr Sibelius was better known for his medical care than as a financial manager and when, three years later, he died looking after his patients in the typhus epidemic that raged during Finland's last great famine, Maria had little choice but to file for bankruptcy. The family remained in Hämeenlinna. All three children showed musical talent, displaying their concert skills on family visits to Loviisa. The birthplace has a photograph from that period which shows the young Jean (violin), Linda (piano), and Christian (cello) during a recital.

Although it is simplistic to think of Sibelius as being solely influenced by the Finnish landscape, he was undoubtedly part of the late 19th-century movement of artists, writers and intellectuals who turned for inspiration to Finland's land, people and past. Yet, after the first performance of his early *Kullervo* symphony, based on Finnish folklore at the height of the National Romantic movement *(see page 77)*, Sibelius withdrew the work and it was not played again until after his death.

The great Sibelius scholar Erik Tawaststjerna insists that Sibelius moved in the mainstream of European music and was influenced by Beethoven, as well as by Bruckner and Tchaikovsky. His relationship to Wagner's music could be described as love-hate.

---

**RIGHT:** bust of Jean Sibelius on display in the Sibelius Museum.

Certainly Sibelius travelled to Bayreuth and Munich in the 1890s and planned an opera, something he did not achieve though some of its proposed music went into *The Swan of Tuonela*. He wrote his First Symphony just before the turn of the 20th century and followed it with the popular Second in 1902, around which time he started to plan the Violin Concerto, now regarded by many as his greatest work. Its first performance in 1904, arranged hurriedly because Sibelius had financial problems, was not a success and it was revised.

Not long after, the family moved to Ainola *(see page 224)*, close to the retreat of his friend the artist Pekka Halonen. The site for Ainola (named

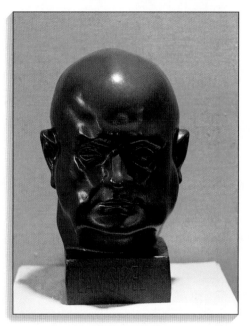

after his wife Aino) was located by the painter Eero Järnefelt, Aino's brother. Another friend, architect Lars Sonck, designed the house, and Sibelius wrote some 150 works there, including the remaining symphonies. Sibelius lived for 53 years at Ainola until his death in 1957, and the small artistic colony spent much time in one another's houses. To compose, Sibelius needed silence: his children went away to friends and the servants crept around on tiptoe.

In his final years, Sibelius left no music. Until his death, there were constant rumours of one more symphony; but, though many believe Sibelius continued to compose, nothing can have satisfied him. The Seventh Symphony was his last. ❏

# FINLAND'S SUMMER FESTIVALS

*In common with other Nordic countries, Finland has a long tradition of festivals which make the most of summer nights in music, song and dance*

The soprano Aino Acte founded Savonlinna in 1912, and it remains the most dramatic setting for any music festival the world over. After this came Jyväskylä, opened in 1955 by the composer Seppo Nummi. The tradition for music festivals continues today, many in rural areas and many which now draw international audiences. One of the most remote is the Kuhmo Chamber Music Festival close to the Russian border, founded in 1970 by cellist Seppo Kimanen. It now draws 150 international musicians to more than 60 concerts.

Other arts festivals include: Tampere (theatre); Kuopio (dance); Pori (jazz); Imatra (big bands); Lieksa (brass bands) and Sodankylä (film).

## FOLK FESTIVALS

One source of traditional festivals was the old-time fire brigades, who got together to play music and dance at annual festivals. Some festivals have their roots in a more sinister past: in 1643, the Ruovesi Witch Trials condemned Antti Lieronen "as a witch most obvious and potent" and burned her at the stake. Today's "trials" include drama and concerts but no one is burned. In 1968 Finland Festivals was formed, to monitor festivals, propose new ideas and guarantee high artistic level. New festivals are born every year.

▷ **CASTLE SETTING**
In all, Savonlinna has seen the world premières of no less than five operas by Finnish composers in a country where the composing and playing of classical music flourishes as never before.

△ **SUMMER MADNESS**
Finland's all too brief summer is certainly cause to celebrate when it arrives – the Helsinki Midsummer Festival attracts hordes of revellers.

△ **SAILING FRENZY**
It's not surprising that a country with so much water at its disposal holds regular rowing and boating regattas in the Lakeland region.

◁ **ONE WORLD**
Finland's festivals are not just local events – international artistes bring their own shows and costumes.

▷ **FOLK TRADITIONS**
Throughout the nine days of Kaustinen Folk Music groups of musicians from many countries hand on old traditions and develop new styles of folk music.

## ROCK, JAZZ AND BLUES FESTIVALS

Finland has a broad rock scene, highlighted by a number of summer rock festivals.

Provinssirock, held in Seinäjoki in early June, traditionally marks the opening of the rock festival season. A four-hour train ride north of Helsinki, Seinäjoki turns into a rock heaven for one weekend. As well as the best of the Finns, Provinssirock attracts big names from abroad, such as REM and David Byrne. As elsewhere, there are beer tents selling brew. (Drugs are low-profile in Finland and you are unlikely to see any.)

The other important summer rock festival is Ruisrock at Turku. The oldest rock festival in Finland, Ruisrock faded for a few years but has now revived and hosts some of the biggest names. Recent guests have included Bob Dylan and Billy Idol.

Even President Mauno Koivisto favours the artists featured in the huge Pori Jazz Festival. Another festival with a family atmosphere is Puisto Blues in Järvenpää, north of Helsinki, at the beginning of June.

◁ **FISH FESTIVAL**
It is not only arts and music that get the festival treatment; food is also celebrated, such as at this Herring Festival on Helsinki's harbour.

▽ **LEARNING THE STEPS**
The Kuopio Dance Festival (*Kuopio tanssii ja soi*) is one of the finest events concentrating on dance from around the world.

# THE WRITER'S DILEMMA

*Finnish literature emerged in the 19th century as an embodiment of the national character. Today, Finnish writers continue to use writing to understand their world*

Eino Leino, poet, novelist and playwright, said of Finnish literature in 1910: "Literature is the country's interpreter. Literature is the nation's mirror. Without literature the nation is like a blind man, like a deaf mute."

The story of the past two centuries of Finnish literature is the story of a country struggling to find its voice and its identity. Mimicking Finland's political development, there have been peaks and troughs, high expectations and disappointments. Writers have expressed the fortunes of their country by veering from romanticism to cynicism and realism. The written portrait of the Finn has covered the spectrum from noble hero to drunken buffoon.

## A blank canvas

The high expectations came first, partly fuelled by the blank canvas on which the first writers of the 19th century worked. Until that time, Finland's literary tradition had been primarily an oral one. Because there was no written precedent, writers had a free hand to invent the Finn on paper, and many made him a hero.

Johan Ludvig Runeberg (1804–77), Finland's national poet, offered just such a romantic vision of his countrymen. In his three collections of Swedish-language poems, *Dikter I–III* (*Poems*), and in his patriotic ballad series, *Fänrik Ståhl Sägner I–II* (*The Tales of Ensign Ståhl*), he created loyal, gracious and noble Finns. They were readily embraced.

In the 1820s, Elias Lönnrot (1802–84) began a project which was to generate yet more national pride. Lönnrot travelled through Finland recording folk poetry. The result was the *Kalevala* of 1835 (now commonly called the "*Old Kalevala*"). A new, longer version was published in 1849.

The *Kalevala* is easily misunderstood as merely "Finland's epic poem", not paying due attention to its literary value. Technically

**LEFT:** Elias Lönnrot, creator of the Finland's national epic poem, the *Kalevala*.

**RIGHT:** Gallén-Kallela's illustrations of the *Kalevala*.

speaking, the *Kalevala* is based on metrical foot, "quadrisyllabic trochee" which makes it rhythmical and easy to recite. There are four pairs of syllables on each line, and two or more lines have a synonomous meaning. Alliteration is also typical, which makes translations impossible – they merely follow the narration. The

poem itself is an heroic epic on the scale of *The Odyssey* or *The Iliad*. But it is also a rag-bag of narratives and light interludes, existing to preserve old customs and songs. The narrative is interrupted by poetic "charms", some of which belong to the realms of Shakespearian comedy. Lönnrot's Finn is a participator in the creation of the world. The characters are classical figures with a Finnish twist. The context – sea, farm, forest – is entirely Finnish.

The *Kalevala* managed to include in its poetry a national fiction-cum-history which stretched back to the beginning of time, and which did not include the humiliating details of real life – never-ending domination by foreign rulers. In Lönnrot's mythical Finland, power lay with the good and the just. Lönnrot compiled the work in the mid-19th century, yet it reads like a piece of literature as old as the classics or, at the very least, as old as the Norse sagas. And, because it is drawn from a dateless oral tradition, it is impossible to question its veracity while under its spell.

At the same time as Lönnrot was compiling the *Kalevala*, other Finnish-language writers such as Aleksis Kivi (1834–72) were celebrating rural life, casting the ordinary people in the role of heroes: true Finns led virtuous lives among the forests, harmonious with nature.

## Twentieth-century works

By the early 20th century, real events began to cast doubts on this unimpeachable national character. Political achievements – especially that of independence – were quickly soured by subsequent developments and crises. It became the job of writers to make sense of events like the Civil War, or the effects of industrialisation, that lay heavy on the nation's conscience. Mainstream Finnish writing concerned itself with events in the world at large.

Notable exceptions include Mika Waltari (1908–79), an escapist writer. His main work, *The Egyptian*, has been translated into more than 25 languages. F. E. Sillanpää, too, wrote

about the mystical rural life and won the Nobel Prize for literature in 1939 – his books include *Meek Heritage* and *The Maid Silja*.

During this time, Swedish-language writers drifted away from the main pulse of Finnish writing, becoming more isolated. Some, like the poet Edith Södergran (1892–1923), nonetheless enjoyed considerable popularity. Christer Kihlman, author of *Den Blå Modern* (*The Blue Mother*) and *Dyre Prins* (*Sweet Prince*), and Tove Jansson's Moomintroll books, show just how idiosyncratic Swedish-Finnish writing has become.

The years after the war expurgated many people's consciences. The fate of refugees from Karelia was one literary theme. Väinö Linna's successful and controversial novel *Tuntematon sotilas* (*The Unknown Soldier*) turned wartime events into a psychological story among a group of Finns from various parts of the country, each reflecting a regional character with a typical dialect.

By the 1960s, the literary trends were those of the rest of Europe – protest poetry, working-class novels, middle-class angst and, because of rural depopulation, a scrutiny of rural life.

## Contemporary voices

Today, Finnish heroes no longer have to act as vessels for the nation's pride. They are as troubled and beset by worries as the heroes of other literatures. Modern writers like Leena Krohn and Pentti Saarikoski reflect Finnish humanity. Veijo Meri is seen as a reformer of Finnish prose with his *Manilla Rope*.

As modern Finnish writers become more international, the *Kalevala* may still be reflected in popular Finnish literature. The bestselling authors, Kalle Päätalo, Laila Hietamies, Arno Paasilinna and Veikko Huovinen place their stories in the same regions where the *Kalevala* was collected. Päätalo's nostalgic rural landscape and Hietamies' lost Karelia both evoke the eternal yearning for youth. Paasilinna and Huovinen both work in a Karelian-style setting and use onomatopoeic words – the backbone of both the *Kalevala* and modern Finnish short stories. Both work on the far side of the Finnish culture where reality and imagination meet, as in the *Kalevala*. ❏

**LEFT:** Viejo Meri, one of Finland's most respected modern writers.

# The Moomins

At first sight Tove Jansson's Moomin books seem like storybooks to buy children as gifts. But the mystical fairytale world of mighty nature and ever-changing seasons inspire even die-hard realists.

Tove Jansson was born in 1914, to an artistic family – both brothers are artists and writers. A tiny Swedish-speaking woman, meek to the point of humility, Jansson has lived much of her life with her female friend on a small island off the southern coast of Finland. Here Jansson created another world like C.S.Lewis and J.R.R. Tolkien. But, where Tolkien was a perfectionist and a scientist, Jansson is a humanist, an artist and a storyteller. Nature is the main element, and nature is always respected.

Moomin books appeal to both children and adults, because their basic philosophy is about acceptance, quest for space and solitude. Some titles, in fact, are too advanced for children, but raise many questions in adults.

The books are all led by the Moomin family characters. The Bohemian Moominmamma takes care of everything, while the Moominpappa is a philosopher, who writes his memoirs and becomes active only when it's time to explore the unknown. The Moomin house is always open to adopted children and strange creatures that seem to appear from the valley. Love and tolerance reign; difference is always accepted. There are no wars, no alcohol is consumed and nothing threatens the idyll except the natural phenomena.

Each character is a sensitively illustrated personality, so every reader will identify oneself with at least one of them. Children fear the monstrous Groke who only appears in winter. He is cold as winter and no one wants to be near him. But even he has human qualities – lonely poor Groke suffers greatly while missing contact with just about anyone. Little My is an adventurous girl, who, along with Moomintroll, is perhaps Tove Jansson's own alter ego. Snufkin is a world traveller who prefers wandering alone. Snitt is a coward; the Fillyjonk is a neurotic pedant. Hemulen is an absentminded botanist and Snork an engineer who does little else than design a light aeroplane. The Snork Maiden, Snork's sister, is extremely feminine. The strange, worm-like electric creatures Hatifnatters

represent foreigners, with whom communication is possible if not easy. All these characters lend themselves to fine psychological drama.

The Moomin life pauses for hibernation when the winter comes, and is reborn at the thaw when Snufkin returns from his world travels, except when the magical winter is brought to life in *Moominland Midwinter*. The four seasons are dominant – from springtime optimism to autumn isolation.

These unpretentious little books have conquered the world, having been translated into over 30 languages. In Finland, there is the Moomin World in Naantali, the Moomin Museum in Tampere and yet another theme park being planned – of all places –

in Hawaii. The Japanese love the Moomin figures, and a TV cartoon series was produced in co-operation with a Japanese company. Finnair has had Moomin figures painted on aeroplanes flying to Japan, and Finnair's flight attendants sell enormous quantities of Moomin paraphernalia to travellers. Several stamps have been issued on Moomin characters, but the commercialised Moomins are not entirely faithful to the originals.

Jansson's world really exists near the village of Pellinki, south of Porvoo. Around this cape, one will find islands, caves and the sea, but the lighthouse that became the Moomin house is no longer there. But the Moomin world is alive anywhere that love and tolerance are understood. ❏

**RIGHT:** the Moomin Valley Museum in Tampere is perennially popular with children and adults.

# FINNS WHO SPEAK SWEDISH

*Finland is officially bilingual, using both Finnish and Swedish, a tradition that goes back centuries between these two neighbouring countries*

Why do so many Finns speak Swedish is a question that is often asked by visitors. The main reason is that for 600 years, Finland was a part of Sweden. In that time it is not so surprising that Swedish became the language for administration, and many Finns adopted the language to survive in the society. Some of their great-grandchildren still use Swedish, the language having been passed down the generations. But the answer isn't quite as simple as that – politics and education have also played their part.

## Early settlers

The earliest inhabitants on the Åland Islands and many other coastal communities were Scandinavian settlers, adventurers and fishermen, who brought their language with them. Many who still live on these islands speak a unique Swedish dialect which may be hard to understand, even by Swedish tourists.

As Finland was a lucrative territory, many Swedes also emigrated, mostly to Nyland ("New Land") and Osterbotten (as opposed to Västerbotten, eastern and western "Bothnia", respectively). Some came as industrialists and founded factories and saw mills. Many of these ancient communities remain, including the cardboard factory in Verla, now a UNESCO World Heritage site.

The military also played a major role in the Swedish "take-over". In many cases, successful soldiers in the Royal Swedish Army were granted privileges in Finland, such as territory and tax-free status, which brought with them a Swedish upper class to many previously remote regions of Finland.

As Swedish soon became the lingua franca in large towns such as Turku, Helsinki and Vyborg, many German, Jewish or Russian burghers living in these areas adopted Swedish, and this usage remains today.

---

**LEFT:** bilingual road signs are a common sight: this sign puts the Swedish language first.

**RIGHT:** a typical Swedish area near Turku.

## A bilingual nation

This is something visitors to Finland find difficult to understand. Swedish-speaking Finns, or Finland-Swedes as they are described by the government, are not immigrants, nor are they Swedes. They may not even have any family connections with Sweden.

When Finland is described as a "bilingual" nation, it means that the two languages are given an official status, very much the same as English and French in Canada – one may assume the right to use either Swedish or Finnish at offices or even in shops in "bilingual" towns. However, this is not always successful – in some cases Finns have to resort to English in order to understand each other.

Swedish as a language is many things in Finland. At one hand, it is a living language (including numerous dialects), used by 300,000 people. It is also a "compulsory" language taught to practically every Finnish child at school. It is an "official" language, which the president uses to address the nation. It is also a "semi-official" language in the sense that the law provides certain minimum services in Swedish, say, regular TV and radio programmes on national channels.

## Linguistic roots

Swedish-speakers are a throwback to the 600 years when Finland was the eastern part of the Kingdom of Sweden. Then, and even during the time when Finland was a Grand Duchy of Russia, from 1808 to independence in 1917, Swedish was the official language, the language of the civil service, of the law, of higher education, at the University of Turku (Abo in Swedish), and of the monied classes.

Fed by students from Turku University, Finnish cultural life was dominated by Swedish-speakers too. It was not until 1828 that the university established a Finnish language lectureship, and not until 1850 that a professorship of Finnish was introduced.

Because the Swedish language held sway in this way, it was the principal language of the nascent Finnish mid-19th-century cultural and political life. Early political activists like the Fennomen, who supported the Finnish language and campaigned for its recognition as an

### SWEDISH-SPEAKING WRITERS

The compiler of the epic poem the *Kalevala*, Elias Lönnrot (1802–84), was born in Nyland in southwest Finland and has a Swedish name. Yet he was a great champion of the Finnish language and folklore and went on to become Professor of Finnish at Helsinki University. He also produced a Swedish-Finnish dictionary, which is credited with establishing a Finnish literary language. Johan Ludwig Runeberg (1804–77) taught at the Porvoo University for 20 years. The opening words of his Swedish-language *Fänrik Ståls Sägner (Tales of Ensign Stål)* became Finland's national anthem *(Vårt Land, or Maamme* in Finnish).

official language, often faced the paradox that they were Swedish-speakers whose love of their country was paramount. A number of 19th-century cultural ambassadors, painters and writers, who searched determinedly for an artistic expression of Finnish nationalism, were also Swedish-speakers.

It was not surprising, therefore, that when Finland gained its independence, the 1919 Constitution decreed that Finland should have two official national languages: Finnish and Swedish. At that time, Swedish-speakers accounted for 12 percent of the Finnish population. Today, the figure has shrunk to around 6 percent.

Swedish-speakers are very much spread out around the country. About half of them live in purely Swedish regions in Nyland, around Turku, on Åland and on the west coast. Regional centres, such as Ekenäs (Tammisaari in Finnish), Borgå (Porvoo) and Jakobstad (Pietarsaari) have their indigenous Swedish culture, and larger towns such as Abo (Turku), Vasa (Vaasa) or the capital Helsinki (which Swedish-speakers call Helsingfors) house about half of the Swedish-speakers.

### DIFFERENT WORDS

Swedish spoken in Finland is not identical to that of Sweden; many local dialect words which have their roots in Finnish are included in Finland's Swedish.

Accusations that Finland-Swedes were more wealthy or disproportionately powerful have rumbled on over the decades.

### Highs and lows

Sadly, the population of Finland-Swedes is decreasing. Figures may be misleading, however. In 1960, there were 21 Swedish-language newspapers (182 Finnish); in 1988, the figure was 14 (with 374 Finnish publications). Finland-Swedes have a choice of papers from either Sweden or Finland. Daily papers from

With encouragement from individuals like Czar Alexander II, who made it official in 1863, Finnish gradually became the dominant language and the language of power. But political disputes over the two languages and their relative prominence have flared up from time to time, especially in the 1920s and 1930s when it became a central political issue. Common comparisons with the Republic of Ireland are not far-fetched – the difference is that, in fact, English has been more dominant than Swedish.

**LEFT:** the League of Nations meets to decide the fate of the Åland Islands' status in 1921.
**ABOVE:** Ålanders enjoying traditional Swedish dancing.

large publishers in Stockholm are always available in Finland's Swedish-speaking centres, and Sweden's culture, politics and daily gossip is popular among Finland-Swedes.

In fact, Finland has been dubbed a model for minority policy. The government spends much more money per capita on Swedish radio and TV programmes, and the largest Swedish daily in Finland, *Hufvudstadsbladet*, manages a circulation of 60,000, which means one paper for each five Swedish-speakers. Some observers note that, as a comparison, Wales has no daily newspaper in the Welsh language – a language that is spoken by more than 15 percent of its population.

As Finland and Sweden entered the European Union in 1995, Swedish became an official language once again, which boosted its significance all over Europe. Finnish-speaking Finns, therefore, readily understand the usefulness of Swedish in both domestic and European communication.

The growing number of "mixed marriages" between Finnish- and Swedish-speakers also doubles the number of bilingual Finns – many families choose to use both languages at home, and Swedish schools are becoming popular once again, even among purely Finnish-speaking families.

### A unique situation

The case of the Åland Islands, which lie off the southwest of Finland almost halfway to Sweden, is unique. Though this is Finnish territory, the roles are reversed. When Finland became independent in 1917, the Ålanders' background and culture were (and are) more clearly Swedish and they voted overwhelmingly in a referendum to become part of Sweden. After much wrangling, the matter went to the infant League of Nations in the early 1920s, complicating what could then have been a relatively simple settlement by deciding that the Åland Islands remain Finnish but that the islanders' use of the Swedish language would be safeguarded.

The official language, therefore, is Swedish, and Swedish culture is preserved by law. However, the 25,000 residents consider themselves to be autonomous, with their own flag and postage stamps. The Ålanders have their own parliament and government to run their internal affairs out of a proportion of the Finnish budget. They also send a member to the main Parliament in Helsinki *(see page 229)*.

The argument goes that as part of Sweden, Ålanders would be "normal" citizens. As part of Finland, they may retain their "special" status. Åland became even more of a special case on 1 July 1999, when tax-free sales became banned within inter-EU travel. Åland is "outside" the Union, however, thus all ferries between Finland and Sweden stop briefly at the Långnäs pier, where popular tax-free sales continue unabated.

### Political representation

The main political party representing mainland Finland-Swedes, the Swedish People's Party (SFP), was founded in 1906. The SFP got 4.6 percent of the vote in the 2003 elections and their – their seats in parliament fell from 11 to 8. However, in spite of this, it could be argued that they were one of the big winners – the nature of Finnish politics (post-vote negotiations as to who should enter Government) meant that the SFP not only remained in Government, but actually secured two ministerial posts.

Frequent coalition governments have resulted in some Cabinet prominence for SFP Members of Parliament. Jan-Erik Enestam held a number of ministerial posts, including Minister of Defence in 1999. The SFP's Elisabeth Rehn was the first female Minister of Defence in the early 1990s, and was a candidate for Finland's president *(see page 63)*.

Talk to Finland-Swedes about the problems of being a linguistic minority and they will often tell you of the difficulties of not being able to express themselves fully in both languages. The plus side is that many, used to switching between two languages, become able linguists, taking on board German, English, French, Danish and Norwegian with ease. And, despite coming from such diverse backgrounds, they benefit from three cultures: Sweden, Finnish Finland and Swedish Finland. ❏

**LEFT:** Swedish People's Party (SFP) leader and Minister of Environment, Jan-Erik Enestam.

# Immigrants

In the heat of the summer of 1999, Romany refugees from Slovakia caught Finns off-guard. Within two weeks over 1,000 had arrived. The government acted immediately, with a new visa compulsion for Slovakian nationals, and the flow soon reversed. The Slovakian "gypsies" became the first news item during the traditionally quiet midsummer weeks.

Finland is no promised land that can take any number of foreigners. It seems that few can arrive without anyone taking notice. The numbers of arrivals are constantly increasing, however. Many Finns, in common with people in most European countries, now realise that labour from outside is required both to keep the service sector ticking over, and to pay taxes into the treasury.

These days Helsinki is fully international, with over 5 percent of the population speaking a foreign language (other than Swedish). It doesn't compare with Stockholm where more than 15 percent are foreigners but the figure is growing. The densely inhabited Kallio suburb in Helsinki is a playground for hard-working immigrants. Bangladeshis run pizza restaurants, Thai women keep massage parlours and ethnic food shops abound.

Finland became a sort of a cul-de-sac when the Soviet Union restricted travel, especially from Russia to Finland. Therefore, the biggest influx of foreigners occurred soon after the Soviet downfall – Russians and Estonians now constitute the largest foreign groups in Finland (35,000) and one percent of all Estonians live in Finland.

Among Asians, the Chinese are the largest ethnic group, working in restaurants or studying. More than 3,000 Vietnamese also live in Finland, most of them originally as refugees. The arrival of the Vietnamese was a media event, many of them hand-picked at refugee camps by Finnish government officials. At the same time Finland gave developmental aid to the Vietnamese government. This was, and still is to some extent, the official refugee policy – a few hundred "quota" refugees who were given full financial support. Other nationals who arrived as refugees came mainly from Chile, or the Kurdish regions in Turkey or Iran.

When the Somalis came, however, the situation changed. Already some 6,000 Somalis live in Finland, a minority well visible in central Helsinki. Rumours abounded about the enormous amounts of tax-payers' money being spent just to clothe them. Gang wars against Somalis occurred, especially during the harsh recession years in the early 1990s when Finland's unemployment figures hovered above 20 percent. The small town of Joensuu became notorious for a "skinhead" gang who terrorised foreigners. Things have now cooled down, although unemployment among Somalis remains high.

Restaurants are typical employers for many Chinese and Indians in Finland, and Turkish kebab

shops are ubiquitous in even smaller towns. Most employers demand full knowledge of Finnish, and most foreigners have low-paid jobs that Finns refuse to accept.

Loneliness or isolation is one of the biggest problems among foreigners. Some refugees will be located in tiny towns where contacts with locals are practically non-existent. Finns seldom "small talk" with strangers, let alone foreigners.

Many immigrants choose Finland over warmer countries: some fall in love with a Finn, Finland has useful social benefit schemes, a very high standard of living and, perhaps most importantly, an increasing number of fellow foreigners – there are now 98,500 immigrants in Finland. ❏

**RIGHT:** Somalian refugees seeking Finnish citizenship at Helsinki airport.

# THE SAMI AND THEIR LAND

*The Sami of north Finland have a distinct culture that, rather than being destroyed*
*by modern life, is increasingly valued by Finns and by tourists*

For the Sami (Lapps), who on the whole prefer to mind their own business and hope other people will mind theirs, the second half of the 20th century has brought mixed blessings, putting pressure on a fragile ecology already under threat. Against that, the many changes have also triggered a much greater awareness of their own identity.

## Early development

Most specialists agree the Sami descend from a people who, following the retreating edge of the continental ice, reached Finland and East Karelia in the latter millennia BC. Their contacts with an indigenous proto-Sami people gave birth to the earliest Sami culture. Later came the Finns, also speaking a Finno-Ugric tongue, and thus sharing a common linguistic heritage originating in the Ural mountains.

The cornerstone of early Sami society was the *siida*, a community of several families and the territories in which they co-operatively hunted, trapped and fished. Place names in southern and central Finland suggest that Sami communities thrived until the Middle Ages. But as the Finnish settlers moved in, so the Sami – those who were not assimilated – moved on, ever northwards. In Finland today they are concentrated in northern Lapland around Utsjoki, Karasjoki, Inari and Enontekiö (*see page 285*). Based on language criteria there are an estimated 6,500 Sami people in Finland, considerably fewer than in Sweden and Norway.

## Land of the midnight sun

The Sami home in Lapland (Lappi) is Finland's northernmost province and covers nearly a third of the country's total area, most of it north of the Arctic Circle. Away from the few towns and scattered communities its extraordinary beauty is still predominantly primeval wilderness. Extensive swamps and forests of conifer and

---

**PRECEDING PAGES:** Sami's midday meal during a reindeer drive. **LEFT:** Skolte Sami woman in Nellim Church. **RIGHT:** a modern Sami girl.

birch rise in the far north to bareheaded fells, the highest topping 1,300 metres (4,270 ft); all this is laced by swift rivers and streams and punctuated by lakes and pools.

You may think of it as the land of the midnight sun which, depending on latitude (and cloud cover), is visible for up to 70 summer

days. In winter there is an almost equivalent sunless period, tempered at times by the flickering veils of the Northern Lights or, around midday, by the lingering dawn effects from the invisible sun or the inescapable, all-pervading whiteness of the snow. Spring is a swift green renaissance in the wake of the big thaw. And autumn flares in colours so spectacular the Finns have a special term for it: *ruska*.

You may also think of it as the land of the Lapps. They, however, prefer their own name for themselves: Sami (pronounced Sah-mi) a preference which is now respected. Today the Sami's territory extends across northern Scandinavia and into the northwest corner of Russia.

## Society and spirit

Inevitably the Sami's fragile, less structured society was threatened by rivalry with the Finnish newcomers over natural resources, by growing contact with Finnish social organisation and, not least, the effects of Finland's innumerable wars. The nomadism associated with the Sami people of Norway and Sweden has never been so widely practised among the predominantly Forest Sami of Finland's Lapland and, gradually, an economy based on hunting and fishing evolved into one dominated by reindeer husbandry as the wild herds once vigorously hunted were semi-domesticated. Early

on, many Sami adopted the more settled life of the Finns, keeping a few cattle and tilling scraps of soil to grow oats and potato, the only viable crops in these latitudes. In reverse, many Finns have opted for the reindeer economy.

Integral to early Sami culture were the shamanist beliefs rooted in the power of nature which so profoundly affected their lives. Everything it was believed, living or inanimate, had a soul and the spiritual world was as real as the material one. The wise man (*noaide*) was skilled in interpreting one world to the other achieving a state of ecstasy with his magic drum and entering the spirit world.

### WORDS AND MUSIC

The religious missions that came to Lapland to convert the Sami not only brought the influence of God, they also brought education. However, the Sami already had a rich oral tradition that ensured a wealth of tales and legends as well as centuries of acquired wisdom were passed from one generation to the next. There was also their simple brand of pictorial art. Also very special to Sami culture – and surviving still – is the *yoik*, a kind of yodelling chant, each a unique improvised tribute to an event, a landscape, an emotion or a person.

Sami culture has always lacked early written sources, and the first books in Sami were exclusively of a religious nature. Later, with education, came grammar books and

dictionaries and, finally, though not until well into the 20th century, the beginnings of a Sami literature.

Ironically, education has brought not only advances but also its own threat to Sami culture as youngsters increasingly abandon traditional occupations to enter almost every branch of trade and the professions. On the other hand, Finland's Sami today have their own publication, *Sápmelias*, founded in 1934, as well as theatre, and arts and crafts organisations. In the field of music, the *yoik* has begun to make strange alliances with modern music forms. And in 1991 for the first time a Finnish Sami writer, Nils-Aslak Valkeapää, was awarded the Nordic Council prize for literature.

Not surprisingly, as soon as the Sami began to penetrate these remote regions, religious missions made every effort to discourage such goings-on; yet, despite drum-burning and other deterrents, shamanism survived well into the 19th century. Its eventual submission was largely due to the teachings of Lars Levi Laestadius whose emotion-charged, fire-and-brimstone form of Christian worship must have struck a familiar chord among the Sami. The old gods gave way to the new and today many of the brightest events on the Lapland calendar are associated with church festivals – notably Lady Day and Easter: popular times for Sami weddings, lasso competitions, reindeer races, and get-togethers for scattered families.

## Into the 20th century

No century has left a greater impact on Lapland than the 20th century. The rebuilding programme following the devastation of World War II marked the beginning of changes that have altered its face forever. Since 1945, Lapland's population has soared to 203,000 (predominantly Finns), though in an area of nearly 100,000 sq. km (38,600 sq. miles) this is hardly overcrowded: the population density is just 2.2 persons per square kilometre.

The administrative capital of Rovaniemi has been virtually rebuilt and expanded to take in a satellite sprawl of light industry. Communities have burgeoned from hamlets into modern mini-townships. A network of new or improved roads penetrates regions only accessible a few decades ago by foot or ski. Rivers, notably the Kemi, have been tamed for their hydro-electric power. Two large man-made lakes, Lokka and Porttipahta, have been created. And a trickle of visitors has grown into a steady stream, spawning a whole range of facilities.

Organisations dedicated to Sami interests go back to the turn of the 20th century but their efforts were uncoordinated until 1956, when the Nordic Sami Council was founded to "promote cooperation on Sami issues between Finland, Norway and Sweden." It was the first body to provide all Sami with a common platform from which to coordinate their aims and inform the world at large. A few years later a

State Commission for Sami Affairs was established by the Finnish government and in 1973 Finland's Sami population acquired a parliamentary assembly, elected by them from among themselves. It has no legislative mandate, but it does provide a forum for promoting Sami concerns. Paramount are their rights to territory and its traditional usage in northern Lapland – age-old rights which have been gradually eroded (though never legally removed).

One may regret the adulteration of a culture under pressure, but people outside Finland are beginning to realise the enriching potential emerging from the Sami's ancient culture. ❑

### A VERSATILE BEAST

The docile reindeer has always represented much more to the Sami than a meal on four legs, its skin contributing to bedding and winter clothing, antlers and bones raw materials for tools and utensils. It has also provided a major means of transport, sledge-hauling across the winter snows, only recently ousted by the noisy, motorised skidoo. Even now, the annual cycle of the reindeer – rutting, herding, separating, slaughtering, calving, marking – moulds the north Lapland calendar. The winter round-ups are among Europe's most colourful events, resembling scenes from a Wild West film transposed to an Arctic setting.

**LEFT:** reindeer round-up at Vuotso, Lapland.
**RIGHT:** Sami man wearing the traditional national dress of the Lapps.

# FROM RALLY DRIVERS TO RUNNERS

*A strong physique and a determined nature have combined to make Finns a force to be reckoned with in the world of national and international sports*

Later on in his life, when asked about the relationship between Finnish independence and the performance of Finnish athletes in the early part of the 20th century, the great Finnish runner Paavo Nurmi commented: "The higher the standard of living in a country, the weaker the results often are in the events which call for work and effort. I would like to warn this new generation: do not let the comfortable life make you lazy! Do not let the new means of transport kill your instinct for physical exercise! Too many young people get used to loafing and driving in cars even for short distances. I believe that I must thank sports for the fact that I am an independent, self-supporting man."

Despite his warnings, Finns still perform remarkably well in sport and achieve international reputations. Soccer players such as Jari Litmanen, now back at Ajax via Barcelona and Liverpool, and Liverpool captain Sami Hyypiä, are among Europe's best known players. Dozens of Finns, such as Teemu Selänne and Saku Koivu, play ice-hockey in America, and Janne Holmén, a marathon runner from the Åland Islands, won gold in the 2002 European Championships, reviving Finland's long distance traditions.

## A sporting tradition

The Finnish sport tradition is unlikely to die out, though, because it is honoured and well established, engrained in every child from the moment he or she is put on skis at the age of two. In the centuries before motorisation, Finns often invented athletic ways to get across their great distances and traverse their vast forests and lakes. The best known was the church boat race, a rowing competition between villagers to see who would arrive at church first.

Sport was associated with religion at other times of the year, too. At Easter, there were competitions in tug-of-war and high and long

jumping, while Christmas was the time for shows of strength by weight-lifters and plough-pullers. Finland has, by virtue of its landscape, always produced a healthy crop of cross-country skiers. Even now, cross-country skiing is as much a form of transport as an enjoyable winter pastime.

Finnish schools today have rigorous sports programmes and, as Finnish officialdom likes to say, sport is the country's biggest youth movement. Whether or not this is strictly true, anyone visiting Finland will nonetheless be both amazed and impressed by the number of sports institutes scattered around even the remotest districts of the country, not to mention the skiers practising on roller skis throughout summer and windsurfers converted to ice surfers in the winter.

In fact, in postmodern Finland, sports has entered a deadly serious state. A recently opened snow tunnel in Vuokatti sports centre, not far from Kajaani, enables skiers to practise

---

**LEFT:** the great long-distance runner Paavo Nurmi lights the Olympic flame at the 1952 Helsinki Games.
**RIGHT:** Eero Mäntyranta, gold-medallist in the 1960s.

in a realistic environment when ordinary people enjoy the few hot summer days.

## Formula One racing

Take any group of rally drivers – men and women who drive their cars into a pulp through forest, desert and farm tracks – and among them you are likely to find a puzzlingly high number of Finns. Finns won eight World Rally Championships between 1991 and 2002, with Tommi Mäkinen, Juha Kankkunen and Marcus Grönholm dominating the sport to an even greater degree than Hannu Mikkola, Ari Vatanen and Timo Salonen did in the 1980s. For-

mula One racing has seen continued success, with Mika Häkkinen crowned World Champion in 1998 and 1999, and his place in the McLaren team being taken by prodigious compatriot Kimi Räikkönen. Rally enthusiasts, from fans to drivers, have marvelled at the way the Finns seem to give their heart and soul to the sport.

No one has satisfactorily explained why Finns should excel in this particular field, but the answers perhaps apply to all successful Finnish athletes: the fact that Finns come from a quiet northerly country that feels a need to make its mark on the world must have something to do with it. Another reason is, of

### FINLAND IN THE OLYMPICS

Outstanding performance in sport is a point of national pride which dates back at least to the Stockholm Olympics of 1912 (the last to be held before World War I), when Finland was still part of Russia. During those games, the Finnish medal winners far outstripped the Russian winners, gaining 23 medals against the Russians' three, although officially Finland and Russia were competing under the same flag.

At the 1912 Games, the Finnish competitors made a point of leaving a 50-metre (150-ft) gap between themselves and the Russians in the Games' opening ceremonies. They also dared to raise a Finnish flag at the

medal ceremonies, the first sign that the yearning for Finnish independence was not to be taken lightly. The gesture was not in vain: the world took notice. Five years later, Finland was an independent republic.

At the 2000 Olympics in Sydney, Finns took two golds – with Arsi Harju (shot put) and Thomas Johansson and Jyrki Järvi (49er class sailing) being propelled into the national spotlight. With the likes of Mikaela Ingberg and Heli Koivula (athletics) and Jere Hård (swimming) making an increasing impact in Europe, the 2004 Athens Olympic Games are anticipated enthusiastically. Winter Olympic events are, however, usually where a Finn's heart truly lies.

course, the landscape: anyone who can orientate himself or herself in the Finnish wilderness already has a strong, built-in sense of navigation (which certainly comes in useful in the more circuitous rally routes) and must therefore have a distinct advantage over someone who comes from a more "civilised", well laid-out country.

Finally, one must look beyond the physical features of the country and examine the Finnish personality. There is one feature of the Finnish character which the Finns themselves call "*sisu*", a quality so central to their being as to make a dictionary definition nearly impos-

## Sprinters

As proof of their durability, Jalmari Kivenheimo was still exercising and running every day even beyond his 100th birthday. His more famous, but not quite as long-lived running mate, Hannes Kolehmainen scored gold in the 1912 Olympics.

But the Finnish runner whose name has been famous for most of the 20th century was just under competition age in 1912: Paavo Nurmi (1897–1973). A multiple world record-breaker and medal-winner (with four gold medals), Nurmi first competed in the 1920 Olympics. Variously known as the Flying Finn, the

sible. Roughly speaking, the word conjures up an enigmatically tough, independent personality. Hand in hand with the toughness is a determined staying power, even under the most adverse conditions.

*Sisu* has certainly played its role not only in sporting achievement but in Finland's most important pursuit: independence itself. From the republic's very early days – in fact, even before Finnish independence – sport and freedom were inseparably intertwined.

---

**LEFT:** champion racing driver, Mika Häkkinen, perhaps Finland's best-known modern sportsman.
**ABOVE:** ski-jumping is one of Finland's favourite sports.

Phantom Finn and the Phenomenal Finn, he is still remembered for his extraordinary running style, speed, and tough character. That champion of the Olympics movement Avery Brundage said of Nurmi: "No one seeing Nurmi's running style can ever forget him. His running rhythm was his endurance secret; it went beyond majestic movement, and the mathematical use of time."

John Virtanen, one of Nurmi's biographers, adds the observation that Nurmi seemed to disregard gravity as he ran. One reason for this was his incredibly long stride, which was measured during a one-mile race at 2.25 meters (7ft 4½ ins).

Nurmi had running in his blood from an early age. Although his father, a religious man, did not approve of running, believing it to be a frivolous pastime Nurmi exerted his independence and spent every spare moment running with boys in his neighbourhood. He ran in competitions at school, and also alone in the woods. John Virtanen suggests that sports competition between Finnish-speaking Finns and Swedish-speaking Finns was particularly keen in Turku, Nurmi's home town in southwest

### SKATING ON WATER

With its network of lakes frozen into ice for much of the winter, all Finnish children grow up as competent on a pair of ice skating blades as on their own feet.

support his family while he was still attending school. But, as he lifted heavy loads and worked under what were no doubt appalling conditions, Nurmi used to tell himself that all physical labour was good for his dream of being a champion runner.

### Snow and ice

Not surprisingly, skiing is one of the top sports in Finland, and the sport most readily associated with this snow-covered nation. Along with its Scandinavian neighbours, Finland has produced cham-

and heavily Swedish-speaking Finland *(see page 203)*, which may have further fired his ambition.

If indeed some of Nurmi's determination was spurred by local ethnic competition, it is interesting to note that later, according to Virtanen, "no ambassador could have been more effective than Nurmi" in attracting positive international attention and even investment to the fledgling Finnish republic while it struggled to build a modern political and economic life for itself.

Nurmi's father died when Paavo was in his early teens, and from then on economic circumstances forced the boy to work to

pion cross-country and downhill skiers, who benefit from an extended winter season in which to perfect their sport.

But skiing is not the only winter sport in which the nation excels. Ice hockey is also one of the most important team sports in Finland. Almost all males participate at school, and the élite are filtered through and chosen for the best teams. Many Finns play in the North American NHL and many foreigners play in Finnish teams.

Ice hockey is also commercialised: one of the leading teams, Jokerit (the Jokers, referring to a deck of cards rather than humour) is run like a large company. Teams in Helsinki, Tampere and Turku are usually the best, and spectators can number well over 10,000 per game. The 2003 World Cup is to be held in Finland, and the Finns hope that they can improve on their recent collection of silver medals, and take gold for the first time since the team triggered a national festival by beating the Swedes in Sweden in 1995.

## Track and field

Pesäpallo is a Finnish version of American baseball, first developed by Tahko Pihkala. The game soon became a "national" hobby, especially in rural Finland. The best teams now participate in the national Super Pesis League, which is well organised and has become increasingly commercial.

Finns also consider athletics as one of the most interesting and most "Finnish" of all sports. Despite Nurmi's legendary performances, long-distance running now only has one male runner, Samuli Vasala, to keep up Finnish hopes, but javelin-throwing is constantly well represented.

Sporting fields are available for schoolchildren and individuals in every town and village. Local governments finance these facilities and the use of equipment is free. Local championships start from elementary school, and reach their peak in the national level at the annual Kaleva Games.

Although summer sports are not generally associated with Finland, the golf scene has boomed in the last decade. For such a large country 94 courses may not seem a great number nationwide, but the wealthy Greater Helsinki area has 12 greens alone serving the capital's golfers. Land is expensive, and practically every golf course is full throughout the summer months. But while the summer golf season is relatively short, the smart Rovaniemi enthusiasts will even play golf on ice in winter.

In February 2003, Mikko Ilonen became the first Finn ever to shoot a best round on golf's European Tour. Tennis has also enjoyed a boom in Finland in recent years, reflecting the success of Jarkko Nieminen in climbing up the ATP ranking.

---

**LEFT:** All-weather, practice skiing tunnel.
**RIGHT:** Finnish football star, Jari Litmanen playing for Ajax against Valenci in the UEFA Championship League.

> ### UNUSUAL GAMES
>
> Less conventional Finnish sports include the annual Wife-carrying Championships at Sonkajärvi (Savo) and Rubber boot-throwing, also in Savo.

## Sport and scandals

Joy turned to national shame during the World Skiing Championships in Lahti in 2001, when many of the Finnish medalists in the cross country disciplines, including stars such as Mika Myllylä and Harri Kirvesniemi, failed doping tests. Both the men's and women's teams were affected, and the national mood afterwards was almost unbelievably sombre. The fact that cross country skiing has such a central part in the national psyche, and that Finland is one of the world

leaders in the battle against drug cheats, made the shame even greater. The scandal reached all levels of society, and completely overshadowed the 1998–99 pesäpallo match fixing fiasco, which saw players winning large sums from betting on pre-arranged results.

Yet sport continues to dominate even the top level of Finnish society: former presidents Kekkonen, Koivisto and Ahtisaari enjoyed cross country skiing, volleyball and golf respectively, prime minister Paavo Lipponen was a good water polo player in his youth, and former rally champion Ari Vatanen is now a member of the European Parliament. Who said Finns don't take their sports seriously? ❏

# FOOD AND DRINK

*Traditional Finnish cuisine makes fine use of its native ingredients, such as fish and game, washed down by strong coffee or locally brewed beer*

Finland is a land of forests and lakes with abundant possibilities for fine dining. Take the trees – Finns have finally found edible substances in each variety: birch gives Xylitol, a sweetener very kind to teeth; spruce spring shoots are used to make sweet jam, a delicacy served with desserts; pine is a good source of tar, an aromatic substance, not oil but extracted from pine in traditional tar-burning pits. The light tar is a soothing aroma, used in Finnish sweets and ice-cream. Pine is also raw material for the Finnish-invented Benecol margarine-style spread that has been found to have cholesterol-lowering qualities.

## Unusual varieties

Finnish food is as innovative as Xylitol or Benecol demonstrate – the years of agricultural conformity are over and the "rural" Keskusta party is kept outside the government. Be it ostrich farms, strawberry wineries or herb producers, Finnish food is becoming more varied by the day – more Finnish restaurants are opening up, and rarities such as bear meat or unusual fungi can be found more regularly on menus. Herbs are pleasant surprises, and often the least likely choices yield the best sensations – try the tiny vendace (*muikku*) with garlic and cream, an unpretentious fish that has more taste than all tropical varieties combined.

It's the taste that Finland is worth visiting for. The changing seasons, endless daylight in summer, deep forests, thousands of lakes, unpolluted environment, all help Finland to produce interesting culinary delights.

This is a country that also produces "non-vegetables" (varieties that are too small to be "accepted" by the European Union directives) but that is often the very point: the "new" potatoes (the first in the season), which are tiny but full of aroma. Small strawberries, blueberries or handpicked fungi from the forests all taste

**PRECEDING PAGES:** smoked fish is a Baltic delicacy.
**LEFT:** selling smoked fish at market.
**RIGHT:** preparing traditional Finnish pies.

better than their fertilised varieties produced in bulk in warmer countries.

Finnish food as we know it today has a short history. Traditionally Finnish food was made up of fat, and was always homemade. Restaurants were non-existent until enough demand justified imitations of exotic meals, say

"Hawaii Cutlet" which consisted of a piece of pork and a slice of tinned pineapple. Hamburgers, kebabs and pizzas satisfy most of the fast food requirements in modern Finland, but tourists should now have no trouble finding genuine Finnish delicacies.

## Water-fed diet

Take fish, for example. Finland has lakes, rivers and the sea, brimming with local species, and many Norwegian varieties are imported. Fish has always been an important diet for Finns, and it is part of a long culinary tradition. Smoked fish must be the speciality, although it may also be grilled, glow-fired, steamed, or basted in the oven. Fried fish is, fortunately, rare in Finnish restaurants.

Salmon soup is another subtle delicacy: only a little bit of salt is added to the liquid, but the main taste comes from the fish. Each way of cooking salmon in Finland gives a distinctive experience, but *graavi lohi* (raw salmon marinated for a day in salt and herbs) is delicious served with potatoes. "*Graavi*" is the Finnish version of *sushi* – but instead of rice and seaweed, small potatoes and dill are used.

### CRAYFISH SEASON

*Rapujuhla* (crayfish parties) are by invitation only, although all fine restaurants serve crayfish during July and August. Much of the red delicacy is imported, as each small creature costs about €3.

various roes and Baltic herring. In winter, turbot is the seasonal variety. But imported fish is always available, and it's up to the chef whether the food is fresh and well-cooked.

## Hunting nation

Much of Finland's tasty elk meat disappears into private deep-freezes during the hunting season, but semi-domesticated reindeer is more common. The Lapland speciality is *poronkäristys* (reindeer casserole), served with mashed potatoes and

While Finnish salmon should not be missed, don't forget to try *siika* as well. This white fish has a more subtle taste, and is also best in the *graavi* variety, with potatoes and dill. *Silakka* (Baltic herring) and *muikku* (vendace) are small fish, very typical in Finnish restaurants, but lamprey is confusingly not fish at all. It is a vertebrate, and is only caught from the rivers of western Finland. Charcoal-grilled and eaten whole, it's another fine experience of Finnish *haute cuisine*.

Fish is very much a seasonal fare. The spring and summer are good for salmon and perch; crayfish dominates in July and August. Autumn is the season for lampreys, white fish, vendace,

cranberry (lingonberry). It's an excellent way to fill oneself up after a week-long trek in Lapland's wilderness but weight-watchers should be wary. Some westerners feel strange about eating meat from an animal that traditionally helps Santa Claus to deliver his gifts, but reindeer herding is an important livelihood for the Samis in Lapland (*see page 109*). The best part of reindeer is fillet steak, usually worth its price.

The best restaurants in Finland will also serve rare game birds during the season. Wild duck is most common. Its hunting season only runs from late summer to autumn, and it is worth trying when available.

Sausage (*makkara*) is also very popular in summer – best grilled with local mustard. Typically Finnish sausage has more flour than meat but quality varies. In Tampere, *mustamakkara* ("black sausage") contains spices, barley and blood in real gut. Blood may also be added to the Åland Island's *svartbröd* ("black bread"), a distinctively sweet brown bread.

## Regional dishes

Regional differences are notable around Finland. The Karelian menu is completely different from, say, western fare. Salted fish, pies and pastries are typical in Karelia (avoid the pre-

a baked rye bread – although it is an acquired taste to some. The northwest coast is renowned for salmon soup and *leipäjuusto*, a bread-like cheese, often eaten with yellow cloudberries (a sour berry that grows on marshlands).

Potato is the staple food, available all year round, but one restaurant, Ursulan Viinitupa (Pohjoisesplanadi 21 in Helsinki), recently introduced barley to replace rice and pasta (which are common in Finland too). Barley is softer, bigger and, some believe, tastier than rice, but sadly quite rare in restaurants. Barley, oats, rye and rice are all used for porridges, which are typical breakfast items in Finnish

packed Karelian pies at supermarkets, which bear no resemblance to their originals). Rye dough is filled with barley or potato and then turned inwards to create the distinctive Karelian pie, baked in the oven and eaten with mashed four-minute eggs and some butter. Another laborious meal is Karelian meat stew (beef) which takes 12 hours to prepare.

The Lakeland provides plenty of fish, as one would expect, and *muikkukukko* is a typical Savo delicacy, consisting of vendace fish inside

**LEFT:** Helsinki harbour is a good place to find fresh fruit, vegetables and fish.
**ABOVE:** traditional salmon and Finnish beer.

### WHERE TO FIND SPECIALITIES

Helsinki is the best place to look for fresh or smoked fish, in supermarkets or markets for self-catering tourists, as small towns rarely serve culinary delights even for locals – there simply isn't enough demand. An exception is a smørgäsbord, or *seisova pöytä*, which can be outstandingly good or simply bad. Many theme restaurants, such as Karelian houses along the eastern border, serve an excellent variety of marinated and smoked fish, pickled herring or "*graavi*" salmon, salads and other vegetables. The larger hotels prepare invariably a great breakfast buffet, and there are also innovative Finnish versions of international buffets.

homes. The authentic Finnish recipes in this particular restaurant are bravely advertised as "homemade" which perhaps hides the elaborate preparation of the ingredients and complex cooking techniques. Some recipes take hours, even days to cook. Although traditional edible beets, such as swede or turnip are seldom considered as "gourmet food" in modern Finland, why not try one that has been on low heat for a day – fully softened swede requires no spices!

Finns, in fact, seldom use spices. Many raw ingredients have a naturally strong flavour that may simply be lured out by the right cooking technique, with no need for additions.

One special element in Finnish cuisine is the abundance of ingredients that are available free on the forested landscape, including a wide range of berries, fungi and herbs. No one owns these foods and Finnish law allows free access to the forests. However berry- and mushroom-picking is hard work and time-consuming and there is always a small price tag, unless you do it yourself. Blueberries are readily available in July, the native sour cranberries (lingonberries) by September. Numerous varieties of delicious edible mushrooms enter restaurant menus by the autumn, quantity depending on the heaviness of the rains.

**SEASONAL FARE**

Christmas food in Finland is very traditional, and still very much loved, in spite of being rather simple by today's standards. Little has changed on the festive menu over the past century: ham, salmon, casseroles, dried codfish always feature and there are plenty of desserts, including ginger biscuits and the popular star-shaped plum tart, *joulutorttu*. At Easter, Finns consume *mämmi* (a malt-based pudding) and drink *sima* (mead), while *tippaleipä* pastries are the May Day speciality. Festival times apart, Finnish food varies both seasonally and geographically, making it an endless source of fascination and providing pleasant surprises for visitors to the country.

## Bread

Ryebread is unique to Finland – Russians and Swedes produce similar but use different recipes and Finnish ryebread is usually less sweet than its counterparts. All are very different to the German variety. It is healthy bread, available as crispbread (rougher and again less sweet that the Swedish variety), soft and fresh or slightly stickier and harder (*jälki-uunileipä*). The latter variety keeps edible longer and is good with cheese and cold milk.

Finnish ryebread is made of sourdough with water, salt and flour added. The distinctive taste is a result of lactic fermentation during the proving process.

## Alcohol

The Finnish *ravintola* may be a restaurant, bar or pub, and most often people go there to drink. Beer is ubiquitous, and one of the "big five" is most usually served: Koff, Lapin Kulta, Karhu, Olvi or Karjala. But there are many more: microbreweries are popping up with more frequency, often located in historical buildings, across the country.

The same goes for wineries, which for the time being seem unique for Scandinavia;

### DESSERTS AND CAKES

Typically, Finns partake of *kahvi* (coffee) and *pulla* (wheat buns) after their meals. Cakes are also abundant; cream cakes topped with strawberries are typical.

## Where to eat

Whether it's culinary delights, fast food, coffee or a pint of lager, you will always find it: there is a restaurant or just a simple kiosk on practically every corner. The kiosk is another Finnish institution that sells chocolate and groceries when other shops are closed.

Helsinki is the best place to savour Finnish delicacies. A La Maison (Salomonkatu 19) has more than a few ways to prepare vegetables. Here, Finnish food is art – each plate is so beautifully arranged that

Finland gave up part of the restricting alcohol policy (a system similar to other Nordic countries) and allowed private wineries, which number at least 20 around Finland. Strawberries, blackcurrants and redcurrants, among others, are used to produce a distinctive red wine – not exactly Burgundy but it is a well-balanced berry drink with a 12 percent strength! In the same way, local producers are now experimenting by adding other berries to stronger alcohol.

one can barely bring oneself to destroy the effect. Havis Amanda (Unioninkatu 23) specialises in fish and seafood. Kanavaranta (Kanavaranta 3) runs its own cooking school and offers four-course meals with a pre-selected accompanying wine, certainly a reliable choice for gourmet dining, competing perhaps only with Savoy (Eteläesplanadi 14), an expert on seasonal varieties.

Lappi (Annankatu 22) is a truly Lappish experience, with a rich menu of Arctic specialities, including reindeer. The other end is represented by Zetor (Kaivopiha), with a rural 1950s decor and plenty of typically Finnish meals on the menu. ❑

**LEFT:** cranberries are just one of the many berries that abound in Finland's forests.
**ABOVE:** Savoy Restaurant in Helsinki.

# IN DEFENCE OF GREENNESS

*Despite the familiar images of Finland's lakes and forests, the country is struggling like the rest of the world to find solutions to environmental problems*

Finns have long looked to their country's natural environment for a sense of national identity. The national anthem celebrates the country's summer landscape; its blue and white flag is said to represent the white snow of winter and the blue lakes of summer; literature, fine art, design and architecture have all drawn on the environment for a Finnish idiom.

As the environmental campaigner Martti Arkko put it in 1990: "We depend on nature and the environment for everything. If we allow our forests and lakes to become polluted, our Finnishness will disappear too. The hearts of the Finnish people lie in the lakes and forests. They are our identity, our capital and riches."

The defence of Finland's lakes is high on the political agenda, looked on as a battle to preserve nationhood and to save the country's greatest assets and, as a race, Finns really care. One of the arguments against joining NATO is a reluctance to allow American army bases to spoil the beauty of Lapland, and an erosion of the principle of *jokameiehenoikeus* – the right of anyone to roam at will, and pick berries, wild fruits or mushrooms in the Finnish countryside.

## Enter the politicians

The environment became a political issue in the 1980s and has continued be into the 1990s. In 1987, the Green League won four parliamentary seats (4 percent of the votes). In the 1991 general election, this figure rose to 10 seats (nearly 7 percent of the votes), and in 1995 and again in 1999 they joined the five-party "rainbow coalition" government. In the 1999 EU Parliament election, they won two seats. A "green" Finland was on the agenda. In 2002, however, the Greens resigned from government in protest at the decision to build a new nuclear power plant in their country.

Public concern for the environment is nothing new in Finland. As in other Nordic coun-

tries, civic organisations have been committed to protecting the countryside for years. The Finnish State Environmental Administration *(Ympäristöhallinto)*, is a state department overseeing nature reserves, protection of wild plants and animals, and even sustainable housing in urban and rural areas. Various other groups,

such as the Finnish Association for Nature and Conservation (SLL) and *Natur och Miljö* (in Swedish speaking areas), also help conserve the Finnish environment.

## Alarming incidents

As long ago as the early days of national independence, the young republic introduced legal protection for the forests and threatened species, and the Forestry Act of 1886, which was intended to curb wasteful uses of the forests, predated the republic by 30 years. Later laws prohibited the devastation of forests and defended threatened forests areas. Yet, when the owners of the private Lake Koijärvi decided

---

**PRECEDING PAGES:** haystacks under an autumn sun.
**LEFT:** Pyhähäkki National Park.
**RIGHT:** Heidi Hautala, Finnish Green MEP.

to drain it, people who protested were prosecuted for civil disobedience.

The Ministry of the Environment was set up in 1983, and the 1980s was the decade when the government surveyed, theorised, and made policies and assessments. Their conclusions appeared in the 1987 National Report on Environmental Protection in Finland, a substantial overview of the state of the environment. It identified many problems and put forward suggestions for controls, concluding: "General environmental protection goals have been comparatively little considered in Finland, especially from a long-term perspective."

fifth nuclear power plant, that industries want and environmentalists don't. Eurajoki, home of two of Finland's nuclear power stations, has been chosen as the location for nuclear waste, but the decision has faced legal hurdles.

Doom-laden though this may sound, we should remember that, by comparison with the really polluted areas of Europe, Finland is a model of purity. Where the country does suffer, perhaps more acutely than others, is from the atmospheric and water pollution of its near-neighbours. Russia is the principal offender, but Poland and what was the GDR have also contributed to the pollution of the Baltic Sea.

Finland's problems are the basic ones shared by industrial nations everywhere: air and water pollution, energy conservation, the despoilation of the natural landscape, endangered species and waste management. Finland has generated more solid municipal waste *per capita* than any other European country, but recycling schemes have increased recently.

The biggest issue concerns emissions and a long-term solution for suitable energy sources. Implementation of the Kyoto Protocol in 1997 is crucial, as Finland's carbon dioxide emissions are one of the largest *per capita* in the EU. Finland is determined to reach the 1990 level by year 2010. The main argument is about the

Since the 1987 report, the government has acted on some of its suggestions. There has been more talk – conferences and summits on the state of the Baltic, on the Arctic, and on acidification – and Finland has put its clean-air and clean-water industrial technology at the disposal of Russia and Eastern Europe.

## Forest threats

Driving through Finland, you might feel there is little cause for concern about its endless green forests and lakes, but the Finns nevertheless brought a Wilderness Act into force in February 1991 to defend the areas which remain in their natural state. The Act designated as "wilderness" 12 areas in Lapland, each road-less and some 150,000 hectares (380,000 acres) in size. Protected zones now account for nearly one-third of Lapland's area. Forestry will be restricted and limited to "natural forestry", where operations are adapted to natural development. No extensive felling, no clearing, and natural regeneration are the prime components.

Finnish forestry accounts for 78 percent of the total land area, some 230,000 sq. km (90,000 sq. miles). It is Finland's largest resource and major export, and forestry and mining provide a large proportion of the country's income. So it is unfortunate that forestry, timber processes and

forestry certificate system was initiated. Overall, forestry has undergone extensive reforms to conform to EU and global requirements for better management.

After Finland joined the EU, the ill-fated Natura protection scheme soured relations between private landowners and the Ministry of Environment. Some landowners have been notorious for clear-felling forests next to a national park, and the programme sparked widespread protests and even more clear felling. The initially popular minister Pekka Haavisto thus lost his seat in the *Eduskunta* (Parliament) in the 1999 election.

mining can cause the most damage to the environment.

Planting, bog-draining for plantations, fertilising and felling have all had severe consequences, changing natural habitats and the balance of Finland's water courses, and over-exploiting the soil. Responsible forest management has been the government's solution but, as the state owns only 27 percent of the forests, it has had to offer incentives for private owners to subscribe to the national plan. In 1998 a

**LEFT:** the image of summer that every Finn wants to preserve.
**ABOVE:** building a road from tyres in Toivakka.

### HUMAN THREATS

The green sanctuaries that are Finland's forests are also Finland's recreational playgrounds. The right of common access permits free access to all the country's forests and allows such activities as the picking of berries and mushrooms, and fishing in the lakes, which are national summer pastimes. But greater use of the forests for recreation also brings more problems: the dispersion of litter and different forms of pollution, such as the noise and emissions of too many vehicles, not to mention the selfish drivers who thoughtlessly plough their cars at speed through uncharted territory.

Finnish lakes are in a better shape than they were some 20 years ago, but fertilising residues from farmland still pose a substantial threat to the environment.

While afforestation and exploitation of the forests have spoiled some habitats, the trees are threatened by air pollution or acidification ("acid rain"). Like other countries, Finland has legal limits designed to control industrial emissions. Policing of these emissions and the question of whether the limits are pitched at an acceptable level are the nub of the issue. Environmentalists push for tighter controls; industry argues for economically "realistic" targets.

## RAISING REINDEER

In Lapland, there is a different cycle of difficulties and paradoxes. The cultural traditions and the livelihood of the Sami, or Lapps, both contribute to environmental damage and are threatened by it. Reindeer herds are a fundamental part of the Sami's lives. Chernobyl was a disaster and meant that hundreds had to be killed. Yet, in that same summer of 1985, the Sami reindeer herds exceeded quotas (introduced to prevent over-grazing and the destruction of young trees) by almost 100,000. Another contradictory factor is the predators – wolves, lynx, eagles, wolverine – protected by the government but seen by the Sami as a threat to their reindeer.

## Making improvements

"Green" policies have for some time been part of everyday Finnish life. Recycling schemes and attempts to improve house insulation continue, and the government has repeated its commitment to public transport. The merits of nuclear power as opposed to fossil fuels are still hotly debated. New worries, such as the damage salt on winter roads may do to the water courses, also rear up regularly. The Baltic Sea is an on-going concern, and global environmental catastrophes continue to preoccupy Finns, as they do people everywhere.

Small-scale Finnish projects, which could solve some of the western world's ecological problems, hit the headlines from time to time. The pioneering idea of building a road out of chopped-up rubber car tyres was intended to have a dual "green" purpose. Firstly, it gave a use for tyres, which are notoriously difficult to dispose of. Secondly, the experiment was an attempt to find a durable road surface able to resist the strains of the fierce winter ice, which calls for frequent road maintenance and endless resurfacing. Other experiments have involved research into biodegradable plastic – especially carrier bags – as a sideline of Finland's oil refineries.

In the world of design, too, specialists have been applying their minds to ecological considerations, with the maximum use of recycled and recyclable materials, the minimum use of energy during the manufacturing process, and the longest possible life for the product.

From a visitor's point of view, Finland may already represent a supremely unspoilt environment. The main selling line of the Finnish Tourist Board has been the country's landscape, supported by photographs of summer in Finland's green forests, its blue waters and its leafy towns. Human habitation appears in its proper context, a tiny sprinkling of buildings in a vast forested terrain.

This is a true picture of Finland, nevertheless. In a country which is the seventh largest in Europe, the 5 million-plus inhabitants are just a blip on the map, highly influential but outnumbered several thousand to one by trees. For this reason, if no other, it is in Finland's interest to protect its natural domain. ❏

**LEFT:** the true Finnish home is in the forest.
**RIGHT:** Finland's lakes and forests.

# A WILDERNESS EXPERIENCE

*It may have been slower to adapt to tourism than its more popular neighbours, but Finland's natural splendour is attracting an increasing number of visitors*

Finland, often forgotten or sometimes ignored, is one of the best-kept secrets in Europe. It's a country with few world-renowned attractions: no fjords, no medieval Orthodox monasteries like its Nordic neighbours. Yet Finland has an indigenous culture with much regional variety, thousands of lakes, rivers and islands, and unlimited possibilities for activities.

Slowly, the world is taking notice. Finland, a member of the European Union and the euro currency area, offers unspoiled wilderness, quaint historical attractions, peace and quiet and free access to practically anywhere – all forests are potentially yours for trekking, berry- and mushroom-picking or short-term camping.

Finland has its share of great European legacy – about 70 medieval stone churches, several imposing castles and plenty of old and new art in museums. Its own traditions are preserved in numerous museums around the country – indeed, there may still be more museums than hotels in Finland!

Statistically, Finland is a very quiet place. In the most recent year for which statistics are available, 657 hotels in the whole of Finland attempted to house tourists – about the same amount as in the city of Prague, and fewer than in many other large cities. Occupancy rates were on average below 50 percent; not even Greater Helsinki managed to get above 60 percent. Many hotels are small: there are only 43,000 hotel rooms in the country, or an average of 65 rooms per hotel. In fact, not all tourists choose hotels. There are campsites, lakeside holiday villages, guesthouses, youth hostels, and some even camp privately in the wild. Supply increases when the summer comes, exactly following the demand.

Finns view tourism as an escape, choosing the elements over Mediterranean warmth. Until recently, the industry has not been taken seriously. Domestic tourism has been slow to pick up and, so far, mass tourism has remained elsewhere, but individuals are beginning to arrive in greater numbers.

## Local attractions

The Finnish Tourist Board lists the Top Twenty tourist attractions, including five spas, three

amusement parks, two churches, one casino and one festival – only eight are conventional tourist attractions such as museums or theme parks. No wonder, tourists are confused. Therein lies the dilemma of the Finnish tourism industry – no one would travel all the way to Finland just to visit third-rate versions of Disneyland, and much of the existing hoopla is around locally popular entertainment.

World-class attractions in the Top Twenty are few – Kiasma, the Museum of Contemporary Art *(see page 173)*, Bomba House in Nurmes *(see page 275)* or the Ateneum Art Museum in Helsinki *(see page 156)* are worth a visit. Little-known wonders attract few visitors, which is

**LEFT:** braving the white waters of Finland's vast network of lakes.
**RIGHT:** light traffic is good news for cyclists.

partly explained by the lack of guidebooks. Indeed, Insight Guides Finland was the first modern guidebook in English when the first edition was published in 1992.

Finns really turned outward towards the end of the 1980s. Prior to this, there weren't even money exchange services available in Helsinki centre at weekends. With a language few can understand, Finns were, and still are, seldom understood. They still have a gauche, slightly perplexed attitude to tourists. Finns don't always smile at you when you'd expect them to, and do when you wouldn't. They remain silent when you want to hear an explanation,

or they talk (in Finnish) when you'd rather enjoy the serenity. In many cases, tourists still experience the unconditional warmth when they are treated as guests, not as customers, especially in farms, only to experience the greediest con artist in a rip-off tourist trap the next moment.

If Finns are eccentrics, so are some of the attractions. The wife-carrying championships are an international media event, as was the first Kutemajärvi sex festival, exclusively for old and stout people. There are offbeat art exhibitions, weird festivals (the annual tango festival is the biggest in the country) and mad habits –

## SPECIAL INTEREST HOLIDAYS

As Finland lacks mass tourism, most visitors have an individual approach to the country, with specific needs. It may seem that Jyväskylä is packed with architecture buffs pointing wide-angled lenses at buildings designed by Alvar Aalto; architecture fans may choose functionalism, Art Nouveau, modern or Neo-classical "tours". Music lovers may choose among hundreds of small or large festivals, or follow Sibelius' footsteps from Hotel Kämp in Helsinki to Ainola to North Karelia. Visitors interested in design can tour various glass factories and pottery studios. Santa Claus can be visited in Rovaniemi. People who want traditional saunas will discover the very roots of Finnishness.

saunas are too hot, and in winter, you're supposed to jump into a hole in the ice!

Savonlinna, the opera festival held in a medieval castle *(see page 92)* has been a success. In Retretti, a man-made cave became an eerie but hectic summer art exhibition *(see page 257)*. Modern architecture shaped the Forest Museum Lusto to become an interesting exhibition on anything wooden – now the region is one of the top destinations in Nordic countries.

## Nature Calls

As Finnish nature is so varied and so accessible, the only limit is imagination. Activity holidays are increasing. Several bird-watching towers have been built near major lakes and bays – the Worldwide Fund for Nature has financed Liminganlahti near Oulu. Individual tourists have about 180,000 lakes to choose from for canoeing, swimming or skiing in winter when ice covers all lakes. Fishing is possible in lakes, rivers, rapids and seashore – a permit is required. Moving from one place to another is possible with skis, dog sleighs or snowmobiles in winter, by bicycle or trekking in summer.

Many tourists seek natural experiences in Finnish national parks. Finland's unique park network is mostly administered by the Forest and Park Service, which controls 29 national

National parks are just the tip of the iceberg. Local municipalities often finance recreational hiking routes for local needs. Many of these can be combined, and thus was born the Karelian Circle Trek, Finland's longest trekking route with approximately 1,000 km (620 miles) of marked trails.

The Karelian Circle Trek offers genuine wilderness routes, variety in four different national parks, and a possibility to combine walking with mountain biking or canoeing. Fishing gear is common, and some even carry a hunting gun. This a friendly wilderness, with no fear of dangerous wild animals, and locals

parks, 14 strict nature reserves and over 350 other protected areas. The organisation rents interesting accommodation in isolated wilderness cottages, often of relatively high quality. It's a network that works from the main information office Tikankontti in Helsinki to excellent park headquarters near the park entrances to assistant wilderness guides who can be reached by a handy mobile phone – and each rentable wilderness hut is now featured on the Internet.

are also friendly. Almost 1 million euros (£600,000/US$960,000) have been spent on this route. Sleeping is possible in bed-and-breakfast locations, free wilderness huts (or ones that have to be reserved in advance) or lean-to structures. Pitching a tent is legal (and free) almost everywhere along this route.

## Organised tours

Small service companies are now popping up around Finland. One of the biggest is Experiences Unlimited, based in Helsinki, which mostly caters to Finnish customers. Owner Timo Heinaro calls himself an adventurer: "Finland lacks the Alps, but with

**LEFT:** the snowmobile is a fast and fun way to get around in winter.
**ABOVE:** ice-breakers are a popular tourist attraction.

innovation, we have been able to avoid the mass tourism and concentrate on small individual groups." Heinaro's company has grown rapidly – 20 percent of his customers are foreigners. "We believe incoming incentive tourism will grow enormously in years to come. Most of all, Finland has genuine experiences available, good infrastructure, reliable facilities: safety and cleanliness are key words."

In Nurmes, the Metsänväki Group recently moved to the new Safari House (tel: 13-480 126, www.bomba.fi) near the famous Bomba tourist centre. The company provides full-range adventure services, including winter outfits for

the shallow, lukewarm water, riding horses across dirt tracks, paddling in the lake, then savouring an enormous buffet with fresh farm produce, game, fish and wonderful cakes. The opportunity for individual freedom is an experience in itself – nothing is actually forbidden – as you have the forest tracks and lakes to enjoy all for yourself.

Naturally, the peace and quiet is not to everyone's taste. One wealthy German arrives regularly at a certain small lakeside cottage in the heart of Finland, enjoys the solitude for two weeks and then returns happily to his hectic business life in Germany.

150 people. Activities may include husky tours, or snowshoe treks to wilderness in winter. Here gateway services are available on the tourist path although real adventure takes place off-road – canoeing, rafting or trekking in summer.

## Farm holidays

As the EU membership decreases chances among Finnish farmers to earn from agriculture alone, many families are now turning their estates into guesthouses. Bed-and-breakfast may be the official term, but most farms provide the visitors with a full range of options. It's an experience that will always be unforgettable – bathing in a lakeside sauna, with a dip in

## Lakeland leisure

Increased tourism along Finland's lake system is bringing the lake steamers back into business. There are now regular passenger routes on several of the lake systems but the oldest and probably the most romantic are those across Saimaa's vast expanses *(see page 253)*. Steam first came to Saimaa, wheezing and belching its thick black smoke, in the 1830s. It revolutionised the timber business, until then reliant on sailing vessels – and, in turn, their dependence on the vagaries of the wind – enabling easier transport of Finland's "green gold" from forest to factory during the short summer months.

The heyday of passenger steamers was in the early years of the 20th century, when the well-to-do of St Petersburg arrived by the night train at Lappeenranta for a leisurely nine-hour steamer trip to Savonlinna, then a new and fashionable spa. In due course the steamers covered the four points of the Saimaa compass, picking up and dropping off the lakeland's scattered inhabitants, along with livestock and every imaginable form of cargo, at communities of all sizes or no size at all. One of the great sights of Savonlinna each morning and evening was the Saimaa fleet of wooden double-deckers. Several still survive.

unmistakable sleek shape and the long-nosed jet slips elegantly down from the sky.

And it's here that Santa Claus himself may be visited 365 days a year, around an ever-growing tourist village by the name of Napapiiri (Arctic Circle). It's a similar attraction to the Equator – one can officially experience the midnight sun to the north of the Arctic line, which is clearly marked across Napapiiri village. This is the biggest tourist trap in the entire country, but a nice reminder of the meek character of the whole country – a theme village built around a character who couldn't possibly be more sympathetic to his guests. ❑

## Christmas visitors

The most recent newcomer to Finland's skies is Concorde, now a regular midsummer and mid-winter visitor to the Arctic Circle with its full complement of passengers eager to "meet" Santa Claus on home territory (see page 138). It is still enough of a novelty to attract a large number of Rovaniemi's citizens. As arrival time approaches, a steady stream of traffic heads out to the airport. There is an appreciative murmur as a distant speck materialises into that

**LEFT:** enjoying a winter break in Espoo.
**ABOVE:** fishing in the rapids near Viitasaari.
**RIGHT:** dry slope bob sleighing.

### TRAVELLING WITH POSTMEN

Finland is a large country. Distances are long but accessibility is easy with public transport. About 90 percent of all Finland's public roads carry regular coach services, including the admirable yellow postbuses which reach deep into areas where few visitors penetrate. Though slower than their more commercial rivals, they provide closer contact with the Finnish ethos. The driver is also the ticket-collector, guide, mentor, friend to country ladies struggling back from market, and postman, delivering mail by a flick of the wrist into rows of roadside postboxes, sometimes far from any visible habitation.

# LAPLAND: THE HOME OF SANTA CLAUS

*Everyone "knows" that Santa Claus comes from Lapland, and today he is fast becoming the biggest tourist attraction in Finland*

Since the beginning of the tourist boom in the 1950s that played on the legend of Santa Claus and Lapland, some 600,000 children in a total of 158 countries write to Finland's Santa every year. Sweden's Jultomten is the biggest competitor to the Finnish Santa, but more than 32,000 letters arrive daily in Lapland in the run up to Christmas, most often from the United Kingdom, Poland or Japan, all expressing their Christmas wishes for that year.

Santa Claus and the Arctic Circle bring 400,000 visitors annually, and there may be 30 nationalities represented any day. Santa "speaks" several European languages – including the essential phrases in Chinese and Japanese.

## PROTECTING A LEGEND

Sinikka Salokorpi is a Santa Claus expert in Finland and has written the official Santa "thesis" for the Ministry of Trade and Industries. It is literally an official publication and includes photos of authentic Santa Claus garments. Although written with a tongue-in-cheek attitude, the booklet defines more than the dress code. It tells us, among other things, that although there is harmony with foreign Santas, the "real" Santa lives in Finland. "It's a commercial battleground – Santa is big business," says Salokorpi.

◁ **FACE TO FACE**
Young children from around the world delight in their visit to the "real" Santa Claus on specialist trips to Lapland.

▷ **RED-NOSED REINDEER**
Although Santa sometimes "uses" helicopters these days, he still uses several reindeer to get around, including Rudolph and friends.

△ **HOME SWEET HOME**
Santa officially "lives" in a small hut at the Korva-tunturi, a 483-metre (1,580-ft) hill at the Finnish-Russian border.

▽ **SANTA TRAIN**
To meet Santa, you must get off the Santa Claus Express train at Rovaniemi and proceed 10 km (6 miles) to Napapiirii.

△ **SANTA TRAINEES**
In reality, there are many working Santas. The Santa Claus Academy started in 1998, and graduates can be hired via the Santa Claus Office.

▷ **CHRISTMAS DREAMS**
Even letters addressed to "Santa, North Pole" or "Reindeer Street" still find their way to the Arctic Circle, Finland.

## SANTA CLAUS THEME PARKS

The Arctic Circle was never an entity until German soldiers marked the spot during World War II, but still no one took much notice until Eleanor Roosevelt paid a visit in 1950; a simple shack was built for the occasion. Mrs Roosevelt became an unofficial sponsor for the growing Santa Claus village, which now includes shops, a Santa Claus Office and, of course, Santa's post office.

The recently founded Santa Park, in co-operation with British theme park experts, is the biggest Santa-related tourist trap in Finland. Just 2 km (1 mile) from the main Arctic Circle area, the "park" found an ingenious location inside an artifical cave. You walk 200 metres (220 yards) inside Syväsenvaara hill and find the Magic Sleigh Ride and other attractions. A digitally produced photo with Santa is available in two minutes – a popular souvenir – but other companies want their share: Christmas paraphernalia and Finnish design is also for sale.

# PLACES

*A detailed guide to the entire country, with principal sites
clearly cross-referenced by number to the maps*

**N**obody has managed to count with any degree of certainty how many lakes and islands there are in Finland – almost enough, it seems, for every Finnish family to have an island or lake of its own, with plenty of space for visitors too. No wonder an ideal Finnish summer is based on a wooden cabin at the edge of lake or sea and a wooden smoke sauna house nearby. With some fishing, swimming, and a small boat tied up alongside, this is Finnish perfection.

There are seemingly endless expanses of untouched landscape, crossed by endless straight roads running between tall trees. Roads like these eat up the distances, though beware in case the sheer ease of navigating the long avenue stretching ahead encourages a tendency to doze off at the wheel.

As the road heads ever further north, you scarcely realise at first that the rolling farmland of the south has moved into those boundless forests and that, gradually, the dark green gives way to the peat and tundra of Lapland, where the midnight sun gives the landscape a red glow in the late evening. This is the territory of reindeer, and the animals of the wilderness areas – bear, wolf and lynx – though their numbers have declined in recent years. In the northwest the ground rises to more than 1,000 metres (3,000 ft) as it reaches towards the Norwegian mountains. Along the west coast of the Gulf of Bothnia, the beaches and surprisingly warm waters are ripe for exploration.

Even the cities are interspersed with greenery. Parks and trees run between the houses and rocky knolls protrude above street level to make possible a church such as Temppeliaukio Church in Helsinki, scooped literally out of the rock, under a beautiful domed roof.

For a country of five million, Finland has produced an astonishing number of architects, artists, sculptors and designers – and it shows. In Helsinki, in particular, almost every corner reveals an intriguing detail: an elegantly carved façade on a block of flats, a statue, a curved window, or a small figurine full of humour that you nearly miss but laugh when you spot it. In older cities such as Turku or Porvoo, where the Swedish influence was strongest, some of the oldest buildings remain. Nowhere else in Scandinavia has so many cultural festivals or such an assortment of artistic events.

Even the seasons seem more distinct. In winter, it is time for snow and skiing and also for the great reindeer round-ups in Lapland. In summer, sea and lake are full of sails and swimmers. Between the two are a sudden bursting spring when everything turns green in a week, and autumn, full of reds and browns as the leaves swirl over the city squares. Finland is emphatically a land for all seasons. ❑

**PRECEDING PAGES:** Helsinki's skyline at sunset; sauna near the lakeland town of Jyväskylä; skiing at Saariselkä in Lapland.
**LEFT:** solitary sauna at Ranssin Kievariin, near Tampere.

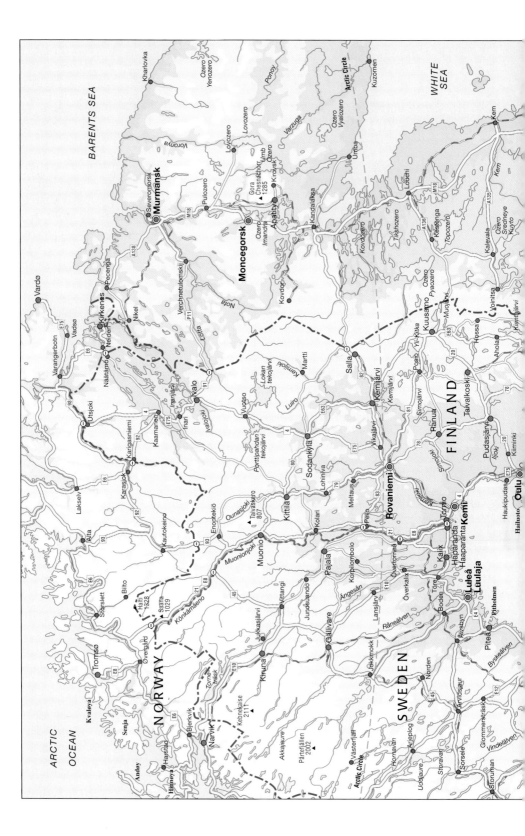

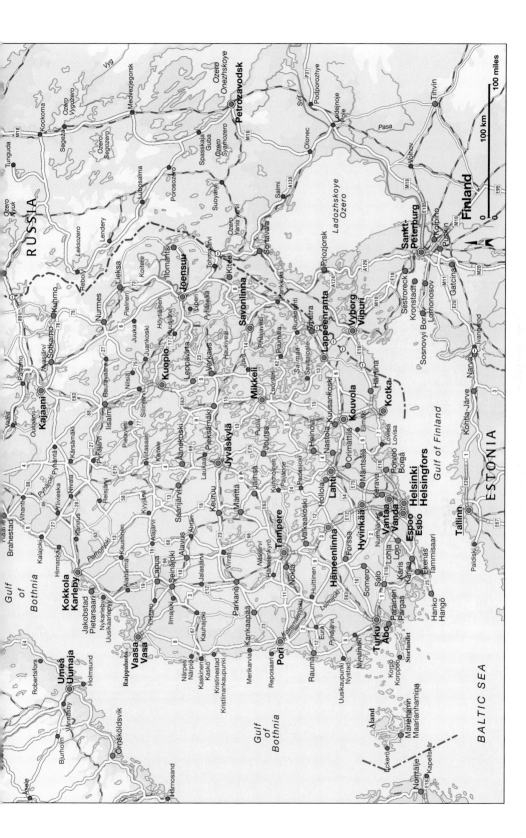

# HELSINKI

Map on page 154

*With its intriguing cultural mix of Russians and Scandinavians, the tiny Finnish capital has a charm as fresh as the breeze that blows over its harbour from the Baltic Sea*

S urrounding the city, the sea appears when you least expect it, its salty tongue lapping at the sides of metropolitan bridges and boulevards, pressing its way into residential areas, creating natural harbours and bays.

In summer, the sea glistens and preens under a tireless sun, driving the light-starved locals wild with its rays. Autumn arrives and, as darkness encroaches and the rains begin to fall, it starts to churn, creating a world of wet and grey where the borders between sea and land are no longer distinct. Only during the long cold winter does the sea finally rest, freezing into an endless expanse on which weekend promenaders can walk dogs or try out their cross-country skis.

To understand Helsinki is to accept that kitsch title "Daughter of the Baltic". It is to the Baltic that Helsinki owes its fortunes, its weather and perhaps even the massive, undulating nature of its architecture. It is also to the Baltic that the city owes much of its relatively short but difficult history.

**PRECEDING PAGES:** Helsinki harbour. **LEFT:** produce on sale at the harbour. **BELOW:** dome of Helsinki Cathedral.

## Helsinki's history

Helsinki was founded in 1550 by King Gustav Vasa of Sweden-Finland to compete with Tallinn in Estonia, whose port was controlled by the Hanseatic League. A first fledgling city was erected on the mouth of the Vantaa River at the innermost point of the Helsinki Bay – a little northeast of where Helsinki stands today. To fill it, Gustav Vasa simply ordered citizens from Porvoo, Ulvila and Rauma to move to the new town.

The new port of "Helsingfors" proved, however, to be not only unpopular but unlucrative as the shallow inner bay became shallower and impossible to navigate. It languished for nearly a century until a visiting governor general named Per Brahe recommended it be moved further towards the open sea. In 1640 a second site was designated on the section of present-day Helsinki called Kruununhaka, and the citizens again moved. On this new site Helsinki finally began to grow, though it still wasn't much more than an outpost for fishermen and farmers. Then the Russian Empire stirred against Sweden, and the town's small fortunes began to go downhill. After battling against the Great Famine in 1697, the Northern War from 1700 to 1721, and the Great Plague in 1710, Helsinki was reduced to ashes and the population to some 150 hardy souls.

Sweden's decision in 1746 to build Suomenlinna Fortress off the shore of Helsinki *(see page 177)*, to protect what remained of its Finnish territory, proved to be the city's saviour. Construction of the fortress drew attention to the port and brought it its first taste of wealth. Merchants constructed a handful of stone houses and, although streets were still unpaved, an interest in European cultural life took root.

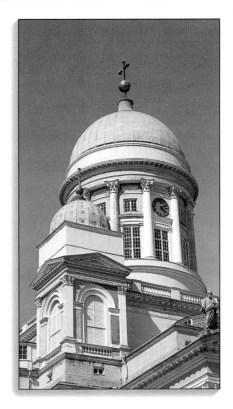

The city was given new life. Russian money and the talents of German architect Carl Ludwig Engel, were poured into the creation of administrative halls and a cathedral. As the city began to enjoy steady prosperity from around 1850, workers' homes were mostly replaced with stone ones. By 1900, Helsinki was a new place. In half a century it grew from a small port with some 20,000 inhabitants into a bona fide capital city. The population soared to 100,000, a railway was built, and gasworks, electricity and water mains all laid down. At the same time, Helsinki became the seat of the nationalist movement. Native architects, such as Eliel Saarinen, then Alvar Aalto, emerged; after independence in 1917, the more Finnish functionalism replaced Jugend (the German version of Art Nouveau) as Helsinki's predominant architectural style.

Unfortunately, nothing could completely protect the city from the massive Russian air raids of 1944 – nor from fervent, and not always lovely postwar reconstruction. But Helsinki's position on the sea resurfaced to help it regain and then increase its stature, not only as a major port but eventually also as the important site for shipbuilding and international meetings it is today.

## Helsinki today

Modern Helsinki is a tranquil but still growing city with some 600,000 occupants – many of whom are second-generation city dwellers. Gone are the marshes and wooden houses, but the faces of the fishermen who sell their catch from the docks are reminders of the city's recent urbanisation. Helsinki isn't a frivolous city but the Finns have let their innate artistry flavour their capital. Statues stand on every other corner, and even the most functional of buildings are notable monuments to Finland's architectural history.

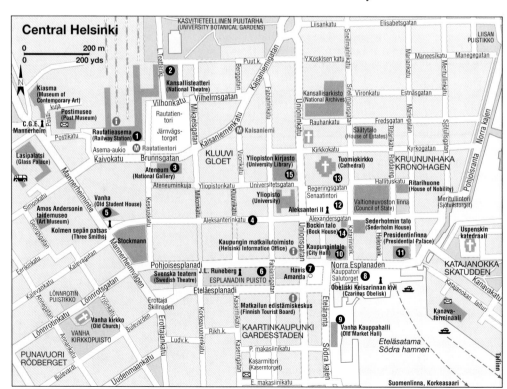

Consider **Rautatieasema**, the **Railway Station** . A busy place that connects Helsinki with numerous commuter cities as well as the rest of Finland, it also contains both a metro station stop and an underground shopping complex. At the same time, the station is a strikingly stylish, round-edged structure in pinkish granite with green trim, a black roof and a 48-metre (160-ft) green clocktower.

Designed by Eliel Saarinen in 1905 but not completed until 1919, it links two of Helsinki's most prevalent styles: National Romanticism and functionalism *(see page 79)*. It also incorporates work by several other well-known Finns. Thanks to Emil Wikström, pairs of solemn-faced, muscular giants hold translucent lanterns on either side of the station's impressive front doors. A large painting by Eero Järnefelt looks over the Eliel Restaurant inside.

The railway station has replaced the harbour as the metropolitan focus. Elielinaukio, between the station and the Post Museum, was completely renovated during Helsinki's "City of Culture" year, and accordingly looks fresh and stylish. It is also a good reference point for a city tour; most places of interest to visitors are within walking distance of here. An extensive network of urban transport also uses the station as its base. The metro stops beneath it, many buses stop beside it and almost all trams stop in front of it.

## Exploring the city

The first thing to do before beginning a tour of Helsinki, however, is to find your directional bearings. These are not immediately obvious because much of central Helsinki lies on a peninsula, jutting southward into the Baltic. Being by the sea, therefore, doesn't automatically mean you are in the south of the city. In fact, the peninsula has only a brief southern shore but extended longitudinal coasts on both its eastern and western sides.

Don't rely on names either, which can be deceiving, particularly if they belong to the time not so long ago when the city was much smaller. The "South" Harbour actually lies on the peninsula's eastern side. It is, however, south of Kruununhaka – the city centre when it was built. Just keep in mind that the railway station is pretty much right in the middle of the peninsula; the tiny *Keskusta*, or centre, runs east-west below it; and the other sections of central Helsinki radiate out around them.

More confusing, probably, is a visitor's initial glance at the city. Helsinki doesn't follow any of the rules of European capitals. It isn't quaint; it isn't regal; it isn't even terribly old. Little more than a century ago, there were still animals wandering in the streets, and almost everything wooden predating 1808 was burnt to the ground. So don't be surprised to step out of the railway station and find yourself face to face with two monolithic commercial complexes side-by-side; one, modern and bedecked with neon signs, called *Kaivopiha*, and the second, nicknamed *Makkaratalo*, or "Sausage House", because of a long tubular balcony winding about its façade. Helsinki is a pragmatist – and for good reason. But Helsinki can also be compelling, not in a flirtatious way but in a quintessentially Finnish way: reserved, modest, yet stylish and wry.

**Map on page 154**

*All Helsinki road signs are shown in both Finnish and Swedish.*

**BELOW:** the guard-house at the Presidential Palace.

The **Kansallisteatteri (National Theatre)** ❷, to the immediate east of the station and at the northern head of the cobbled railway square, is impressive. This little castle in white granite with green trim and a red roof was conceived in national romantic style. Productions are in Finnish but the pensive statue of Aleksis Kivi, Finland's national writer, in front of it, transcends language.

Directly across the square from the theatre is the **Ateneum** ❸ (Kaivokatu 2; tel: 9-173 361; open Tues–Sun; entrance fee). Built in 1887, the Ateneum's gilt yellow-and-white façade might seem reminiscent of St Petersburg but it is the site of Finland's National Gallery of Art, one of the first manifestations of Finland's struggle for independence. The museum's collection of Finnish paintings, sculpture and graphic art covers the years 1750 to 1960 and includes works by such famous Finns as Akseli Gallén-Kallela and Albert Edelfelt.

The Ateneum lies on the east side of Makkaratalo. Wedged in between Kaivopiha and the north-south running **Mannerheimintie** (Helsinki's main thoroughfare and the longest street in Finland) is the handsome though slightly faded Seurahuone Hotel. Inside, the red-velveted, high-ceilinged Café Socis is a perennial favourite with locals and resident foreigners, especially late at night.

## Shops and students

Behind these buildings stretch three blocks containing one of Helsinki's most important shopping districts. **Aleksanterinkatu** ❹ (better known as Aleksi), running parallel to the railway station, is the main thread of this area, but intersecting streets also contain shops. Kaivopiha's fountain-crowned square has its own special shopping identity; outdoor racks sell postcards and novelties, and at weekends there are often street fairs and art markets.

**BELOW:**
Wikström's massive figures at Helsinki Railway Station.

Steps from this square lead up to Mannerheimintie and **Vanha (Old Student House)** ❺. Built in 1870, Vanha's own stairs are a favourite meeting-place for young trendies in leather jackets, and its interior now houses a "progressive" performance hall, smoky drinking room, exhibition quarter and library. Student organisations, as well as a cinema and ticket service, have been moved to the New Student House, on the other side of the Kaivopiha steps.

Map on page 154

Vanha lies on the intersection of Aleksi and Mannerheimintie, and a trio of naked men with fine pectorals – the Three Smiths' Statue – dominate the triangular square beneath it. As soon as the snow melts in spring, musicians use this square to serenade the passing crowds, ice cream stands open for business and even some café tables appear.

Finland's largest department store, **Stockmann**, lies on the other side of Three Smiths' Square from Vanha. Beside it, on Keskuskatu, is Scandinavia's largest bookshop, Akateeminen Kirjakauppa *(see page 313)*. This is a great place to browse in, though an expensive one given the high price of hardback books in Finland. Upstairs is a stylish café designed by Alvar Aalto.

*Traditional Finnish dolls are popular souvenirs.*

## Place to meet

The bookshop faces another Helsinki landmark, **Esplanadin puisto (Esplanade Park)** ❻. Planned by Ehrenström (also responsible for the 19th-century city plan), it was first laid out in 1831 and runs east-west between Mannerheimintie and South Harbour.

The **Svenska teatern (Swedish Theatre)**, an elegant semi-circular stone building dating from 1866, commands Esplanade Park's western head on Mannerheimintie. Back to back with it and facing into the long and narrow park is

**BELOW:** a quiet day in Helsinki's harbour.

a family-type restaurant called Teatteri. Its terrace is always filled with relaxed beer drinkers in warm weather.

An old-fashioned promenade leads from here across the length of the park; between well-sculpted patches of lawn, past the central statue of J. L. Runeberg, Finland's national poet, to the Kappeli Restaurant at its eastern end. This park is still a popular meeting place and is the scene of the Christmas Fair and the Night of the Arts in August. On May Day Eve it is given over to general lunacy. Kappeli is also an important spot for a rendezvous, though in recent years it has lost its sheen. The tall, lacy windows and a whimsical roof give it a Chekhovian, gazebo-like feel – the older parts of the café date from 1867. Like all self-respecting restaurants in Helsinki, Kappeli has a summer terrace. This mars its beauty but allows patrons to simultaneously enjoy fresh air, drinks and a range of musical performances (Jun–Sept) from the bandstand opposite.

Flanking the bandstand are two pretty little "ponds" graced by statues of cavorting fish boys and water nymphs. But they cannot compete with the **Havis Amanda fountain** ➐ on the small square that separates the eastern end of the park from the South Harbour amid a constant swirl of traffic and trams. The sensuous bronze Amanda created quite a stir when she was first erected in 1908. Surrounded by four sea lions spouting water, she represents the city of Helsinki rising from the sea, innocent and naked. On May Day Eve, at least, she gets something to wear – a white student cap – while a champagne-happy chaos of clustering human cap-wearers cheer. This square is also the site of an outdoor produce, handicrafts and flower market.

Two boulevards stretch east-west alongside either side of the park. Nowadays, the fine 19th-century stone buildings along Pohjoisesplanadi mostly house

**BELOW:** enjoying the sunshine in Esplanadi.

design shops like Marimekko and Aarikka, the latter featuring, among other things, Aarikka's distinctive wooden jewellery. Number 19 is an exception. The **Helsinki Information Office** and the **City Tourist Board** occupy its first floor. Both offer extensive selections of maps and brochures.

More venerable houses line the Southern Esplanadi, most of which function in some type of official or commercial capacity. The oldest is Engel's Empire-style former Council of State, dating from 1824. During the period of Russian rule, it was the palace of the governor general.

Map on page 154

## Going to market

The **Kauppatori (Central Market Square)** ❸, across from Havis Amanda on the South Harbour, exudes a much earthier type of appeal. A busy market makes its home here year round, from 7am to 2pm Mondays through Saturdays and, again, from 3.30pm to 8pm during summer weekday evenings. Going to market is still an important part of daily routine in Helsinki, partly because agrarian life is a comparatively recent experience for many residents. Shoppers, baskets tossed over their arms, wander from stand to stand looking for the perfect new potato or bunch of dill.

Peninsular Helsinki has no less than four open-air markets. Of these, the Central Market is both the one most aimed at visitors and the most expensive, but locals on lunch-breaks from nearby shops and offices and housewives from the affluent southern suburbs still favour it. A multitude of ruddy-faced merchants gather to serve them and, after the ice melts, boat owners also get involved, tying their vessels to the end of the harbour and selling fish and root and other vegetables straight from their prows.

**BELOW:**
Kappeli Restaurant, a popular haunt in summer.

## ART NOUVEAU

At first sight they are just city buildings, but the elements are unique: interesting windows, heavy ornamentation, grey granite, natural colours and castle-like features. Some of the most famous tourist attractions in Helsinki are Art Nouveau – the National Museum, or the Hvitträsk House in Kirkkonummi. But Art Nouveau, or Jugend as it is called in Finland, is far more common in Helsinki than first seems to be the case.

Art Nouveau is also called National Romanticism. Its roots go back to the great epic *Kalevala*, which inspired the composer Sibelius and the artist Gallén-Kallela. Architects Gesellius, Saarinen and Lindgren soon followed suit, going back to the roots of Karelianism, forests, bedrock – the key elements of Finnishness.

One of the best areas to look for their designs is Katajanokka. Eira is another area – see Lars Sonck's hospital at Laivurinkatu 27. Lord Hotel (Lönnrotinkatu 29) by Lindahl and Thomé is typically Art Nouveau with a granite façade, as is their Otava House (Uudenmaankatu 10), Pohjola House at Aleksanterinkatu 44 (by Gesellius *et al.*) or the Tarjanne's National Theatre. Even Saarinen's railway station has hints of Art Nouveau. Arrive before your train leaves and take a look.

*Home-grown vegetables are a popular buy at the Central Market.*

**BELOW:**
a typical Helsinki shopping complex.

The north part of the market square is reserved for Finland's delicious fresh produce. Offerings very much follow the seasons and, in summer, become irresistible: sweet baby peas and mounds of deeply flavoured berries. No wonder that, by July, every Helsinki dweller can be seen clutching a small paper bag filled with something juicy and colourful. The coffee tent attracts locals and tourists; even presidents have been known to pop out from the nearby palace for a quick snack. Try one of the sweet rolls or warm meat pastries.

Further down, around the bellicose **Obeliski Keisarinnan kivi** – whose imperial, doubled-headed golden eagle was ripped off during the Russian Revolution and not restored until 1972 – the market turns away from food. Some of these stands proffer interesting goods and handicrafts, but if you are looking for authenticity you should know that most Finns stopped wearing fur hats quite a while ago. Women wearing high heels might also want to bear in mind that the spaces between the cobblestones are particularly treacherous here.

The water in this part of South Harbour is overrun by gulls and geese and not that clean, but don't let that stop you from sitting with the locals on its storied docks in the sun, and enjoying a punnet of Finland's fabulous strawberries.

However, if it is cold or raining, you might prefer to duck into the yellow-and-red brick **Vanha Kauppahalli (Old Market Hall)** ❾. Having traded for more than 100 years, the Old Market Hall is not only Helsinki's most centrally located *kauppahalli* but its oldest. It knows its advantage. The interior is polished to the gills, and the price of even simple *piirakka* can be high. As well as reindeer cold-cuts and rounds of Oltermanni cheese, you can buy ready-made snacks from an excellent Russian-style kebab stand or at the small market café.

## Civic triumphs

The Central Market sprawls like a spectre of the masses before some of Helsinki's most important administrative buildings. An austere row lies directly across at the end of Pohjoisesplanadi: the long blue City Hall, designed by Engel in 1833, with a Finnish flag flying above it; the sensible brown Swedish Embassy, importantly placed, and with a Swedish flag; the Supreme Court, dating from 1883; and the Presidential Palace.

The **Kaupungintalo (City Hall)** ❿ started out with a different purpose. Until 1833 it was home to the Seurahuone Hotel (now across from the railway station). Its first opening was celebrated by a masquerade ball, so that women could attend – although they had to leave by 4.30am.

The **Presidentinlinna (Presidential Palace)** ⓫ was designed in 1818 as a private home and turned into a tsarist palace by Engel in 1843. The Finnish president no longer lives here, but the new official residence Mäntyniemi, not far from Seurasaari, is occasionally open for visitors.

Helsinki's third major landmark, **Senaatintori (Senate Square)** ⓬, stands one block north of here, back along Aleksi. There seems to be something fateful about Senate Square. As early as the 17th century, the same spot housed a town hall, church and central square. It was flattened by the next century's continual

battles, but the merchants made rich by Suomenlinna soon rebuilt it, erecting the city's first stone buildings about its southern perimeter. The 1808 fire destroyed everything wooden, but Russia straightaway commissioned architect C. L. Engel to rebuild the square as the municipal centre of their new city plan for Helsinki. Eventually, so many important institutions made their home here that Senate Square became a sort of national centre.

The square is still a very impressive spot. Encompassing some 7,000 sq. metres (8,300 sq. yards), it is covered by no less than 400,000 grey-and-red cobblestones of Finnish granite. Nowadays, the Senate Square functions principally as a byway. The main building of Helsinki University, which occupies the square's entire western border, has a new entrance at the back that lures student activity away. The current Council of State, directly opposite, receives few visits from the average citizen. The former Town Hall, on the south side, is used for entertaining official guests, and the flux of boutiques around it cater mostly for visitors.

But the city remembers. Senaatintori becomes the centre of activity on important occasions such as Independence Day in December, when the windswept square is a sea of candles held by students who march here from Hietaniemi Cemetery in the mid-winter dark. Locals gather again one month later to listen to the mayor's traditional New Year's Eve speech and watch fireworks, and again for May Day. The University often uses it for commemorative events.

An extremely self-important statue of Tsar Alexander II, erected in 1894, stands in the centre of all this. At his feet, four additional figures tell the square's story: *Lex*, or law (facing the government palace); *Lux*, or light (facing the sun); *Labour* (facing the university); and *Pax*, or peace (facing the cathedral).

Map on page 154

**BELOW:** gypsies selling traditional lace at the harbour market.

*Statue of Tsar Alexander, standing proud on Senaatintori (Senate Square).*

**BELOW:** capital city Christmas shopping by tram.

The **Tuomiokirkko (Helsinki Cathedral)** , up a bank of treacherously steep steps on the northside, is a point of pride for Finns, and the exterior – with its five green cupolas, numerous white Corinthian columns and sprinkling of important figurines posing on its roof – is certainly impressive. The interior, however, is startlingly severe. Apart from the gilded altarpiece and organ, only statues of Luther, Agricola and Melanchthon disturb its white symmetry.

## Engel's triumph

A walk around Senate Square can also reveal a lot about Helsinki's history. The city's oldest stone building, dating from 1757, is the small blue-grey Sederholm House on the corner of Aleksi and Katariinankatu. Across the street is the **Bockin talo (Bock House)** ❹, also 18th-century, which became the meeting place for Helsinki's City Council in 1818, as a plaque by its door proclaims. It also served briefly as the governor general's residence after Engel had it embellished with Ionic pillars and a third floor.

The rest of the square is pure Engel, making it not only a beautiful but an unusually consistent example of Neo-classical design. In 1832, the oldest part of the main building of Helsinki University (it was extended later to cover the entire block) was completed under the architect, on the western side of the square. Ten years earlier, he had designed the Council of State, along the entire eastern side of the square. The Finnish Government still has its seat here. Engel drew the plan for the cathedral as well, although he died 12 years before its completion in 1852.

Across Unioninkatu, the **Yliopiston kirjasto (University Library)** ❺ is decidedly ornate. Not only do white Corinthian columns line every inch of its

yellow façade, but inside the splendour continues. In the central room, more columns (now marble with gold tips) support a dark-wood second tier, beneath a painted cupola ceiling. Yet this is still a working library, and visitors are expected to leave their coats at the door, sign in and, above all, respect the quiet. Nor are all the rooms open to visitors – look out for some prohibition signs. But don't let this discourage you from enjoying the public parts of this most beautiful of Engel's works, dating from 1844.

Maps
Centre 154
Districts
166–7

## Outside the centre

After exploring Helsinki's *Keskusta* (centre), venture into one of the surrounding districts, each of which has its own very particular character, though borders are not always clearly defined.

One of the most attractive is **Katajanokka**, which lies on a small promontory sticking out into the sea a few blocks east from Senate Square. Katajanokka is connected to the centre by two short bridges where locals like to cast their fishing rods. A restaurant complex opened a few years ago, injecting new life into this area. After a snowstorm or on a brilliant spring day, its elegant streets are the picture of serenity. Unfortunately, the first thing you see crossing the Kanavakatu Bridge on to Katajanokka is one of Alvar Aalto's least successful efforts: the dirty white marble Enso Gutzeit Office Building (the "sugar cube"), dated 1962. Fortunately, Katajanokka has better sights to offer.

The **Uspenskin katedraali (Uspensky Cathedral)** ⓰, across the street at the top of a sudden grassy knoll, gives supreme proof of this. Russian Orthodox, built in 1868, dedicated to the Virgin Mary and undeniably glamorous, Uspensky makes a striking exception to Helsinki's general architectural style. Its red-

**BELOW:** façade of the University of Helsinki Library.

brick conglomeration of cross-tipped spires and onion-shaped domes has undoubtedly helped convince many filmmakers to use Helsinki as a surrogate Moscow (for example, in *Reds* and *Gorky Park*). Uspensky's interior is also both impressive and atmospheric, with a glittering iconostasis. The cathedral opens daily (except Mondays in winter) but on Sundays for short periods only. Services in Church Slavic are held at least twice weekly.

Appropriately enough, a Russian restaurant called the Bellevue sits at the base of the cathedral, across from Katajanokka Park. The Bellevue, however, has a slightly unorthodox political history. The restaurant was founded the year Finland declared independence from Russia (1917). It also has on one of its golden walls a thank-you note received in 1990 from America's former First Lady, Barbara Bush.

The Russian motif is echoed elsewhere on Katajanokka, and flirtatious basilic motifs appear over many doorways. Red brick also gets more use, particularly in the recently built residences on the tip of the promontory. But central Luotsikatu is one street where Jugendian (Art Nouveau) style rules. Many of the buildings on this and nearby streets were designed by the architectural team of Gesellius, Lindgren and Saarinen at the turn of the 20th century and abound with little pleasures. Don't miss the charming griffin doorway at No. 5.

Turning north from Luotsikatu on to Vyökatu takes you to the northern waterfront. A narrow flight of stone steps leads down to an ageing gateway, which until 1968 blocked the way to the **Merikasarmi (Naval Barracks)**. These long, yellow buildings have since been restored and now house the Finnish Foreign Ministry. Some have been reconstructed but follow Engel's original design. The public is welcome to stroll along the avenues that run between them.

**BELOW:** the ornate interior of Uspensky Cathedral.

The southern side of Katajanokka sees more public activity. This is where the huge Viking Line ships come in from Stockholm three times a day, disembarking crowds of passengers. Conversions have already been completed on the block of old warehouses at Pikku Satamakatu, beside the Viking Line Terminal and the so-called Wanha Satama now entertains a clutch of eating spots (including the cheerful Café Sucre), exhibition halls and stores. Two more warehouses nearby have also been earmarked for renovation but the Customs and Bonded Warehouse, however, should not change. Even if you don't have any business to attend to here, it's worth passing by to view its inventive Jugendian style, as designed by Gustaf Nyström in 1900.

*The tubular Sibelius Monument by Eila Hiltunen honours Finland's finest composer.*

## The old city

Following Kanavakatu back west will return you to Helsinki's oldest district, **Kruununhaka ⓱**, whose name means "the Crown's Paddock" and not so many centuries ago was primarily a home for cows. Senate Square is at the lower end of this area, which is now favoured by the well-heeled and boasts a large collection of antique furniture, book and clothing shops and art galleries.

Central Helsinki's second oldest building lies in the southeastern corner of this district, at the juncture of Aleksanterinkatu and Meritullintori. The modest squat structure was erected in 1765 as a Customs Warehouse, but now houses everyday offices. Other venerable left-overs of an earlier age hover nearby, such as the deep red Lord Mayor's Residence at No. 12 Aleksanterinkatu (next to Helsinki's Theatre Museum) with its gorgeous blown-glass windowpanes, and the mid-19th-century, neo-Gothic Ritarihuone ("House of Nobility") situated one block north on Hallituskatu.

**BELOW:** striking architecture of the Katajanokka area.

A few particularly nice pedestrian streets crown the crest of hilly Kruununhaka. Solid stone buildings in yellow, brown, rust and grey cut into exposed rock cliffs, insulating the end of the district from the Siltavuori Strait flowing directly below.

They also shelter the city's oldest extant wooden buildings at Kristianinkatu 12, the **Ruiskumestarin talo (Burgher's House) ⓲** (tel: 9-135 1065; open Wed–Sun; entrance fee). The Burgher's House was built in 1818, shortly after the Great Fire, by a wealthy merchant who unfortunately wasn't quite wealthy enough to use stone as a building material. A high wooden fence encloses it with a second mustard-coloured house and a weatherbeaten red shed, all cuddled round a small earth-floored courtyard filled with the pungent scent of wood smoke. In structure, the main house remains exactly as it was when first built, and its beautiful wooden floors are completely original. The furniture, however, has been assembled from different periods starting from 1860. To complete the period atmosphere, guides dress in old-fashioned garb.

## Into Greater Helsinki

If it's a warm day, you may want to head east down to **Tervasaari ⓳**. This little island, now connected to Kruununhaka by a man-made isthmus, used to be the city's storage place for tar – an important early export

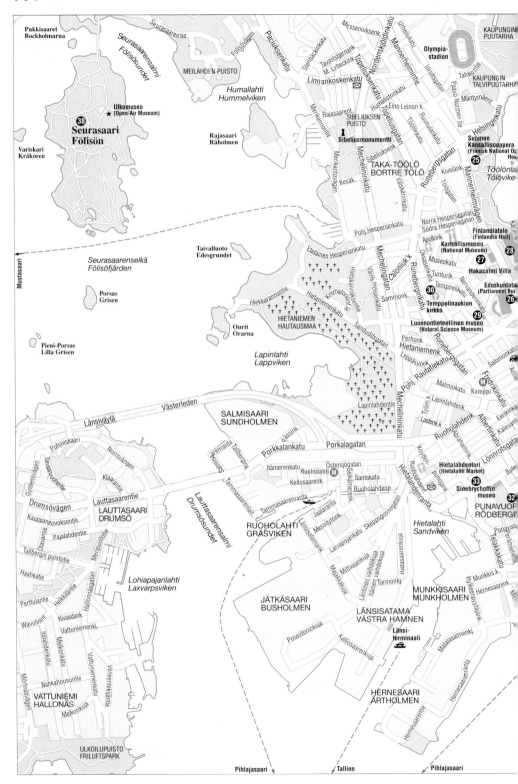

Pukkisaaret
Bockholmarna

Seurasaarentie

Seurasaarensalmi
Fölisösundet

Paciuksenkatu

MEILAHDEN PUISTO

Humallahti
Hummelviken

Ulkomuseo
★ (Open-Air Museum)

**38**

**Seurasaari**
**Fölisön**

Rajasaari
Råholmen

Variskari
Kråkören

Mustasaari

Seurasaarenselkä
Fölisöfjärden

Taivalluoto
Edesgrundet

Porsas
Grisen

Pieni-Porsas
Lilla Grisen

Ourit
Orarna

Lapinlahti
Lappviken

Västerleden

Länsiväylä

Pohjoiskaari

Norrsvängen

SALMISAARI
SUNDHOLMEN

Taivaanvuohentie

Klaarantie

Gyldensvägen

Lauttasaarentie
LAUTTASAARI
DRUMSÖ

Drumsövägen

Lauttasaarensalmi
Drumsösundet

Kauppaneuvoksentie

Pajalahdentie

Otavantie

Tallbergin puistotie

Haahkatie

Lohiapajanlahti
Laxvarpsviken

Perttulantie

Heikkiläntie

Kiviaidank.

Wavulimt.

Vattunkuja

Vattuniemenkj.

Meripuistotie

Hallonnäspatan

Melkonkatu

Itälahdenkatu

Vattuniemenkatu

Nahkahousuntie

Mörtnäsvägen

Veneentekijäntie

VATTUNIEMI
HALLONÄS

Melkonkuja

ULKOILUPUISTO
FRILUFTSPARK

Messeniuksenk.

Stenbäckinkatu

Töölönkatu

Nordenskiöldinkatu

Mannerheimintie

Topeliuksenkatu

M.L. Lybeckink.

Taivaststjernank.

Urheilukatu

Paavo Nurmen tie

KAUPUNGIN
PUUTARHA

Olympia-
stadion

Irrottasatan

Tahkontie

KAUPUNGIN
TALVIPUUTARHA

Linnankoskenkatu

Humalistonkatu

Eino Leinon k.

Mäntymäent

SIBELIUKSEN
PUISTO

Rajasaarent.

Merikannontie

Merikantovägen

Kesäk.

MECHELININKATU

TAKA-TÖÖLÖ
BORTRE TÖLÖ

Sibeliusmonumentti

Sibeliuksenk.

Helsinginkatu

Töölönlahti

Runebergsgatan

Kivelänk.

Mannerheimvägen

Suomen
Kansallisooppera
(Finnish National O)
Ho
**25**

Töölönla
Tölövike

Norra Hesperiagatan
Södra Hesperiagatan

Finlandiatalo
(Finlandia Hall)

Apollonk.

Oksasenkatu

Kansallismuseo
(National Museum)
**27**

**28**

Museokatu

Hakasalmi Villa

Pohj. Hesperiankatu

Eteläinen Hesperiankatu

Krematorntie

Caloniuk.k

Hietakannaksentie

Runeberginkatu

Tunturik.

Nervanderinkatu

Temppelik.

**30**

Eduskuntatalo
(Parliament Bui)
**26**

HIETANIEMEN
HAUTAUSMAA

Hiekkarannantie

Hietaniementie

Vaini. mosenkatu

Sammonk.

Sandudsgatan

Temppelinaukion
kirkko
**29**

Luonnontieteellinen museo
(Natural Science Museum)

Mechelingatan

Perhonk.

Runeberginkatu

Hietaniemenk.

Lepäsuonk.

Pohj. Rautatiekatu

Salomonkatu

Malminkatu

Fredrikinkatu

Kamppi
**M**

Anna

Työnk.

Lapinlahdenk.

Albertinkatu

Eerikink.

Kalevani

Lastenk.k

Lapinlahdentie

Ruoholahdenk.

Abrahamink.

Lönnrotsgatan

Mechelininkatu

Porkkalankatu

Porkalagatan

Pässink.

Itämerenkatu

Österjögatan

Ruoholahti
**M**

Ruoholahdenranta

Santakatu

Hietalahdentori
(Hietalahti Market)

Puntink.

Hietalahdenranta

Sinebrychoffin
museo

**33**

**32**

PUNAVUOF
RÖDBERGE

Kellosaarenk.

Ruoholahdenp.

Säbelnranta
Tallbergink.

Tammasaarenlaht.

Tammasaarenranta

RUOHOLAHTI
GRÄSVIKEN

Jaalaranta

Messitytönk.

Laivapojankatu

Länsisatamank.

Skeppsgossegatan

Hietalahti
Sandviken

Punavuor.

Telakkakatu

Munkkis.k.

JÄTKÄSAARI
BUSHOLMEN

Majakkakuja

Mittaajankuja

Länt. vahdekuja

Itäinen vahdekuja

Itäinen Tarmonk.

LÄNSISATAMA
VÄSTRA HAMNEN

MUNKKISAARI
MUNKHOLMEN

Hernesaarenk.

Hernesaarenkatu

Poseidoninkuja

Kallosaarenkuja

Länsi-
terminaali

Matalasalmenkj.

HERNESAARI
ÄRTHOLMEN

Hernesaarenranta

Hernesaarenrinne

Pihlajasaari

Tallinn

Pihlajasaari

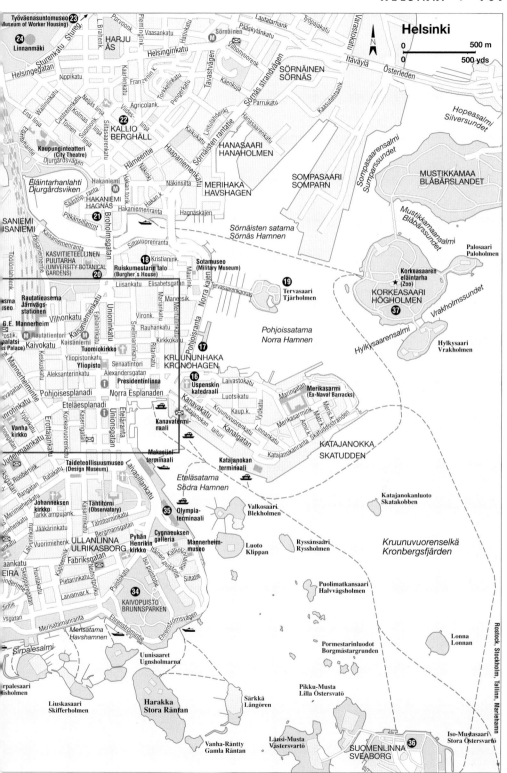

**Helsinki**

0      500 m
0      500 yds

Työväenasuntomuseo ㉓
Museum of Worker Housing)

㉔ Linnanmäki

HARJU
ÅS

Helsinginkatu

Porvoonk.

Fleminginkatu

Vaasankatu

Sörnäinen

Pääskyläniank

Lautatarhank

Työpajakatu

Varasto

Itäväylä
Österleden

SÖRNÄINEN
SÖRNÄS

Vilhonvuorenk.

Sörnäs strandvägen

Hopeasalmi
Silversundet

KALLIO
BERGHÄLL
㉒

Kaupunginteatteri
(City Theatre)

Eläintarhanlahti
Djurgårdsviken

HANASAARI
HANAHOLMEN

Hämeentie

Haapaniemenkatu

Sörnäisten rantatie

Näkinsilta

MERIHAKA
HAVSHAGEN

SOMPASAARI
SOMPARN

Sompasaarensalmi
Sumparssundet

MUSTIKKAMAA
BLÅBÄRSLANDET

HAKANIEMI
HAGNÄS
㉑

Hakaniementori

Hagnäskajen

Sörnäisten satama
Sörnäs Hamnen

Mustikkamaansalmi
Blåbärssundet

SANIEMI
ISANIEMI

Palosaari
Paloholmen

KASVITIETEELLINEN
PUUTARHA
(UNIVERSITY BOTANICAL
GARDENS) ⑳

⑱ Kristianink.

Ruiskumestarin talo
(Burgher's House)

Sotamuseo
(Military Museum)

Korkeasaaren
eläintarha
(Zoo)

KORKEASAARI
HÖGHOLMEN
㊲

Vrakholmssundet

⑲ Tervasaari
Tjärholmen

Hylkysaarensalmi

Hylkysaari
Vrakholmen

Rautatieasema
Järnvägs-
stationen

G. E. Mannerheim

Rautatientori

Tuomiokirkko

Pohjoissatama
Norra Hamnen

KRUUNUNHAKA
KRONOHAGEN
⑰

Yliopisto
Senaatintori

Presidentinlinna

Norra Esplanaden

Eteläesplanaden

⑯ Uspenskin
katedraali

Merikasarmi
(Ex-Naval Barracks)

Vanha
kirkko

Kanavatermi-
naali

KATAJANOKKA
SKATUDDEN

Taideteollisuusmuseo
(Design Museum)

Makasiini
terminaali

Katajanokan
terminaali

Katajanokanluoto
Skatakobben

Johanneksen
kirkko

Tähtitorni
(Observatory)

㉟ Olympia-
terminaali

Eteläsatama
Södra Hamnen

Valkosaari
Blekholmen

ULLANLINNA
ULRIKASBORG

Pyhän
Henrikin
kirkko

Cygnaeuksen
galleria

Mannerheim-
museo

Luoto
Klippan

Ryssänsaari
Ryssholmen

Kruunuvuorenselkä
Kronbergsfjärden

EIRA

㉞

KAIVOPUISTO
BRUNNSPARKEN

Puolimatkansaari
Halvvägsholmen

Lonna
Lonnan

Mensatama
Havshamnen

Uunisaaret
Ugnsholmarna

Pormestarinluodot
Borgmästargrunden

Sirpalesalmi

rpalesaari
isholmen

Liuskasaari
Skifferholmen

Harakka
Stora Räntan

Särkkä
Längören

Pikku-Musta
Lilla Östersvatö

Vanha-Räntty
Gamla Räntan

Länsi-Musta
Västersvartö

Iso-Mustasaari
Stora Östersvartö

SUOMENLINNA
SVEABORG
㊱

Rostock, Stockholm, Tallinn, Mariehamn

(Tervasaari means "tar island"). Modern times have turned it into a nice park for summer sunning, with a dog run and laid-back terraced restaurant.

Although Finland has not won, strictly speaking, any of the wars it has fought, the **Sotamuseo** (**Military Museum**), on Maurinkatu 1, is worth seeing, especially as wars have been so tragic for the nation that eventually managed to defend its independence against Soviet aggression (tel: 9-1812 6381; open Sun–Fri; entrance fee).

Walking west now brings you down to Kaisaniemenkatu, the street that begins in front of the railway station and frames the west of Kruununhaka. An attractive park squeezes between it, the station and Kaisaniemi Bay.

Kaisaniemen puisto is a sort of multi-purpose park, with sloping stretches of grass, a variety of playing fields that turn into ice-hockey rinks in winter, an open-air restaurant and the **Kasvitieteellinen puutarha ⑳ (University Botanical Gardens**, Unioninkatu 44; tel: 9-191 24453; gardens open daily, 7am–8pm, greenhouses open Tues–Sun, 11am–5pm; entrance fee). Designed by a landscape gardener from St Petersburg in the 1830s, these gardens offer a very peaceful place for a stroll right in the middle of the town.

## Blue-collar heritage

A long bridge separates the Kruununhaka area and the park from the tiny district of **Hakaniemi ㉑** and larger Kallio, which were traditionally Helsinki's "worker" communities. Indeed, Lenin briefly lived beside spacious Hakaniemen tori (Hakaniemi Square) before the Russian Revolution. Lately, an increasing trendiness and the large student population has lent Hakaniemi a bohemian feel. From 7am until 2pm, Monday through Saturday, however, a no-nonsense

**BELOW:** the Burgher's House, one of the city's oldest buildings.

market takes over the square and the Hakaniemi Market Hall on its edge. Both are noticeably more natural than those at the Central Market, and the hall has an upstairs devoted to dry goods including stands run by the ubiquitous Marimekko and Aarikka companies.

Map on pages 166–7

**Kallio ㉒** was first built up in haphazard fashion during the early 19th century. It was eventually given a city plan and rebuilt after the fashion of St Petersburg, but you still need to know where to wander to find attractive areas. One of its prettiest blocks, Torkkelinkatu, rises above the whimsical Kallio Library on Viides Linja. The nearby Kallio Church is an important Art Nouveau structure in grey granite from 1912. Its bells ring a tune by Sibelius.

The northern border of Kallio hides the **Työväenasuntomuseo (Museum of Worker Housing) ㉓** (Kirstinkuja 4; tel: 9-146 1039; open May–Sept: Wed–Sun; entrance fee). This museum comprises four wooden tenements built by the city for its workers and used from 1909 until 1987. Household scenes have been recreated with great effect in eight apartments, using intimate knowledge of the former inhabitants. In flat C-6, for example, where an abandoned wife and her trouble-making son lived, a bottle of alcohol stands beneath the man's seat at the table. All the apartments displayed are single rooms that housed entire families. This meant that, by day, the beds had to be tucked away in some fashion, but, in flat 9-E in 1925, those of a widow and five of her six children are left unmade. Only the eldest daughter had gone to work, folding her bed against the wall and leaving steel hair curlers on the table. This family's story is particularly poignant; after the woman's husband died (it is said by suicide), she saved until she was able to buy a cross for his grave and, with no money left to hire a car, carried it on her back all the way to Malmi Cemetery.

*Helsinki has adopted the European love of pavement cafés.*

**BELOW:**
a 1920s room in the Museum of Worker Housing.

Helsinki's amusement park, **Linnanmäki** , perches on a wooded hill a short walk north from here (access from Helsinginkatu or Tivolitie; tel: 9-773 991; open May–Aug: daily, noon–10pm; entrance fee). A traditional funfair that ploughs its profits back into children's charities, this is the most visited attraction in Finland.

## Töölö Bay

Kallio lies north of the railway station along the east side of Töölö Bay. Several other of Helsinki's 50-odd museums lie on the bay's western side, in a neighbourhood called **Töölö**. Like Kallio, Töölö came into its own after the turn of the 20th century. Though it is not especially chic today, many of its streets offer priceless examples of Jugendian (Art Nouveau) architecture.

To get to Töölö from Kallio, you can follow a pleasant park around the bay's north end, over the train tracks. This way passes some important places for locals: the City Theatre, the City Conservatoire, the Olympic Stadium (beside which is an overly popular outdoor swimming pool) and the enormous, ultra-modern **Suomen Kansallisooppera (Finnish National Opera House)** which opened in 1993 *(see page 81)*.

To take the alternative route to Töölö, start by walking one block west of the railway station to Mannerheimintie, as far as the four-storey mall Forum Shopping Centre, where there are shops, fast-food restaurants, a bar and two cafés. Turn north, and one-and-a-half blocks further on a bronze statue of General Mannerheim on horseback presides over the busy intersection between Mannerheimintie, Arkadian, Postikatu and Salomon streets. Töölö lies directly across the traffic bridge from here.

**BELOW:** the Ilmatar and Sotka statue in Sibelius Park.

Beneath the bridge, the old Railway Yard has been converted into a fashionable art gallery and a clutch of international food and goods stores.

Map on pages 166–7

## Architectural trio

The **Eduskuntatalo (Parliament Building)** ❷⓺, directly across the street, atop an important row of steps, is decidely less casual. Fourteen columns of grey granite mark its stern façade, built between 1925–30 after J.S. Sirén's design.

Statues of former Finnish presidents scatter the area between the Parliament Building and the **Kansallismuseo (National Museum)** ❷⓻. The Gesellius-Lindgren-Saarinen trio designed this museum in 1906 to reflect Finnish history in its very construction. Although National Romantic in style, the heavy grey building also incorporates snatches of old Finnish church and castle architecture. The main tower imitates that of the Turku Cathedral *(see page 208)*.

The museum's decoration and collection offer more on Finland. The stone bear by the entrance is the work of Wikström and the frescos on the foyer ceiling, depicting scenes from Finland's national epic the *Kalevala* are by Gallén-Kallela. The entertaining jumble of artefacts inside runs from early archaeological finds up to present-day items. The City Museum branch in the fine Hakasalmi Villa (tel: 9-169 3444) houses a special exhibition on Helsinki's history, and has one of the cosiest of Helsinki's many cafés on its front lawn.

**Finlandiatalo (Finlandia Hall)** ❷⓼, next door, is undoubtedly the most famous building in Töölö – if not all of Helsinki. Alvar Aalto designed it both inside and out, completing the main section in 1971 and the congress wing in 1975. It now houses the Helsinki Philharmonic Orchestra and is used for any number of concerts and events.

*Streetside snack of Finnish pastries.*

**LEFT:** *Attack* by Edvard Isto (1899). **BELOW:** detail of the Barbara Altar from Kalanti Church (both in the National Museum).

The striking white building was specifically devised to blend environmentally with the backdrop of Hesperia Park and Töölö Bay, especially in the winter. Ironically, Finlandiatalo is having ecological troubles. The Carraran marble of its façade did not just turn grey, it warped disastrously from the Finnish winter weather. A new layer of similar white marble now replaces the old one, but it is anyone's guess how long that will last. Meanwhile, the hall has had a second, widely-discussed problem: the acoustics of the concert hall were poorly conceived and electrical experiments have been going on in an effort to try to improve them. Regardless, the hall serves as an indisputable bastion for modern Finnish culture.

A number of other important cultural spots are clustered around the Parliament House. The **Sibelius Academy**, Helsinki's renowned musical conservatory, is just around the corner. Concerts are given here by some of the top students (tel: 9-405 411 for information).

Across the street at Pohjoinen Rautatiekatu 13 is the **Luonnontieteellinen museo (Natural Science Museum)** ❷, whose numerous showcases and vivid dioramas offer a colourful lesson on Finnish wildlife. Its Neo-Baroque building is easily identified by the bronze cast of an elk on its lawn ( tel: 9-191 28800; open daily; entrance fee).

Nestling, literally, into a small hill behind all of this on the winding streets of Töölö, is the ultra-modern church, **Temppelinaukion kirkko** ❸. It is not only an architectural oddity – built as it is directly into the cliffs, with inner walls of stone – but it is also the site of many excellent concerts during the year. A service for English speakers is held here weekly (open daily, but on Sunday for worshippers only).

**BELOW LEFT AND RIGHT:** architectural glories along the beautiful Bulevardi.

## Helsinki's new heart

The whole neighbourhood is evolving based on a plan by Alvar Aalto, which is finally being realised in perhaps ways the great designer would not have anticipated. In spring 1998 **Kiasma** ㉛, a new museum of contemporary art, opened its impressive doors, on Mannerheiminaukio, just across from the Parliament building and adjacent to Finlandia Hall, this remarkable machine-like structure by American architect Steven Holl is a symbol of a new Helsinki, whose city centre is shifting to this area. The curving asymmetrical building harmoniously interacts with its surroundings – the oddly-shaped windows afford good views of the key landmarks of Helsinki. The bold exhibitions vary from astounding to macabre (open Tues–Sun; entrance fee) .

A triangle of "functionalist" architecture has emerged with a new role in life: Kiasma, closest to the railway station, Lasipalatsi ("Glass Palace") across Mannerheimintie and the former Tennispalatsi ("Tennis Palace") at the other end of the bus station area. Lasipalatsi is one such functionalist structure that has been rejuvenated with utmost care to create a welcoming media centre with an Internet library, two TV studios (for live programming), a cinema, other media companies and fine cafés and restaurants. Tennispalatsi, formerly an eyesore for the aesthetically minded, was used during the 1952 Olympic Games, and now houses Finland's largest cinema complex (14 screens) and two museums. The bus station is poised for further development. Several new hotels are also opening in Töölö at the close of the 20th century, as further proof that this is fast becoming the city's new "heart".

In 1999 Finland chaired the European Union and in 2000 Helsinki not only celebrates its 450th anniversary but is simultaneously honoured as the

Map on pages 166–7

*A whole range of buskers take to the streets in the city's brief summer.*

**BELOW:** the small boat harbour.

European City of Culture – a monumental year for such a comparatively new and diminuitive capital city.

## Gracious avenue

Another district in southwestern Helsinki worth exploring is **Punavuori** ㉜, a plush area beneath Töölö towards the end of the peninsula. The main street here is Bulevardi, which begins at a perpendicular angle from Mannerheim-intie (just a couple of blocks before its end) and leads down to Hietalahti shipyard. Drop in at Bulevardia restaurant (Bulevardi 34, tel: 9-742 55544) for lunch, dinner or a glass of wine on the summer terrace. It has been a favourite artists' hangout for decades.

**Bulevardi** is one of Helsinki's most beautiful avenues. Most of the buildings date from between 1890 and 1920 and were formerly home to Helsinki's turn-of-the-century patricians. Vanha Kirkko (The Old Church), however, between Annan and Yrjön streets, is a stray from Engel. Dating from 1826, it was the first Lutheran church to be built in the new "capital".

The former National Opera House lies a few blocks further west on Bulevardi. This delightful red building was erected in 1870 as a theatre for Russian officers and for decades it housed the national opera, until the building of the new opera house *(see page 170)*. The inside is plush and ornate, but much too small for classic opera productions. It functions better as a musical theatre and school.

As you reach the end of Bulevardi, you will come to the former Sinebrychoff Brewery, which was established in 1819 and is the oldest brewery in Finland. The Sinebrychoff Museum of Foreign Art (tel: 9-173 361; open Wed–Mon) is housed at Bulevardi 40, and includes Old Masters and miniatures. Don't miss

**BELOW:**
the strikingly
modern National
Opera House.

the **Hietalahdentori** ㉝, best known for its flea market. The goods are usually just unwanted records and clothes, but this market is one of the best places in Helsinki to watch large numbers of locals in action during the day.

Bulevardi does, however, also harbour many fashionable art galleries and boutiques, which spill into neighbouring streets. Two blocks south and parallel to Bulevardi, the Iso-Roobertin pedestrian street has many youth orientated shops and restaurants. Another two blocks further on, is the Johannes Church. This rather regal affair with important stiletto spires is the largest church in Helsinki and a particularly popular place for choral concerts, with excellent acoustics. Across the street, at Korkeavuorenkatu 23, the **Taideteollisuusmuseo (Design Museum)** is an essential stop, as it is a showcase for Finland's famed skills in design, including Aalto furniture and Lapponia jewellery *(see pages 81–2)*. The museum is open daily, tel: 9-622 0540.

In the same block is the **Suomen rakennnustaiteen museo (Museum of Finnish Architecture)**, at Kasarmikatu 24 (tel: 9-856 75100; open Tue–Sun; entrance fee), which has an excellent archive of architectural drawings, and changing exhibitions focusing on Finnish architectural movements (including National Romantic, Neo-classic, Jugendian, Functionalist and Modern).

## High-class life

Heading directly south from here you come upon Eira, perhaps Helsinki's most exclusive neighbourhood. On the southernmost end of the peninsula the coastline below Eira is lined by parkland. After the ice melts, small boats dock all along the coastline and half the world seems to be cycling by. While the sea is still frozen, you can actually walk out to some of the closer offshore islands.

*Neo-classical stone detail, near the Eira district of Helsinki.*

**BELOW:** Helsinki's shopping area, Aleksanterinkatu.

Towards the northeast and the centre, this strip of green grows into Helsinki's best park: **Kaivopuisto** ❸. In summer, the city sponsors numerous free concerts here and Kaivopuisto overflows with happy sun-bathing locals. Kaivohuone, a former spa in the park, is also one of the city's most popular places to meet and hear music. The recently refurbished nightclub features hot Finnish bands, but due to complaints about noise on its terrace, it can currently rock 'n' roll only on agreed evenings.

Embassies fill the well-heeled Ullanlinna district. Most noticeably, the Russian Embassy commands almost a block opposite St Henrik's, one of Helsinki's two Catholic churches. Above them rises **Observatory Hill** (the Finnish name *Tähtitorninmäki* literally means "star tower hill"). From here you can look down over the city centre and Katajanokka to the north.

The **Mannerheim-museo** (tel: 9-635 443; open Fri–Sun; entrance fee; guided tour obligatory) is tucked away between embassies at Kalliolinnantie 14. It was the home of General C.G.E. Mannerheim, perhaps the most respected figure in Finland's history *(see page 49)*. His achievements include a two-year expedition to Asia, when he travelled 14,000 km (8,700 miles) on horseback along the Silk Road. Some of his souvenirs from his lengthy travels are on display here.

Not far away is **Cygnaeuksen galleria** (Kalliolinnantie 8; tel: 9-4050 9628; open Wed–Sun; entrance fee), a tiny, exquisite wooden summer home of the poet Cygnaeus. Inside the house is a remarkable 19th-century collection of Finnish painting and sculpture.

Directly below to the east is the **Olympiaterminaali (Olympia Quay)** ❸, stopping place for huge Silja liners and a reminder that the sea has brought prosperity to Helsinki, the "Daughter of the Baltic".

**BELOW:**
an 1842 stable in the Seurasaari open-air museum.

## Helsinki's Islands

Literally hundreds of islands dot the Helsinki coastline. Some, like Lauttasaari and Kulosaari, have been so integrated by bridges and metro lines that they are almost indistinguishable from the mainland. Others are reserved for weekend cottages, reached over the ice in winter or by motorboat in summer.

Suomenlinna ㊱ ("Finland's castle") is undoubtedly the most important of the latter. In reality it consists of five islands, over which the ruins of a naval fortress and its fortifications are spread. Suomenlinna has played an integral part in Helsinki's life since its construction started in 1748, under Count Augustin Ehrensvärd. It is a unique architectural monument, which has been listed by UNESCO as a World Heritage Site.

Suomenlinna has a complicated identity. It began as a naval post, and still houses Finland's Naval War Academy, but it is hardly just a military enclave. A thriving local artists' community, which uses restored bastions as studios and showrooms, is more visible. Fishing boat repairers and restoration workers also live on the island.

Getting to the island is both cheap and easy. Water buses leave from Market Square every half hour, year round, and cost the same as a metro ticket. They dock on Iso Mustasaari and from here, a hilly path leads up through **Jetty Barracks** (Rantakasarmi), which now house art exhibitions and an interesting restaurant and microbrewery by the name of Panimo (tel: 9-228 5030).

Continuing past wooden houses, the Lutheran church sometimes stages concerts. This part of Suomenlinna has permanent residents living both in new houses and formerly Russian-era military houses. This island also has three museums. The **Nukke-ja lelumuseo (Museum of Dolls and Toys)** (tel: 9-668 417; open daily in summer, Sat–Sun in spring and autumn; entrance fee) contains thousands of dolls and toys from the Helsinki region from the 1830s to the 1960s, collected during the last 30 years. It is a private collection, the achievement of Piippa Tandefelt, an energetic lady who also prepares apple pies for the museum café.

The large **Suomenlinna Museum** (tel: 9-4050 9691; open daily in summer, Sat–Sun in spring and autumn; entrance fee) is the main historical exhibition of the islands. A fine, multivision programme is shown regularly. The building also houses the main information centre (tel: 9-648 1880) for Suomenlinna. The Military Museum exhibits heavy equipment – authentic artillery and other war machines, with roots in Swedish, Russian and Finnish history.

Crossing the bridge leads to the rambling remains of the **Kruunulinna Ehrensvärd (Ehrensvärd Crown Castle)** and gardens. The castle courtyard is the best preserved section of the fortress and contains the 1788 sarcophagus of the Count himself. His former home is now a museum, with old furniture, arms and lithographs (tel: 9-6841 1850; open May–Sept: daily; Oct–Apr: Sat–Sun; entrance fee).

The rest of Suomenlinna is split between residences and the fortress fortifications, which spread across Susisaari and the southernmost island of Kustaan-miekka. From the highest outcrop on this windswept

Map on pages 166–7

**BELOW:**
Kaivopuisto Park.

**TIP**

One of the most
popular eating places
on Susisaari is the
Cafe Piper, in a park
just south of the
Ehrensvärd Crown
Castle. The cafe has a
delightful setting, and
offers al fresco dining
with a view.

last island, close to an atmospheric summer restaurant called Walhalla, it is
sometimes possible to see Estonia, some 80 km (50 miles) away. The might of
passing ferries, on their way to Estonia or Sweden, is a view that one could
write home about. There is also the Rannikotykisto museo (Coast Artillery
Museum), and the Vesikko Submarine.

**Korkeasaari** ❸ (tel: 9-169 5969, open daily; entrance free) is another "tourist
island" but has neither Suomenlinna's complexity nor its charm. Finland's only
zoo completely dominates this rocky outcrop just a few steps away from the
mouth of Sörnäinen Harbour. You can reach it by boat from Hakaniemi or from
the Market Square. Helsinki Zoo, perhaps not surprisingly, specialises in "cold
climate animals" although there's a very interesting enclosure, which is home
to South American animals. However, if you want to learn about indigenous
Finnish fauna, you'd probably do just as well at the Natural Science Museum
*(see page 172)*.

**Seurasaari** ❸ (tel: 9-484 712) is also strictly a visitors' island, but eminently
more atmospheric. A pretty, forested place, its northeastern side has been made
into an Ulkomuseo (Open-Air Museum), containing wooden buildings from
provinces all over Finland. The transplanted houses on Seurasaari date from
the 17th to 19th centuries and include farmsteads and a church. Bonfires are held
near here to celebrate traditional festivities for Midsummer and Easter, during
which local Finnish children dress up as "Easter witches". The other side of
the island is a national park.

The island is connected to the Helsinki shore by a wooden footbridge, so
there's no need for a boat. Just take either bus No. 24 from the centre or cycle
along the Meilahti coastal drive (which takes you past Sibelius Park and the sil-

**BELOW:** old ships
and historic
buildings within
Helsinki's harbour.

very tubular Sibelius Monument) to the bridge. Admission to the island is free but, to enter any of the houses, you'll need to buy a ticket. Houses are open in June, July and August daily until 5pm, and two weeks before and after the summer season until 3pm.

Less well known are the smaller islands that form a string around Helsinki's southern peninsula. Across the "Olympic Harbour" are Luoto and Valkosaari, popular restaurant islands with romantic villas. A long pier outside Kaivopuisto *(see page 176)* offers a boat service to Särkkä, another island with a popular restaurant, and Harakka. Uunisaari is accessible at the southern end of the street Neitsytpolku. It's a popular recreational island with a beach, a sauna and a restaurant. The Finnish Sauna Society situated on the beautiful island of Lauttasaari offers wood-fired saunas and massage (tel: 9-686 0560; open 11.30am–4pm for men, 4.30–8pm for women).

Helsinki's favourite island for swimming is undoubtedly **Pihlajasaari**. Literally meaning Rowan Island, Pihlajasaari actually comprises two islands, with a sandy beach, café and changing cabins on the larger island's western shore. Helsinki's only nudist beach is on the smaller island, which also hides wartime bunkers. Boats to Pihlajasaari depart in summer every 15 to 30 minutes just, outside Café Carousel in Eira.

The very special **Harakka** island is now a wildlife reserve but, up until 1990, was reserved for military purposes and is still absolutely pristine. A network of paths (marked by signposts giving information in Finnish and Swedish) circle the tiny island and visitors are asked not to stray from these paths or remove plants. You can reach Harakka by boat in the summer or, in winter, by crossing the ice from Eira *(see page 175)*. ❏

Map on pages 166–7

**BELOW:** boats plying the Baltic waters around the capital.

# The Baltic States

A s the Finnish economy started to grow stronger in the 1970s, affluent Finns and Swedes enjoyed more leisure time and discovered the 24-hour mini cruise and the opportunity to take a "quick" foreign holiday. For foreign visitors also, the ferries around the Baltic create an easy and unusual way to combine a visit to different countries.

The ships ply the Baltic sea lanes to and from Sweden, via the Åland Islands, and several sail under the Swedish flag. Any preconceived ideas about car ferries will vanish as soon as you board one of these magnificent ships operated by either of the top players, Viking Line (red) and Silja Line (white). They are fun, value for money, and cruise through the most beautiful seascapes in the world.

Some of the most popular ferry trips from Helsinki are across the Bay of Finland to the attractive cities of the former Soviet Union. Most popular of all is the two-day excursion to St Petersburg: visas are not needed, accom-

modation is provided on the boat and there are no money worries; Russians would rather have your dollars, pounds or yen than their own devalued rouble. Disputes between Finnish tourist companies and the Russian authorities over visa prices are becoming increasingly common and it is worth checking in advance on the current state of affairs. Largely built by European architects in the 18th century, St Petersburg is the least Russian of Soviet cities. Situated on 40 islands in the Neva river delta, its Italianate palazzi and numerous waterways draw comparisons with Venice and Amsterdam.

It is European art that draws the crowds to the city's Hermitage gallery, for the highlights of the collection are concentrated in the rooms devoted to Western painting, from private collections nationalised after the Revolution: masterpieces by Rembrandt, Poussin, Cézanne, Van Gogh and Matisse.

St Petersburg is a rewarding city for walking and absorbing the street life. The city is particularly lively during the "white nights" of June, when everyone comes out to watch the lingering sunsets. A walk from the Hermitage, through the archway of the General Staff building, will take you to Nevsky Prospect, the city's main thoroughfare. Men still play chess here and street musicians perform. Also visit the enclosed market off Nevsky for a slice of daily life. The Kafe Literaturnoya (18 Nevsky) has a Viennese atmosphere: coffee and cakes, and occasional poetry readings or chamber concerts. Pushkin ate his last meal here in 1837, before fighting a fatal duel.

Arts Square, round the corner, offers music at the Philharmonia Bolshoy and the Glinka Maly halls, and opera and ballet at the Mariinsky Theatre. Gostiny Dvor (35 Nevsky) is the largest department store, where home-produced consumer goods sit beside increasingly popular imports from the West.

A trip to Petrodvorets, 28 km (18 miles) west of the city is a must. This is Peter the Great's answer to Versailles and he invited all the European rulers to attend its gala opening. The centrepiece of the Great Cascade is a statue of Samson tearing open the jaws of a lion which symbolises Peter's

**LEFT:** young Estonian girl in national dress.
**RIGHT:** medieval city of Riga, in Latvia.

victory over the Swedes in 1709. Equally revealing of his character are the trick fountains: be careful when choosing a seat – some will send up a shower of water.

Tallinn, the capital of Estonia, is the other ferry destination, and from here you can set off to explore all three newly independent Baltic states: Estonia, Latvia (capital Riga) and Lithuania (capital Vilnius). Tallinn lies directly opposite Helsinki, 80 km (50 miles) across the water, and large numbers of Finnish tourists (many of them former Estonian refugees who fled in the final years of World War II) visit the city – more, it has to be said, for the lively nightlife than for its beautiful medieval old town. Cobbled alleys ascend from the 14th-century castle and the Gothic architecture reminds you that Tallinn was once an important port of the Hanseatic League.

Riga, a city founded by merchants, has a very similar history. The 13th-century Romanesque cathedral is lined with the tombs of bishops, knights and landmeisters. The organ is the fourth largest in the world, and most evenings you can hear performances of Bach or Mozart. In Vilnius, three things impinge on every visitor: the ubiquitous jewellery shops selling amber, for which Lithuania has long been famous; the medieval streets clustering below the castle and the festive atmosphere that prevails here now that the longed-for independence has finally come.

The increasing popularity of the trips and, in turn, the increased size of the ferries is, however, causing valid concern for the erosion of the shorelines, the islands of the inner archipelago and the seabed. Another environmental concern is the pollution caused by heavy traffic near ferry terminals. The ferries carry around 900,000 passenger cars, 30,000 coaches and 170,000 trailers a year. At the same time the ships are a vital link in Finnish-Swedish trade and one of Finland's lifelines to Europe. Much of Finland's foreign trade travels by ferry.

But on a still summer night, as pinpoints of light appear on islands beside the ferry's white wake, these issues are unlikely to trouble a passenger leaning over the deck rail and gazing out to a darkening sea. ❏

# WEST OF HELSINKI

*Many of the artists and architects who created Helsinki's image
chose to reside in the city's western suburbs, which are also still
home to a few rural and traditional communities*

The 19th-century search for a rural Finnish identity has left a selection of museums and buildings dotting the landscape of what are, now, glorified suburbs of the capital, albeit many with country settings. If you have the time to leave the city for a day, many of the places mentioned in this chapter are worth a visit and offer a different view to the city centre.

## A garden "city"

Passing through Inkoo and Kirkkonummi, the next city of any size you'll come to is **Espoo ❶**. While Espoo is, strictly speaking, a "city", its main impression is of a huge, spread-out municipality. A bastion of wealthier Finns who work in Helsinki, Espoo is a strange mix of rural farm areas and genteel, leafy suburbs that give you, when taken in total, a large and colourful palette of Finnish residential architectural styles.

Espoo's Tapiola area is renowned as the planned garden suburb of the 1950s, in which leading architects of the age aimed to create a harmonious mix of housing, from flats to family houses, set around a central pool. Yet despite all the sleek newness, the area has been settled since 3500 BC, and Espoo's parish church dates from the 15th century. In addition, many artists and architects have made their homes in the area. Only a handful of wooden houses and scenic rapids now mark the original settlements, however the river paths are beautifully tended and lead to some surprisingly authentic Finnish countryside only moments away from Helsinki's centre.

**PRECEDING PAGES:**
golden wheatfields.
**LEFT:** church
steeples on the
western road.
**BELOW:** an
agricultural life.

## Finland's national artist

At the beginning of the route from Helsinki to Turku is **Tarvaspää ❷**, the home of Finland's national artist, Akseli Gallén-Kallela *(see page 278)*. He was already well established when, between 1911–13, he built a studio-home around the Linudd Villa on the old Alberga Manor ground. The studio has been converted into the **Gallén-Kallela Museum**, at Gallén-Kallen-latie 27 (tel: 9-541 3388; open daily in summer, closed Mon in winter, entrance fee).

Today, Helsinki reaches almost to Tarvaspää yet the latter is still set in forest and field (although next to a noisy highway). The studio was designed by Gallén-Kallela himself, whose forceful personality is etched throughout, along with his own hard physical work. Architect Eliel Saarinen, a close friend, participated informally in the studio project as technical adviser.

The museum, contains some 100 illustrations for the *Kalevala* which decorated the Finnish Pavilion at the Paris Exhibition in 1900. The paintings are on display at the Ateneum in Helsinki *(see page 156)* and

Turku Art Museum, where Gallén-Kallela's work sometimes features in temporary exhibitions. Also on view are paintings for his frescos in the Jusélius Mausoleum in Pori *(see page 238)*, which commemorated Sigrid Jusélius, the 11-year-old daughter of a Pori businessman. Working on these frescos was a poignant task for the painter because his own young daughter had died a few years earlier. There are also relics of his times in Africa, Paris and elsewhere.

The Gallen-Kallela Museum is a peaceful oasis, where concerts are occasionally held. It consists of a studio wing, tower and main building, with a coffee house and a terrace restaurant; guided tours are available by appointment.

To get there by car, leave Road 1 (E3) 200 metres (250 yards) past Turunväylä (Tarvontie). Almost at once, a road marked Tarvaspää takes you to the museum. Alternatively, travel on tram 4 and enjoy the scenic 2-km (1-mile) walk from the last stop, or take bus 33 from Munkkiniemi.

## Art Nouveau in the woods

Another artistic mecca that it would be a shame to miss is Eliel Saarinen's home at **Hvitträsk** ❸, some 20 km (14 miles) west of Helsinki in Kirkkonummi municipality (tel: 9-405 09630; open Jun–Oct: daily; Nov–May: Tue–Sun; entrance fee; guided half-day tours by arrangement in summer). It can be easily reached by Road 1 (E3), taking junction 3 left for Jorvas, and follow the signs for Hvitträsk. It can also be reached by bus (number 166 from platform 62 at Helsinki bus station) or train (L train: Luoma and Masala or S train: Masala).

You would expect the studio home of three of Finland's most famous architects to be at one with its surroundings but Hvitträsk surpasses the term. The stone and timber buildings seem to blend into the forest, the great cliffs and

**BELOW:** self-portrait of Akseli Gallén-Kallela on display at Tarvaspää.

the lake (White Lake) that gives the house its name. Inside, architecture, interior designs and furniture all blend together. The partnership of Eliel Saarinen, Herman Gesellius and Armas Lindgren was responsible for many important buildings and, in all, the big, main studio, now a museum, saw the planning of 70 projects. Hvitträsk celebrated one of the architects' earliest triumphs, the Finnish Pavilion at the Paris World Exhibition in 1900. The dining-room ceiling, like the pavilion decoration, is Gallen-Kallela's work. Saarinen, who disliked long meetings, designed the hard black table and chairs; reproductions of his furniture designs are still on sale today.

The early working harmony did not always extend into the private life of the little community, however. Proximity, perhaps, turned the gaze of Saarinen's first wife, Matilda, towards his partner Gesellius and she simply crossed the garden and changed houses. Apparently bearing no grudge, Saarinen married Gesellius' sister, Loja, two years later. But the triumvirate broke up in 1906 and by 1916 Saarinen was working at Hvitträsk on his own.

In 1922, after gaining a major prize in a competition in New York, Saarinen moved to the United States, was made Dean of the Cranbrook Academy of Art and became as well known abroad as in Finland. He continued to visit Hvitträsk each year until his death in 1950, and his grave overlooks the lake.

Map on pages 194–95

*The flat landscape and quiet, rural roads make the area ideal for cyclists.*

## Leased to Russia

The whole Kirkkonummi municipality was once a large rural Swedish-speaking area. However, at the end of World War II, Finland was forced to lease the Porkkala Peninsula in the south to the Soviet Union as a naval base, a situation that remained until 1955 *(see page 55)*. The Russian cemetery here, on a typical

**BELOW:**
Hvitträsk, once home to Finland's finest architects.

Map on pages 194–95

Soviet scale, is an ageless reminder of that time, when 7,000 Finns had to leave their homes at 10 days' notice.

Today Porkkala has a Finnish naval garrison in **Upinniemi**, with a remarkable Sea Chapel, designed by Marianne and Mikko Heliövaara, shaped like a boat with open sails and overlooking the sea. Some of the best bird migration routes pass over the Porkkala Peninsula and spring and autumn draw ornithologists galore to watch flocks of cranes, swans and geese. In summer, sailing boats and beach cabins dot the spectacular Baltic coastline.

Back on Road 1 and heading west, the area of lake and ridge is part of the Salpausselkä Ridge, formed at the end of the Ice Age. The next major stop is **Sammatti ❹**, just south of the road. Look out for the sign to **Paikkari Cottage**, (Paikkarin torppa), the home of Elias Lönnrot, who collected the old legends and tales for the *Kalevala (see page 95)*. The building is typical of a worker's home in 19th-century southwest Finland. Outside, Lönnrot's statue is by Halonen and Räsänen. Not far away stands Lammi House where the writer died.

At **Salo ❺**, some 115 km (80 miles) from Helsinki in the heart of the apple-growing Salojoki Valley, it is worth turning off the main road to go into the town centre, which has old houses and beautiful gardens, Uskela Church, another of C.L. Engel's works, and a fine valley view. Many of the world-famous Nokia mobile phones are manufactured in Salo *(see page 82)*.

## Tyrant's carriage

At Piikkiö, only 15 km (10 miles) from Turku, turn right for the **Pukkilan kartano-ja ajokalumuseo (Pukkila Manor House Museum and Vehicle Museum) ❻**, where the rococo-style mansion is furnished as the home of a state official. The Carriage Museum in the former byre has 30 different carriages, including that of the Governor General Bobrikov, assassinated in 1904.

The town church dates back to 1755, built partly of stones from the ruins of **Kuusiston Castle ❼**. This medieval bishop's castle is worth a detour to the Kuusisto peninsula, just west of Piikkiö – take the road to Pargas (Parainen) and branch on to a secondary road to the ruins. The 14th century castle stood stoutly until Gustav Vasa ordered its demolition in 1528, but enough remains to have encouraged recent attempts at restoration.

Having come this far, you may like to continue to **Pargas (Parainen) ❽**, which has a beautiful view over the islands of the archipelago and is famous for its large limestone quarries. Pargas has one of the most stunning medieval greystone churches in Finland, Harmaa Kivikirkko, dedicated to St Simon. Built in the 1320s, it is unusual for the spreading brick columns that support the interior and contrast with the light blue trim of the pews. Notice, too, the panel paintings of Old Testament figures running around the porch where the organ sits. Pargas has a good marina, and a charming series of wooden buildings scattered around the church which form a kind of extended folklore museum; weaving still goes on here.

From here it is a short drive northwest to the old city of Turku *(see page 203)*.   ❑

**BELOW:** a coat of arms shows the Swedish influence.
**RIGHT:** wildflowers bloom in Finland's springtime.

# THE TRADITIONAL FINNISH SAUNA

*An old Finnish proverb says: "First you build the sauna, then you build the house"; even today there's nothing so uniquely Finnish as a sauna*

There are some things along the way which a traveller does not forget – and a real Finnish sauna is one of them. Although its origin is obscure, the sauna came to Finland over 2,000 years ago, and it is a rare Finn who admits to not liking one. Official statistics estimate that there are over 625,000 saunas in Finland, not counting those in private houses or summer cottages that dot the shoreline of the country's lakes *(see page 250)*. The actual figure could easily be over 1 million in a country of just 5 million people – but then, the sauna is a national institution.

## BUSINESS AND PLEASURE

The sauna outgrew its rural roots long ago. Today, be it city or village, you will find public saunas, and it is safe to assume that every new apartment block has a sauna for its tenants. Many companies also have saunas for their employees.

A Finnish sauna is not a meeting place for sex, as it is in some countries; codes of behaviour are strict. Titles and position are, they say, left hanging in the changing room with the clothes. It is is not unusual for board meetings and government cabinet meetings to be held in a sauna – perhaps because it's "not done" to swear or raise one's voice. A sauna also leaves you relaxed yet alert.

▽ **FRIENDS AND FOLIAGE**
Tying up birch leaves for the sauna is a social event in summer.

▽ **MORAL CODE**
Despite the nudity, a Finnish sauna is a moral place. Generally, saunas are same-sex only; a mixed sauna is solely a family affair.

▽ **HOT GOSSIP**
There is more to the sauna than just getting clean. It is a happening – a time to meet friends or rivals, to talk and socialise.

## HOW TO TAKE A SAUNA

There is no "right way" to take a sauna – temperature and style vary. The ideal temperature is between 80–100° C (175–210° F) although it can be a cooler 30° C (85° F) on the bottom platform, reserved for children. A common practice is to brush oneself with a wet birch switch, called the *vihta*. This not only gives off a fresh fragrance but increases blood circulation and perspiration.

How long you sit in the sauna is entirely up to you. When you have had enough, you move on to stage two: cooling off. A cold shower is the most common way but, if the sauna is by a lake or the sea, a quick plunge into the cool water is stimulating.

The final stage is to dry off, which should be done naturally, to avoid further perspiration. It is also time for a beer or coffee and a snack to complete the ritual.

△ **STEAM HEAT**
Water thrown over the hot stones creates a dry steam *(löyly)*, which makes the heat tolerable and stimulates perspiration.

◁ **COOLING OFF**
In the winter, brave souls jump through holes in the ice or roll around in the snow – not recommended practice for people with high blood pressure.

◁ **SAUNA FASHIONS**
The sauna has become such an integral part of Finnish life, that there are even "designer" outlets specially geared towards sauna accessories.

▷ **ANCIENT USES**
In olden days in rural Finland the sauna was not just the place in which to get clean, but also where babies were born and sausages smoked.

# SOUTHERN FINLAND

*From Swedish-speaking farming communities to bastions built to protect the Finn-Russian border towns, the south coast has an atmosphere quite distinct from the rest of the country*

Map
on pages
194–95

o follow the south coast of Finland from west to east is to follow a route once travelled by Nordic kings and princes to St Petersburg. It is mainly flat, coastal country covered with farmland and densely grown forest. And, because proximity to the sea has always given extra value to land – in addition to the beneficial, warming effects of the Gulf of Finland – this area is heavily settled – in Finnish terms.

It is also heavily Swedish-speaking. From Pargas *(see page 188)* south of Turku at the head of the Turunmaa island chain, through Ekenäs (Tammisaari), Karis (Karjaa), and further east through a cluster of small villages on the approach to Kotka, you will hear a great deal of Swedish and read it as the first language on signposts. This is all part of the democracy of bilingualism in Finland: in any town with a majority of Swedish speakers, the Swedish name normally takes precedence.

**LEFT:** models of ships traditionally grace the windows of Loviisa's wooden houses.
**BELOW:** Hanko's church.

## Farms and fortresses

The landscape changes only very subtly from west to east. As most of Finland is above the 60th parallel, its southernmost reaches are the major farming areas. The land is low, and tends to be misty in the early morning and late evening. Although it is not as rich in lakes as the country north of here, it is sufficiently irrigated by local meandering rivers and streams.

The green of new wheat and the yellow of rape seed dominate in late spring; then the wheat matures and the wildflowers burst into bloom. The grassy strips at the roadside are first overrun with cowslip and lupin, a midsummer flower with tall purple, pink, and white spindles. When the lupin fades, *maitohorsma* takes over; also a tall, spindly flower, the splash of its magenta petals fill not just the road edges but entire forests and fields. Autumn is slightly more colourful in the west, where the linden adds its bright hue to the gold of the birches. The west is also hillier than the east. Set against this backdrop are clusters of old farm buildings, stained dark red; most larger coastal towns have old sections whose buildings are painted in an array of pastel shades. Manor houses in the region are painted a rich ochre or brilliant yellow.

The eastern portion of the coast, past Helsinki, is riddled with fortifications. For the Swedes, then the Russians, and finally the independent Finns, the Russian border has been a crucial dividing line. From 1944 to 1956, the Soviets had a military base at Porkkala, an elbow-shaped peninsula west of Helsinki.

The Finnish-Soviet borders still have a no-man's land running between them, and although travel between the two countries has become far easier and

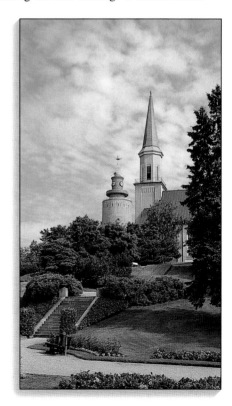

more popular since the break-up of the USSR, there is no mistaking the sterner attitude of the Russian customs guards and immediate deterioration of road conditions as soon as one crosses over the border to the east.

## Exploring the islands

Richly vegetated but sparsely populated, the archipelago of **Turunmaan** is quieter than the Ålands in terms of tourism *(see page 229)*, and the islands are reached more quickly from the mainland. They are linked by a series of bridges and then ferries. Ferries also service some of the smaller islands that spin off south from the main chain. Local buses connect the larger towns.

Turunmaa's finest harbour is on the northeast spur of **Nagu**. An old wooden house overlooking the marina has been made into a guesthouse-style hotel, with a French brasserie and a chic restaurant, L'Escale, next door. Also to be found in Nagu is the Borstö Folk Museum and the 14th-century St Olof's Church (open Jun–Aug: daily).

As you approach Pargas (Parainen) from west or south you come to **Sattmark**, on the island of Stortervolandet. This tiny log cabin was once a sailor's quarters. It now serves light meals in its prettily furnished rooms and down on the dock that runs below and behind it.

**Salo** is the first large market town to the east on the mainland. Set off by a triad of churches – the Lutheran Uskela (1832), the Greek Orthodox Tsasouna at its foot, and the stunningly modern Helisnummen (Helisnummi Church) about 4 km (2½ miles) outside the town – Salo still has a very lively market, held every day except Sundays. Along the Uskela river there are some beautiful residential garden districts.

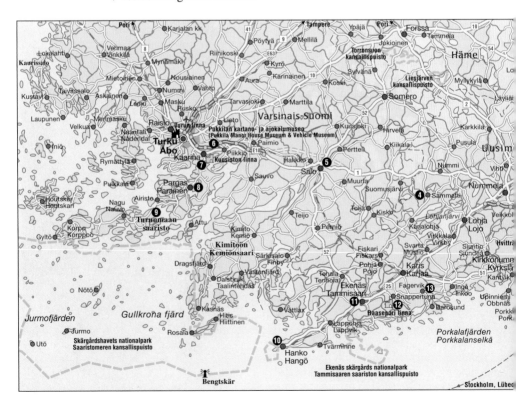

## Marina life

Due south of Salo is **Hanko (Hangö)** ❿, Finland's southernmost town. Known not only for its annual July regatta and its long beaches, Hanko has some of the most jocular architecture to be found in Finland. A long parade of turreted and deeply-eaved houses follows the stretch of beach – in varying states of repair.

Hanko's Linnoitusmuseo (Frontline Museum) outlines the town's strategic history, such as the destruction of the fortifications during the Crimean War (open May–Sept:daily except Mon; in winter, Sat, Sun and Wed afternoons only). Hanko was also the port from which 300,000 Finns emigrated between 1880 and 1930 to escape raging epidemics and famine. It is still a large customs port, with a lively summer milieu centered on its large marina, which hosts boats from dozens of foreign ports. On land, there is a parachuting school, public tennis courts, and a tall watchtower from which to view the busy sea lanes.

**Ekenäs (Tammisaari)** ⓫ is the next main coastal stop along the route of kings. It is a finely laid-out old town, with cobbled streets named after different crafts trades, and is a great place for a stroll; some artisans still set up shop here in summer. Just to the south is the Tammisaaren saariston kansallispuisto, a national park, resplendent with marshes, forests and water birds.

There is an extremely active boating life in and around Ekenäs, and numerous outdoor concerts in summer: Ekenäs is considered by many as the major cultural centre of Finland's Swedish-speaking people. The Knippan boardwalk restaurant and the steeple of the old granite church (1680) are the town's main landmarks. There's also a pretty camping ground within walking distance. For an historical background on the town, visit Porvaristalo, the Ekenäs Museum on Gustav Wasas Gata 13 (tel: 19-263 3161, open daily throughout the summer).

Map on pages 194–95

**TIP**

Information on archipelago boat tours is available from the tourist information office at Bulevardi 10 in Helsinki (tel: 19-220 3411) or on the marina (summer only).

GULF OF FINLAND

Southern Finland

0        20 km
0              20 miles

## Historic villages

A few kilometres eastward is **Snappertuna** (no connection with fish), a farming village of Swedish-speaking Finns and the town closest to the splendid 13th-century castle at **Raasepori** , enfolded in a wooded valley. Most of the fortification is in good condition and you can freely tour its ramparts and impressive interior spaces, refurbished in wood.

The Outdoor Theatre in the Raseborg dale stages dramatic and musical evenings, and if you visit in July you may catch a re-enacted medieval duel. (These tend to be comic rather than grave historic events; British factions are often featured.)

Further east beyond Snappertuna is **Fagervik**, the site of a tremendous old manor overlooking a protected sea inlet. Its granite and wood buildings make a fine backdrop for a picnic or horse ride. There are also good walking paths here; the so-called King's Road signposts point out landmarks.

North and east of Helsinki is **Vantaa**, another city with endless open space. The Vantaa rivermouth, a wide wash of water just to the east of the capital, is the home of the "*Vanhakaupunki*", or "old city", upon which Helsinki was founded in the 16th century (*see page 153*).

**Porvoo (Borgå)** is one of Finland's most important historical towns. The Swedish King Magnus Eriksson gave Porvoo a Royal Charter in 1346; from this point on it became a busy trading post and, ultimately, it was the place where the Diet of Porvoo (1809) convened to transfer Finland from Swedish to Russian hands (*see page 33*). The striking **Porvoo Cathedral** (open daily, closed Mon in winter; entrance free), where this momentous event took place, dates back to the 15th century.

**BELOW:**
near Porvoo, the Alikartano Manor House is dedicated to the Finnish explorer, Nordenskjöld.

Map on pages 194–95

While its rich history made the town important, Porvoo's artists give it its real character. The **Edelfelt-Vallgren Art Museum** (Välikatu 11; tel: 19-574 7589; open May–Aug: daily; Sept–Apr: Wed–Sun; entrance fee) occupies a 1792 merchant's house, formerly the Town Hall, on Rahtihuoneentori (The Town Hall Square). It features paintings by Albert Edelfelt – one of Finland's finest 19th-century artists *(see page 77)* – and works by sculptor Ville Vallgren, as well as a fine Art Nouveau furniture collection. The Albert Edelfelt Atelier in Haikko, 6 km (4 miles) south of Porvoo, also exhibits much of Edelfelt's work. The town is also alive with the work of current artists and writers.

For scenery, Porvoo also has few rivals: its trim riverbanks are lined with fishing cottages and the pastel-coloured houses of the old town provide a charming backdrop.

East of Porvoo, the landscape becomes more rural and less populated, with only the occasional village to break up the vast spread of wheatfields and forests. In summer, the grassy hillocks bristle with wildflowers. There are just two more towns and one sizeable city, all in fortification country. **Loviisa** ⑯, a pretty, provincial town with an esplanade headed by the New Gothic Church, is the smallest of these. A town museum tells the local history, including the role of the Rosen and Ungern bastions, built in the 18th century to protect the important trade route between Vyborg and Turku.

The frequency of rivers (originating in the great lake area immediately to the north) and Orthodox churches now begins to increase. After the old towns of Ruotsinpyhtää and Pyhtää is the broad Kotka Delta. At first sight Kotka can appear unappealingly industrial, yet on closer inspection it is one of the most beautifully situated cities in Finland.

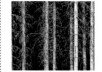

*Vast tracts of forest make up much of the landscape of southern Finland.*

**BELOW:** bicycles are a good way of exploring the southern coast.

## Delta fishing

It is around **Kotka** ⏰ that the Kymi river breaks up into five branches before rushing off into the sea, making for perfect salmon and trout fishing. The closest of the spray of islands along the coast can be reached by bridges, the rest by ferry. Kotka centre is based on an esplanade. One street to the northwest, at Kirkkokatu and Koulukatu, is the main Lutheran church, with tremendous brick buttresses; the imposing Orthodox church complex and park runs along Papinkatu. Kotka has frequent boat services to nearby islands, some of which have old fortifications. The pleasant Sapokka harbour has one of the finest parks in Finland; there is even a high artifical waterfall.

Apart from the Kotka islands, the **Kymenlaakso** (Kymi river valley) extends further inland, where there are gorgeous forest paths. Details are available from the Kotka tourist office at Kirkkokatu 3, tel 5-234-4424.

The famous fishing lodge of Tsar Alexander III, is at **Langinkoski** ⏱ (signposted from Langinkoskentie; tel: 5-228 1050; open May–Aug: daily; entrance fee). The tremendous log building was crafted by the Finns for the Tsar; its furnishings are now preserved as a museum.

Several nature paths begin from Langinkoski – if you walk north for 5 km (3 miles), you'll pass Kyminlinna fortification, over Hovinkoski river through Kyminkartano (manor) to **Keisarin Kosket**. These "tsar's rapids" course around Munkkisaari Island, with its Orthodox chapel (Tsasouna). A pilgrimage of the faithful is made here every 14 August. The spot is also ideal for fishing and rapids shooting. On the bank is Keisarin Kosket Lodge, an Orthodox monastery site from 1650 to 1850, with café, boats, and cabins for hire; fishing licences are also sold (tel: 5-210 7400 for details).

**BELOW:** the Tsar's fishing lodge at Langinkoski, near Kotka.

Map on pages 194–95

In summer, **Kärkisaari**, just to the west of Kotka, makes for a lovely excursion. The former youth hostel here has been turned into one of the most stylish B&B locations in the country. The food, including the tasty pastries, are well worth sampling. The long swimming dock leads into the island-filled inlet of the Gulf of Finland. On the adjacent peninsula is Santalahti, with caravan and cabin facilities; the crescent-shaped beach has grassy knolls at the edge of a sandy bay.

The Kotka Tourist Board can point out nature-protected paths and rivers, as well as arrange other trips and activities (with guides, if needed).

## Towards Russia

Kotka is only 70 km (45 miles) from the nearest Russian city, Viipuri (Vyborg) and 270 km (170 miles) from St Petersburg; all varieties of Finland-Russia trips can be arranged with the Kotka Tourist Board, but remember to plan overnight trips in advance so that your visa will be ready.

**Hamina** ⓭ is the last of the large Finnish towns before you reach the border. Its concentric plan is part of a huge fortification, and its military nature is also preserved by the presence of thousands of young Finnish men based here for national service. Pastel-coloured wooden houses contrast prettily with red brick barracks and magazines. Three old churches are to be found in Hamina, as well as several quaint museums. One of the large bastion sections has been turned into a covered concert venue. The acoustics of the "Bastioni" are excellent and the site awe-inspiring.

Further east lies **Vaalimaa**, the busiest border station on your way to Russia. Huge supermarkets sell goodies to Russians and Finns – more than 1 million people cross the border here annually. ❑

*Old cannons on the Finno-Russian border are reminders of former tensions between the nations.*

**BELOW:** the planned town of Hamina, with military fortifications.

# WESTERN FINLAND

*The western area of Finland is known by many as the "essential triangle", encompassing three major cities and various tributes to the industries and artists that have formed the modern nation*

Map
on page
204

I n many countries, a city conjures up images of busy streets clogged with cars and tall buildings. A Finnish city certainly has its motor traffic but it is also a spreading area of lake, forest and green spaces between the buildings that sometimes feels as though it were in the heart of rural Finland. A round trip of some 500 km (310 miles) from the capital Helsinki to the west of Finland, takes in the three largest cities and is one of the best ways to get a feel of the country in a couple of weeks. Our route leads to Turku, the old capital in the centre of Swedish-speaking Finland, and then on to Tampere, the industrial capital, where water set the first 18th-century mills rolling.

Along the way are most of the elements, past and present, that make Finland what it is today. In the south, there are coasts and lakesides, some lakes so vast that it is difficult to decide whether they are lake or sea. Beautiful old houses restored as museums and hotels lie along the route, as do historic castles with magnificent banqueting halls and dungeons, and statues that reflect Finland's history, sometimes warring, sometimes at peace. Further north, the lakes become more frequent, and it is tempting to leave the car and travel as the Finns of old did, using waterways such as the Silverline route which winds through the lake system between Tampere and Hämeenlinna. You can go north by the Poet's Way to Virrat, and swim, fish or sail on lake or sea.

This is a good opportunity to get to know something about Finland's arts and culture, remarkable in a country of only five million, and see the Finns' famed skill in design at glassworks at studios that welcome visitors and offer distinctive articles that could only be Finnish. Above all, between the cities lies the long Finnish road through forests and old villages, to make it a tour filled with flowers and fresh air.

**PRECEDING PAGES:** misty headlands. **LEFT:** the *Sigyn* barque. **BELOW:** making lace at the Handicrafts Museum.

## Turku

**Turku** ❶ is the "other" face of Finland, the view from the southwest, closest to Scandinavia and the rest of Europe, not just in trade but also in culture. Its atmosphere is a mixture of river and sea: the River Aura divides the modern city in two; the Baltic, curling round the river mouth, has countless islands in an archipelago that stretches southwest until it runs into the Åland Islands, halfway between Finland and Sweden *(see page 229)*.

It is also a city of paradoxes. Turku (Åbo in Swedish) feels like a capital even though it never held that title in a sovereign country but only as the principal city and home of the Viceroy in the Swedish-Finnish kingdom. It is Finland's oldest city and yet many of the buildings go back only to the Great Fire of 1827 which destroyed a town then largely made of wood. Islands, river and sea make

Turku a summer paradise, yet it is also the birthplace of Finnish culture and the country's religious centre.

The Swedes were the first known nation to arrive at the mouth of the Aura River when King Erik sailed in with an English bishop and an expeditionary force in 1155. As Bishop Henrik, the bishop later became the first Finnish patron saint. Even earlier, Finnish tribes from the southeast had settled and traded along the river valleys of southwest Finland, and sailors and merchants came and went to the first settlement, up-river at Koroinen.

The Swedes called their growing town Åbo and in 1229 Pope Gregory IX agreed to transfer the See of the Bishop of Finland to Koroinen. By 1300, a new cathedral downstream on Unikankare (the "Mound of Sleep") was ready for consecration, and Turku became the spiritual centre of Finland.

Around the same time, the solid lines of a castle began to rise near the mouth of the River Aura as the heart of royal power in Finland, where the Swedish governor lived and visiting dignitaries paid their respects. It was also a fighting

castle, standing firm under a winter siege in the mid-14th century in one of the bloody struggles for the Swedish throne. In all, the castle was besieged six times. In the 16th century, Gustav Vasa survived another winter siege and proclaimed his young son (later Johan III) as the Duke of Finland.

After Duke Johan returned in 1552, with his wife, the Polish princess Katarina Jagellonica, Turku Castle entered its most colourful phase of royal glory. Katarina brought glamour, in her Polish courtiers, her velvet and lace, and even her spoons, forks and knives, and introduced a splendid court life that was already common in most of Europe but had not yet reached Finland. In summer, the court visited the island of Ruissalo, just off the coast, as Finns do today. But this gracious life did not last. After Gustav Vasa's death, feuds broke out between his three sons, and the eldest brother, Erik XIV, besieged the Duke. The castle surrendered in three weeks and Johan and Katarina were bundled into captivity. Though later, as Johan III, Duke Johan gained his revenge on Erik whom he imprisoned in Turku Castle, court life never again achieved such heights.

## Exploring the old city

Today, the massive façades, honey-coloured under the sun, grey in winter, of **Turunlinna (Turku Castle)** Ⓐ (Linnankatu 80; tel: 2-262 0300; open daily; entrance fee) look towards the modern town centre, some 3 km (2 miles) away. Many of its rooms have been preserved as the Turku Historical Museum, with portraits of Duke Johan and his wife. The old chapel has regained its original role and the magnificent banqueting halls are the scene of civic celebrations.

Turku had the first university in Finland, founded by the 17th-century Governor General of Finland, Count Per Brahe. He travelled the length and

Maps
Area 204
City 206

**BELOW:** impressive vaulted ceiling of Turku Cathedral.

*Panelled cabinet at Turku Castle.*

breadth of his governorship and his name is commemorated in many towns and buildings. His greatest contribution to Turku, however, was **Åbo Akademi** Ⓑ which, after its ceremonial opening in 1640, made Turku the centre of culture and learning as well as religion. When Finland became a Russian Grand Duchy, the Tsar ordered the Academy to be transferred to the new capital to become the University of Helsinki but the Old Academy Building remains. In 1918, independent Finland created a second Akademi as Turku's Swedish-language university, and also founded the University of Turku.

After the Great Fire in 1827, market and town moved away from the cathedral to the west bank of the Aura, much of it designed and built to the plan of that industrious German, Carl Ludwig Engel, who visualised a city of rectangular blocks intersected by broad streets, a plan still clear in modern Turku. The way to start a walking tour is among the bright stalls, piled with fruit and flowers, in the market square. On one side, the Hotel Hamburger Börs is one of Turku's best, with busy bars, cafés and restaurants packing its ground floor. The hotel faces across to the green, cap-like dome of the Orthodox Church, an Engel design built in 1838 on the orders of Tsar Nicholas I. The yellow building to the southwest is the Swedish Theatre, also by Engel.

During the days of the Grand Duchy, the **Ortodoksinen kirkko (Orthodox Cathedral)** Ⓒ served a Russian community but it is now attached to Istanbul. Its present congregation of 2,000 includes converts and one or two families who moved from Karelia during the World War II resettlement. Inside, it has all the rich beauty one would expect, the dome held up by ornate pillars. Paintings tell the story of St George and the Dragon, and Empress Alexandra (wife of the Roman Emperor Diocletianus) to whom the church is dedicated.

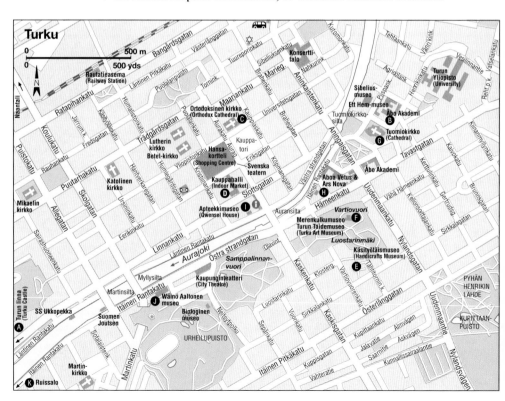

## Shopping

A cluster of shops such as Pentik, Aarikka and Sylvi Salonen, along Yliopis-tonkatu (Universitetsgatan) to the west, is a happy hunting ground for gifts and mementoes, with a selection of handicrafts, wood and chinaware and other typically Finnish goods. Between here and Eerikinkatu (Eriksgatan) is the **Hansakortteli (Hansa Shopping Centre)**, enticingly weatherproof in a Finnish winter. Just across from Hansa, Mezzo is another indoor shopping complex with a variety of restaurants, cafés and shops.

More exciting is the 19th-century **Kauppahalli (Indoor Market)** , across the street in Eerikinkatu. There is something about the smell of a market hall that lures you in, a mixture of cheese, meat, fish, sweets and a tang of exotic spices. The stalls stretch along the entire length, with tempting arrays of *munkki*, a sort of doughnut, and *pulla*, a cake-like bread. At Turun Tee ja Mauste you can smell some of more than 200 teas before you buy and pick up oddities such as ginger tea for Christmas or tea spiced with cloves – good for cold weather, the Finns say. Nearby, a stall sells typical wooden tulips and leaves, painted in bright colours. Made by a sheltered workshop, they are half the usual cost.

Turning down Aurakatu towards the Auransilta (bridge) you pass the **Tourist Information Office**. The bridge gives the first view of the numerous restaurant boats and the sleek white hull and complicated rigging of the *Suomen Joutsen*, the "Swan of Finland", which once plied the ocean between South America and Europe. Along the banks, people sit at open-air restaurants and, below the bridge, there is dancing every summer Tuesday from 6 to 8pm.

Over the bridge, on the right-hand side, there is a statue of long-distance runner Paavo Nurmi, Turku's most famous son.

*Map on page 206*

*Paavo Nurmi (1897–1973) is said to have been the greatest long-distance runner of all time. He won a total of nine gold and three silver Olympic medals, and set 31 world records. He also carried the Olympic Torch in the 1952 Helsinki Games.*

**BELOW:** guides in traditional dress at the Pharmacy Museum.

*An employee at the Handicrafts Museum wears traditional 18th-century costume.*

**BELOW:** the *Icy Sea* memorial on Mill Bridge.

## Historic buildings

The entrance to one of Turku's most interesting areas is just a short walk from here. This is Luostarinmäki (Cloister Hill), the site of an early convent. There's a certain rough justice in the fact that the only part of the wooden city to survive the Great Fire of 1827 was this hill, for it housed those too poor to buy houses in the 18th-century city and they moved here to build their own community. That escape has left an inheritance that, unlike most Nordic open-air museums, stands where it was founded and is not a collection of re-located buildings. The name, **Käsityöläismuseo (Handicrafts Museum)** **Ⓔ**, (tel: 2-262 0350; open daily summer, Tues–Sun winter; entrance fee). is a slight misnomer because this old area is much more; the woman spinning today in the dark interior of a wooden house is a museum worker but she is spinning in the same way and in the same place as the early inhabitants, and the 18th-century costumes seem quite natural. There are traditional sweets, every sort of craft, tin, copper and goldsmith's, and a baker's which sometimes sells pretzels made in the traditional way. Seamstresses and tailors sew and the old way of life is revealed in the community houses where different families lived in the same building, sharing their kitchen and their bathhouse, or by the truckle bed of a university student who lived with a family, giving service in return for his keep. The main house near the entrance has an excellent self-service restaurant with good homemade food.

Coming down the hill, detour via the Observatory on Vartiovuori, another Engel building, now the **Merenkulkumuseo (Turku Art Museum)** **Ⓕ** until year 2004, when it will return to its former location on Puolalanmäki. Nearby is an anti-aircraft gun memorial from World War II, when ordinary Finns raised money for defensive guns – Turku bought nine.

**Tuomiokirkko (Turku Cathedral)** **Ⓖ** (open daily; entrance free), also on this side of the river, was the focal point of old Turku. Look down from the balcony for the best view of the high arches of the main aisle, with its side chapels. The balcony also has the Cathedral Museum (entrance fee), with valuable collections opened to the public in the 1980s after the most recent restoration. Among the most interesting chapels is the Kankainen Chapel where the stained-glass window by Wladimir Swetschkoff shows Queen Karin Månsdotter, wife of the luckless Erik XIV, who was eventually poisoned after his imprisonment.

Don't miss the statue of Mikael Agricola near the cathedral's south wall. The architect of the Reformation in Finland, he was born on a farm in Pernå east of Helsinki and took the name Agricola meaning "farmer's son" when he went to study in Rome. In the Cathedral Park Governor Per Brahe stands in a classically proud pose, not far from Åbo Akademi, a block or two to the north. The main buildings of the present Swedish-language university and the University of Turku are also nearby.

Not far away stands the magnificent **Rettig Palace**, formerly a secretive residence of Hans von Rettig, tobacco industrialist, shipowner and one of the richest men in Turku. After his death in 1979 the building was opened to the public. And what a building! Now called **Aboa Vetus and Ars Nova** **Ⓗ**, the main house exhibits modern art and the garden has become a museum of medieval Turku (Itäinen Rantakatu 4–6; tel: 2-250 0552; open daily summer, Tues–Sun winter; entrance fee).

**Map on page 206**

## Along the river

In Turku you are never far from the River Aura and can cross and recross its five main bridges or take the little ferry that still carries pedestrians and cycles across free of charge.

For a riverbank tour, the first stop is **Apteekkimuseo (Qwensel House)** ❶, Turku's oldest wooden building, named after and built by Judge W.J. Qwensel, who bought the plot as long ago as 1695. Perhaps the best kept secret in town, the backyard of this house has a café with 18th-century decor and recipes. From the waterside, low bushes trace the name TURKU/ÅBO, and Qwensel House now houses the rare **Pharmacy Museum** (Läntinen rantakatu 13; tel: 2-262 0280; open daily; entrance fee), which keeps traditions alive by growing herbs in the backyard. A recent innovation, leaving from the front of the museum, is the horse-cab *Musta-Hilu* which provides a leisurely and unusual view of the city. (Children can also have the Koiramäki tour of the city in a special red and yellow bus with guides in costume. This daily summer tour is, as yet, only conducted in Finnish.)

Walking past Myllysilta (Mill Bridge), in Borenpuisto Park, the dramatic statue entitled *Icy Sea* is dedicated to Turku's seamen. August Upman (inscribed on the pedestal) was a pioneer of winter navigation. Past the next bridge, Martinsilta, the SS *Ukkopekka* was the last steamship to sail Finland's coastal waters. Depending on how far you care to walk, you can continue on this side as far as Turku Castle and the modern harbour areas that show how important the sea still is to Turku, with merchant tugs and tankers and the terminals of the Viking and Silja Lines.

On your way to the harbour at Linnankatu 74 is the Maritime Centre, also known as **Forum Marinum** (open daily Jun–Aug; one entrance fee covers all ships). The Maritime Museum and many of Turku's museum ships will find their final home here, including the smaller barque *Sigyn*, launched in Göteborg in 1887, and sailing as far as the East Indies and South America. Her last home port was the Åland Islands and her last voyage from there in 1949. *Sigyn* is unique as the last barque-rigged ocean-going vessel.

Heading back towards the centre you come to the austere outlines of the **Wäinö Aaltonen museo (Wäinö Aaltonen's Museum)** ❼ (Itäinen Rantakatu 38; tel: 2-262 0853; open Tue–Sun; entrance fee). Designed by Aaltonen's architect son and daughter-in-law, the building contains much of his work including the massive statues of *Peace*, hands raised, and *Faith*, a mother and child. In a self-portrait, this private man placed a text in front of his face to hide his feelings. Outside the City Theatre is Aaltonen's statue of Aleksis Kivi, one of the first authors to write in Finnish.

The windmill on Samppalinnanmäki overlooking the river is the last of its kind in Turku. Here also, stopwatch in hand, Paavo Nurmi trained against his

**TIP**

Numerous boat restaurants dot the riverside. At last count, there was a full dozen of them, each serving a variety of beers and fully packed on sunny summer days. In 1999 alone, three new boats were added.

**BELOW:** Pentti-Oskari Kangas, captain of the SS *Ukkopekka.*

own best times, and the polished granite stone on the slopes is Finland's independence memorial, unveiled in 1977 on the 60th anniversary. On this river walk, you will notice the waterbuses by Auransilta Bridge and below Martinsilta Bridge. A sightseeing cruise is the best way to get a feel for this water city.

## Ruissalo Island

Boat services will take you several times daily to **Ruissalo Island** , also reached in a few minutes by crossing a bridge. It is a green and leafy island, a place for botanists and birdwatchers as well as cyclists and walkers. Ruissalo has the area's best beaches, including a nudist beach – something still rare in Finland, not because of any national prudery but because the Finns, with their lonely cabins on isolated lakesides, had not realised one might need permission to bathe without a swimsuit.

The island is also a surprise place for art lovers, for Ruissalo boasts one of the best art centres in Finland. The 19th-century **Villa Roma** is typical of the "lace villas" (so-called because of their latticed balconies and windows) built by wealthy merchants. Its owner, the Procultura Foundation (tel: 2-589 300), shows summer exhibitions of top-quality Finnish art, from glass to painting to textiles. There are toy and home museums, and a café. A good restaurant is Honkapirtti, a Karelian-style pinewood building built in 1942–43 by infantry soldiers near the front during the Continuation War. In summer, the island is home to Ruisrock, the world's oldest annual rock festival *(see page 93)*.

One of the most civilised ways to see the archipelago is a supper cruise aboard the SS *Ukkopekka* which retains something of its steamship past and its original engine. As the passengers strive for window tables, the *Ukkopekka* moves

**BELOW:** the Convent Church in Naantali.

smoothly down the river and out to sea. The bearded skipper, Captain Pentti-Oskari Kangas, is everyone's image of a sea captain and a couple of musicians sing old Finnish sailing songs as the islands glide by. If the timing is right, a fisherman may sail out to the *Ukkopekka* with the fish he has caught and smoked that day. The steamship cruises to different islands and towns, including Captain Kangas' home town of Naantali, north of Turku.

## Naantali

**Naantali** is now a famous sailing harbour, packed with visiting boats. It is also a historic 200-year-old town, with old houses that are still lived in today. There is a beautiful greystone convent church, with a new organ that attracts famous organists, particularly during the June Music Festival when some 15,000 visitors crowd into the tiny town. At its start in the 1980s, the sceptics thought that little Naantali's festival "would die in 10 years". Now reaching into its third decade, it is proving them wrong. The harbour is also popular with artists, and galleries include the Purpura, which specialises in Finnish artists and supports an artist-in-residence scheme.

Naantali, around 20 minutes by the new road from Turku, could also be a detour on the way to Tampere, but the more direct routes leave the city on Road 40 (motorway at first). This leads to **Aura ❷**, some 30 km (20 miles) north, where from Road 9 you have a fine view of the Aurakoski (rapids). Road 9 continues northeast through rich farmland with a possible detour right at the Helsinki-Pori crossroads (Road 2) for a short drive to the Humppila Glassworks, where at a glass-walled demonstration forge you watch glass-blowers at work. The Glass Village at Nuutajärvi, a little further north on the left of the

**Maps**
**Area 204**
**City 206**

*Finland's president has a summer home near Naantali, at Kultaranta, whose gardens are open to the public. Many foreign dignitaries take a sauna in former President Kekkonen's unusual house above the rocky coast.*

**LEFT:** the largest bell in Finland at Tampere's Orthodox Cathedral.
**BELOW:** the "prism" at the Sara Hildén Museum.

road, was formed around Finland's oldest glassworks from 1793, and is also well worth a brief stop. An alternative route, Road 41, slightly to the west goes through Oripää, a gliding centre, where the Moorish style building is the studio-home of sculptor Viljo Syrjämaa, and from Vammala, the road goes through the flat, fertile land of the Loimijoki valley. A 5-km (3-mile) detour on the secondary road to Ellivuori is well worthwhile; just north of Nokia are more magnificent rapids at the start of the waterway system that leads to Tampere.

## Tampere

Citizens of Tampere call their city the Manchester or the Pittsburgh of Finland, depending on whether they are talking to someone from Great Britain or the United States, yet anything less like a classic industrial city is hard to imagine.

Tampere ❸ lies on a narrow neck of land between two lakes, great stretches of water so large that you feel you are close to a sea rather than way inland. Linking the lakes, the rushing waters of the Tammerkoski River first brought power, industry and riches to Tampere. Though it still provides some energy, the Tammerkoski is so clean nowadays that it attracts growing numbers of anglers, out for trout. At weekends, the two lakes are bright with rainbow sails and the white wakes of motor boats, packed with picnickers, track their course to one of the islands or to a summerhouse along the lakeside.

Despite a changing pattern of industry, Tampere has managed to retain many bygone factories and workers' houses without allowing them to turn into slums, and the tall red-brick chimneys that do remain are symbols of both past and present, for Tampere's factories are still high on the list of Finland's leading manufacturers and exporters.

**BELOW:** one of the Pirkka statues on the Hämeensilta Bridge.

## THE INDUSTRIAL HEARTLAND

With its over-abundance of forests (two thirds of the country is covered with mostly pine and birch trees), it's hardly surprising that Finland should find itself at the forefront of international paper production, with the rise of the Industrial Revolution in the mid-19th century. It is still a thriving industry – more than 60 percent of the paper produced in Finland is exported around the world – and factories lining the waterways are still a familiar sight, as is the distinctive, not altogether pleasant odour these factories pump into the air. But in these days of "green thinking" environmental concerns have begun to be raised, not just in Finland but the world over, about the preservation of the country's forest land, and increasingly recycled paper is being used and marketed as a more attractive and ecological option.

Tampere's other major industry in the 19th century was the production of textiles, set up by the Scotsman James Finlayson, but the city was also known for shoe-making, wood production and engineering among other processes. Today, industry is still at the forefront of Tampere life and, in keeping with its innovative past, it is at Finland's cutting edge of high-technology, including highly respected training institutions.

There are some 200 lakes in and around the city. The two largest, Näsijärvi to the north and Pyhäjärvi to the south, are the meeting point of two famous waterway routes. To the south, the Silverline threads its way though a labyrinth of lakes towards Hämeenlinna, passing Valkeakoski, another industrial town in a splendid rural setting, and stopping at the beautiful Aulanko Forest Park among other places *(see page 223)*.

The romantically named Poet's Way boat, SS *Tarjanne*, steers north through narrow, winding waters to Ruovesi and Virrat. The whole journey takes nine hours and gives a two-day taste of Finland's lakes, with an overnight stay at either Virrat or Ruovesi. A little further north, Ahtäri has one of Finland's best native zoos. The national poet, J. L Runeberg began his best-known work, *Tales of Ensign Ståhl*, in Ritoniemi Mansion at Ruovesi and, near the village, Akseli Gallén-Kallela *(see page 78)* built his first "Kalela" studio-home, which is open to the public.

Tampere was officially founded in 1779 by King Gustav III of Sweden-Finland but, since the Middle Ages, the Pirkkala area to the south of the centre had been settled by farmers, attracted by the waterways which made transport easy. From around the 13th century, when the Swedes granted them rights to collect taxes from the Lapp people, they prospered richly. These earliest *tamperelaiset* (Tampere people) are commemorated on the Hämeensilta Bridge in four statues by Wäinö Aaltonen, *The Merchant*, *The Hunter*, *The Tax Collector* and *The Maid of Finland*, characters who come from the ancient legends of the Pirkka. Also clear from the bridge is the tall chimney of one of Tampere's earliest industries, the paper-makers Frenckell from 1783. The old mill is now a theatre with two stages.

**Maps**
**Area 204**
**City 214**

*Bronze statue by Wäinö Aaltonen on Hämeensilta Bridge, Tampere.*

**BELOW:** the spectacular interior of Tampere Hall.

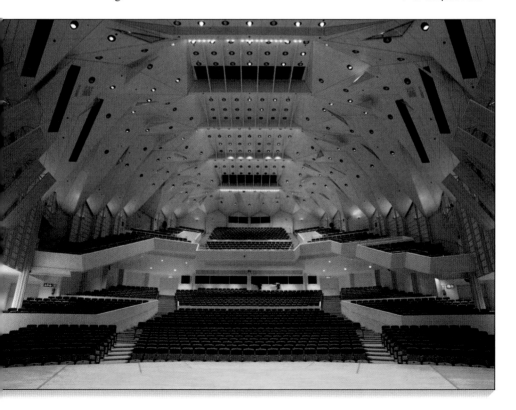

The Tammerkoski has largely lost its working factories, and hotels, shopping centres and museums have taken their place. The venerable and well restored Grand Hotel Tammer, the Cumulus Koskikatu and Hotel Ilves all have splendid views of the Tammerkoski rapids, and, from the top of the Ilves' 18 storeys, the panorama takes in the quay where the Silverline boats berth, the leisure craft, the red brick of the old factories and the magnificent stretches of lake. A minute or two away on the riverside, the **Verkaranta Arts and Crafts Centre** sells good-quality craftwork. Above it on the town side is the Tourist Information Office. Below the hotel, the Koskikeskus covered shopping centre has some 100 shops. There is also a Market Hall at Hämeenkatu 19.

## Old memories, new buildings

Across a footbridge over the rapids, one of the oldest factory areas stands on Kehräsaari (Spinning Island). In the Independence (Civil) War, the victorious White Army crossed the Tammerkoski here to capture Tampere. Today, its factories and boutiques are grouped around cobbled courtyards. Nearby, the only factory still working on the river, Tako, makes carton paper. Keep an eye out too for the old factory chimney with a bomb shield on the top, a reminder that Tampere was bombed fiercely in the 1918 Civil War, when it was an important "Red" stronghold, and again during World War II with eight heavy raids.

Culture and education centre on Tampere, but it is modern culture and scientific and technical education. The architecture is also largely 20th-century, typified by the **Kirjasto (City Library)** (Pirkankatu 2; open Mon–Sat), an astonishing building said to be based on the open wings and spread tail feathers of a wood grouse, though you might see it more as a series of mushrooms.

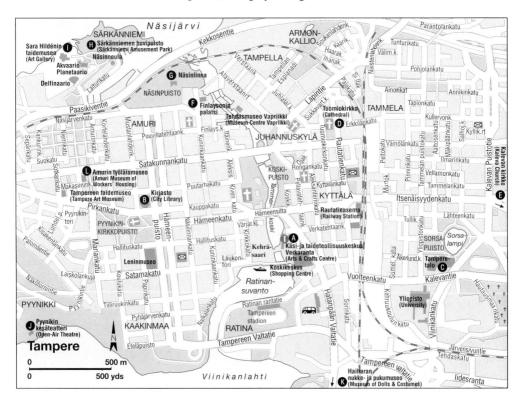

In the mid-1980s the library and the Tampere City Building Office won several awards for its husband and wife architects, Reima and Raili Pietilä. Finns are great readers and borrow, on average, 20 books each per year. Adults as well as children are intrigued by the Moomin Valley section that has the original fantasy characters, the Moomins, created by Tove Jansson *(see page 97)*.

Map on page 214

Tampere's pride is the **Tampere-talo (Tampere Hall) ⊙**, a spectacular blue-white building designed by Esa Piiroinen and Sakari Aartelo in 1990. Light streaming in picks out the main foyer's fountains, which commemorate the Tammerkoski rapids as the source of prosperity. The main hall holds 2,000, a small auditorium 500 and, if you arrive on a festival morning, from the stage comes the sound of one of the choirs or orchestras in rehearsal. Lit for an opera such as *Parsifal*, the large hall is magnificent, and Tampere people are happy to tell you that their hall is bigger than Helsinki's Finlandia *(see page 171)*, and the acoustics are much better. The hall is used for conferences and congresses and there is a whole beehive of meeting rooms and a café, the Café Soolo.

*Sugar snap peas are one of Finland's most popular home-grown vegetables and sold in all city markets.*

## Tampere's churches

Lars Sonck was only 30 when he won a national competition with his design for the **Tuomiokirkko (Tampere Cathedral) ⊙**, which was then St John's church, completed in 1907 at the height of the National Romantic movement. It stands in its own park at Tuomiokirkonkatu 3 (open daily; entrance free), a few blocks east of the river, and contains some of the best of Finnish art, including Magnus Enckell's altar fresco of the Resurrection and his circular window that forms a cross and wreath of thorns. Hugo Simberg painted *The Wounded Angel*, a shattered form carried by two boys, and *The Garden of Death* – despite its

**BELOW:**
the 16th-century
Messykylä church.

*Finland's glassware ranges from the practical to the decorative.*

name, not a gloomy picture. His note on the back of a working sketch reads: "A place where souls go before entering heaven." Around the gallery, his *Garland of Life* shows 12 boys carrying a green garland of roses, symbolising humanity's burden of life. This great church seats 2,000 and, softly lit, makes a beautiful setting for a Sunday evening concert, with every seat taken.

The **Kalevan kirkko (Kaleva Church) Ⓔ**, east on the Kaleva road (open daily; entrance free), stands solid in the centre of a green park, like a silo rising out of a field. No wonder it's nicknamed "the silo of souls". Inside, the stark appearance changes to dramatic, with a soaring light that pulls your gaze upwards. A striking feature of this church, another Pietilä design from 1966, is the organ, its 3,000 pipes shaped like a "sail". Behind the altar the wooden statue is intended to be a reed – "a bruised reed He shall not break".

Tampere's oldest church is a rare example from the 15th century, **St Michael's** at Messukylä, around 5 km (2 miles) east along the Iidesjärvi (lake) on the old Lahti road (open daily May–Aug only; entrance free). The oldest and coldest part is the vestry that once stood beside an even earlier wooden church. A moment of high excitement in 1959 revealed extensive wall paintings, now restored, from the 1630s. The church's most valuable wooden sculpture is believed to be the royal saint King Olav of Norway, whose tomb in Trondheim became a place of pilgrimage during the Middle Ages.

## Industrial heritage

**BELOW:** re-created room at the Workers' Museum.

Tampere's industrial history is also rich and, as though to prove how international the city was nearly two centuries ago, one of the most important industries, textiles, was founded by a Scotsman, James Finlayson. He arrived in 1820

from Russia to build a heavy engineering works at the north end of the Tam-merkoski, with the first water-powered spinning mill. When he sold to Rauch and Nottbeck in 1836 it grew to become one of the biggest textile factories in the Nordic countries, but in those early days Mrs Finlayson was not too proud to sell the mill's products in the market. James Finlayson was an industrialist in the Quaker mould and Finlaysons became almost a town within a city, with its own police, health programme and hospital, factory school, and a church: the yellow building with a wooden door near the factory complex. Visitors now find a completely refurbished area of bustling activity, with a microbrewery, the restaurant Plevna, a 10-screen cinema complex and museum devoted to the workers' movement.

The other main company, Tampella, on the eastern side of the river, started as a foundry in 1850. Recently renovated and renamed Vapriikki (from the Swedish word *fabrik*, or factory), the enormous edifice housed some of the EU meetings during Finland's presidency. The factory halls are transforming into a Museum Centre with the technology museum being the flagship.

After Finlayson returned to Scotland, the new owners continued the traditions and the name, and lived in a mansion house nearby, known as the **Finlaysonin palatsi (Finlayson Palace) ⑦** and built by Alexander von Nottbeck. It became a famous house, visited by Tsar Alexander II and his court, and there are portraits of both Alexander I and II on the central staircase, grand enough to feel you should be sweeping down it in full evening dress. The palace is now a club, with live music in the evenings. The restaurant serves food during the day and is also popular for art exhibitions and social functions. The surrounding park is open daily, admission free.

Map on page 214

**BELOW:** Iittala glassware is among the most respected in the country.

**TIP**

The multi-purpose ticket, the "Särkänniemi key" (a wristband), provides entry to all attractions in Särkänniemi, including the Sara Hildén Art Gallery, but lower price individual tickets can be bought.

The greater part of Tampella has moved further out of town but, as many of its old buildings deserve preservation, the aim is to convert them to apartments, offices and similar uses. One former Tampella factory on a peninsula above Lake Näsijärvi is now the Lapinniemi Spa Hotel, the first of a style of hotels which concentrate on health, with massage and other treatments in an atmosphere of good food and comfort.

Another Nottbeck home was **Näsinlinna G**, an old mansion on a hill in Näsinpuisto Park overlooking the lake, an easy walk from the Finlayson buildings. Don't miss Emil Wikström's Pohjanneito Fountain on your way through. To illustrate how knowledge and skill are passed from generation to generation, on one side a grandmother explains handiwork to a little girl, on the other a boy shows an old man how water power has made work easier. On top is the Maid of the North from the *Kalevala* sitting on a rainbow, spinning golden thread.

The Nottbeck house is now **Hämeen museo (Häme Museum)**, a collection of items from the the old province of Häme. There are often exhibitions of traditional arts, such as *ryijy* rug-making, an ancient Scandinavian technique which probably arrived from Sweden. These rugs were not only warm and beautiful, they were practical too, serving as money to meet the tax collectors' demands.

### Tampere's amusements

From Näsilinna, across the northern harbour entrance is an even higher viewpoint, the Näsinneula Observation Tower at the centre of **Särkänniemi Park H**, with its Aquarium, Dolphinarium, Planetarium and Children's Zoo (tel: 3-248 8111; aquarium, planetarium and dolphinarium open daily; amusement park open daily early May–mid-Aug). A new attraction, white-water adventure (*Koskiseikkailu*) has been carved into the rock with a little help from concrete: German-made rafts travel a long and potentially wet ride. The tower is the highest in Finland and there is no better way to get an overview of Tampere than from the open-air platform over 120 metres (400 ft) up or from the revolving restaurant above it. Looking immediately below, the funfair's scenic railways, roundabouts and ferris wheels look like a child's toys whirling and climbing on their metal girders. The restaurant is good and medium-priced; it takes 50 minutes to complete a revolution and is open until midnight.

If your tastes run to modern art rather than funfairs, or if you like both, don't miss the **Sara Hildénin taidemuseo (Sara Hildén Art Gallery) I** in a beautiful building close by, which claims to have Tampere's best lake view. Sara Hildén was a businesswoman and art collector who specialised in Finnish and foreign art of the 1960s and 1970s, and there are also visiting exhibitions and concerts (tel: 3-214 3134; open daily; entrance fee).

Between the lakes, the western part of the isthmus rises in a raised beach to a tree-clad ridge which joins the lakes in a series of steps down through the woods. This is the Pyynikki Ridge, born 10,000 years ago during the last Ice Age round the old bowl of an ancient sea. It was once the home of the town's bishop, and its old viewing tower is a popular place

**BELOW:**
Häme Castle.

for looking over both lakes and towards the **Pyynikin kesäteatteri (Pyynikki's Open-air Theatre)** ❿ down near Lake Pyhäjärvi. In a remarkable example of lateral thinking, the theatre auditorium revolves rather than the stage – truly theatre in the round as the audience turns to face each new scene, with perhaps fairies from *A Midsummer Night's Dream* perched high in the trees. The theatre, open from mid-June to mid-August, is especially beautiful when the bird cherries are drenched in white blossom. There is also a restaurant and café.

**Haiharan nukke-ja pukumuseo (Museum of Dolls and Costumes)** Ⓚ (tel: 3-222 6261; open Tues–Sun summer, Wed–Sun winter) moved recently from the Haihara manor house to the imposing Hatanpää manor, just south of Tampere's centre. The last owner, Gunvor Ekroos, built up a huge private collection of some 1,000 dolls, including one from 12th-century Peru, as well as puppet theatres and many exhibits that illustrate the history of play and old magic skills. On her death, the collection became the Haihara Museum Foundation with 5,000 dolls, and many more items that illustrate the life of the upper classes from the rococo era to modern times. An arboretum nearby is worth a visit.

## Full circle

Further west is Pispala (Bishop's Village), now considered a very prestigious place to live. In fact, it was built two generations ago by factory workers. As a sign of progress, their children left and went to live in central Tampere but now the grandchildren of the original builders are eager to return and restore. The **Amurin työläismuseo (Amuri Museum of Workers' Housing)** Ⓛ (Makasininkatu 12; tel: 3-3146 6690; open Tue–Sun, early May–mid Sep; entrance fee) shows how these houses would have looked between 1910 and 1970. There

Map on page 214

**BELOW:** altar detail at Hattula Church.

are 25 houses and two shops, all giving the impression that the owners might return at any moment.

If you have the time to spare, the unusual **Lenin Museum** (Hämeenpuisto 28; tel: 3-276 8100; open daily; entrance fee) is also worth a visit. Exhibits document Lenin's stays in Finland after the failed 1905 revolution, including the occasion he met Stalin for the first time here in Tampere.

Whatever else you miss in this water city, do not miss a boat journey. If the Silverline or the Poet's Way take up too much time, try an excursion (City Information Office has details) or hop on a boat to Viikinsaari or another island. In half an hour you are on one of the beaches, you can birdwatch or botanise under cool forest trees, and picnic away from everyone else. Hard to believe that, strictly speaking, you are still in Finland's leading industrial city.

## Back to Helsinki

Many of the elements that make up Finland – history, industry, agriculture, lakeland, forest, design and the arts – follow you along Road 3 from Tampere to Helsinki. The first stops are Valkeakoski and Sääksmäki, yet more of those Finnish industrial centres that contrive to place themselves in beautiful surroundings between two lakes.

In the Middle Ages, **Valkeakoski** ❹ was no more than a hamlet, later a mining village in the important parish of Sääksmäki; but, even then, it had the rapids that meant water power, first to grind corn and then to make paper. In contrast, the 19th-century National Romantic movement also brought artists to Sääksmäki, and these two ingredients still combine today. For a feeling of Valkeakoski's industrial history, go to the wooden outdoor

**BELOW:**
Sibelius's lakeside home, Ainola.

museum of **Kauppilanmäki**, typical of the early paper-mill workers' homes up to 1920. The workers' hall, with its union flags, was the centre of political thought as well as home to the community entertainment.

The old **Voipaalan kartano** (**Voipaala Manor**) on Rapola Hill has become an art centre. The museum was once the studio of the sculptor Elias Ilkka, who owned the manor and the farm where the Valkeakoski Summer Theatre performs. On the hill above is an ancient hill fort and a view of the church of **Sääksmäki ❺**, a short walk away. This early parish had an even older church but the present greystone building dates back to the 15th century. An accident on April Fools' Day 1929 resulted in a fire, but everyone thought the alarm was a joke. The church was restored in 1932 but some wall paintings by the windows remain from the old church, as do the altarpiece and two wooden statues.

Just over the bridge, detour right towards Toijala and then right again to **Visavuori ❻**, the studio home of one of Finland's best-known sculptors, Emil Wikström (1864–1942). Aged 29, he had just won a competition to design the frieze for Helsinki's House of Estates, when he designed his house on the peninsula overlooking the lake. Here he worked in the wood-lined studio, spending his nights observing the stars in his rooftop observatory (tel: 3-543 6528; open May–Sept: daily, Oct–Apr: Tues–Sun; entrance fee).

Of all Finland's well-known glassmakers, **Iittala ❼** is probably the most famous, with austere designs, beautiful functional glassware, and *objets d'art* such as glass birds and fruit shapes so perfect that you immediately want to hold them – a practice not recommended in the museum which houses past and present designs by such eminent people as Alvar Aalto and Timo Sarpaneva, designer of the "i-collection" which became Iittala's trademark. Helped by an

Map on page 204

*Gooseberries are part of the summer's yield in Finland.*

**BELOW:** strawberry-picking is a favourite activity in summer months.

*The old army camp ground near the Tank Museum, with the Lion of Parola statue, recalls Tsar Alexander II's signing of the Language Charter in 1863, in nearby Hämeenlinna, to give Finnish equal status with Swedish.*

expert glass-blower who does most of the work, you can try your talents on a misshapen paperweight. Even better is the Iittala shop where seconds are often indistinguishable to the inexpert eye and less than half the price of perfect work.

There is no escape from modern history at the **Panssarimuseo (Parola Tank Museum)** ❽ (tel: 3-1814 4524; open daily May–Sept; entrance fee), set up by the Association of Armoured Troops and Veterans, survivors of the Finnish campaigns during World War II. Some Winter War tanks go back to 1910, and the Continuation War terrace has some captured Soviet tanks, their hammer and sickle replaced by the still-sinister swastika, after Finland found itself fighting on the same side as the Germans. For military historians this little known museum is fascinating, a tribute to the Finnish tank operators, but even the most casual visitor is intrigued by the armoured train in the woods above. The Finns had two of these mighty trains, adapted and armed with 76mm guns and machine-guns. To reach Parola, take Road 57, marked Hattula, off the main road, and then, just past the next crossroads, branch left again to Parola.

Continue back on Road 57 to **Hattulan Pyhän Ristin kirkko (Hattulan Church of the Holy Cross)** ❾, one of Finland's best known and oldest churches. It was built in 1320 beside the lake of Hattula when Catholicism had not long come to this region after the Swedes built Häme Castle, about 6 km (4 miles) further south. Inside, your eyes are immediately drawn upwards by the delicate colours of the intricate 16th-century frescos which cover ceilings and walls. They were later lime-washed and not re-discovered and restored until the mid-19th century. Today, Hattula has regained the atmosphere of a medieval church and its most valuable statue is a wooden St Olav, the 15th-century Norwegian royal saint (open daily 15 May–15 August; entrance fee).

**BELOW:** the town of Hämeenlinna.

Aulangon puisto (Aulanko Forest Park) , just off Road 3, is ideal for a break. The forest had a fortress long before the days of Christianity but the man who made Aulanko what it is today was Colonel Hugo Standertskjöld, in the 1930s the governor of Häme province. He had made his fortune as an arms dealer in Russia and returned to build a new manor and beautify the forest park with ornamental lakes, follies and the Observation Tower overlooking Aulanko-järvi (lake). The Bear Cave nearby has an appealing family group of bears carved by Robert Stigell. Jean Sibelius, born in Hämeenlinna, is said to have commented on Aulanko: "I was thinking of these scenes from my childhood when I composed *Finlandia*." Aulanko is a stopping place for the Silverline boats and the modern hotel, with golf courses and tennis courts, the outdoor theatre and lake excursions attract a quarter of a million visitors a year.

**Map on page 204**

*Silk threads in a rainbow of colours are part of the unique Silk Museum in the heart of Aulanko.*

## Castle and composer

Hämeenlinna ⓫ has two claims to fame: Häme Castle (tel: 3-675 6820; open daily; entrance fee) and the fact that it is the birthplace of Jean Sibelius.

In the early 13th century, when Earl Birger led the first Swedish foray into this ancient countryside, Swedish governors were ever-conscious of the closeness of Russia and obsessed with the need for defence. His first task was to build a square, walled defensive "camp" with towers at its corners, which still form the heart of the castle. Over the next 700 years, Häme was remodelled to suit the moods of kings and politicians, and Swedish, Finnish and Russian history is intertwined in the old red-brick walls. The castle area also includes the **Prison Museum** (tel: 3-621 2977; open daily) and the **Artillery Museum** (tel: 3-682 4600; open May–Sept: daily, Oct–Apr: Sat–Sun; entrance fee).

**BELOW:** the Silk Museum in Aulanko Forest Park.

Map on page 204

*In Hyvinkää, in Rantapuisto Park, is Finland's largest statue, the gigantic yellow arches of the Triad Monument.*

**BELOW:** in summer and autumn the markets are full of brilliant berries.
**RIGHT:** Naantali harbour.

Hämeenlinna itself was granted town status in 1639 by Count Per Brahe, but it was already an important settlement on the Oxen Trail between Turku and Häme Castle. This centuries-old route has served soldier, merchant and traveller alike, though pack animals and carts have given way to motor cars and the track has become a modern road. With its busy centre and shady park, Hämeenlinna makes an excellent base for touring.

Sibelius was born in December 1865 in the little timberboard house of the town physician, Christian Gustaf Sibelius. The three Sibelius children were musical and one room in the house, now the **Sibelius Home Museum** (Hallituskatu 11; tel: 3-621 2755; open daily; entrance fee) shows Sibelius's upright piano from some 20 years later and an old photograph of the young family trio performing at the Loviisa Spa Casino, where they gave summer concerts. The big dining room is now used for occasional recitals, and the house is full of memorabilia of the composer's childhood *(see page 91)*.

The **Suomen Lasimuseo/Finnish Glass Museum** (Tehtaankatu 23; tel: 19-741 7555; open May–Aug: daily, Sept–Dec, Feb–Apr: Tues–Sun; entrance fee) is the most popular place to visit in **Riihimäki** ⑫, just off Road 3 some 35 km (26 miles) south of Hämeenlinna. The building is an authentic glassworks from 1914, still active in the 1930s. The ground-floor exhibition traces the history of glass-making, from the early days of Finnish independence when the industry concentrated on mundane items such as window panes, to the 1930s which saw both the beginning of glassmaking as a fine art and, at the opposite end of the scale, more mass production. Recently, there has again been a partial return to individual glass-blowing and handmade glass, all shown in the upstairs collection of glass of every sort.

## Lake dwellers

Heading south through Hyvinkää to Järvenpää, you are only 45 km (30 miles) from Helsinki. The area's Lake Tuusulanjarvi attracted late 19th-century artists away from their city haunts, to build studio-villas on the eastern side, just beyond **Järvenpää** ⑬.

The first of the artist-intellectuals were writer Juhani Aho and his artist wife, Venny Soldan-Brofeldt. Within a year they were followed by artist Pekka Halonen, whose work had already been inspired by the beautiful **Lake Tuusulanjärvi** ⑭ and by the farming life around him, as was another incomer, portrait painter Eero Järnefelt, famous for his rural and folk scenes. When Sibelius and his wife Aino moved to the lake shores, the Halonens' home, Halosenniemi (open May–Sept: Tues–Sun), became a meeting point for convivial saunas, recitals and the drinking of Halonen's homemade rhubarb wine.

**Ainola** ⑮ was the Sibelius home for 53 years (tel: 9-287 322; open daily, summer only; entrance fee). Designed by Lars Sonck, it is still furnished as it was in Sibelius's time – the drawing room holds the composer's piano. Outside in summer, the garden is quiet and peaceful. Sibelius died at Ainola in 1957 at the age of 91; his wife died in 1969 at the age of 97. Underneath the apple trees their grave is a square flat stone, with always a few floral tributes close by. ❏

# THE ÅLAND ISLANDS

Map
on page
230

*Separated from the mainland and inhabited by Swedish-speakers,
the Åland Islands are nevertheless very firmly a part of the
Finnish landscape and heritage*

The Åland Islands (Ahvenanmaa in Finnish) are a collection of granite-bound skerries spraying out to the west of the Finnish coast. Most people outside Scandinavia have never heard of them, though they are a part of a unique, autonomous political set-up that gives the 25,000 Swedish speakers here their own particular identity. They have had their own flag since 1954 and their own postage stamps since 1984.

## Geography and culture

In 1917 the Ålands were the western limit of the Grand Duchy of Russia that Finland then was, and the Russians began sending reinforcements to the islands. But, while Finland was celebrating independence from Russia in 1918–19, Ålanders were petitioning to become part of Sweden. Although the League of Nations assigned the islands as a demilitarised, semi-autonomous entity to Finland (with Swedish as the official language), today's Ålanders hold no grudge. Like mainland Finns, Ålanders take tremendous pride in a Finnish athlete or team beating the Swedish competition. Yet they certainly don't think of themselves as ordinary Finns. Ålanders have inhabited their islands for thousands of years, and have a strong ethnic culture and a formidable pride in their identity. The fact that they did not become associated with Sweden seems, if anything, to have nurtured even greater pride in their uniqueness.

From June to August, the archipelago is a place of breeze-ruffled inlets edged with tiny, sunkissed beaches of glacier-worn granite. Some are shaded by the shadows of umbrella pines. Fishing villages huddle at the edges of rocky promontories, dwarfed to child-size when one of the larger Sweden-Finland ferries, or even one of the grander private yachts, sails past. Winters here are sodden and windy and rarely cold enough for any real snow. Although the islands attract fleets of oversize sailing and motor yachts, and with them crowds of well-to-do boat owners, the feeling here is never élitist, merely restful.

The Ålanders have scraped a living from the soil and extracted it from the sea for centuries. In the days before motorised sailing, it took about six weeks to journey over water to Helsinki, where Ålanders traded sealskins and oil. They also profited from their local apples, herring and loaves of sweet black bread known as "*svartbröd*", which goes especially well with herring.

Today, Ålanders earn their living in a slightly less gruelling fashion. Fifteen percent are directly employed in tourism and another 15 percent in tourist-related services. Seal hunting has dropped out of the picture, but farming, fishing and construction are still

**PRECEDING PAGES:** canoeing on the Åland waters. **LEFT:** Åland district coat of arms. **BELOW:** museum ship, *Pommern.*

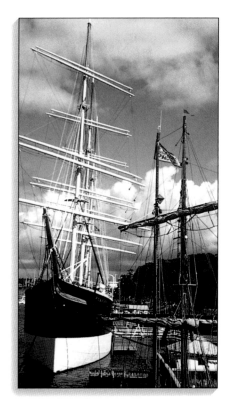

important. One unique Åland product you'll see is the Finnish potato crisp, made from Åland-grown spuds.

The grand-scale shipbuilding that once went on here has mostly died out, but a large part of Finland's merchant navy is still owned by Åland shippers, and Ålanders have recently revived their traditional boat-building skills with three ocean-going, wooden sailing ships that you may be lucky enough to see in Mariehamn. The Finland-Sweden ferries provide hundreds of jobs, but some Ålanders still work on merchant and freight ships, following the shining trails of the old Åland grain ships that plied worldwide routes as far as the Antipodes. Ålanders also continue to follow some extraordinary customs. Many of these centre on weddings: until very recently, brides from certain islands wore black and a few brides still wear the traditional high crown of birch leaves and wild-flowers. A real Åland wedding can go on for days. On a rotating biannual sched-ule, the Ålands host another tradition, the international Island Olympics. Participants are mainly from British islands such as the Isle of Man, the Shet-land and Orkney islands, and, from further afield, the Falklands. A decade ago Estonian coaches arrived penniless from the Baltic isle Saaremaa, and demanded US dollars to feed their athletes (they got food coupons).

*With rare exceptions, the Ålanders' life has not been the privileged world of the Swede-Finn gentry on the mainland. Despite the language differences, Ålanders are more akin to the mainland Finn, with the same simple livelihoods – farm-ing, fishing, forestry and shipping.*

## Mariehamn and around

An enjoyable way to visit the Åland Islands is by taking the Viking Line ship from Turku (*see page 203*) to Mariehamn, which provides a scenic cruise through the thousands of islands and skerries.

**Mariehamn ❶** is the capital of the main island, Åland, and has 11,000 inhab-itants; the original town on this site was called Ytterna, and some of its old

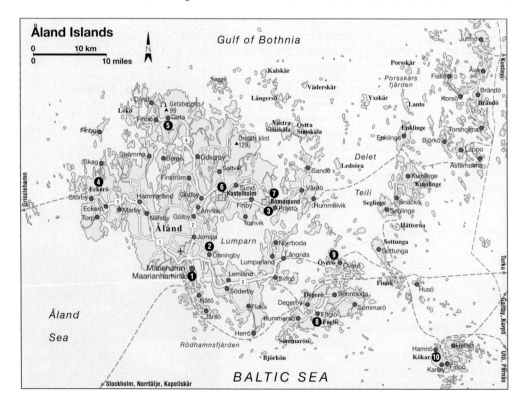

buildings can still be seen in south Mariehamn. Mariehamn is the only town-sized settlement, but there are dozens of villages, many dating back centuries, such as **Onningby** ❷ at Jomala, much favoured by painters, including the acclaimed Finnish artist Victor Westerholm, who had a summer house here. The smallest islands are either wholly uninhabited, or inhabited perhaps only by a single family.

The main ring of islands, connected by a ferry service, includes Åland, Föglö, Kökar, Sottunga, Kumlinge and Brändö. A splendid way to tour the islands is by bicycle and ferry. You'll find many Finnish and Swedish families doing so, particularly in July. From Åland, there is a daily bike ferry to **Prästö** ❸; you can hire bicycles from the Mariehamn harbours.

In Mariehamn west harbour is the four-masted museum ship *Pommern* – built in Glasgow in 1904 and still in its original state – which together with a visit to the nearby Maritime Museum will give you the lowdown on the archipelago's seagoing history (tel: 018 531421; open daily Apr–Oct; entrance fee).

On the cultural side is the **Ålands Museum**, located at Stadshusparken (tel: 18-25000; open daily, May–Aug; entrance fee), a museum and art gallery with exhibitions on prehistoric and Ice and Bronze Age Åland life. From more recent times are displays on folk customs and archaeological finds from the islands' many medieval churches.

The **Lilla Holmen Bird Reserve** (entrance free), below the east harbour, is an island park filled with roving peacocks and roosters, mixed in with Angora rabbits and guinea pigs (caged). There is also a café and short strip of beach. A more interesting excursion is made by foot or bicycle to the Ramsholmen Nature Reserve on the nearby island of Jomala.

Map on page 230

*A decorative maypole celebrates the start of spring on the Åland Islands.*

**BELOW:** boats plying the waters near Mariehamn.

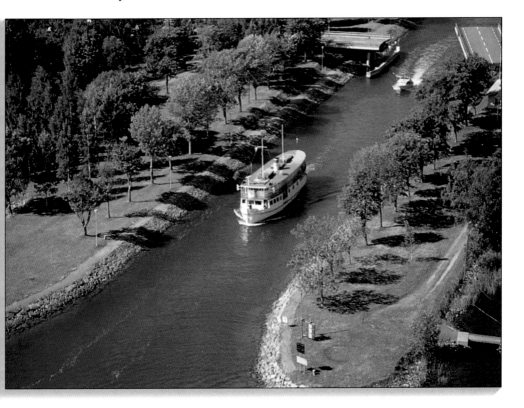

**TIP**

Mariehamn has a
summer boat hotel,
great for budget
travellers (Botel Alida,
tel: 18-13755). On
smaller islands
accommodation is in
campsites, cottages or
guesthouses. A tours
and lodgings agency
is Ålandstrafiken
(tel: 18-25155, fax:
18-17815).

### Eckerö

On the main island, the countryside stretches out for dozens of miles in all directions from Mariehamn, alternating between wide open fields and sea vistas to dense, pungent forests crowded with pines and birches. The scenery is particularly beautiful along the straits that cut into **Eckerö ❹**, straits which resemble rivers at their narrower points. Eckerö Harbour is set off by the cherry-red boathouses clustered along its bays and promontories. Due to its western exposure, you can watch the midnight sun in Eckerö from its evening dip towards the sea till its early dawn rising.

Several museums in Eckerö are worth a visit. The large Russian-era **Posthus (Post House)** has two small museums, both open daily in summer, which detail the dangerous voyages made by postmen delivering mail between here and Sweden. In mid-June the **Postrodden** or mailboat race leaves from Eckerö, a re-enactment of the once arduous journey to Stockholm to deliver post. Participants sail over in 18th-century costume, and stay at the old postal workers' hotel at Storby. At the attractive fishing harbour, **Jakt och Fiskemuseum** (tel: 18-38299; open May–Aug: daily, Sept–Apr: Sat–Sun; entrance fee) has especially rewarding exhibitions on hunting and fishing,

Eckerö is closest to the Swedish mainland (Grisslehamn) and so is a popular car ferry departure point. The journey takes two hours.

Moving across the north to **Geta ❺** you'll find a tremendous landscape of shelves of granite laced with natural grottoes dug out aeons ago by glaciers and then eroded by the sea. There is a small café at the end of the Geta road; the grotto path is to the right. The teetering piles of stones that edge the path are said to be remains from old bread ovens.

**BELOW:**
Kastelholm Castle
in the east Ålands.

### East Åland

Saltvik, Sund, Lumparland and Lemland on the east side of the islands are farming areas. With its numerous, forest-fringed inlets and natural protection from the open sea, Lumparland Sound is a fine spot to fish or picnic, or arrange a cottage stay.

In Åland's northeast are the historic Kastelholm and Bomarsund fortresses. **Kastelholm ❻** in Tosarby Sund (tel: 18-432150; open last two weeks Apr: Mon–Fri; May–Sept: daily; fee for guided tours) was once the administrative centre of the islands, and dates from the 1300s. The Russians began fortifying it in 1829; ultimately the site was destroyed by fire, but it is now under extensive restoration. Adjacent are the Cultural History Museum and Jan Karlsgärden Open-Air Museum (open May–Sept: daily; entrance fee). Five km (3 miles) to the north of Kastelholm is the 13th-century granite church of Sund.

About 13 km (8 miles) east of Kastelholm is **Bomarsund ❼**, built by the Russians as a huge fortified area, surrounded by a stone wall and knocked out by British and French firepower during the Crimean War. The 1856 Peace of Paris that followed included Tsar Alexander's declaration that the islands would have no more military reinforcements. Ålanders are, even today, exempt from national service in Finland.

## Bird island

To the southeast of Åland lies the second most populated island, **Föglö** ❽. The ferry takes about 30 minutes from Svinö (a bus from Mariehamn to Svinö takes about 40 minutes) and lands at the enchanting port town of **Degerby**, once an important vodka smugglers' destination as well as an important customs post. In the eastern part of the island is a natural bird reserve, inspiration for the three golden birds on Föglö's coat of arms.

Degerby's cross-shaped Maria Magdalena Church was once a key landmark for sailors crossing the north Baltic. It dates from the 12th century and was renovated at great expense in 1859. On the altar is a precious silver crucifix from the 1500s (excavated in the 1960s), preserved in a lucite casing. The church's sacristy holds an extraordinary collection of priests' robes.

The Maria Magdalena cemetery has many headstones carrying the name Perón; any Föglö resident named Perón is related to the family of the late Argentine president. One version of the unlikely story explaining this link claims that an Argentine seaman became involved in work at the Degerby customs station, found a Degerby wife, and never left.

Föglö has wonderful possibilities for touring by bike, with its empty roads and lack of any really steep terrain. From Degerby you can ride to **Överö** ❾, the northernmost island in the Föglö group, in just over an hour, using a series of car bridges that stretch to the last strait before Överö. To cross this, you must go on board the cable ferry, which, like the inter-island ferries, is considered an extension of the road system and so is free.

Unless you decide to rent a private cottage along the Föglö straits, the only choice for accommodation will be the charming **Enigheten Guesthouse** at Degerby, a preserved farmhouse manor run by volunteers (tel: 018-50310).

## Archaeological treasures

**Kökar** ❿ is a bare island and most of its vistas look towards the open sea. By the rocky coast at Hamnö is a fascinating medieval church, founded by Franciscan fathers and renovated in 1784. The soil around the church has yielded up rich archaeological treasures including a medieval graveyard, Estonian coins, and the church's original baptismal font, now located near the altar. Other finds are displayed in the stone chapel in the churchyard. Near the font is the memorial stone of the Franciscan-trained native son Stephanus Laurentii, who in 1496 was made Finland's first Doctor of Theology.

The **Kökar Museum** (open Jun–Aug: daily; entrance fee) has a collection of old photos whose written commentary has been hand-corrected by locals who perhaps recognise a wrongly identified grandparent. There are also farm tools, costumes and narratives about the Germans' failed attempts to shoot down Kökar's beacon tower during World War II.

The amenities here include only two food shops, one café, one bank and two taxis. However, there is a handsome old guesthouse, **Antons** (tel: 018-55729), on a family estate with its own beach, campsite, and bicycle hire. ❑

Map on page 230

*The seafaring islands decorated their ships with glamorous models.*

**BELOW:** medieval churches abound on the islands.

# THE WEST COAST

*Dotted with islands, the beautiful Gulf of Bothnia preserves its rich centuries-old maritime heritage and retains its harmonious blend of Finnish and Swedish culture and language*

Map on page 238

T he west coast of Finland is a fascinating mixture of past and present. There are plenty of reminders of days gone by: old wooden houses; museums that focus on the great days of sailing ships and the export of tar; and monuments to fierce battles when Sweden and Russia tussled over the body of Finland, caught fast between its powerful neighbours. The present is represented by modern industry which, fortunately, is usually well clear of historic town centres. The hinterland is either flat or gently undulating, largely an area of farms and forest with a sprinkling of lakes – in other words, typically Finnish.

As this is the part of Finland closest to Sweden, Swedish was the language of many communities on the southern part of this coast during the centuries when Finland was dominated by the Swedes. Even today, many still speak Swedish as a first language and some towns have both Swedish and Finnish names.

## An industrial heritage

The first main town north of Turku *(see page 203)* on Road 8 is **Uusikaupunki (Nystad) ❶**, typical of this coastline. At the end of the 19th century, it boasted Finland's second biggest sailing fleet. An earlier high point came on 30 August 1721, when the Peace Treaty of Nystad ended the "Great Hate", a particularly bloody period in Russo-Swedish hostilities. The town's fortunes declined with the arrival of the steamship but revived with the coming of new industries in the 1960s. The Saab-Valmet car assembly plant offers tours and a motor museum exhibits rally-winning vehicles. The harbour is now used only by pleasure boats plying the archipelago; the old salt warehouses are now antiques shops and restaurants.

Nevertheless, maritime memories remain. The **Kulttuuruhistoriallinen museo** (Ylinenkatu 11; tel: 2-8451 5399; open Jun–Aug: Tues–Sun; entrance fee) is in the house of F.W. Wahlberg, a former shipowner and tobacco manufacturer. Vallimäki Hill has a pilot's cottage, in use from 1857 to 1967, which is now a small museum. The church, completed in 1629, received a vaulted roof in the 1730s and the 1775 steeple also served as a fire watchtower. Myllymäki Park is a reminder that many retired sailors became millers and the countryside was once dotted with windmills; four windmills and a tower remain.

**Rauma ❷** is one of six Finnish towns founded in the Middle Ages and today is the largest medieval town in Scandinavia, listed as a UNESCO World Heritage Site. The 600 or so wooden buildings, painted in traditional pastel shades, are still private homes. Although the dwellings and shops are 18th- and 19th-century, the pattern of narrow streets dates back to the 16th century.

**PRECEDING PAGES:** windmills at Uusikaupunki. **LEFT:** inside Rauma church. **BELOW:** boats are a way of life.

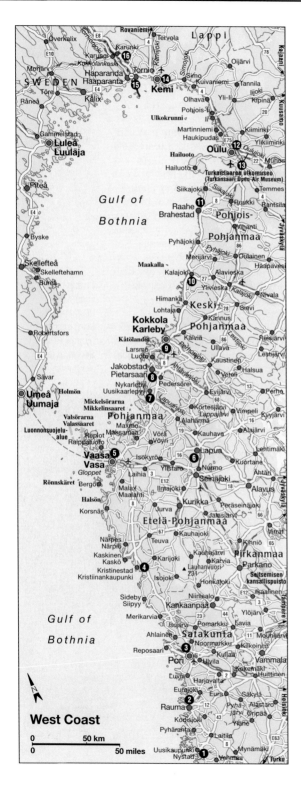

West Coast

0        50 km

0              50 miles

Like most west coast towns, Rauma expanded and prospered in the days of sailing ships and the **Marela Museum** at Kauppiaankatu 24 (open daily; entrance fee) is the home of a former merchant and master shipper, Abraham Marelin. Much of the interior – panelling, stoves and doors – is original and the museum has an interesting display of period costumes. Kirsti's, an early 20th-century sailor's home, provides another maritime connection, continued by the Rauma Museum in the Old Town Hall.

The museum's other main attraction is lace, for bobbin lace-making has been associated with Rauma since the mid-18th century. Nobody knows how lace came to the town, but by the 1850s it was a major industry and almost every woman in the town a skilled lacemaker. The bubble burst when lace bonnets went out of fashion, but since the 1950s there has been a revival, with a lace week in summer, and many Rauma ladies have acquired the old skill. Lace is sold in specialist shops.

## Pori

Pori ❸, some 47 km (37 miles) north, of Rauma, was founded by Duke Johan of Sweden in 1558, as a port at the mouth of the Kokemäenjoki river. Since then the sea has receded and the land has risen, a phenomenon common to the Gulf of Bothnia coastline; so today Pori is 10 km (6 miles) from the sea. In the intervening years, the town burnt down nine times – something of a record even for Finland. The last conflagration in 1852 led to the stylish rebuilding of the present centre. With a population of 77,000, it is, above all, an industrial centre and port.

Post-1852 buildings include the Jennélius Palace, now the Town Hall, built in the style of a Venetian Palace. The Pori Theatre, completed in 1884, has been restored and is now looked on as one of the most beautiful in Finland. More off-beat is the strange **Jusélius Mausoleum** (tel: 2-623 8746; open May–Aug: daily, Sept–Apr: Mon–Sat;

entrance free) at Käppärä Cemetery, built by a Pori businessman in memory of his young daughter. Its interior is one of Akseli Gallén-Kallela's masterpieces (*see page 78*), restored by the artist's son in the 1930s.

The **Satakunnan museo** (Hallituskatu 11, tel: 2-621 1078; open Tues–Sun; entrance fee), dating from 1888, is the largest Finnish cultural history museum with over 60,000 items on display, plus an archive of 110,000 photographs and 10,000 books. The museum has a particularly fascinating section on Pori itself.

The **Porin taidemuseo** (Eteläranta; tel: 2-621 1080; open Tues–Sun; entrance fee), an art museum in a skilfully converted warehouse, is also worth a visit.

Kirjurinluoto Island in the river has a natural park with a summer theatre on which centres the great annual **Pori Jazz Festival**. Of all Finland's famous summer festivals *(see page 92)*, Pori Jazz is both one of the best known and one of the earliest, with modest beginnings in 1966. It now lures in jazz musicians from many parts of Europe and beyond and, for a hectic week in July, this old town is alive with jazz day and night. An annual audience of between 40,000–60,000 bumps up the town's population by more than a half.

*A former shipowner's home preserved as a Maritime Museum at Kristinestad shows the importance of local naval life.*

The 20-km (12-mile) peninsula leading from Pori to Reposaari (island) has a long sandy beach on the side away from the port and shipyard, Yyteri. It is one of Finland's best resorts, with a big hotel and congress centre. A new golf course has been created in response to a huge surge of interest in the game in Finland.

## Beside the sea

**Kristinestad (Kristiinankaupunki)** ❹ was founded by the enthusiastic Swedish governor, Count Per Brahe, in 1649. A master of diplomacy, he gave the town the name of both his wife and Queen Kristina of Sweden-Finland.

**BELOW:**
old and new on
the Pori riverbank.

This Swedish influence is still noticeable and even today around 58 percent of the population is Swedish-speaking and uses the town's Swedish name rather than its Finnish name.

Despite its illustrious beginnings, Kristinestad remained quiet until the 19th century, when it became the home port of one of the country's largest merchant fleets and a ship-building centre. The importance of this is shown clearly in the **Merimuseo** (Kauppatori 1; tel: 6-221 2859; open May–Sept; Tues–Sun; entrance fee), set in the house of former shipowner, S.A. Wendelin and displaying his maritime memorabilia. But, as elsewhere, the shipowners were caught out by the switch from sail to steam. The building of a railway in 1912 failed to halt the decline and many citizens emigrated to the United States.

Kristinestad is now a modest sort of place beside the water with an interesting townscape, including an impressive Town Hall by E.B. Lohrmann dated 1856. During Swedish rule every traveller into the town paid customs duty and the wooden customs house built in 1720 is now the tourist information office. Another customs house, at the northern end, is even older – built in 1680 – and the oldest street is the quaintly named Catwhipper's Lane. Ulrika Eleonora's Church (1700), named after another Queen of Sweden-Finland, was restored and reconsecrated in 1965. It is typical of a coastal church with votive ships, donated by sailors, hanging from the ceiling.

The **Lebellin kaupiaantalo** (Rantakatu 51; tel: 6-221 2159; open Tues–Sun; entrance fee) is worth seeing. Labell was a Polish aristocrat and soldier who married the mayor's daughter and took her name. He lived in the Labell family home which had been gradually extended, with the result that its 10 rooms now represent a variety of styles spanning the 18th and early 19th centuries.

**BELOW:** farming life at Bragegården Open-Air Museum in Vaasa.

## Vaasa and around

**Vaasa (Vasa) ❺** is a marker along the coast and an obvious division between north and south. Its origins lie in Old Vaasa, established in the 14th century when the present site was below sea level. It has had a history of devastation by wars and fire, the last of which in 1852 left little but smouldering ruins.

Today, Vaasa (population 56,000) is a handsome town with wide, attractively laid-out streets and a large market square, a mixture of Jugendstil and modern architecture. Axel Setterberg designed the Orthodox church, which is surrounded by late 19th-century buildings of the Russian Grand Duchy, and the Court of Appeal (1862). The Town Hall (1883) is the work of Magnus Isaeus and is equally imposing. But for the best view of the town, clamber up the 200 steps in the tower behind the police station headquarters.

Vaasa is well endowed with museums reflecting the region's life, the most important being the **Pohjanmaan museo**, which covers local history and art (Museokatu 3; tel: 6-325 3800; open daily; entrance free Wed). The **Bragen ulkomuseo** (Hietalahden puisto; tel: 6-312 7166; open Jun–Aug: Tues–Sun; Jun–Aug; entrance fee), an open-air museum, shows how Ostrobothnian farmers lived at the end of the 19th century, and a strong culture is clear in several art museums and three professional theatres. The **Auto-ja Moottorimuseo** (Varastokatu 8, opposite the bus station; tel: 6-317 6271; open daily, May–Aug, 11am–5pm; entrance fee), has a private collection of vintage vehicles all lovingly restored, such as the glossy black 1939 American Pontiac.

This area is also rich in political history. In the Civil War of 1918 the whole area around Vaasa was a "White" stronghold. Nearby **Lapua ❻**, on Road 16 inland from Vaasa, was the birthplace of the anti-Communist Lapua Movement

Map on page 238

*Traditional lace-making skills survive in Rauma.*

**BELOW:** enjoying the sea life on the west coast.

which reached its zenith in 1930, when 12,000 people from all over Finland poured into Helsinki on the "Peasants' March", and forced the Finnish Government to ban Communism.

From an adjoining island linked by a causeway, ferries leave on three routes to Sweden, and there is **Wasalandia**, the town's colourful amusement park with the usual range of exciting rides (open May–Aug: daily; Sept–Apr: Sat–Sun; entrance fee). Nearby is an enclosed tropical "water world".

Offshore islands, which necessitate a short ferry crossing, add to the charms of Vaasa, as does the collection of old farm buildings at Stundars, 16 km (10 miles) from the town. North of Vaasa, the flat, farming country recalls parts of Sweden, with the Swedish influence being especially clear in the architecture.

## Travelling north

St Birgitta's Church at **Nykarleby (Uusikaarlepyy)** ❼, built in 1708, is one of the most beautiful in Ostrobothnia. Its ceiling paintings are by Daniel Hjulström and Johan Alm, while the windows behind the altar are much more recent, painted by Lennart Segerstråhle in 1940. The 1876 Thelin organ is another prized possession. The town, founded in 1620 by Sweden's great warrior king, Gustav II Adolf, faces a beautiful archipelago.

Nykarleby also has its place in history. On 13 September 1808, a Swedo-Finnish force beat off an attack by a Russian army at the battle of Jutas just outside the town. The event is commemorated by a monument to Major General G. C. von Döbeln and in a poem by J. L. Runeberg, Finland's national poet. After this brief fame, Nykarleby did not develop to the same extent as some other coastal towns (today the population is 8,000). Though a narrow-gauge

**BELOW:** the fun park at Wasalandia.

Map
on page
238

railway line opened at the turn of the 20th century, it did little to promote trade and industry and closed in 1916. Today the 55-year-old steam engine *Emma* puffs along on summer weekends.

Pushing further north, **Jakobstad (Pietarsaari) ❽** takes its Swedish name from a famous military commander, Jacob de la Gardie, and was founded by his widow in the mid-17th century. Much of the town was destroyed in the Russo-Swedish war of the early 18th century. Nevertheless, Jakobstad became the pre-eminent Finnish shipbuilding centre, producing ships that opened new trade routes around the world. In the 18th century, no shipowners were more powerful in the town than the Malms. One of the family was reputedly Finland's richest man, who, on his death, left 6½ million gold marks – a vast fortune in those days. **Malmin talo**, his house, is now a museum (open daily; entrance fee).

One of the town's best known sailing ships *Jakobstads Wapen*, a 1767 galleass, was designed by Fredrik Henrik af Chapman, one of the most famous naval architects of the 18th century. An exact copy of the ship has been completed from original drawings. Until it was closed in 1998, Jakobstad played host to Europe's oldest tobacco factory, the former office block surmounted by what claims to be Finland's largest clock. In the older part of the town, proud owners have carefully restored some 300 or so wooden houses.

## Kokkola

From Pietarsaari to Kokkola, take the attractive route called the "road of seven bridges", which runs from island to island across the archipelago.

Like Nykarleby, **Kokkola (Karleby) ❾** was founded by King Gustav II Adolf in 1620, and went through the familiar cycle of growth, prosperity, decline

**BELOW:**
Finns get their sea legs early in life.

*Fox pelts hanging up to dry in Oulo.*

**BELOW:** the west coast thrives on its fishing industry.

and a second period of expansion from the 1960s with new industries and a new port, established at Ykspihlaja (Yxpila) away from the town centre. Today it has a population of 35,600 of which 20 percent is Swedish-speaking. One man, Anders Chydenius (1729–1803), had a decisive effect on Kokkola's development. He was a clergyman, Member of Parliament and one of Finland's first exponents of economic liberalism. At that time, the tar which should have brought prosperity to his town and coast had to be sold abroad through Stockholm, the then Sweden-Finland capital, which made most of the profits. Largely due to Chydenius's efforts, Stockholm's monopoly was broken and from 1765, one after another, the towns gained "staple" rights – the all-important freedom to sell and ship tar directly to foreign customers.

Kokkola's Town Hall was designed by C. L. Engel, who has left his mark on so many Finnish towns, but the town's most unusual trophy is in a small building in Englantilainen (the English Park). It relates to a bizarre episode in 1854 during the Crimean War. Beside the "English Boat", an inscription explains the "skirmish of Halkokari": "In 1854 in connection with the Crimean War, the British Fleet conducted raids along the coast of the Gulf of Bothnia. Two English frigates sent nine boats on a raid at Kokkola. Each was equipped with a cannon and a crew of about 30. After one hour's battle the enemy had to retreat. One boat ran ashore and was captured. Nine members of the crew were killed and 22 taken prisoner. In all, English casualties numbered between 100 and 150 men dead and wounded." The port has one of the largest harbours on the Gulf of Bothnia. Behind the old harbour and a beach is a memorial to the battle.

On the 230-km (140-mile) north road between Kokkola and Oulu, there are only two places of any consequence. The sand dunes around the mouth of the

river **Kalajoki** ⑩ have made the town of the same name into a holiday area with fishing, bathing and sailing. Further north is **Raahe (Brahestad)** ⑪ which, as its Swedish name implies, was founded by Count Per Brahe in 1649. Shipping used to be its dominant industry, but today it is the Rautaruukki Steelworks, fortunately outside the centre. In summer, guided works tours are popular and there are also summer boat trips around the offshore islands.

## Tar city

**Oulu** ⑫, with a population of more than 110,000, is the largest city in northern Finland. It owes its existence to the Oulu river and King Karl IX of Sweden and its fortunes to tar, essential for wood sailing ships. After excessive Central European tar-burning in the 18th century led to a decline in the coniferous forests, the industry moved to the Baltic. Ostrobothnia was soon one of the most important areas for tar.

Making tar occupied the whole northern area; every village east of Oulu had its smouldering pits, and barrels by the thousand came down to the coast in long narrow boats, some 12 metres (40 ft) long. In 1781, Oulu merchants set up a Tar Exchange and in the 19th century the town was the leading tar exporter in the world. Prosperity ended abruptly in 1901 when the Tar Exchange went up in flames. The demand for tar disappeared with the sailing ships.

Old tar pits and tar boats can be found at the **Turkansaaren ulkomuseo ⑬**, over a footbridge to a small island in the Oulujoki (river) 14 km (8 miles) east of Oulu, off Road 22. Established in 1922, this open-air museum has an interesting collection of 19 Ostrobothnian buildings, including a church, farm buildings and windmills. It is well worth a visit (tel: 8-5586 7191; open Jun–Sept: daily: entrance fee).

Map on page 238

After the era of tar and sail, Oulu languished in the doldrums but the establishment of a university in the 1960s was a turning point. It attracted hi-tech companies to the area and led to the creation of the Finnish Technical Research Centre. This emphasis on the latest technology has been responsible for one of Oulu's notable attractions, **Tietomaa** (Nahkatehtaankatu 6; tel: 8-5584 1340; open daily; entrance fee), a science centre opened in 1988. The wealth of exhibits is not so much for looking at as for trying out. This hands-on approach appeals to both adults and children alike. Exhibits range from an aircraft simulator to a means of checking on the world's weather and population. In all, Oulu has seven museums, from those concentrating on geology and zoology to the oldest wooden house in the city (1737). The elegant **Oulun Taidemuseo** (Kasarmintie 7; tel: 8-558 47450; open Tues–Sun; entrance fee) has a permanent exhibition of Finnish contemporary art plus temporary exhibitions.

An 1822 fire led to a new city centre and cathedral, designed by Engel. The city also benefits from a number of islands linked by bridges, the Oulu river and some green oases, such as Hupisaaret Park. Visit *Koskikeskus* (Rapids Centre) on the mouth of the River Oulujoki, with 12 fountains and surrounding islands. The island of **Linnansaari** has castle ruins and there are recreational facilities on Raatinsaari and Mustasaari.

**BELOW:**
Oulu's Ainola Museum in winter.

## Towards Sweden

From Oulu to Kemi on the Swedish frontier, road and railway cross numerous rivers draining into the Gulf of Bothnia and the scenery undergoes a subtle change. This is no longer the west coast but the approach to Lapland.

**Kemi** ⓮ is called the seaport of Lapland or, rather optimistically, the "Pearl of the Gulf of Bothnia". Largely destroyed in World War II, the town is now a port and industrial centre. The open-air Kemin museo is in Peripuisto Park. The **Kemin Jalokivigalleria** (tel: 16-220 300; open daily; entrance fee) has a collection of 3,000 gemstones and copies of some of Europe's most famous Crown Jewels, including the Crown of the King of Finland – who never reigned. If you are this far north in winter, you can take an excursion (15 Dec–30 Aug: Thur–Sat) on an 1961 icebreaker, *Sampo*, which displays its remarkable power to force its way through ice up to 2 metres (6 ft) thick. You may also visit the annual Lumilinna (Snow Castle), a remarkable icy castle which houses exhibitions, a restaurant and even a few chilly hotel rooms!

Kemi lies at the mouth of the Kemijoki (river) and just on the border a little way north is **Tornio** ⓯, near the mouth of the Tornionjoki. As Tornio (population 23,000) ends, the Swedish town of Haparanda begins and, since its founding in 1621, this border position has made Tornio the scene of much bitter fighting, the last time during World War II.

Fortunately, the town's three major churches have survived and Tornio Church, with its separate bell tower, is one of the most beautiful in Finland. Completed in 1686, it is dedicated to the Swedish Queen Eleonora. Alatornio Church on the outskirts is a vast edifice, the largest in northern Finland and able to hold a congregation of 1,400. It is a splendid example of Jaakko Rijf's

**BELOW:** a traditional Finnish picnic on the rocky coast.

Map on page 238

Neo-classical style. Tsar Alexander I ordered the building of an Orthodox Church in 1825. After Finnish Independence in 1917, the building lay empty until 1987 when it was restored, reconsecrated and re-opened to serve the 150 Orthodox Christians who live locally.

The fine **Aineen taidemuseo** (Torikatu 2; tel: 16-432 438; open Tues–Sun; entrance fee) houses the Aine Kuvataide Foundation art collection and an historical museum of western Lapland. On a fine day, the best place to get a view of the town is from the observation platform on top of the water tower.

## Golf and fishing

**Tornio Golf Club** on the Finnish-Swedish border is the oddest in Europe. During a round of 18 holes, you play nine in Sweden and nine in Finland – and there's a one-hour time difference between the two. It opens from 1 June to 31 October, and it is a rare delight to play a night round in summer, thanks to the midnight sun. After the ninth hole in Finland – just after midnight – you will cross the border and continue in Sweden – yesterday!

If you travel 9 miles (15 km) north of Tornio off Road E78, you will come to **Kukkolankoski ⓰**, the longest (3,500 metres/3,830 yards) free-flowing rapids in Finland. At the highest point the fall is 18.8 metres (45 ft). They have been famous for fish since the Middle Ages. Today, as they balance precariously on a crude boardwalk out over the fast-flowing river, fishermen still use the old techinque of a longhandled net. At the nearby Café Myllypirtti freshly grilled and skewered white fish is the main item on the menu, an authentic taste to end the 1,000-km (600-mile) drive north along a coast that has always depended for its living upon sea, ships and river. ❑

*Furry mascot at Kemi's spectacular Snow Castle.*

**BELOW:** rocky shores near Kemi.

# ENJOYING THE FINNISH SUMMER

*Summer is the best time in Finland and those Finns who live abroad always return for the days of endless sun, fresh fruits and warm weather*

On Friday afternoons in summer almost all the capital's dwellers leave Helsinki in the weekly rush hour. But once into the heartland of the country, the traffic eventually dissolves as it turns off at intervals on to what seem to outsiders like invisible dirt tracks. Thousands of these roads lead to yet more thousands of summer cottages. Here, Finns live their parallel lives.

## LIFE AT THE SUMMER COTTAGE

Daily life at a *mökki* (summer cottage) is a mixture of Bohemian, Chekhovian and certainly Finnish. Families pay visits to relatives and friends; food is eaten and coffee drunk. Days are long and families often eat leisurely meals together, unlike in city homes where everyone is too busy. Cottage gardens yield salad vegetables and new potatoes, but the nearby *kyläkauppa* (village shop) is a steady source of bottled drinks and ready-made food. So important is the influx of summer visitors in small villages that in summer months sales (and population) may triple.

Finns don't stay at the cottage every day: aside from summer sports, such as fishing, cycling, swimming and sailing, summer festivals are always on the agenda *(see page 92)*. Every town and village tries the same formula – pick a theme and build a reputation as a "must-do" event.

A summer in Finland is a totally different experience from winter snow: it is

▷ **THE SIMPLE LIFE**
A good *mökki* should be rustic, yet equipped with modern amenities. Part of the attraction is the simple life but electricity is needed for appliances.

△ **NATURE'S GARDEN**
The vast tracts of Finnish forest provide berries and mushrooms for summer cooking, as well as trekking and canoeing adventures.

◁ **PARK LIFE**
For those who don't

△ **WATER IDYLL**
Most of the 188,000 lakes

## PAYING FOR A ROOM WITH A VIEW

Most Finns rent rather than own their *mökki* – a lakeside location is preferred but it is not cheap, and buying a nice house near water is impossible for most Finns. The cottages are usually inherited. "If I sold this cottage, I could easily move to a big house in Tampere," says a divorced woman in her late 30s. "But I would never forgive myself for selling this," she says, referring to her lakeside property with two tiny islands.

Less than an hour's drive from big towns such as Tampere, Finns may enjoy unrestricted freedom, with no noise and no pollution. The law requires that no new house is built on the lakeshore, so most cottages are hidden and the lakeview remains unmarred by unscrupulous investors.

However, wealthy urbanites masquerading as jovial countrypeople do not impress the locals – the cultural gap between town and country is widening.

### △ ROW YOUR BOAT

The simple rowing boat has a variety of uses: leisurely fishing trips that may take half a day, or just for getting from one lakeside to another.

### ◁ SUNSET PARTY

After swimming and saunas, friends cool off on the pier, feeling the evening's breeze blowing, and admiring the colours of the nearly-setting sun.

# LAKELAND

*Finland's central region of lakes, surrounded by lush pine forests, is perhaps the most immediate image most people have of the country, and a tour of the waterways will not disappoint*

Map on page 254

Helsinki

I f you could flood the whole of Scotland and dot it with some 33,000 islands and peninsulas, you would have the equivalent of the Saimaa Lake area alone. Add on the Päijänne system and you could cover Wales as well.

The Great Lakes of Saimaa and Päijänne in Central Finland are among the best known and most popular places to visit in the country and are the target for thousands of visitors who long only to be in, on, or beside them. But people do nothing to make this watery landscape appear crowded because there is so much of it – lakes and lakelets, smooth curving bays with yellow-grey beaches or ragged and broken shores, rushing torrents squeezed between high banks or flooding over hidden rocks, and rivers linking the different waters.

Where the land intervenes, Finnish engineers turned their skills as long ago as the 19th century to building canals to connect the stretches of water. Today, boats big and small can journey the length and breadth of both lake systems, calling at the small, strategically placed towns, where people have lived for centuries, and the even smaller villages, or stopping along the endless lake-sides which have never been settled.

Sometimes, the land is flat beside the water or crunched up into ridges where rocks and trees point upwards. This varied landscape owes its beauty to the Ice Age when glaciers carved out the shape of lake and ridges, the most famous being at Punkaharju, an 8-km (5-mile) chain of ridges which winds between the lakes. Far inland, Saimaa has its own resident species of seal, the Saimaa marble seal, whose ancestors were trapped in the lake system long ago when the glaciers cut off the route to the sea.

There are two perfect ways to get to know the Great Lakes: from the water by passenger steamer or smaller craft, or by doing as the Finns do and renting a lakeside cabin, to fish, swim, canoe or simply sunbathe.

## The Saimaa system

The famous Saimaa waterway was the historic buffer zone between the kingdom of Sweden-Finland and Tsarist Russia, at times changing hands with dizzying frequency. Subsequently it became part of the longest of any western nation's frontier with the Soviet Empire. The effects of these shifting borders are recurring themes as you travel the area.

It would be hard to visualise landscapes more fragmented or more liquid than the Saimaa waterway. A series of large and lesser lakes are linked by rivers, straits and canals, and framed by an amazing complexity of headlands, ridges, bays, islands and skerries, to form Europe's largest inland waterway system. Up to a quarter of the Saimaa region's total area of 70,000 sq. km (27,000 sq. miles) is covered by water.

**PRECEDING PAGES:** sunset at Aulanko. **LEFT:** peacefulness in Lakeland. **BELOW:** water-skiing is a popular lake sport.

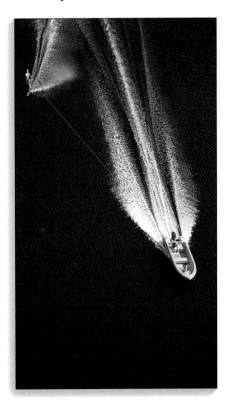

Saimaa's waters provided natural highways for goods and people long before railways and, especially, roads probed into its remoter reaches. To a large extent, they still do. No lakeside home is without its rowing boat, usually with outboard engine. Tugboats hauling their floating timber trains, up to half a kilometre long, from forest to factory, are common sights.

Embryonic tourism dates from the 19th century as the well-to-do of Tsarist St Petersburg boarded the then new-fangled railway to explore the Grand Duchy of Finland on the neighbouring fringes of their empire. They went to take the waters in the handful of newly created spas, to marvel at such natural wonders as the foaming cascades of Imatra and to hunt and fish in the richly stocked forests and waters.

The best approach is via industrial **Kouvola** ❶, about 140 km (86 miles) northeast of Helsinki and a junction of road and rail routes into Saimaa. Although not the most interesting town in Finland, Kouvola's Kaunisnurmi quarters, formerly a railway staff colony, house quaint handicraft shops and

several museums. Kouvola is also a jumping-off point to the unspoiled lake regions of Iitti and Jaala, northwest of Kouvola. Jaala's UNESCO-listed World Heritage site Verla is a perfectly preserved cardboard factory.

There are much shorter ways to your destination of Kuopio but, to capture the spirit of Saimaa, ignore these and first head east on Road 6. About 80 km (50 miles) on, you reach Lappeenranta, South Karelia's main town.

Map on page 254

## Finn-Russian control

Like almost every Finnish community, **Lappeenranta** ❷ combines work and play. There is a great deal of industry and some excellent holiday facilities – for most kinds of watersports, for example. Its spa amenities have undergone a recent renaissance too, though their origins lie in the Tsarist 1820s. The town is the southern terminus for Saimaa's venerable lake fleet.

This was historically also a major military town, heavily fortified by the Swedes in the 18th century, only to be rebuilt by the Russians after they destroyed it. The Linnoitus (fortress) is the oldest and most interesting part, where you will find Finland's oldest Orthodox Church (1785), the **Etelä-Karjalan (South Karelian) Museum** (tel: 5-616 2255; open Jun–Aug: daily, Sept–May: Tues–Thur, Sat–Sun; entrance fee), with a fascinating exhibit on the old city of Vyborg, and the **Ratsuväkimuseo (Cavalry) Museum** (tel: 5-616 2257; open daily, summer only; entrance fee), detailing the history and distinctive red uniforms of Finland's proud soldiers. There are also a number of handicrafts workshops and quite a lot of military hardware.

*The 19th century re-created in Lappeenranta.*

Lappeenranta is only a few miles from the border with its large eastern neighbour; but it was not so in the days when Vyborg (Viipuri) and substantial portions of huge Lake Ladoga formed part of the Grand Duchy and (during its first decades) of the Republic of Finland. It was certainly not so in 1856 when the Saimaa Canal was completed, thus linking Saimaa with the Gulf of Finland through entirely Finnish territory and encouraging the development of a string of inland ports, Lappeenranta among them.

**BELOW:** a boat is an essential part of life in Lakeland.

Victorian travellers hailed the canal as one of the greatest engineering feats of the 19th century and, soon after leaving Lappeenranta, Road 6 crosses its watery slit or, rather, that of its successor. Post-World War II reparations transferred over half the canal into Soviet domains, after which it lay disused and in growing disrepair until the 1960s. After lengthy negotiations and the privilege of paying for its restoration, the Finns regained use of the canal, which reopened in 1968. Recently, attacks on Finnish tourists in Viipuri have led to the cancellation of day trips to the town, but check with local tourist offices to see if they have resumed.

## Niagara of Finland

Despite the overwhelming predominance of lake and forest, parts of Saimaa's southern shores are undeniably industrial. Just a few miles ahead, centred on **Imatra** ❸, lies the most concentrated industrial area of Finland. It also has some claim as a famed beauty spot, and was described by one early 20th-century

British visitor, with shameless exaggeration, as the "Niagara of Finland". Nevertheless, the very fine rapids of **Imatrankoski** were responsible for the presence of the grand old (now much-restored) Imatran Valtionhotelli, built to cater to the sightseers who flocked here, including many distinguished and high-born guests.

It was the eventual taming of the rapids, of course, which triggered off the industrial boom. Happily their full power and splendour can still be seen on certain days in summer; check with the local tourist office for there is no other good reason to linger here.

About 50 km (30 miles) on from Imatra, Road 6 passes within a few hundred metres of the Russian border; multilingual frontier-zone notices and watch towers did not quickly succumb to the best efforts of *glasnost*. Soon after, around Parikkala, the road turns north away from the border. Switching to Road 14, you soon come to one of Finland's best loved beauty spots.

## Forests and lakes

**Punkaharju** ❹ is one of countless ridges bequeathed to Finland by the last Ice Age. In places it is just wide enough to carry the road; elsewhere it widens to carry magnificent pine and birch woods framing the ever-changing permutations of lake and sky, island and skerry, bedrock granite and the "green gold" forests. The light is ever-changing too, to combine all the main elements of essential Finnish scenery.

In addition to the narrow ridge, the Punkaharju islands include a large research forest (Tutkimuspuisto) and a protected nature reserve, associated with the superb Forestry Museum, Lusto. An architectural achievement in its own right,

**BELOW:** Lappeenranta was a favourite with 19th-century Russians.

Lusto has a complete exhibition on Finland's forests and anything associated with them – design, wilderness trekking, forestry industry and research (tel: 15-345 1030; open May–Sept: daily, Oct–Apr: Tues–Sun; entrance fee). Bicycles may also be hired here.

Tucked away amongst Punkaharju's ridges are well-equipped holiday centres and the **Kesämaa (Summerland) Leisure Centre** for family fun. One attraction in the area that definitely should not be missed is the Art Centre of **Retretti** (tel: 15-775 2200; open daily, Jun–Aug: daily; entrance fee). Part of the centre is housed in caverns literally blasted out of the living rock to provide 800 sq. metres (8,600 sq. ft) of exhibition space and an atmospheric underground area. Artificial pools and waterfalls also provide stunning settings for changing exhibitions of Finnish art and design. An underground concert hall can cater for over 1,000 spectators. Olavi Lanu is the sculptor responsible for the striking human and other shapes that populate Retretti's surrounding pinewoods. The annual Retretti art exhibition, featuring four usually quite different, internationally acclaimed artists, is something of a media event in Finland.

In summer, a regular lake steamer sails between Punkaharju/Retretti and Savonlinna: the trip is a delightful mini-odyssey through the islands, taking over two hours compared with a 20-minute spin along the highway. Road travellers, however, should make a short detour on Road 71 to **Kerimäki** ❺, a typically scattered Finnish rural community harbouring the world's largest wooden church, built in 1848 with a congregation capacity of 3,500 people – larger than the town's population – and a 25-metre (82-ft) cupola (tel: 15-578 9111; open daily, Jun–Aug: daily; entrance free). Classical music concerts are staged here in summer.

Map on page 254

*The Imatrankoski rapids are an impressive sight.*

**BELOW:** a boating regatta on the Saimaa system.

## Savonlinna

**Savonlinna** ❻ – the name means "the castle of Savo" – sprawls over a series of interlinked islands. It is the most charming of Finland's main lakeland towns and the best base in Saimaa for making trips. It has the medieval castle of Olavinlinna, as well as spa facilities, excellent lake sports amenities, varied sightseeing and a great deal of culture. Castle and culture combine particularly successfully in the annual International Opera Festival, one of Finland's leading events, which takes place throughout July *(see page 92)*. Tickets for, and accommodation during, the festival should be booked well ahead (tel: 15-476 750; fax: 15-476 7540).

Olavinlinna (open daily; tours obligatory; entrance fee) occupies an islet a short walk from the town centre. With its massive granite walls, ramparts and shooting galleries topped by three great round towers (surviving from the original five), its Knights Hall and grim dungeon, it has everything you might expect from a medieval castle. Originally built by the Danish-born nobleman Erik Axelsson Tott in 1475, it was intended to be a main defence against the Russians, but so frequently did the eastern border shift that Olavinlinna often lay too far from the battlefield.

As an operatic setting the castle is simply splendid, whether it's for *Aïda* in Italian, *Faust* in French or *The Magic Flute* in Finnish. Opera-goers often come in their best finery and most are wisely armed with blankets, for Finnish summer nights are predictably cool. After the performance, with daylight fading at last, Olavinlinna is softly illuminated to provide a memorably romantic backdrop as you stroll back past elegant boutiques and coffee shops in the town, still open and welcoming.

*Savonlinna is a useful port for backpackers touring the country.*

**BELOW:** Olavinlinna Castle is the dramatic setting for the Savonlinna Opera Festival.

Savonlinna itself developed from a small trading centre by the castle, its growth greatly hampered by wars and fires. The coming of steam and the opening of the Saimaa Canal gave the necessary stimulus, for the town's situation made it a natural junction for lake traffic that in due course spread to the four points of the Saimaa compass.

The days have long gone when the venerable Saimaa fleet was powered by wood-burning engines but, converted to diesel, a number of the attractive double-decked wooden vessels continue to ply Saimaa's waters. One of the sights of Savonlinna is the morning departure and evening return of these romantic vessels to the passenger harbour, right by the open-air market on Kauppatori in the centre of town. Another, near the castle, is the museum ship *Salama*, a steam schooner built in 1874, shipwrecked in 1898 and raised from the lake in 1971. The *Salama* is one of three converted old ships that form the inland navigation section of the **Savonlinnan maakuntamuseo (Savonlinna Provincial Museum)**, on Riihisaari (tel: 15-571 712; open Jul–Aug: daily, Sept–Jun: Tues–Sun; entrance fee).

## The northern route

From Savonlinna to Kuopio by lake steamer is a full day's journey, as opposed to a few hours by road, yet it is only by travelling on the lakes that you can fully experience the scenery: from forest and meadow through reed bed or granite shore, timber-built farms and summer cottages huddled along the lakefronts, to islands emerging suddenly from headlands; and watch the reflections tossed from huge sky to broad lake and back again in endlessly varying light and colour tones.

Map on page 254

**BELOW:** a cruise boat at Lahti.

*The Päämajamuseo preserves General Mannerheim's headquarters as they were during World War II.*

Road travellers have a choice of continuing west from Savonlinna on Roads 14 and 5 to Mikkeli and thence further west still into the Päijänne lake system *(see page 263)*; or staying with Saimaa to its northern limits beyond Kuopio. **Mikkeli** 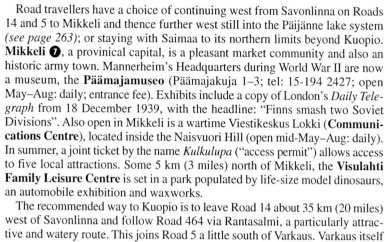, a provinical capital, is a pleasant market community and also an historic army town. Mannerheim's Headquarters during World War II are now a museum, the **Päämajamuseo** (Päämajakuja 1–3; tel: 15-194 2427; open May–Aug: daily; entrance fee). Exhibits include a copy of London's *Daily Telegraph* from 18 December 1939, with the headline: "Finns smash two Soviet Divisions". Also open in Mikkeli is a wartime Viestikeskus Lokki (**Communications Centre**), located inside the Naisvuori Hill (open mid-May–Aug: daily). In summer, a joint ticket by the name *Kulkulupa* ("access permit") allows access to five local attractions. Some 5 km (3 miles) north of Mikkeli, the **Visulahti Family Leisure Centre** is set in a park populated by life-size model dinosaurs, an automobile exhibition and waxworks.

The recommended way to Kuopio is to leave Road 14 about 35 km (20 miles) west of Savonlinna and follow Road 464 via Rantasalmi, a particularly attractive and watery route. This joins Road 5 a little south of Varkaus. Varkaus itself is industrial (music specialists should note its **Mekaanisen Musiikin Museo** at Pelimanninkatu 8; tel: 17-558 0643 – unique in the Nordic countries), but the little town of **Joroinen** 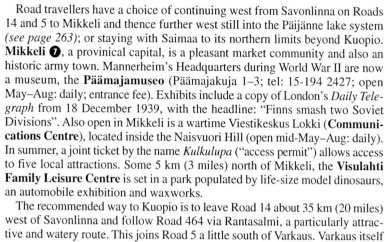, 15 km (10 miles) to the south, is very typical of a smaller Finnish community. In contrast with its own modernity are the fine old farms and manor houses dotted about these fertile landscapes, some used as settings for the music festival which is arranged here each summer.

Road 5 is the direct way to Kuopio, 75 km (45 miles) north of Varkaus. West of Varkaus along Road 23 the pleasant rural community of Pieksämäki lies on Saimaa's western fringes on another approach route to Päijänne. Northeastwards from Varkaus, Road 23 leads to Joensuu in North Karelia *(see page 271)*, passing close by two major religious houses: the Orthodox monastery of **Valamon luostari** 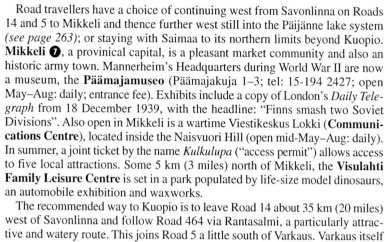 and the Convent of Lintula. On all three counts of history, culture and scenery these merit a visit, a recommended possibility being by special monastery cruises from Kuopio in summer.

The clue to the monastery's history lies in its name. Valamo is the large island on Lake Ladoga on which an Orthodox religious foundation was established in the Middle Ages, attracting a growing number of pilgrims over the centuries, though latterly its fortunes declined. During the Finn-Russian Winter War of 1939–40, the surviving handful of elderly monks was forced to leave and eventually accorded the present site of Uusi ("New") Valamo (tel: 17-570 111), originally an old manor house and outbuildings. One of these outbuildings was adapted as the monks' first place of worship, embellished by the precious 18th-century icons and other sacred objects which they had brought with them.

Valamon luostari has since experienced something of a renaissance. An injection of younger blood ensures its continuance; there is a fine new church completed in 1977, a cafeteria, a wine shop, souvenir shop and a modern hotel to cater for the growing num-

**BELOW:** Finland's summer may be brief, but it is full of wildflowers.

ber of visitors and pilgrims. The **Lintulan luostari** (**Convent of Lintula**) (tel: 17-563 106), a few kilometres away, has a similar but shorter history. The pious inhabitants of both contribute to their upkeep by working the land in these delightful lakeside settings though you may find the rather humbler aspects of Lintula more conducive to spiritual thought.

Map on page 254

## Kuopio to Iisalmi

**Kuopio** ❿ is a thoroughly nice town and one of Finland's liveliest, with a crowded summer calendar including the International Dance and Music Festival in June *(see page 92)*. Its daily market is one of the most varied outside Helsinki, and hard to miss as it fills most of Kuopio's central *Tori* (Market Place). Here you can try freshly baked *kalakukko* (fish and pork in a rye crust), traditional local fare that is definitely an acquired taste; or in due season you may be tempted by the varied edible fungi or succulent mounds of berries straight from the forests or bogs. There is a smaller market on summer evenings at the passenger harbour (east side of the town).

Like many Finnish country towns that developed in the 18th and 19th centuries, central Kuopio follows the grid-iron pattern, a chessboard of parallel streets more familiar to Americans than Europeans. This was designed to provide plenty of firebreaks between the then predominantly wooden buildings though, alas, it failed in its purpose all too often. Most of those that survived have been replaced by modern buildings but the **Kuopion kortellimuseo**, a few blocks south of the market place (Kirkkokatu 22; tel: 17-182 625; open summer: daily, winter: Tues–Sun; entrance fee), preserves a number of original dwellings complete with authentic furniture, warehouses, and even gardens

**LEFT:** Kuopio's bustling market area.
**BELOW:** the annual wine festival in Kuopio.

*Admiring the lake views from the Puijo Tower.*

dating from the 18th century to the 1930s – a quiet oasis showing how much of small-town Finland used to look.

A little to the east of the market place the **Kuopion museo** at Kauppakatu 23 (tel: 17-182 603; open Sun–Fri; entrance fee) houses excellent regional collections of a cultural and natural history order in a castle-like building that is a typical example of Finnish early 20th-century National Romantic style. Among several famous Finns associated with Kuopio, statesman Johan Vilhelm Snellman worked and married here in the 1840s. The conjugal home at Snellmaninkatu 19 is also a small, but less detailed museum of the period (open May–Aug: daily; entrance free).

On the edge of the town centre, the **Ortodoksinen kirkkomuseo** (Karjalankatu 1; tel: 17-287 2244; open Tue–Sun; entrance fee) is unique in western Europe, housing collections of icons (many from the 18th century, some from the 10th century) and sacred objects brought here from Valamo and Konevitsa in Karelia and a few from Petsamo in the far north, all territories ceded to the Soviet Union. A little further on is Puijo hill topped by **Puijon torni**, over 75 metres (250 ft) high (tel: 17-255 5100, open Jun–Jul: daily; entrance fee). The vistas from the tower's viewing platforms and revolving restaurant are beautiful, with lakes and forests merging into purple distances. Try and time your visit for an hour or two before sundown – the colours are out of this world.

By the time you reach **Iisalmi** ⓫, 80 km (50 miles) north of Kuopio on Road 5, you are almost exactly halfway between Helsinki and the Arctic Circle, and you are still – just – in the Saimaa region. Should you launch a canoe from Iisalmi's lake shore, it would be either level paddling or gently downhill all the way to the Gulf of Finland – over 400 km (250 miles) away.

**BELOW:**
the daunting ski jump in Lahti.

Iisalmi is a pleasant small provincial town, birthplace of writer Juhani Aho in 1861 (the family home is a museum on the outskirts of town), and site of one of Finland's innumerable battles against the Russians (1808; the Finns won this one, even though they were outnumbered seven-to-one).

**Evakkokeskus**, a Karelian-Orthodox Cultural Centre at Kyllikinkatu 8, displays valuable relics recovered from territory now in Russia, along with 80 models of churches and chapels since destroyed there. You can dine at Kuappi, "the smallest restaurant in the world", or, if it's full, at Olutmestari, the nearby beer hall with an attractive terrace in summer. Iisalmi's Olvi brewery has an excellent brewery museum upstairs.

## The Päijänne system

Päijänne is Finland's longest and deepest lake – 119 km (74 miles) long as the crow flies, though many times that if you follow its wondrously intricate shoreline. At opposite ends of the lake system are two of Finland's more substantial towns, Lahti and Jyväskylä. The watery topography between the two defeated the railway engineers, but they are linked to the west of Päijänne by one of Europe's main highways, E24, and to the east of it by a network of slower more attractive routes. Alternatively in summer there is the leisurely 10½-hour waterborne route.

Further removed from troublesome historical border areas than many regions of Finland, this central district has been subjected less to conflict and change. Tourism also reached it later, though it has made up for it since, capitalising on the lovely well-watered, deeply wooded landscapes. Sports, education, industry and architecture are among its major themes.

Map on page 254

**BELOW:**
Hollola Church.

**TIP**

Lahti is home to the world's only skiing museum, which includes exhibits on Finnish Olympic medallists and a video about the development of the sport.

**BELOW:** the popular view of Finland – endless lakes and forests.

**Lahti** lies 103 km (64 miles) north of Helsinki on Road 4 (E75). It straddles part of one of Finland's more distinctive topographical features, the extensive ridge system called Salpausselkä, which is regularly the setting for major world skiing championships. Here, too, is the **Lahden Urheilukeskus** , the town's sports center, with some of Finland's best winter sports facilities including three ski jumps (50-, 70- and 90-metre, open daily for visitors). It is the venue for the annual Finlandia Ski Race and the Ski Games *(see page 315)*.

From the viewing platform on top of the highest ski jump, the town spreads at your feet. Beyond, the gleaming sheets of Vesijärvi (lake) are linked, by the Vääksy Canal a few miles to the north, to the much greater waters of Päijänne. Lahti is a modern place, one of its few older buildings being the Kaupungintalo (Town Hall,1912) designed, as were so many Finnish public buildings of the period, by Eliel Saarinen. Three blocks to the north is the market, a lively morning spot, and two blocks further north, at Kirkkokatu 4, the highly individualistic **Ristinkirkko (Church of the Cross)**, built in 1978 (open daily). This was the last church in Finland designed by Alvar Aalto, powerful in its simplicity and a fine main venue for the Lahti Organ Festival every summer.

The **Lahden Historiallinen museo** in Lahti Manor, an exotic late 19th-century building at Lahdenkatu 4 (tel: 3-814 4536; open daily; entrance fee), has very good regional ethnographical and cultural history collections, as well as unique art and furniture collections. For living history, though, go a few kilometres northwest to the area known as Tiirismaa. Here is south Finland's highest hill (223 metres/730 ft), some of her oldest rocks and the tourist centre of **Messilä** combining an old manor house, crafts centre and Summerland fun park. Sixteen km (10 miles) further on (not actually in Hollola) the 15th-century

greystone Hollola Church has some good wooden sculptures and is among the largest and finest of about 80 churches surviving from that period in Finland. Near it are a good rural museum and some excellent coffee houses.

Map on page 254

## Fishing and bird-watching

From Lahti it's only 35 km (21 miles) northeast on Road 5 to the pleasant little town of **Heinola** ⓭, on the way passing Suomen urheiluopisto, the top Finnish Sports Institute at Vierumäki. Taking the popular summer lake route, it is an astonishing – and lovely – 4½ hours by steamer, 3½ hours by hydrofoil. A glance at the map reveals the contortions needed for lake traffic plying this route, first negotiating the Vääksy Canal north into Päijänne, and later squeezing southeast through narrow straits into the wider waters that lead to Heinola.

There are more narrow straits at Heinola, where the scurrying waters of **Jyrängönkoski** (rapids) provide good sport for local canoeists and for fishermen casting for lake and rainbow trout. You can also try for the latter, with rather more likelihood of success, from the teeming tanks of Siltasaari Fishing Centre by the rapids where, for a few euros, you can rent a rod and have your catch smoked to eat on the spot or take away.

Heinola blossomed into yet another spa town in Tsarist times. There are a number of wooden buildings dating from the turn of the 20th century, including a Chinese pavilion on the ridge-top park, now a restaurant, redolent of a more leisurely age. Not far away, the pond of Kirkkolampi is a focal point of the well-arranged **Kirkkolammen lintutarha** – bird sanctuary and hospital – with four aviaries (open daily, entrance free). The town's main church, an octagonal wooden building from the early 19th century, has a separate bell tower designed by that prolific architect, C.L. Engel.

From Heinola, Road 5 continues northeast to Mikkeli in western Saimaa. From here you could branch north on to Road 4 (E75) for Jyväskylä, but there is a slower and more attractive way. For this, leave Lahti north on Road 24 and after 25 km (15 miles), soon after crossing the Vääksy canal at Asikkala, branch right on to minor Road 314. This soon carries you along the several miles of Pulkkilanharju (ridge), another relic from the last Ice Age which vies with that of Punkaharju for narrowness and magnificence of lake and forest views. You continue by a series of asphalted but lesser roads via Sysmä and Luhanka, twisting along or across the complex succession of headlands, bays, capes and interlinked islands that make up Päijänne's contorted eastern shore. At **Luhanka** ⓮, the Mäkitupalaismuseo (Peltola Cotters Museum) throws light on the unenviable lot of the 19th-century "cotters": smallholders who effectively mortgaged their working lives to wealthy landowners in return for a scrap of land whose lease could be revoked at the owner's will.

To rejoin Road 9 (E63) at Korpilahti for the final leg to Jyväskylä you can now use an enormous bridge across Kärkistensalmi, one of Päijänne's many narrow straits. Road 24, of course, provides a more direct main road link all the way from Lahti to Jyväskylä in 174 km (107 miles). A particular beauty spot inside a

**BELOW:** Jyväskylä outdoor market.

Map on page 254

*One of many Alvar Aalto buildings in Jyväskylä.*

**BELOW:** selling local fish at Jyväskylä.

national park, a little off this route is the long, slender island of **Kelvenne** ⓕ, about 60 km (37 miles) north of Lahti, with its lakes, lagoons and curious geological formations. You can reach it from Kullasvuori camping area at Padasjoki. Road 24 also bypasses Jämsä and joins Road 9 to the south of the town, avoiding the industrial district of Jämsänkoski.

## Language and architecture

**Jyväskylä** ⓖ (population: 75,000) has contributed much, as an educational centre, to the country's cultural development: at a time when the Finnish language was still regarded by the Swedish-speaking ruling classes as the "peasants' language", the first Finnish-language secondary school opened here in 1858, and a teachers' training college opened a few years later. It now also has a lively university whose campus is the work of Alvar Aalto. Indeed it was in Jyväskylä that this renowned architect embarked on his career, and there are no fewer than 30 major buildings by him around the area, as well as the **Alvar Aalto museo** (7 Alvar Aallonkatu; tel: 14-624 809; open Tues–Sun; entrance fee) which has exhibits on his architecture and his furniture designs.

As with many Finnish towns whose older buildings have been largely lost, Jyväskylä is predominantly modern and it has a popular congress centre. From the observation platform of the Water Tower on the ridge running through the town you can gaze across it to the lakes. There are sports facilities on the same ridge and even more out at Laajavuori, a winter and summer sports centre on the northwest outskirts of town. Jyväskylä caters for most sports but is internationally best known as the venue for the 1,000 Lakes Rally in August, which draws 400,000 spectators to Finland's premier motor racing event. In June, the Jyväskylä Arts Festival chooses a different theme each year, examining its every aspect in seminars, exhibitions, concerts and theatre performances.

For a glimpse into the region's past, go to the excellent **Keski-Suomen museo** (tel: 14-624 930; open Tues–Sun; entrance fee), next to the Alvar Aalto Museum. Or, with a little more time, head 32 km (20 miles) west on Road 23 to **Petäjävesi** and **Keuruu,** a further 28 km (17 miles). Both have charming 18th-century wooden churches in typical central Finland rural settings – the one in Petäjävesi is listed by UNESCO as a World Heritage site. Road 23 continues west to Virrat at the northern end of the Poet's Way route (see page 213).

North of Jyväskylä, Road 4 (E4/75) continues through yet more forested lake-strewn landscapes harbouring a growing scattering of holiday and leisure centres. After 35 km (21 miles) Road 13 forks left to Saarijärvi, focal point of a pleasant holiday area. Just before it, turn south on Road 630, then shortly east to **Summassaari** ⓗ where a Stone Age village has been reconstructed. A short distance beyond Saarijärvi in **Kolkanlahti** ⓘ is the elegant 19th-century house, now a museum, where Finland's national poet, J. L. Runeberg, worked as a tutor in the 1820s.

Back on Road 4 (E4/75), before long you bypass Äänekoski, of no particular interest, as the highway leads ever northwards towards the Arctic Circle. ❏

# Canoeing

One of the more testing annual events on the European canoeing calendar is the Arctic Canoe Race which takes place every summer north of the Arctic Circle from Kilpisjärvi to Tornio along 537 km (334 miles) of the border rivers between Finland and Sweden. Another is the six-day 700-km (430-mile) Finlandia Canoe Relay each June, usually through the complex Saimaa system.

With 187,888 lakes (at the last count) and innumerable rivers to choose from, it's surprising that canoeing has only become popular in Finland in recent years. There is now, however, a growing range of packages whereby you can canoe well-tried routes of varying lengths, the cost based on whether you are part of a group or by yourself, the hire of canoe, paddles, provision of map and/or guide, with the option of camping equipment or farmhouse accommodation.

A particularly well-tried series of routes forms an overall 350-km (217-mile) circuit beginning and ending at Heinola. This needs 10–15 days but can also be fragmented into more manageable two- to five-day sections. Another, along 320 km (200 miles) of the Ounasjoki river in Lapland from Enontekiö to Rovaniemi, features sections of true Arctic wilderness; the rapids are mainly Grade I but it's possible to portage round the most daunting of these. Yet another follows a 285-km (200-mile) lake-and-river route taken by the old tar boats from Kuhmo to Oulu.

If you're attracted to the idea of pioneering across the lakes the possibilities are legion. Any of the 19 road maps which cover the entire country on a scale of 1:200 000 will be sufficient for general planning, but absolutely essential for more detail are the special inland waters charts, for example, for Saimaa on a scale of 1:40 000/1:50 000.

It's not until you are in your canoe, however, that navigation problems become clear. From the low level of a canoe one island of rock and pinewood looks very like another. Across wide expanses of water there are few helpful landmarks. You will then appreciate those other vital aids to canoeing the Finnish lakes: a compass and a pair of binoculars.

The greatest inconvenience – at times amounting to hazard – you are likely to encounter is wind. Squalls can blow up quickly and, across these expanses, waters are soon whipped up into turbulence. Head for shelter at the first sign.

Camping may prove more difficult than you might expect in seemingly empty landscapes. Much of the shoreline is either rocky or fringed by reed beds. Once landed, finding space enough between trees can be a problem even for a small tent and, where a clearing does exist, it has probably been created to accommodate a cottage or farm. The right to pitch your tent anywhere has been abused by some foreigners and is no longer promoted, so seek permission to camp whenever possible.

But, of course, there is often no one to ask. It is one of the joys of canoeing in Finland that you may travel for days without sign of humanity other than a tugboat hauling its train of timber, or a fisherman. ❑

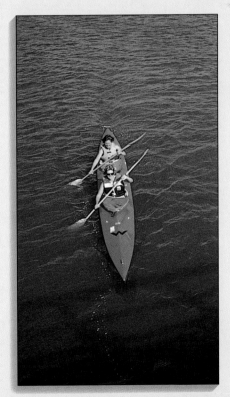

**RIGHT:** kayaking the rapids and waters of Finland's lake regions is a popular sport.

# KARELIA AND KUUSAMO

Map on page 272

*The ancient, rural communities of eastern Finland are considered the cultural heartland of the country, the region of myths and legends immortalised in the epic poem, the* Kalevala

Eastern Finland, which stretches broadly to the eastern frontier, is a changeover zone between the great Finnish Lakelands area and Lappi or Lapland. Few people live in this wild territory but the character of Karelia and its distinctive Orthodox churches have charm, tradition and colour.

Finland's most famous and perhaps most photographed scenery stretches below the lofty summit of the Koli Heights above Lake Pielinen, which also has good winter skiing. The "Bard and Border Way" takes the traveller to the frontier sights, including battlegrounds from World War II. Hiking in the wild, shooting the rapids and winter sports are the specialities of this region.

## Festival centres

**Joensuu ❶** at the mouth of the River Pielisjoki is the "capital" of North Karelia. It has a relaxed and welcoming air, for the majority of the inhabitants are Karelians, people who have a well-earned reputation for good humour and ready wit, traits particularly in evidence at the bustling marketplace.

At the end of June each year, Joensuu plays host to the Festival of Song, centred on the Joensuu Song Bowl, which has a stage large enough for an 11,000-strong choir. The **Pohjois-Karjalan museo** exhibits articles from prehistory, history and the folk culture of this part of Karelia. The museum (tel: 13-267 5222, open daily; entrance fee) is housed in a new tourist centre, Carelicum, opposite the market square at Koskikatu 5, which also has a tourist information office (tel: 13-267 5223), a souvenir shop, a café and other cultural venues. There is also the **Taidemuseo**, (Kirkkokatu 23, tel: 13-228 653; open Tues–Sun; entrance fee) with an icon collection and Finnish paintings from the 19th and 20th centuries. The **Yliopiston kasviti-eteellinen puutarha** – University Botanical Gardens (Heinäpurontie 70; open Tues–Sun; entrance fee) feature a range of plant species and a butterfly section. In many places in Joensuu, you will find restaurants serving Karelian specialities, such as the Restaurant Puukello, on the island of Ilosaari at the rapids, which offers Karelian roasts and pies with salted fish.

Before turning north, go as far east as you can in Finland to **Ilomantsi ❷**. Take Road 6 south out of Joensuu and then Road 74 east for the 70-km (50-mile) drive. Ilomantsi was the scene of heavy fighting in World War II, and in the village of Hattuvaara to the northeast the **Taistelijan talo (Warrior's House)** marks the spot where fighting ended in 1944. Trips to the easternmost point of Finland (and the EU) are arranged via Hattuvaara. On a more peaceful note, since the 14th century Ilomantsi has also been a stronghold of the Orthodox Church and the main

**PRECEDING PAGES:** relaxing in the wild. **LEFT:** whitewater rafting at Kainuu. **BELOW:** wild flowers gathered as decoration.

church is dedicated to St Elias. Easter is the most impressive festival, but the area is full of old rites and rituals.

For more light-hearted music and colour, it would be hard to beat the village of **Rääkkylä** ❸, a few miles south of Joensuu on a secondary road along the southern end of Lake Pyhäselkä. Its renowned folk band has won the national championship and many other awards and some of the young musicians play that most Karelian of instruments, the kantele, a stringed instrument similar to a zither.

## Shooting the rapids

Heading north from Joensuu, take Route 6 out of the town towards Eno. Where the road divides, take the right fork eastward (Route 73) which leads along the eastern shore of Lake Pielinen to **Lieksa** ❹. The roads through this countryside are tarred and well maintained but they are neither broad highways nor motorways and sometimes seem little different from the minor roads and lanes that lead off into the forest. But usually driving is simple, with main routes numbered and villages signposted.

The **Ruuankoski rapids** are a sight not to be missed from Lieksa. For some 33 km (21 miles) the Ruunaa plunges through six sets of foaming rapids and drops around 15 metres (50 ft) on the way. Equipped with lifejacket and waterproofs, shooting the rapids is safe under the careful supervision of a proficient guide.

Lieksa, one of the many forest centres in Finland, is less than 20 years old and has a population of only 19,000 (and a few bears) in an area larger than London. The **Pielisen museo (Pielinen Outdoor Museum)** has numerous buildings from different ages which document the settlement of the surrounding area – the oldest is from the 17th century (tel: 13-689 4151; open May–Sept: daily; entrance fee). The town's attractive church was built in 1982 by the husband and wife team Raili and Reima Pietilä.

At Vuonisjärvi, 29 km (18 miles) from the centre is **Paateri**, the studio of Eeva Ryynänen, a well-known wood sculptor who has decorated the area with her work, including a spectacular wooden Wilderness church (open late May–early Sept: daily; entrance fee). **Kaksinkantaja**, 38 km (24 miles) from the centre, has an exhibition of bear skulls and stuffed animals by Väinö Heikkinen, a famous bear hunter (open Jun–Aug: daily; entrance fee). Heikkinen, however, only speaks Finnish.

Lieksa may not be the most prepossessing of towns, but it is an important centre for visitors to this part of Finland's wilderness, which stretches as far as the Russian border. Capercaillie, elk, bear, reindeer and even wolves roam these dense pine forests. The best way to get an idea of its sheer size is from the viewing platform of the town's 47-metre (150-ft) tall water tower.

"Never go hiking on your own," is the warning motto of this region, and inexperienced walkers in particular should take guided tours, which can be arranged for individuals or groups. Most walks involve camping and the local shops in Lieksa can provide all the equipment and maps that are needed. Expeditions include the "Bears' Walk" along the Russian border, lake fishing in summer, and ice fishing in winter.

Trout, landlocked salmon (a relic of the Ice Age), coarse fish and bream all swim in these unpolluted waters. Join a guided fishing expedition if you would like to try your hand at catching them. A package will include the services of a guide, transport, accommodation and licences. Otherwise, you can buy a fishing licence from any local post office, or a regional fishing licence from a tourist office. Lieksa's main tourist office is on the town's main street, Pielisentie (tel: 13-689 4050; open daily).

Map on page 272

*Exhibits at the Museum of North Karelia, Joensuu.*

**BELOW:** a typical Karelian house.

# Karelians

I f Finland has a soul, that soul lives in Karelia. When Finns have gone to war, it has concerned Karelia. A Karelian theme runs through most of the music of Sibelius and his *Karelian Suite* reaches sublime heights of elegy and patriotism.

The Karelians were one of the earliest of the Finnish communities. They are evident in Bronze and Iron Age discoveries and their true origins are lost in myth and legend. The *Kalevala*, that great epic saga of ancient life in the far north, is really about the Karelians. This long poem, which in the 18th and 19th centuries became the cornerstone of the struggle for national culture, tells how with magic and sword the northern heroes fought for survival against the powers of evil. It recounts weddings, rituals, bear hunts and journeys into the mysterious Otherworld, and finally the heroes' joy as they celebrate in song the salvation of the land of Kalevala from its enemies. Although the *Kalevala*

depicts a pre-Christian period, the last poem predicts the decline of paganism, with the maid Marjatta giving birth to a son. The son is baptised and becomes king of Karelia.

The Karelians emerge into recorded history as a people living in the area of forest and lakes stretching from the present-day southeastern Finnish-Russian border to the White Sea. The Karelians came under Russian influences, although in no sense did they become russified. Slash and burn was their way of converting the impenetrable woodland into productive fields and they used the ash as a fertiliser. With these techniques came the production of grain and the need to dry it through steam heat, adapted first for grain-drying and then for relaxation. Thus, the sauna was born.

Orthodox religion is also a feature of the Karelian people, although it is accorded the title Greek Orthodox rather than Russian. There are 60,000 adherents and many churches in southeast Finland today. Karelian dialect, however, has almost died out.

The terrible Winter War of 1939–40 was fought to save Karelian land and has become the Finns' great *cause célèbre* but it was only one war out of some 200 which were fought for Finnish Karelia. As a result of the settlement forced on Finland at the end of the Continuation War, some 400,000 Karelians had to be re-settled in the 1940s. The Karelian Isthmus was lost, along with all of East Karelia, now settled by Russians. Since then, people of Karelian origin can be found in all parts of Finland. They tend to be lively and talkative, in contrast to the more taciturn nature of other Finns.

True Karelia today exists only as a fragment of its former self. The border has all but cut it out of the Finnish body politic, its people have dispersed. A line roughly parallel to the border from Lieska down to the Isthmus delineates modern Finnish Karelia. Yet even in this small region something distinctive remains. Perhaps it is their delicious food, or perhaps it is the grandeur of the forest. But the Karelian legacy is more than a lost homeland. Sauna, saga and Sibelius – these are the Karelians' true memorials. ❑

**LEFT:** Young Karelians generally dress in national costume only for festivals these days.

## The national landscape

From Lieksa, the same Road 73 leads to **Nurmes ❺** in about an hour, keeping close to the shores of Lake Pielinen. First mentioned in documents in 1556, Nurmes only became a city as recently as 1974. Nicknamed "the town of the birch", Nurmes sits on a ridge between two lakes at the northern end of the Pielinen lake system; it is a beautiful town, with wooden houses built in authentic early-Karelian style.

**Bomba House** is a traditional Karelian house at Ritoniemi, about 2 km (1 mile) from the town, surrounded by a recently built "Karelian village" which provides visitors not only with comfortable accommodation but also with delicious meals of local specialities. Bomba House's menu includes an assortment of local pies, the tiny fish vendace, cold smoked whitefish, warm smoked lamb, hearty meat casseroles, fried wild mushrooms, baked cheese with Arctic bramble jam – all designed to get the taste buds working overtime.

It would be a pity to miss Finland's most gracious way to travel and Nurmes is the place to leave the car and take a leisurely steam boat ride down Lake Pielinen to that famous beauty spot, the hills of **Koli**. The lake scenery is wonderful, and you may meet Finland's largest inland waterway ferry as well as numerous other boats, big and small.

The Koli Hills rise halfway down the western side of the lake, the highest **Ukko-Koli (Old Man Koli) ❻**, reaching 347 metres (1,100 ft). Scramble up to the top (there are steps) and spread out below you is a view that has inspired some of the greatest artists, including Albert Edelfelt and Eero Järnefelt, whose paintings immortalised Koli around the turn of the 20th century and did much to stimulate the national awakening of the time *(see page 77)*. Sibelius, too, wove the Koli Hills into his symphonies and, looking down, it is not hard to understand why this countryside is always called Finland's "national landscape". The legend goes that Sibelius loved the area so much that he had a grand piano carried to the top of this hill to celebrate his marriage.

## The wilderness way north

Finland's wilderness way north has three of the country's glories – sauna, salmon and scenery, the last embodied in its national parks although not confined to them. You will meet these three great assets at almost every turn in Finland but never so frequently and in such abundance as in the region that starts north of Nurmes, roughly along the line of the Oulu waterway – lake and river – that almost bisects Finland, and stretches north to Rovaniemi and Lapland proper *(see page 287)*.

To many however, the biggest attraction of this area are the traditional saunas. There is purportedly one sauna for every four people in Finland and visitors will find them everywhere – in hotels, private homes, on board ships, at motels, holiday villages and forest camps. Every Finn is proud of the sauna, the one word which the Finnish language has offered to the rest of the world, and nothing better complements the end of a long northern day in the open air to refresh and revitalise body and soul *(see page 190)*.

Map on page 272

*Traditional Bomba House in Nurmes, a typical Karelian village.*

**BELOW:** salmon leaping upstream.

On the stove or in the stream there is only one really classic fish in this area and that is the Atlantic salmon. Though Finland has no sea border with the Atlantic, thanks to the Ice Age, this region, like others, retains an Atlantic legacy in the salmon that swim in the large natural landlocked lakes and in the smaller stocked waters.

National parks are protected areas where nature is left as untouched as possible but some amenities are provided for visitors; marked trails, camp sites, and cabins are set in the larger parks, with hotel accommodation just outside the parks proper. With so much unspoiled territory, it may hardly seem necessary for Finland to designate national parks but it has 25, some of the best along this wilderness way north.

From the east of the country, the natural way in to the area is from Nurmes on Road 75 to Kuhmo, or via Road 6 north, either turning right on to Road 76 just before Sotkamo to reach Kuhmo or continuing left on Road 6 for Kajaani on Oulujärvi (lake) to the west. From the west coast the natural route would be from Oulu *(see page 244)* along the waterway connecting the Oulu river, lake, Kajaani and Kuhmo.

## A natural world

Even before you reach the Oulu area, if your choice is Road 6 north you might like to detour to the remote national park, **Tiilikkajärven Kansallispuisto ❼**, near Rautavaara. After Valtimo, some 25 km (16 miles) north of Nurmes, turn left on to Road 5850 towards Rautavaara, and some 50 km (32 miles) on you come to the park. It was established to conserve the uninhabited area of Lake Tiilikka and the surrounding bogs.

**BELOW:** Orthodox Archbishop Paavali blesses the opening of Bomba House near Nurmes.

Another national park, the **Hiidenportin Kansallispuisto**  is southeast of Sotkamo and best reached also from Road 6. Turn right off Road 6 onto Road 5824, and some 25km (16 miles) on you come to the park on the left. This is a rugged area, with the narrow Hiidenportti Gorge, a large rift valley with rock sides dropping some 20 metres (70 ft) to the floor of the gorge. Both the park and the neighbouring Peurajärvi hiking and fishing area have designated trails, marked with orange paint, and camp sites. At Peurajärvi, permits are sold that allow anglers to catch one salmon each. Though you could wriggle through a complicated series of minor roads on the Sotkamo route from here, unless you are feeling adventurous, it is probably easier to go back to Road 18.

Both in and outside the parks, the further north you go, the more likely you are to find reindeer. These semi-domesticated animals are the main source of income for many people living in these parts and it is very important to take special care on roads when reindeer are around.

*The Kuhmo region is famous for its herds of rare forest reindeer, some 500 of which roam the forests in winter.*

## The Finnish frontier

**Kuhmo**  is a frontier town surrounded by dense forests in the wilderness area of Kainuu. The largest municipal area in Finland, it covers 5,458 sq. km (2,100 sq. miles). Close to the Russian border and remote and empty though the area is, Kuhmo has established an international reputation through the annual Kuhmo Chamber Music Festival, first held in 1970 *(see page 92)*. Fifty km (30 miles) east in Saunajärvi is the Winter War Memorial marking Finland's desperate 100-day struggle in 1940 against overwhelming odds. Travel agents in Kuhmo arrange trips across the border to Russian Karelian villages, but visas are required and take at least 10 days to arrange.

**BELOW:** the lynx is one of the wild animals that lives in the Karelian forests.

At one time this whole area was devoted to making tar, by a lengthy process of cutting, leaving and then burning forest trees to extract the sticky liquid that formed the basic ingredient. Once it was in barrels, peasants loaded their small boats for the slow journey down through lake and river to the port of Oulu where, in a rare symbiosis, shipbuilders bought it for their own craft and entrepreneurs shipped it abroad. In the 19th century Finland was the biggest exporter of tar in the world.

A fascinating recreated **Kalevala Village** in a wooded park on the outskirts of Kuhmo displays numerous local folk traditions (tel: 8-652 0114; open Jun–Aug: daily; entrance fee). The aim is to give modern-day visitors some idea of Finnish culture as it was immortalised by the folklorist Elias Lönnrot and artists such as Akseli Gallén-Kallela. The result is a "living" demonstration of the daily culture of ancient times as portrayed in Finland's epic poem, the *Kalevala (see page 95)*.

The village also serves as the scene for numerous events based on other folk literature, including plays, celebrations and performances by theatre groups. Guided tours teach visitors about primitive hunting and fishing skills and how tar was made in the Finnish wilds. The village has models of ingenious traps to catch birds and animals, including bears, and examples of how the old fishing families and peasants lived. The large Hotel Kalevala serves a tasty buffet lunch during the holiday season (tel: 8-655 4100).

North of Kuhmo, near the village of Lentiira is Lentiiran Lomakylä, one of the most welcoming and comfortable holiday village chalet complexes by the lake. With a wood-fired sauna and cold beer included, this must surely be Finnish tourist hospitality at its very best (tel: 8-650 141).

**BELOW:** Karelia abounds with berries in summer, such as these bilberries.

## AKSELI GALLÉN-KALLELA

Akseli Gallén-Kallela (1865–1931) is considered by many to be Finland's national artist. After studying at the Finnish Society of Fine Arts, Kallela made his debut in the 1880s to popular acclaim, with his realistic images of everyday Finns. Between 1884–8 Kallela lived in Paris and painted images of Parisian bohemian life, but he was soon to be drawn back to his native country. Kallela had become fascinated with Elias Löhnrot's epic collection of poetry, the *Kalevala* and wanted to capture in paint its mythical heroes. Returning to Finland, Kallela devoted his time to researching themes from the *Kalevala*. In 1890 he married Mary Slöör and they honeymooned in Eastern Finland and Karelia, the regions of the folk poems. The *Kalevala* paintings were to become the best-known of Kallela's works. From 1911–15 he was the chairman of the Finnish Artist Society and from 1919–31 he was the vice chairman of the Kalevala Society. However, Kallela was also a keen traveller. In 1909–10 the family lived in East Africa (present-day Kenya), and Kallela painted some 150 works, and gathered collections of ethnographic and zoological material. In the 1920s, they lived in the United States for three years, during which time Kallela created studies for the *Great Kalevala*, sadly unfinished.

## Political past

A long straight road through some of Finland's darkest forests leads west out of Kuhmo to Sotkamo and then onwards to **Kajaani** ❿, the area's main town, on the eastern edge of Oulujärvi (lake) and once the collecting point for barrels of tar ready for their journey to the coast.

Kajaani was founded in 1651 by the Swedish governor-general Count Per Brahe in the shelter of an existing fortress designed as a bastion against Russia. But in 1716, the fortress fell and the whole town was razed during the disastrous war between Sweden and Russia. The town still has the ruins of the 1604 castle. The Town Hall is yet another designed by the well-travelled German architect, C. L. Engel, who was responsible for so much of early Helsinki *(see page 162)*. The old tar boat canal and the lock keeper's house by the river Kajaani are still visible. Famous residents have included Elias Lönnrot, who at one time lived in Kajaani, and the town is also known as the home of Finland's longest-serving president, Urho Kekkonen.

The Tsar's Stable in **Paltaniemi** ⓫ is a relic of a visit by Tsar Alexander I. Also in Paltaniemi is the birthplace of the poet Eino Leino, and the city has a Cultural and Congress Centre. Heading some 20 km (12 miles) from the centre, Ruuhijarvi Wilderness Village has peaceful fishing grounds and old hunting lodges which are open all year.

The road from Kajaani to Oulu hugs the shores of Lake Oulu, plunging first into thickly wooded hill country. Before entering Oulu, the route goes through Muhos which has the second-oldest church in Finland, dating from 1634. Oulu continues the tradition of tar making and the Lakelands town still lights tar pits on midsummer's eve.

Map on page 272

*As the landscape becomes more Arctic, so, too, does the wildlife.*

**BELOW:** tundra takes over the landscape near the Arctic Circle.

Map
on page
272

Distances are long in this scantily populated area where Finns come to walk and fish and look at nature. The only other main centre, Kuusamo, almost at the Russian border, is some 360 km (225 miles) northeast across the breadth of the country along Road 20. Before Kuusamo, if you feel like a detour, turn left at Pudasjärvi and take Road 78 for 90 km (55 miles) to **Ranua ⓬**, which claims the world's northernmost zoo. Next to it is a piece of Santa Claus nonsense called the Murrr-Murrr-Linna (Castle) and featuring Santa's animal workshop.

## Rushing water and wind

**Kuusamo** is marvellous wilderness country, with tundra as far as you can see in any direction, forest, racing rivers with water foaming through gorges and canyons, some bare, others a dense dark green. The main sound in these parts is a mixture of rushing water and wind high in the pines. There are dozens of rapids, some suitable for canoeing, others for fishing. The Oulanka-joki and Iijoki (rivers) are excellent for family canoeing trips, but the Kitka-joki calls for experienced canoeists only.

There are literally thousands of excellent fishing spots in both rivers and lakes. The "Russian" brown trout rise in the rivers from Lake Paanajärvi in greater numbers each year thanks to efficient tending of the fishing grounds. This is also berry country, with blueberries, raspberries, lingonberries and cloudberries all growing in great profusion on the Arctic tundra. The only snag is the number of mosquitoes: they multiply rapidly in the northern summer so take plenty of protection.

In both summer and winter, this vast unspoiled area is given over to recreation. In the middle, Karhuntassu Tourist Centre has been specially built to provide information on every activity, accommodation and most other aspects of the region, and there are other more distant centres. In winter, the area is excellent for skiing and the skidoo or snowmobile comes into its own. Snowmobiling is both an exhilarating and a practical way to get around this snowbound landscape, though many consider this modern convenience outweighed by its noise and fumes.

There are two national parks near here. The largest, **Oulangan Kansallispuisto ⓭**, to the north stretches over an largely untouched region of 270 sq. km (105 sq. miles), bordering the Oulanka river. It is a landscape of ravines and rushing torrents, sandbanks and flowering meadows. Karhunkierros, the most famous walking route in Finland, stretches some 100 km (60 miles) through the Oulanka canyon to the **Rukatunturi Fells ⓮**. A few kilometres will give the flavour of the trail but to cover the whole route, staying at camp sites or forest cabins en route, takes several days. In winter the area is given over to winter sports with some 28 ski pistes. A smaller national park, Riisitunturi, lies to the southwest of Oulanka, another untouched wilderness of spruce dominated by hills and bogs.

Almost imperceptibly on the way north, the landscape and culture have changed from the traditions of Karelia to the ancient ways of the Sami people. From here on, without doubt the land is Lappi. ❑

**BELOW:**
hunting and fishing are two sports often combined.

# Hunting

The great bull elk of Finland, standing 1.8 metres (6 ft) high at the shoulder, gazes through the northern forest. Crowned by massive horns, this elk is not the sluggish, lumbering giant it looks. Silent as night, wary, elusive, fast and with highly developed senses, this titan of the tundra and one time co-habitant of the dinosaur tests man's hunting skills to the utmost.

The justification for shooting elk is the paramount need to protect both food and the young timber that is so important to Finland's economy. The elk breeds so well in modern Finland that an annual cull of around 50,000 animals is necessary. But while a hunter is justified, he is no pest controller. Justification is one thing; motivation is another. It is the thrill of the chase that brings the elk hunter with his .300 calibre rifle and his pack of dogs to the forest in October for the short elk-hunting season.

Sub-Arctic tundra make pursuit of the elk arduous and competitive, modern arms notwithstanding. The trees are dense, the cover is thick; trained dogs aid the hunter in his quest. An elk is big enough to disregard a dog. Sometimes the elk will take off, but not out of fear. A dog can hold an elk at bay simply because it is disinclined to move.

If the quarry moves, the dogs will hunt it mute by scent. The signal for the hunter who is following is the renewed barking of the dog, for this means the elk is standing still and the approach can begin. Now comes the most critical part of the day, for if an elk is tolerant of a dog, it is most decidedly intolerant of man. The ground is covered in material which, to quote an old advertising slogan, "snaps, crackles and pops". The hunter must proceed with light footsteps, and may have to crawl on his belly for the final approach. It is sudden movement that attracts attention and a day's effort may be ruined by one false move.

If culling is the justification behind elk hunting, it is also the *raison d'être* for wolf hunting. Wolves still prowl the border area of Finland and Russia. Once in Finland,

wolves kill domestic reindeer, protected by a close season in the east and in the south protected year round.

Hunting wolves is a difficult affair but Finnish hunters use an ingenious method of encirclement, also found in other parts of Eastern Europe. From large spools strapped to their backs, the men lay a line of string with red flashes through the woods. It can take up to two days to set the lines but some curious instinct tells a wolf not to cross them; it's the opposite of a red rag to a bull. The helpers then drive the wolves to where the hunters are waiting. The guns now have some advantage, though the cunning and speed of wolves saves them from the bullet and only a few wolves are shot each year.

You can make hunting tours with guides in several parts of Finland, with elk hunting – lasting three or four days – the most popular. Hunting usually means living in a hut or cabin, invariably clean and bright. After many hours in the open, nothing could be better than the ritual of the sauna to give a sense of total well-being.     ❑

**RIGHT:** waiting for prey requires patience, skill and silence.

# LAPLAND

*Synonymous with Christmas and bleak Arctic landscapes, it comes as a surprise to many visitors that Lapland is also a thriving region of agricultural and fishing communities*

Map on page 286

Helsinki

**T**wo main roads bore their way northwards through the province of Lapland (Lappi). Road 4, sometimes called the Arctic Road, links Kemi with Rovaniemi before continuing northeastwards through ever more sparsely inhabited landscapes to cross into Norway at Utsjoki. The other is Road 21 (E78) which follows the Tornio Valley upstream from Tornio, continuing beside various tributaries that form the border with Sweden, eventually to cross into Norway near Kilpisjärvi. This is the river route of the Arctic Canoe Race and the road that accompanies it is also sometimes known as the "Way of the Four Winds", after the four points of the Sami traditional male headgear. Bridges and ferries provide links with Sweden.

## Arctic landscape

Respectively the two routes cover 540 km (336 miles) and 457 km (284 miles). Either will show you superficially a great deal of Arctic countryside, but from neither will you glean anything but the faintest hint of what Lapland is all about. For that you must leave the main roads – preferably the minor ones too – and set out on foot or in a canoe or, in winter, a pair of skis. It's not even necessary to go very far for there are silent spaces to be found within a few hundred yards of the most modern hotel, which seem barely to have been touched since the last Ice Age, but of course the experience deepens with distance and duration. The vital need for proper clothing and equipment, however, can't be over-stressed: climatic changes occur with ferocious suddenness and, for all its magnificence, the Arctic wilderness can be a ruthless place.

As you progress northwards the trees become spindlier, the forests sparser, the habitations fewer, the hills more numerous and gradually higher until you reach the sweeping undulations of the bare-topped fells of northern and northwestern Lapland. Beyond the tree line vegetation crouches and crawls – dwarf juniper and willow and miniature birch clinging to the fellsides among the mosses and the lichens, the miniscule campions and tiny saxifrages. In summer take plenty of mosquito repellent; every paradise must have its serpent.

In 1944 the German army followed a scorched-earth policy as it retreated north into Norway, so any old buildings that survive are mostly away from the main roads. But despite the monumental changes wrought on the province by the second half of the 20th century *(see page 127)* at least some elements of an age-old way of life endure. One notable village that has managed to escape destruction and modern development is Suvanto, north of Kemijärvi, not far from Pelkosenniemi.

**PRECEDING PAGES:** reindeer herds. **LEFT:** spectators at Inari's reindeer races. **BELOW:** winter golf at Rovaniemi.

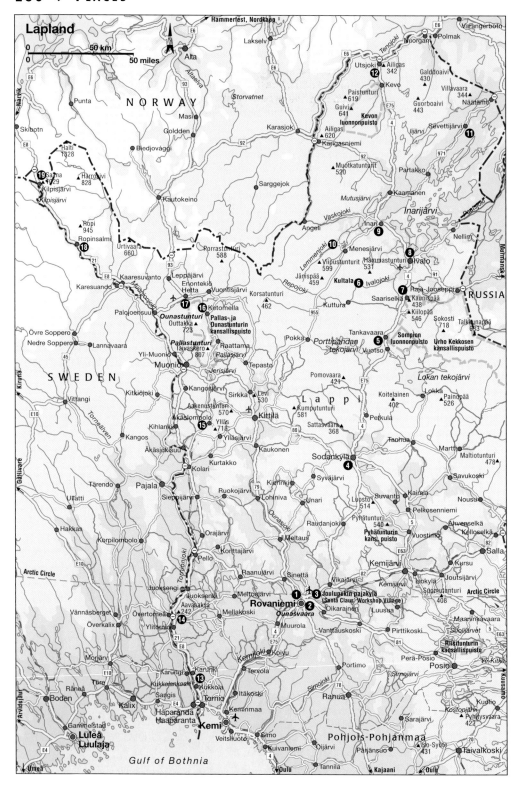

Lapland

## Rovaniemi

From Kemi, Road 4 follows the valley of the Kemijoki in which a rash of timber-based industries has spawned a succession of communities. You reach **Rovaniemi ❶** within 115 km (70 miles). This, the administrative capital of Lapland, all but nudges the Arctic Circle and is the launching point for most trips into the province. The town, well placed at the confluence of the Ounasjoki and Kemijoki rivers, has been completely rebuilt since World War II, almost quadrupling its population (now about 34,500) in the process. In early summer timber is still floated down the Ounasjoki from the forests of central Lapland.

The reconstruction plan for Rovaniemi was made by Alvar Aalto who also designed the fine Lappia Hall complex on Hallituskatu, containing the Provincial Museum, a theatre and congress facilities and, next to it, the Library. The odd-looking **Arktikum House** (The Arctic Centre), half-buried underground and thus offering a sensation of Midnight Sun through the glass ceiling, has exhibits illustrating Arctic history and culture (tel: 16-317 840; summer: daily, winter: Tues–Sun;entrance fee).

Also in the Arktikum building, the Provincial Museum gives a good introduction to Lapland's flora and fauna, Sami traditions and Rovaniemi's history, but you'll get a better feel of bygone living from the 19th-century farm buildings at the **Pöykkölä Museum**, by the Kemi river 3 km (2 miles) to the south on Road 78 (tel: 16-348 1095; open Jun–Aug: daily; entrance fee). **Rovaniemi Art Museum** (Lapinkävijäntie 4; tel: 16-322 2822; open Tues–Sun; entrance free) has a collection of modern Finnish art. Not far from Lappia Hall the main Lutheran Church has a modern altar fresco, *The Source of Life*, by Lennart Segerstråle.

Rising up from the confluence of the Ounasjoki and Kemijoki are the wooded slopes of **Ounasvaara ❷**, now a well-developed skiing area and site of annual international winter games. It's also a favourite gathering place on Midsummer Night.

## Land of Santa Claus

Eight km (5 miles) from the town on Road 4, soon after the turn-off for Rovaniemi airport, **Joulupukin Pajakylä** (**Santa Claus' Workshop Village**) ❸ straddles the Arctic Circle (Napapiiri). Its post office annually handles thousands of letters from children worldwide, and there are some good shops, a puppet theatre, art exhibitions, a glass factory, a few reindeer and, of course, Santa Claus *(see page 138)*.

**Santa Park** (tel: 016-333 0000; open Dec, Jun–Aug: daily, Jan–May, Sept–Nov: Sat–Sun; entrance fee) was recently opened in a man-made cave inside the Syväsenvaara Hill some 2 km (1 mile) south of the Arctic Circle. A miniature train takes visitors to the site, which was planned in co-operation with British theme park designers, and provides various fun rides for children.

A number of fell areas east of Road 4 in southern Lapland have been developed for winter and summer tourism. One of the best is centred on Pyhätunturi, about 135 km (84 miles) northeast of Rovaniemi. Another, just north of it, is Luostotunturi, south of

Map on page 286

*Sami textiles reflect their lifestyles, such as their dependence on reindeer.*

**BELOW:** when roads are few, locals take to the water.

Sodankylä. At the **Scandic Hotel**, Luosto (tel: 16-624 400; fax: 16-624 410) you can stay overnight in a cosy log cabin with an Arctic-style built-in bed and blazing fire. Popular hiking and skiing routes span between these two centres.

You will have noticed the landscapes – predominantly forested – becoming progressively emptier. However, there are reindeer aplenty and the occasional elk, so do drive slowly; keep your eyes open and your camera handy – they say white reindeer bring good luck.

**Sodankylä ❹**, 130 km (80 miles) from Rovaniemi, is the first substantial place along this route, a long established community reputed to be the coldest in Finland. It is the home of the Midnight Sun Film Festival held each June. Next to its 19th-century stone church, its wooden predecessor is Lapland's oldest church, dating from 1689. Road 5 comes into Sodankylä from the southeast and minor roads wander off east and west to link tiny scattered communities.

## Gold country

Northwards, there's little to detain you for the next 60 (100 km) miles or so until, a few miles beyond Vuotso, you reach **Tankavaara ❺**. Gold panning has been practised in various parts of Lapland for well over a century, and at Tankavaara there is an entertaining Kultakylä (Gold Village, tel: 16-626 171; fax: 16-626 261); its Kultamuseo (Gold Prospectors' Museum) not only chronicles man's historical endeavours to find gold, but for a modest fee gives tuition and allows you to pan for gold for an hour, a day, even several days, in an authentic wilderness setting. At nearby **Kultala ❻** (*kulta* is Finnish for gold) in trackless wilderness to the northwest, on the banks of the Ivalojoki, you can also see an 1870 goldwashing station.

**TIP**

For staying in Saariselkä, contact the Tourist Office at Honkapolku 3, (tel: 16-668 400; fax: 16-668 405) or try the Saariselkä Fell Hotel, with fine rooms and excellent Lappish cuisine (tel: 16-68 111; fax: 16-668 771).

**BELOW:** snow sculpture is a popular pastime.

About 40 km (25 miles) further north there is a great deal more self-catering accommodation, together with modern hotels, spas and sports facilities, centred on Laanila and **Saariselkä** ❼, an immensely popular winter sports centre among the élite of Helsinki's business life. Saariselkä's landscape marks a difference, scattered about the forests and slopes of a huge area of primeval fell towards the Russian border. It is an excellent area for skiing, and has plenty of wilderness huts. Much of this region is designated as a national park named after Urho Kekkonen, Finland's longest-serving president.

## Ivalo and Inari

In another 23 km (14 miles) you pass the turn-off for Ivalo airport, Finland's northernmost. **Ivalo** ❽ itself straggles along the east bank of the Ivalojoki. It's the largest community in northern Lapland, with all the usual facilities, though in terms of Sami culture it is much less important than Inari. There is, however, an attractive little wooden Orthodox church tucked away in the woods, serving the Skolt Sami, a branch of the Sami people who formerly lived in territory ceded to the Soviet Union in 1944. They have different costumes, language and traditions to Finnish Sami, and some now breed sheep rather than, or as well as, reindeer. A number of Skolt Sami families live in Nellim, about 45 km (29 miles) northeast of Ivalo towards the Russian border.

Ivalo's Lutheran Church stands near the bridge which carries Road 4 over the Ivalojoki; then it's a further 39 km (27 miles) to **Inari** ❾ – much of it a delightful route along parts of the contorted shores of Lake Inari. Inari village is an excellent base for wilderness exploration; you can lodge at the traditional Hotel Inarin Kultahovi (tel: 16-671 221). Though smaller and rather more scat-

Map on page 286

*Thick animal skin boots protect against the snow and ice.*

**BELOW:** the colours of summer in Lapland.

tered than Ivalo, this is nevertheless the administrative centre for a vast if sparsely populated area, and a traditional meeting place for colourfully costumed Sami people for weddings and other festivities, especially during the church festivals of Lady Day and Easter.

Focus of many Sami festivities is the simple modern church near the lake shore. **Lake Inari** is Finland's third largest, covering 1,300 sq. km (808 sq. miles) and is dotted with about 3,000 islands, some of them considered sacred according to Sami tradition. It is a wild, lonely beautiful lake, the theme of numerous haunting songs and many legends. Boat trips and sightseeing flights are available during the summer to the holy Ukko island, particularly revered by the local Sami).

Inari's excellent **Saamelaismuseo (Siida Lappish Museum)** (tel: 16-665 212; open summer: daily, winter: Tues–Sun;; entrance fee) comprises a new museum building and an open-air section (*skansen*) with old buildings and equipment illustrating the traditionally nomadic way of life. There are also some exhibits on early Skolt Sami culture and modern Sami life. The Siida building also houses the Ylä-Lapin luontokeskus (Nature Centre for Upper Lapland), which sells fishing permits and assists in hiking plans for those wishing to explore the wilderness. From the museum a marked trail covering a return journey of some 15 km (9 miles) leads to a remote 18th-century wooden church at Pielppajärvi, one of Lapland's oldest surviving buildings. It's a beautiful spot that is also accessible by boat.

Be sure, however, to leave enough time for shopping at Inari's many fine handicraft shops that include a silversmith's shop and the acclaimed studio of knife-maker Petteri Laiti.

**BELOW:** drying reindeer meat.

## SLEDGING

The easiest way to get across Lapland's vast, icy and largely flat landscape has always been on skis or sledges; the latter less exhausting for longer distances. There are many different types of sledging, but the most popular and readily associated with northern Finland is the dog sledge. Four or six husky dogs, hardy beasts naturally acclimatised to snow and ice, are harnessed to the front of a sledge, with passengers standing on the back runners. Unlike horses, the huskies are not readily controllable, so keeping the sledge stationary or stopping the sledge is done with a hook wedged deep in the snow. Once the hook is withdrawn, the dogs lurch forward.

Reindeer sledging, as epitomised by images of Santa and his sleigh each Christmas, is another method of getting around, with the advantage that these animals can cover longer and more snowy distances, although they journey slower than the dogs.

Many centres in Lapland now offer the chance of sledging excursions for tourists – contact tourist information offices in main towns for more details. It is essential that the right equipment is worn: thermals, waterproofs, hats and goggles are necessary to combat the dampness and icy bitterness of the snow.

## Towards Norway

The minor Road 955 from Inari leads 40 km (25 miles) southwest to **Menesjärvi**, a Sami settlement from which one can continue by road then river boat or on foot up the wild and beautiful **Lemmenjoki Valley**  ("river of love") to a remote gold prospectors' camp. The extensive national park area, though less isolated than it once was, is still a very lonely area of rocky canyons and primeval forest where you are wise to hire a guide. From Menesjärvi, Road 955 continues across Lapland to join Road 79 at Kittilä.

Around Inari and north of it, the road passes a number of attractive holiday centres, mostly of the self-catering variety. After 26 km (16 miles) you come to Kaamanen from which a minor road branches northeast 100 km (60 miles) to **Sevettijärvi** ⓫, the modern main settlement for the Skolt Sami. An interesting time to visit is during the Easter Orthodox festival. While there, visit the Sami graveyard, with its unusual turf-covered graves. Just a couple of kilometres north of Kaamanen you have a choice: to go north by minor road to Utsjoki, 94 km (58 miles) away on the border with Norway; or bear northwest along Road 4 to the Norwegian border 41 miles (66 km) away at Karigasniemi.

Either way, the landscapes get hillier, wilder and emptier. You will also pass the coniferous tree line, beyond which only the hardier dwarf birch survive on the lower fell slopes, their gnarled and weathered forms looking curiously biblical in this barren Arctic countryside.

The more beautiful route is the minor one to Utsjoki, passing a series of lakes close to the eastern fringes of the Kevo Nature Park, where Turku University runs an experimental station. **Utsjoki** ⓬ is an important Sami community – good for fishing and hiking – close to Finland's northernmost point. Its church

Map on page 286

*Hiking on the fells requires proper clothing and equipment but the scenery makes it worthwhile.*

**BELOW:** northern flat bread has a distinctive taste.

(1860) is one of the few pre-World War II churches still standing in Lapland. The village and road follow the Utsjoki downstream to join with the Tenojoki, a famed salmon river.

Both Utsjoki and Karigasniemi are dominated by "holy" fells called *Ailigas*, the one dominating Karigasniemi reaching over 620 metres (2,000 ft). From these border points you can also join the Norwegian road system for a variety of routes eventually returning into western Lapland at Kilpisjärvi or Enontekiö.

## Western Lapland

Your route through western Lapland is likely to begin at Tornio about 80 km (50 miles) south of the Arctic Circle *(see page 246)*. The earlier stretches of the Way of the Four Winds or Road 21 (E78) present a very different face of Lapland from the Arctic Road, for the lower section of the Tornio valley is much more populated, and served by Finland's northernmost railway branch to Kolari.

In its southern stages the road passes through a string of small communities mainly based, in these marginally milder and more fertile conditions, on agriculture and dairy farming. The Tornionjoki is also a good salmon river; at **Kukkola ⓭** look out for the Kukkolankoski rapids. About 70 km (43 miles) north of Tornio, beyond Ylitornio, is the 242-metre-high (794-ft) **Aavasaksa Hill ⓮**, the most southerly point from which the midnight sun can be seen, attracting considerable throngs for Midsummer Eve festivities. A few miles nearer Juoksenki, you cross the Arctic Circle. The scenery now gets wilder as you pass between Pello and Kolari. A little south of the latter Tornionjoki is replaced by a tributary, the Muonionjoki, at the Fenno-Swedish border.

**BELOW:** reindeer on the hoof.

# Fell country

About 10 km (7 miles) north of Kolari a worthwhile detour by minor Road 940 to the right leads to **Akäslompolo** ⓯. This well-equipped tourist resort and skiing centre is scattered about the shores of a small lake set amongst magnificent forested hills and bare-topped fells; the highest is Ylläs, at 718 metres (2,355 ft), served by chair lifts. A marked trail follows the chain of fells stretching northwards from here, eventually leading in about 150 km (90 miles) to the Pallastunturi fell group. It's a glorious trail if you come properly equipped, with overnight shelter available in untended wilderness huts – these are even marked on the 1:200 000 road maps.

From Akäslompolo you can continue north along minor roads and in 31 km (19 miles) turn left on to Road 79. This is the main road from Rovaniemi, providing an alternative approach to western Lapland. After a further 10km (7 miles) Road 957 to the right is highly recommended as the best approach to Enontekiö. A further branch left off this route leads from Road 79 to the lonely hotel complex of Pallastunturi, magnificently cradled in the lap of five of the 14 fells which make up the Pallastunturi group (the highest being Taivaskero at 807 metres/2,647 ft).

From here the choice of fell walks includes the long-distance 60-km (37-mile) trail north from Yllästunturi across the fells to Enontekiö. Road 957 brings you to the upper Ounasjoki valley via the small community of Raattama to **Ketomella** ⓰ where there's a car ferry across the river. Until fairly recent times this part of the valley was accessible only on foot or by boat or sledge, so a number of venerable farm buildings have survived, highly photogenic as they lean, tipsy with age. Along the entire route you get lovely views of first the

Map on page 286

*Signposts won't let you forget quite how far north you've travelled.*

**BELOW:** sparkling meltwaters at Windelhed.

Map on page 286

Pallas, then the Ounas fells. At the junction at Peltovuoma you turn west for Enontekiö and, eventually, Palojoensuu, back on Road 21.

## Enontekiö

Enontekiö ⑰, sometimes known as Hetta, is the attractively sited administrative centre of this extensive but sparsely populated area. The village sprawls along the northern shore of Ounasjärvi (lake), looking across to the great rounded shoulders of the Ounastunturi fells – the highest of which is Outtakka at 723 metres (2,372 ft). Once completely isolated, now it's accessible by air and road from all directions, with a road link north into Norway.

Most of Enontekiö's buildings are modern, including the pretty wooden church which has an altar mosaic depicting Sami people and reindeer. There's a good range of accommodation available, from camp sites to top-class hotels, all set up for the avid fishermen, hikers and canoeists for whom this makes an excellent holiday centre. It's also a main centre for the Sami of western Lapland, most of whom live in lone farmsteads or tiny communities in and around the area. Here, too, there are major traditional Sami gatherings at certain times of the year (see page 107).

From Palojoensuu, Road 21 continues northwest along the Muonionjoki and Könkämäeno valleys, the scenery becoming ever wilder and more barren. A little north of Kaaresuvanto you cross the coniferous tree line and pass the last of the spindly pines. At Järämä, 10 km (6 miles) further from the tiny settlement of Markkina, German soldiers built fortifications during a standstill in the Lapland War of 1944. Many of these bunkers have been restored and are now open to the public.

**BELOW:** if you are wrapped up warm enough, snow can be great fun.
**RIGHT:** snow skis are the most practical form of travel.

## Lakes and mountains

A little south and north of **Ropinsalmi** ⑱ there are good views respectively of Pättikkäkoski and Saukkokoski, two of the more testing rapids of the Arctic Canoe Race. The mountains reach ever greater heights; the highest, Halti, soars up to 1,328 metres (4,357 ft) on the Norwegian border at Finland's northwesternmost point.

More accessible and distinctive is **Saana** ⑲, 1,029 metres (3,376 ft) above the village and the resort of Kilpisjärvi. Kilpisjärvi is an excellent launching pad for wilderness enthusiasts. There is a lake of the same name whose western shore forms the border with Sweden, and a marked trail which takes about a day leads to the boundary stone marking the triple junction of Finland-Sweden-Norway. The Mallan luonnonpuisto, a nature reserve to the north of the lake requires a permit for entry, but once you are within it there is a pleasant 15-km (9-mile) trek.

The rest of these immense, empty, rugged, acres are as free to all comers as the elements – and as unpredictable. Never set off without proper equipment and provisions and, unless you are experienced in such landscapes, a guide; always inform someone where you are heading and when you expect to return. Simple advice, but it cannot be said often enough. ❑

# INSIGHT GUIDES
# Travel Tips

# INSIGHT GUIDES Phonecard

One global card to keep travellers in touch. Easy. Convenient. Saves you time and money.

## It's a global phonecard

Save up to 70%* on international calls from over 55 countries

Free 24 hour global customer service

Recharge your card at any time via customer service or online

## It's a message service

Family and friends can send you voice messages for free.

Listen to these messages using the phone* or online

Free email service - you can even listen to your email over the phone*

## It's a travel assistance service

24 hour emergency travel assistance – if and when you need it.

Store important travel documents online in your own secure vault

For more information, call rates, and all Access Numbers in over 55 countries, (check your destination is covered) go to www.insightguides.ekit.com or call Customer Service.

JOIN now and receive US$ 5 bonus when you join for US$ 20 or more.

## Join today at

## www.insightguides.ekit.com

When requested use ref code: **INSAD0103**

## OR SIMPLY FREE CALL
## 24 HOUR CUSTOMER SERVICE

| | |
|---|---|
| UK | 0800 376 1705 |
| USA | 1800 706 1333 |
| Canada | 1800 808 5773 |
| Australia | 1800 11 44 78 |
| South Africa | 0800 997 285 |

## THEN PRESS ⓪

For all other countries please go to "Access Numbers" at www.insightguides.ekit.com

* Retrieval rates apply for listening to messages. Savings based on using a hotel or payphone and calling to a landline. Correct at time of printing 01.03
(INS001)

*powered by* ⊕ *ekit*

"The easiest way to make calls and receive messages around the world"

# CONTENTS

# Getting Acquainted

## The Place

**Area:** 338,000 sq km (130,500 sq miles).
**Capital:** Helsinki.
**Population:** 5 million.
**Language:** 93 percent of the population speak Finnish; six percent Swedish and one percent other languages, including Sami.
**Religion:** Largely Evangelical Lutheran, with one percent Finnish Orthodox and 12 percent unaffiliated.
**Time zone:** Greenwich Mean Time (GMT) + 2 hours; Eastern Standard Time (EST) + 7 hours.
**Currency:** euro (€/EUR).
**Weights and measures:** metric.
**Electricity:** 220 AC (two-pin plug).
**International dialling code:** 358.

## Geography

Finland is set on the Baltic Sea between Sweden to the west and Russia to the east. A tiny arm of Norway is flung over the top of Finland to join with Russia. About one-third of Finland's landmass is above the Arctic Circle, which defines the area known as Lapland, or Lappi.

Finland is 65 percent covered by forest, 10 percent by lakes, and 8 percent by cultivated land (17 percent conurbations, industrial use, etc.). The last Ice Age left a great deal of flat land but, towards the north, glaciers pushed ridged mountains into the landscape, creating the famous rolling hills or *tunturi* of Lapland. The highest peak is Haltiatunturi, at just over 1,400 metres (4,000 ft) above sea level. The lakes are concentrated in south central Finland.

## Economy

Finland is a country that had modest agricultural and textile trades before the end of World War II. A few older companies founded in the 19th century, such as the family-owned Ahlstrom Oy, which began as metalworks and has now diversified into the paper and boiler industries, have survived into the 21st century.

Finland's obligation to pay war damages to the Soviet Union after World War II gave it the impetus to develop its modern industry because it was able to pay off much of its debt in manufactured goods. Pulp and paper products and machinery, the forestry industry, and a few electronics and engineering giants, such as Nokia mobile telephones and Neste oil refining, are now the lords of Finnish industry.

The rest of the economy is made up of service industries and agriculture. Although Finnish farmers are still very protected when it comes to government subsidies and over-production payments, farming is rapidly losing its appeal with the younger generations and, as a result, just 10 percent of the population is now involved in the farming industry.

## Government

Finland is a parliamentary democracy, with a president, a prime minister, and a 200-member, single-chamber parliament. The president is elected directly, while the prime minister is chosen by a conference of parties participating in the current government.

Coalition governments led by Social Democrats have dominated Finland's short history as an independent republic. In 2000, Social Democrat Tarja Halonen was elected president for a six year term. The unusual coalition government, consisting of Social Democrats, the conservative Kokoomus, the Greens, the Left-Wing Alliance and the Swedish People's Party, was formed after the 1995 election, and the same parties continued to rule the country after the 1999 election.

The Swedish-speaking Aland Islands, off the west coast, have an MP in the national Parliament (*Eduskunta*) in Helsinki. However the Alands are semi-autonomous, following a post-World War I League of Nations ruling, so have their own Parliament (*Landsting*), which administers regional matters.

There are 461 Finnish municipalities. The municipalities look after social services and welfare, as well as education.

## People

Finland is the sixth-largest land area in Europe. The population is sparse, however, with only 16 inhabitants per sq km (6 people per sq mile); in total there are five million inhabitants, about 40 percent of whom live in rural areas. Approximately one million Finns live in Greater Helsinki. The other cities' populations are sparse, however. There are approximately 100,000 foreign residents living in Finland.

## Etiquette

In general Finns are courteous, particularly to foreign guests. However, they do not squeak "Sorry!" any time they brush past you on the street, not even if they tread on your toes. This is because the Finns have failed to come up with a normal word for "Sorry" or "Excuse Me". For graver offences or extreme politeness, there is the word *Anteeksi*, but for minor offences, a simple "Oops" is usually enough.

If you are going to a Finn's house for dinner, bringing a plant or flowers for the host or hostess and, if you plan to drink, a bottle of wine, is the norm. However, if you bring spirits to a casual gathering, it is not considered rude to bring an already opened bottle. This is in homage to the very high cost of alcohol in Finland.

# Planning the Trip

## Passports and Visas

Citizens of most Western countries do not need visas to travel to Finland; a valid passport will suffice. EU citizens may enter with a valid ID card. The Nordic countries only stamp you in once for a three-month tourist stay, so if you arrive via, say Sweden, you won't need to be stamped at the Finnish border.

It is difficult for non-EU citizens to work in Finland; if you want to work, though, contact a Finnish Embassy or Consulate outside Finland well before you go. An employer's letter is usually needed in advance of the work permit being granted.

## Customs

The following items are permitted to be brought into Finland.

### Cigarettes/tobacco

Any visitor over 16 years of age may bring in 200 cigarettes or 250 gm (½ lb) of tobacco products duty free.

### Alcohol

Any visitor aged 20 or over can bring in 15 litres of beer, 2 litres of other mild alcohol (drinks containing not more than 22 percent by volume of ethyl alcohol) and 1 litre of strong alcohol (spirits). For visitors 18–19 years of age, the quantity limit is the same, but must not include strong alcohol.

In addition, visitors can bring in up to 1,100 markkas worth of gifts or items intended for one's own use. Food stuffs are limited to no more than 2.5 kg (around 5 lbs) of butter and 15 kg (33 lbs) of other

foods; no more than one third of this may be edible fats.

## Animal Quarantine

Pets vaccinated against rabies are in most cases allowed into Finland (pets must have been vaccinated at least 30 days and less than 12 months before entry). Double checking these requirements and your vaccination certificates is crucial because Finland is sometimes rabies-free, sometimes not, and these rules change from year to year.

## Money

Since early 2001, Finland, in common with 11 other EU member states, has used euro (€) notes and coins. Finns themselves have had longer to get used to the change, with salaries and prices being displayed in both marks and euros for some time prior to the official changeover.

There are 100 cents (Finnish: *sentti*) to the euro. Coins come in denominations of 1, 2, 5, 10 and 50 cents, and 1 and 2 euros. Controversially,

Finnish shops and businesses are not obliged to accept 1 or 2 cent coins, and prices are rounded off to the nearest factor of 5. Notes come in denominations of 5, 10, 20, 50, 100, 200 and 500 euros; the lowest amount withdrawable from a cash machine is €20 (about £14 or US$20.)

### Credit Cards and Travellers' Cheques

Credit cards are widely accepted in Finland. MasterCard/ Access, Visa, Diner's Club and American Express are accepted in all but the most humble establishments.

Travellers' cheques and common currencies can be exchanged easily in banks.

Most cash machines (ATMS) marked OTTO will give euros if you have a bank card with an international PIN number (Visa, Cirrus, Plus, MasterCard, Maestro, and so on).

## Public Holidays

- New Year's Day (1 Jan)
- Epiphany (6 Jan)
- Good Friday (Mar/Apr – variable)
- Easter Day (Mar/Apr – variable)
- May Day Eve (30 April)
- May Day (1 May)
- Ascension Day (May)
- Whitsun (late May or early June)
- Midsummer (21–22 Jun)
- All Saints' Day (late Oct)
- Independence Day (6 Dec)
- Christmas Eve (24 Dec)
- Christmas Day (25 Dec)
- Boxing Day (26 Dec)

## What to Bring

The best advice on packing for Finland is to bring layers of clothes, no matter what the season. While it is famous for frigid winters – when gloves, long underwear, hats, woollen tights and socks, and several layers of cotton topped by wool and something waterproof are recommended – Finland is less known for its very sunny temperate summers. As a result, sun block and a sun hat are as essential at these times as warm clothes are in the winter

In winter, bring heavy-duty footwear not only to keep out the damp but to avoid the heartbreak of good shoes ruined by salt and gravel put down to melt the ice on the pavements. Spring and autumn are rainy, and summers are usually pleasantly dry and sunny, but occasionally wet.

## Getting There

### By Air

Finnair is the national carrier of Finland and operates international and national routes. Both Finnair and British Airways connect London and Helsinki with daily flights. Finnair (and many other airlines, including Lufthansa) fly direct between Helsinki and most European capitals, and Finnair also links with several North American cities including New York. You may be able to find value-for-money package fares and charter flights from New York or London, but they are rare; watch newspaper advertisements for offers.

From Helsinki, Finnair and Air Botnia fly numerous domestic routes to more than 20 cities, including several to North Finland airports, and have cross-country flights between some of them. It was announced in 2003 that budget airline Ryanair were to begin flying between Tampere and Stockholm, with flights between Tampere and London, and other parts of Europe, to begin later on in the year. Check www.ryanair.com for latest details.

### By Sea

The best routes to Finland by boat are from Sweden and Germany. **Silja Line** and **Viking Line** have daily routes between Stockholm and Helsinki. These ferries are luxurious with restaurants, saunas, swimming pools, tax-free shops and children's playrooms. Silja's refurbished Finn-jet boat makes the trip in summer to and from Germany in 24 hours.

It's less expensive to travel by ferry from Stockholm to Turku or Naantali in western Finland and then overland to Helsinki rather than by direct ship to Helsinki. Viking provides very cheap train or

bus tickets for the overland trip; the ferry ticket is also cheaper as the voyage is shorter. One can also travel to Finland's Aland islands by boat from Stockholm or Turku – Viking has a daily service to Marie-hamn. Silja runs services between Vaasa and Sweden's Umeå but this service does not have tax-free sales so it may discontinue in future.
**Silja Line**
Tel: 0203-74552.
**Viking Line**
Tel: 09-12351/0-1942
262662 (UK).

### By Rail

It's a long haul to Finland from just about anywhere by rail, because you inevitably finish the long rail trip north with a 15-hour journey by boat and train from Stockholm to Helsinki. From Britain, the handiest route is Sealink from Harwich to the Hook of Holland, overland to Copen-hagen, then the connecting train to Stockholm and boat/boat and train to Helsinki. Total travel time is about 45 hours. This is cheaper than an Apex flight only if you get a special fare rail ticket; residents of Nordic countries now qualify for Interail tickets regardless of age.

Rail travel to north Finland requires completion by bus as Finnish rail lines only run as far as Rovaniemi and Kemijärvi (in winter to Kolari).

### Disabled Travellers

For disabled people, travelling should not pose tremendous problems in Finland. Most newer buildings have access for disabled people, in terms of ramps and lifts. Check the Finland Hotel guide which indicates by symbols which hotels have access and facilities for disabled people. With careful planning, transport should also go smoothly; when ordering a taxi, specify your needs (wheelchair is "pyörätuoli"). Public transport may be a bit more problematic, although some city buses "kneel", making it easier to board. If you have queries related to disabled travel in Finland, contact:
**Rullaten ry**
Pajutie 7C 02770 Espoo
Tel: 09-805 7393
Fax: 09-855 2470.

There are agencies specialising in holidays for the disabled and one travel agency in Helsinki arranges a major tour on request: the 7-day historical/architectural/cultural "Triangle Tour" of the three major cities (Helsinki, Tampere, Turku). It can be organised by contacting
**Area Travel**
Mannerheimintie 102, 00251
Helsinki
Tel: 09-818 383.

### Travelling with Children

Overall, Finland is a family- and child-orientated society, and hence one that is generally safe for children. Public conveniences usually include baby-changing areas and most restaurants can provide high chairs. Children are almost always accepted in all hotels. In Helsinki, the Tourist Board can pro-vide a list of qualified child-minders. In the cities, public transport is geared for use by those with prams, as well as wheelchairs, and getting around with children is easier than in almost any other country.

### Sailing Around the Baltic

Visas have usually been required for travel to the former Soviet Union though, in the light of events, this may change. You can get visas in Finland from Finnish travel agents but it is safer to allow 10 working days for processing. Most Western nationalities may enter Estonia, Latvia and Lithuania without a visa, and daytrips to Tallinn (Estonia) are extremely popular and recommended. There may be over 20 departures on an average summer day, so discounts are not unusual. Tickets are available at harbours on Katajanokka, Olympia-laituri and Länsisatama, Helsinki.

**Kristina Cruises**
Tel: 05-211 44
Fax: 05-211 4500
Offer a summer St Petersburg trip, lasting three to four days, with lodging on board and guides for the city. Passengers without visas may go on this trip but, once in St Petersburg, they must remain with the guided tours.

For information in the UK on sea or other options for travel to the former Soviet Union, contact:
**Voyages Jules Verne**
Tel: 020-7616 1000
www.vjv.co.uk.

# Practical Tips

## Business Hours

In larger cities, stores are generally open from 9am–5pm, with late-night opening on Thursdays. In Helsinki, many shops now open until 9pm on weekdays and until 6pm on Saturday. Larger foodstores will usually be open 9am–8pm weekdays and 9am–4pm Saturday. The only really late-opening places are in the tunnel under the Helsinki railway station, open weekdays 10am–10pm and weekends noon–10pm.

Larger shopping outlets, such as Stockmann's department store and the shops in the Forum shopping mall diagonally across from it on Mannerheimintie in Helsinki, are open weekdays 9am–8pm, Saturdays 9am–5pm.

Banking hours are 9.15am–4.15pm Mon–Fri. Some exchange bureaux open later, particularly at travel points such as airports and major harbours, as well as on international ferries.

## Media

### Newspapers and Books
No one has yet been able to come up with a good explanation as to why papers published on the Continent cannot arrive in Finland on their day of publication. But, with the exception of the *International Herald Tribune*, which arrives on the afternoon of its publication date, you'll have to wait a day-and-a-half for British newspapers to get to Helsinki. The papers are sold at Helsinki railway station, in at least two bookstores (Suomalainen Kirjakauppa at Aleksanterinkatu 23, and Akateeminen Kirjakauppa at Pohjoisesplanadi 39, where you can also get books in English) and at the larger hotels in other cities, as well as at main airports.

### Radio and Television
For news in English, you can tune in to the Finnish national broadcasters' YLE Capital FM (97.5 FM) in most of Southern Finland. This broadcasts hours of programmes in Spanish, French and Russian, but mainly English, using American, Canadian, Australian and South African stations as well as the BBC and Ireland's RTE. For up-to- date schedules, contact YLE on 9-1480 4316. YLE 1 also broadcasts news in English on weekdays at 08.10, and the BBC's World Service and other English-language channels are usually available in hotels.

## Postal Services

Post offices are open 9am–5pm. Services include stamps, registered mail and *poste restante*. The *poste restante* address in Helsinki is Mannerheimintie 11, 00100 Helsinki. It's on the railway square side of the post office and is open Mon–Sat 8am–1pm, Sun 11am–10pm.

When post offices are closed, there are stamp machines outside and in the railway station. Insert the necessary coin and you get the equivalent in stamps. The machines are orange and mounted on the walls, as are the post boxes.

## Telephones

The Finnish telephone system is being overhauled and existing area codes are gradually changing. Callers from outside Finland should dial the international code, then the country code followed by the area code, omitting the initial zero (0).

The best way to call overseas cheaply is at the post and telegraph office in a main city. Look for the "*Lennätin*" section, which means telecommunications. To make a normal direct call at a *Lennätin*, use any booth with a green light and pay the cashier after your call. You must dial 00 to get a line outside of Finland, then the country code and number (for example, 00 44 for the UK; 00 1 for US numbers). If you want to reach an operator in your own country to make a reverse charge call (call collect), ask for the Finland Direct pamphlet, which lists the numbers. For the UK operator, dial 9-800 1 0440, US 9-800 1 0010/ATT. Dial 020222 for overseas call assistance from a Finnish (English-speaking) operator. The front of the white pages telephone directory also has directions for foreigners.

Don't forget that hotels usually add surcharges for telephone calls made from your room.

### Mobile Phones
Finland is a nation of mobile phone users. The most typical mobile phone system is GSM900, which covers practically all of Finland. Roaming services are available with most existing operators around the world. US mobile phone operators do not use GSM at all, so to use your phone in Finland, the chip has to be removed and replaced with a GSM chip – enquire at your local phone store for more information. The two Finnish operators are **Radiolinja** (numbers starting with 050) and **Sonera** (040). Sweden's **Telia** operator is also expanding rapidly, as competition increases.

## Doing Business

Doing business in Finland does not differ greatly from doing business elsewhere in Europe, with a few exceptions.

**Business Hours:** Everything is done earlier. Lunch is earlier (as early as 11am, with 1pm the outside limit), and many offices operate from 8am–4pm as opposed to 9am–5pm; in summer offices often close as early as 3pm.

**Business Style:** There is a marked lack of bombast. Finns tend not to dress anything up, but rather present things as they are, warts and all. In other words, they are terribly honest, and do not go in much for exaggeration of any kind, whether it relates to a person or a business deal. Hence, their way of selling things might seem a bit subdued compared to other countries.

**Business Entertaining:** You are as likely to be invited on a ski outing or sailboat ride as on a night out on the town. These days, Finns tend not to drink at lunch, but after hours drinking is still de rigueur, and as people on business accounts are about the only ones who can afford long spells of drinking, if you get an invitation, enjoy it while you can.

**Business Etiquette:** It is ill-advised to be late for business meetings; Finns tend to be very punctual and courteous, though quite formal. Handshakes are used for meeting business as well as casual acquaintances; most people have business cards, and all have mobile phones, which they are delighted to use, so do not be put off by the fact that office hours seem short; there is almost always a mobile phone link to the person in question.

**Holidays:** Finally, try to avoid business in July and early August. The Finnish summer is short and sacred, and you'll find some offices nearly deserted of staff at these times. (Conversely, this is a good time for tourists, to whom hotels offer bargains to compensate for the lost business trade.) Other blackout periods are the spring skiing break in late February (Southern Finland) or early March (Northern Finland) plus two weeks at Christmas, and a week at Easter.

## Health

You'll have little to worry about healthwise in Finland. However, you may have an uncomfortable time if you coincide with the mosquito season, which descends on the northern and central parts of the country in July and into August. Enquire in Finland about the most effective mosquito repellents from chemists, who know their own brand of insect best.

If you need medical treatment in Finland, it is generally free, or dispensed at a nominal charge (a hospital visit will be charged at €22, or €26 if an overnight stay is required). Almost any Terveysasema

(health clinic) or Sairaala (hospital) will treat you; you can also schedule regular appointments at a Terveysasema (listed as such in telephone directories). The Emergency section is generally called Ensiapu.

Visitors needing hospital care in Helsinki should contact:

**Meilahti Hospital**, Haartmaninkatu 4, Helsinki, tel: 0 9-4711 (for surgery and medicine);

**Helsinki University Hospitals' Töölö Hospital**, Topeliuksenkatu 5, tel: 0 9-4711 (orthopaedic specialists). In other cities, consult hotels for hospital emergency numbers.

Pharmacies (Apteekki) charge for prescriptions, but not outrageously. There is usually at least one pharmacy open in larger towns on a late-night basis. In Helsinki, the Apteekki at Mannerheimintie 96 is open 24 hours; tel: 02032-0200 for around-the-clock on-call numbers.

## Emergency Numbers

**National emergency number:** 112
**Police:** 10022
**Helsinki house-call doctors:** 0400-414 350
**Emergency dental services:** 09-310 47450

## Tourist Information

Finland has over 50 main tourist information offices, marked with an "i" for information. Summer tourist offices spring up along harbours and lakes where need dictates.

All-Finland information is available from the **Finnish Tourist Board** (see box). In Helsinki, you can book hotels through the Hotel Booking Centre at Asema-aukio 3, 00100 Helsinki, tel: 0 9-2288 1400; fax: 0 9-2288 1499. A full listing of all tourist offices can be obtained at the Helsinki and Rovaniemi offices.

### Tourist Publications

Useful publications in Helsinki include Helsinki Happens, an English-language guide to cultural and tourist events, free from the tourist office and most hotels; City,

## Main Tourist Offices

**Finnish Tourist Board**
Eteläesplanadi 4, 00130 Helsinki, tel: 09-4176 9300, fax: 4176 9301; postal address: PO Box 249, 00130 Helsinki.
**Helsinki City Tourist Office**
Pohjoisesplanadi 19, 00100 Helsinki, tel: 09-169 3757; fax: 169 3839.
**Rovaniemi Tourist Information**
Koskikatu 7, 96200 Rovaniemi, tel: 016-346 270; fax: 347 351.
**Tampere City Tourist Office**
Verkatehtaankatu 2, FIN-33101 Tampere; tel: 03-3146 6800, fax: 3146 6463.
**Turku City Tourist Office**
Aurakatu 4, 20100 Turku, tel: 02-262 7444; fax 262 7500.

a weekly newspaper featuring a calendar of cultural events and restaurant listings; Helsinki This Week and brochures put out by the Tourist Board.

## Security & Crime

Vandalism is the only noticeable sign of crime in this safe country. Occasional pickpocketing is known on the Helsinki metro and at main railway stations; it appears that alcoholics, on the hunt for money for their next drinking bout, are often the perpetrators. Be on your guard in these places.

## Religious Services

The Lutheran Church is the state church of Finland, with over 90 percent of Finns counted as Lutherans. There is a small Greek Orthodox population, and just two Catholic churches in Finland.

In Helsinki, services in English are held at the Temppeliaukio church, the church in the rock on Lutherinkatu (see page 172); there are both Lutheran and ecumenical services here. There is also one synagogue and one mosque in Helsinki, for those of Jewish or Muslim faith.

# Getting Around

## On Arrival

Finland's main international airport, Helsinki-Vantaa, is connected by Finnair bus and local bus to Helsinki; fares are usually a little more on the Finnair bus. There is also a "shared" taxi stand at the airport, with a reasonable fare available to any destination in the centre of the city.

## Public Transport

### By Air

Finnair and Air Botnia both operate domestic flight services. Fares are relatively inexpensive; in July, fares are very cheap. It is a good idea to fly if, for example, you want to get to Lapland from the south without spending days on the road.

The Finnair Holiday Pass costs about €460 and is good for up to 10 flights in 30 days; it's not valid on "Blue Flights", usually the most popular business travel times. The pass is available to any foreign resident who flies to Finland, and can be obtained from Finnair and some travel agents in Britain and the US; check with the Finnish Tourist Board in your country nearest you. Finnair Holiday Youth Passes, to which roughly the same conditions apply, cost around €230.

Also available are discounts for groups, families and senior citizens.

### By Rail

The Finnish rail network is limited, but service is adequate in most cases and very good between major points like Turku and Helsinki. Finnrail passes are available for 3-day, 5-day, and 10-day periods; first-class passes are also available. In summer, a special *Loma-Lippu* (Holiday Ticket) is available for about €135 (7 travel days in a month) or about €67 (three travel days). One may start a "day" the previous day after 7pm, and continue during one "day" as far as the train goes if the departure time is before midnight.

For more information, contact:
**Finnish State Railways**
Vilhonkatu 13
PB 488, 00101 Helsinki
Tel: 0307-20 902
Fax: 0307-21 051.

### Water Transport

Ferries and passenger boats in Finland play a strong role where international destinations are concerned *(see page 180)* but there are some lakeland ferry routes worth pursuing. There are the **Silverline and Poet's Way**, which begin in Tampere and cover much of the western lakelands, tours in the **Päijänne** region and over Finland's largest lake, **Saimaa**, in eastern Finland. Many other operators run trips on the lakes; for more information, contact the central or regional tourist boards *(see page 304)*.

Helsinki's only real commuter island is Suomenlinna, with ferries travelling back and forth roughly every half-hour (schedule depends on season). Most of these ferries are part of the public transport network of Helsinki. Other Helsinki islands closer to the coast are connected by road.
**Silverline and Poet's Way**
Tel: 03-212 4804
**Lake Päijänne Cruises**
Tel: 014-263 447
**Roll Risteilyt**
Tel: 017-266 2466

### Bus and Coach

Finland is greatly dependent on buses for transporting the bulk of its passenger traffic. There are coach services on 90 percent of Finland's public roads (40,000 long-distance departures a day) which also cover the areas that trains don't, particularly in the north and in smaller places throughout the country. The head office for long-distance bus traffic is **Matkahuolto**, Lauttasaarentie 8, 00200 Helsinki, tel: 0 9-682701; fax: 692 2082.

There is no penalty for buying a ticket on the coach but you cannot

## Getting Around Helsinki

Walking around Helsinki city centre is recommended, but if you want to travel by public transport, trams are the most efficient way to get around. Buy a **Helsinki Card** at the Tourist Office on Pohjoisesplanadi (also available from hotels and R-kiosks) for one, two or three days; with this you get free entry to museums and free transport on buses, trams, metro and trains, as well as assorted discounts at restaurants and concerts.

The 3T tram doubles as a sightseeing route; it covers a figure-eight around most of Helsinki. Catch it in front of the railway station, for example, between 6am and 1.15am. On buses and trams, you cancel your ticket in the same way; machines are on vehicles.

Bus and tram routes are usually not shown at the stops, only end destinations, so try to get journey advice before you set out. Most run from 6am until midnight, but ask the Tourist Board about night buses in Helsinki and to Espoo and Vantaa.

Helsinki has a single metro line that runs east-west, serving local commuters in and out of town. It is fast and clean, but shuts down at 11.20pm so is not suitable for late-night travel. Services resume again at around 6am. Tickets, which are good for one hour including transfers to buses and trams, should be cancelled at the special machines at stations before the journey begins. Trains run at either 5- or 10-minute intervals.

get group discounts (for three adults or more on trips over 75 km/47 miles) from the coach ticketseller. Senior citizens and full-time students (university and lower) are also eligible for discounts, but must purchase, for €5, a coach card entitling them to this discount – at least 30 percent. Bring a photo and ID. Accompanied children under four travel free.

Visitors can reserve long-distance coach seats (for a small fee) by calling Matkahuolto or visiting the main bus station, situated at the corner of Mannerheimintie and Simonkatu in Helsinki.

## Driving

Finland's roads are not too plagued by traffic although they do get very busy between the capital and the countryside on Fridays and Sundays during the summer. There are few multi-lane motorways. Most are two-lane only.

Pay attention to road signs showing elk and reindeer zones. Collisions with these animals are usually serious. Use caution at all hours, but especially at dusk when elk are most active.

For winter driving, studded tyres should ideally be used from November to March and are strongly recommended throughout December at all times.

Foreign cars entering Finland should have a nationality sticker. In most cases, your own insurance with a green card will suffice in Finland, but check ahead to be sure. If you are driving a foreign car and are involved in an accident, contact the **Finnish Motor Insurers' Bureau**, tel: 09-680 401.

Don't risk driving while drunk in Finland. The limit is low (0.5 percent blood alcohol and about to be lowered to 0.2 percent) and the fines very steep; imprisonment is also possible in some cases. Taxis are available throughout the country, even in the backwaters; do as the Finns do and use them if you've been drinking.

### Rules of the Road

Drive on the right, overtake on the left. All cars must use their lights outside built-up areas. Elsewhere, lights must be used at dusk or at night or in bad weather (UK cars must sweep their lights right). Wearing of seat-belts is also compulsory.

Traffic coming from the right has right of way. Exceptions are on roads marked by a triangle sign; if this is facing you, you must give right of way; similarly if you are on a very major thoroughfare it is likely that the feed-in streets will have triangles, giving you the right of way. On roundabouts (rotaries), the first vehicle to reach the roundabout has right of way.

Speed limits are signposted, and range from 30 kmph (18 mph) in school zones to 100 kmph (62 mph) on motorways.

## Taxis

Finnish taxis run throughout the country, with fares starting at around €3. Helsinki city centre and the centres of other large cities, as well as most major airports, bus and railway stations, have taxi stands. Otherwise local telephone books list the number of the nearest dispatcher (under *Taksi* in the White Pages). Finding the closest one is worthwhile, especially in Helsinki, as taxis charge from embarkation point (plus an order fee). You can also hail a cab on the street, but this is a rarer way of getting a taxi in Finland than those mentioned above.

## Bicycles

Finland is a good cycling country with its well-engineered cycle paths and gently rolling landscape. The number of outfits renting cycles has grown. Two major hire points are the youth hostel at Helsinki's Olympic Stadium and Ro-No rentals on both harbours of Mariehamn *(see page 230)* in the Åland islands (a popular summer cycling destination).

The **Finnish Youth Hostel Association** also offers planned route tours at good-value prices (which can also include accommodation). Also ask the Finnish Tourist Board *(see page 304)* about other firms that run planned cycling tours in the country.
**Finnish Youth Hostel Association**, Yrjönkatu 38B 00100 Helsinki. Tel: 09-565 7150 Fax: 09-565 71510.

## Hitchhiking

Thumbing is still a time-honoured way to get a cheap ride in Finland, but you may have to wait a long time to get picked up, particularly at weekends and in the furthest reaches of Lapland where traffic can be pretty thin. Hitchhiking is prohibited on Finland's motorways; the smaller secondary routes are a better bet. As with any country in the world however, safety can never be guaranteed on the road, and this mode of transport is not recommended.

# Where to Stay

## Choosing a Hotel

You can pretty much depend on Finnish accommodation being clean and in good shape, but prices are high. There are bargains to be hunted out, however. Big discounts (up to 60 percent) are available at most hotels on weekends, and in summer when they lose their business and conference trade.

Budget accommodation includes youth and family hostels, farmhouses, *gasthaus* accommodation, family villages, camping, various forms of self-catering, and so on. During the summer holidays, some student residences become Summer Hotels, opening on 1 June. The local Tourist Boards and booking centres will provide up-to-date prices, including details of weekend and summer discounts.

General information is available from the **Finnish Tourist Board** in your home country, or the head office in Helsinki *(see page 304).*

Helsinki has its own hotel booking centre at the railway station: **Hotel Booking Centre**, Asemaaukio 3, tel: 09-2288 1400; fax 09-175 524. E-mail: hotel@helsinkiexpert.fi

## Chain Hotels

Finland has many large hotel chains of its own, as well as foreign chains. Big hotel chains, such as Sokos Hotels or Cumulus, offer fairly comfortable standard services in most big towns. Some chains, such as Radisson SAS, have emerged recently to offer perhaps even more comfortable services. Most of these hotels are very reliable in providing extremely clean rooms and (their own) chain restaurants with identical menus

countrywide. Some of the best known are:
**Best Western Finland**
Köydenpunojankatu 7, 00180 Helsinki.
Tel: 09-622 64900
**Restel Hotel Group**
Hämeentie 19, PO Box 72, 00501 Helsinki.
Tel: 09-73 352
**Sokos Hotels (sok)**
Fleminginkatu 34, PO Box 60, 00511 Helsinki.
Tel: 09-188 2800
Fax: 09-131 00222
**Summer Hotels**
Yrjönkatu 38, 00100 Helsinki.
Tel: 09-693 1347.

To get discounts, enrol in the Finncheque scheme, in which some 250 hotels participate. By spending around €34 on a Finncheque, you get a night's free accommodation in these hotels. The system is a co-operation between several chains; further details from the Tourist Office in Helsinki *(see page 304).*

## Price Guide

The following price categories indicate the cost of a double room in high season:
€€€: €226–€300
€€: €151–€225
€: €75–€150

## Hotel Listings

Hotels are listed in alphabetical order by region, with the most expensive first.

### HANKO

**Pensionat Garbo**
Raatimiehenkatu 8, 10900 Hanko.
Tel: 019-248 7897.
This charming little house is like a museum of Hollywood superstars – each themed room features a diva from the silver screen. An unusual choice, with just 10 rooms. €€
**Villa Maija**
Appelgrenintie 7, 10900 Hanko.
Tel: 019-248 2900.
This fine 19th-century villa is one of

many on this attractive street. Open all year. €€

### HELSINKI

#### Expensive
**Scandic Grand Marina**
Katajanokanlaituri 7, 00160 Helsinki.
Tel: 09-16661
Fax: 09-664 764.
Designed in 1911 by noted Finnish architect Lars Sonck, this hotel on the island of Katajanokka was once a warehouse. Each of the 462 rooms is exquisitely decorated and well-equipped, with specially designed accommodation for non-smokers, allergy sufferers and the disabled. Five restaurants, two conference halls and a heated garage. €€€
**Klaus Kurki**
Bulevardi 2–4, 00120 Helsinki.
Tel: 09-618911.
Located on a handsome street just a few steps away from the Esplanadi. Early 20th-century carved granite exterior. Cosy interior, recently decorated in Continental style. Bar, restaurant and terrace. €€€
**Scandic Hotel Kalastajatorppa**
Kalastajatorpantie 1, Helsinki.
Tel: 09-45811
Fax: 09-458 1668.
In a park about 7 km (4 miles) from the city centre bordered by the Gulf of Finland, this countryside resort hotel is spacious and ultra-modern, with 235 rooms, many with a sea view. Tennis courts, sauna, private beach and two indoor swimming pools. Business services. €€€

#### Moderate
**Hotel Anna**
Annankatu 1, Helsinki.
Tel: 09-616 621
Fax: 09-602-664.
This quiet, comfortable hotel has 60 rooms with all the amenities, in a quiet shopping quarter in the city centre. €€
**Radisson SAS Royal**
Runeberginkatu 2, 00100 Helsinki.
Tel: 09-69 580.
The Helsinki SAS has sunny, open

dining and bar areas and the usual good service. About a 10-minute walk from the centre, across from the bus station. €€

**Rivoli Hotel Jardin**
Kasarmikatu 40, Helsinki 00100.
Tel: 09-681 500
Fax: 09-656 988.
An intimate, charming hotel with 54 tastefully furnished rooms with all the amenities. City centre location. Breakfast buffet included. Sauna, open-air terrace. €€

**Sokos Hotel Torni**
Yrjönkatu 26, 00100 Helsinki.
Tel: 09-131 131.
Known as the tallest building in town at 13 storeys, Torni is a gracious hotel with an old and new section. The older section is in Art Deco style, and the rooms have original features. Try for rooms overlooking the courtyard. The "new" section, with bar-lookout tower, has functional decor outside; its interior has been renovated to a high standard of comfort. €€

## Price Guide

The following price categories indicate the cost of a double room in high season:
€€€: €226–€300
€€: €151–€225
€: €75–€150

### Inexpensive

**Academica**
Hietaniemenkatu 14, 00100 Helsinki.
Tel: 09-1311 4334
Fax: 09-441-201.
This is a basic summer hotel which is a student quarter during the university term. Small modern rooms have their own kitchen. Family rooms and extra beds also available. Residential but central location. €

**Eurohostel**
Linnankatu 9, 00160 Helsinki.
Tel: 09-622 0470
Fax: 09-655 044.
On Katajanokka Island by the ferry terminals, this no-frills hostel is convenient for those travelling by ship, and is just a 10-minute walk from the marketplace and city

centre. The 135 rooms (singles, twins and triples) have shared facilities including kitchen. Two laundrettes, sauna and café. €

**Stadium Hostel**
Olympic Stadium
Pohjoinen Stadiontie 3B.
Tel: 09-477 8480.
There are several other summer hostels, but this one is open all year. About 3 km (2 miles) north of the centre, with easy access by bus and tram. €

## IMATRA

**Scandic Hotel Imatran Valtionhotelli**
Torkkelinkatu 2, 55100 Imatra.
Tel: 05-68881.
This imposing Art Nouveau castle, next to the Imatrankoski hydro-electric power station (with daily waterfall shows in summer) is one of the most notable hotel buildings in Finland. The rooms in the main building are expensive but more attractive than the annexe. €€€

## JOENSUU

**Sokos Hotel Kimmel**
Itäranta 1, 80100 Joensuu.
Tel: 013-277 111.
The largest hotel in Joensuu, this edifice is opposite the railway station and perhaps the town's liveliest spot in the evenings. €€€

## JYVASKYLA

**Hotel Yöpuu**
Yliopistonkatu 23, 40100 Jyväskylä.
Tel: 014-333 900.
Although Jyväskylä has many large hotels, this 26-room hotel is one of the best choices, with an old-world ambience and a fine restaurant. €€€

## KOTKA

**Sokos Hotel Seurahuone**
Keskuskatu 21, 48100 Kotka.
Tel: 020-1234666.

This very central hotel has superb rooms and a fine restaurant. €€€

## KUOPIO

**Scandic Hotel Kuopio**
Satamakatu 1.
Tel: 017-195 111.
This large hotel on the waterfront is one of the finest in town. €€€

**Sokos Hotel Puijonsarvi**
Minna Canthinkatu 16.
Tel: 017-170 111.
This chain hotel features modern architecture and clean rooms. €€€

**Hotelli-Kylpylä Rauhalahti**
Katiskaniementie 8.
Tel: 017-473 473.
This fine spa hotel includes a hostel wing with clean apartments for budget travellers. A smoke sauna bath is open for visitors on Tuesdays and Fridays – reputedly the largest of its kind in southern Finland. A traditional dinner is also available on those evenings. €–€€

## LAPPEENRANTA

**Scandic Hotel Patria**
Kauppakatu 21
53100 Lappeenranta.
Tel: 05-677 511.
This modern hotel is situated close to the harbour and the fortress area. There are 130 rooms, and several restaurants and saunas. €€€

## OULU

**Kylpylähotelli Eden**
Nallikari, Oulu.
Tel: 08-884 2000.
This hotel offers spa facilities in the Nallikari beach area. €€€

## PUNKAHARJU

**Punkaharjun Valtionhotelli**
58450 Punkaharju 2.
Tel: 015-739 611.
This scenic region, not far from Savonlinna, offers an opportunity to stay in Finland's oldest hotel. It's a

wooden Russian-style villa with lots of atmosphere and 24 rooms. €€

## RAUMA

**Kalatorin Majatalo**
Kalatori 4
Tel: 02-837 86150.
A small pleasant hotel in a renovated Art Deco warehouse. There are just 20 rooms and a restaurant. €€

## ROVANIEMI

**Rantasipi Pohjanhovi**
Pohjanpuistikko 2
96200 Rovaniemi.
Tel: 016-33 711
Fax: 016-313 997
This legendary and luxurious hotel is known for its dance and concert evenings. Pleasantly located on the Kemijoki riverfront, with a swimming pool, nightclub, casino, and a range of travel services and outdoor activities. €€€

## SAVONLINNA

**Spa Hotel Casino**
PL 60, 57101 Savonlinna.
Tel: 015-739 50.
This large hotel complex has very clean rooms, a large spa section and some inexpensive hostel beds available in summer. The hotel is located on an island opposite the central railway halt, access via a wooden bridge. €€€
**Perhehotelli Hospitz**
Linnankatu 20, 57130 Savonlinna.
Tel: 015-515 661.
This cosy hotel has a superb location close to the Olavinlinna castle. It's an extremely well-run family hotel with a nice garden on the waterfront. Often fully booked in summer. €€

## TURKU

*Expensive*
**Scandic Marina Palace**
Linnankatu 32, 20100 Turku.
Tel: 02-336 300
Fax: 02-251-6750.

Situated by the Aura River in a picturesque location, near the museum quarter and harbour sights. Atrractive rooms and well furnished, with all amenities. Restaurants, bar and meeting rooms. €€€
**Ateljee Hotel**
Humalistonkatu 7
20100 Turku.
Tel: 02-233 6111
Fax: 02-233 6699.
The building was designed by Alvar Aalto (see page 80) and two of the rooms contain furniture by the master. There are 230 well-equipped rooms. Many artists have taken up permanent residence and display their works here; guests can visit them in their ateliers. €€
**Sokos City Börs**
Eerikinkatu 11 (across the market square), 20100 Turku.
Tel: 02-337 381
Fax: 02-231 1010.
A slightly cheaper but excellent alternative to Hamburger Bors. €€
**Sokos Hamburger Börs**
Kauppiaskatu 6
20100 Turku.
Tel: 02-337 381
Fax: 02-231 1010.
Centrally located on the Marketplace; excellent restaurants include French Fransmanni and German-style Hamburger Hof. €€
**Park Hotel**
Rauhankatu 1, 20100 Turku.
Tel: 02-273 2555
Fax: 02-251 9696.
This elegantly restored Jugenstil building (1902) was once a private mansion. Each of the well-furnished rooms is different; some have a park view. €€
**Scandic Hotel Julia**
Eerikinkatu 4, 20110 Turku.
Tel: 02-336 000
Fax: 02-336 02211.
Popular hotel centrally located near the market square. Acclaimed restaurant. Attentive service and comfortable rooms. €€
**Seaport Hotel Turku**
Matkustajasatama, 20100 Turku.
Tel: 02-283 3000
Fax: 02-283 3100.
One of the more imaginatively restored hotels in Finland, once a 19th-century warehouse. Its red-

brick facade is in original neo-Gothic style with beautiful wooden beams inside. Views of harbour or castle. Modern bathrooms. €

## TAMPERE

**Cumulus Koskikatu**
Koskikatu 5, 33100 Tampere.
Tel: 03-242 4111
Fax: 03-242 4399.
Built in 1979 and vibrantly modern throughout; the bar and dining facilities are excellent. €€
**Sokos Hotel Ilves**
Hatanpäänvaltatie 1
33100 Tampere.
Tel: 03-2626 262
Fax: 03-2626 263.
An 18-storey building with views over the harbour and Tammarkoski Rapids. Stylish with swimming pool, and saunas. €€
**Sokos Hotel Tammer**
Satakunnankatu 13
33100 Tampere.
Tel: 03-262 6265
Fax: 03-2626 266.
A tribute to Finnish Art Deco, set in a green, hilly part of the city. €€
**Victoria**
Itsenäisyydenkatu 1
33100 Tampere.
Tel: 03-242 5111.
Fax: 03-242 5100.
This simple, hostel-style hotel has clean, modern rooms and a lively bar and restaurant in the basement, the Tunneli. Group discounts. €

## Hostels

Finland has a widespread network of some 115 youth and family hostels, which vary from small farmhouses, to manors, camping and special centres. They usually have family rooms (2–4 visitors) or dormitories (5–10). Some 70 of these hostels are open year-round, the remainder in summer only. Details of hostels and the Finnish Youth Hostel cheque system are available from the **Finnish Youth Hostel Association**, Yrjönkatu 38B, 00100 Helsinki, tel: 09-656 7150; fax: 09-565 71510.
E-mail: info@srm.inet.fi

# Where to Eat

## What to Eat

Finnish cuisine has broadened and improved enormously in recent years, as more foods are imported and farming and greenhouse methods are refined. Those items once unheard of above 60° north latitude can now be seen in the markets, such as Finnish-grown cucumbers and red tomatoes.

You'll also find that there are some excellent Finnish cooks who, given the right mix of fresh produce and good meats and fish, can produce a superb meal. The wild game dishes are a real treat and are usually served with exquisite mushroom and berry sauces. In summer, you are strongly recommended to try Finnish crayfish, or ravut *(see page 120)*. However, if you eat only in cafeteria-style restaurants, you may get bored with the monotony of the offerings.

A lot of Finns eat a large hot lunch and then a smaller cold meal in the evening, although this is not to say that you can't have wonderful evening meals in Helsinki and other cities. International cuisines have crept in slowly over the years, and you'll now find Chinese, Italian, and French-style restaurants in almost all major towns. The best Russian cuisine outside of Russia is still found all over Helsinki.

## Choosing a Restaurant

It is difficult to find a really cheap meal in Finland, but you can find places where you will definitely get value for money – in other words, where portions are generous and quality is high. Fixed-price lunches are often very good deals and are usually advertised on signboards outside restaurants. Many places have English translated menus.

For on-the-run, really cheap eats, go to a *nakki* (sausage) kiosk. Hot dogs and sausages are the main fare, and you can usually get French fries and drinks as well. Other slightly more expensive quick meals can be had at any one of the ubiquitous hamburger chains like McDonalds, Hesburger or Carrols. Pizza is also popular in Finland.

Many of the hotels in the three main cities of Helsinki, Turku and Tampere, and elsewhere, have good restaurants, ranging from gourmet to wine bars and cafés, including restaurants that specialise in particular ethnic cuisines.

## Restaurant Listings

Restaurants are listed in alphabetical order by region, with the most expensive first.

## HELSINKI

### Expensive
**Havis Amanda**
Unioninkatu 23.
Tel 09-666 882.
This very fine seafood restaurant offers seasonal fish and seafood varieties, and seldom disappoints – even a connoisseur. €€€
**Kanavaranta**
Kanavaranta 3E & F.
Tel: 09-622 2633.
Reputedly Finland's leading chefs prepare genuine Finnish treats. Try the four-course Seasonal Menu with carefully selected wines for perhaps the finest culinary experience in Finland. €€€
**Torni**
Yrjönkatu 26
00100 Helsinki.
Tel: 09-131 131.
Hotel Torni's gourmet restaurant in this traditional hotel. Also try the Ateljee Bar on the 13th floor for light meals and drinks (outdoor seating in summer) offering the best view in Helsinki. €€€ (bar €)

**Walhalla**
Suomenlinna.
Tel: 09-668 552.
Open to the public in summer and the rest of the year by arrangement, the restaurant is set in the archways of the old fortress on historic Suomenlinna island *(see page 177)*. It offers some of the finest Finnish cuisine in the country. Try the snow grouse or reindeer specialities. €€€

### Moderate
**Kynsilaukka Garlic Restaurant**
Fredrikinkatu 22.
Tel: 09-651 939.
The chef brings fresh market produce and high imagination to the garlic-centred dishes served here. Comfortable and friendly; small and large portions. €€
**Lappi**
Annankatu 22.
Tel: 09-645 550.
An authentic Lapland experience is a bonus when sampling anything made of reindeer, tasty fish, salted fungi and exotic berries. Try the Lappish plate to savour a full range of northern specialities. €€
**Talon Tapaan A La Maison**
Salomonkatu 19.
Tel 09-685 6606.
An unpretentious restaurant with a genuine Finnish menu. Reservations are essential. Finnish Symphony is a costly *hors d'oeuvre* but worth it. €€

## KUOPIO

The small *muikku* (whitefish) is a must in Kuopio, although more famous is the *kalakukko* (loaf of rye bread crust filled with fish and pork) that can be found at the market.
**Musta Lammas**
Satamakatu 4.
Tel: 017-5810 458.
A pleasant restaurant, considered Kuopio's best. The dining hall is vaulted and quite pleasant. €€€
**Vapaasatama Sampo**
Kauppakatu 13.
Tel: 017-261 4677.
Kuopio's most famous restaurant,

formerly a "sailors' pub", this traditional restaurant serves excellent fish (*muikku* is the most popular meal) in what still seems to be a very informal pub. €€

**Wanha Satama**
Tel: 017-197 304
This rustic and lively pub-restaurant by the passenger harbour serves very tasty *muikku* fish with garlic and mashed potatoes. €€

## SAVONLINNA

The market is busy and popular in this opera town. Prices are a bit steep during the opera festival *(see page 92)*, but the market is also at its liveliest then.

**Majakka**
Satamakatu 1
Tel: 015-531 456.
A popular restaurant near the market serving good, fresh fish and meat. €€

**Sillansuu**
Verkkosaarenkatu 1.
Tel: 015-531 451.
This pub near the market bridge is considered to be one of the best in Finland. €€

## TAMPERE

**Astor**
Aleksis Kivenkatu 26.
Tel: 03-260 5700.
A popular spot for food and drink with live piano music every night and an even livelier crowd. Reindeer meat and a good variety of fish available. €€€

**Näsinneula**
Näsinneula, Särkänniemi.
Tel: 03-248 8234.
This is the revolving restaurant in the Näsinneula Observation Tower, where you dine 168 metres (635 ft) above the scenic landscape of Tampere. Fine Finnish cuisine is a speciality. €€€

**Eetvartti**
Sumeliuksenkatu 16.
Tel: 03-3155 5300.
This is the restaurant of the Pirkanmaa Hotel and Restaurant School. You can dine very well on

fare cooked by the students at low prices for high quality. €

**Plevna**
Itäinen katu 8.
Tel: 03-260 1200.
Lively pub/café and brewery, which specialises in steaks and grilled sausages. A variety of beers are brewed on the premises. €

**Salud**
Tuomiokirkonkatu 19.
Tel: 03-366 4460.
Salud is by nature a Spanish restaurant and Tampere's most popular place to wine and dine. €

## TURKU

Summer in Turku is not perfect without a proper session in one of the dozen boat restaurants on Aurajoki River. Most people stop for beer, but food is also on offer.

**Enkeliravintola**
Kauppiaskatu 16.
Tel 02-231 9088.
Decorated with angels in all shapes and sizes, this very fine restaurant serves good food in a unique atmosphere. €€€

**Pinella**
Porthaninpuisto.
Tel: 02-251 0001.
An archway-flanked building with a Victorian verandah greets you at this famous Turku restaurant. There are two dining areas, one featuring seafood and meat, the other Dutch fare. €€

**Samppalinna**
Itäinen Rantakatu.
Tel: 02-311 165.
Continental cuisine including roast mutton and a host of specialities such as salmon soup, all served in a splendid Victorian building. €€

## VAASA

**Gustav Wasa**
Raastuvankatu 24.
Tel: 06-326 9200.
This cellar restaurant serves excellent meat portions, and some fish. The pleasantly rustic dining hall was a coal-storing cellar until 1967. €€€

**Price Guide**

The following price categories indicate the cost of a meal for one, without drinks:
€€€:  over €37
€€:  €15–€37
€:  under €15

**Waild-Kanttarellis**
Kauppapuistikko 15.
Tel: 06-361 0000.
This restaurant, and its bar annexe Hullu Pullo, are both attractions in themselves with their incredible decor. The menu has many kinds of fish and meat €€

**Drinking Notes**

Alcohol is expensive in Finland due to high taxes, and beer and wine are no exceptions. The Finnish *tuoppi* is about 30 percent larger than the British pint; a *pieni tuoppi* is about two-thirds of that quantity. If you don't specify, you will be served a large, strong (number 4 = 4.5 percent alcohol) beer. You must say if you want the 3.5 percent beer, known as *keski-olut*, or medium beer. Number 1 beer is the weakest *(ykkös-olut)*, at just over 1 percent alcohol.

Wine in Finland is imported and very costly in restaurants, but there is more choice in Alko (the state alcohol monopoly) these days. The range of prices begins with Eastern European wines (about €7 a bottle) and goes up precipitously.

Spirits and wine can be bought only from Alko (Stockmann's department store in Helsinki has an Alko unit on the ground floor). Medium and lower alcohol beer can be bought in supermarkets. Most restaurants serve alcohol as long as they serve food. A restaurant marked *B-oikeudet* is licensed only to serve beer and wine. Most bars and taverns are open until at least midnight in Helsinki; some stay open until 3 or 4am.

# Culture

## Museums

Finland is a country of small museums. The grandest in scale is the Ateneum in Helsinki, which could fit neatly into London's National Gallery at least three times. Art dominates the museum scene, with the greatest variety of venues in Helsinki. In total, there is probably more contemporary art to be seen than older art.

Admission prices are generally steep, but Helsinki sells the Helsinki Card, *(see box, page 305)* which includes free entrance to many museums on presentation. Turku recently introduced a similar card.

Museum opening hours are almost always reduced in winter. Most museums close on Monday.

## Classical Music & Opera

Most larger cities have a steady itinerary of concerts throughout the year, but music festivals abound in Finland in summer, and many of these are held in stunning settings *(see page 92)*. The most famous of these are held in July: the Savonlinna Opera Festival at Olavinlinna Castle in eastern Finland, the Kuhmo Chamber Music Festival, also in eastern Finland and the Kaustinen Folk Festival in western Finland. The festivals feature Finnish and international performers.

Finnish opera has a great following, and much of it features Finnish composers and performers.

### Helsinki Events

In late summer are the Helsinki *Juhlaviikot* (festival weeks) featuring broad-ranging programmes with artists from Finland and abroad, set at different venues around the city. Information from:
**Helsinki Festival Office,**
Rauhankatu 7E,
00170 Helsinki
Tel: 09-135 4522.

Also, try the weekday evening series of concerts at the unique Temppeliaukio (Church-in-the-rock) in Töölö, Helsinki *(see page 172)*.

During the rest of the year, main events are at Finlandia Concert Hall, many by the Radio Symphony Orchestra and the Helsinki Philharmonic Orchestra. The national opera (and ballet) company's hall in Helsinki opened in 1992 *(see page 171)*.

### Turku Events

Turku is a lively musical city, with concerts given by the Turku City Orchestra, a series of concerts in the Sibelius Museum, and others in the cathedral and the castle. The Turku Musical Festival is one of the oldest in Finland and ranges from medieval music to first performances. Held in mid-August, it attracts visiting composers and international musicians.

Further information is available from the **Foundation for the Turku Music Festivals**, Uudenmaankatu 1, 20500 Turku, tel: 02-2511 162.

### Tampere Events

Tampere has always had its share of music. Since 1975 the city has held an international choir festival each year and the Tampere Biennale, started in 1986, is a festival of new Finnish music, arranged in cooperation with the Association of Finnish Composers. For information contact:
**Tampere Biennial,**
Tullikamarinaukio 2
33100 Tampere
Tel: 03-314 66136.
Since the opening of the Tampere Hall, interest has soared. The auditorium is one of the great concert halls of the world and the acoustics are acknowledged to be far better than those of Helsinki's Finlandia Hall. The small auditorium is used for chamber music, and the

## Jazz and Rock

In Tampere there is an annual jazz festival called Jazz Happening. For information on dates and concerts, contact **Tampere Jazz Happening,** Tullikamarinaukio 2, 33100 Tampere, tel: 03-314 66136.

There is also Ruisrock on the island of Ruissalo, Finland's oldest and highly popular rock festival *(see page 92)*.

Hall is also a conference venue. Tampere holds numerous concerts in its cathedral, churches and halls.

## Theatre

### Helsinki

The Finnish National Theatre and Svenska Teatern in Helsinki both enjoy long traditions of performance in, respectively, Finnish and Swedish. Unfortunately, there is no foreign-language theatre to speak of, but you may be interested in touring the theatre buildings themselves, or even going to a play you know well enough to overcome the language barrier.

The listings guides in Helsinki will list theatre events *(see page 304)*. Equivalent guides in Turku and Tampere also carry listings.

### Turku

Plays performed are of a high standard but rarely in languages other than Finnish or Swedish. In winter, there is the Turku City Theatre on the bank of the River Aura and the Swedish Theatre on the corner of the Marketplace – the oldest theatre in Finland still in use.

### Tampere

Tampere rivals Helsinki for year-round theatrical events but, again, the difficulty is language. One exception is the Pyynikki Outdoor Summer Theatre *(see page 219)* where you can see plays from mid-June to mid-August, with synopses in English. This is particularly worthwhile if you want to enjoy the setting at the edge of the Lake

Pyhäjärvi. Booking is necessary, tel: 03-216 0300.

The Tampere Theatre Festival in August includes many international companies who produce plays in their own languages.

Further information is available from **Tampere International Theatre Festival**, Tullikamarinaukio 2, 33100, Tampere, tel: 03-2228 536.

## Cinema

Finns do not dub their films, and you can enjoy as good a selection of movies here as in any other European city of moderate size. **Nordia** (Yrjönkatu 36, tel: 09-1311 9550) in Helsinki shows a mix of commercial successes and slightly artier films, while the **Suomen Elokuva-arkisto** at the Orion Film Archive (Eerikinkatu 15–17, tel: 09-615 400) has endless stocks of older films, both Finnish and foreign. **Andorra** (Eerikinkatu 11, tel: 09-612 3117) is owned by the Kaurismäki director brothers of such films as *Drifting Clouds* (see page 90).

Film showings are usually at 6pm and 8.30pm. The kiosk outside the east entrance to Helsinki railway station has comprehensive listings, as do the newspapers; listings are also available at the Tourist Board. Seats are reserved at the time you buy the tickets, and box offices usually open 30–45 minutes before show time but at some cinemas may be purchased even earlier.

Tampere has a cinema centre, **Finnkino Plevna**, in the Finlayson area (Itäinen katu 4). In Turku most cinemas are found in the Hansa Shopping Centre *(see page 207).*

# Nightlife

## Pubs, Bars and Clubs

Nightlife can be a difficult thing to get the hang of in Finland. In Helsinki, you will see hordes of revellers bar-crawling their way across town into the early hours; most are old acquaintances just getting drunk together. There are several clubs which attract the best music acts, for example the university-owned Tavastia. Occasionally a good jazz or rock act will make it to Helsinki but the city is certainly not on the itinerary of most major performers.

The official drinking age is 18 and over but some clubs may have a minimum age limit of 21. Entrance fees can be anything from free to outrageous. Nightclubs can be expensive and good dance floors are hard to find. More easily found is the casual camaraderie of the few places that attract a sprinkling of foreigners, such as the pubs O'Malley's and Vanha.

A few of the better bars and night spots in Finland's three main cities, Helsinki, Tampere and Turku, are listed as follows:

### HELSINKI

**Highlight Café**
Frederikinkatu 42.
A sports theme pub with American-style food set in this beautifully restored former church. It is owned by Jari Kurri, a former NHL ice hockey champion.
**Corona Bar**
Eerinkatu 11.
Tel: 09-642002.
This popular spot attracts a young hip crowd who come to talk, drink beer and play pool.

**Kuu**
Töölönkatu 27.
Tel: 09-2709 0973.
An intimate, older, small bar with local jazz groups now and again. Excellent Finnish cuisine.
**O'Malleys**
Yrjönkatu 28.
Tel: 09-131 131.
Irish, mellow, small and usually crowded tavern. Some live music.
**Storyville**
Museokatu 8.
Tel: 09-408 007.
Jazz club featuring local and international musicians. A cosy spot to have a late drink. Cover charge.
**Tavastia**
Urho Kekkosenkatu 4.
Tel: 09-694 8511.
This university-owned club attracts some of Helsinki's best live music. Rocking atmosphere; downstairs is a usually packed self-service bar, waiter service upstairs.
**Vanhan Kellari**
Vanha Yliopisto
Mannerheimintie 3.
Tel: 09-684 4900.
University students' union-owned, Vanhan, which is set in a neo-classical building, flows with the traffic of devoted beer-drinkers the year round. Occasional live music.
**Zetor**
Kaivopiha.
Tel: 09-666 966.
This "tractor-style" rock 'n' roll disco has to be seen to be believed. Experience the surrealism of the Finnish countryside.

### TAMPERE

Tampere's nightlife is very evident on the town's main street, Hämeenkatu. Bar-hopping is very easy, although more "traditional" pubs are elsewhere. Try:
**Salhojankadun Pub**
Salhojankatu
**Ohranjyvä**
Näsilinnankatu 15.
**Plevna**
(Itäinen katu 8) and Vanha Posti (Hämeenkatu 13A).
Serves good locally brewed beer.

## TURKU

**Panimoravintola Koulu**
Eerikinkatu 18.
Tel: 02-274 5757.
Just next to the market square, this old former school building has a brewery and many former classrooms refurbished as pubs or restaurants.
**Puutorin Vessa**
Puutori.
Tel 02-233 8123.
This unusual pub was once a public toilet. After a very, very thorough cleaning, it is now the funniest theme pub in town.
**Old Bank**
Aurakatu 3.
Tel: 02-274 5700.
Once a very fine bank, this pub serves more beer varieties than any other pub in town.
**Uusi Apteekki**
Kaskenkatu 1.
Tel: 02-250 2595.
Literally "new pharmacy", this pub is set in an old chemist shop and sells over 20 different beers.

# Children

## Attractions

Just a 15-minute train ride from downtown Helsinki is an ideal spot for engaging children and grown-ups: **Heureka**, the Finnish Science Centre in Vantaa-Tikkurila, has a range of permanent and temporary "hands-on" exhibitions, a planetarium and an IMAX theatre fAssesible to disabled visitors. Tel: 09-85799.

Further from Helsinki, the main amusement park in southern Finland is **Lystiland Children's Fun Park**, just north of Karjaa town centre. It features a miniature train tour on an enchanted forest trail.

In Naantali, **Moomin World (Muumimaailma)** is open from June to August (entrance fee). It is a theme park with characters from Tove Jansson's books – as you would expect – very much in evidence.

There are several good spots in the Lakeland region for travellers with children. At **Messilä Vacation Centre** in Hollola near Lahti, there are all manner of supervised activities for children, including horse- and pony-riding. In winter, there are skiing activities (Alpine and Nordic) for children and adults.

A bit north from Hollola, towards Hartola, is the fascinating little **Musta and Valkea Ratsu Dollhouse and Puppet Theatre** on road 52 (signposted), 19230 Onkiniemi, tel: 03 718-6959.

In Outokumpu, north of Savonlinna, is **The Land of the Mountain Troll**, an amusement park and mineral and mining exhibition, and Mikkeli has the **Visulahti**

**Tourist Centre** (tel: 015-18281), including a dinosaur theme amusement park and waxworks. A little further from Mikkeli is an arboretum which includes a small menagerie. Contact **Mikkeli Tourism**, tel: 015-194 3900.

Rovaniemi, near the Arctic Circle is where you will find **Santa Claus' Village** (see page 139). Rumour has it that Father Christmas stays here when he is visiting from his secret hideaway in Korvatunturi-fell. There is a post office as well as a shopping centre which stocks gifts from Lapland. Take the Santa Claus Express train at Rovaniemi and get off at Napapiirii (a 10-km/6-mile journey). Open daily year round.

When in the **Åland Islands**, you might want to check out the amusement park by the west harbour, the *Pommern* ship museum (at the west harbour), and Lilla Holmen bird park on the east harbour. Here you will see peacocks, ducks, and beautiful angora rabbits.

# Shopping

## What to Buy

### Finnish Design

If people know anything at all about Finnish design, they usually think of the smooth contemporary lines associated with Finnish architecture imposed on jewellery, woodwork, clothing, glassware and sculpture. To see the best of the design, you might want to go first to the Applied Arts Museum in Helsinki.

Lapponia Aarikka and Kaleva Koru jewellery are expressly Finnish, the first being a mainly contemporary collection and the second a collection based on designs from the Finnish epic poem *Kalevala*, rendered in silver, gold, and also in more affordable brass.

Aarikka also puts out some of the finer woodwork products, including chopping boards, Christmas decorations, toys and wooden jewellery.

The most impressive ceramic work is commissioned by Arabia, one of the older Finnish firms. Their factory (about 20 minutes' tram ride from downtown Helsinki) has a small museum upstairs, and first- and second-quality goods on sale downstairs.

Pentik is known for its ceramics as well as beautifully crafted leather clothing.

Iittala *(see page 221)* makes beautiful glassware at their factory, from drinking glasses to candle holders.

Marimekko is the quintessential Finnish clothing designer, with items made of brightly coloured fabrics for men, women and children, as well as textiles for home use.

All these companies can be found both in their own stores and in department stores in most Finnish towns of any size, including Pohjoisesplanadi in Helsinki.

## Shopping Areas

### Helsinki

Apart from mainstream department stores and boutique shopping in Helsinki, there are several market squares that sell both fresh food and a range of other consumer goods of greatly varying quality, from second-hand clothes and records to designer jewellery, Lapp mittens, and fur hats.

**Kauppatori** is the main Helsinki market, followed by Hietalahdentori and Hakaniementori, all near the centre. Note that markets have extended hours in summer and are open until about 8pm, but close briefly from about 2pm.

Otherwise, the **Esplanade** is the hub of shopping delights in Helsinki. You'll find relatively few foreign retail outlets in Finland, but in recent years a few have managed to establish themselves, such as Hennes & Mauritz (H&M), Ikea, Body Shop and Benetton.

### Tampere

Tampere has most of the medium-sized department stores found in Helsinki and Turku. This area also has a host of interesting smaller boutiques.

A good collection is at **Kehräsaari Boutique Centre**, Laukontori 1, Keräsaari, in a converted textile mill. Visit also the **Verkaranta Arts and Crafts Centre** at Verkatehtaankatu 2, for a good selection of handicrafts and toys. T

The main Tampere Market Hall is at Hämeenkatu 19, open Monday to Saturday.

### Turku

Turku has its own Stockmann's at **Yliopistonkatu** 22. Also on Yliopistonkatu are **Pentik** (No. 25), famous for ceramics, and (No. 27B) **Aarikka**, for handmade wooden crafts and decorations.

For more crafts, look into **Sylvi Salonen**, specialising in linens and decorative objects at Yliopistonkatu 29, or **Neoviska**,

For handmade *ryijy* (rya) rugs and other textiles head for **Juhana Herttuan** at Puisto 10

Check locally for market days at the lovely main market (the market opens in summer from 4–8pm). The **Hansa Shopping Centre** is also in Turku *(see page 207).*

## Department Stores

The king of department stores in Finland is Stockmann's; it is the place Finns go to when they want to hunt down some elusive item, or some exotic gift. To the outsider it will probably seem merely a large, pleasant place to shop, but to Finns it is something of an institution; branches are also in Tampere, Turku and Tapiola (Espoo). Stockmann's also owns the Akateeminen Kirjakauppa, Finland's best-known bookstore. Another good department store to look out for throughout Finland is Sokos, with its fine food hall.

# Sport

## Participant Sports

Finland is known as a sporting nation, a reputation which it lives up to in every Olympic Games by producing a high number of medal winners at both summer and winter games. The devotion to training is constant; it is not unusual on a hot summer's day to see squadrons of muscular youths out on roller-skis to make sure they do not lose their touch for the coming winter.

### Cycling

Bicycling is big in Finland. The countryside is ideal for cyclists, dead flat on the west coast leading to gently rolling hill areas; for suggested cycle routes, contact: **Finnish Youth Hostel Association**, Yrjönkatu 38B 00100 Helsinki Tel: 09-656 7150 Fax: 09-656 71510.

### Sailing

Boating exists in all forms, and most harbours have guest marinas where one can dock for reasonable overnight fees. Canoeing is also popular in the Lakelands region.

### Other Sports

For information on any sport in Finland, please contact **Suomen Urheilu ja Liikunta (Finnish Sports Federation)**, Radiokatu 20 00240 Helsinki (Ilmala) Tel: 09-348 121 Fax: 09-348 12602.

## Spectator Sports

There is a near endless list of spectator sports in Finland, but a shortlist of the most popular must include ski-jumping, regatta sailing and hockey.

### Summer

One of the biggest sailing events of the year is the Hanko Regatta, which takes place in early July off Finland's south coast. Kotka also sponsors a yearly Tall Ships event.

The biggest inland sailing regatta is on Lake Päijänne, also in July. Details are available from the **Finnish Yachting Association**, Radiokatu 20, 00093 Helsinki Tel: 020-733 8881 Fax: 020-733 8888.

Before mid-June is the **Finlandia Canoeing Relay**, held in the large Lakeland region – the venue changes annually. It lasts five days and covers over 545 km (350 miles), with day and night action.

### Winter

**Lahti**, about 105 km (65 miles) north of Helsinki, is the best place to watch ski-jumping.

For winter spectator sports, the **Finlandia Ski Race** in mid-February is one of the top events. This 75-km (47-mile) event attracts the best Finnish skiers and ample spectator opportunities.

For information, contact: **Finlandia Ski Race Office** Urheilukeskus 15110 Lahti Tel: 03-816 813 Fax: 03-751 2079.

As is the case with participant sports, all general sport queries can be directed to the Suomen Urheilu ja Liikunta (Finnish Sports Federation).

## Skiing in Finland

Finns are particularly famous as cross-country runners and skiers, as well as ski jumpers. You'll find facilities for any of these sports excellent; in most major urban areas there are maps of the non-auto paths set aside for such pastimes. Ask for the *Ulkoilukartta* (outdoor map) from tourist boards.

One can ski cross-country anywhere in Finland, but Lapland is a favourite spot for this very Nordic sport, as well as for downhill skiing (try to avoid school holiday weeks). Unlike Norway and even Sweden, Finland has very little in the way of mountains, except in the far north, where the Lappish hills, the highest over 1,400 metres (4,000 ft), are called *tunturi*.

There are many participant cross-country ski events as well; information is available from **Suomen Latu (Finnish Ski Trek Association)**, Fabianinkatu 7, 00130 Helsinki, tel: 09-4159 1100; fax: 09-663 376.

# Language

## Getting By

**Good morning** *Hyvää huomenta*
**Good day** *Hyvää päivää*
**Good evening** *Hyvää iltaa*
**Today** *Tänään*
**Tomorrow** *Huomenna*
**Yesterday** *Eilen*
**Hello** *Päivää or terve*
**How do you do?** *Kuinka voit*
**Goodbye** *Näkemiin or hei hei*
**Yes** *Kyllä or joo*
**No** *Ei*
**Thank you** *Kiitos*
**How much does this cost?**
*Paljonko tämä maksaa?*
**It costs...** *Se maksaa...*
**How do I get to..?** *Miten pääsen..?*
**Where is...?** *Missä on...?*
**Right** *Oikealla*
**To the right** *Oikealle*
**Left** *Vasemmalla*
**To the left** *Vasemmalle*
**Straight on** *Suoraan*
**What time is it?** *Paljonko kello on?*
**It is (the time is)** *Kello on*
**Could I have your name?** *Saisinko nimesi?*
**My name is...** *Nimeni on...*
**Do you speak English?** *Puhutko englantia?*
**I only speak English** *Puhun vain englantia*
**Can I help you?** *Voinko auttaa sinua?*
**I do not understand** *En ymmärrä*
**I do not know** *En tiedä*

## Eating Out

**Breakfast** *Aamiainen*
**Lunch** *Lounas*
**Dinner** *Illallinen*
**To eat** *Syödä*
**To drink** *Juoda*
**I would like to order...** *Haluaisin tilata*

**Could I have the bill?** *Saisko laskun?*
**Could I have the key?** *Saisko avaimen?*
**Toilet** *Vessa*
**Gentlemen** *Miehet (Swedish: Herrar)*
**Ladies** *Naiset (Swedish: Damer)*
**Vacant** *Vapaa*
**Engaged** *Varattu*
**Entrance** *Sisäänkäynti*
**Exit** *Uloskäaynti*
**No entry** *Pääsy kielletty*
**Open** *Avoinna, Auki*
**Closed** *Suljettu, Kiinni*
**Push** *Työnnä*
**Pull** *Vedä*

## Shopping

**Clothes** *Vaatteet*
**Overcoat** *Päällystakki*
**Jacket** *Takki*
**Suit** *Puku*
**Shoes** *Kengät*
**Skirt** *Hame*
**Blouse** *Pusero*
**Jersey** *Puuvilla or villapusero*
**Handicraft** *Käsityö*
**Grocers** *Ruoka kauppa*
**Shop** *Kauppa*
**Food** *Ruoka*
**To buy** *Ostaa*
**Off licence** *Alko*
**Launderette** *Pesula*
**Dry cleaning** *Kemiallinen pesu*
**Dirty** *Likainen*
**Clean** *Puhdas*
**Stain** *Tahra*
**Money** *Raha*

## Days of the Week

**Monday** *Maanantai*
**Tuesday** *Tiistai*
**Wednesday** *Keskiviikko*
**Thursday** *Torstai*
**Friday** *Perjantai*
**Saturday** *Launantai*
**Sunday** *Sunnuntai*

## Numbers

| | |
|---|---|
| 1 | *yksi* |
| 2 | *kaksi* |
| 3 | *kolme* |
| 4 | *neljä* |
| 5 | *viisi* |
| 6 | *kuusi* |

## Useful Words

**Chemist** *Apteekki*
**Hospital** *Sairaala*
**Doctor** *Lääkäri*
**Police station** *Poliisilaitos*
**Parking** *Paikoitus*
**Phrase book** *Turistien sanakirja*
**Dictionary** *Sanakirja*
**Car** *Auto*
**Bus, Coach** *Bussi, Linja-auto*
**Train** *Juna*
**Aircraft** *Lentokone*
**Cheers** *Kippis, (Swedish: skål)*
**To rent** *Vuokrata*
**For sale** *Myytävänä*
**Free, no charge** *Ilmainen*
**Room to rent** *Vuokrattavana huone*

| | |
|---|---|
| 7 | *seitsemän* |
| 8 | *kahdeksan* |
| 9 | *yhdeksän* |
| 10 | *kymmenen* |
| 11 | *yksitoista* |
| 12 | *kaksitoista* |
| 13 | *kolmetoista* |
| 14 | *neljätoista* |
| 15 | *viisitoista* |
| 16 | *kuusitoista* |
| 17 | *seitsemäntoista* |
| 18 | *kahdeksantoista* |
| 19 | *yhdeksäntoista* |
| 20 | *kaksikymmentä* |
| 30 | *kolmekymmentä* |
| 40 | *neljäkymmentä* |
| 50 | *viisikymmentä* |
| 60 | *kuusikymmentä* |
| 70 | *seitsemän-kymmentä* |
| 80 | *kahdeksan-kymmentä* |
| 90 | *yhdeksänkym-mentä* |
| 100 | *sata* |
| 200 | *kaksisataa* |
| 1,000 | *tuhat* |

# Further Reading

## General Interest

**A Guide to Finnish Architecture** by Kaipia & Putkonen (Otava). A fascinating town-by-town guide to individual buildings, with plenty of photos and illustrations.

**Facts about Finland** (Otava). The most comprehensive coverage of Finland's history and culture, by a range of Finnish authors.

**Finnish Sauna, Design, Construction and Maintenance** (the Finnish Building Centre). Among the many books on Finnish sauna, this one is the most practical, and is popular among home builders.

**Food from Finland** by Anna-Maija and Juha Tanttu (Otava). An excellent guide to Finnish food, including recipes and colourful features on raw ingredients, such as berries and fungi.

**Finland – Nature's Table** (Crea Video Oy). Another excellent cookbook that covers not only raw ingredients but a very colourful image of Finland's nature.

**Helsinki Jugendstil Art Nouveau Promenades** by Henry Moorhouse (Taide Publishing). This handy little guide is a good introduction to Helsinki's finest buildings, with illustrations and street maps.

**A Short History of Finland** by Singleton & Upton (Cambridge University Press). As the name suggests, this book covers Finland's history in brief, and is perhaps the best-written account of the past two millennia.

**The Year of the Hare** by Arto Paasilinna (Peter Owen, 1996). A good example of a contemporary Finnish humorous novel.

**The Egyptian** by Mika Waltari (Buccaneer Books). The novel that made Finnish writer Waltari's name – a great epic of Sinuhe, the Egyptian.

## Other Insight Guides

Other Insight Guides which highlight destinations in this region include Denmark, Russia, Norway and Sweden.

**Insight Guide: Norway** takes readers on a compelling journey through the Land of the Midnight Sun, from the fjords and mountains to the forests and lakes.

Sweden is one of Europe's last green lungs. Apa Publications assembled expert writers and talented photographers to produce **Insight Guide: Sweden**, which tells you what is and what is not worth seeing from vibrant cities of Stockholm and Gothenburg to distant, snowy Lapland, home of the Sami.

## Feedback

We do our best to ensure the information in our books is as accurate and up-to-date as possible. The books are updated on a regular basis, using local contacts, who painstakingly add, amend and correct as required. However, some mistakes and omissions are inevitable and we are ultimately reliant on our readers to put us in the picture.

We would welcome your feedback on any details related to your experiences using the book "on the road". Maybe we recommended a hotel that you liked (or another that you didn't), as well as interesting new attractions, or facts and figures you have found out about the country itself. The more details you can give us (particularly with regard to addresses, e-mails and telephone numbers), the better.

We will acknowledge all contributions, and we'll offer an Insight Guide to the best letters received.

Please write to us at:
**Insight Guides
PO Box 7910
London SE1 1WE
United Kingdom**
Or send e-mail to:
**insight@apaguide.co.uk**

# ART & PHOTO CREDITS

Marja Airio/Rex Features 61
AKG-Images London 18
Aland Tourist Board 101, 231
Delany Brendan/FTB 59L, 59R
Marcus Brooke 256
Central Art Archive/Hannu
Aaltonen 74/75
Fritz Dressler back flap bottom,
161, 226/227
Jämsä Esuo/FTB 242
Finnish Tourist Board (FTB) 135,
187, 239
Robert Fried back cover left, back
flap top, 23, 99, 175T, 176, 206T,
208T, 213T, 215T, 217T, 218,
221T, 222, 223, 223T, 233T, 267,
287T, 293T
Sari Gustafsson/Rex Features 87
Blaine Harrington 175
Mary Ann Hemphill 140/141,
160T, 162T, 165T, 198, 210, 231T
Esa Hiltula 114
Jim Holmes spine, all back cover
pictures except back left, 2B, 4B,
4/5, 5BL, 5BR, 14, 28, 76, 91, 97,
120, 121, 123, 131, 133, 137L,
137R, 153, 155, 157, 169T, 171T,
173T, 179, 182/183, 187T, 192,
199T, 208, 217, 232, 233, 239T,
240, 241T, 252, 255T, 257T, 258T,
260T, 266T, 273T, 275T, 278, 296
Michael Jenner 71, 84/85, 155T,
157T, 261L, 261R, 262T
Layne Kennedy 142/143, 146,
178, 197T, 244T, 247
Matti Kolho/Kuvasuomi 1, 56, 70,
72, 119, 132, 241, 244, 246, 253,
258, 264, 268/269, 280, 281

Kainulainen/Rex Features 63
Lyle Lawson front flap bottom, 6/7,
8/9, 12/13, 20, 24, 25, 26, 27,
29, 32, 33, 35, 43, 46, 48, 49,
52, 53, 54, 62, 64/65, 66/67,
68, 69, 79, 80, 81, 95, 106, 107,
109, 116/117, 124/125, 126,
128, 130, 134, 144/145, 152,
156, 158, 159, 160, 163, 164,
165, 168, 169, 170, 171L, 171R,
172L, 172R, 173, 184, 185, 188,
189, 193, 196, 197, 202, 203,
205, 207, 211L, 211R, 212, 213,
215, 216, 219, 220, 221, 224,
225, 234/235, 236, 237, 239,
243, 248/249, 255, 259, 260,
262, 263, 265, 266, 271, 273,
284, 285, 288, 290, 291
Tony Marshall/Empics 115
Ville Myllynen/Rex Features 102
National Board of Antiquities
16/17, 30/31, 36, 100
National Museum of Architecture
34
National Museum of Finland 22,
77, 94
Nurmes Tourist Board 287
Anita Peltonen 228
Rex Features 19, 57, 60, 73, 78,
82, 83, 86, 87, 88, 89, 96, 103,
112, 118, 127, 129, 136, 174,
181, 186, 247T, 289T, 291T
Robert Harding Picture Library
2/3, 10/11, 122, 150/151, 177,
200/201, 279, 282/283, 293
Screen International 90
TM Foto 111
Topham Picturepoint 21, 37, 38,

39, 40/41, 42, 44, 45, 47, 50/51,
55, 58, 98, 104/105, 108, 110,
113, 199, 245, 270, 274, 275,
276, 277, 289, 292
Turku Tourist Board 209
Williams Paul/FTB 162

## Picture Spreads

**Pages 92/93**
*Top row from left to right:* Rex
Features, Rex Features, Matti
Kolho/Lebrecht Collection, Topham
Picturepoint. *Centre row:* all Rex
Features. *Bottom row left to right:*
Michael Jenner, Rex Features,
Michael Jenner.
**Pages 138/139**
*Top row from left to right:* Topham
Picturepoint, Robert Harding Picture
Library, Rex Features, Esa Hiltula.
Centre row: Rex Features. *Bottom
row left to right:* Robert Fried, Rex
Features, Robert Fried.
**Pages 190/191**
All photography by: Layne Kennedy
except for *top left:* Esa Hiltula and
*top centre right:* Robert Harding
Picture Library
**Pages 250/251**
All Photography by: Layne Kennedy
except for *top centre left:* Esa
Hiltula and *top centre right:* Robert
Harding Picture Library.

**Map Production:** Geodata
© 2003 Apa Publications GmbH & Co.
Verlag KG (Singapore branch)

INSIGHT GUIDE
FINLAND

*Cartographic Editor* **Zoë Goodwin**
*Design Consultants*
**Carlotta Junger, Graham Mitchener**
*Picture Research* **Hilary Genin,
Britta Jaschinski**

# Index

*Numbers in italics refer to photographs*

# Insight Guides Website
## *www.insightguides.com*

Insight Guides Website

Insight Guide
**South Africa**

This 370-page book includes a section detailing South Africa's history, 22 features covering aspects of the country's life and culture, ranging from living without Apartheid to spectacular wildlife, a region by region visitor's guide to the sights, and a comprehensive Travel Tips section packed with essential contact addresses and numbers. Plus many quality photographs and 15 maps.

UK:  £16.99  ISBN:  981-234-223-0
US:  $22.95  ISBN:  0-88729-445-6

(Note: cover shown may differ in some markets.)

Close Window

*Don't travel the planet alone. Keep in step with Insight Guides' walking eye, just a click away*

# INSIGHT GUIDES
*The world's largest collection of visual travel guides*

# INSIGHT GUIDES

## The classic series that puts you in the picture

| | | | |
|---|---|---|---|
| **A**laska | Dominican Rep. & Haiti | London | Rio de Janeiro |
| Amazon Wildlife | Dublin | Los Angeles | Rome |
| American Southwest | **E**ast African Wildlife | **M**adeira | Russia |
| Amsterdam | Eastern Europe | Madrid | **S**t Petersburg |
| Argentina | Ecuador | Malaysia | San Francisco |
| Arizona & Grand Canyon | Edinburgh | Mallorca & Ibiza | Sardinia |
| Asia, East | Egypt | Malta | Scandinavia |
| Asia, Southeast | England | Mauritius Réunion | Scotland |
| Australia | **F**inland | & Seychelles | Seattle |
| Austria | Florence | Melbourne | Sicily |
| **B**ahamas | Florida | Mexico | Singapore |
| Bali | France | Miami | South Africa |
| Baltic States | France, Southwest | Montreal | South America |
| Bangkok | French Riviera | Morocco | Spain |
| Barbados | **G**ambia & Senegal | Moscow | Spain, Northern |
| Barcelona | Germany | **N**amibia | Spain, Southern |
| Beijing | Glasgow | Nepal | Sri Lanka |
| Belgium | Gran Canaria | Netherlands | Sweden |
| Belize | Great Britain | New England | Switzerland |
| Berlin | Great Railway Journeys | New Orleans | Sydney |
| Bermuda | of Europe | New York City | Syria & Lebanon |
| Boston | Greece | New York State | **T**aiwan |
| Brazil | Greek Islands | New Zealand | Tenerife |
| Brittany | Guatemala, Belize | Nile | Texas |
| Brussels | & Yucatán | Normandy | Thailand |
| Buenos Aires | **H**awaii | Norway | Tokyo |
| Burgundy | Hong Kong | **O**man & The UAE | Trinidad & Tobago |
| Burma (Myanmar) | Hungary | Oxford | Tunisia |
| **C**airo | **I**celand | **P**acific Northwest | Turkey |
| California | India | Pakistan | Tuscany |
| California, Southern | India, South | Paris | **U**mbria |
| Canada | Indonesia | Peru | USA: On The Road |
| Caribbean | Ireland | Philadelphia | USA: Western States |
| Caribbean Cruises | Israel | Philippines | US National Parks: West |
| Channel Islands | Istanbul | Poland | **V**enezuela |
| Chicago | Italy | Portugal | Venice |
| Chile | Italy, Northern | Prague | Vienna |
| China | Italy, Southern | Provence | Vietnam |
| Continental Europe | **J**amaica | Puerto Rico | **W**ales |
| Corsica | Japan | **R**ajasthan | Walt Disney World/Orlando |
| Costa Rica | Jerusalem | | |
| Crete | Jordan | | |
| Cuba | **K**enya | | |
| Cyprus | Korea | | |
| Czech & Slovak Republic | Laos & Cambodia | | |
| **D**elhi, Jaipur & Agra | Las Vegas | | |
| Denmark | Lisbon | | |

# ⵣ INSIGHT GUIDES

**The world's largest collection of
visual travel guides & maps**

# EYEWITNESS TRAVEL

# WASHINGTON, DC

Main contributors:
**Susan Burke and Alice L. Powers**

DK

LONDON, NEW YORK,
MELBOURNE, MUNICH AND DELHI
www.dk.com

**Project Editor** Claire Folkard
**Art Editors** Tim Mann, Simon J.M. Oon
**Senior Editor** Helen Townsend
**Editors** Emily Anderson, Felicity Crowe
**US Editor** Mary Sutherland
**Designers** Gillian Andrews, Eli Estaugh,
Elly King, Rebecca Milner
**DTP Designers** Sam Borland, Maite Lantaron
**Picture Researchers** Brigitte Arora, Katherine Mesquita
**Production** Mel Allsop

**Contributors**
Susan Burke, Alice L. Powers, Jennifer Quasha, Kem Sawyer

**Photographers**
Philippe Dewet, Kim Sayer, Giles Stokoe, Scott Suchman

**Illustrators**
Stephen Conlin, Gary Cross, Richard Draper, Chris Orr & Associates, Mel Pickering,
Robbie Polley, John Woodcock

Printed and bound by L. Rex Printing Company Limited, China

First published in the UK in 2000 by
Dorling Kindersley Limited,
80 Strand, London WC2R 0RL, UK

14 15 16 17 10 9 8 7 6 5 4 3 2 1

Reprinted with revisions 2002, 2003, 2004, 2005, 2006, 2008,
2009, 2010, 2011, 2012, 2013, 2014

Copyright © 2000, 2014 Dorling Kindersley Limited, London
A Penguin Random House Company

All rights reserved. No part of this publication may be reproduced,
stored in a retrieval system, or transmitted in any form or by any
means, electronic, mechanical, photocopying, recording, or otherwise,
without the prior written permission of the copyright owner.

A CIP catalogue record is available from the British Library.

ISBN 978-1-40932-692-2

Floors are referred to throughout in accordance with
American usage; ie the "first floor" is at ground level.

MIX
Paper from
responsible sources
FSC™ C018179
www.fsc.org

**The information in this
DK Eyewitness Travel Guide is checked annually.**
Every effort has been made to ensure that this book is as up-to-date as possible
at the time of going to press. Some details, however, such as telephone numbers,
opening hours, prices, gallery hanging arrangements and travel information are
liable to change. The publishers cannot accept responsibility for any consequences
arising from the use of this book, nor for any material on third party websites, and
cannot guarantee that any website address in this book will be a suitable source of
travel information. We value the views and suggestions of our readers very highly.
Please write to: Publisher, DK Eyewitness Travel Guides, Dorling Kindersley,
80 Strand, London, WC2R 0RL, UK, or email: travelguides@dk.com.

Front cover main image: The United States Capitol

◀ Iwo Jima Statue, with the Washington Monument and the United States Capitol in the background

# Contents

## How to Use this Guide 6

Fountain in Dumbarton Oaks

## Introducing Washington, DC

View toward the Lincoln Memorial from
Arlington National Cemetery

Columns from the US Capitol building, now in the National Arboretum

Map seller outside the National Gallery of Art on the Mall

The George, a boutique hotel

Quirky decor at Acadiana restaurant

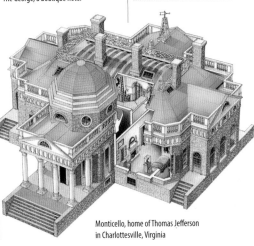
Monticello, home of Thomas Jefferson in Charlottesville, Virginia

# HOW TO USE THIS GUIDE

This guide helps you to get the most from your stay in Washington, DC. It provides detailed practical information and expert recommendations. *Introducing Washington, DC* maps the city and the region, sets it in its historical and cultural context, and gives an overview of the main attractions. *Washington, DC Area by Area* is the main sightseeing section, giving detailed information on all the major sights, with

photographs, illustrations and maps. *Farther Afield* looks at sights outside the city center, and *Beyond Washington, DC* explores other places within easy reach of the city. Carefully researched suggestions for restaurants, hotels, entertainment, and shopping are found in the *Travelers' Needs* section, while the *Survival Guide* contains useful advice on everything from changing money to traveling on Washington's Metrorail system.

## Washinton, DC Area by Area

The center of Washington has been divided into five sightseeing areas. Each section opens with a portrait of the area, summing up its character and history and listing all of the

sights to be covered. Sights are numbered and clearly located on an *Area Map*. After this comes a large-scale *Street-by-Street Map* focusing on the most interesting part of the area.

Finding your way about the area section is made easy by a numbering system. This refers to the order in which the sights are described on the pages that complete the section.

**Color-coding** on each page makes the area easy to find in the book.

**Recommended restaurants** in the area are listed and plotted on the map.

**A locator map** shows you where you are in relation to surrounding areas. The area of the *Street-by-Street Map* is highlighted.

**Numbered circles** pinpoint all the listed sights on the area map. The Octagon Museum, for example, is **8**

**1 Area Map**
For easy reference, the sights in each area are numbered and located on an area map. To help the visitor, the map also shows Metrorail stations.

**Octagon Museum 8** is shown on this map as well.

**Stars** indicate the sights that no visitor should miss.

**A suggested route** for a walk takes in the most attractive and interesting streets in the area.

**2 Street-by-Street Map**
This gives a bird's-eye view of the heart of each sightseeing area. The numbering of the sights ties in with the area map and the fuller descriptions on the pages that follow.

## Washington, DC at a Glance

Each map in this section concentrates on a specific theme: *Museums and Galleries in Washington, DC* and *Monuments and Memorials in Washington, DC*. The top sights are shown on the map.

**Each sightseeing area** is color-coded.

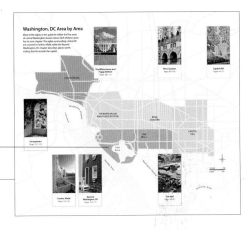

**Washington, DC Area by Area**

Most of the sights in this guide lie within the five areas of central Washington shown here. Each of these areas has its own chapter. The sights surrounding central DC are covered in Further Afield, while the Beyond Washington, DC chapter describes places worth visiting that lie outside the capital.

**Practical Information** lists all the information you need to visit every sight, including a map reference to the *Street Finder* at the back of the book.

**Numbers** refer to each sight's position on the area map and its place in the chapter.

## 3 Detailed information on each sight

All important sights in each area are described in depth in this section. They are listed in order, following the numbering on the *Area Map*. Practical information on opening hours, telephone numbers, websites, admission charges, and facilities available is given for each sight. The key to the symbols used can be found on the back flap.

**The Visitors' Checklist** provides the practical information you will need to plan your visit.

**Stars** indicate the most interesting architectural details of the building, and the most important works of art or exhibits on view inside.

**The façade** of each major sight is shown to help you spot it quickly.

**Numbered circles** point out key features of the sight listed in a key.

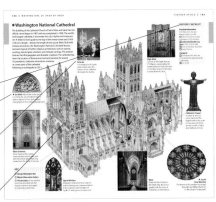

## 4 Washington, DC's major sights

These are given two or more full pages in the sightseeing area in which they are found. Historic buildings are dissected to reveal their interiors; and museums and galleries have colour-coded floor plans to help you find important exhibits.

# INTRODUCING WASHINGTON, DC

# GREAT DAYS IN WASHINGTON, DC

Washington boasts not only world-renowned works of art and majestic monuments, but picturesque neighborhoods and beautiful gardens. Here are itineraries for some of the best of the attractions and unexpected treasures, arranged first under themes and then by length of stay. All the sights can be reached on foot or by public transportation. Feel free to dip into the itineraries as you wish. Price guides on pages 10–11 show the daily cost for two adults or for a family of two adults and two children including lunch.

The White House, the Presidential residence

## Black History

**Two adults** allow at least $20

- Frederick Douglass House
- Mary McLeod Bethune Site
- U Street landmarks
- African American Civil War Museum and Memorial

## Monumental City

**Two adults** allow at least $40

- Lincoln Memorial
- World War II Memorial
- Corcoran Gallery of Art
- The White House

### Morning

Start your day at the **Lincoln Memorial** (see pp86–7), six blocks south of the Foggy Bottom Metro stop. Inside, on the north and south walls, you will find inscriptions of President Lincoln's **Gettysburg Address** (see p165). In front of the memorial, to the left of the Reflecting Pool, is the moving **Vietnam Veterans Memorial** (see p85). Engraved on black granite are the names of Americans who died in the war. Then make your way through the shady Constitution Gardens back to the Reflecting Pool. To the right is the **Korean War Veterans Memorial** (see p85) and nearby is the **World War II Memorial** (see p84). Here you can see the Freedom Wall, its inscriptions, and the bas-reliefs showing the US at war. After this memorial, move on to

17th Street where there are several historic buildings including the **Organization of American States** and the **Daughters of the American Revolution** (see p116). Drop into the **Corcoran Gallery of Art**, one of the country's first art galleries (see p115). Have lunch here, or head to a café near Pennsylvania Avenue.

### Afternoon

Stroll down Pennsylvania Avenue, passing the red brick Renwick Gallery, Blair House (where presidential guests stay), and **The White House** (see pp110–11). Walk around the White House to the Visitor Center at 1450 Pennsylvania Avenue. Afterwards, visit the **US National Archives** (see p92) to see historic documents including the *Declaration of Independence* and the *Bill of Rights*. End your day with a tour of **Ford's Theater** (see p98) where Lincoln was shot, followed by a meal in **Chinatown** (see pp98–9) or **Penn Quarter** (see pp88–105).

### Morning

If traveling by car, spend the morning at the **Frederick Douglass House**, an estate in Anacostia (see p147). Douglass was a fugitive slave who became a famous abolitionist. Almost all of the furnishings here are original (look out for the walking stick collection). Cross the river to **The Shaw Neighborhood** (see p143) with its lovely Victorian houses, where prominent African-Americans lived in the 1940s. Visit the **Mary McLeod Bethune Council House** (see p142), home of the civil rights leader and founder of the National Council of Negro Women.

Lunch at **Ben's Chili Bowl** (see p189) on U Street, a place that was once the Minnehaha silent movie theater.

Lincoln Theatre, the venue for many of Duke Ellington's performances

◄ An 1801 aquatint view of Washington

Georgetown's pretty gardens and houses, a delightful neighborhood to stroll through

**Afternoon**
Stroll along U Street, once known as Black Broadway. Audiences went wild when Duke Ellington performed at the **Lincoln Theatre** *(see p142)*. He lived nearby at numbers 1805 and 1816 13th Street. Visit the **African American Civil War Museum and Memorial**, honoring black soldiers *(see p135)*. End the day in style in Georgetown with dinner and jazz at **Blues Alley** *(see pp198–9)*.

## Art and Shopping

**Two Adults** allow at least $35
- National Gallery of Art
- Lunch on the Mall
- Georgetown Shopping
- Washington Harbor

**Morning**
To experience the full scope of art covered at the **National Gallery of Art** *(see pp60–63)*, visit both the West Building (13th–19th century European and American art) and the East Building (modern and contemporary art). Don't miss the Matisse Cut-Outs in the tower of the East Building. Have a coffee break at the Espresso Bar on the Concourse level. Outside, in the Garden Court (north side of East Building), find the Andy Goldsworthy installation entitled *Roof*, a

study of domes. Wander through the enchanting Sculpture Garden to the Pavilion Café, a charming spot for lunch.

**Afternoon**
Now head to cobblestoned **Georgetown** *(see pp122–9)*. You could take the 90-minute walk *(see pp150–51)*, but if shopping is your ultimate goal, go to M Street or Wisconsin Avenue for numerous galleries and shops and a range of stylish goods – lamps, Italian ceramics, prints and cutting-edge fashion. To finish, have tea in the Garden Terrace at the **Four Seasons Hotel** *(see p179)*, or have a drink at **Washington Harbor** while watching the boats *(see p124)*, then stroll through the Georgetown waterfront park next to the harbor.

## A Family Day

**Family of Four** allow at least $55
- Visit the National Zoo
- National Air and Space Museum
- Washington Monument

**Morning**
Start early at the **National Zoo** *(see pp140–41)*, checking at its Visitor Center for feeding times, talks, and training sessions (entry is free). See Clouded

Leopards and Giant Pandas on the Asia Trail and the Sumatran Tigers in Great Cats. At the Great Ape House orangutans scale a 400-ft (130-m) "O Line." Have lunch at the Mane Restaurant or at one of the snack bars.

**Afternoon**
Go by metro to the **National Air and Space Museum** *(see pp66–7)*. Discover facts such as the cruising speed of the *Spirit of St. Louis*, or the reason Skylab was covered with a coating of gold. Catch a film at the IMAX theatre, where you can experience flying without leaving the ground. Then head for the **Washington Monument** *(see p80)* and take the elevator to the top for the spectacular view (advance booking required). Finish off at the **Kennedy Center** *(see pp120–21)* in Foggy Bottom, for free entertainment on the Millennium Stage at 6pm.

Washington Monument, for a fabulous view of the city

The Martin Luther King, Jr. memorial, surrounded by cherry blossom

## 2 days in Washington, DC

- Marvel at the White House
- Watch first-class entertainment at the Kennedy Center
- Discover great paintings at the National Gallery of Art

**Day 1**
**Morning** Start the day with a roam around the nation's legislative heart, the **US Capitol** *(pp52–3)*, admiring its Neo-Classical architecture. Then stroll the grand mile-long **National Mall** *(pp56–87)*, lined on either side with an amazing choice of museums. Stop at the **National Museum of American History** *(pp76–9)* to see the First Ladies exhibition, the flag that inspired the national anthem, and Abraham Lincoln's top hat. Afterward, join the line for the elevator taking you to the top of the city's tallest landmark, the **Washington Monument** *(p80)*.

**Afternoon** Marvel at one of the world's most recognizable homes, the **White House** *(pp110–13)*, residence of the US president, then take a virtual tour at the **White House Visitor Center** *(p113)*. End the day with a show at the legendary **Kennedy Center** *(pp120–1)*, renowned for its music, theater, and ballet productions.

**Day 2**
**Morning** While away a few hours exploring the trove of great painting at the **National Gallery of Art** *(pp60–3)*. Then head to

the **National Air & Space Museum** *(pp64–7)*, which showcases exhibits ranging from the Wright brothers' first airplane to the latest space rockets.

**Afternoon** Walk along **Tidal Basin** *(p81)*, which is particularly pretty when the cherry trees are in blossom. Take in the striking monuments honoring past presidents, including the **Jefferson Memorial** *(p81)* and **Franklin D. Roosevelt Memorial** *(pp86–7)*. A short distance from here is the awe-inspiring **Lincoln Memorial** *(p87)*, which looms large over the Reflecting Pool. Make your way to the **Smithsonian Museum of American Art & National Portrait Gallery** *(pp100–103)*, which houses portraits of all the American presidents.

## 3 days in Washington, DC

- Learn about the nation's history at the many memorials
- Shop along Wisconsin Avenue in Georgetown
- Enjoy the view from the Washington Monument

**Day 1**
**Morning** Stroll the scenic **Tidal Basin** *(p81)*, passing the **Jefferson Memorial** *(p81)*, **Franklin D. Roosevelt Memorial** *(pp86–7)*, and the statue of civil rights leader **Martin Luther King, Jr.** *(p85)*. Visit the imposing **Lincoln Memorial** *(p87)*, and then spend time exploring the

poignant **Vietnam Veterans Memorial** *(p85)* and **World War II Memorial** *(p84)*. Next, ascend the **Washington Monument** *(p80)*, for far-reaching views.

**Afternoon** Stand in awe of the **White House** *(pp110–13)* and explore the **White House Visitor Center** *(p113)* for a chance to see the rooms where history is made. Nearby, the **Smithsonian Museum of American Art & National Portrait Gallery** *(pp100–103)* tells the nation's story through paintings and photos. End the day with an evening show at the infamous **Ford's Theatre** *(p98)*, the scene of Abraham Lincoln's assassination.

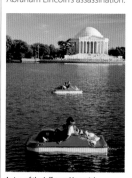

A view of the Jefferson Memorial from across Tidal Basin

**Day 2**
**Morning** After a tour of the soaring Rotunda and statuary hall of the **US Capitol** *(pp52–3)*, witness history in action at the **US Supreme Court** *(p50)*. Then stop at the impressive **Library of Congress** *(pp48–9)* to admire the stunning Great Hall and Main Reading Room. For something different, head to the **National Gallery of Art** *(pp60–3)*, which houses a remarkable collection of painting and sculpture.

**Afternoon** Explore the riveting **Newseum** *(p95)*, documenting events from the past and present in both print and digital formats. Then pop into the enormous **National Museum of Natural History** *(pp72–3)*. The Dinosaur Hall and Ocean Hall are a must. Wind down after a busy day with a performance at the **Kennedy Center** *(pp120–1)*.

## Day 3
**Morning** Head to the **National Mall** *(pp56–87)* for a variety of world-class museums. Highlights include the **National Air & Space Museum** *(pp64–7)*, the **National Museum of American History** *(pp76–9)*, and the **Hirschhorn Museum** *(pp68–9)* for modern art.

**Afternoon** Visit the city's most historic quarter, **Georgetown** *(pp122–9)*, to meander its pretty streets lined with Federal townhouses and browse the shops on **Wisconsin Avenue** *(pp124–5)*. Follow with a tour of the splendid **Dumbarton Oaks** estate *(p129)*, and then dine at one of the riverside restaurants at **Washington Harbor** *(p124)*.

### 5 days in Washington, DC

- Visit George Washington's estate at Mount Vernon
- Pay your respects at Arlington Cemetery
- Explore the portraits at the Smithsonian Museum

## Day 1
**Morning** See American history in the making at the **US Capitol** *(pp52–3)*, and then take in some culture at the **National Gallery of Art** *(pp60–3)*. Ride the elevator to the top of the **Washington Monument** *(p80)* for magnificent views of the city and the **World War II Memorial** *(p84)*.

**Afternoon** A walk along **Tidal Basin** *(p81)* will lead you to the **Jefferson Memorial** *(p81)*, **Franklin D. Roosevelt Memorial** *(pp86–7)*, and **Lincoln Memorial** *(p87)*. Look out for the statue of civil rights leader **Martin Luther King, Jr.** *(p85)* en route. Nearby is the **Vietnam Veterans Memorial** *(p85)*. After, head to the **Smithsonian Museum of American Art & National Portrait Gallery** *(pp100–3)*, which displays portraits of all the US presidents.

## Day 2
**Morning** Admire the rooms of the **White House** *(pp110–13)* at the **White House Visitor Center**

*(p113)*, then see it for real. Nearby, the **Corcoran Gallery** *(p115)* has fine modern and African-American art alongside European and American masterworks.

**Afternoon** Discover **Dumbarton Oaks** estate *(p129)* for a leisurely walk in the circular garden. Then continue to **Georgetown** *(p122–9)*, to look around its shops on **Wisconsin Avenue** *(pp124–5)*. Afterward, take a stroll along the historic **Chesapeake and Ohio Canal** *(pp124–5)* towpath. Round off the day with a show at the **Kennedy Center** *(pp120–1)*.

## Day 3
**Morning** Visit the stately quarters of the nation's tribunal, the **US Supreme Court** *(p50)*, and marvel at the colossal reading rooms in the **Library of Congress** *(pp48–9)*. The historic treasures of the **National Archives** *(p92–3)*, including the original Declaration of Independence and the US Constitution and Bill of Rights, are worth a closer look.

**Afternoon** Watch history come to life in the newsreels of the **Newseum** *(p95)*. Next, pick between the **National Museum of American History** *(pp76–9)*, the **National Air & Space Museum** *(pp64–7)*, or the **Hirschhorn Museum** *(pp68–9)*, which line the **National Mall** *(pp56–87)*. Later, visit **Ford's Theatre** *(p98)* and explore the trendy restaurants in the **Penn Quarter** *(pp86–105)*.

## Day 4
**Morning** Immerse yourself at the heart-rending **United States Holocaust Memorial Museum**

A pretty, tree-lined street in Washington's historic quarter, Georgetown

*(pp82–3)*. Then, for something lighter, see the Hall of Mammals and the Dinosaur Hall at the **National Museum of Natural History** *(pp72–3)*.

**Afternoon** Head out for a tour of the magnificent **Washington National Cathedral** *(pp144–5)*. At night, choose one of the ethnic restaurants in **Adams-Morgan** *(p139)* or dine in one of the restaurants at lively **Washington Harbor** *(p124)*.

## Day 5
**Morning** Spend the morning at **Mount Vernon** *(pp162–3)*, George Washington's beautiful riverside estate, and tour the mansion, grounds, and gardens.

**Afternoon** Take a moving trip to **Arlington National Cemetery** *(pp132–3)* for the tombs of John F. Kennedy and the nation's war heroes. Follow this with a visit to **Old Town Alexandria** *(pp160–61)*, whose streets are lined with boutiques, restaurants, and historic sights aplenty.

The impressive Neo-Classical architecture of the US Capitol

# Putting Washington, DC on the Map

Washington, DC is situated near the East Coast of North America,
surrounded by the state of Maryland and separated from Virginia by
the Potomac River. It covers an area of 108 sq km (67 sq miles) and has
a population of 600,000. As the capital of the United States, and seat
of federal government, the city is a major focus of American life. It is a
very popular tourist destination, attracting millions of visitors each
year. The beautiful countryside of Maryland and Virginia is also easily
reached from the capital city.

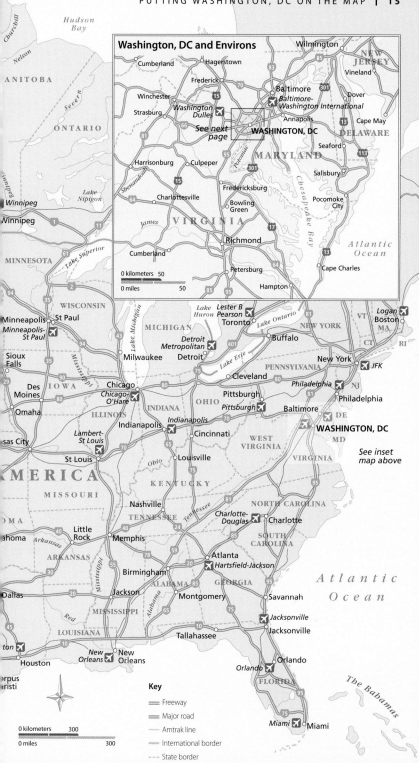

**Washington, DC and Environs**

Hudson Bay

Churchill

Nelson

MANITOBA

ONTARIO

Severn

Winnipeg

Winnipeg

Lake Nipigon

Cumberland        Hagerstown

Frederick

Winchester                    Baltimore
                              Baltimore-
Strasburg    Washington      Washington International
             Dulles
                 See next    Annapolis
                 page        WASHINGTON, DC

Harrisonburg    Culpeper     MARYLAND

                Fredericksburg

Charlottesville    Bowling
                   Green

James        VIRGINIA

Cumberland    Richmond

                Petersburg

Hampton

0 kilometers 50

0 miles 50

Wilmington

NEW JERSEY

Vineland

Dover

Cape May

DELAWARE

Seaford

Salisbury

Pocomoke City

Chesapeake Bay

Atlantic Ocean

Cape Charles

MINNESOTA        Lake Superior

WISCONSIN

Minneapolis    St Paul
Minneapolis-
St Paul

Sioux Falls

Des Moines        IOWA

Omaha

as City

MERICA

MISSOURI

OMA

ahoma        Little Rock

Dallas

Red

ton

Houston

orpus
aristi

MICHIGAN        Lake Huron    Lester B Pearson    Toronto    Lake Ontario

Lake Michigan        Detroit Metropolitan        Lake Erie

Milwaukee        Detroit

Chicago
Chicago-O'Hare        INDIANA        OHIO        Cleveland

Lambert-St Louis        Indianapolis        Indianapolis    Cincinnati

St Louis        ILLINOIS

Ohio                Louisville

KENTUCKY        WEST VIRGINIA

Nashville        VIRGINIA

TENNESSEE

Memphis        Tennessee

ARKANSAS        Charlotte-Douglas    Charlotte

Birmingham        Atlanta    SOUTH CAROLINA

Jackson        Hartsfield-Jackson

MISSISSIPPI        Montgomery    Savannah

ALABAMA    GEORGIA

LOUISIANA

New Orleans    New Orleans        Tallahassee    Jacksonville
                                              Jacksonville

Orlando    Orlando

FLORIDA    Miami    Miami

VT

NEW YORK        Logan    Boston    MA

Buffalo

CT        RI

New York        JFK

PENNSYLVANIA

Pittsburgh        Philadelphia    NJ
Pittsburgh                Philadelphia

Baltimore        DE

**WASHINGTON, DC**

MD

*See inset map above*

NORTH CAROLINA

Atlantic Ocean

The Bahamas

**Key**

— Freeway

— Major road

— Amtrak line

— International border

--- State border

0 kilometers 300

0 miles 300

**For additional map symbols** *see back flap*

# Greater Washington, DC

The city of Washington was created not only as a new capital for the United States but also as the seat of government, independent from the other states. It was laid out in a diamond-shaped area with a grid system of roads. One side of the square was lost after land was ceded back to Virginia in 1846. Although the city has sprawled beyond its original limits, officially the District of Columbia remains within the boundaries indicated. Washington is an easy city to get around, with an efficient modern metro system.

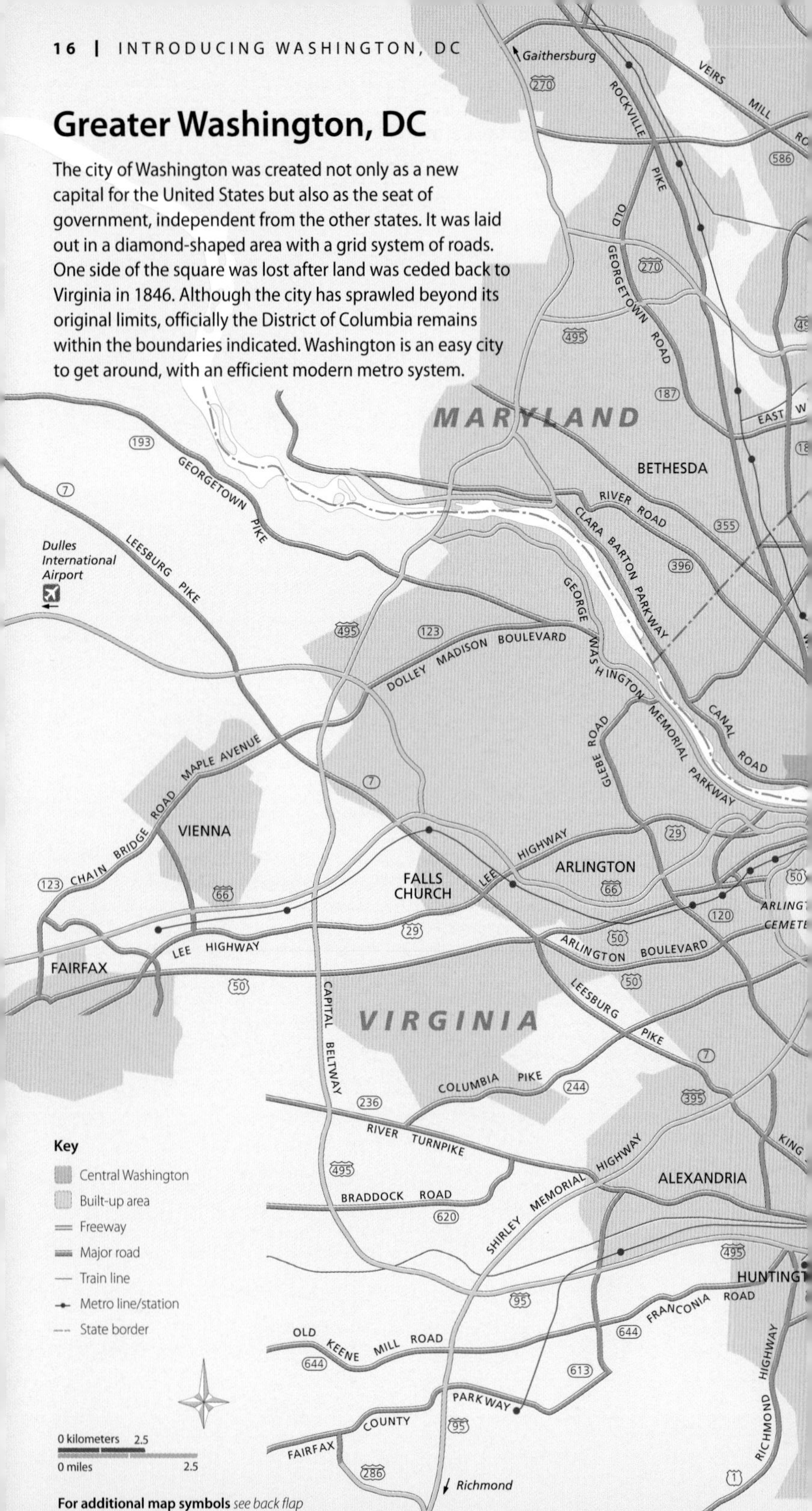

Gaithersburg

VEIRS

MILL

270

ROCKVILLE PIKE

586

OLD GEORGETOWN ROAD

270

495

187

EAST W

**MARYLAND**

18

193

BETHESDA

7

RIVER ROAD

355

Georgetown Pike

CLARA BARTON PARKWAY

Dulles International Airport

LEESBURG PIKE

396

495

123

DOLLEY MADISON BOULEVARD

GEORGE WASHINGTON MEMORIAL PARKWAY

CANAL ROAD

MAPLE AVENUE

CHAIN BRIDGE ROAD

GLEBE ROAD

7

LEE HIGHWAY

29

**VIENNA**

**ARLINGTON**

123

66

66

120

ARLING

CEMETE

**FALLS CHURCH**

ARLINGTON BOULEVARD

50

**FAIRFAX**

LEE HIGHWAY

29

50

LEESBURG PIKE

7

**VIRGINIA**

CAPITAL BELTWAY

COLUMBIA PIKE

244

395

236

KING

RIVER TURNPIKE

495

SHIRLEY MEMORIAL HIGHWAY

**ALEXANDRIA**

BRADDOCK ROAD

620

**HUNTING**

FRANCONIA ROAD

95

**Key**

Central Washington

Built-up area

Freeway

Major road

Train line

Metro line/station

State border

OLD KEENE MILL ROAD

644

644

613

RICHMOND HIGHWAY

PARKWAY

COUNTY

95

0 kilometers 2.5

0 miles 2.5

**FAIRFAX**

286

Richmond

1

**For additional map symbols** *see back flap*

# THE HISTORY OF WASHINGTON, DC

Native Americans settled in what is now the District of Columbia as long as 6,000 years ago. Archeologists have discovered traces of three villages in the area; the largest was called Nacotchtanke. Its people, the Anacostines, settled along the Potomac River and a smaller tributary now named the Anacostia River.

## English Settlement

In December 1606 Captain John Smith of the Virginia Company, under the charge of King James I of England, set sail from England for the New World. Five months later he arrived in the Chesapeake Bay and founded the Jamestown colony. A skilled cartographer, Smith was soon sailing up the Potomac River. In 1608 he came to the area that would later become Washington.

The English settlers who followed supported themselves through the fur trade, and later cultivated tobacco and corn (maize). The marriage in 1614 between John Rolfe, one of the settlers, and Pocahontas, daughter of the Indian chief Powhatan, kept the peace between the English and the Indians for eight years. Struggles over land ownership between the English and the Powhatan Indians, whose ancestors had lived there for centuries, led to massacres in 1622. The English finally defeated the Indians in 1644, and a formal peace agreement was made in 1646.

The first Africans arrived in the region on board a Dutch ship in 1619 and worked as indentured servants on plantations. They were given food and lodging as payment for serving for a fixed number of years. However, within the next 40 years the practice changed so that blacks were purchased for life, and their children became the property of their master. As the number of plantations grew, so did the number of slaves.

In the late 1600s another group of settlers, this time Irish-Scottish, led by Captain Robert Troop, established themselves here. Along the Potomac River two ports, George Town (later known as Georgetown) and Alexandria, soon became profitable centers of commerce. Here planters had their crops inspected, stored, and shipped. In both towns streets were laid out in rectangular patterns. With rich soil, plentiful land, abundant labor, and good transportation, the region rapidly grew in prosperity.

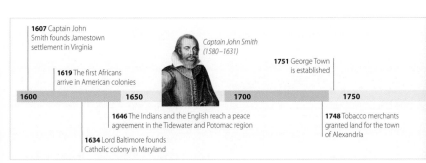

**1607** Captain John Smith founds Jamestown settlement in Virginia

**1619** The first Africans arrive in American colonies

*Captain John Smith (1580–1631)*

**1751** George Town is established

**1600**  **1650**  **1700**  **1750**

**1646** The Indians and the English reach a peace agreement in the Tidewater and Potomac region

**1634** Lord Baltimore founds Catholic colony in Maryland

**1748** Tobacco merchants granted land for the town of Alexandria

◀ George Washington by Rembrandt Peale, painted 1824–5

## Revolutionary Years

Some 100 years after the first settlers arrived, frustration over British rule began to grow, both in the Potomac region and elsewhere in the 13 American colonies. In 1775, the colonies began their struggle for independence. On April 19, shots were fired at Lexington, Massachusetts by American colonists who wanted "no taxation without representation," thus beginning the War of Independence.

On July 4, 1776, the Declaration of Independence was issued as colonists attempted to sever ties with Britain. Revolt led to revolution, and the newly formed United States won an important victory at Saratoga, New York in 1777. The French came to the aid of the Americans and finally, on October 19, 1781, the British, led by Lord Cornwallis, surrendered at Yorktown, Virginia. This ended the war and assured the independence of the United States. The peace treaty was signed in Paris on September 3, 1783. Britain agreed to boundaries giving the US all territory to the south of what is now Canada, north of Florida, and west to the Mississippi River.

The Continental Congress, a legislative body of representatives from the newly formed states, appointed a committee to draft the country's first constitution. The result was the Articles of Confederation, which established a union of the newly created states but provided the central government with little power. This later gave way to a stronger form of government, created by the delegates of the Federal Constitutional Convention in Philadelphia in May, 1787. George Washington was unanimously chosen to be president. He took office on April 30, 1789.

Meeting in New York of first delegates of Congress to discuss location for a new capital city

## A New City

The Constitution of the United States, ratified in 1788, allowed for the creation of a seat of government, not to exceed 10 square miles, which would be ruled by the United States Congress. This area was to be independent and not part of any state. At the first meeting of Congress in New York City in 1789, a dispute arose between northern and southern delegates over where the capital should be located. Secretary of the Treasury Alexander Hamilton and Secretary of State Thomas Jefferson worked out an agreement whereby the debts incurred by northern states during the Revolution would be taken over by the government, and in return the capital would be located in

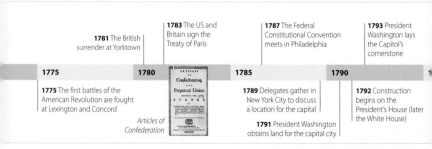

**1781** The British surrender at Yorktown

**1783** The US and Britain sign the Treaty of Paris

**1787** The Federal Constitutional Convention meets in Philadelphia

**1793** President Washington lays the Capitol's cornerstone

1775     1780     1785     1790

**1775** The first battles of the American Revolution are fought at Lexington and Concord

*Articles of Confederation*

**1789** Delegates gather in New York City to discuss a location for the capital

**1791** President Washington obtains land for the capital city

**1792** Construction begins on the President's House (later the White House)

the south. George Washington chose an area that incorporated land from both Maryland and Virginia, and included the towns of Alexandria and Georgetown. It was to be known as the city of Washington. At Suter's Tavern in Georgetown, Washington convinced local residents to sell their land for £25 an acre. He chose a surveyor, Andrew Ellicott, and his assistant Benjamin Banneker, a free African-American, to lay out the streets and lots. Washington also invited Major Pierre Charles L'Enfant to create a grand design for the new capital city *(see p69)*.

Ellicott's engraved map of 1792, based on L'Enfant's plan

In 1800 the government was moved to Washington. President John Adams and his wife Abigail took up residence in the new President's House, designed by James Hoban, which was later renamed the White House by Theodore Roosevelt. The city remained empty of residents for many years while the building works took place.

The British attack on Washington, DC in August 1814

## War of 1812

Tension with Britain over restrictions on trade and freedom of the seas began to escalate during James Madison's administration. On June 18, 1812, the US declared war on Britain. In August 1814, British troops reached Washington and officers at the Capitol fled, taking the Declaration of Independence and the Constitution with them. First Lady Dolley Madison escaped from the White House with Gilbert Stuart's portrait of George Washington. On August 24, the British defeated the Americans at Bladensburg, a suburb of Washington. They set fire to the War Department, the Treasury, the Capitol, and the White House. Only a night of heavy rain prevented the city's destruction. The Treaty of Ghent, which finally ended the war, was signed on February 17, 1815 in the Octagon.

**1814** The British set fire to Washington

**1802** Robert Brent appointed first mayor of Washington

**1812** US declares war on Britain

**1815** President Madison signs the Treaty of Ghent with Britain

| 1800 | 1805 | 1810 | 1815 |

**1800** The seat of government is transferred from Philadelphia to Washington

**1804** President Jefferson initiates the Lewis and Clark expedition which resulted in the discovery of America's West Coast

*The signing of the Treaty of Ghent*

The Baltimore and Ohio Railroad's "Tom Thumb" locomotive racing a horse-drawn car

## Rebirth

With the end of the War of 1812 came a period of renewed optimism and economic prosperity in Washington. Washingtonians wanted to make their city a bustling commercial capital. They planned to build the Chesapeake and Ohio Canal to connect Washington to the Ohio River Valley and thus open trade with the west. Construction on the Baltimore and Ohio Railroad line also got under way. As the population grew, new hotels and boarding-houses, home to many of the nation's congressmen, opened up. Newspapers, such as the *National Intelligencer*, flourished.

In 1829, James Smithson, an Englishman, bequeathed a collection of minerals, books, and $500,000 in gold to the United States, and the Smithsonian Institution was born.

Construction began on three important government buildings, each designed by Robert Mills (1781–1855): the Treasury Building, the Patent Office, and the General Post Office building. Also at this time, the Washington National Monument Society, led by George Watterston, chose a 600-ft (183-m) obelisk to become the Washington Monument, again designed by the architect Robert Mills.

## Slavery Divides the City

Racial tension was beginning to increase around this time, and in 1835 it erupted into what was later known as the Snow Riot. After the attempted murder of the widow of architect William Thornton, a botany teacher from the North was arrested for inciting blacks because plant specimens had been found wrapped in the pages of an abolitionist newspaper. A riot ensued, and in the course of the fighting a school for black children was destroyed as well as the interior of a restaurant owned by Beverly Snow, a free black. As a result, and to the anger of many people, black and white, laws were passed denying free blacks licenses to run saloons or eating places.

Nothing has been more divisive in Washington's history than the issue of slavery. Many Washingtonians were slaveholders; others became ardent abolitionists. The homes of several abolitionists and free blacks, as well as black churches, were used as hiding places for fugitive slaves. On an April night in 1848, 77 slaves attempted to escape the city, and boarded a small schooner on the Potomac River. But the following night they were captured and brought back to Washington, where they

**1828** President John Quincy Adams breaks ground for the Chesapeake and Ohio Canal

*James Smithson (1765–1829)*

**1844** The invention of the telegraph speeds the distribution of news from Washington

| 1825 | 1830 | 1835 | 1840 | 18 |

**1829** James Smithson leaves a fortune worth more than $500,000 to the United States

**1827** The Washington Abolition Society is organized

**1835** Baltimore and Ohio Railroad links Washington and Baltimore. Racial tension leads to the Snow Riot

**1846** Construction on the Smithsonian Castle begins. Alexandria is retroceded to Virginia

were sold at auction. The incident served only to heighten the tension between pro-slavery and anti-slavery groups. Slavery was abolished in Washington in 1862.

## The Civil War

In 1860, following the election of President Abraham Lincoln, several southern states seceded from the Union in objection to Lincoln's stand against slavery. Shots were fired on Fort Sumter in Charleston, South Carolina on April 12, 1861, and the Civil War began. By the summer, 50,000 volunteers arrived in Washington to join the Army of the Potomac under General George B. McClellan. Washington suddenly found itself in the business of housing, feeding, and clothing the troops, as well as caring for the wounded. Buildings and churches became makeshift hospitals. Many people came to nurse the wounded, including author Louisa May Alcott and poet Walt Whitman.

Thousands of northerners came to help the war effort. They were joined by hordes of black people heading north to escape

Black residents of Washington celebrating the abolition of slavery in the District of Columbia

slavery, so that by 1864 the population of Washington had doubled that of 1860, reaching 140,000.

After skirmishes on July 12, 1864, witnessed by Lincoln himself at Fort Stevens, the Confederates retreated. By March 1865 the end of the war appeared to be close at hand. Parades, speeches, and band concerts followed Confederate General Robert E. Lee's surrender on April 9, 1865. Yet the celebratory mood was short-lived. Disturbed by the Union Army's victory, John Wilkes Booth assassinated President Lincoln at Ford's Theatre during the third act of *Our American Cousin* on April 14, 1865. Lincoln was taken to the house of tailor William Petersen, across the street from the theater, where he died the next morning (see p98).

Victory parade through Washington, DC to celebrate the end of the Civil War in April 1865

**1851** Major expansion of the Capitol begins

**1859** Senate wing of the Capitol is completed

**1857** House of Representatives wing of the Capitol is completed

**1861** Civil War begins when shots are fired on Fort Sumter, South Carolina

**1862** Slavery is abolished in the District of Columbia

**1850**    **1855**    **1860**    **1865**

**1848** 77 slaves attempt to escape from Washington by schooner. Ground is broken for the Washington Monument

**1863** The Emancipation Proclamation is issued

**1865** General Robert E. Lee surrenders to the Union. President Lincoln is assassinated

*President Lincoln*

**1860** President Abraham Lincoln elected

## Post Civil War

The Freedmen's Bureau was created to help provide African Americans with housing, food, education, and employment. In 1867 General Oliver Otis Howard, commissioner of the bureau, used $500,000 of the bureau's funds to purchase land to establish a university for African Americans. He was president of this institution, later named Howard University, from 1869 to 1873.

On February 21, 1871, a new "territorial government" was formed to unite Georgetown, the city of Washington, and the County of Washington into the District of Columbia. A governor and a board of public works were appointed by President Ulysses S. Grant. Alexander "Boss" Shepherd, a member of the board of public works, paved streets, installed streetlights, laid sidewalks, planned parks, and designed an advanced sewerage system. But the District's debts rose uncontrollably. As a result, Congress quickly tightened its reins and established home rule. It took over some of the District's debts, and appointed three commissioners to work within a set budget.

Washington became a city of contrasts, attracting both rich and poor. One of the most distinguished literati in the city was Henry Adams, best known for his autobiographical work, *The Education of Henry Adams*. He lived on Lafayette Square next door to John Hay, Secretary of State and also a man of letters. One of Washington's most prominent African Americans, Frederick Douglass, lived at Cedar Hill, across the river in Anacostia. Born a slave in Maryland, he escaped north to freedom where he started an abolitionist newspaper. During the Civil War he became an adviser to President Lincoln.

Many lived well, including the growing middle class, which moved to the new suburbs of Mount Pleasant and LeDroit Park, yet a large number of the poor made their home in Washington's hidden alleys.

The Library of Congress under construction

## A New Century

In 1901 Senator James McMillan of Michigan spearheaded a plan to improve the design of Washington by partaking in the "city beautiful" movement, in vogue at the time. L'Enfant's plan was finally completed, and the Mall between the Washington Monument and the US Capitol was laid out. Architects Daniel Burnham, Charles F. McKim, and others planned the building of a memorial to honor President Abraham Lincoln.

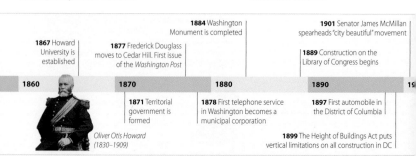

**1867** Howard University is established

**1877** Frederick Douglass moves to Cedar Hill. First issue of the *Washington Post*

**1884** Washington Monument is completed

**1901** Senator James McMillan spearheads "city beautiful" movement

**1889** Construction on the Library of Congress begins

| 1860 | 1870 | 1880 | 1890 | 19 |

**1871** Territorial government is formed

**1878** First telephone service in Washington becomes a municipal corporation

**1897** First automobile in the District of Columbia

Oliver Otis Howard (1830–1909)

**1899** The Height of Buildings Act puts vertical limitations on all construction in DC

Suffragettes demanding a hearing for imprisoned leader Alice Paul

When the US entered World War I in 1917, growing numbers of women came to Washington to fill the posts vacated by men. Suffragists took to the streets to campaign for the right to vote. The National Women's Party, led by Alice Paul, picketed the White House to urge President Wilson to endorse a constitutional amendment to give women the vote.

African Americans in Washington were not only banned from voting but also faced discrimination in housing and education. After a local black battalion was excluded from a World War I victory parade, tension mounted. On July 20, 1919, riots erupted on the streets and did not stop for four days. Although discrimination continued, the 1920s were a period of commercial, artistic, and literary success for the black community. The area around U Street and Howard University attracted small businesses, theaters, nightclubs, and

restaurants. It became home to many successful musicians and writers; Duke Ellington and the opera star Madame Evanti lived here, as did poets Langston Hughes and Paul Dunbar. Alain Locke, a professor of philosophy at Howard, and Jean Toomer, author of *Cane*, were also residents.

## Roosevelt Ushers in a New Deal

Following the stock market crash of 1929, federal workers received salary cuts, and many other Washingtonians lost their jobs. As a result, President Roosevelt created the "New Deal," an ambitious public works program to reduce unemployment. People were paid to do a range of tasks, from planting trees on the Mall to completing some of the city's edifices, such as the Supreme Court, the government office buildings of the Federal Triangle, and the National Gallery of Art.

Roosevelt's wife, Eleanor, was a champion of the poor and a tireless reformer. In 1939, when Marian Anderson, the African American singer, was denied permission by the Daughters of the American Revolution to perform at Constitution Hall, Eleanor Roosevelt arranged for her to sing at the Lincoln Memorial instead, to a crowd of 75,000.

President Franklin D. Roosevelt with First Lady Eleanor

Marian Anderson (1897–1993)

**1906** Teddy Roosevelt's daughter, Alice, is married in the White House

**1908** Opening of Union Station, designed by Daniel Burnham

**1918** Washington celebrates Armistice Day

**1919** Race riots continue for four days

**1917** US enters World War I

**1920** The 19th amendment, granting suffrage to women, is ratified

**1929** The Great Depression begins

**1933** New Negro Alliance is formed to improve the status of blacks

**1939** Marian Anderson performs at the Lincoln Memorial

1910　1920　1930　1940

After the US entered World War II in December 1941, Washington's population soared. Women from all across the country arrived in the capital, eager to take on government jobs while the men were overseas. They faced housing shortages, and long lines as they waited to use rationing coupons for food and services. The city also offered a respite for soldiers on leave. Actress Helen Hayes, a native Washingtonian, opened the Stage Door Canteen where celebrities provided food and entertainment.

Soldiers on patrol after the death of Martin Luther King, Jr.

## The Civil Rights Movement

In 1953 the Supreme Court's ruling in the Thompson Restaurant case made it illegal for public places to discriminate against blacks. With the passage of other anti-discrimination laws, life in Washington began to change. In 1954, the recreation department ended its public segregation. In the same year, on May 17, the Supreme Court ruled that "separate educational facilities are inherently unequal."

On August 28, 1963, more than 200,000 people arrived in the capital for the "March on Washington" to support civil rights. From the steps of the Lincoln Memorial, Marian

Anderson sang again and Reverend Martin Luther King, Jr. shared his dream in words that would echo for generations *(see p93)*.

In November 1963, the nation was stunned by the assassination of President John F. Kennedy in Dallas, Texas. An eternal flame was lit at his funeral in Arlington Cemetery by his widow, Jaqueline. Five years later, on April 4, 1968, Martin Luther King was shot. Killed at the age of 39, he is revered as a hero and a martyr.

The opening of the Kennedy Center for Performing Arts in 1971 indicated the growing international character of the city. Several art museums with impressive collections (the East Wing of the National Gallery of Art, the Hirshhorn, the National Museum of American Art, and the National Portrait Gallery) also opened to enrich the city's cultural life. The construction of the Metro helped alleviate traffic problems. The embassies, the foreign banking community (the World Bank, the International Monetary Fund, and the Inter-American Development Bank), and the increasing number of immigrants, provided a cosmopolitan flavor.

John F. Kennedy, Jr. salutes his father's casket at Arlington Cemetery in 1963

**1940** First plane lands at National Airport

**1945** The first atomic bomb is dropped on Hiroshima, ending World War II

**1940**

**1941** The National Gallery of Art opens. After Japan attacks Pearl Harbor, the US enters World War II

*Dr. Martin Luther King, Jr. (1929–68)*

**1950**

**1973** Washingtonians gain the right to elect a mayor

**1963** Martin Luther King gives "I Have a Dream" speech

**1969** 250,000 anti-Vietnam War protesters march

**1960**

**1964** Washington residents vote in a presidential election for the first time

**1976** Metro opens. National Air and Space Museum opens

**1974** President Richard Nixon resigns following criminal investigation

**1970**

**1978** Marion Barry elected mayor for the first of four terms

**1982** Dedication of the Vietnam Veterans Memorial, designed by Maya Ying Lin

19

## Home Rule

Residents of the District of Columbia have never been given full representation in American politics, as they have no congressman. (Until the 23rd Amendment of 1961 they could not even vote for president – the 1964 election was the first in which they took part.) In 1967, with people clamoring for a greater say in local government, President Lyndon Johnson replaced the system of three commissioners, set up by Congress in 1871, with an appointed mayor and a city council with greater responsibility in policy and budget issues. The result was the city's first elected mayor in over 100 years, Walter E. Washington. Residents were permitted to elect a non-voting delegate to Congress in 1971, and the Home Rule Act of 1973 allowed the people to elect both mayor and city council.

In 1978 Marion Barry succeeded as mayor. Born in Mississippi and raised in Tennessee, he came to Washington in 1965 to work for civil rights. He was the city's mayor for 16 of the next 20 years, but toward the end of his tenure, a large deficit and dissatisfaction with city politics developed. Middle-class families, both white and black, continued to flee the increasingly crime-ridden city for the safety of the suburbs. In 1995 Congress stripped the mayor

Walter E. Washington campaigning for re-election

of much of his power and appointed a five-person "financial control board" to oversee the city's affairs. The election in 1998 was won by Anthony Williams, an outsider who offered a fresh outlook and financial stability. Congress returned to the mayor much of the authority it had taken away. Within months of taking his new office it appeared that Mayor Williams was turning the city around. The budget was operating with a surplus, the population had stabilized, and unemployment was down.

A new administration under Adrian

Fireworks lighting the Washington Monument during the 2000 celebrations

Fenty, elected in 2006, transformed the city's image. No longer dubbed the crime capital of the US, Washington, DC has once again become a mecca for tourists and a safer, cleaner place for its residents. In 2010, Fenty was defeated by moderate democrat Vincent Gray.

In 2009 Barack Obama became the first African-American president in US history – a momentous occasion.

**1993** Opening of the US Holocaust Memorial Museum

*President Bill Clinton (1946–)*

**2005** George W. Bush inaugurated for a second term as US president

**2011** Rare 5.8 magnitude earthquake hits DC

**2012** Barack Obama re-elected for a second term as president

| 1990 | 2000 | 2010 | 2020 |

**2001** September 11 Terrorist attack on the Pentagon

**2010** Vincent Gray elected mayor

**2009** Barack Obama becomes the first African-American elected president

# The American Presidents

The presidents of the United States have come from all walks of life; at least two were born in a log cabin – Abraham Lincoln and Andrew Jackson. Others, such as Franklin D. Roosevelt and John F. Kennedy, came from privileged backgrounds. Millard Fillmore attended a one-room schoolroom and Jimmy Carter raised peanuts. Many, including Ulysses S. Grant and Dwight D. Eisenhower, were military men, who won public popularity for their great achievements in battle.

**Benjamin Harrison**
(1889–93)

**Chester A. Arthur**
(1881–5)

**Millard Fillmore**
(1850–53)

**Zachary Taylor**
(1849–50)

**Franklin Pierce**
(1853–7)

**James K. Polk**
(1845–9)

**W.H. Harrison**
(1841)

**Rutherford B. Hayes**
(1877–81)

**George Washington**
(1789–97) was a Revolutionary War general. He was unanimously chosen to be the first president of the United States.

**James Madison**
(1809–17), known as the Father of the Constitution, was co-author of the Federalist Papers.

**Andrew Johnson**
(1865–9)

| 1775 | 1800 | 1825 | 1850 | 1875 |

| 1775 | 1800 | 1825 | 1850 | 1875 |

**John Adams**
(1797–1801), a lawyer and historian, was the first president to live in the White House.

**James Monroe**
(1817–25)

**John Quincy Adams** (1825–9)

**John Tyler**
(1841–5)

**James A. Garfield**
(1881)

**Martin Van Buren**
(1837–41)

**Ulysses S. Grant**
(1869–77)

**Thomas Jefferson**
(1801–9), architect, inventor, landscape designer, diplomat, and historian, was the quintessential Renaissance man.

**James Buchanan**
(1857–61)

**Grover Cleveland**
(1885–9)

**Andrew Jackson**
(1829–37) defeated the British at the Battle of New Orleans in the War of 1812.

**Abraham Lincoln**
(1861–5) won the epithet, the Great Emancipator, for his role in the abolition of slavery. He led the Union through the Civil War.

**Grover Cleveland**
(1893–7)

**William McKir**
(1897–1)

**Key to Timeline**

- Federalist
- Democratic Republican
- Whig
- Republican
- Democrat

**Woodrow Wilson** (1913–21) led the country through World War I and paved the way for the League of Nations.

**Harry S. Truman** (1945–53) made the decision to drop the atomic bombs on Hiroshima and Nagasaki in 1945.

**John F. Kennedy** (1961–3) was one of the most popular presidents. He sent the first astronaut into space, started the Peace Corps, and created the Arms Control and Disarmament Agency. His assassination rocked the nation.

**Richard Nixon** (1969–74) opened up China and sent the first men to the moon. He resigned after the Watergate scandal (see p119).

**Franklin D. Roosevelt** (1933–45) started the New Deal, a reform and relief program, during the Great Depression. He was elected to four terms.

**Jimmy Carter** (1977–81)

**George Bush** (1989–93)

**George W. Bush** (2001–09)

| 1900 | 1925 | 1950 | 1975 | 2000 | 2025 |
|---|---|---|---|---|---|

| 1900 | 1925 | 1950 | 1975 | 2000 | 2025 |
|---|---|---|---|---|---|

**William H. Taft** (1909–13)

**Dwight D. Eisenhower** (1953–61)

**William J. Clinton** (1993–2001)

**Herbert Hoover** (1929–33)

**Gerald Ford** (1974–7)

**Calvin Coolidge** (1923–9)

**Ronald Reagan** (1981–9), a one-time movie actor and popular president, cut taxes, increased military spending, and reduced government programs.

**Warren Harding** (1921–3)

**Barack Obama** (2009–), a senator from Illinois, is the first African-American president in the history of the US.

**Lyndon B. Johnson** (1963–9) escalated the Vietnam conflict, resulting in widespread protests.

**Theodore Roosevelt** (1901–9) created many national parks and oversaw the construction of the Panama Canal.

### The Role of the First Lady

In the 19th century, the First Lady acted primarily as hostess and "behind-the-scenes" adviser. Later, when Eleanor Roosevelt held her own press conferences, the role of First Lady changed greatly. Jackie Kennedy gave support to the arts, Rosalynn Carter attended Cabinet meetings, Barbara Bush promoted literacy, and Hillary Clinton ran her own political campaign. Michelle Obama follows in this vein, campaigning for charitable causes, including the prevention of childhood obesity.

Eleanor Roosevelt at a press conference in the 1930s

# How the Federal Government Works

In September 1787, the Constitution of the United States of America was signed *(see p93)*. It was created as "the supreme Law of the Land," to ensure that it would take precedence over state laws. The powers of the federal government were separated into three distinct areas: the legislative branch to enact the laws, the executive branch to enforce them, and the judicial branch to interpret them. No one branch, however, was to exert too much authority, and the system of checks and balances was instituted. Provisions were made for amending the Constitution, and by December 1791 the first ten amendments, called the Bill of Rights, were ratified.

### Checks and Balances

The system of checks and balances means that no one branch of government can abuse its power.

**The Executive Branch:** The President can recommend and veto legislation and call a special session of Congress. The President appoints judges to the courts and can grant pardons for federal offenses.

**The Judicial Branch:** The Supreme Court interprets laws and treaties and can declare an act unconstitutional. The Chief Justice presides at an impeachment trial of the President.

**The Legislative Branch:** Congress can override a presidential veto of a bill with a two-thirds majority. Presidential appointments and treaties must be approved by the Senate. Congress also oversees the jurisdiction of the courts and can impeach and try the President and federal judges.

**The Senate,** sitting in session in the US Capitol.

## The Executive Branch

The President, together with the Vice President, is elected for a four-year term. The President suggests, approves, and vetoes legislation. The Executive also develops foreign policy and directs relations with other countries, serves as Commander-in-Chief of the armed forces, and appoints ambassadors. Secretaries to the Cabinet, composed of various heads of departments, meet regularly to advise the President on policy issues. Several agencies and councils, such as the National Security Council and the Office of Management and Budget, help determine the executive agenda.

Seal of the President

**Ulysses S. Grant** served as the US President from 1869 to 1877.

```
EXECUTIVE BRANCH
      |
   PRESIDENT
      |
VICE PRESIDENT
      |
   CABINET
```

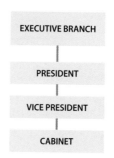

**Henry A. Wallace** served as Vice President under Franklin D. Roosevelt, from 1941 to 1945.

**The White House** is the official residence of the US President.

**Madeleine Albright,** the first woman to serve as Secretary of State, was appointed in 1997.

## The Judicial Branch

The Supreme Court and other federal courts determine the constitutionality of federal, state, and local laws. They hear cases relating to controversies between states and those affecting ambassadors or citizens of different states. They also try cases on appeal. The Supreme Court consists of nine justices appointed for life by the President.

**The Supreme Court** is the highest court in the United States and is the last stop in issues of constitutionality.

**Thurgood Marshall** was the first African American to be a Supreme Court Justice. He held the position from 1967 to 1991.

**JUDICIAL BRANCH**

**9 SUPREME COURT JUSTICES**

**OF WHOM ONE IS CHIEF SUPREME COURT JUSTICE**

**Earl Warren** was Supreme Court Justice from 1953 to 1969. He wrote the unanimous opinion in Brown v. Board of Education (1954). (See p50).

**Oliver Wendell Holmes,** Supreme Court Justice from 1902 to 1932, was a strong advocate of free speech.

## The Legislative Branch

The Congress of the United States consists of two bodies, the House of Representatives and the Senate. Representatives to the House are elected by the voters in each state for a two-year term. The number of Representatives for each state is determined by the state's population. The Senate is composed of two Senators from each state, elected for six-year terms. Congress regulates commerce and is empowered to levy taxes and declare war. This branch also makes the laws: bills discussed, written, and revised in legislative committees must be passed first by the House and by the Senate before being approved by the President.

**Daniel Webster** served both in the House of Representatives (1813–17) and in the Senate (1822–41).

**LEGISLATIVE BRANCH**

**HOUSE OF REPRESENTATIVES**

**SENATE**

**Sam Rayburn** was a popular and distinguished Speaker of the House.

**Edward Kennedy,** leader of the United States' most famous political family, served in the Senate from 1962 until his death in 2009.

**The US Capitol** is home to both the House of Representatives and the Senate.

# WASHINGTON, DC AT A GLANCE

Washington is more than just the political capital of the United States. It is also the home of the Smithsonian Institution, and as such is the cultural focus of America. Its many superb museums and galleries have something to offer everyone. Always one of the most popular sights, the president's official residence, the White House, attracts millions of visitors each year. Equally popular is the

National Air and Space Museum, which draws vast numbers of visitors to its awe-inspiring displays of air and spacecraft. Also of particular interest are Washington's many monuments and memorials. The huge Washington Monument, honoring the first US president, dominates the city skyline. In contrast, the war memorials, dedicated to the thousands of soldiers who died in battle, are quietly poignant.

## Washington's Top Ten Attractions

The White House *See pp104–13*

**National Air and Space Museum**
*See pp64–7*

**National Gallery of Art**
*See pp60–63*

**Kennedy Center**
*See pp120–21*

**Vietnam Veterans Memorial**
*See p85*

**Washington National Cathedral** *See pp144–5*

**Arlington National Cemetery** *See pp132–3*

**Washington Monument** *See p80*

**Lincoln Memorial**
*See p86*

**US Capitol**
*See pp52–3*

◀ Statue of General Grant in front of the United States Capitol

# Museums and Galleries in Washington, DC

Few cities can claim to have as many museums and galleries in such a concentrated area as Washington. The Mall forms the main focus because it is lined with museums. Most of these are part of the Smithsonian Institution *(see p74)*, which is funded by the government. They cover a wide range of exhibits, from great works of art to space shuttles, to mementos of major events in American history. Admission to most of the museums and galleries is free.

**National Museum of American History**
This statue of a toga-clad George Washington is one of millions of artifacts in this museum of American history *(see pp76–9)*.

Georgetown

The White House and Foggy Bottom

Tidal Basin

*P o t o m a c   R i v e r*

**Corcoran Gallery of Art**
This Beaux Arts building houses a collection of American and European art and sculpture, including some of the best works by US artists of the 19th and 20th centuries *(see p115)*.

**US Holocaust Memorial Museum**
Photographs, videos, and re-created concentration camp barracks bring to life the brutality of the Holocaust and illustrate the terrible fate of Jews and others in World War II Nazi Germany *(see pp82–3)*.

**Smithsonian American Art Museum and the National Portrait Gallery**
This Neo-Classical building houses the world's largest collection of American paintings, sculpture, photographs, and crafts *(see pp100–3).*

**National Museum of Natural History**
A huge African elephant is the focal point of the building's main foyer. The museum's fascinating exhibits trace the evolution of animals and explain the creation of gems and minerals *(see pp72–3).*

Penn Quarter

The Mall

Capitol Hill

**National Gallery of Art**
The futuristic East Building houses the 20th-century art in this collection, while the 1930s West Building is home to older works *(see pp56–63).*

0 meters 500
0 yards 500

**National Air and Space Museum**
Washington's most popular museum has exhibits from aviation and space history, including the Wright Brothers' first airborne plane and the Apollo 14 space module *(see pp64–7).*

# Monuments and Memorials in Washington, DC

As the political center of the United States, and home of its president, Washington has a great number of monuments and memorials honoring America's key figures and historic events. The most well-known among these are the Washington Monument and the Lincoln Memorial – sights of great interest to all who visit the city. For those who wish to remember the countless men and women who lost their lives fighting for their nation, there are poignant monuments, set in tranquil parks, where visitors can reflect in peace.

**Korean War Veterans Memorial**
Created in 1995, the 19 stainless steel, larger than life-size statues of this memorial recall the thousands who died in the Korean War *(see p85)*.

**Georgetown**

**The White House and Foggy Bottom**

**Lincoln Memorial**
This emotive and inspirational marble figure has often been the focus of civil rights protests *(see p87)*.

*Potomac River*

0 meters 500
0 yards 500

**Iwo Jima Statue (US Marine Corps Memorial)**
This iconic memorial depicts US Marines capturing the Japanese island of Iwo Jima at the end of World War II *(see p136)*.

**Vietnam Veterans Memorial**
Visitors to this dramatic memorial are confronted by a sobering list of names on the V-shaped granite walls *(see p85)*.

**Martin Luther King, Jr. Memorial**
Surrounded by cherry blossom trees and including an inscription on the wall, this is the first memorial on the Mall to an African-American *(see p85)*.

**Washington Monument**
One of the most enduring images of Washington, this 555-ft (170-m) marble obelisk can be seen from all over the city. Built in two stages, the monument was finally completed in 1884 *(see p80)*.

Penn Quarter

Capitol Hill

The Mall

**Jefferson Memorial**
This Neo-Classical building houses a bronze statue of President Jefferson, the key player in America's struggle for independence *(see p81)*.

**Franklin D. Roosevelt Memorial**
This vast memorial, in the form of a 7-acre park, includes statuary, waterfalls, and ornamental gardens *(see pp86–7)*.

# WASHINGTON, DC THROUGH THE YEAR

A wide variety of events takes place in Washington, DC all through the year. In late March or early April, when the famous cherry blossoms bloom, the city really comes to life. Parades and outdoor festivals begin, and continue through the summer as more and more people come to explore the DC area in June, July, and August. The White House is a focus for many visitors, and it plays host to annual events such as the Easter Egg Roll in the spring and the Garden Tours in the spring and fall. Some of the more popular events are listed below; for further details on these and other events in the city, contact the Destination DC tourist office (see p207).

## Spring

The air is clear in springtime in Washington, DC, with crisp mornings and warm, balmy days. The cherry tree blossoms surrounding the Tidal Basin are world famous and should not be missed, although the area does get very busy. Memorial Day is a big event in DC; it marks the official beginning of summer, and is celebrated in many ways.

### March

**Washington Home and Garden Show**, Walter E. Washington DC Convention Center, 801 Mount Vernon Place, NW (7th St and New York Ave, NW). **Tel** (202) 249-4039. A vast array of garden items.
**St. Patrick's Day** (Sun before Mar 17), Constitution Ave, NW. Parade celebrating Irish culture. There are also celebrations in Old Town Alexandria.
**Cherry Blossom Kite Festival** (last Sat), Washington Monument. **Tel** (202) 633-1000. Kite designers fly their best models and compete for prizes.

### April

**National Cherry Blossom Festival** (late Mar–early Apr), Constitution Ave, NW. **Tel** 1-877-442-5666. Parade and concerts to celebrate the blooming of Washington's famous trees.
**White House Egg Roll** (Easter Mon), White House Lawn. www.whitehouse.gov/easteregg roll. Children's races with eggs.
**White House Spring Garden Tours** (second weekend), White House gardens. **Tel** (202) 456-7041. Tour of the Jacqueline Kennedy Garden and more.
**Thomas Jefferson's Birthday** (Apr 13), Jefferson Memorial. **Tel** (202) 426-6821. Military drills, speeches, and wreath-laying.
**Shakespeare's Birthday Celebration** (end of Apr), Folger Shakespeare Library, 201 E Capitol St, SE. **Tel** (202) 544-4600. A day of music, plays, food, and children's events.

Mother-and-daughter team in the Easter Egg Roll at the White House

### May

**Flower Mart** (first Fri & Sat), Washington National Cathedral. **Tel** (202) 537-6200. Flower booths, music, and crafts.
**Memorial Day Weekend Concert** (last Sun), West Lawn of Capitol. **Tel** (202) 619-7222. National Symphony Orchestra performs. **Memorial Day** (last Mon), Arlington National Cemetery. **Tel** (703) 607-8000. US Navy Memorial. **Tel** (202) 737-2300. Vietnam Veterans Memorial. **Tel** (202) 619-7222. Wreath-laying, speeches, and music to honor war veterans.
**Memorial Day Jazz Festival** (last Mon), Old Town Alexandria. **Tel** (703) 746-5592. Live, big-band jazz music.
**Twilight Tattoo Military Pageant** (7pm every Wed, May & Jun), Fort McNair. **Tel** (202) 685-2888. Military parade presenting the history of the US Army.

Cherry tree blossoms surrounding Jefferson Memorial at the Tidal Basin

## Average Daily Hours of Sunshine

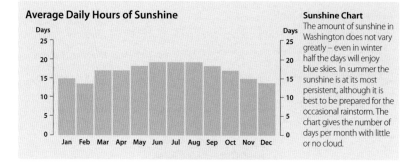

**Sunshine Chart**
The amount of sunshine in Washington does not vary greatly – even in winter half the days will enjoy blue skies. In summer the sunshine is at its most persistent, although it is best to be prepared for the occasional rainstorm. The chart gives the number of days per month with little or no cloud.

## Summer

In June, July, and August, visitors come to Washington, DC from far and wide. The streets and parks are packed with people enjoying the sunshine. Many attractions become overcrowded, so it is important to call ahead and make reservations at this time of year.

The summer months can also be extremely hot and humid; even so, parades and outdoor fairs are usually very popular. Independence Day on July 4 is particularly exciting, with a parade during the day and fireworks at night.

### June

**Taste of Georgetown** *(second Sat)*, Wisconsin Ave, NW. **Tel** (202) 298-9222. Washington's finest restaurants showcase their talents.
**Smithsonian Festival of American Folklife** *(late Jun–early Jul)*, The Mall. **Tel** (202) 633-6440. A huge celebration of folk culture, including music, dance, games, and food.
**Capitol Pride** *(mid-Jun)*, Pennsylvania Ave, NW. Street festival and parade celebrating the gay communities of DC.
**DC Caribbean Carnival** *(last Sat in Jun)*, Georgia Ave, NW. A colorful parade of more than 3,000 masqueraders, plus food, dance, and music.

### July

**Independence Day** *(Jul 4)*, Constitution Ave & US Capitol, other areas. Concert on west front of the Capitol. A parade along Constitution Avenue,

Fireworks over Washington, DC on the Fourth of July

with fireworks from the base of the Washington Monument. Other areas such as Old Town Alexandria and Mount Vernon have parades and fireworks.
**Bastille Day** *(Jul 14)*. A celebration involving food, music, and dance. Events are held in the French Embassy and selected cafés and restaurants.
**Mary McLeod Bethune Celebration** *(Jul 10)*, Bethune Statue, Lincoln Park, E Capitol St, SE, between 11th St & 13th St. **Tel** (202) 673-2402. Memorial wreath-laying, gospel music, and speeches.

**Capital Fringe Festival** *(Jul)*, venues all over the city. Modeled on Edinburgh's Fringe festival, the focus is on theater, dance, puppetry, and the spoken word. Film and visual arts also feature.
**Screen on the Green** *(Beginning at dusk: Mon evening Jul–Aug)*, The Mall. **Tel** 1-877-262-5866. A Washington summer tradition. Classic movies are shown on giant screens.

### August

**Shakespeare Free for All** *(mid-Aug)*, Sidney Harmon Hall, 610 F St, NW. www. shakespearetheatre.org. Nightly performances by the Shakespeare Theater Company, free of charge.
**Arlington County Fair** *(mid-Aug)*, Thomas Jefferson Center, Arlington, VA. **Tel** (703) 829-7471. www.arlingtoncountyfair.us. Food, crafts, music, and fairground rides.
**National Frisbee Festival** *(late Aug)*, Washington Monument. **Tel** (202) 619-7222. A weekend celebrating the game of Frisbee, including a free Frisbee contest for champions and amateurs alike.

A frenzy of Frisbee throwing at Washington's National Frisbee Festival

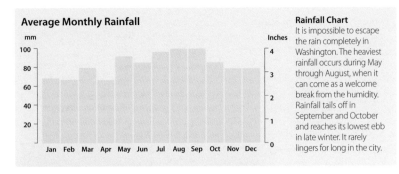

## Average Monthly Rainfall

**Rainfall Chart**
It is impossible to escape the rain completely in Washington. The heaviest rainfall occurs during May through August, when it can come as a welcome break from the humidity. Rainfall tails off in September and October and reaches its lowest ebb in late winter. It rarely lingers for long in the city.

A school band performing in front of the Lincoln Memorial

## Fall

With the air turning cooler, Labor Day (the first Monday in September) bids goodbye to the summer. The fall (autumn) season covers September, October, and November in Washington, when the temperatures steadily drop. A particularly enjoyable event at this time of year is Halloween, when children dress up as their favorite creatures or characters to go trick-or-treating.

Halloween
Jack-O'-Lantern

### September
**Labor Day Weekend Concert** *(Sun before Labor Day)*, West Lawn of the US Capitol. **Tel** (202) 619-7222. National Symphony Orchestra performs a concert.
**Fiesta DC** *(Sep)*, Columbia Heights neighborhood. A celebration of Latino culture.
**International Children's Festival**, Wolf Trap Park, Vienna, VA. **Tel** (703) 255-1900.

Musical and dance performances are held from around the world.
**National Book Fair** *(Sep)*, National Mall. **Tel** (202) 707-5000. A two-day event where more than 80 award-winning authors, illustrators, and poets talk about their books and participate in book signing.
**Adams-Morgan Day Festival** *(second Sun)*. Giant street party with music, food, and crafts.
**Colonial Market and Fair**, Mount Vernon, VA. **Tel** (703) 780-2000. Craft demonstrations and 18th-century entertainment.

### October
**Columbus Day** *(second Mon)*, Columbus Memorial, Union Station. **Tel** (202) 289-1908. Speeches and wreath-laying in honour of the man who discovered America.
**White House Fall Garden Tours** *(mid-Oct)*. **Tel** (202) 456-7041. A chance to walk the grounds of the President's home.
**Boo at the Zoo** *(end Oct)*,

Washington National Zoo. **Tel** (202) 397-7328, or buy tickets at the zoo. Halloween celebration for children.
**Halloween** *(Oct 31)*. Young people trick-or-treating, dressed as ghosts, clowns, and witches. Dupont Circle and Georgetown are popular areas.

### November
**Veterans Day Ceremonies** *(Nov 11)*, Arlington National Cemetery. **Tel** (703) 607-8000. Services, parades, and wreath-layings take place at various memorials around the city, commemorating United States military personnel who died in war. There are special Veterans Day ceremonies also at the Vietnam Veterans Memorial. **Tel** (202) 426-6841, and at the US Navy Memorial **Tel** (202) 737-2300).
**Kennedy Center Holiday Festival** *(late Nov–New Year's Eve)*. **Tel** (202) 467-4600. Musicals, ballet, and classical concerts for the holiday season.

Military guard on Veterans Day in Arlington National Cemetery

## Average Monthly Temperature

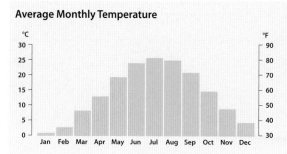

**Temperature Chart**
Washington's climate varies greatly. In winter the air is bitterly cold, with temperatures rising little above freezing. In July and August, however, it becomes very hot and extremely humid. The best time to visit the city is in the spring or fall, when the weather is pleasantly mild and the air is clear.

## Winter

Temperatures can plummet below freezing during the winter months of December, January, and February. Hence the city is generally quieter at this time of year, making it a good time to see the most popular sights. Over the Christmas period, Washington becomes busy again with festive events to get people into the holiday spirit. Decorations are visible across the city, and many places offer Christmas tours.

Toward the end of winter, a number of famous birthdays are celebrated, including those of Martin Luther King, Jr. and Presidents Abraham Lincoln and George Washington.

### December
**National Christmas Tree Lighting** *(mid-Dec)*, Ellipse south of the White House. www.thenationaltree.org. The President turns on the lights on the National Christmas tree (advance tickets only).

**Washington National Cathedral Christmas Services** *(throughout Dec)*. **Tel** (202) 537-6200. Holiday celebrations with festive music.
**Christmas at Mount Vernon** *(weekends late Nov–mid-Dec)*, Mount Vernon, VA. **Tel** (703) 780-2000. Experience an 18th-century Christmas.

### January
**Robert E. Lee's Birthday** *(mid-Jan)*. Tours of the Lee-Fendall house in Alexandria. **Tel** (703) 548-1789.
**Martin Luther King, Jr.'s Birthday** *(third Mon)*. Commemorative events.
**Restaurant week** *(mid-Jan)*. Many of Washington's top restaurants offer prix fixe lunch or dinner specials.

### Febuary
**Chinese New Year** *(first two weeks)*, N St, Chinatown. **Tel** *(202) 789-7000*. Parades, dancing, and live music.
**African American History Month** *(throughout Feb)*. Various events are held across the city:

contact the Smithsonian (**Tel** (202) 633-1000) and the National Park Service (**Tel** (202) 619-7222). **George Washington's Birthday Parade** *(around Feb 15)*, Old Town Alexandria, VA. **Tel** (703) 838-4200.
**Abraham Lincoln's Birthday**, *(Feb 12)*, Lincoln Memorial. **Tel** (202) 619-7222. Wreath-laying ceremony followed by a reading of the Gettysburg Address.

Girl Scouts watching George Washington's Birthday Parade

### Federal Holidays
**New Year's Day** (Jan 1)
**Martin Luther King, Jr.'s Birthday** (3rd Mon in Jan)
**Presidents' Day** (3rd Mon in Feb)
**Easter Monday** (Mar or Apr)
**Memorial Day** (last Mon in May)
**Independence Day** (Jul 4)
**Labor Day** (1st Mon in Sep)
**Columbus Day** (2nd Mon in Oct)
**Veterans Day** (Nov 11)
**Thanksgiving** (4th Thu in Nov)
**Christmas Day** (Dec 25)

The National Christmas tree outside a snow-covered White House

United States Capitol at sunrise ▶

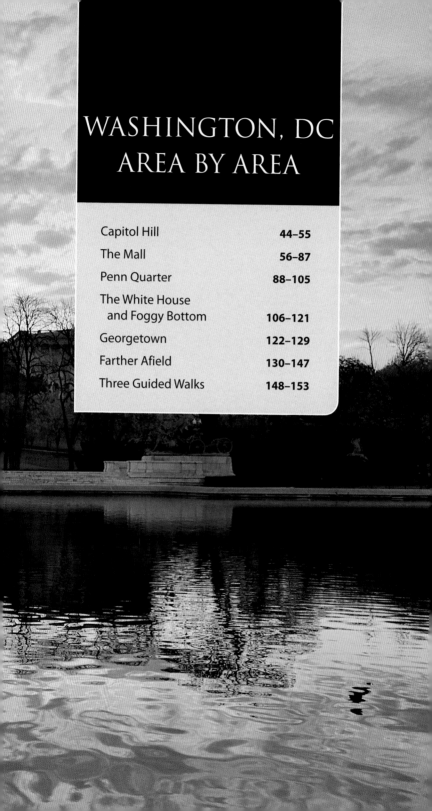

# WASHINGTON, DC AREA BY AREA

# CAPITOL HILL

Soon after the Constitution was ratified in 1788, America's seat of government began to take root on Capitol Hill. The site was chosen in 1791 from 10 acres that were ceded by the state of Maryland. Pierre L'Enfant *(see p21)* chose a hill on the east side of the area as the foundation for the Capitol building and the center of the new city.

In more than 200 years, Capitol Hill has developed into a bustling microcosm of modern America. Symbols of the country's cultural development are everywhere, from its federal buildings to its centers of commerce, shops, and restaurants, as well as its multicultural residential areas.

The Capitol Hill area is frequented by the most powerful people in the United States. While access to official government buildings is strictly controlled for reasons of security, ordinary citizens may still find members of Congress greeting tour groups in the halls of the Capitol or dining at local restaurants.

## Sights at a Glance

### Historic Buildings
1 Library of Congress pp48–9
2 Folger Shakespeare Library
3 US Supreme Court
4 Sewall-Belmont House
5 United States Capitol pp52–3
13 Union Station

### Museums and Galleries
14 National Postal Museum

### Market
12 Eastern Market

### Monuments and Memorials
6 Robert A. Taft Memorial
7 National Japanese American Memorial
8 Ulysses S. Grant Memorial

### Parks and Gardens
9 US Botanic Garden
10 Bartholdi Park and Fountain

### Church
11 Ebenezer United Methodist Church

### Restaurants *see p183*
1 Acqua Al 2
2 Banana Café
3 Belga Café
4 Bistro Bis
5 Bullfeathers
6 Cava Mezze
7 Dubliner
8 Ethiopic
9 Five Guys
10 Good Stuff Eatery
11 Market Lunch
12 The Monocle
13 Montmartre
14 Sonoma
15 Tortilla Coast
16 Toscana Café
17 Tunnicliff's
18 We, the Pizza

See also Street Finder map 4

0 meters 500
0 yards 500

◀ United States Capitol with cherry blossom in foreground

**For keys to symbols** see back flap

# Street-by-Street: Capitol Hill

The cityscape extending from the Capitol is an impressive combination of grand classical architecture and stretches of grassy open spaces. There are no skyscrapers here, only the immense marble halls and columns that distinguish many of the government buildings. The bustle and excitement around the US Capitol and US Supreme Court contrast with the calm that can be found by the reflecting pool or in a quiet residential street. Many of the small touches that make the city special can be found in this area, such as the antique lighting fixtures on Second Street, the brilliant bursts of flowers along the sidewalks, or the brightly painted façades of houses on Third Street near the Folger Shakespeare Library.

**5** ★ **US Capitol**
The famous dome of the nation's seat of government is one of the largest in the world.

**6** **Robert A. Taft Memorial**
A statue of Taft (1889–1953) stands in front of the bell tower that was erected to honor his principles and achievements.

**Ulysses S. Grant Memorial**
General Grant (1822–85), the Union leader in the American Civil War, is the central figure in a remarkable group of bronze equestrian statuary.

**8** **US Botanic Garden**
Established in 1820, the Botanic Garden contains thousands of exotic and domestic plants.

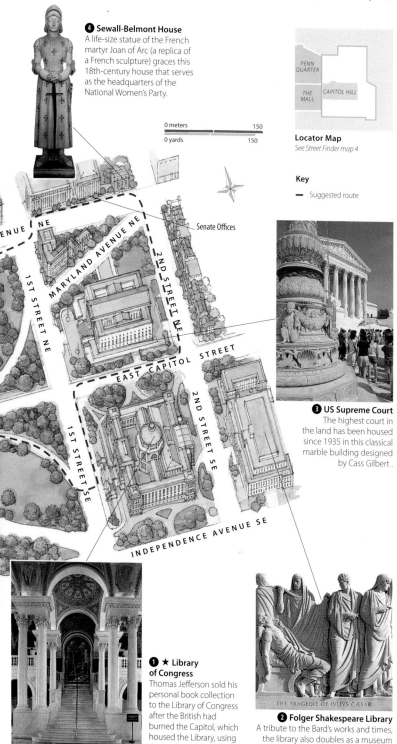

**4 Sewall-Belmont House**
A life-size statue of the French martyr Joan of Arc (a replica of a French sculpture) graces this 18th-century house that serves as the headquarters of the National Women's Party.

| 0 meters | | 150 |
| 0 yards | | 150 |

Senate Offices

**Locator Map**
*See Street Finder map 4*

**Key**

— Suggested route

ENUE NE

MARYLAND AVENUE NE

2ND STREET NE

1ST STREET NE

EAST CAPITOL STREET

2ND STREET SE

1ST STREET SE

INDEPENDENCE AVENUE SE

**3 US Supreme Court**
The highest court in the land has been housed since 1935 in this classical marble building designed by Cass Gilbert .

**1 ★ Library of Congress**
Thomas Jefferson sold his personal book collection to the Library of Congress after the British had burned the Capitol, which housed the Library, using the books as kindling.

THE TRAGEDIE OF IVLIVS CÆSAR

**2 Folger Shakespeare Library**
A tribute to the Bard's works and times, the library also doubles as a museum displaying Elizabethan treasures.

# ❶ Library of Congress

Congress first established a reference library in the US Capitol in 1800. When the Capitol was burned in 1814, Thomas Jefferson offered his own collection as a replacement, his belief in a universality of knowledge becoming the foundation for the Library's acquisition policy. In 1897 the Library of Congress moved to an Italian Renaissance-style building designed by John L. Smithmeyer and Paul J. Pelz. The main building, the Thomas Jefferson Building, is a marvel of art and architecture, with its paintings, mosaics, and exhibitions, such as Creating the United States and Thomas Jefferson's Library. The Library of Congress has the world's largest collection of books, with over 650 miles (1,050 km) of bookshelves housing 35 million volumes.

Front façade of the Jefferson Building

★ **Main Reading Room**
Eight huge marble columns and 10-ft (3-m) high female figures personifying aspects of human endeavor dwarf the reading desks in this room. The domed ceiling soars 160 ft (49 m) above the reading room floor.

**African & Middle Eastern Reading Room**
This is one of 10 reading rooms in the Jefferson Building where visitors can use books from the Library's collections.

**KEY**

① Exhibition Area

② Asian Reading Room

**Mosaic of Minerva**
This beautiful marble mosaic figure of Minerva of Peace, created by Elihu Vedder, dominates the staircase landing near the Visitors' Gallery, overlooking the Main Reading Room.

## VISITORS' CHECKLIST

**Practical Information**
**Map** 4 E4.
101 Independence Avenue SE.
**Tel** (202) 707-8000.
**W** loc.gov
**Open** 8:30am–4:30pm Mon–Sat.
**Closed** Jan 1, Thanksgiving, Dec 25.
(202) 707-0919 (group tours).
For reading rooms access, visitors must be over 18 and have a user card, obtained by presenting a driver's license or passport and completing a registration form.

**Transport**
**M** Capitol South.
32, 34, 36, 96.

★ **Gutenberg Bible**
The 15th-century Gutenberg Bible was the first book printed using movable metal type. This is one of only three perfect vellum copies.

Main Entrance

**Neptune Fountain**
The bronze statue of Neptune, the Roman god of the sea, forms a striking feature at the front of the Jefferson Building.

★ **Great Hall**
Splendid marble arches and columns, grand staircases, imposing bronze statues, stained-glass skylights, mosaics, and murals all combine to create a magnificent entrance hall.

## ❷ Folger Shakespeare Library

201 E Capitol St, SE. **Map** 4 F4.
**Tel** (202) 544-4600. Ⓜ Capitol South.
**Open** 10am–5pm Mon–Sat. **Closed**
Federal hols. 📷 ♿ Tickets for plays,
concerts, and readings available from
box office. 🆆 **folger.edu**

Inspired by Shakespeare's own era, this library and museum celebrate the works and times of the Elizabethan playwright.

The research library was a gift to the American people in 1932 from Henry Clay Folger who, as a student in 1874, began to collect Shakespeare's works. Folger also funded the construction of this edifice, built specifically to house his collection. It contains 310,000 Elizabethan books and manuscripts, as well as the world's largest collection of Shakespeare's writings, including a third of the surviving copies of the 1623 First Folio (first editions of Shakespeare's works). One of these first editions is displayed in the oak-paneled Great Hall, along with books and engravings.

The Folger hosts many cultural events. For example, there are regular performances of Shakespeare's plays in the library's 250-seat reconstruction of an Elizabethan theater. There is also an annual series of poetry readings, as well as numerous lectures and talks throughout the year. The Folger Consort early music ensemble, performs concerts of 12th- to 20th-century music.
In the grounds of the library,

The Great Hall in the Folger Shakespeare Library

The impressive Neo-Classical façade of the US Supreme Court

the Elizabethan Garden has plants and flowers that are featured in Shakespeare's plays. Shakespeare's birthday is celebrated every April with jugglers, music, theater shows, and a tour of the library.

## ❸ US Supreme Court

1st St between E Capitol St and
Maryland Ave, NE. **Map** 4 E4.
**Tel** (202) 479-3000. Ⓜ Capitol South.
**Open** 9am–4:30pm Mon–Fri.
**Closed** Federal hols. 📷 🖥 ♿
Lectures. 🆆 **supremecourtus.gov**

The Supreme Court forms the judicial and third branch of the US government *(see pp30–31)*. It was established in 1787 at the Philadelphia Constitutional Convention and provides the last stop in the disposition of the nation's legal disputes and issues of constitutionality. Groundbreaking cases settled here include *Brown v. Board of Education*, which abolished racial segregation in schools, and *Miranda v. Arizona*, which declared crime suspects were

entitled to a lawyer before being interrogated. The Court is charged to guarantee "Equal Justice Under Law," the motto emblazoned over the entrance.

As recently as 1929 the Supreme Court was still meeting in various sections of the US Capitol building. Then, at Chief Justice William Howard Taft's urging, Congress authorized a separate building to be constructed. The result was a magnificent Corinthian edifice, designed by Cass Gilbert, that opened in 1935. Sculptures depicting the allegorical figures of the Contemplation of Justice and the Guardian of the Law stand beside the steps while on the pediment above the entrance are figures of Taft (far left) and John Marshall, the fourth Chief Justice (far right).

Visitors can watch the court in session Monday to Wednesday from October to April. Admission is on a first-come, first-served basis. When court is not in session, public lectures on the Supreme Court are held every hour on the half-hour in the Courtroom (contact for confirmation).

Hallway of the 18th-century Sewall-Belmont House

## ❹ Sewall-Belmont House

2nd St and Constitution Ave, NE. **Map** 4 E4. **Tel** (202) 546-1210. Ⓜ Capitol South, Union Station. **Open** noon–5pm Wed–Sun. **Closed** Federal hols. Donations welcome. 🅿️ 📷 🌐 **w** sewallbelmont.org

Robert Sewall, the original owner of this charming 18th-century house, rented it out to Albert Gallatin, the Treasury Secretary under President Thomas Jefferson, in the early 1800s. It was here Gallatin entertained a number of wealthy contributors whose financial backing brought about the Louisiana Purchase in 1803, which doubled the size of the United States. During the British invasion in 1814, the house was the only site in Washington to resist the attack. While the US Capitol was burning, American soldiers took refuge in the house from where they fired upon the British.

The National Women's Party, who won the right to vote for American women in 1920, bought the house in 1929 with the help of feminist divorcee Alva Vanderbilt Belmont. Today, the house is still the headquarters of the Party, and visitors can admire the period furnishings and suffragist artifacts. The desk on which the, as yet unratified, Equal Rights Amendment of 1923 was written by Alice Paul, leader of the Party, is here.

## ❺ US Capitol

*See pp52–3.*

## ❻ Robert A. Taft Memorial

Constitution Ave and 1st St, NW. **Map** 4 E4. Ⓜ Union Station. ♿

This statue of Ohio senator Robert A. Taft (1889–1953) stands in a park opposite the US Capitol. The statue itself, by sculptor Wheeler Williams, is dwarfed by a vast, white bell tower (the Carillon), that rises up behind the figure of the politician. The memorial, designed by Douglas W. Orr, was erected in 1959 as a "tribute to the honesty, indomitable courage, and high principles of free government symbolized by his life." The son of President William Howard Taft, Robert Taft was a Republican, famous for sponsoring the Taft-Hartley Act, the regulator of collective bargaining between labor and management.

## ❼ National Japanese American Memorial

Louisiana and New Jersey Avenues at D St, NW. **Map** 4 E3. Ⓜ Union Station.

This memorial, designed by Davis Buckley, commemorates the story of the 120,000 Japanese Americans interned during World War II and the more than 800 Japanese

Statue of Robert Taft

Americans who died in military service. The names of these servicemen are carved upon a curving granite wall, while etched on the top are the names of the ten detention camps where Japanese American civilians were confined. An 18-foot long aluminum gong may be rung by visitors, serving as a call to reflection and remembrance.

## ❽ Ulysses S. Grant Memorial

Union Square, west side of US Capitol in front of Reflecting Pool. **Map** 4 E4. Ⓜ Capitol South, Union Station. **Open** Visitor center: 9am–5pm daily. ♿

This dramatic memorial was sculpted by Henry Merwin Shrady and dedicated in 1922. With its 13 horses, it is one of the world's most complex equestrian statues. The bronze groupings around General Grant provide a graphic depiction of the suffering of the Civil War. In the artillery group, horses and soldiers pulling a cannon are urged on by their mounted leader. The infantry group storms into the heat of battle, where a horse and rider have already fallen under the charge.

Shrady worked on the sculpture for 20 years, using soldiers in training for his models. He died two weeks before it was dedicated.

The artillery group in the Ulysses S. Grant Civil War Memorial

# ❺ United States Capitol

The US Capitol is one of the world's best-known symbols of democracy. The center of America's legislative process for 200 years, its Neo-Classical architecture reflects the democratic principles of ancient Greece and Rome. The cornerstone was laid by George Washington in 1793, and by 1800 the Capitol was occupied. The British burned it down in the War of 1812, but restoration began in 1815. Many architectural and artistic features, such as the Statue of Freedom and Brumidi's murals, were added later. An impressive Capitol Visitor Center, located below the East Plaza, offers improved visitor access and facilities.

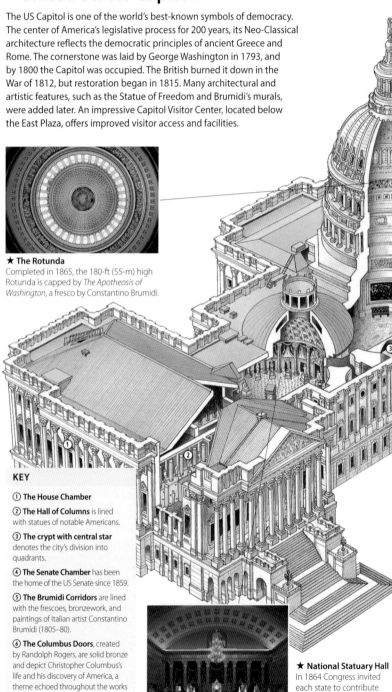

**★ The Rotunda**
Completed in 1865, the 180-ft (55-m) high Rotunda is capped by *The Apotheosis of Washington*, a fresco by Constantino Brumidi.

**KEY**

① **The House Chamber**

② **The Hall of Columns** is lined with statues of notable Americans.

③ **The crypt with central star** denotes the city's division into quadrants.

④ **The Senate Chamber** has been the home of the US Senate since 1859.

⑤ **The Brumidi Corridors** are lined with the frescoes, bronzework, and paintings of Italian artist Constantino Brumidi (1805–80).

⑥ **The Columbus Doors**, created by Randolph Rogers, are solid bronze and depict Christopher Columbus's life and his discovery of America, a theme echoed throughout the works of art in the Capitol.

**★ National Statuary Hall**
In 1864 Congress invited each state to contribute two statues of prominent citizens to stand in this hall.

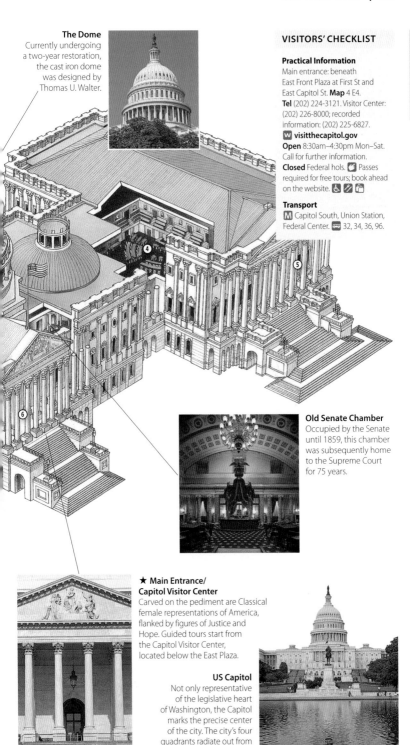

**The Dome**
Currently undergoing a two-year restoration, the cast iron dome was designed by Thomas U. Walter.

**VISITORS' CHECKLIST**

**Practical Information**
Main entrance: beneath East Front Plaza at First St and East Capitol St. **Map** 4 E4.
**Tel** (202) 224-3121. Visitor Center: (202) 226-8000; recorded information: (202) 225-6827.
**w** visitthecapitol.gov
**Open** 8:30am–4:30pm Mon–Sat. Call for further information.
**Closed** Federal hols. ☑ Passes required for free tours; book ahead on the website. & ☑ ☑

**Transport**
Ⓜ Capitol South, Union Station, Federal Center. ☒ 32, 34, 36, 96.

**Old Senate Chamber**
Occupied by the Senate until 1859, this chamber was subsequently home to the Supreme Court for 75 years.

**★ Main Entrance/ Capitol Visitor Center**
Carved on the pediment are Classical female representations of America, flanked by figures of Justice and Hope. Guided tours start from the Capitol Visitor Center, located below the East Plaza.

**US Capitol**
Not only representative of the legislative heart of Washington, the Capitol marks the precise center of the city. The city's four quadrants radiate out from the middle of the building.

## ❾ US Botanic Garden

1st St and Independence Ave, SW. Entrance: 100 Maryland Ave, SW. **Map** 4 D4. **Tel** (202) 225-8333. Ⓜ Federal Center SW. **Open** 10am–5pm daily. Ⓖ Ⓦ usbg.gov

The 80-ft (24-m) tall Palm House is the centerpiece of the Botanic Garden Conservatory. The appearance of the 1933 building has been preserved but modernized, creating a spacious venue for the collection of tropical and subtropical plants, and the comprehensive fern and orchid collections. Other specialties are plants native to deserts in the Old and New Worlds, plants of economic and healing value, and endangered plants rescued through an international trade program.

The Botanic Garden was originally established to cultivate plants that could be beneficial to the American people. The garden was revitalized in 1842, when the Wilkes Expedition to the South Seas brought back an assortment of plants from around the world, some of which are still on display.

A National Garden of plants native to the mid-Atlantic region was created on 3 acres (1 ha) of land west of the Conservatory. It includes a Water Garden, a Rose Garden, and a terraced lawn. Visitors can dial (202) 730-9303 from their cell phones for an audio tour as they walk through.

## ❿ Bartholdi Park and Fountain

Independence Ave and 1st St, SW. **Map** 4 D4. Ⓜ Federal Center SW. Ⓖ Ⓦ usbg.gov/bartholdi-park

The graceful fountain that dominates this jewel of a park was created by Frédéric August Bartholdi (sculptor of the Statue of Liberty) for the 1876 Centennial. Originally lit by gas, it was converted to electric lighting in 1881 and became a nighttime attraction. Made of cast iron, the symmetrical fountain is decorated with figures of nymphs and tritons.

The elegant Bartholdi Fountain, surrounded by miniature gardens

Surrounding the fountain are tiny model gardens, planted to inspire the urban gardener. They are themed, and include Therapeutic, Romantic, and Heritage plants, such as Virginia sneezeweed, sweet william, and wild oats.

## ⓫ Ebenezer United Methodist Church

4th St and D St, SE. **Tel** (202) 544-1636. **Map** 4 F5. Ⓜ Eastern Market. **Open** 10am–2pm Tue–Fri. **Closed** Federal hols.

Ebenezer Church, established in 1819, was the first black church to serve Methodists in Washington. Attendance grew rapidly, and a new church, Little Ebenezer, was built to take the overflow. After the Emancipation Proclamation in 1863 (see p23), Congress decreed that black children should receive public education. In 1864, Little Ebenezer became the District of Columbia's first school for black children. The number of members steadily increased and another church was built in 1868, but this was badly damaged by a storm in 1896. The replacement church, which was constructed in 1897 and is still here today, is Ebenezer United Methodist Church. A model of Little Ebenezer stands next to it.

## ⓬ Eastern Market

7th St and C St, SE. **Map** 4 F4. Ⓜ Eastern Market. **Open** 7am–7pm Tue–Fri, 7am–6pm Sat, 9am–5pm Sun. **Closed** Jan 1, Jul 4, Thanksgiving, Dec 25 & 26. Ⓖ at West end. Ⓦ easternmarket-dc.org

This block-long market hall has been a fixture in Capitol Hill since 1871, and the provisions sold today still have an Old World flavor. Big beefsteaks and fresh pigs' feet are plentiful, along with gourmet sausages and cheeses from all over the world. The aroma of fresh bread, roasted chicken, and flowers pervades the hall. On Friday afternoons

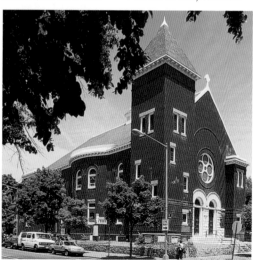

The redbrick, late-19th-century Ebenezer United Methodist Church

Flowers for sale on the sidewalk outside the Eastern Market

and Saturdays, the covered stalls outside are filled with crafts and farmers' produce, while on Sundays they host a flea market. The markets draw large crowds.

Eastern Market was designed by local architect Adolph Cluss. It is one of the few public markets left in Washington, and the only one that is still used for its original purpose.

## ⓭ Union Station

50 Massachusetts Ave, NE. **Map** 4 E3.
**Tel** (202) 289-1908. Ⓜ Union Station.
**Open** daily. 🅿 🛗 ♿ &
Ⓦ unionstationdc.com

When Union Station opened in 1908, its fine Beaux Arts design (by Daniel H. Burnham) set a standard that influenced architecture in Washington for 40 years. The elegantly proportioned white granite structure, its three main archways modeled on the Arch of Constantine in Rome, was the largest train station in the world. For half a century, Union Station was a major transportation hub, but as air travel became increasingly popular, passenger trains went into decline.

By the late 1950s, the size of the station outweighed the number of passsengers it served. For two decades, the railroad authorities and Congress debated its fate. Finally, in 1981, a joint public and private venture set out to restore the building.

Union Station reopened in 1988, and today is the second most visited tourist attraction

in Washington. Its 96-ft (29-m) barrel-vaulted ceiling has been covered with 22-carat gold leaf. There are around 100 specialty shops and a food court to visit, and the Main Hall hosts cultural and civic events throughout the year. The building still serves its original purpose as a station, however, and over 100 trains pass through daily.

## ⓮ National Postal Museum

2 Massachusetts Ave, NE. **Map** 4 E3.
**Tel** (202) 633-5555. Ⓜ Union Station.
**Open** 10am–5:30pm daily.
**Closed** Dec 25. 🗂 🛗 &
Ⓦ postalmuseum.si.edu

Opened by the Smithsonian in 1990, this fascinating museum is housed in the former City Post

Vintage stamp depicting Benjamin Franklin

Office building. Exhibits include a stagecoach and a postal rail car, showing how mail traveled before modern airmail.

"Mail Call", a permanent exhibition, explores the history of the military postal system. The Philatelic Gallery displays one of the best stamp collections in the world. "Binding the Nation" explains the history of the mail from the pre-Revolutionary era to the end of the 19th century. Other exhibits illustrate how the mail system works and how a stamp is created.

At postcard kiosks, you can address a postcard electronically, see the route it will take to its destination, and drop it in a mailbox on the spot.

Columbus Memorial, sculpted by Lorado Taft, in front of Union Station

# THE MALL

In L'Enfant's original plan for the new capital of the United States, the Mall was conceived as a grand boulevard lined with diplomatic residences of elegant, Parisian architecture. L'Enfant's plan was never fully realized, but it is nevertheless a moving sight – this grand, tree-lined expanse is bordered on either side by the Smithsonian museums and features the Capitol at its eastern end and the Washington Monument at its western end. This dramatic formal version of the Mall did not materialize until after World War II. Until then the space was used for everything from a zoo to a railroad terminal to a wood yard.

The Mall forms a vital part of the history of the United States. Innumerable demonstrators have gathered at the Lincoln Memorial and marched to the US Capitol. The Pope said Mass, African-American soprano Marian Anderson sang at the request of first lady Eleanor Roosevelt, and Dr. Martin Luther King, Jr. delivered his famous "I have a dream" speech here. Every year on the Fourth of July (Independence Day), America's birthday party is held on the Mall, with a fireworks display. On summer evenings, teams of locals play softball and soccer on its fields.

## Sights at a Glance

### Museums and Galleries
1. National Gallery of Art pp60–63
2. National Air and Space Museum pp64–7
3. Hirshhorn Museum
4. Arts and Industries Building
5. National Museum of African Art
6. National Museum of the American Indian
7. National Museum of Natural History pp72–3
8. Smithsonian Castle
9. Arthur M. Sackler Gallery
10. Freer Gallery of Art
11. National Museum of American History pp76–8
12. Washington Monument
13. United States Holocaust Memorial Museum pp82–3

### Official Buildings
14. Bureau of Engraving and Printing

### Monuments and Memorials
15. Jefferson Memorial
17. World War II Memorial
18. Vietnam Veterans Memorial
19. Korean War Veterans Memorial
20. Martin Luther King, Jr. Memorial
21. Franklin D. Roosevelt Memorial
22. Lincoln Memorial

### Parks and Gardens
16. Tidal Basin

### Restaurants see p184
1. The Atrium Café
2. Cascade Café
3. CityZen
4. Mitistam Café
5. Pavilion Café

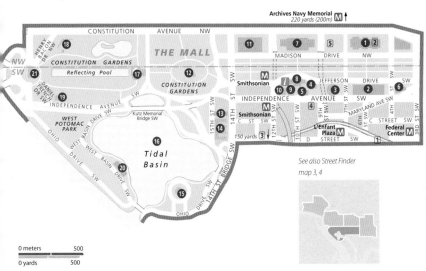

See also Street Finder map 3, 4

| 0 meters | 500 |
| 0 yards | 500 |

◀ America by Air Gallery, National Air and Space Museum

**For keys to symbols** see back flap

# Street-by-Street: The Mall

This 1-mile (1.5-km) boulevard between the Capitol and the Washington Monument is the city's cultural heart; the many different museums of the Smithsonian Institution can be found along this green strip. At the northeast corner of the Mall is the National Gallery of Art. Directly opposite is one of the most popular museums in the world – the National Air and Space Museum, a soaring construction of steel and glass. Both the National Museum of American History and the National Museum of Natural History, on the north side of the Mall, also draw huge numbers of visitors.

**❼ ★ National Museum of Natural History**
The central Rotunda was designed in the Neoclassical style and opened to the public in 1910.

**❽ Smithsonian Castle**
The main information center for all Smithsonian activities, this building once housed the basis of the collections found in numerous museums along the Mall.

**❾ Arthur M. Sackler Gallery**
This extensive collection of Asian art was donated to the nation by New Yorker Arthur Sackler.

**⓫ ★ National Museum of American History**
From George Washington's uniform to this electric streetcar, US history is documented here.

MADISON DRIVE NW

1 2 T H STREET

JEFFERSON DRIVE SW

Washington Monument

**❺ National Museum of African Art**
Founded in 1965 and situated underground, this museum houses a comprehensive collection of ancient and modern African art.

**❿ Freer Gallery of Art**
Asian art, including this 13th-century Chinese silk painting, is a highlight, in addition to a superb Whistler collection.

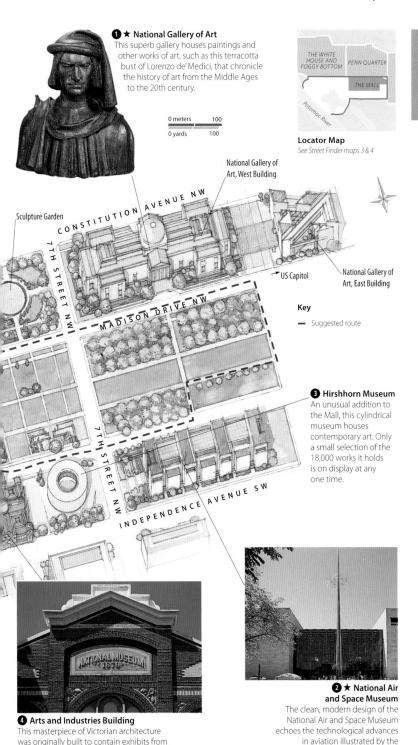

**❶ ★ National Gallery of Art**
This superb gallery houses paintings and other works of art, such as this terracotta bust of Lorenzo de' Medici, that chronicle the history of art from the Middle Ages to the 20th century.

0 meters 100
0 yards 100

**Locator Map**
*See Street Finder maps 3 & 4*

THE WHITE HOUSE AND FOGGY BOTTOM

PENN QUARTER

THE MALL

Potomac River

Sculpture Garden

CONSTITUTION AVENUE NW

National Gallery of Art, West Building

National Gallery of Art, East Building

US Capitol

7TH STREET NW

MADISON DRIVE NW

7TH STREET NW

INDEPENDENCE AVENUE SW

**Key**
— Suggested route

**❸ Hirshhorn Museum**
An unusual addition to the Mall, this cylindrical museum houses contemporary art. Only a small selection of the 18,000 works it holds is on display at any one time.

**❹ Arts and Industries Building**
This masterpiece of Victorian architecture was originally built to contain exhibits from the Centennial Exposition in Philadelphia.

**❷ ★ National Air and Space Museum**
The clean, modern design of the National Air and Space Museum echoes the technological advances in aviation illustrated by the spectacular exhibits inside.

# ❶ National Gallery of Art

In the 1920s, American financier and statesman Andrew Mellon began collecting art with the intention of establishing a new art museum in Washington. In 1936 he offered his collection to the country and offered also to provide a building for the new National Gallery of Art. Designed by architect John Russell Pope, the Neoclassical building was opened in 1941. Other collectors followed Mellon's example and donated their collections to the Gallery, and by the 1960s it had outgrown the West Building. I.M. Pei designed the innovative East Building, which was opened in 1978. The building was paid for by Andrew Mellon's son and daughter.

★ **Ginevra de' Benci**
This depiction of a thoughtful young Florentine girl by Leonardo da Vinci (c.1474) is his only painting in the US.

**The Alba Madonna**
Painted c.1510 by Raphael, this work is considered one of the major achievements of the Renaissance.

★ **Woman with a Parasol – Mme Monet and her Son**
(1875) This painting by Claude Monet of his wife hangs in the West Building.

### Key to Floor Plan

- 13th–15th-century Italian
- 15th–16th-century Netherlands and Germany
- 16th-century Italian and Spanish
- 17th-century Dutch and Flemish
- 17th–18th-century Spanish, Italian, and French
- 18th–19th-century Spanish and French
- 19th-century French
- American paintings
- British paintings
- Sculpture, Decorative Arts, Drawings and Prints
- Special exhibitions
- Non-exhibition space

West Garden Court

Micro Gallery

Sculpture Garden

Ground Floor

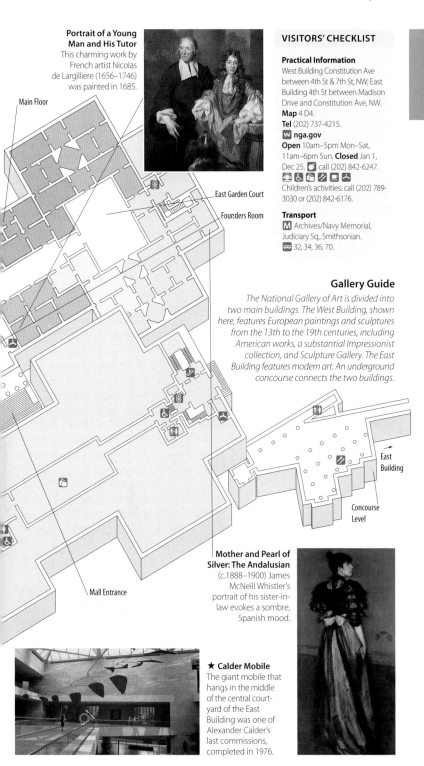

**Portrait of a Young Man and His Tutor**
This charming work by French artist Nicolas de Largilliere (1656–1746) was painted in 1685.

Main Floor

East Garden Court

Founders Room

**VISITORS' CHECKLIST**

**Practical Information**
West Building Constitution Ave between 4th St & 7th St, NW; East Building 4th St between Madison Drive and Constitution Ave, NW. **Map** 4 D4.
**Tel** (202) 737-4215.
W **nga.gov**
**Open** 10am–5pm Mon–Sat, 11am–6pm Sun. **Closed** Jan 1, Dec 25. call (202) 842-6247.
Children's activities: call (202) 789-3030 or (202) 842-6176.

**Transport**
M Archives/Navy Memorial, Judiciary Sq., Smithsonian.
32, 34, 36, 70.

**Gallery Guide**
*The National Gallery of Art is divided into two main buildings. The West Building, shown here, features European paintings and sculptures from the 13th to the 19th centuries, including American works, a substantial Impressionist collection, and Sculpture Gallery. The East Building features modern art. An underground concourse connects the two buildings.*

East Building

Concourse Level

Mall Entrance

**Mother and Pearl of Silver: The Andalusian**
(c.1888–1900) James McNeill Whistler's portrait of his sister-in-law evokes a sombre, Spanish mood.

**★ Calder Mobile**
The giant mobile that hangs in the middle of the central court-yard of the East Building was one of Alexander Calder's last commissions, completed in 1976.

# Exploring the National Gallery of Art

The National Gallery's West and East Buildings are an unusual pair. The West Building, designed by John Russell Pope, is stately and Classical, with matching wings flanking its rotunda. Built of Tennessee marble, it forms a majestic presence on the Mall. Its collection is devoted to Western art from the 13th to the early 20th century. The East Building, completed in 1978, occupies a trapezoidal plot of land adjacent to the West Building. The triangular East Building is as audacious as the West one is conservative, but together they are harmonious. The interior of the East Building is a huge, fluid space, with galleries on either side housing works of modern art. The Sculpture Garden, adjacent to the West Building, has a fountain area that becomes an ice rink in winter.

Detail of *Christ Cleansing the Temple* (c.1570), by El Greco

Giotto's *Madonna and Child*, painted between 1320 and 1330

## 13th- to 15th-Century Italian Art

The Italian galleries house paintings from the 13th to 15th centuries. The earlier pre-Renaissance works of primarily religious themes illustrate a decidedly Byzantine influence.

The Florentine artist Giotto's *Madonna and Child* (c.1320–30) shows the transition to the Classical painting of the Renaissance. *Adoration of the Magi*, painted around 1480 by Botticelli, portrays a serene Madonna and Child surrounded by worshipers in the Italian countryside. Around the same date Pietro Perugino painted *The Crucifixion with the Virgin, St. John, St. Jerome and St. Mary Magdalene*. Andrew Mellon bought the triptych from the Hermitage Gallery in Leningrad. Raphael's *The Alba Madonna* of

1510 was called by one writer "the supreme compositional achievement of Renaissance painting." Leonardo da Vinci's *Ginevra de' Benci* (c.1474–8) is thought to be the first ever "psychological" portrait (depicting emotion) to be painted.

## 16th-Century Italian Art

This collection includes works |by Tintoretto, Titian, and Raphael. The 1500s were the height of Italian Classicism. Raphael's *St. George and the Dragon* (c.1506) typifies the perfection of technique for which this school of artists is known. Jacopo Tintoretto's *Christ at the Sea of Galilee* (c.1575/1580) portrays Christ standing on the shore while his disciples are on a storm-tossed fishing boat. The emotional intensity of the painting and the role of nature |in it made Tintoretto one of the greatest of the Venetian artists.

## 17th- to 18th-Century Spanish, Italian, and French Art

Among the 17th- and 18th-century European works are Jean-Honoré Fragonard's *Diana and Endymion* (c.1753–6), which was heavily influenced by Fragonard's mentor, François Boucher. El Greco's *Christ Cleansing the Temple* (pre-1570) demonstrates the influence of the 16th-century Italian schools. El Greco ("The Greek") signed his real name, Domenikos Theotokopoulos, to the panel.

## 17th-Century Dutch and Flemish Art

This collection holds a number of Old Masters including works by Rubens, Van Dyck, and Rembrandt. An example of Rembrandt's self-portraits is on display, which he painted in oils in 1659, ten years before his death.

Oil painting, *Diana and Endymion* (c.1753), by Jean-Honoré Fragonard

Several paintings by Rubens in this section testify to his genius, among them *Daniel in the Lions' Den* (c.1615). This depicts the Old Testament prophet, Daniel, thanking God for his help during his night spent surrounded by lions. In 1617, Rubens exchanged this work for antique marbles owned by a British diplomat. Rubens also painted *Deborah Kip, Wife of Sir Balthasar Gerbier, and her Children* (1629–30). Not a conventional family portrait, the mother and her four children seem withdrawn and pensive, suggesting unhappiness and perhaps even foreboding tragedy. Van Dyck painted Rubens's first wife, *Isabella Brant* (c.1621) toward the end of her life. Although she is smiling, her eyes reveal an inner melancholy.

## 19th-Century French Art

This is one of the best Impressionist collections outside Paris. Works on display include Paul Cézanne's *The Artist's Father Reading "L'Evénement"* (1866), Auguste Renoir's *A Girl with a Watering Can* (1876), *Four Dancers* (c.1899) by Edgar Degas, and Claude Monet's *Woman with a Parasol – Madame Monet and Her Son* (1875) and *Palazzo da Mula, Venice* (1908). Post-Impressionist works include Seurat's pointillist *The Lighthouse at Honfleur* (c.1886), in which thousands of dots are used to create the image, and Van Gogh's *Self Portrait*. The latter was painted in St Rémy in 1889 when he was staying in an asylum and shows his mastery at capturing character and emotion. Toulouse-Lautrec's painting, *Quadrille at the Moulin Rouge* (1892), depicts a dancer provocatively raising her skirts above her ankles.

Miss Mary Ellison by Mary Cassatt (1880)

Geometric skylights in the plaza from the West Building to the East Building

## American Painting

This important collection of American artists shows evidence of European influence, but in themes that are resolutely American. James McNeill Whistler's *Mother of Pearl and Silver: The Andalusian* (1888–1900) has a European sophistication. Mary Cassatt left America for exile in Europe and was heavily influenced by the Impressionists, especially Degas. *Boating Party* (1893–4) is an example of one of her recurrent themes: mother and child. *Children Playing on a Beach* (1884) is also a good example of her child paintings, and *Miss Mary Ellison* of her portraiture. Winslow Homer's *Breezing Up (A Fair Wind)* (1873–6) is a masterpiece by the American Realist. His painting is a charming depiction of three small boys and a fisherman.

## Modern and Contemporary Art

The enormous East Building houses modern and contemporary art. I.M. Pei's "H"-shaped building contains a vast atrium which is edged by four balconies and adjacent galleries. Architecturally, this space provides a dramatic focus and spatial orientation for visitors to the East Building.

Centered in the atrium is *Untitled*, a vast red, blue, and black creation by Alexander Calder. It was commissioned in 1972 for the opening of the museum in 1978. At the entrance to the East Building is Henry Moore's bronze sculpture *Knife Edge Mirror Two Piece* (1977–8).

Also in the East Building are a research center for schools, offices for the curators, a library, and a large collection of drawingsand prints.

Both the East and West buildings also host traveling exhibits. These are not limited to modern art, but have included the art of ancient Japan, American Impressionists, and the sketches of Leonardo da Vinci. The East Building's galleries are surprisingly intimate.

## Sculpture Garden

Located across the street from the West Building at 7th Street, the elegant Sculpture Garden holds 17 sculptures. The late 20th-century works include pieces by Louise Bourgeois, Roy Lichtenstein, and Joan Miró. Although different, the sculptures do not compete with each other because they are spread out. Transformed into an ice rink in winter and a venue for free jazz concerts in summer, the garden functions both as an outdoor gallery and as a pleasant oasis within the city. The pavilion houses a year-round café.

# ❷ National Air and Space Museum

The Smithsonian's National Air and Space Museum opened in 1976. The soaring architecture of the building on the Mall, designed by Hellmuth, Obata, and Kassabaum, is well suited to the airplanes, rockets, balloons, and space capsules of aviation and space flight. A second site, the Steven F. Udvar-Hazy Center, located near Dulles International Airport, opened in 2003 to celebrate the 100th anniversary of the Wright brothers' first powered flight. The museum is the largest air and space museum complex in the world and is home to the retired Discovery space shuttle.

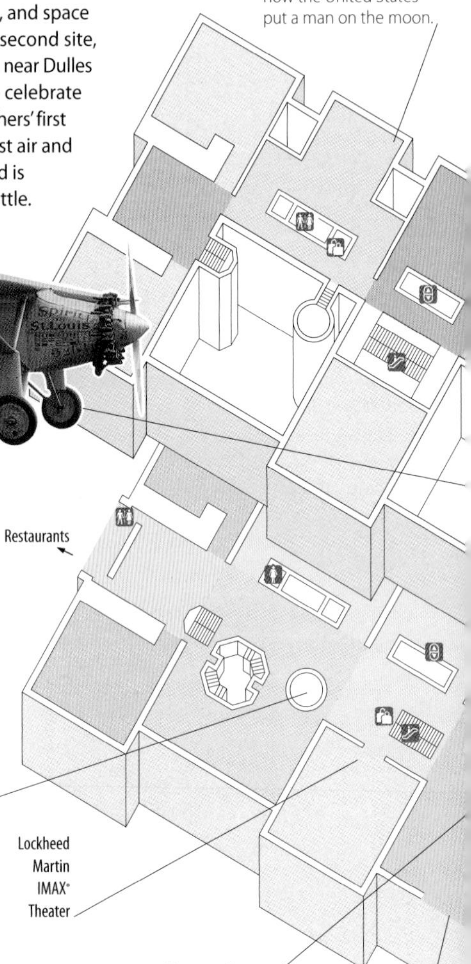

**Apollo to the Moon**
Full of artifacts, this exhibit tells the story of how the United States put a man on the moon.

★ **Spirit of St. Louis**
At the age of 25, pilot Charles Lindbergh made the first solo transatlantic flight in this plane, landing in France on May 21, 1927.

Restaurants

**Skylab Orbital Workshop**
This was an orbiting workshop for sets of three-person crews, who conducted research experiments.

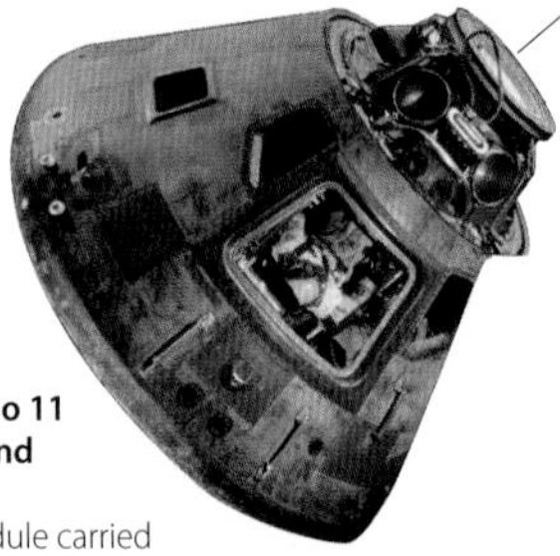

Lockheed Martin IMAX® Theater

Mall Entrance

**Key to Floor Plan**

- Milestones of Flight
- Exploring the Moon
- Aviation in World Wars I and II
- The Space Race Barron Hilton
- Pioneers of Flight
- Other exhibitions
- Explore the Universe
- Temporary exhibition space
- Wright Brothers
- Developments in Flight

★ **Apollo 11 Command Module**
This module carried astronauts Buzz Aldrin, Neil Armstrong, and Michael Collins on their historic mission to the moon in July 1969, when Neil Armstrong took his famous first steps.

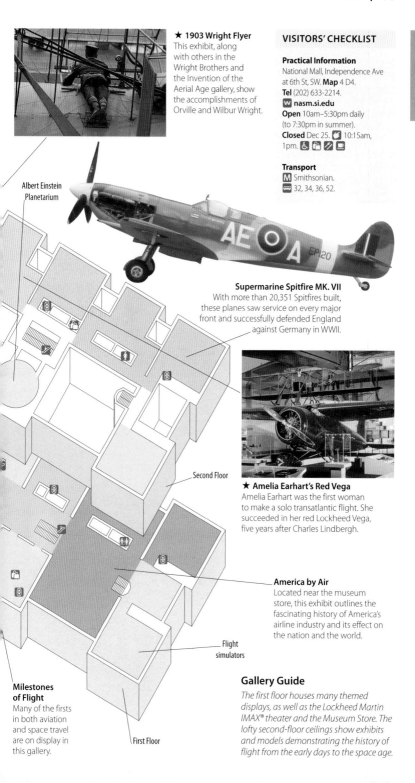

### ★ 1903 Wright Flyer
This exhibit, along with others in the Wright Brothers and the Invention of the Aerial Age gallery, show the accomplishments of Orville and Wilbur Wright.

### VISITORS' CHECKLIST

**Practical Information**
National Mall, Independence Ave at 6th St, SW. **Map** 4 D4.
**Tel** (202) 633-2214.
**w** nasm.si.edu
**Open** 10am–5:30pm daily (to 7:30pm in summer).
**Closed** Dec 25. 10:15am, 1pm.

**Transport**
**M** Smithsonian.
32, 34, 36, 52.

**Albert Einstein Planetarium**

**Supermarine Spitfire MK. VII**
With more than 20,351 Spitfires built, these planes saw service on every major front and successfully defended England against Germany in WWII.

**Second Floor**

### ★ Amelia Earhart's Red Vega
Amelia Earhart was the first woman to make a solo transatlantic flight. She succeeded in her red Lockheed Vega, five years after Charles Lindbergh.

**America by Air**
Located near the museum store, this exhibit outlines the fascinating history of America's airline industry and its effect on the nation and the world.

**Flight simulators**

**Milestones of Flight**
Many of the firsts in aviation and space travel are on display in this gallery.

**First Floor**

### Gallery Guide
*The first floor houses many themed displays, as well as the Lockheed Martin IMAX® theater and the Museum Store. The lofty second-floor ceilings show exhibits and models demonstrating the history of flight from the early days to the space age.*

# Exploring the National Air and Space Museum

The National Air and Space Museum on the Mall has a massive exhibition space of 23 galleries. The most visited museum in the world, it has to cope not only with millions of visitors but also with the range and sheer size of its artifacts, which include hundreds of rockets, planes, and spacecraft. In 2003 the museum opened a sister exhibition space: a huge new state-of-the art facility, the Steven F. Udvar-Hazy Center, located near Dulles Airport. Now with two sites, more of NASM's historic collections are on display for the public to enjoy.

F4B-4    9241    U.S. MARINES

The Boeing F4B Navy fighter

from an era when flight was new and daring. The **Pioneers of Flight** gallery celebrates the men and women who have challenged the physical and psychological barriers faced when leaving the earth. Adventurer Cal Rogers was the first to fly across the United States, but it was not non-stop. In 1911 he flew from coast to coast in less than 30 days, with almost 70 landings. His early biplane is one of the exhibits. (Twelve years later, a Fokker T-2 made the trip in less than 27 hours.) Amelia Earhart was the first woman to fly the Atlantic, just five years after Charles Lindbergh. Her red Lockheed Vega is displayed. Close by is *Tingmissartoq*, a Lockheed Sirius seaplane belonging to Charles Lindbergh. Its unusual name is Inuit for "one who flies like a bird." Some of the greatest strides in aviation were made in the period between the two world wars, celebrated in the **Golden Age of Flight** gallery. The public's intense interest in flight resulted in races, exhibitions, and adventurous exploration. Here a visitor can see planes equipped with skis for landing on snow, with short wings for racing, and a "staggerwing" plane on which the lower wing was placed ahead of the upper.

## Milestones of Flight

Entering the National Air and Space Museum from the Mall entrance, first stop is the soaring **Milestones of Flight** gallery, which gives an overview of the history of flight. The exhibits in this room are some of the major firsts in aviation and space technology, as they helped to realize man's ambition to take to the air.

The gallery is vast, designed to accommodate the large aircraft – many of which are suspended from the ceiling – and spacecraft. Some of these pioneering machines are surprisingly small, however. Charles Lindbergh's *Spirit of St. Louis*, the first aircraft to cross the Atlantic with a solo pilot, was designed with the fuel tanks ahead of the cockpit so Lindbergh had to use a periscope to look directly ahead. John Glenn's Mercury spacecraft, *Friendship 7*, in which he orbited the earth, is smaller than a sports car.

Near the entrance to the gallery is a moon rock – a symbol of man's exploration of

space. Also in this gallery is the *Apollo 11* Command Module, which carried the first men to walk on the moon. The Wright brothers' *Flyer* (in gallery 209) was the first plane to sustain powered flight on December 17, 1903, at Kitty Hawk, North Carolina.

## Developments in Flight

Travelers now take flying for granted – it is safe, fast, and, for many, routine. The National Air and Space Museum, however, displays machines and gadgets

The propeller-driven Douglas DC-3 aircraft in the America by Air gallery

Rockets on display in the Space Race gallery

The F4B Navy fighter, used by US Marine Corps squadrons, was developed between the world wars and is on display in the **Sea-Air Operations** gallery. Flight then progressed from propeller propulsion to jets. The **Jet Aviation** gallery has the first operational jet fighter, the German Messerschmitt Me 262A. *Lulu Belle*, the prototype of the first US fighter jet, was used in the Korean War of 1950–53.

**America by Air** traces the development of commercial air-travel, from the air mail age to the "glass cockpit," and beyond. This is a fun, family-friendly gallery with hands-on exhibits.

## Aviation in World Wars I and II

One of the most popular parts of the museum is the **World War II Aviation** gallery, which has planes from the Allied and the Axis air forces. Nearby is an example of the Japanese Mitsubishi A6M5 Zero Model 52, which was a light, highly maneuverable fighter plane.

The maneuverability of the Messerschmitt Bf 109 made it Germany's most successful fighter. It was matched, and in some areas surpassed, by the Supermarine Spitfire of the Royal Air Force, which helped to win control of the skies over Britain in 1940–41.

## The Space Race

The animosity that grew between the United States and the Soviet Union after World War II manifested itself in the Space Race. America was taken by surprise when the Soviets launched *Sputnik 1* on October 4, 1957. The US attempt to launch their first satellite proved spectacular failure when the *Vanguard* crashed in December 1957. The satellite is on display here.

In 1961, Soviet cosmonaut Yuri Gagarin became the first man to orbit the earth. The Americans countered with Alan Shepard's manned space flight in *Freedom 7* later the same year. The first space walk was from the *Gemini IV* capsule by American astronaut Edward H. White in 1965.

On July 20, 1969, the race reached a climax when the world watched as Neil Armstrong walked on the moon. His original spacesuit from the Apollo 11 mission is on display. Other exhibits from the Space Race include the *Skylab 4* command module, and *Gemini 7*, a two-person spacecraft that successfully orbited the earth in 1965.

Gemini IV capsule

The Space Hall gallery shows the result of the final détente between the superpowers with the Apollo-Soyuz Test Project. This was a purposefully collaborative space mission meant to symbolize a new era of cooperation. It was the last Apollo flight. When the American *Apollo* module docked alongside the Soviet *Soyuz* spacecraft in 1975, it was the start of the end of the Space Race.

## Progress in Air and Space Technology

Mankind's fascination with flight is in part a desire to see the earth from a great distance and also to get closer to other planets. In the Independence Avenue lobby is artist Robert T. McCall's interpretation of the birth of the universe, the planets, and astronauts reaching the moon.

The Hubble Telescope, launched from the *Discovery* shuttle in April 1990, provides pictures of extremely distant astronomical objects. Launched in 1964, the *Ranger* lunar probe also took high-quality pictures of the moon, and then transmitted them to Cape Canaveral.

**Moving Beyond Earth** gives an insight into recent human spaceflight and future possibilities. A space shuttle model and other launch vehicle models, as well as astronaut gear, are on display. Visitors can also experience aspects of spaceflight through interactive computer kiosks.

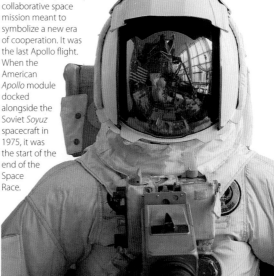

The spacesuit worn by Apollo astronauts in 1969

Fountain in the central plaza of the Hirshhorn Museum

# ❸ Hirshhorn Museum

Independence Ave and 7th St, SW. **Map** 3 C4. **Tel** (202) 633-1000. Ⓜ Smithsonian, L'Enfant Plaza. **Open** 10am–5:30pm daily (Sculpture Garden: 7:30am–dusk). **Closed** Dec 25. Ⓦ hirshhorn.si.edu

When the Hirshhorn Museum was still in its planning stages, S. Dillon Ripley, then Secretary of the Smithsonian Institution, told the planning board that the building should be "controversial in every way" so that it would be fit to house contemporary works of art.

The Hirshhorn certainly fulfilled its architectural mission. It has been variously described as a doughnut or a flying saucer, but it is actually a four-story, not-quite-symmetrical cylinder. It is also home to one of the greatest collections of modern art in the United States.

The museum's benefactor, Joseph H. Hirshhorn, was an eccentric, flamboyant immigrant from Latvia who amassed a collection of 6,000 pieces of contemporary art. Since the museum opened in 1974, the Smithsonian has built on Hirshhorn's original donation, and the collection now consists of 3,000 pieces of sculpture, 4,000 drawings and photographs, and approximately 5,000 paintings. The works of art are arranged chronologically. The main, lower floor displays newly acquired work. It is also home to the "Black Box," a space dedicated to film, video, and other digital works by emerging international artists. The second floor hosts temporary exhibitions, of which there are at least three a year. These are usually arranged thematically, or as tributes to individual artists, such as Lucien Freud, Alberto Giacometti, or Francis Bacon. The third floor houses the permanent collection, which includes works by artists such as Alexander Calder, Arshile Gorky, Willem de Kooning, and John Singer Sargent. In addition, visitors should not miss the outdoor sculpture garden, across the street from the museum. It includes pieces by Alexander Calder, Auguste Rodin, Henri Matisse, and many others.

The outdoor Full Circle Café, located in the plaza at the center of the building, makes a pleasant spot in which to enjoy lunch during the summer months.

**Arts and Industries Building's fountain**

# ❹ Arts and Industries Building

900 Jefferson Drive, SW. **Map** 3 C4. **Tel** (202) 633-1000. Ⓜ Smithsonian. **Closed** to the public. ♿ 📷 Ⓦ si.edu

The ornate, vast galleries and the airy rotunda of the splendid Victorian Arts and Industries Building were designed by Montgomery Meigs, architect of the National Building Museum (see p105). The Arts and Industries Building was extraordinary because of its expanse of open space and abundance of natural light.

The museum served a wide-ranging variety of functions after its completion on March 4, 1881. In its opening year, it was the site of President James A. Garfield's inaugural ball; it also displayed artifacts from Philadelphia's 1876 Centennial Exposition, including a complete steam train; later, it was home to a collection of the First Ladies' gowns, as well as Lindbergh's famous airplane the Spirit of St. Louis, before these exhibits were moved to other Smithsonian museums on the Mall. A working carousel is located in front of the building, on the Mall (closed in winter).

Concerns over its deteriorating condition led to the building's closure in 2004. However, it has since been allocated $25 million for renovation work and is due to reopen in late-2014.

The Hirshhorn Museum's sculpture garden, a green space in which to contemplate pieces by Calder, Rodin, Matisse, and others

Tribal masks at the National Museum of African Art

## ❺ National Museum of African Art

950 Independence Ave, SW. **Map** 3 C4.
**Tel** (202) 633-4600. **M** Smithsonian.
**Open** 10am–5:30pm daily.
**Closed** Dec 25. 🦽 ♿ 🏠 🏛
**W** nmafa.si.edu

Washington's National Museum of African Art is one of the most peaceful spots on the Mall. Perhaps because it is mostly underground, with a relatively low above-ground presence, it is often missed by visitors. The entrance pavilion, situated in the Enid A. Haupt Garden directly in front of the Smithsonian Castle, leads to three subterranean floors, where the museum shares space with the adjacent Ripley Center and the Arthur M. Sackler Gallery (see pp74–5).

The museum was founded in 1964 by Warren Robbins, a former officer in the American Foreign Service (he was a cultural attaché and public affairs officer), and was the first museum in the US to concentrate entirely on the art and culture of the African continent. It was first situated in the home of Frederick Douglass (see p147), on Capitol Hill. For several years Robbins had to finance the museum himself, gradually acquiring more space in the form of a collection of town houses near the original building. Eventually financial support was forthcoming as

the importance of the collection was recognized. The Smithsonian Institution acquired Robbins' collection in 1979, and the works were finally moved to their current home on the Mall in 1987.

The 9,000-piece permanent collection includes both modern and ancient art from Africa, although the majority of pieces date from the 19th and 20th centuries. Traditional African art of bronze, ceramics, and gold are on display, along with an extensive collection of masks. There is also a display of *kente* cloth from Ghana – brightly colored and patterned cloth used to adorn clothing as a symbol of African nationalism. The Eliot Elisofon Photographic Archives (Eliot Elisofon was a famous photographer for *Life* magazine) contain 300,000 prints and some 120,000 ft of edited and unedited film footage, as well

A Benin bronze head at the NMAA

as videos and documentaries on African art and culture. The museum now also holds 525 pieces of the Walt Disney-Tishman African Art Collection. The Warren M. Robbins Library has approximately 32,000 books in its collection, mainly on African art, history, and culture. The library, however, also has children's literature and videos. It is open to the public by appointment only.

To display its vast archive of exhibits, the museum runs a rolling program of themed exhibitions. It also hosts performing arts events featuring dance, music, and the spoken word. Year-round there is a full calendar of educational tours, lectures, and workshops, including many for children. At the bi-monthly Music of Africa workshop, children over six can play African musical instruments and learn about different rhythms and playing techniques.

## History of the Mall

In September, 1789, French-born Pierre L'Enfant (1754–1825) was invited by George Washington to design the capital of the new United States. While the rest of the city developed, the area planned by L'Enfant to be the Grand Avenue, running west from the Capitol, remained swampy and undeveloped. In 1850, landscape gardener Andrew Jackson Downing was employed to develop the land in accordance with L'Enfant's plans. However, the money ran out, and the work was abandoned. At the end of the Civil War in 1865, President Lincoln, eager that building in the the city should progress, instructed that work on the area should begin again, and the Mall began to take on the park-like appearance it has today. The addition of many museums and memorials in the latter half of the 20th century established the Mall as the cultural heart of Washington.

Aerial view, showing the Mall stretching down from the Capitol

# ❻ National Museum of the American Indian

Built from Minnesota Kasota limestone, the National Museum of the American Indian was established in collaboration with Native American communities throughout the western hemisphere. It is the only national museum dedicated to the Native peoples of the Americas, and is the eighteenth museum of the Smithsonian Institution. The original collections of artifacts were assembled by George Gustav Heye (1874–1957), a wealthy New Yorker, at the turn of the 20th century. The exhibitions showcase the spiritual and daily lives of diverse peoples and encourage visitors to look beyond stereotypes.

**★ Our Peoples**
American Indians, including the Blackfeet and Kiowa, tell their own stories and histories, focusing on both the destruction of their culture and their resilience.

**George Heye (1874–1957)**
Collector and world traveler George Gustav Heye and his wife, Thea, accompanied a Zuni delegation in New York c.1923.

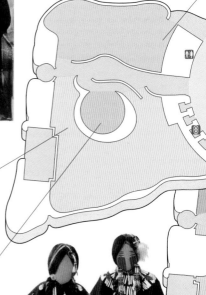

**★ Lelawi Theater**
In this circular theater a spectacular multimedia presentation is shown every 15 minutes. "Who We Are" highlights the diversity of American Indian life from the Arctic, to the Northwest Coast, to Bolivia.

**★ Our Universes**
Eight groups of American Indians, from the Santa Clara Pueblo in New Mexico to the Lakota in South Dakota, share their world views, philosophies of creation, and spiritual relationship with nature.

**Window on Collections: Many Hands, Many Voices**
Over 3,500 objects are on display, including dolls, beaded objects, and artwork.

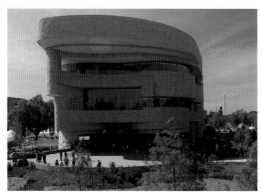

**Exterior of Museum**
The museum's curvilinear limestone exterior gives it a natural, weathered effect. It is set in a landscape of flowing water, hardwood forest, meadowland, and croplands, to reflect the American Indian's connection to the land.

## VISITORS' CHECKLIST

**Practical Information**
National Mall, 4th St & Independence Ave, SW.
**Map** 4 D4. **Tel** (202) 633-1000.
W **nmai.si.edu**
**Open** 10am–5:30pm daily.
**Closed** Dec 25.

**Transport**
M L'Enfant Plaza (Maryland Ave exit). 30, 32, 34, 35, 36.

**Window on Collections**
Interactive technology allows for a self-guided tour of the exhibits. Shown here is a peace medal that once belonged to Powder Face, an Arapaho.

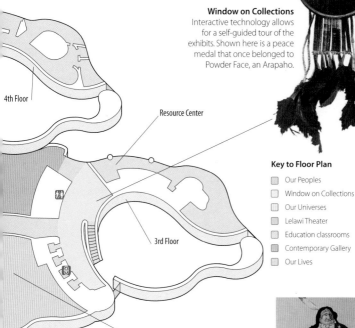

4th Floor

Resource Center

3rd Floor

**Key to Floor Plan**
- Our Peoples
- Window on Collections
- Our Universes
- Lelawi Theater
- Education classrooms
- Contemporary Gallery
- Our Lives

## Gallery Guide

*Begin your visit with the "Who We Are" multimedia presentation at the Lelawi Theater (4th floor). The three permanent exhibitions on this level are "Our Universes," "Our Peoples," and "Window on Collections," while "Our Lives" is on the 3rd floor. On the ground level is a shop and the Mitsitam café.*

**Our Lives**
Examines the lives and identities of Native Americans and the consequences of legal policies that determine who is an American Indian. Here Fritz Scholder (b.1937) explores "nativeness" in this work *The American Indian.*

# ❼ National Museum of Natural History

Second Floor

The National Museum of Natural History, which opened in 1910, preserves artifacts from the earth's diverse cultures and collects samples of fossils and living creatures from land and sea. Visiting the museum is a vast undertaking, so sample the best of the exhibits and leave the rest for return visits. The O. Orkin Insect Zoo, with its giant hissing cockroaches and large leaf-cutter ant colony, is popular with children, while the Dinosaur Hall delights young and old. The stunning Hall of Mammals displays 274 specimens, and looks at how they adapted to changes in habitat and climate over millions of years.

**★ O. Orkin Insect Zoo**
This popular exhibit explores the lives and habitats of the single largest animal group on earth and features many live specimens.

**Butterflies and Plants: Partners in Evolution**
This permanent exhibition, which includes live butterflies, innovatively combines traditional and experiential learning.

First Floor

**The Kenneth E. Behring Family Hall of Mammals**
has 22,500 sq ft (2,090 sq m) of displays explaining the diversity of mammals.

**African Elephant**
The massive African Bush Elephant is one of the highlights of the museum. It is the centerpiece of the Rotunda and creates an impressive sight as visitors enter the museum.

## Gallery Guide

*The first floor's main exhibitions feature mammals and marine life from different continents. Dinosaurs and myriad cultural exhibits are also displayed on this level. The Gems and Minerals collection and the O. Orkin Insect Zoo are on the second floor.*

★ **Hope Diamond**
At 45.52 carats, the Hope Diamond is the largest deep blue diamond in the world and is famed for its stunning clarity and color. It is more than one billion years old and once belonged to King Louis XIV of France in the 17th century.

The Johnson IMAX® Theater

## VISITORS' CHECKLIST

**Practical Information**
Constitution Ave and 10th St, NW.
**Map** 3 C4.
**Tel** (202) 633-1000 (recorded message after museum hours).
🌐 mnh.si.edu
**Open** 10am–5:30pm daily (7:30pm in summer). **Closed** Dec 25. Butterfly Pavilion: 🦋 Free Tue. 🎬 10:30am & 1:30pm Mon–Fri. 🏛 ♿ 🛍 📷 ☕

**Transport**
Ⓜ Smithsonian, Federal Triangle.
🚌 32, 34, 36.

### Key to Floor Plan

- African Cultures and Ice Age
- Bones, Egyptian Mummies, and the Insect Zoo
- Discovery Room
- Fossils, Dinosaurs, and Early Life
- Geology, Gems, and Minerals
- Human Origins
- Kenneth E. Behring Family Hall of Mammals
- Ocean Hall
- Rotunda
- Special Exhibition space
- Non-exhibition space

**Easter Island Stone Head**
Originally erected by the hundreds on Easter Island avin the South Pacific, these huge stone statues were built in memory of the dead.

**Ice Age Mammals,** such as the saber-toothed cat and the woolly mammoth, flourished between about 1.6 million and 10,000 years ago.

Ground Floor

**A cast of a nest of dinosaur eggs** sheds light on the life of *Maiasaura*, a kind of duckbilled dinosaur, who lived around 70 million years ago.

★ **Dinosaur Hall**
Featuring reconstructions of fossils that lived up to 230 million years ago, including this skeleton of *Triceratops horridus*, the Dinosaur Hall is one of the most popular areas of the museum.

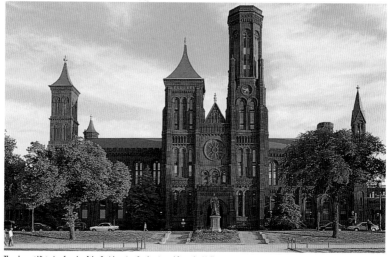

The elegant Victorian façade of the Smithsonian Castle, viewed from the Mall

### ❽ Smithsonian Castle

1000 Jefferson Drive, SW. **Map** 3 C4.
**Tel** 633-1000. Ⓜ Smithsonian.
**Open** 8:30am–5:30pm daily.
**Closed** Dec 25. 🎟 ♿ 📷 🅆 si.edu

This ornate Victorian edifice served as the first home of the Smithsonian Institution, and was also home to the first Secretary of the Smithsonian, Joseph Henry, and his family. A statue of Henry stands in front of the building.

Constructed of red sandstone in 1855, the Castle was designed by James Renwick, architect of the Renwick Gallery

The tomb of James Smithson

(see p115) and St Patrick's Cathedral in New York. It is an outstanding example of the Gothic Revival style. Inspired also by 12th-century Norman architecture, the Castle has nine towers and an elaborate cornice. Today it is the seat of the Smithsonian administration and houses its Information Center. Visitors can visit the Crypt Room and see the tomb of James Smithson, who bequeathed his fortune to the United States. The South Tower Room was the first children's room in a Washington museum. The ceiling and colorful wall stencils that decorate the room

were restored in 1987.

Outside the castle is the Smithsonian rose garden, filled with beautiful hybrid tea roses. The garden was a later addition that now connects the Castle to the equally ornate Arts and Industries Building (see p68).

### ❾ Arthur M. Sackler Gallery

1050 Independence Ave, SW.
**Map** 3 C4. **Tel** 633-1000.
Ⓜ Smithsonian. **Open** 10am–5:30pm daily. **Closed** Dec 25. 🎟 12:15pm.
♿ 📷 🛍 🅆 asia.si.edu

Dr. Arthur M. Sackler, a New York physician, started collecting Asian art in the 1950s. In 1982, he donated more than

### James Smithson (1765–1829)

Although he never once visited the United States, James Smithson, English scientist and philanthropist, and illegitimate son of the first Duke of Northumberland, left his entire fortune of half a million dollars to "found at Washington, under the name of the Smithsonian Institution, an establishment for the increase and diffusion of knowledge among men." However, this was only if his nephew and heir were to die childless. This did happen and hence, in 1836, Smithson's fortune passed to the government of the United States, which did not quite know what to do with such a vast bequest. For 11 years Congress debated various proposals, finally agreeing to set up a government-run foundation that would administer all national museums. The first Smithson-funded collection was shown at the Smithsonian Castle in 1855.

James Smithson

10th-century Indian sculpture of the goddess Parvati in the Arthur M. Sackler Gallery

1,000 artifacts, along with $4 million in funds, to the Smithsonian Institution to establish this museum. The Japanese and Korean governments also contributed $1 million each toward the cost of constructing the building, and the museum was completed in 1987.

The entrance is a small pavilion at ground level that leads down to two subterranean floors of exhibits. The Sackler's 3,000-piece collection is particularly rich in Chinese works, and highlights include a stunning display of Chinese bronzes and jades, some dating back to 4000 BC. There are also 7th-century ceramics from the Ming dynasty and an extensive range of sculpture from India and southeast Asia.

Over the years the gallery has built on Arthur Sackler's original collection. In 1987 it acquired the impressive Vever Collection from collector Henri Vever, which includes such items as Islamic books from the 11th to the 19th centuries, 19th- and 20th-century Japanese prints, Indian, Chinese, and Japanese paintings, and modern photography. The gallery also hosts international traveling exhibitions of Asian art from museums such as the Louvre in Paris.

The Sackler is one of two underground museums in this area; the other is the National Museum of African Art (see p69), which is part of the same complex. The Sackler is also connected by underground exhibition space to the Freer Gallery of Art. The two galleries share a director and administrative staff as well as the Meyer Auditorium, which hosts dance performances, films, and chamber music concerts. There is also a research library in the Sackler devoted to Asian art.

## ⑩ Freer Gallery of Art

Jefferson Drive and 12th Street, SW. **Map 3** C4. **Tel** 633-1000. Ⓜ Smithsonian. **Open** 10am– 5:30pm daily. **Closed** Dec 25. ♿ 📷 Ⓦ **asia.si.edu**

The Freer Gallery of Art is named after Charles Lang Freer, a railroad magnate who donated his collection of 9,000 pieces of American and Asian art to the Smithsonian, and funded the building of a museum to house the works. Freer died in 1919 before the building's completion. When the gallery opened in 1923 it became the first Smithsonian museum of art.

Detail of a screen by Thomas Wilmer Dewing

Constructed as a single-story building in the Italian Renaissance style, the Freer has an attractive courtyard with a fountain at its center. There are 19 galleries, most with skylights that illuminate a superb collection of Asian and American art. Since Freer's original donation, the museum has tripled its holdings. In the Asian Art collection are examples of Chinese, Japanese, and Korean art, including sculpture, ceramics, folding screens, and paintings. The gallery also has a fine selection of Buddhist sculpture, and painting and calligraphy from India.

There is a select collection of American art in the Freer as well, most of which shows Asian influences. Works by the artists Childe Hassam (1859–1935), John Singer Sargent (1865–1925), and Thomas Wilmer Dewing (1851–1938) are all on display. The most astonishing room in the museum is James McNeill Whistler's "The Peacock Room." Whistler (1834–1903) was a friend of Freer's who encouraged his art collecting. Whistler painted a dining room for Frederick Leyland in London, but Leyland found that it was not to his taste. Freer purchased the room in 1904; it was later moved to Washington and installed here after his death. In contrast to the subtle elegance of the other rooms, this room is a riot of blues, greens, and golds. Whistler's painted peacocks cover the walls and ceiling.

The attractive courtyard of the Freer Gallery of Art

# ⓫ National Museum of American History

The National Museum of American History preserves a collection of artifacts from the nation's past. Among the 3 million holdings are the First Ladies' gowns, a 280-ton steam locomotive, the National Quilt Collection, and the original Star-Spangled Banner that flew over Fort McHenry in 1814. The museum's west wing will be under renovation until 2015. Some galleries may be closed and exhibits may be moved around.

Second Floor

**★ The First Ladies**
Always a popular exhibition, this is a selection of gowns worn by America's First Ladies, such as this floral chine dress worn by Frances Cleveland, a fashion icon in the late 1800s.

Mall
Entrance

**★ Star-Spangled Banner**
This flag is the symbol of America. It inspired Francis Scott Key to write the lyrics that became the US national anthem. Visitors can view the flag through a window wall.

**Key to Floor Plan**
- ☐ Transportation and Technology
- ☐ Science and Innovation
- ☐ American Ideals
- ☐ American Lives
- ☐ American Wars and Politics
- ☐ Entertainment, Sports and Music
- ☐ Non exhibition space

**On the Water: Stories from Maritime America**
Visitors can explore the history of maritime America through documents, objects, stories, audiovisual programs, and interactive exhibits.

**Lincoln's Top Hat**
Lincoln was wearing this hat when he was assassinated on April 14,1865 while at Ford's Theatre. It has a molded paper base that is embedded with shaved fur fibers.

Third Floor

### VISITORS' CHECKLIST

**Practical Information**
14th St and Constitution Ave.
**Map** 3 B4. **Tel** (202) 633-1000 (recorded message outside opening hours).
**W** americanhistory.si.edu
**Open** 10am–5:30pm daily (Jun–Aug: to 7:30pm).
**Closed** Dec 25.

**Transport**
**M** Smithsonian-Federal Triangle.
32, 34, 36.

★ **The Price of Freedom: Americans at War**
A fascinating look at the ways in which wars have shaped American history, from the Colonial era to the present day, including this famous painting by Louis M. D. Guillaume, *The Surrender of the Arm of Northern Virginia* (1867).

Constitution Avenue Entrance

On the Water: Stories from Maritime America

★ **America on the Move**
This first floor exhibition allows visitors to travel back in time through the history of transport in America, including this famous Ford Model T, bicycles, trains, and more.

### Gallery Guide
*The first floor features the transportation and science exhibits. Highlights of the second floor include the Star-Spangled Banner. The third floor offers an eclectic selection including the American Presidency: A Glorious Burden, The First Ladies exhibit, and military displays.*

First Floor

# Exploring the National Museum of American History

The collections at the National Museum of American History are very diverse. Whether you head straight for the First Ladies' gowns or spend time viewing the collections of money, medals, musical instruments, and presidential artifacts, planning is the key to a successful visit. The museum is gradually being transformed with the continuing renovation of the 120,000 sq ft (11,148 sq m) west exhibition wing. The center core and east wing remain open to the public.

The museum's modern façade on Madison Drive

### First Floor

**Stories on Money** explores the museum's collection of American coinage and currency. The exhibition "America's Money" examines the changes from Colonial America to the Gold Rush, and the present day, focusing on the renaissance of American coinage.

"The Power of Liberty" exhibit features an array of coins from the United States and around the world, depicting Liberty and the female freedom movement. The exhibition consists of 1.5 million objects, including a Colonial shilling from 1690 and a unique $20 gold coin from 1849.

**America on the Move** is the museum's largest single exhibition and tells the story of how trains, streetcars, and automobiles have shaped American lives. Exhibits include the locomotive that pulled Franklin D. Roosevelt's funeral train, a 40-ft (12-m) section of pavement from the legendary Route 66, a 1903 Winton, Ford's *Model T*, and a Hot Rod.

**On the Water: Stories from Maritime America** is an 8,000-sq-ft (743-sq-m) exhibition

chartering American maritime history and exploring life and work on the nation's waterways. The exhibits on display build on the Smithsonian's unparalleled National Watercraft Collection of rigged ship models, patent models, documents and images to bring the sights, sounds, and stories from the oceans, inland rivers, and coastal communities to museum visitors.

The maritime influence on American history is one of the most compelling chapters in the national story. Maritime trade established major cities, created connections between people and places and opened the continent. From 18th-century sailing ships, 19th-century steamboats and fishing craft to today's mega containerships, America's maritime connections are shown through interactive displays, documents and film.

Elsewhere on the first floor visitors can explore **Lighting a Revolution**, which looks at electricity and electrical invention in the 20th century, and illuminates the differences in the process of invention between Thomas Edison's time and our own.

For those with an interest in all things mechanical, the **Power Machinery Hall** is a must. This exhibition features examples of the machines that made America a world leader in industrial production, and contains models and actual examples of engines, turbines, pumps, and more. Perhaps the most famous machine of all is the **John Bull Locomotive** in the East Wing, the oldest operative self-propelled locomotive in the world. The **Invention at Play** is a family-orientated exhibit exploring the similarities between the way children and adults play, and the impact play has on invention. Visitors can also "meet" the inventors.

### Second Floor

**American Stories** showcases the historic and cultural journey of American history through more than 100 objects from the museum's vast collection including, Dorothy's ruby

1950 Buick Super sedan displayed in America on the Move

The kitchen of 16 Elm Street, rebuilt in the museum as it was in the 1940s

slippers, the rarely displayed walking stick used by Benjamin Franklin, Abraham Lincoln's gold pocket watch, Muhammad Ali's boxing gloves, and a fragment of Plymouth rock.

Through a chronological look at the people, inventions, issues, and events that shaped the American experience, American Stories serves as an introduction to American history.

The West Wing also contains **Within These Walls...** This exhibition tells the story of American history through the domestic lives of the families who lived at 16 Elm Street in Ipswich, Massachusetts, from the mid-1760s to 1945. This extraordinary house saw American colonists forging a new way of living, the birth of a revolution, community activists united against slavery, a family on the home front in World War II, and more.

**Communities in a Changing Nation: The Promise of 19th-Century America** takes a look at America's history through the lives of different communities – industrial workers in Bridgeport, Connecticut; Jewish immigrants in Cincinnati, Ohio; and slaves and free blacks in South Carolina. Through hundreds of photographs, objects, and illustrations, visitors can learn about the challenges and successes that made up the

lives of these different groups of people.

In the East Wing of the second floor, visitors can see the **Star-Spangled Banner** that flew over Fort McHenry in 1814 and inspired Francis Scott Key to write the lyrics that was later to become the national anthem. Also on the second floor is the **National Museum of African-American History and Culture Gallery**, exploring the role of visual images in the fight for civil rights and racial justice.

Teddy Bear, dating from 1903

## Third Floor

One of the museum's most popular exhibits, where fashion meets history: **The First Ladies** is a collection of gowns worn by some of the nation's most iconic presidential wives. The collection includes Michelle Obama's white chiffon gown worn to the 2009 inaugural ball. It was made by a relatively unknown designer, Jason Wu.

The largest exhibition on this floor is **The Price of Freedom: Americans at War** in the East Wing. It

explores the nation's military history, from the French and Indian War in the 1750s to recent conflicts in Afghanistan and Iraq. The exhibition features a restored Vietnam-era Huey helicopter, uniforms from the Civil War, a World War II jeep, and General Colin Powell's battle dress uniform from Operation Desert Storm.

The gunboat *Philadelphia* is located on the third floor. Sunk by the British in 1776, the 54-ft (16-m), 29-ton timber boat rested on the bottom of Lake Champlain until it was found and recovered in 1935.

The **American Presidency: A Glorious Burden** displays over 400 objects that represent the lives and office of the presidency. Artifacts include the portable desk on which Thomas Jefferson wrote the Declaration of Independence, and the top hat worn by President Lincoln the night he was shot.

Also here is a delightful teddy bear. The name of the bear was inspired by President Theodore "Teddy" Roosevelt, who, while out hunting one day, refused to shoot a bear cub that had been captured for him. A cartoon appeared in the *Washington Post* the next day, which inspired the production of a range of bears, named Teddy Bears.

Office of War information poster

# ⑫ Washington Monument

Constructed of 36,000 pieces of marble and granite, the Washington Monument remains one of the most recognizable monuments in the capital. Funds for this tribute to the first president of the United States initially came from individual citizens. A design by Robert Mills was chosen, and construction began in 1848. When the money ran out, the building work stopped for 25 years. Then, in 1876, President Ulysses S. Grant approved an act authorizing the completion of the project. (A slight change in the color of stone marks the point where construction resumed.) The Monument has 897 steps to the top. The earthquake of August 2011 caused damage to the Monument, which is currently closed for renovation.

**VISITORS' CHECKLIST**

**Practical Information**
Independence Ave at 17th St, SW.
**Map** 2 F5 & 3 B4.
**Tel** (202) 426-6841.
W nps.gov/wamo
Book free timed tickets at:
W recreation.gov
**Closed** for renovation; scheduled to reopen in 2014. Call ahead to check. ♿ 📷

**Transport**
Ⓜ Smithsonian. 🚌 13, 52.

Viewing window

Elevator taking visitors to top

**The Original Design**
Although the original design included a circular colonnade around the monument, lack of funds prohibited its construction.

**The two-tone stonework** indicates the point at which construction stopped in 1858 and then began again in 1876.

**The Marble Capstone**
The capstone weighs 3,300 pounds (2,000 kg) and is topped by an aluminum pyramid. Restoration of the monument was carried out in 1934 as part of President Roosevelt's Public Works Project (see p25).

**Commemorative stones** inside the monument are donations from individuals, societies, states, and nations.

50 flagpoles surrounding the monument represent each state

**View of the Monument** The gleaming white stone of the restored monument makes it clearly visible from almost all over the city. The views from the top of the monument across Washington are stunning.

**The foundation** of the monument is more than 36 ft (10 meters) deep. The width of the base of the shaft is 55 ft (17 meters).

The colonnaded, domed Jefferson Memorial, housing the bronze statue

so the standing statue of Jefferson had to be cast in plaster. After World War II, the statue was recast in bronze and the plaster version was moved.

Etched on the walls of the memorial are Jefferson's words from the Declaration of Independence and other writings. The statue of Jefferson is 19 ft (6 m) high and weighs 10,000 lb. It shows him looking towards the White House.

### ⓭ United States Holocaust Memorial Museum

*See pp82–3.*

### ⓮ Bureau of Engraving and Printing

14th and C St, SW. **Map** 3 B5.
**Tel** 1-877-874-4114. Ⓜ Smithsonian.
⏱ 8:30am–3:30pm Mon–Fri (Apr–Aug: 8:30am–7:30pm). **Closed** Week after Christmas, Federal hols. ♿ 🅿
Ⓦ **moneyfactory.gov**

Until 1863, individual banks were responsible for printing American money. A shortage of coins and the need to finance the Civil War led to the production of standardized bank notes, and the Bureau of Engraving and Printing was founded. Initially housed in the basement of the Treasury Building (*see p114*), the bureau was moved to its present location in 1914. It prints over $140 billion a year, as well as stamps, federal documents, and White House invitations. Coins are not minted here, but in a federal facility in Philadelphia.

The 40-minute tour includes a short film, and a walk through the building to view the printing processes and checks for defects. Also on display are bills that are out of circulation, counterfeit money, and a special $100,000 bill. The Visitor Center has a gift shop, videos, and exhibits.

### ⓯ Jefferson Memorial

South bank of the Tidal Basin.
**Map** 3 B5. **Tel** (202) 426-6841.
Ⓜ Smithsonian. **Open** 24 hours daily.
**Closed** Dec 25. Interpretive talks & Interpretive tours: 10am–11pm hourly. ♿ 🅿 Ⓦ **nps.gov/thje**

Thomas Jefferson (*see p168*) was a political philosopher, architect, musician, book collector, scientist, horticulturist, diplomat, inventor and the third American president, from 1801 to 1809. He also played a significant part in drafting the Declaration of Independence in 1776.

The idea for the memorial came from President Franklin Delano Roosevelt, who felt that Jefferson was as important as Lincoln. Designed by John Russell Pope, this Neo-Classical memorial was dedicated in 1943 and covers an area of 2.5 acres (1 ha). At the time, metal was strictly rationed

Statue of Jefferson

### ⓰ Tidal Basin

Boathouse: 1501 Maine Ave, SW.
**Map** 2 F5 & 3 A5. Ⓜ Smithsonian.
Paddle-boats: **Tel** (202) 479-2426.
**Open** Mar–Oct: 10am–6pm. ♿
Ⓦ **tidalbasinpaddleboats.com**

The Tidal Basin was built in 1897 to catch the overflow from the Potomac River and prevent flooding. In 1912, hundreds of cherry trees, given by the Japanese government, were planted along the shores of the man-made lake. However, during the two weeks when the cherry trees bloom (between mid-March and mid-April) chaos reigns around the Tidal Basin. The area is filled with cars and busloads of people photographing the sight. The only way to avoid this gridlock is to see the blossoms at dawn. The Tidal Basin reverts to a relatively quiet park after the blossoms have fallen and the hordes depart. Paddle-boats can be rented from the boathouse on Maine Avenue.

The banks of the Tidal Basin, with Jefferson Memorial in the distance

# ⑬ United States Holocaust Memorial Museum

The US Holocaust Memorial Museum, opened in 1993, bears witness to the systematic persecution and murder in Europe of six million Jews and others deemed undesirable by the Third Reich, including homosexuals and the disabled. The exhibition space ranges from the intentionally claustrophobic to the soaringly majestic. The museum contains 2,500 photographs, 1,000 artifacts, 53 video monitors, and 30 interactive stations that contain graphic and emotionally disturbing images of violence, forcing visitors to confront the horror of the Holocaust. While Daniel's Story is suitable for children of eight years and up, the permanent exhibition is not recommended for the under 12s.

**★ Hall of Remembrance**
The Hall of Remembrance houses an eternal flame that pays homage to the victims of the Holocaust.

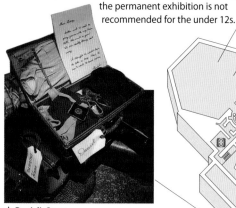

Second Floor

First Floor

14th Street Entrance

**★ Daniel's Story**
This exhibit, aimed at children between the ages of eight and 12, tells the history of the Holocaust from the point of view of an eight-year-old Jewish boy in 1930s Germany.

**Key to Floor Plan**

- ▢ Concourse Level
- ▢ First Floor
- ▢ Second Floor
- ▢ Third Floor
- ▢ Fourth Floor

**★ Hall of Witness**
The soaring central atrium features the Hall of Witness. The Museum aims to preserve the memory of those who died.

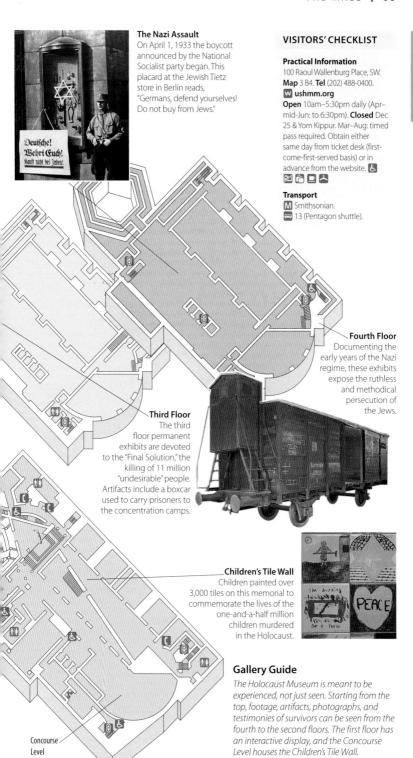

**The Nazi Assault**
On April 1, 1933 the boycott announced by the National Socialist party began. This placard at the Jewish Tietz store in Berlin reads, "Germans, defend yourselves! Do not buy from Jews."

**VISITORS' CHECKLIST**

**Practical Information**
100 Raoul Wallenburg Place, SW.
**Map** 3 B4. **Tel** (202) 488-0400.
**ushmm.org**
**Open** 10am–5:30pm daily (Apr–mid-Jun: to 6:30pm). **Closed** Dec 25 & Yom Kippur. Mar–Aug: timed pass required. Obtain either same day from ticket desk (first-come-first-served basis) or in advance from the website.

**Transport**
Ⓜ Smithsonian.
🚌 13 (Pentagon shuttle).

**Fourth Floor**
Documenting the early years of the Nazi regime, these exhibits expose the ruthless and methodical persecution of the Jews.

**Third Floor**
The third floor permanent exhibits are devoted to the "Final Solution," the killing of 11 million "undesirable" people. Artifacts include a boxcar used to carry prisoners to the concentration camps.

**Children's Tile Wall**
Children painted over 3,000 tiles on this memorial to commemorate the lives of the one-and-a-half million children murdered in the Holocaust.

**Gallery Guide**
*The Holocaust Museum is meant to be experienced, not just seen. Starting from the top, footage, artifacts, photographs, and testimonies of survivors can be seen from the fourth to the second floors. The first floor has an interactive display, and the Concourse Level houses the Children's Tile Wall.*

Concourse Level

The National WWII Memorial looking west towards the Lincoln Memorial

## ⑰ National WWII Memorial

17th St, NW, between Constitution Ave & Independence Ave. **Map** 2 E5. **Tel** (202) 426-6841. Ⓜ Smithsonian or Federal Triangle. **Open** 9:30am–11:30pm daily. **Closed** Dec 25. ♿ Ⓦ nps.gov/nwwm The online Registry of Remembrances: Ⓦ wwiimemorial.com

Sixteen million Americans served in World War II, and of them, 400,000 died. The 4,000 gold stars, the "Field of Stars," on the Freedom Wall commemorate these war dead, and in front of the wall is the inscription: "Here We Mark the Price of Freedom." Millions more ordinary citizens contributed in some way to the war effort. The National World War II Memorial on the National Mall honors their service and sacrifice.

The establishment of the memorial, however, was not without controversy as to both location and scale. After a bill was first introduced in 1987 it took a further six years before the legislation made its way through Congress. President Clinton signed the bill into law on May 25, 1993 and then there followed a great debate over where it should be located. The Rainbow Pool site was chosen in October 1995 with the condition that the east-west vista from the Washington Monument to the Lincoln Memorial be preserved. Further delays followed because the Commission of Fine Arts criticized the mass and scale of the initial plans and asked that further consideration be given to preserving the vista. Work finally began in 2001.

Design and construction was awarded to the firm of Leo A. Daly, and the design architect

Ceremonial entrance shield

was Friedrich St. Florian (former dean of Rhode Island School of Design).

Two 43-ft (13-m) pavilions stand on either side of the Rainbow Pool, marking the north and south entrances, and represent the Atlantic and Pacific theaters of war. Fifty-six granite pillars, one for each of the country's states and territories during that time, are adorned with bronze wreaths of oak leaves and wheat, which symbolize the nation's agricultural and industrial strength. Bas-relief panels created by sculptor Ray Kaskey line both sides of the 17th St entrance. They depict the many contributions Americans made to the war effort: from enlistment and embarkation to the Normandy landings, from Rosie the Riveter to medics in the field.

Words spoken by presidents and generals are inscribed throughout the memorial, including these by General Douglas MacArthur marking the war's end: "Today the guns are silent…The skies no longer rain death – the seas bear only commerce – men everywhere walk upright in the sunlight. The entire world is quietly at peace."

The memorial was officially opened to the public in April 2004 and on May 29 some 150,000 people, many of them veterans, joined in the dedication ceremony.

The Freedom Wall lined with 4,000 stars commemorating the US war dead

# ❶ Vietnam Veterans Memorial

21st St & Constitution Ave, NW.
**Map** 2 E4. **Tel** (202) 426-6841.
Ⓜ Smithsonian. **Open** 24 hours daily.
🕐 10am–11pm daily on the hour.
♿ 🖥 nps.gov/vive

Maya Lin, a 21-year-old student at Yale University, submitted a design for the proposed Vietnam Veterans Memorial as part of her architecture course. One of 1,421 entries, Maya Lin's design was simple – two triangular black walls sinking into the earth at an angle of 125 degrees, one end pointing to the Lincoln Memorial, the other to the Washington Monument. On the walls would be inscribed the names of more than 58,000 Americans who died in the Vietnam War, in chronological order, from the first in 1959 to the last in 1975.

Lin received only a B grade on the course, but she won the competition. Her design has become one of the most moving monuments on the Mall. Veterans and their families leave tokens of remembrance – soft toys, poems, pictures, and flowers – at the site of the fallen soldier's name.

**The Vietnam Women's Memorial**

To mollify those opposed to the abstract memorial, a statue of three soldiers, sculpted by Frederick Hart, was added in 1984. Further lobbying led to the Vietnam Women's Memorial, erected close by in 1993.

# ❷ Korean War Veterans Memorial

21st St & Independence Ave, SW.
**Map** 2 E5. **Tel** (202) 426-6841.
Ⓜ Smithsonian, Foggy Bottom.
**Open** 24 hours daily. ♿
🖥 nps.gov/kwvm

The Korean War Veterans Memorial is a controversial tribute to a controversial war. Although 1.5 million Americans served in the conflict, war was never officially declared. It is often known as "The Forgotten War." Intense debate preceded the selection of the memorial's design. On July 27, 1995, the 42nd anniversary of the armistice that ended the war, the memorial was dedicated.

Nineteen larger-than-life stainless steel statues, a squad on patrol, are depicted moving towards the American flag as their symbolic objective. Their ponchos are a

Names on the wall at the Vietnam Veterans Memorial

reminder of the war's notoriously miserable weather conditions. On the south side is a polished black granite wall etched with the images of more than 2,400 veterans. An inscription above the Pool of Remembrance reads: "Our nation honors her sons and daughters who answered the call to defend a country they never knew and a people they never met."

# ❸ Martin Luther King, Jr. Memorial

1964 Independence Ave, SW.
**Map** 2 E5. **Tel** (202) 483-3373.
Ⓜ Smithsonian, Foggy Bottom.
**Open** 9am–10pm daily. ♿
🖥 mlkmemorial.org

Set among the famous cherry blossom trees of the Tidal Basin (see p81) is the Martin Luther King, Jr. Memorial. The Mall's first memorial to an African-American, dedicated on August 26, 2011, commemorates the life and work of Dr. King. Designed by Chinese sculptor Lei Yixin, the memorial consists of two massive stone tablets – one features excerpts from King's speeches, while the other shows the figure of Martin Luther King emerging from the stone. The choice of a non-American sculptor proved controversial, as did King's somewhat stern expression.

The poignant statues of the Korean War Veterans Memorial

# ㉑ Franklin D. Roosevelt Memorial

Franklin Roosevelt once told Supreme Court Justice Felix Frankfurter, "If they are to put up any memorial to me, I should like it to be placed in the center of that green plot in front of the Archives Building. I should like it to consist of a block about the size of this," pointing to his desk. It took more than 50 years for a fitting monument to be erected, but Roosevelt's request for modesty was not heeded. Opened in 1997, this memorial is a mammoth park of four granite open-air rooms, one for each of Roosevelt's terms, with statuary and waterfalls. The president, a polio sufferer, is portrayed in a chair, with his dog Fala by his side.

**The statue of Roosevelt** by Neil Estern, is one of the memorial's most controversial elements as it shows the disabled president sitting in a wheelchair hidden by his Navy cape.

**A relief of Roosevelt's funeral cortège** was carved into the granite wall by artist Leonard Baskin. It depicts the coffin on a horse-drawn cart, followed by the crowds of mourners walking behind.

## KEY

① **The fourth room** honors Roosevelt's life and legacy. A statue of his wife, Eleanor, stands in this room.

② **Third room**

③ **Second room**

④ **The first room** commemorates FDR's first term and includes a bas-relief of his inaugural parade.

⑤ **The Visitor Center** includes an information area and a bookstore. The wheelchair that FDR used after he had polio is also on display.

**Dramatic waterfalls** cascade into a series of pools in the fourth room. The water reflects the peace that Roosevelt was so keen to achieve before his death.

## VISITORS' CHECKLIST

**Practical Information**
West Basin Drive, SW. **Map** 3 A5.
**Tel** (202) 426-6841.
**w** nps.gov/fdrm
**Open** 24 hours daily.
**Closed** Dec 25. 🚻 📷
Interpretive programs and talks.

**Transport**
M Smithsonian and 25-minute walk. 🚌 13.

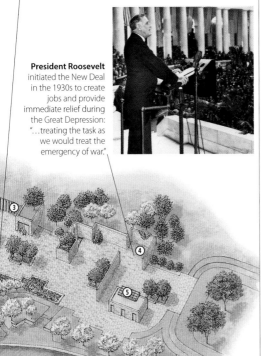

***Breadline*, a sculpture of figures** waiting in the breadline, by George Segal, recalls the hard times of the Great Depression, during which Roosevelt was elected and reelected three times.

**President Roosevelt** initiated the New Deal in the 1930s to create jobs and provide immediate relief during the Great Depression: "…treating the task as we would treat the emergency of war."

## ㉒ Lincoln Memorial

Constitution Ave, between French & Bacon Drives. **Map** 2 E5. **Tel** (202) 426-6841. M Smithsonian, Foggy Bottom, and 20-minute walk. **Open** 24 hours daily. 🚻 📷 Call (202) 747-3420 to listen to interpretive programs. **w** nps.gov/linc

Many proposals were made for a memorial to President Abraham Lincoln. One of the least promising was for a monument on a swampy piece of land to the west of the Washington Monument. Yet this was to become one of the most awe-inspiring sights in Washington. Looming over the Reflecting Pool is the seated figure of Lincoln in his Neo-Classical "temple" with 36 Doric columns, one for each state at the time of Lincoln's death.

Before the monument could be built in 1914, the site had to be drained. Solid concrete piers were poured for the foundation so that the building could be anchored in bedrock. Architect Henry Bacon realized that the original 10-ft (3-m) statue by Daniel Chester French would be dwarfed inside the building, so it was nearly doubled in size. As a result, it had to be carved from 28 blocks of white marble.

Engraved on the south wall is Lincoln's Gettysburg Address *(see p165)*. Above it is a mural painted by Jules Guerin depicting the angel of truth freeing a slave. Dr. Martin Luther King, Jr.'s famous address, "I Have a Dream" *(see p99)*, was given from the steps of the memorial.

Lincoln Memorial, reflected in the still waters of the pool

# PENN QUARTER

Bordered by the Capitol to the east and the White House to the west, Washington's Penn Quarter was the heart of the city at the start of the 20th century. F Street, the city's first paved road, bustled with shops, bars, newspaper offices, and churches, as well as horses and carriages. Penn Quarter was also an important residential neighborhood. The upper classes kept elegant homes, while middle-class merchants lived above their shops. By the 1950s suburbia had lured people away, and in the 1980s Penn Quarter was a mixture of boarded-up buildings and discount shops. The 1990s saw a dramatic change and the beginnings of regeneration, as the Verizon Center attracted new restaurants and stores.

## Sights at a Glance

### Museums and Galleries

**5** Newseum
**13** National Museum of Women in the Arts
**14** Carnegie Library Building
**18** Smithsonian American Art Museum and the National Portrait Gallery pp100–103
**19** International Spy Museum
**22** National Building Museum

### Statues and Fountains

**1** Mellon Fountain
**8** Benjamin Franklin Statue

### Aquarium

**10** National Aquarium

### Historic and Official Buildings

**2** National Archives
**6** Ronald Reagan Building
**7** Old Post Office
**11** Willard Hotel
**12** National Theatre
**15** Ford's Theatre
**16** Martin Luther King Memorial Library
**20** Verizon Center

### Districts, Streets, and Squares

**4** Pennsylvania Avenue
**9** Freedom Plaza
**17** Chinatown

### Memorials

**3** US Navy Memorial
**21** National Law Enforcement Officers' Memorial

### Restaurants see pp184–5

1 Acadiana
2 Austin Grill
3 Brasserie Beck
4 Carmines
5 Chipotle
6 District Chophouse & Brewery
7 District of Pi
8 Fogo de Chao
9 Full Kee
10 Graffiato
11 Jaleo
12 Luke's Lobster
13 Merzi
14 Oceanaire
15 Old Ebbitt Grill
16 Oyamel
17 Paul Bakery
18 Poste
19 Proof
20 Rasika
21 Rosa Mexicano
22 The Source
23 Teaism
24 Zaytinya

| 0 meters | | 500 |
| 0 yards | | 500 |

*See also Street Finder map 3, 4*

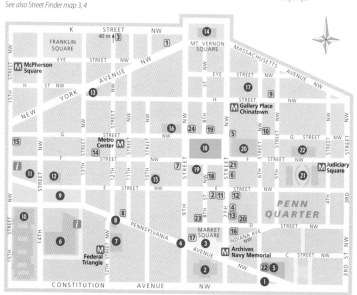

◀ The flag-festooned Old Post Office

**For keys to symbols** see back flap

# Street-by-Street: Penn Quarter

By the mid-20th century, Pennsylvania Avenue, the main route for presidential inaugural parades, had become tawdry and run down. It is now a grand boulevard worthy of L'Enfant's original vision. Pennsylvania Avenue links the White House to the US Capitol and is home to some of the city's main sights. Opposite the US Navy Memorial is the US National Archives, housing original copies of the Constitution and the Declaration of Independence. To the east are the Mellon Fountain and the National Gallery of Art. The Ronald Reagan Building was the site of the 1999 NATO summit.

**❹ ★ Pennsylvania Avenue**
Part of L'Enfant's original plan for the city, Pennsylvania Avenue was the first main street to be laid out in Washington. The thoroughfare reflects the architect's grandiose plans.

**❽ Benjamin Franklin Statue**
This inventor, statesman, writer, publisher, and man of genius is remembered as "printer, philosopher, philanthropist, patriot".

FBI Building

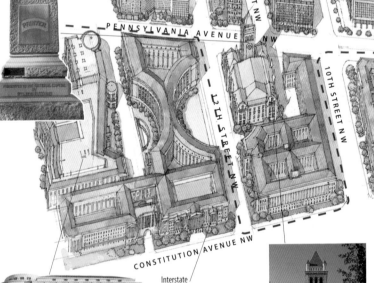

11TH STREET NW

10TH STREET NW

PENNSYLVANIA AVENUE NW

12TH STREET NW

CONSTITUTION AVENUE NW

Interstate Commerce Commission

**❻ Ronald Reagan Building**
Built in 1997, this impressive edifice echoes the Classical Revival architecture of other buildings in the Federal Triangle.

**❼ Old Post Office**
This majestic granite building was completed in 1899 and was the city's first skyscraper. The elegant clock tower measures 315 ft (96 m) in height.

**③ US Navy Memorial**
The memorial at Market Square contains a huge etching of the world surrounded by low granite walls.

**Locator Map**
*See Street Finder Maps 3 & 4*

**Key**
— Suggested route

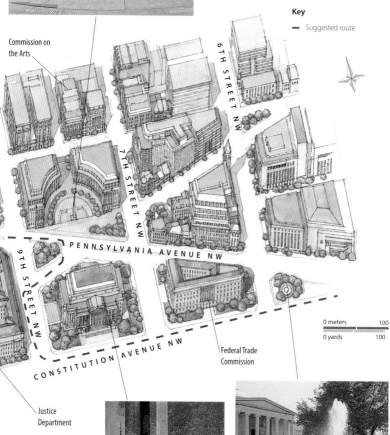

Commission on the Arts

6TH STREET NW

7TH STREET NW

PENNSYLVANIA AVENUE NW

9TH STREET NW

CONSTITUTION AVENUE NW

Federal Trade Commission

Justice Department

| 0 meters | 100 |
| 0 yards | 100 |

**② ★ US National Archives**
The Rotunda houses the National Archives' most precious documents, known as the "Charters of Freedom," including the Bill of Rights. A copy of England's Magna Carta is also on display.

**① Mellon Fountain**
Located by the National Gallery of Art's West Building, this fountain is named after Andrew Mellon, an industrialist and art collector who founded the gallery in the 1930s.

The cascading water of the Classical-style Mellon Fountain

# ❶ Mellon Fountain

Constitution Ave & Pennsylvania Ave, NW. **Map** 4 D4. Ⓜ Archives-Navy Memorial.

Situated opposite the National Gallery of Art *(see pp60–63)*, this fountain commemorates the man who endowed the gallery with its collection. Andrew Mellon was Secretary of the Treasury and a financier and industrialist. At his death, his friends donated $300,000 to build the fountain, which was dedicated on May 9, 1952.

The three bronze basins with their cascades of water were inspired by a fountain seen in a public square in Genoa, Italy. On the bottom of the largest basin, the signs of the Zodiac are engraved in bas-relief. The Classical lines of the fountain echo the architectural style of the National Gallery of Art West Building.

# ❷ National Archives

7000 Constitution Ave, between 7th St & 9th St, NW. **Map** 3 D3. **Tel** 1-866-272-6272. Ⓜ Archives-Navy Memorial/Penn Quarter. **Open** Mar 15–Labor Day: 10am–7pm daily; Sep–Mar: 10am–5:30pm daily. **Closed** Sun, Thanksgiving, Dec 25. 📷 💿 ♿ Ⓦ archives.gov

In the 1930s, Congress recognized the need to preserve the country's paper records before they deteriorated, were lost or were destroyed. The National Archives building, created for this purpose, was designed by John Russell Pope, architect of the National Gallery of Art and the Jefferson Memorial; it opened in 1934. This impressive library houses the most important historical and legal documents in the United States.

Statue outside the US National Archives

On display are all four pages of the *Constitution of the United States*, as well as the *Declaration of Independence*, the *Bill of Rights*, and a 1297 copy of the *Magna Carta*, which is on indefinite loan from Ross Perot.

Also in the National Archives are millions of documents, photographs, motion picture film, and sound recordings going back over two centuries. There is enough material, in fact, to fill around 250,000 filing cabinets. The National Archives and Records Administration (NARA) acataloging, managing, and conserving all this material. Much of the Archives' information is now stored on computer. A permanent exhibition, "Public Vaults," offers people an interactive opportunity to explore a representative sample of the Archives' vast collection. The National Archives is of great importance as a research center. The Central Research Room is reserved for scholars, who can order copies of rare documents for study purposes. Copies of military records, immigration papers, slave transit documents, death certificates, and tax information are also available.

The impressive Neoclassical façade of the National Archives Building

# The Constitution of the United States

In 1787, delegates from the 13 original American states convened in the city of Philadelphia to redraft the Articles of Confederation *(see p20)*. It soon became clear that an entirely new document was required, rather than a revised one. Weeks of debate grew into months, as delegates drafted the framework for a new country. Cooperation and compromise finally led to the creation of the Constitution, a document that outlines the powers of the central government and the makeup of Congress. One of the main issues, how to elect the representatives, was finally determined to be by direct voting by the people. Once signed, the new Constitution was sent to the states for review. Federalists and anti-Federalists debated fervently over its content in pamphlets, speeches, and articles. In the end, the majority of states ratified the Constitution, giving up some of their power in "order to form a more perfect union."

The Preamble of the Constitution of the United States

Signatures on the US Constitution

### Signing of the Constitution

*After many months of debate by the delegates to the Federal Convention, the Constitution was completed and signed by 39 of the 55 state delegates on September 17, 1787, at Assembly Hall in Philadelphia. The oldest delegate was 81-year-old Benjamin Franklin. James Madison, another signatory, played a major role in achieving the ratification of the new Constitution during the two years after it was signed.*

James Madison

## The Constitution Today

*The seven articles of the Constitution (of which the first three lay out the principles of government; see pp30–31) still determine the laws of the United States today. In addition there are Amendments. The first ten form the Bill of Rights, which includes such famous issues as the right to bear arms and the freedom of religion and of speech.*

### Swearing Allegiance
The pledge of allegiance to the flag was written in 1892 to mark the 400th anniversary of Columbus's discovery of America. Today it is recited daily by schoolchildren and by immigrants taking up American citizenship.

### Public Demonstration
Citizens demonstrate their right to free speech by protesting against the Persian Gulf War.

A view down tree-lined Pennsylvania Avenue toward the US Capitol

### ❸ US Navy Memorial

Market Square, Pennsylvania Ave between 7th St & 9th St, NW. **Map 3** C3. Ⓜ Archives-Navy Memorial/Penn Quarter. ♿ Naval Heritage Center: 701 Pennsylvania Ave, NW. **Tel** (202) 737-2300. **Open** 9:30am–5pm daily. **Closed** Jan 1, Thanksgiving, Dec 25. 📷 🌐 navymemorial.org

The memorial to the US Navy centers on the statue of a single sailor. Sculpted in bronze by Stanley Bleifeld in 1990, the figure provides a poignant tribute to the men and women who have served the US Navy.

The sculpture stands on a vast map of the world – the outlines of the countries are laid into the ground and protected by low walls. Four waterfalls and a group of flagpoles complete the memorial. There are free summer concerts by military bands in the square. Behind the memorial is the **Naval Heritage Center**, with historical exhibits and portraits of famous naval personnel, including John F. Kennedy. A free film "At Sea," is shown daily at noon.

The lone sailor of the US Navy Memorial

### ❹ Pennsylvania Avenue

Pennsylvania Ave. **Map** 3 A2 to 4 D4. Ⓜ Federal Triangle, Archives-Navy Memorial.

When architect and urban designer Pierre L'Enfant drew up his plans in 1789 for the capital city of the new United States, he imagined a grand boulevard running through the center of the city, from the presidential palace to the legislative building. For the first 200 years of its history, however, Pennsylvania Avenue fell sadly short of L'Enfant's dreams. In the early 19th century it was simply a muddy footpath through the woods. Paved in 1833, it became part of a neighborhood of boarding houses, shops, and hotels.

During the Civil War, the area deteriorated quickly into "saloons, gambling dens, lodging houses, quick-lunch rooms, cheap-jack shops, and catch penny amusement places" according to the *Works Progress Administration Guide to Washington*. When President John F. Kennedy's inaugural parade processed down Pennsylvania Avenue in 1961, Kennedy took one look at "America's Main Street" with its shambles of peep shows, pawn shops, and liquor stores and said, "It's a disgrace – fix it." This command by Kennedy provided the impetus to re-evaluate the future of Pennsylvania Avenue.

Almost 15 years later, Congress established the Pennsylvania Avenue Development Corporation – a public and private partnership that developed a comprehensive

### Presidential Inaugural Parades

The tradition of inaugural parades to mark a new president's coming-to-office started in 1809, when the military accompanied President James Madison from his Virginia home to Washington, DC. The first parade to include floats was held in 1841 for President William Henry Harrison. In 1985, freezing weather forced Ronald Reagan's inaugural ceremony indoors to the Capitol Rotunda. A record crowd of approximately 1.8 million attended the 2009 parade for Barack Obama. The Army Band traditionally leads the procession down Pennsylvania Avenue from the US Capitol to the White House.

President Franklin D. Roosevelt's third inaugural parade in 1941

The multistory building housing the Newseum

outside and modern on the inside. Completed in 1997, it was the most expensive federal building project ever undertaken. Designed by Pei Cobb Freed & Partners, architects of the US Holocaust Memorial Museum *(see pp82–3)* and the National Gallery of Art's East Wing, the building houses a mix of federal, trade, and public spaces. It is named after President Ronald Reagan, who authorized the construction in the late 1980s. On the east end of the atrium is the largest neon sculpture in North America – "Route Zenith," a creation of Keith Sonnier. Outside the building is the Oscar Straus Memorial Fountain, with sculpture by Adolph Alexander Weinman.

In summer the four-acre Woodrow Wilson Plaza, graced by sculptures by such artists as Martin Puryear and Stephen Rodin, is the venue for free concerts from noon to 1:30pm every weekday.

The building is the home of the Washington DC Visitor Information Center due to its location in the heart of the capital. The Center provides tour information and tickets to shows and events.

plan of revitalization. Today, Pennsylvania Avenue is a clean, tree-lined street. Parks, memorials, shops, theaters, hotels, museums, and assorted government buildings border the street on either side, providing a suitably grand and formal setting for all future presidential inaugural parades.

who have lost their lives in the line of duty. On the front of the building is an inscription of the First Amendment listing the five freedoms – religion, speech, press, assembly, and petition.

Sculpture from the Oscar Straus Memorial Fountain

## ❺ Newseum

555 Pennsylvania Ave, NW. **Map** 4 F4. **Tel** 888-639-7386. **M** Archives-Navy Memorial. **Open** 9am–5pm daily. **Closed** Jan 1, Thanksgiving, Dec 25. 🅿 ♿ 🍴 🚭 🌐 newseum.org

This award-winning interactive news and media museum is housed in a beautiful building with a balcony that affords splendid views of the city. The Newseum features seven levels, 14 galleries, and 15 theaters that explore how and why news is made. The galleries span five centuries of news history and include up-to-the-second technology and hands-on exhibits. The gallery of Pulitzer Prize-winning photographs is one of the highlights. Among the iconic images on display are the 1945 photograph documenting the raising of the US flag after the Battle of Iwo Jima and a 1969 photograph portraying the execution of a prisoner in Saigon, Vietnam. Other galleries deal with the history of the Berlin Wall and the events of 9/11. There is also an interactive newsroom where visitors can play the role of a reporter or broadcaster, and a moving memorial to journalists

## ❻ Ronald Reagan Building

1300 Pennsylvania Ave, NW. **Map** 3 B3. **Tel** (202) 312-1300. **M** Federal Triangle. **Open** 5am–2am daily. **Closed** Federal hols. 🍴 11am Mon, Wed & Fri from 14th St entrance (to book ahead call 312-1647). Visitor Center: **Tel** 289-8317. 🚭 🅿 ♿ 🌐 itcdc.com

The Ronald Reagan Building is a modern 3.1 million sq ft limestone structure that is Classical in appearance on the

Mock-Classical entrance to the immense Ronald Reagan Building

Food court in the spectacular galleried hall of the Old Post Office

## ❼ Old Post Office

1100 Pennsylvania Ave, NW. **Map** 3 C3. **Tel** (202) 289-4224. Ⓜ Federal Triangle. **Open** Mar–Aug: 9am–8pm Mon–Sat, 10am–6pm Sun; Sep–Feb: 9am–5pm Mon–Sat, 10am–6pm Sun. **Closed** Jan 1, Thanksgiving, Dec 25. tower only (call 606-8691). **W oldpostofficedc.com**

Built in 1899, the Old Post Office was Washington's first skyscraper. Soaring 12 stories above the city, it was a fireproof model of modern engineering with a steel frame covered in granite. The huge interior had 3,900 electric lights and its own generator, the first one to be used in the city. Its fanciful Romanesque architecture was fashionable at the time it was built, and the breathtaking hall, with its glass roof and balconies, remains a spectacular mixture of light, color, and gleaming metal.

In the 15 years following its construction, the Post Office became an object of controversy. Its turrets and arches, once praised by critics, were derided. The *New York Times* newspaper said the building looked like "a cross between a cathedral and a cotton mill." Government planners thought the Post Office building clashed with the Neo-Classical architecture that dominated the rest of Washington. When the postal system moved its offices in 1934, there seemed to be no reason to keep the architectural relic. Only a lack of funds during the Great Depression of the 1930s *(see p25)* prevented the Old Post Office from being torn down.

The building was occupied intermittently by various government agencies until the mid-1960s, when its decrepit condition again drew a chorus in favor of demolition. A Washington preservation group, Don't Tear It Down, promoted the historical significance of the Old Post Office, and it was spared once more.

The renovated building housed a complex of shops and restaurants, commonly known as the Old Post Office Pavilion, until its purchase in 2013 by business magnate Donald Trump, who is renovating the area once again. It is scheduled to reopen in 2016.

## ❽ Benjamin Franklin Statue

Pennsylvania Ave & 10th St, NW. **Map** 3 C3. Ⓜ Federal Triangle.

Donated by publisher Stilson Hutchins (1839–1912), it was unveiled by Benjamin Franklin's great-granddaughter in 1889. The words "Printer, Philosopher, Patriot, Philanthropist" are inscribed on the four sides of the statue's pedestal in tribute to this man of diverse talents. Postmaster general, writer, and scientist, Benjamin Franklin was also a key member of the committee that drafted the 1776 Declaration of Independence. As a diplomat to the court of Louis XVI of France, he went to Versailles in 1777 to gain support for the American cause of independence from Britain. Franklin returned to France in 1783 to negotiate the Treaty of Paris that ended the American Revolution *(see p20)*.

## ❾ Freedom Plaza

Pennsylvania Ave between 13th St & 14th St, NW. **Map** 3 B3. Ⓜ Federal Triangle, Metro Center.

Freedom Plaza was conceived as part of a Pennsylvania Avenue redevelopment plan in the mid-1970s. Designed by Robert Venturi and Denise Scott Brown, and completed in 1980, the plaza displays Pierre L'Enfant's original plan for Washington in black and white stone embedded in the ground. Around the edge are engraved quotations about the new city from Walt Whitman and President Wilson, among others.

Freedom Plaza provides a dramatic entry to Pennsylvania Avenue *(see pp94–5)*. On the north side of the plaza, where

The large-scale reproduction of L'Enfant's city plans, Freedom Plaza

Pennsylvania Avenue leads into E Street, are the **Warner Theatre** and the **National Theatre**. South of the plaza is the Beaux Arts **District Building** (housing government employees). The Freedom Plaza is a popular site for festivals and political protests.

# ⑩ National Aquarium

Commerce Building, 14th St & Constitution Ave, NW. **Map** 3 B3. **Tel** (202) 482-2825. Ⓜ Federal Triangle. **Open** 9am–5pm daily. **Closed** Thanksgiving, Dec 25. 🅿 🌊 ♿ Ⓦ nationalaquarium.org

Originally located in 1873 at Woods Hole, Massachusetts (a major center for marine biology), the National Aquarium was moved to Washington in 1888 in order to make it more accessible. Since 1931 it has been located in the US Department of Commerce Building, and today the aquarium is home to around 1,200 specimens and 200 different species.

Green Turtle at the National Aquarium

The Aquarium has a wide range of freshwater and saltwater fish on display, such as nurse sharks, piranhas, and moray eels, and also a number of reptiles and various species of amphibians, all displayed in simulated "natural environments."

There are daily public feedings of the sharks and piranhas at 2pm, as well as talks.

# ⑪ Willard Hotel

1401 Pennsylvania Ave, NW. **Map** 3 B3. **Tel** (202) 628-9100, 800-827-1747. Ⓜ Metro Center. ♿ Ⓦ intercontinental.com

There has been a hotel on this site since 1816. Originally called Tennison's, the hotel was housed in six adjacent two-story buildings. Refurbished in 1847, it was managed by hotel keeper Henry Willard, who gave his name to the hotel in 1850. Many famous people stayed

here during the Civil War (1861–65), including the writer Nathaniel Hawthorne, who was covering the conflict for a magazine, and Julia Ward Howe who wrote the popular Civil War standard *The Battle Hymn of the Republic*. The word "lobbyist" is said to have been coined because it was known by those seeking favors that President Ulysses S. Grant went to the hotel's lobby to smoke his after-dinner cigar.

The present 330-room building, designed by the architect of New York's Plaza Hotel, Henry Hardenbergh, was completed in 1904. It was the most fashionable place to stay in the city until the end of World War II, when the surrounding neighborhood fell into decline. For 20 years it was boarded up and faced demolition. A coalition, formed of preserva-tionists and the Pennsylvania Avenue Development Corporation, worked to restore the Beaux Arts building, and it finally reopened in renewed splendor in 1986.

No other hotel can rival the Willard's grand lobby, with its 35 different kinds of marble, polished wood, and petal-shaped concierge station. There is a style café, a bar, and a restaurant called The Willard Room.

Façade of the National Theatre on E Street

# ⑫ National Theatre

1321 Pennsylvania Ave, NW. **Map** 3 B3. **Tel** (202) 628-6161, 800-447-7400. Ⓜ Metro Center, Federal Triangle. ♿ Ⓦ nationaltheatre.org

The present National Theatre is the sixth theater to occupy this Pennsylvania Avenue site and the oldest cultural institution in the city. The first four theaters burned down, and the fifth one was replaced by the current building in 1922. The National Theatre hosts Broadway-bound productions and touring groups. The National is known as an "actor's theater" because of its excellent acoustics (even a whisper on stage can be heard in the top balcony). It is haunted by the ghost of 19th-century actor John McCullough, murdered by a fellow actor and buried under the stage. There are free performances for children every Saturday at 9:30am and 11am.

Peacock Alley, one of the Willard Hotel's luxuriously decorated corridors

## ⑬ National Museum of Women in the Arts

1250 New York Ave, NW. **Map** 3 C3.
**Tel** (202) 783-5000, 800-222-7270.
Ⓜ Metro Center. **Open** 10am–5pm
Mon–Sat, noon–5pm Sun.
**Closed** Jan 1, Thanksgiving, Dec 25.
📷 for groups (call 783-7996). 🅿 ♿
💻 📷 Ⓦ nmwa.org

This museum of women's art houses works that span five centuries, from the Renaissance to the present day. The collection was started in the 1960s by Wilhelmina Holladay and her husband, who gathered paintings, sculpture, and photography from all over the world.

The museum operated out of the Holladays' private residence for several years, until it acquired a more permanent home in this Renaissance Revival landmark building, formerly a Masonic Temple. The collection has as its highlights masterpieces by female American artists. Some of the outstanding works on display from the 19th century include *The Bath* (1891) by Mary Cassatt and *The Cage* (1885) by Berthe Morisot. Among the works by 20th-century artists are Elizabeth Cutlett's *Singing their Songs* (1992) and *Self-Portrait Between the Curtains, Dedication to Trotsky* (1937) by Mexican artist Frida Kahlo. The museum shop sells a range of gifts, also created by women.

Impressive exterior of the National Museum of Women in the Arts

## ⑭ Carnegie Library Building

801 K St (Mount Vernon Sq), NW.
**Map** 3 C2. **Tel** (202) 393-1420.
Ⓜ Gallery Place–Chinatown, Mt
Vernon Sq. Kiplinger Research Library:
**Tel** 383-1829. **Open** 10am–5pm Tue–
Sat. **Closed** Jan 1, Jul 4, Thanksgiving,
Dec 25. ♿ 💻 📷 Ⓦ historydc.org

The Carnegie Library Building was once Washington's central library. It hosts various events and exhibitions, and in 2003 the Washington Historical Society moved its headquarters to the building and the City Museum of Washington, DC was created.

The state-of-the-art Kiplinger Research Library and Reading Room houses extensive collections of historic materials, including rare publications, prints, maps, photographs, manuscripts, and memorabilia. There are also lectures, workshops, and videos. Washington Perspectives, an overview exhibit, features a giant map of the city set into the floor.

Painting of John Wilkes Booth poised to shoot Abraham Lincoln

## ⑮ Ford's Theatre

511 10th St between E St & F St, NW.
**Map** 3 C3. **Tel** (202) 426-6924.
Ⓜ Gallery Place-Chinatown, Metro
Center. **Open** 9am–5pm daily (except
matinee or rehearsal days – call
ahead). ♿ Petersen House:
**Closed** Dec 25. **Open** 9:30am–5:30pm
daily with free timed ticket. **Closed**
Dec 25. 📷 Ⓦ fordstheatre.org

John T. Ford, a theatrical producer, built this small jewel of a theater in 1863. Washington was a Civil War boomtown, and the theater, located in the thriving business district, enjoyed great popularity. The fate of the theater was sealed, however, on April 14, 1865, when President Abraham Lincoln was shot here by John Wilkes Booth while watching a performance. Across the road from the theater, **Petersen House**, where the wounded president died the next morning, has been preserved as a museum.

After the tragedy, people stopped patronizing the theater, and Ford was forced to sell the building to the federal government a year later. It was left to spiral into decay for nearly a century until the government decided to restore it to its original splendor.

The theater now stages small productions. The Presidential Box is permanently decorated in Lincoln's honor.

Exterior of Ford's Theatre, site of the shooting of President Lincoln

### ⓰ Martin Luther King Memorial Library

901 G St at 9th St, NW. **Map** 3 C3. **Tel** (202) 727-0321. Ⓜ Gallery Place–Chinatown, Metro Center. **Open** noon–9pm Mon–Tue, 9:30am–5:30pm Wed–Sat, 1–5pm Sun. **Closed** Federal hols. ♿ Ⓦ dclibrary.org/mlk

Washington's Martin Luther King Memorial Library is the only example of the Modernist architecture of Ludwig Mies van der Rohe in the city. A prominent figure in 20th-century design, van der Rohe finalized his plans for the library shortly before his death in 1969. It was named in honor of Dr. Martin Luther King Jr. at the request of the library's trustees when it opened in 1972, replacing the small and out-dated Carnegie Library as the city's central public library.

Architecturally, the building is a classic example of van der Rohe's theory of "less is more." It is an austere, simple box shape with a recessed entrance lobby. Inside, there is a mural depicting the life of Dr. Martin Luther King Jr., the leader of the Civil Rights Movement, painted by artist Don Miller.

The library sponsors concerts and readings, as well as a program of children's events.

The "Friendship Archway" spanning H Street in the heart of Chinatown

### ⓱ Chinatown

5th St to 8th St & H St to I St, NW. **Map** 3 C3 & 4 D3. Ⓜ Gallery Place-Chinatown.

The small area in Washington known as Chinatown covers just six square blocks. Formed around 1930, it has never been very large and today houses about 500 Chinese residents. The area was reinvigorated with the arrival of the adjacent Verizon Center *(see p104)* in 1997. H Street is particularly lively, with many shops and a selection of good restaurants.

The "Friendship Archway," a dramatic gateway over H Street at the junction with 7th Street, marks the center of the Chinatown area. Built in 1986, it was paid for by Washington's sister city, Beijing, as a token of esteem, and is based on the architecture of the Qing Dynasty (1649–1911). Its seven roofs, topped by 300 painted dragons, are balanced on a steel and concrete base, making it the largest single-span Chinese arch in the world. It is lit up at night.

During the Chinese New Year celebrations in late January or early Febuary, the area comes alive with parades, dragon dances, and live musical performances *(see p61)*.

---

### Dr. Martin Luther King, Jr.

A charismatic speaker and proponent of Mahatma Gandhi's theories of non-violence, Dr. Martin Luther King, Jr. was a black Baptist minister and leader of the civil rights movement in the United States.

Born in Atlanta, Georgia in 1929, King's career in civil rights began with the 1955 Montgomery, Alabama bus boycott – a protest of the city's segregated transit system. The movement escalated to protests at schools, restaurants, and hotels that did not admit blacks. King's methods of non-violence were often met with police dogs and brutal tactics.

The culmination of the movement was the March on Washington on August 28, 1963, when 200,000 people gathered at the Lincoln Memorial in support of civil rights. The highlight of this event was King's "I Have a Dream" speech, calling for support of the movement. A direct result was the passing by Congress of the civil rights legislation in 1964, and King was awarded the Nobel Peace Prize the same year. In 1968 he was assassinated in Memphis, Tennessee, triggering riots in 100 American cities, including Washington.

Dr. King speaking at the Lincoln Memorial

# ⑱ Smithsonian American Art Museum and the National Portrait Gallery

Nowhere in Washington is the city's penchant to copy Greek and Roman architecture more obvious than in the former US Patent Office Building, now the home of the Smithsonian American Art Museum and the National Portrait Gallery (NPG). The wonderfully ornate 1836 building was converted into the twin museums in 1968. The American Art Museum contains a permanent collection of works by more than 7,000 American artists. The NPG is America's family album, featuring paintings, photographs, and sculptures of thousands of famous Americans.

Façade of the building, housing the main entrance to both galleries

## ★ Achelous and Hercules

*This painting (1947) by Thomas Hart Benton (1889–1975) is a mythological analogy of early American life. Interpreted in many ways, it is widely accepted that Hercules is man taming the wild, then enjoying the results of his labors.*

### KEY

① **An African-American** is depicted climbing over a fence to the idealized equality of America.

② **Hercules** tries to capture the bull.

③ **Achelous**, the river god, appears as a bull being wrestled by Hercules, representing the struggle of the American people.

④ **Hercules** is about to break off the bull's horn.

⑤ **The horn** is transformed into a cornucopia, or horn of plenty, symbolizing America as a land of abundance and opportunity.

⑥ **The man** working in the field represents the people of America, enjoying the fruits of the land after laboring.

**★ Among the Sierra Nevada, California**
Albert Bierstadt painted this Western landscape in 1867–8. He was later criticized by some for not offering a topographically correct view of the West.

### Mary Cassatt
This portrait by Edgar Degas, painted c.1882, depicts his fellow artist Mary Cassatt playing cards.

### "Casey" Stengel
This bronze sculpture of the baseball great was created by Rhoda Sherbell in 1981 from a 1965 cast.

### John Singleton Copley
This self-portrait of the artist, who was largely known for his depictions of others, was painted c.1780.

**VISITORS' CHECKLIST**

**Practical Information**
Smithsonian American Art
Museum: 8th St & F St, NW.
**Map** 3 C3.
**Tel** (202) 633-7970.
W **americanart.si.edu**
**Open** 11:30am–7pm daily.

National Portrait Gallery:
8th St & F St, NW.
**Map** 3 C3.
**Tel** (202) 633-8300.
W **npg.si.edu**
**Open** 11:30am–7pm daily. ▢

**Transport**
Ⓜ Gallery Place-Chinatown.

### Old Bear, a Medicine Man
This vibrant painting by George Caitlin dates from 1832. Native Americans were a popular choice of subject matter for this artist.

### ★ Manhattan
This 1932 oil painting by Georgia O'Keeffe was created for an exhibition at New York's Museum of Modern Art. It portrays her vision of the city's architectural landscape.

### In the Garden
This charming depiction of the poet Celia Thaxter is by the artist Childe Hassam and was painted in 1892.

# Exploring the Smithsonian American Art Museum

The Smithsonian American Art Museum was established in 1829 and is the first federal art collection. It began with gifts from private collections and art organizations that existed in Washington, DC before a bequest from British scientist James Smithson enabled the foundation of the Smithsonian Institution "for the increase and diffusion of knowledge" in 1846. The museum is a center for America's cultural heritage, with more than 42,000 artworks spanning 300 years.

## 19th- and Early 20th-Century Art

Some of the highlights in this collection from the last two centuries are the Thomas Moran Western landscapes and those of Albert Bierstadt. This subject matter can be seen in *Among the Sierra Nevada, California* (1867–8), Bierstadt's evocative depiction of the landscape.

Many of the American artists such as Albert Pinkham Ryder, Winslow Homer, and John Singer Sargent, were contemporaries to the Impressionists. Homer's *High Cliffs, Coast of Maine* (1894) is a dramatic meeting of land and sea. Seascapes were also a popular subject for Ryder. *Jonah*, painted c.1885, illustrates the Bible story of Jonah and the whale, depicting Jonah floundering in the sea during a storm, overlooked by God.

The museum holds hundreds of paintings of Native Americans, many of them works by George Caitlin. This was also a popular subject for Charles Bird King and John Mix Stanley. American Impressionists are also well represented in the museum, including Mary Cassatt, William Merritt Chase, John Henry Twachtman, and Childe Hassam. Hassam's paintings, inspired by the French Impressionists, are refreshing yet tranquil. The calm seascape of *The South Ledges, Appledore* (1913) is typical of his style.

## American Modernists

The enormous canvases of the Modernists provide a dramatic contrast to the landscapes and portraits of the 19th and 20th centuries. Franz Kline's black slashes on a white canvas in *Merce C* (1961), which was inspired by his involvement with dancer Merce Cunningham, are the antithesis of the delicacy of the Impressionists. Kenneth Noland's geometrical compositions resemble firing targets. Other Modernists here include Georgia O'Keeffe, Robert Rauschenberg, and David Hockney.

## American Folk Art

The collection of American folk art includes some truly amazing pieces of work, created from a wide range of materials. James Hampton's *Throne of the Third Heaven of the Nations' Millennium General Assembly* (c.1950–64) is one of the star pieces in the collection.

Robert Rauschenberg's *Reservoir* (1961), mixed media on canvas

## Contemporary Art

Roy Lichtenstein's 6.5-ton (5,900-kg) sculpture *Modern Head* (1989) greets visitors at the main entrance to the museum, and reflects the Smithsonian's dedication to the acquisition of modern and contemporary works. Inside are works by Jenny Holzer, Nam June Paik, and Edward Kienholz, among others. Karen LaMonte's *Reclining Dress Impression with Drapery* (2009) is a glorious, almost luminous, life-size sculpture in rippling cast glass.

## Luce Foundation Center

The three-story Luce Foundation Center for American Art holds about 3,300 artworks from the museum's collection. The items on display include paintings and sculptures, contemporary craft objects, folk art, and jewelry.

*Throne of the Third Heaven of the Nations' Millennium General Assembly* by James Hampton

# Exploring the National Portrait Gallery

The National Portrait Gallery keeps generations of remarkable Americans in the company of their fellow citizens. The gallery's mission is to collect and display images of "men and women who have made significant contributions to the history, development and culture of the people of the United States." Through the visual and performing arts, the lives of leaders such as George Washington and Martin Luther King, Jr., artists such as George Gershwin and Mary Cassatt, and activists such as Rosa Parks and Sequoyah are celebrated.

Ronald Reagan, an oil on canvas by Henry C. Casselli, Jr. painted in 1989

## Overview of the Collection

The National Portrait Gallery illuminates America's family album, magnificently combining history, biography, and art in its collections. The portraits are fascinating not only because they reveal their subjects but also because they illustrate the times in which they were produced. There are more than 20,000 images in the permanent collection, which includes paintings, photographs, sculptures, etchings, and drawings. Both heroes and villains are represented. Portraits taken from life sittings are favored by the gallery.

Portrait of Pocahontas by an unidentified artist

country's religious or cultural history. Athletes include the famous baseball player Babe Ruth and baseball manager Casey Stengel. Among figures from the world of entertainment are portraits of actresses Judy Garland, Tallulah Bankhead, and Mary Pickford. John Wayne also features among the Hollywood stars, as do Buster Keaton, Clark Gable, and James Cagney. There are also bronze busts of the poet T.S. Eliot and the humorist Will Rogers. Religious leaders, business magnates, pioneers in women's rights and civil rights (such as Dr. Martin Luther King, Jr.), explorers, and scientists are portrayed in a whole range of media, including oils, clay, and bronze. There are also many photographic portraits, including some of Marilyn Monroe, which were taken during a morale-boosting visit the actress made to soldiers during the Korean War.

## The Great Hall

The third-floor Great Hall is a crazy quilt of tiles and ceiling medallions. A frieze showing the evolution of technology in America also runs around the room. Once a display area for new inventions, it is a reminder of the building's past as the Patent Office.

## 20th-Century Americans

The National Portrait Gallery's collection is not limited to the political history of the country. There is also a large collection of portraits of American people notable for their achievements in the arts, sports, or in the

## America's presidents

In 1857, Congress commissioned George Peter Alexander Healy to paint portraits of the presidents. The chronologically ordered portrayal of all of the country's leaders remains the heart of the National Portrait Gallery's exhibitions.

Two portraits of George and Martha Washington are featured prominently in the Portrait Gallery. The most famous portrait of George Washington is Gilbert Stuart's "Landsdowne," painted from life in 1796. Abraham Lincoln posed for photographer Alexander Gardener several months before he was assassinated (see p98).

The exhibition also features modern-day presidents, such as Bill Clinton and George W. Bush. Shepard Fairey's iconic portrait of Barack Obama, an image seen throughout the latter's presidential campaign, is also here.

Diana Ross and The Supremes, photographed by Bruce Davidson in 1965

The unique and innovative International Spy Museum

### ⑲ International Spy Museum

800 F St, NW. **Map** 3 C3. **Tel** (202) 393-7798, EYE-SPY-U. Ⓜ Gallery Place-Chinatown, Metro Center. **Open** Apr–Oct: 9am–7pm; Nov–Mar: 10am–6pm. **Closed** Jan 1, Thanksgiving, Dec 25. ⚑ ▢ ⌂ ⌖ group tours by reservation. Ⓦ **spymuseum.org**

The Spy Museum is the first museum in the world devoted to international espionage. Its huge collection includes the German Enigma cipher machine from World War II, a Soviet shoe transmitter, a wristwatch camera, and a lipstick pistol, displayed in a variety of themed exhibits. A visit to the museum

begins with a film on the real life of a spy, revealing what motivates people to enter this clandestine world. The "School for Spies" exhibit displays over 200 artifacts used by spies to disguise and protect themselves during operations. "The Secret History of Histories" traces the art of spying from biblical times

World War II cipher machine, essential for breaking enemy codes

to the early 20th century. "Spies Among Us" examines the making and breaking of codes during World War II. Other permanent exhibits such as "Weapons of Mass Disruption" explore technology and cyber attacks, while "War of the Spies" looks at espionage from the Cold War to the present day, featuring spy planes, listening and tracking devices, and the lives of spies, such as Aldrich Ames and Robert Hanssen.

### ⑳ Verizon Center

601 F St, NW. **Map** 4 D3. **Tel** (202) 628-3200. Ⓜ Gallery Place-Chinatown. Team Store: **Open** 10am–5:30pm daily (later on event days). ⚑ for National Sports Gallery. ♿ ✎ ⌂ Ⓦ **verizoncenter.com**

Opened in 1997, the Verizon Center is a sports and enter-tainment complex that houses many shops and restaurants.

The 20,000-seat Verizon stadium is the home of Washington's basketball teams, the Wizards (men's team), Georgetown Hoyas, and the Mystics (women's), as well as the ice hockey team, the Capitals. The presence of the complex has revived the surrounding area beyond recognition. Half of the arena's seats are below ground level, in a vast but harmonious structure. It hosts rock concerts as well as sports events and exhibitions.

### Penn Quarter Renaissance

During the 1990s, Washington's Penn Quarter was transformed from a derelict historic area to prime real estate. The construction of the Verizon Center and renewed appreciation for the restoration of dilapidated Victorian buildings helped to accelerate this process. As a result of losing its shabby image, Penn Quarter also lost many of the artists who carved studios out of the high-ceilinged, low-rent spaces, but their influence can still be seen in the large number of art galleries and exhibitions in the area. Some of the non-profit organizations and small businesses that leased offices in the big, aging buildings were forced to relocate due to an increase in rent. Soaring prices also closed a number of traditional Chinese restaurants around the Verizon Center, which have been replaced by upscale eateries. Today Penn Quarter is a safer area for those on foot, with a buzzing selection of nightly activities available, including sports events, theater shows, concerts, and lively restaurants.

A contemporary office building linking two Victorian façades on 7th Street

Majestic lion statue alongside a marble wall at the police memorial

# ㉑ National Law Enforcement Officers Memorial

E St, NW, between 4th St & 5th St, NW. **Map** 4 D3. **Tel** (202) 737-3400. Ⓜ Judiciary Square. Visitor Center: 605 E St, NW. **Open** 9am–5pm Mon–Fri, 10am–5pm Sat, noon–5pm Sun. **Closed** Jan 1, Thanksgiving, Dec 25. 🚻 ♿ 📷 🖥 nleomf.org

Dedicated by President George Bush in 1991, the National Law Enforcement Officers Memorial honors the 18,600 police officers who have been killed since the first known death in 1792. Spread over three acres in the center of Judiciary Square, the memorial's flower-lined pathways are spectacular in springtime. The names of the fallen officers are inscribed on marble walls. Each path is guarded by a statue of an adult lion shielding its cubs, symbolic of the US police force's protective role.

# ㉒ National Building Museum

401 F St at 4th St, NW. **Map** 4 D3. **Tel** (202) 272-2448. Ⓜ Judiciary Square, Gallery Place-Chinatown. **Open** 10am–5pm Mon–Sat, 11am–5pm Sun. **Closed** Jan 1, Thanksgiving, Dec 25. 📷 🎞 ♿ 🖥 🖼 nbm.org

It is fitting that the National Building Museum, dedicated to the building trade, should be housed in the architecturally audacious former Pension Bureau building. Civil War General Montgomery C. Meigs saw Michelangelo's Palazzo Farnese on a trip to Rome and decided to duplicate it as a Washington office building, albeit twice as big and in red brick as opposed to the stone masonry of the Rome original.

Completed in 1887, the building is topped by a dramatic terracotta frieze of the Civil War measuring 3 ft (1 m) in height. The daring exterior of the building is matched by its flamboyant interior. The vast concourse, measuring 316 ft by 116 ft (96 m by 35 m), is lined with balconies containing exhibitions. The roof is supported by huge columns, constructed of brick, plastered, and faux-painted to give the appearance of marble. The Great Hall has been the impressive venue for many presidential balls.

In 1926 the Pension Bureau relocated to different offices, and

Ornamental plinth in the grounds of the museum

there was a move to demolish Meigs' building. Instead it was occupied by various government agencies for a time and was even used as a courthouse for a while.

The building was eventually restored, and in 1985 opened in renewed splendor as the National Building Museum. A privately owned collection, the museum has a display on the architectural history of the city – "Washington: Symbol and City." It includes an excellent illustration of Pierre L'Enfant's original plans for the capital, as well as other photographs, models, and interactive exhibits demonstrating how the city grew and changed. The temporary exhibits in the museum often highlight controversial issues in design and architecture. There is a small café in the courtyard, and a gift shop. For children under six, the "Building Zone" offers some hands-on fun including giant lego blocks, bulldozers, and a playhouse.

The splendid, colonnaded Great Hall in the National Building Museum

# THE WHITE HOUSE AND FOGGY BOTTOM

The official residence of the President, the White House is one of the most distinguished buildings in DC and was first inhabited in 1800. Although burned by the British during the War of 1812, most of today's building remains as it was planned. Other buildings surrounding the White House are worth a visit, such as the Daughters of the American Revolution building and the Corcoran Gallery. East of the White House is the Foggy Bottom area, which was built on swampland. Notable edifices here include the Kennedy Center, the State Department building, and the notorious Watergate Complex, focus of the 1970s Nixon scandal.

## Sights at a Glance

### Galleries
**5** Renwick Gallery
**7** Corcoran Gallery of Art

### Squares
**3** Lafayette Square
**17** Washington Circle

### Historic Buildings
**4** Hay-Adams Hotel
**6** Eisenhower Old Executive Office Building
**8** Octagon Museum
**9** Daughters of the American Revolution
**15** George Washington University
**18** Watergate Complex

### Official Buildings
**1** The White House pp110–13
**2** Treasury Building
**10** Organization of the American States
**11** Department of the Interior

**12** Federal Reserve Building
**13** National Academy of Sciences
**14** State Department

### Performing Arts Center
**19** Kennedy Center pp120–21

### Church
**16** St. Mary's Episcopal Church

See also Street Finder map 2, 3

| 0 meters | 500 |
| 0 yards | 500 |

### Restaurants see pp185–7

1 Ancora
2 Aroma
3 Bayou
4 Blue Duck Tavern
5 The Bombay Club
6 City Bites
7 Cone E. Island
8 Firefly
9 Founding Farmers
10 Georgia Brown's
11 Johnny Rockets
12 Marcel's
13 McFadden's
14 One Fish, Two Fish
15 Potbelly Sandwich Shop
16 The Public Bar
17 Rasika West End
18 Roof Terrace Restaurant
19 Vidalia
20 Westend Bistro

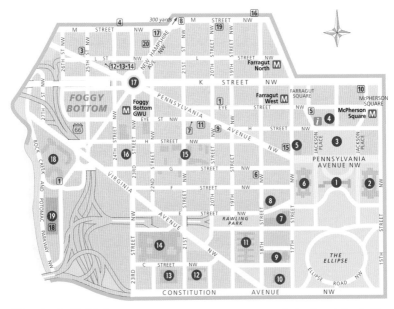

◀ The south portico of The White House

For keys to symbols see back flap

# Street-by-Street: Around The White House

The area surrounding the White House is filled with grand architecture and political history, and the vistas from the Ellipse lawn are breathtaking. It is worth spending a day exploring the area and seeing some of its buildings, such as the Treasury Building with its statue of Alexander Hamilton (the first Secretary of the Treasury) and the Eisenhower Old Executive Office Building. The buildings of the Daughters of the American Revolution and the OAS both offer the visitor an insight into the pride the nation takes in its past.

**❻ Eisenhower Old Executive Office Building**
Although it was poorly received on its completion in 1888, this attractive building now houses staff of the Executive branch.

**❺ Renwick Gallery**
The gallery is part of the Smithsonian American Art Museum. The inscription above the entrance of the building reads "Dedicated to Art.

**❽ Octagon Museum**
At one time James Madison's home, this building has had a varied history functioning as a hospital and a school, among other things.

**❼ ★ Corcoran Gallery of Art**
A treasure trove of fine art, the Corcoran Gallery counts works by Rembrandt, Monet, Picasso, and de Kooning among its many exhibits.

**❾ DAR Building**
This beautiful Neoclassical building is one of three founded by the historical organization, the Daughters of the American Revolution.

**Key**
— Suggested route

**❿ OAS Building**
The central statue of Queen Isabella of Spain stands in front of this Spanish Colonial-style mansion. Built in 1910, it houses the Organization of American States.

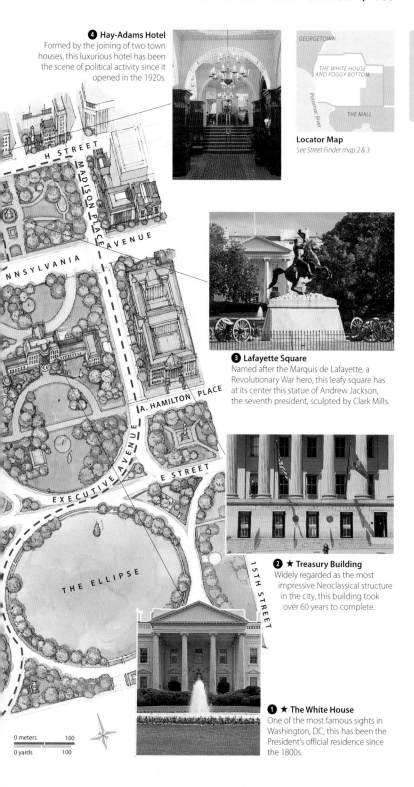

**4 Hay-Adams Hotel**
Formed by the joining of two town houses, this luxurious hotel has been the scene of political activity since it opened in the 1920s.

**Locator Map**
*See Street Finder map 2 & 3*

**3 Lafayette Square**
Named after the Marquis de Lafayette, a Revolutionary War hero, this leafy square has at its center this statue of Andrew Jackson, the seventh president, sculpted by Clark Mills.

**2 ★ Treasury Building**
Widely regarded as the most impressive Neoclassical structure in the city, this building took over 60 years to complete.

**1 ★ The White House**
One of the most famous sights in Washington, DC, this has been the President's official residence since the 1800s.

0 meters 100
0 yards 100

# ❶ The White House

In 1791 George Washington chose this site as the location for the new President's House. Irish-born architect James Hoban was selected to design the building, known as the Executive Mansion. In 1800, President and Mrs. John Adams became the first occupants, even though the building was not yet completed. Burned by the British in 1814, the restored edifice was occupied again in 1817, by James Monroe. In 1901, President Theodore Roosevelt changed the official name of the building to the White House and in 1902 ordered the West Wing to be built. The East Wing was added in 1942 on the instruction of President Franklin D. Roosevelt, completing the building as it is today.

**The White House**
The official residence of the US president for over 200 years, the White House façade is familiar to millions of people around the world.

**★ State Dining Room**
Able to seat as many as 140 people, the State Dining Room was enlarged in 1902. A portrait of President Abraham Lincoln, by George P.A. Healy, hangs above the mantel.

## KEY

① **The West Terrace** leads to the West Wing and the Oval Office, the President's official office.

② **The Stonework** has been painted over and over to maintain the building's white façade.

③ **Blue Room**

④ **The Green Room** was first used by Thomas Jefferson as a dining room.

⑤ **Treaty Room**

⑥ **The East Room** is used for large gatherings, such as concerts and press conferences.

⑦ **The East Terrace** leads to the East Wing.

**★ Red Room**
One of three reception rooms on the state floor, the Red Room is furnished in red in the Empire Style (1810–30).

**Lincoln Bedroom**
President Lincoln used this room as his Cabinet Room. Today it is used as a guest bedroom furnished in Lincoln-era decor.

## VISITORS' CHECKLIST

**Practical Information**
The White House: 1600 Pennsylvania Ave, NW. **Map** 3 B3.
W **whitehouse.gov**
**Open** 7:30–10am Tue–Sat only for groups with congressional or embassy appointments. Contact Visitor Center for information.
**Closed** federal hols and official functions. 🎫 obligatory; call (202) 456-7041 for more information.

White House Visitor Center: 1450 Pennsylvania Ave, NW.
**Tel** (202) 208-1631.
W **nps.gov/whho**
**Open** 7:30am–4pm daily.
**Closed** Jan 1, Thanksgiving, Dec 25. 🏠 ♿ 🎫

**Transport**
Ⓜ Federal Triangle.

★ **The Vermeil Room**
This yellow room houses six paintings of first ladies, including this portrait of Eleanor Roosevelt by Douglas Chandor.

**Diplomatic Reception**
This room is used to welcome friends and ambassadors. It is elegantly furnished in the Federal Period style (1790–1820).

## White House Architects

After selecting the site, George Washington held a design competition to find an architect to build the residence where the US president would live. In 1792 James Hoban, an Irish-born architect, was chosen for the task. It is from Hoban's original drawings that the White House was initially built and all subsequent changes grew. In 1902 President Teddy Roosevelt hired the New York architectural firm of McKim, Mead, and White to check the structural condition of the building and refurbish areas as necessary. The White House underwent further renovations and refurbishments during the administrations of Truman and Kennedy.

James Hoban, architect of the White House

# Exploring the White House

The rooms in the White House are beautifully decorated in period styles and filled with valuable antique furniture, china, and silverware. Hanging on their walls are some of America's most treasured paintings, including portraits of past presidents and first ladies. Those not lucky enough to be granted permission to tour the White House can experience a virtual tour at the White House Visitor Center.

## The Library

Originally used as a laundry area, this room was turned into a "gentleman's ante-room" at the request of President Theodore Roosevelt in 1902. In 1935 it was remodeled into a library. Furnished in 1962 in the style of the late Federal period (1800–1820), the library was redecorated in 1962, and then again in 1976. It had its latest update in 2006 when it was painted in classic cream and red tones. Today, it is often used for media tapings.

Portraits of four native-American chiefs, painted by Charles Bird King, are displayed in the library. The chandelier was crafted in the early 1800s and was originally owned by the family of James Fenimore Cooper, author of *The Last of the Mohicans*.

## The Vermeil Room

The Vermeil Room is named after the collection of vermeil, or gilded silver, that is on display in the cabinets. On show are 18th-, 19th-, and 20th-century tableware, including pieces crafted by English Regency silversmith Paul Storr (1771–1836) and French Empire silversmith Jean-Baptist Claude Odiot (1763–1850). The collection was bequeathed to the White House in 1958 by Margaret Thompson Biddle.

Several portraits of first ladies hang on the walls: Elizabeth Shoumatoff's painting of Claudia (Lady Bird) Johnson, Aaron Shikler's portrait of Jacqueline Kennedy in her New York apartment, and an unusual painting of Eleanor Roosevelt, caught in various moods, by Douglas Chandor. Also on display are portraits of Lou Hoover, Mamie Eisenhower, Pat Nixon, and Nancy Reagan.

## The China Room

Edith Wilson created this room in 1917 to display examples of tableware used in the White House. Today it is used as a reception room. The rich red color scheme is suggested by the stunning portrait of Grace Coolidge, painted in 1924 by Howard Chandler Christy. The Indo-Isfahan rug dates from the early 20th century.

The red and cream color scheme of the China Room

## The Blue Room

President James Monroe chose the French Empire-style decor for this magnificent, oval-shaped room in 1817. The Classically inspired furniture and accompanying motifs, such as urns, acanthus leaves, and imperial eagles, typify the style. The settee and seven chairs were created by Parisian cabinetmaker, Pierre-Antoine Bellangé.

A portrait of Thomas Jefferson by Rembrandt Peale, dating from 1800, hangs in this elegant room, along with a portrait of President John Adams, painted in 1793 by artist John Trumball. The Blue Room has always been used as a reception room, except for a brief period during the John Adams administration.

## The Red Room

This room was decorated in the Empire style by Jacqueline Kennedy in 1962 and was refurbished in 1971, and again in 2000. Much of the wooden furniture in the room, including the beautiful inlaid round table, was created by cabinetmaker Charles-Honoré Lannuier in his New York workshop. Above the mantel hangs a portrait of Angelica Singleton Van Buren, the daughter-in-law of President Martin Van Buren, which was painted by Henry Inman in 1842. The room is used as a parlor or sitting room; it has also been used for small dinner parties.

## The State Dining Room

As a result of the growing nation and its international standing, the size of official dinners in the White House increased. Finally in 1902 the architects McKim, Mead, and White were called in to enlarge the State Dining Room. The plaster and paneling was modeled on the style of 18th-century Neo-Classical English houses. The mahogany dining table was created in 1997. The pieces of French giltware on the table were bought by President Monroe in 1817.

The dining room was re-decorated in 1998, when the Queen Anne-style chairs, which date from 1902, were reupholstered.

## The Lincoln Bedroom

Used today as the guest room for the friends and family of the President, the Lincoln Bedroom is decorated in the American Victorian style, dating from around 1860. Used by Lincoln as an office and cabinet room, this room became the Lincoln Bedroom when President Truman decided to fill it with furniture from Lincoln's era. In the center is a 6 ft- (1.8 m-) wide rosewood bed with an 8 ft- (2.5 m-) high headboard. The portrait of General Andrew Jackson next to the bed is said to have been one of President Lincoln's favorites.

## The Treaty Room

Beginning with Andrew Johnson's presidency in 1865, the Treaty Room served as the Cabinet Room for 10 presidential Administrations. The room contains many Victorian pieces bought by President Ulysses S. Grant, including the original table used by the Cabinet. The cut-glass chandelier that hangs here was made in Birmingham, England around 1850. The

### The White House Visitor Center

The White House Visitor Center has interesting exhibits about the history of the White House and its decor, as well as royal gifts on display. There are also seasonal lectures by renowned speakers on aspects of history in and out of the White House. The Center has a monthly Living History program with actors portraying historic figures. The gift shop carries an extensive range, including the annual White House Christmas ornament. Tours of the state rooms of the White House are extremely limited at this time. Guided tours can only be booked by special arrangement through a member of Congress or, if a non-US citizen, through an embassy. Requests need to be made at least 30 days in advance.

Façade of the White House Visitor Center

chandelier has 20 arms, each one fitted with a frosted glass globe.

### The East Wing

The East Wing houses offices rather than ceremonial rooms. The walls of the Lobby are adorned with portraits of presidents. Both the East Landing and the East Colonnade, which fronts the East Terrace, look out onto the Jacqueline Kennedy Garden. The Terrace, which links the East Wing to the Residence, houses the White House movie theater. It was once Theodore Roosevelt's coatroom.

The interior of the Oval Office, located in the West Wing

### The West Wing

In 1902, the West Wing was built by the architectural firm McKim, Mead, and White for a total cost of $65,196. In this wing, the former Fish Room was renamed the Roosevelt Room by President Nixon, in honor of presidents Theodore and Franklin Roosevelt who created this wing. Their portraits still hang in the room.

Also in the West Wing are the Cabinet Room, where government officials meet with the president, and the Oval Office, added in 1909, where the president meets with visiting heads of state. Over the years, many presidents have personalized this room in some way.

The Victorian-era interior of the Treaty Room

The colonnaded portico of the Neo-Classical Treasury Building

## ❷ Treasury Building

15th St & Pennsylvania Ave, NW.
**Map** 3 B3. **Tel** (202) 622-2000. **M**
McPherson Square. 🎫 Tours for US
citizens only, by appointment through
congressman. ♿ **W treasury.gov**

The site of this massive, four-story Greek Revival building, home to the Department of the Treasury, was chosen by President Andrew Jackson. The grand, sandstone-and-granite edifice was designed by architect Robert Mills, who also designed the Washington Monument (see p80). A statue of Alexander Hamilton, the first Secretary of the Treasury, stands in front of the southern entrance to the building.

The official guided tour, shows visitors the restored historic rooms, including the 1864 burglar-proof vault, the Andrew Johnson suite (Johnson's temporary office after the assassination of President Lincoln in 1865), and the marble Cash Room.

Between 1863 and 1880, US currency was printed in the basement, and during the Civil War it was used as storage space for food and arms. Today, the building is home to the Department of the Treasury, which manages the government's finances and protects US financial systems.

## ❸ Lafayette Square

**Map** 2 F3 & 3 B3. **M** Farragut West, McPherson Square. **W nps.gov**

Set behind the White House is Lafayette Square, named after the Marquis de Lafayette (1757–1834), a hero of the American Revolutionary War (see p21). Due to its proximity to the White House, this public park is often the scene of peaceful demonstrations. It is home to 19th-century former mansions and the historic church of St. John's (the "Church of the Presidents"), built in 1816 by Benjamin Latrobe, who designed Decatur House, 748 Jackson Place, which was home to famous figures such as Henry Clay and Martin

Liberty Bell beside the Treasury

Van Buren, and is open to the public. In the center of the Square is a huge statue of President Andrew Jackson (1767–1845) seated on a horse. Cast in bronze by Clark Mills, it was the first equestrian statue of its size to be built in the US and was dedicated in 1853.

At each of the square's four corners stand statues of men who took part in America's struggle for liberty. The southeast corner has the bronze figure of French compatriot Lafayette. In the southwest corner is a statue of another Frenchman, Jean-Baptiste Donatien de Vimeur, Comte de Rochambeau (1725–1807). This was a gift from France to the American people and accepted by Theodore Roosevelt in 1902. A statue of Polish general, Thaddeus Kosciuszko (1746–1817), who fought with the American colonists in the Revolutionary War, stands in the northeast corner. Baron von Steuben (1730–94), a German officer and George Washington's aide at the Battle of Valley Forge, is honored at the northwest end.

## ❹ Hay-Adams Hotel

1 Lafayette Square, NW. **Map** 2 F3 & 3 B3. **Tel** (202) 638-6600, 1-800-424-5054. **M** Farragut North, Farragut West. **W hayadams.com**

Situated close to the White House, the historic Hay-Adams Hotel is an Italian Renaissance landmark in Washington. Its plush interior is adorned with European and Oriental antiques.

It was originally two adjacent houses, built by Henry Hobson Richardson in 1885, belonging to statesman and author John Hay and diplomat and historian Henry Adams. A popular hotel since its conversion in 1927 by developer Harry Wardman, the exclusive Hay-Adams remains one of Washington's top establishments (see p179), well situated for all the major sights. Afternoon tea and drinks are available in the Lafayette Restaurant.

Federal-style 19th-century houses overlooking tranquil Lafayette Square

## ❺ Renwick Gallery

Pennsylvania Ave at 17th St, NW.
**Map** 2 F3 & 3 A3. **Tel** (202) 633-1000.
Ⓜ Farragut West. **Open** 10am–
5:30pm daily. **Closed** Dec 25. 🄴 🄳
🄿 🆆 **americanart.si.edu**

Forming part of the Smithsonian
American Art Museum *(see p102)*,
this red-brick building was
designed and constructed by
James Renwick Jr. in 1858. It
originally housed the art collection
of William Wilson Corcoran until
this was moved to the current
Corcoran Gallery of Art in 1897.

The building was later bought
by the Smithsonian. Refurbished
and renamed, the Renwick
Gallery opened in 1972, primarily
to conserve and display the
Smithsonian's collection of 20th-
century and contemporary
American arts, crafts, and design.

The museum is currently closed
for a two-year renovation and
refitting of the interior, including
a bold re-imagining of the Grand
Salon as a digital display space,
with state-of-the-art projection
and audio systems that create
extraordinary effects.

## ❻ Eisenhower Old Executive Office Building

17th St at Pennsylvania Ave, NW.
**Map** 2 F4 & 3 A3. Ⓜ Farragut West.
**Closed** to the public. 🄳 Sat.
Call (202) 395-5895 to book. 🄴
🆆 **nps.gov**

Formerly known simply as the
Old Executive Office Building,
this structure stands on the
West side of the White House.

Imposing façade of Eisenhower Old
Executive Office Building

The magnificent Renwick Gallery, a fine example of French Empire style

It was once the home of the War,
Navy, and State Departments.
Built over 17 years between
1871 and 1888 by Alfred B.
Mullett, its exuberant French
Second Empire design, which
was inspired by
the 1852 expansion of
the Louvre in Paris,
generated much
criticism at the time.

The building has
long been the site
of historic events,
such as the meeting
between Secretary
of State Cordell Hull
and the Japanese
after the bombing
of Pearl Harbor.

Lion statue guarding the
Corcoran Gallery

Today the building houses
government agencies, including
the White House Office, the
Office of the Vice President, and
the National Security Council.

## ❼ Corcoran Gallery of Art

500 17th St, NW. **Map** 2 F4 & 3 A3.
**Tel** (202) 639-1700. Ⓜ Farragut West,
Farragut North. **Open** 10am–5pm
Wed–Sun (to 9pm Thu, except
Thanksgiving). **Closed** Jan 1, Dec 25.
🄲 🄳 🄴 🄼 🄿 🄰 🄰
🆆 **corcoran.org**

One of the first fine art museums
in the country, the Corcoran
Gallery of Art opened in 1874.
It outgrew its original home
(what is now the Renwick Gallery
building) and moved to this
massive edifice designed in 1897
by Ernest Flagg. A privately

funded art collection, the
Corcoran was founded by
William Wilson Corcoran – a
banker whose main interest
was American art. Many of
the European works in the
collection were added
in 1925 by art collector
and US senator
William A. Clark.

The Corcoran
Gallery of Art is
filled with works
by European and
American masters
that span the
centuries. These
include 16th- and
17th-century works,
19th- century French
Impressionist paintings by
Monet and Renoir, and other
19th-century works by Eakins,
Homer, and Hassam. The gallery
also contains the largest
collection of paintings by Jean-
Baptiste Camille Corot outside
France. There is a fine collection
of modern and African-American
art, which includes sculpture,
paintings, textiles, and photographs, as well as a permanent
collection highlighting modern
and contemporary art since
1945 with artists such as Rob
Fischer and Andy Warhol.

Within the building is the
only accredited art school in
Washington. A café within the
beautiful atrium serves a selection of delicious soups, cakes
and drinks. The Corcoran also
has a shop selling an excellent
selection of books, postcards,
and other items.

## ❽ Octagon Museum

1799 New York Ave, NW. **Map** 2 F4 & 3 A3. **Tel** (202) 626-7312. Ⓜ Farragut West and Farragut North. **Open** by appointment. **Closed** Jan 1, Thanksgiving, Dec 25. 📷 🎥 1–4pm Thu & Fri. ♿ (first floor only). Ⓦ theoctagon.org

Actually hexagonal in shape, the Octagon is a three-story red-brick building, designed in the late-Federal style by Dr. William Thornton (1759–1828), first architect of the US Capitol. The Octagon was completed in 1801 for Colonel John Tayloe III, a rich plantation owner from Richmond County, Virginia, and a friend of George Washington.

When the White House was burned in the War of 1812 against Britain *(see p21)*, President James Madison and his wife, Dolley, lived here from 1814 to 1815. The Treaty of Ghent that ended the war was signed by Madison on the second floor of the house on February 17, 1815.

In the early 1900s, the building was taken over by the American Institute of Architects. The American Architectural Foundation, established in 1970, set up a museum of architecture in the Octagon. The building has been restored to its historically accurate 1815 appearance, and has some original furnishings and fine architectural features, such as a circular entrance hall. Ongoing restoration work and private events cause occasional suspension of tours (check website or call ahead).

The circular main entrance to the attractive Octagon Museum

South portico of the DAR Memorial Continental Hall

## ❾ Daughters of the American Revolution

1776 D St, NW. **Map** 2 F4 & 3 A3. **Tel** (202) 628-1776. Ⓜ Farragut West. **Open** 9:30am–4pm Mon–Fri, 9am–5pm Sat. **Closed** 1 week in Jul, Federal hols. 🎥 9am–3pm Sat (book in advance for groups of 5 or more). ♿ Caters for children. Ⓦ dar.org/museum

Founded in 1890 as a non-profit organization, the Daughters of the American Revolution (DAR) is dedicated to historic preservation and promoting education and patriotism. In order to become a member, you must be a woman with blood relations to any person, male or female, who fought in or aided the Revolution. There are currently over 160,000 members in 3,000 regional branches throughout the USA and in nine other countries.

The DAR Museum is located in the Memorial Continental Hall, designed for the organization by Edward Pearce Casey and completed in 1910.

The 13 columns in the south portico symbolize the 13 original states of the Union. Entrance to the museum is through the gallery, which displays an eclectic range of pieces from quilts to glassware and china.

The 33 period rooms that form the State Rooms in the museum house a collection of over 50,000 items, from silver to porcelain, ceramics, stoneware, and furniture. Each room is decorated in a unique style particular to an American state from different periods during the 18th and 19th centuries. An attic room filled with 18th- and 19th-century toys will delight children. Also, there is a huge genealogical library, consisting of approximately 125,000 publications.

DAR Museum banners proclaiming Preservation, Patriotism, Education

Fountain in the courtyard of the OAS building

# ❿ Organization of American States

17th St & Constitution Ave, NW.
**Map** 2 F4 & 3 A4. **Tel** (202) 458-3000.
**Open** 9am–5:30pm Mon–Fri. **Closed** Sat & Sun, Federal hols. Art Museum of the Americas: 201 18th St, NW. **Tel** (202) 458-6016. **Open** 10am–5pm Tue–Sun. **Closed** Good Friday, Federal hols. Ⓜ Farragut West. 🎧 Call (202) 458-6016. Ⓦ **museum.oas.org**

Dating back to the First International Conference of the American States, held from October 1889 to April 1890 in Washington, the Organization of American States (OAS) is the oldest alliance of nations dedicated to reinforcing the peace and security of the continent, and maintaining democracy. The Charter of the OAS was signed in Bogotá, Colombia, in 1948 by the US

and 20 Latin American republics. Today there are 35 members. The building houses the Columbus Memorial Library and the **Art Museum of the Americas**, which exhibits 20th-century Latin American and Caribbean art.

# ⓫ Department of the Interior Building

19th St, between C St & E St, NW.
**Map** 2 F4 & 3 A3. **Tel** (202) 208-3100. Ⓜ Farragut West. **Closed** for renovations; phone for opening times. 🚻 📷 Ⓦ **doi.gov/interiormuseum**

Designed by architect Waddy Butler Wood and built in 1935, this huge limestone building is the headquarters of the Department of the Interior. The building has a long central section, with six wings that extend off each side. In total it covers more than 16 acres of floor space, and has 2 miles (3 km) of corridors.

The Department of the Interior was originally formed of only the Departments of Agriculture, Labor, Education, and Energy, but it expanded to oversee all federally owned land across the United States. Visible inside, but only when taking the official guided tour, are 36 murals painted by Native American artists in the 1930s, including one of the singer Marian Anderson performing at the Lincoln Memorial in 1939 (see pp86–7).

Displays in the small **Department of the Interior Museum**, located on the first floor, include an overview of the Department's history, and some intricate dioramas of American wildlife and important historical events, such as the 1929 Kinloch Mine explosion. Also on view are paintings by 19th-century surveyors, and crafts by Native Americans, including a great collection of basketry.

The south façade of the immense Department of the Interior Building

Portrait, in crayon, by Saint Memin of Colonel John Tayloe III

## The Tayloe Family

John Tayloe III (1771–1828), a colonel in the War of 1812, was responsible for the construction of the unusual Octagon building. He and his wife Ann, the daughter of Benjamin Ogle (the governor of Maryland), had their primary residence at Mount Airy, an estate and tobacco plantation in Richmond County, Virginia. The Tayloes decided they wanted to build a second house where they could spend the inclement winter seasons. President George Washington, a close friend of Tayloe and his father, was at the time overseeing the building of the US Capitol and was eager for people to move into the new city. The president encouraged Tayloe and his family to choose a plot in Washington rather than in the more popular Philadelphia. The family heeded his advice and the triangular-shaped corner plot for the Octagon was chosen. Tayloe's vast wealth enabled him to employ the services of William Thornton, the original designer of the US Capitol building, and spend a total of $35,000 on the construction of the house.

## ⓬ Federal Reserve Building

Constitution Ave & 20th St NW.
**Map** 2 E4 & 3 A4. **Tel** (202) 452-3778
for art exhibitions. Ⓜ Foggy Bottom.
**Open** by appointment.
**Closed** Federal hols. &
ⓦ federalreserve.gov

Known to most people as "the Fed," this building is home to the Federal Reserve System. This is the US banking system under which 12 Federal Reserve banks in 12 districts across the country regulate and hold reserves for member banks in their districts. Dollar bills are not printed here, however, but at the Bureau of Engraving and Printing *(see p81)*.

The four-story, white marble edifice opened in 1937 and was designed by Paul Philippe Cret, architect for the OAS building *(see p117)* and the Folger Shakespeare Library *(see p50)*. Small art exhibitions are held in the building throughout the year.

Marble eagle above the entrance to "the Fed"

## ⓭ National Academy of Sciences

2101 Constitution Ave, NW. **Map** 2 E4.
**Tel** (202) 334-2000. Ⓜ Foggy Bottom.
**Closed** for restoration until 2014. &
ⓦ nationalacademies.org

Established in 1863, the National Academy of Sciences is a non-profit organization that conducts over 200 studies a year on subjects such as health, science, and technology, and educates the nation by providing news

The gleaming, white marble exterior of the Federal Reserve Building

of scientific discoveries. Among the past and present Members of the Academy are nearly 200 Nobel Prize winners, most notably Albert Einstein. To be elected as a member is considered a great honor for a scientist.

The three-story white marble building, designed by Bertram Grosvenor Goodhue, was completed in 1924. Inside is a gold dome adorned with portraits of Greek philosophers and panels illustrating various scientists. A 700-seat auditorium hosts a series of free chamber recitals throughout the year. On the building's upper floors are the offices of the National Research Council, the National Academy of Sciences, and the National Academy of Engineering.

Nestled among the trees in front of the Academy is the much-admired bronze statue of Albert Einstein, sculpted by Robert Berks. The same artist created the bust of President John F. Kennedy, which can be seen in the Grand Foyer of the Kennedy Center *(see pp120–21)*. The huge

statue of Albert Einstein reaches 12 ft (4 m) in height and weighs 7,000 pounds (4 tons). It was erected in 1979.

## ⓮ State Department

23rd St & C St, NW. **Map** 2 E4 & 3 A3.
**Tel** (202) 647-4000. Ⓜ Foggy Bottom-GWU. 📷 daily by appointment; must show photo ID; reserve up to 3 months in advance. **Closed** Federal hols. & ⓦ state.gov

As the oldest executive department of the United States government, established in 1781, the State Department handles all foreign policy.

Covering an expanse of 2.5 million sq ft (232,250 sq m) over four city blocks, the State Department building rises eight stories high. Workplace of the Secretary of State, the State Department, and the United States Diplomatic Corps, the building plays host to some 80,000 guests and 60,000 visitors every year. The State Department's Diplomatic Reception Rooms were lavishly refurbished in the late 1960s, and now contain antiques worth over $90 million.

## ⓯ George Washington University

2121 I (Eye) St, NW. **Map** 2 E3.
**Tel** (202) 994-1000. Ⓜ Foggy Bottom-GWU. Lisner and Betts Auditoriums:
**Tel** (202) 994-6800. ⓦ gwu.edu

Founded in 1821, George Washington University, known as "GW" to many people, is

Sculpture of Albert Einstein outside the National Academy of Sciences

named after the first president of the United States. George Washington is the largest university in Washington, DC. There are nine schools offering both undergraduate and graduate studies. Strong subjects on offer include International Affairs, Business Administration, Medicine, Law, and Political Science.

As a result of its location, the university has many famous alumni, including Colin Powell (US Secretary of State in George W. Bush's administration) and Jacqueline Bouvier (who married John Kennedy) as well as a number of children of past presidents, including Lynda Johnson, Margaret Truman, and D. Jeffrey Carter.

The on-campus Lisner, Morton and Betts auditoriums host a series of plays, dances, lectures, and concerts.

St. Mary's Episcopal Church, built for freed slaves

## 16 St. Mary's Episcopal Church

728 23rd St, NW. **Map** 2 E3. **Tel** (202) 333-3985. **M** Foggy Bottom-GWU. **Open** 9:30am–3pm Mon–Thu. 10am Sun, 12:10pm Wed. **W** stmarysfoggybottom.org

Opened on January 20, 1887, the red-brick, Gothic St. Mary's Episcopal Church was the first church in Washington to be built specifically for freed slaves.

St Mary's was designed by James Renwick, the architect of the Renwick Gallery (see p115), the Smithsonian Castle (see p74), and St. Patrick's Cathedral in New

The distinctive curved walls of the infamous Watergate Complex

York City. The church was placed on the city's register of protected historic buildings in 1972.

## 17 Washington Circle

**Map** 2 E3. **M** Foggy Bottom-GWU.

One of several circles and squares created by Pierre L'Enfant's original design of the city (see p21), Washington Circle lies at the northern edge of Foggy Bottom. It forms the point where Pennsylvania Avenue and New Hampshire Avenue meet K Street and 23rd Street. The circle boasts an imposing bronze statue of George Washington astride his horse, designed by artist Clark Mills and unveiled in 1860. The statue faces east, looking toward the White House and the US Capitol.

## 18 Watergate Complex

Virginia Ave between Rock Creek Parkway and New Hampshire Ave, NW. **Map** 2 D3. **M** Foggy Bottom-GWU.

Located next to the Kennedy Center (see pp120–21), on the bank of the Potomac River, the impressive, Italian-designed Watergate Complex was completed in 1971. The four rounded buildings that make up the complex were designed to contain shops, offices, apartments, hotels, and diplomatic missions.

In the summer of 1972 the complex found itself at the center of international news. Burglars, linked to President Nixon, broke into "the offices of the Democratic National Committee, sparking off the Watergate scandal that led to the president's resignation.

### The Watergate Scandal

On June 17, 1972, during the US presidential campaign, five men were arrested for breaking into the Democratic Party headquarters in the Watergate Complex. The burglars were employed by the re-election organization of President Richard Nixon, a Republican.

President Nixon addressing the nation while still in office

Found guilty of burglary and attempting to bug telephones, the men were not initially linked to the White House. However, further investigation, led by Washington Post reporters Woodward and Bernstein, uncovered the extent of the President's involvement, including the possession of incriminating tapes and proven bribery. This led to an impeachment hearing, but before Nixon could be impeached, he resigned. Vice-President Gerald Ford succeeded him.

# ⓳ The Kennedy Center

In 1958, President Dwight D. Eisenhower signed an act to begin fund-raising for a national cultural center that would attract the world's best orchestras, opera, and dance companies to the US capital. President John F. Kennedy was an ardent supporter of the arts, taking the lead in fund-raising for it. He never saw the completion of the center, which was named in his honor. Designed by Edward Durrell Stone, it was opened on September 8, 1971. This vast complex houses several huge theaters; the Opera House, the Concert Hall, the Eisenhower Theater, and the Family Theater; on the roof are the Jazz Club, the Terrace Theater, and the Theater Lab.

**Don Quixote Statue**
This bronze and stone statue by Aurelio Teno was a gift to the center from Spain.

**The Eisenhower Theater**
This is one of the three main theaters. A bronze bust of President Eisenhower by Felix de Weldon hangs in the lobby.

**Millennium Stage**
The Millennium Stage provides free performances in the Grand Foyer every evening at 6pm.

### KEY

① **East Roof Terrace**

② **The Hall of Nations** houses the flag of every country with which the US has diplomatic relations.

③ **The Concert Hall** is the largest auditorium, seating more than 2,400 people. It is the home of the National Symphony Orchestra.

**The Hall of States**
The flags of each of the 50 American states, the five US territories, and the District of Columbia hang here.

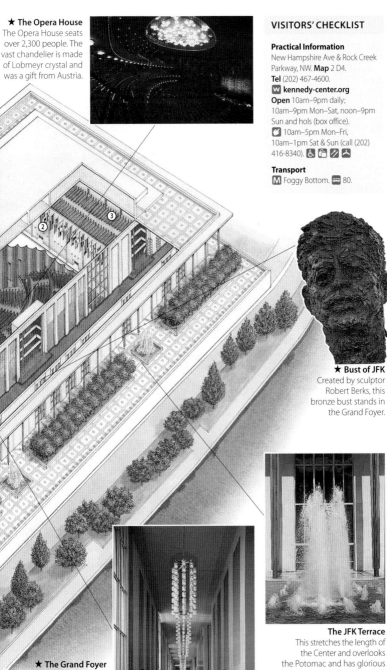

★ **The Opera House**
The Opera House seats over 2,300 people. The vast chandelier is made of Lobmeyr crystal and was a gift from Austria.

**VISITORS' CHECKLIST**

**Practical Information**
New Hampshire Ave & Rock Creek Parkway, NW. **Map** 2 D4.
**Tel** (202) 467-4600.
🌐 **kennedy-center.org**
**Open** 10am–9pm daily; 10am–9pm Mon–Sat, noon–9pm Sun and hols (box office). 🕐 10am–5pm Mon–Fri, 10am–1pm Sat & Sun (call (202) 416-8340). ♿ 🏛 ✏ ✈

**Transport**
Ⓜ Foggy Bottom. 🚌 80.

★ **Bust of JFK**
Created by sculptor Robert Berks, this bronze bust stands in the Grand Foyer.

**The JFK Terrace**
This stretches the length of the Center and overlooks the Potomac and has glorious views up and down the river. Quotes by John F. Kennedy are engraved into the marble walls.

★ **The Grand Foyer**
This enormous room stretches 630 ft (192 m) and provides an impressive entrance into the Opera House, the Concert Hall, and the Eisenhower Theater.

# GEORGETOWN

Georgetown developed well before Washington, DC. Native Americans had a settlement here, and in 1703 a land grant was given to Ninian Beall, who named the area the Rock of Dumbarton. By the mid-18th century immigrants from Scotland had swelled the population, and in 1751 the town was renamed George Town. It grew rapidly into a wealthy tobacco and flour port and finally, in 1789, the city of Georgetown was formed. The harbor and the Chesapeake and Ohio Canal were built in 1828, and the streets were lined with townhouses. The birth of the railroad undercut Georgetown's economy, which by the mid-1800s was in decline. But by the 1950s the cobblestone streets and charming houses were attracting wealthy young couples, and restaurants and shops sprang up on Wisconsin Avenue and M Street. Today Georgetown retains its quiet distinction from the rest of the city, and is a pleasant area in which to stroll for a few hours (*see pp150–51*).

## Sights at a Glance

### Historic Buildings
**5** Old Stone House
**7** Washington Post Office
**9** Georgetown University
**10** Tudor Place
**13** Dumbarton Oaks

### Streets, Canals, and Harbors
**1** Washington Harbor
**2** Wisconsin Avenue
**4** Chesapeake and Ohio Canal
**6** M Street
**8** N Street

### Churches and Cemeteries
**3** Grace Church
**11** Mt. Zion Church
**12** Oak Hill Cemetery

### Restaurants see pp187–9
1  1789
2  Bandolero
3  Booeymonger
4  Café Bonaparte
5  Café Divan
6  Café Milano
7  Café la Ruche
8  Chadwick's
9  La Chaumiere
10  Clyde's
11  Das Ethiopian Cuisine
12  El Centro D.F.
13  Filomena
14  Five Guys
15  Johnny Rockets
16  Kafe Leopold

17  Martin's Tavern
18  Le Pain Quotidien
19  Patisserie Poupon
20  Paolo's
21  Paul
22  Peacock Café
23  Pizzeria Paradiso
24  Puro
25  Sea Catch
26  Sequoia
27  Serendipity 3
28  ShopHouse Southeast Asian Kitchen
29  Sweetgreen
30  The Tombs
31  Tony and Joe's Seafood Café
32  Unum

See also Street Finder map 1–2

Vine-covered walls of Dumbarton Oaks Summerhouse

For keys to symbols see back flap

Fountain at Washington Harbor

### ❶ Washington Harbor

3000-3020 K St, NW. **Map** 2 D3.

Washington is a city where few architectural risks have been taken. However, the approach used by architect Arthur Cotton Moore for Washington Harbor, which is a combination residential and commercial building on the Potomac River, is unusually audacious.

Moore's creation is a structure that hugs the waterfront and surrounds a semi-circular pedestrian plaza. The architect borrowed motifs from almost every type of design, such as turrets and flying buttresses. The harbor has a pleasant boardwalk, a huge fountain, and tall, columned lampposts. Under the ground are steel gates that can be raised to protect the building from floods. The top floors of the harbor are apartments. On the bottom floors are office complexes, restaurants, and shops. Sightseeing boats dock at the river's edge for trips to Mount Vernon and Alexandria. The spring of 2011 saw severe flooding to the harbor, which caused considerable damage. However, with new floodgates in place, Hurricane Sandy did not damage the waterfront in 2012.

### ❷ Wisconsin Avenue

Wisconsin Ave. **Map** 1 C2.
Ⓜ **Foggy Bottom.**

Wisconsin Avenue is one of two main business streets in Georgetown and is home to a wide variety of shops and restaurants. It is also one of the few streets in Washington that pre-dates L'Enfant's grid plan (see p69). It starts at the bank of the Potomac and runs north through Georgetown right to the city line, where it continues as Rockville Pike. On the

## ❹ The Chesapeake and Ohio Canal

When it was constructed in 1828, the C&O Canal featured an ingenious and revolutionary transportation system of locks, aqueducts, and tunnels that ran along its 184 miles (296 km) from Georgetown to Cumberland, Maryland. With the arrival of the railroad in the late 19th century, the canal fell out of use. It was only as a result of the efforts of Supreme Court Justice William Douglas that the Chesapeake and Ohio Canal was finally declared a protected national park in 1971. Today visitors come to enjoy its recreational facilities and also to study its fascinating transportation system. A 15-mile (20-km) walking and biking trail along the canal connects Georgetown with Great Falls Park (see p166).

**Georgetown**
The attractive federal houses of Georgetown line the banks of the canal for about 1.5 miles (2 km).

Great Falls
14 miles

Williamsport
75 miles

CANAL ROAD NW

Chesapeake and Ohio Canal

**The Francis Scott Key Memorial Bridge** was named after the the composer of the American national anthem, *The Star-Spangled Banner*.

Potomac

**Canal Trips**
The towpath trail runs north to Great Falls and historic Williamsport, where boat trips can be taken and costumed guides add colour to the waterside.

junction of Wisconsin Avenue and M Street is the landmark gold dome of PNC Bank (formerly the Riggs National Bank).

During the French and Indian Wars, George Washington marched his troops up the avenue on his way to Pittsburgh to engage the British.

The gold dome of PNC Bank

## ❸ Grace Church

1041 Wisconsin Ave, NW.
**Map** 1 C3. **Tel** (202) 333-7100.
**Open** call office in advance (office open 10am–6pm Mon, Tue, Fri). ♿
**W** gracedc.org

Built in 1866, Grace Church was designed to serve the religious needs of the boatmen who worked on the Chesapeake and Ohio Canal and the sailors of the port of Georgetown. Set on a tree-filled plot south of the canal and M Street, the Gothic Revival church, with its quaint exterior, is an oasis in Georgetown.

The building has undergone few extensive alterations over the years and has a certain timeless quality. The church's multi-ethnic congregation makes great efforts to reach out to the larger DC community and

Sign for Grace Church

works with soup kitchens and shelters for the homeless. The church also sponsors the "Thank God It's Friday" lunchtime discussion group, and holds a poetry coffee house on the third Tuesday of the month. Classical concerts, including chamber pieces, organ, and piano works, are held here regularly. There is also a popular annual festival devoted to the music of the German composer J.S. Bach.

### Rowing on the Canal
Boating is popular on the C&O and is best between Georgetown and Violette's Lock – the first 22 miles (35 km) of the canal.

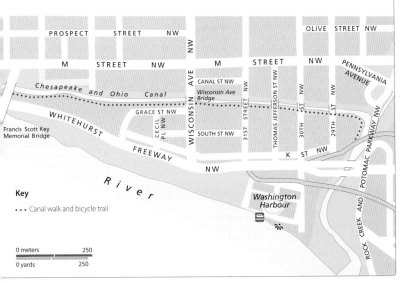

PROSPECT STREET NW
OLIVE STREET NW
M STREET NW
M STREET NW
PENNSYLVANIA AVENUE
Chesapeake and Ohio Canal
CANAL ST NW
Wisconsin Ave Bridge
GRACE ST NW
Francis Scott Key Memorial Bridge
WHITEHURST
FREEWAY
WISCONSIN AVE
CECIL PL NW
SOUTH ST NW
31ST STREET NW
THOMAS JEFFERSON ST NW
30TH ST NW
29TH ST NW
K ST NW
River
NW
ROCK CREEK AND POTOMAC PARKWAY NW

**Key**
••• Canal walk and bicycle trail

Washington Harbour

0 meters    250
0 yards     250

For additional map symbols *see back flap*

## ❺ Old Stone House

3051 M St, NW. **Map** 2 D2. **Tel** (202) 426-6851. **Open** noon–5pm daily. 🚌 30, 32, 34, 36, 38. ♿ call (202) 895-6070. ♿ limited
**W** nps.gov/olst

The Old Stone House may be the only building in Washington that pre-dates the American Revolution. It was built in 1765 by Christopher Layman, and the tiny two-story cottage has a large garden, which is a welcome respite from the shops of busy M Street.

There is a legend that still persists about the Old Stone House – that it was the Suter's Tavern where Washington and Pierre L'Enfant made their plans

for the city. However, most historians today now believe that they met in a tavern located elsewhere in Georgetown.

Over the years, the building has housed a series of artisans, and in the 1950s it even served as offices for a used-car dealership. In 1960 the National Park Service restored it to its pre-Revolutionary War appearance. Today park rangers give talks (noon–5pm) about what Georgetown would have been like during the Colonial days. The Old Stone House is technically the oldest house in DC, although The Lindens, which is now in Kalorama, was built in the mid-1750s in Massachusetts and later moved to Washington.

The picturesque Old Stone House

## ❻ M Street

M St, NW. **Map** 1 C2.
🚌 30, 32, 34, 36, 38.

One of two main shopping streets in Georgetown, M Street is also home to some of the most historic spots in the city. On the northeast corner of 30th and M Streets, on the current site of a bank, stood Union Tavern. Built in 1796, the tavern played host to, among others, Presidents George Washington and John Adams, Napoleon's younger brother Jerome Bonaparte, author Washington Irving, and Francis Scott Key, the composer of the "Star Spangled Banner." During the Civil War, the inn was turned into a temporary hospital where Louisa May Alcott, the author of *Little Women*, nursed wounded soldiers. In the 1930s the tavern was torn down and replaced by a gas station. Dr. William Thornton, architect of the US Capitol and Tudor Place *(see p128)* lived at 3219 M Street.

On the south side of M Street is Market House, which has been the location of Georgetown's market since 1751. In 1796 a wood frame market house was constructed and later replaced by the current brick market in

**Only the two end houses** in this group of fine Federal homes (numbers 3327–3339) are still in their original state.

## ❼ N Street

N St, NW. **Map** 1 C2. 🚌 30, 32, 34, 36.

N Street is a sampler of 18th-century American Federal architecture – a style favored by leaders of the new nation as being of a lighter and more refined design than the earlier Georgian houses.

At the corner of 30th and N Streets is the Laird-Dunlop House. Today it is owned by Benjamin Bradlee, the former editor of the *Washington Post*.

An excellent example of a Federal house is the Riggs-Riley House at 3038 N Street, most recently owned by Averill and Pamela Harriman. At 3041–3045 N Street is Wheatley Row. These houses were designed to provide not only maximum light from large windows but also maximum privacy as they were placed above street level.

**Known as Wheatley Row**, these three well-designed Victorian town homes were built in 1859.

1865. In the 1930s the market became an auto supply store, and in the 1990s the New York gourmet food store Dean and Deluca opened a branch here.

Today M Street is home to a collection of fashionable stores and restaurants. Young buyers shop for alternative music at Smash and alternative clothing at Urban Outfitters. National chainstores such as Banana Republic, Pottery Barn, and Starbucks have branches along M Street. The fashionable Cady's Alley at 3318 M Street, is a haven of trendy boutiques, high end furnishing, and antique retailers.

Clyde's restaurant at number 3236 is a Georgetown institution, famous for its "happy hour."

The elegant façade of the Post Office in Georgetown

Attractive houses lining the bustling M Street

## ❼ Washington Post Office, Georgetown Branch

1215 31st St, NW. **Map** 2 D2. 🚌 30, 32, 34, 36. **Open** 9am–5pm Mon–Fri, 9am–2pm Sat.

Built in 1857 as a customhouse, the still-functioning Georgetown Branch of the Washington Post Office is interesting both historically and architecturally. A customhouse was a money-producing venture for the Federal government, and the US government's investment in such an expensive building provides evidence of Georgetown's importance as a viable port for many years. Architect Ammi B. Young, who was also responsible for the design of the Vermont State Capitol building in 1832 and the Boston Custom House in 1837, was called to Washington in 1852. He designed several other Italianate buildings in the capital, but this post office is his finest work. The granite custom-house was converted to a post office when Georgetown's fortunes declined.

The building underwent a renovation in 1997 that increased its accessibility but retained the integrity of Young's simple, functional design.

---

**The Thomas Beall House** (number 3017) was built in 1794 by one of Georgetown's most prominent families. It has since been occupied by the Secretary of War during World War I, and by Jackie Kennedy, who lived here for a year after the death of JFK.

**Number 3025–3027**, with its raised mansard roof, shows the influence of the French during this period.

**The Laird-Dunlop House** (number 3014) was built by John Laird who owned many of Georgetown's tobacco warehouses. Laird modeled his home on those in his native Edinburgh. It was subsequently owned by President Lincoln's son, Robert.

Unusual flat roof

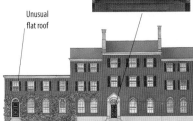

## ❾ Georgetown University

37th St & O St, NW. **Map** 1 B2. **Tel** (202) 687-0100. **Open** varies, depending on university schedule. ◻ ◻
ⓦ georgetown.edu

Georgetown University was the first Catholic college to be established in America. Founded in 1789 by John Carroll, and affiliated with the Jesuit Order, the university now attracts students of all faiths from over 100 countries around the world.

The oldest building on the campus is the Old North Building, completed in 1872, but the most recognizable structure is the Healy Building, a Germanic design topped by a fanciful spiral. The university's most famous graduate is President Bill Clinton.

The Gothic-inspired Healy Building, Georgetown University

## ❿ Tudor Place

1644 31st St, NW. **Map** 1 C2. **Tel** (202) 965-0400. **Open** 10am–4pm Tue–Sat, noon–4pm Sun. **Closed** Jan, Easter Sunday, Memorial Day, Jul 4, Labor Day, Thanksgiving, Dec 24, 25. ◻ ◻
◻ ⓦ tudorplace.org

The manor house and large gardens of this Georgetown estate, designed by William Thornton, offer a unique glimpse into a bygone era.

Martha Washington, the First Lady, gave $8,000 to her granddaughter, Martha Custis Peter, and her granddaughter's husband. With the money, they purchased eight acres and commissioned Thornton, the

Stone dog in the garden of Tudor Place

architect of the Capitol (see pp52–3), to design a house. Generations of the Peters family lived here from 1805 to 1984. It is a mystery as to why this stuccoed, two-story Georgian structure with a "temple" porch is called Tudor Place, but it was perhaps illustrative of the family's English sympathies at the time.

The furniture, silver, china, and portraits provide a glimpse into American social and cultural history; some of the pieces on display come from Mount Vernon (see pp162–3).

## ⓫ Mt. Zion Church

1334 29th St, NW. **Map** 2 D2. **Tel** (202) 234-0148. ◻ 11am Sun. ◻ ◻

This church is thought to have had the first black congregation in DC. The first church, at 27th and P Streets, was a "station" on the city's original Underground Railroad. It provided shelter for runaway slaves on their journey

Altar in Mt. Zion church

north to freedom. The present redbrick building was completed in 1884 after the first church burned down.

Mt. Zion Cemetery, the oldest black burial ground in Washington, is located a short distance away, in the middle of the 2500 block of Q Street.

## ⓬ Oak Hill Cemetery

3001 R St, NW. **Map** 2 D1. **Tel** (202) 337-2835. **Open** 9am–4:30pm Mon–Fri, 1–4pm Sun (weather permitting). **Closed** Federal hols.
ⓦ oakhillcemeterydc.org

William Wilson Corcoran (see p115) bought the land and Congress then established Oak Hill Cemetery in 1849. Today, about 18,000 graves cover the 25-acre site, which is planted with huge oak trees.

Members of some of the city's most prominent families are buried here, their names featuring throughout the city's history, including Magruder, Thomas, Beall, and Marbury.

At the entrance to the cemetery is an Italianate gatehouse that is still used as the superintendent's lodge and office. Northeast of the gatehouse is the Spencer family monument, designed by Louis Comfort Tiffany. The granite low-relief of an angel is signed by Tiffany. Also notable is

### The Founding of the United Nations

In 1944, a conference held at the Dumbarton Oaks estate laid the groundwork for establishing the United Nations. President Franklin Roosevelt and the British Prime Minister, Winston Churchill, wanted to create a "world government" that would supervise the peace at the end of World War II. Roosevelt proposed that a conference be held in Washington, but at the time the State Department did not have a room big enough to accommodate all the delegates. As a solution, Robert Woods Bliss offered the use of the music room in his former home, Dumbarton Oaks, for the event.

The structure of the United Nations was settled at the Dumbarton Oaks Conference and then refined at the San Francisco Conference a year later when the United Nations' charter was ratified. The UN Headquarters building, the permanent home of the organization, was built in New York on the East River site after John D. Rockefeller donated $8.5 million toward its construction.

The conference members in the music room of Dumbarton Oaks

the Gothic chapel designed by James Renwick. Nearby is the grave of John Howard Payne, composer of "Home, Sweet Home," who died in 1852. The bust that tops Payne's monument was originally sculpted with a full beard, but Corcoran requested a stonemason to "shave the statue" and so now it is clean shaven.

### ⑱ Dumbarton Oaks

1703 32nd St, NW. **Map** 2 D2. **Tel** (202) 339-6401 (call ahead to check times). **Open** House: 2–5pm Tue–Sun. Gardens: 2–6pm Tue–Sun (to 5pm Nov–Feb). **Closed** Federal hols. 🌳 gardens only. 🎥 for groups call (202) 339-6409. 🏛 🚻 house only. 🔗 **doaks.org**

In 1703, a Scottish colonist named Ninian Beall was granted around 800 acres of land in this area. In later years the land was sold off and in 1801, 22 acres were bought by Senator William Dorsey of Maryland, who proceeded to build a Federal-style brick home here. A year later, financial difficulties caused him to sell it, and over the next century the property changed hands many times.

By the time pharmaceutical heirs Robert and Mildred Woods Bliss bought the run-down estate in 1920, it was overgrown and neglected. The Blisses altered and expanded the house, with the architectural

advice of the prestigious firm McKim, Mead and White (see p111), to meet 20th-century family needs. They engaged their friend, Beatrix Jones Farrand, one of the few female landscape architects at the time, to lay out the grounds. Farrand designed a series of terraces that progress from the formal gardens near the house to the more informal landscapes farther away from it.

Fountain in Dumbarton Oaks

In 1940 the Blisses moved to California and donated the whole estate to Harvard University. It was then converted into a library, research institution, and museum. Many of the 1,400 pieces of Byzantine Art on display were collected by the

Blisses themselves. Examples of Greco-Roman coins, late Roman and early Byzantine bas-reliefs, Egyptian fabrics, and Roman glass and bronzeware are just some of the highlights. In 1962 Robert Woods Bliss donated his collection of pre-Columbian art. In order to house it, architect Philip Johnson designed a new wing, consisting of eight domes surrounding a circular garden. Although markedly different from the original house, a separate wing is well suited to the dramatic art collection it houses, which includes masks, stunning gold jewelry from Central America, and Aztec carvings.

Swimming pool in the grounds of Dumbarton Oaks

# FARTHER AFIELD

North of the White House is Dupont Circle, a neighborhood of museums, galleries, and restaurants. The Embassy Row, Kalorama, Adams-Morgan, and Cleveland Park neighborhoods are a walker's paradise, especially for visitors interested in architecture. Arlington,

Virginia, across the Potomac River, was one of DC's first suburbs. Arlington National Cemetery was founded in 1864 to honor those who died for the Union. The Pentagon was built 80 years later by Franklin D. Roosevelt and is the area's most famous landmark.

## Sights at a Glance

**Museums and Galleries**

7 African American Civil War Memorial and Museum
10 National Geographic Museum
11 The Phillips Collection
12 Textile Museum
17 Mary McLeod Bethune Council House
18 Hillwood Estate Museum
29 Anacostia Museum

**Historic Districts, Streets, and Buildings**

2 The Pentagon
4 Southwest Waterfront
6 Heurich Mansion
9 Dupont Circle
13 Woodrow Wilson House
14 Embassy Row
15 Kalorama
16 Adams-Morgan
19 Lincoln Theatre

21 *Washington National Cathedral pp144–5*
27 Howard University
28 Frederick Douglass House

**Monuments**

3 Air Force Memorial
8 Iwo Jima Statue
24 Basilica of the National Shrine of the Immaculate Conception

**Parks and Gardens**

5 Theodore Roosevelt Island
20 *National Zoological Park pp140–41*
22 Cleveland Park
23 Rock Creek Park
25 National Arboretum
26 Kenilworth Park and Aquatic Gardens

**Cemetery**

1 *Arlington National Cemetery pp132–3*

**Key**

▢ Central Washington
▢ Greater Washington
→ Metro line
═ Freeway (motorway)
▬ Major road
— Minor road
–·– State Border

0 kilometers      2.5
0 miles             2.5

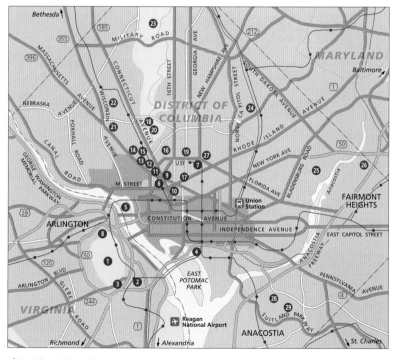

◄ Amphitheater, Arlington National Cemetery

**For additional map symbols** *see back flap*

# ❶ Arlington National Cemetery

For 30 years, Confederate General Robert E. Lee (1807–70) lived at Arlington House. In 1861 he left his home to lead Virginia's armed forces, and the Union confiscated the estate for a military cemetery. By the end of the Civil War in 1865, 16,000 soldiers were interred in the consecrated Arlington National Cemetery. Since then, around another 300,000 veterans have joined them. Simple headstones mark the graves of soldiers who died in every major conflict from the Revolution to the present. The focus of the cemetery is the Tomb of the Unknowns, which honors the thousands of unidentified soldiers who have died in battle.

**Confederate Memorial**
This bronze and granite monument honors the Confederate soldiers who died in the Civil War. It was dedicated in 1914.

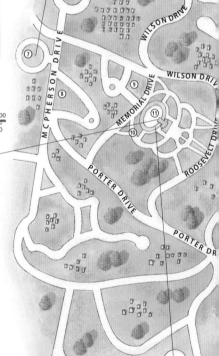

**Sea of Graves**
More than 330,000 service members and their families are buried on the 624 acres of Arlington Cemetery.

| 0 meters | 200 |
| 0 yards | 200 |

★ **Tomb of the Unknowns**
This tomb contains four vaults – for World War I and II, Vietnam, and Korea. Each vault held one unidentified soldier until the Vietnam soldier was identified by DNA analysis and reburied in his home town.

**Memorial Amphitheater**
This marble amphitheater is the setting of the annual services on Memorial Day *(see p38)* when the nation's leaders pay tribute to the dead who served their country. It has also hosted many military ceremonies.

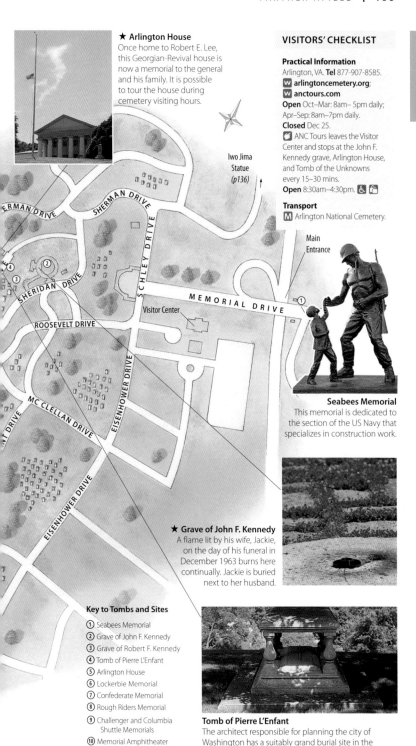

★ **Arlington House**
Once home to Robert E. Lee, this Georgian-Revival house is now a memorial to the general and his family. It is possible to tour the house during cemetery visiting hours.

Iwo Jima Statue (p136)

**VISITORS' CHECKLIST**

**Practical Information**
Arlington, VA. **Tel** 877-907-8585.
ⓦ arlingtoncemetery.org;
ⓦ anctours.com
**Open** Oct–Mar: 8am– 5pm daily;
Apr–Sep: 8am–7pm daily.
**Closed** Dec 25.
ⓒ ANC Tours leaves the Visitor Center and stops at the John F. Kennedy grave, Arlington House, and Tomb of the Unknowns every 15–30 mins.
**Open** 8:30am–4:30pm. Ⓚ Ⓟ

**Transport**
Ⓜ Arlington National Cemetery.

Main Entrance

MEMORIAL DRIVE

Visitor Center

**Seabees Memorial**
This memorial is dedicated to the section of the US Navy that specializes in construction work.

★ **Grave of John F. Kennedy**
A flame lit by his wife, Jackie, on the day of his funeral in December 1963 burns here continually. Jackie is buried next to her husband.

**Key to Tombs and Sites**
① Seabees Memorial
② Grave of John F. Kennedy
③ Grave of Robert F. Kennedy
④ Tomb of Pierre L'Enfant
⑤ Arlington House
⑥ Lockerbie Memorial
⑦ Confederate Memorial
⑧ Rough Riders Memorial
⑨ Challenger and Columbia Shuttle Memorials
⑩ Memorial Amphitheater
⑪ Tomb of the Unknowns

**Tomb of Pierre L'Enfant**
The architect responsible for planning the city of Washington has a suitably grand burial site in the cemetery (*see p69*).

View of the Pentagon building's formidable concrete façade from the Potomac River

## ❷ The Pentagon

1000 Defense Pentagon, Hwy 1-395, Arlington, VA. **Tel** (703) 697-1776. Ⓜ Pentagon. Tours by appointment for US citizens only. For information call the above number. Ⓦ **pentagon.afis.osd.mil**

President Franklin Roosevelt decided in the early 1940s to consolidate the 17 buildings that comprised the Department of War (the original name for the Department of Defense) into one building. Designed by army engineers, and built of gravel dredged from the Potomac River and molded into concrete, the Pentagon was started on September 11, 1941 and completed on January 15, 1943, at a cost of $83 million. As the world's largest office building, it is almost a city in itself. Yet despite its size, the Pentagon's unique five-sided design is very efficient, and it takes only seven minutes to walk between any two points.

The Pentagon is the headquarters of the Department of Defense, a Cabinet-level organization consisting of three military departments, the Army, Navy, and Air Force, as well as 14 defense agencies. Leading personnel are the Secretary of Defense and the Chairman of the Joint Chiefs of Staff.

On September 11, 2001, the building was damaged in a terrorist attack. A memorial to the 184 people who died in the Pentagon and on Flight 77 was dedicated on September 11, 2008.

## ❸ Air Force Memorial

Off Columbia Pike. **Tel** (703) 979-0674. Ⓜ Pentagon City & Pentagon. **Open** Apr–Oct: 8am–11pm daily; Nov–Mar: 8am–9pm daily. 📷 by appt. Ⓦ **airforcememorial.org**

Located on a promontory overlooking the Pentagon, this memorial honors the service and sacrifices of the men and women of the United States Air Force and its predecessor organizations. Central to the bold, graceful design, intended to evoke flight, are three stainless steel spires which soar skyward, the highest reaching 270 ft (82 m). President George W. Bush accepted the Memorial on behalf of the American people in October 2006.

A stall at the waterfront's fish market

The elegant Air Force Memorial

## ❹ Southwest Waterfront

Ⓜ Waterfront. Fish Market: **Open** 7:30am–8pm daily. Ⓦ **swdcwaterfront.com**

In the 1960s, urban planners tested their new architectural theories on Washington's southwest waterfront along the Potomac River. Old neighborhoods were torn down, and apartment high-rises put up in their place. Eventually new restaurants developed along the waterfront, and Arena Stage, a popular regional theater company, built an experimental theater here. The area enjoyed a regeneration, and today it is a relaxed place to eat or just take a stroll.

The fish market, a remnant of the old waterfront cultures located off Maine Avenue. Today it is still a thriving business, drawing customers from all over Washington and enjoying its reputation as one of the most vibrant spots in the area. Customers can buy lobster, crabs, oysters, and all kinds of fresh fish from the vendors selling from their barges on the river. There are also several good restaurants along the waterfront that specialize in freshly caught local fish and seafood. Arrive early during the summer months as this is a popular place to dine.

## September 11

On September 11, 2001, one of four airplanes hijacked by terrorists was flown into the Pentagon, resulting in huge loss of life and causing the side of the building to collapse. Crews at the Pentagon

worked tirelessly to rebuild the damaged 10 percent of the building (400,000 to 500,000 square feet). It was estimated that repairs would take three years to finish but they were completed in less than a year. The west wall has a dedication capsule and a single charred capstone. A memorial has been erected.

The damaged Pentagon after the September 11 attack

when it relocated to the City Museum in the Carnegie Library Building *(see p98)*. The Heurich Mansion is a fine example of an upper-middle-class family house in Washington in the late 1800s.

The ornate carving in Heurich's Beer Hall

## ❺ Theodore Roosevelt Island

GW Memorial Pkwy, McLean, VA.
**Map** 1 C4. **Tel** (703) 289-2500.
Ⓜ Rosslyn. **Open** 6am–10pm daily.
🎫 by appt only. 🆆 nps.gov/this

A haven for naturalists, Theodore Roosevelt Island's 91 acres (37 ha) of marshlands and 2 miles (4 km) of nature trails are home to a variety of wildlife including red-tailed hawks, great owls, groundhogs, and wood ducks, as well as many species of trees and plants. President Theodore Roosevelt (1858–1919), a great naturalist himself, is honored with a 17-ft (5-m) tall memorial in bronze, and four granite tablets, each inscribed with quotes by the president.

The island is just one of several sites that form part of the George Washington Memorial Parkway. Enjoy a quiet stroll or visit one of the parkway's other historical sites. Remember to

carry drinking water, especially during the summer months.

There is a carpark on the George Washington Memorial Parkway (northbound) from where you can access the footbridge leading to the island. Bicycles are not permitted on the island.

## ❻ Heurich Mansion

1307 New Hampshire Ave, NW.
**Tel** (202) 429-1894. Ⓜ Dupont Circle.
🎫 11:30am & 1pm Thu & Fri,
11:30am & 2pm Sat. Wed by appt.
**Closed** Federal hols. 🏛 donation.
♿ 🆆 heurichhouse.org

Brewer Christian Heurich built this wonderful Bavarian fantasy for his family just south of Dupont Circle in 1894. The turreted mansion built in the Romanesque Revival architectural style was home to the Historical Society of Washington, DC until 2003,

## ❼ African American Civil War Memorial and Museum

Museum: 1925 Vermont Ave, NW.
Memorial: 10th St and Vermont Ave,
NW. **Tel** (202) 667-2667. Ⓜ U Street.
**Open** 10am–6:30pm Mon–Fri,
10am–4pm Sat (call for tours), noon–4pm Sun. 🆆 afroamcivilwar.org

Opened in January 1999, the African American Museum uses photographs, documents, and audiovisual equipment to explain the still largely unknown story of African Americans' long struggle for freedom. The Museum's permanent exhibition is entitled "Slavery to Freedom; Civil War to Civil Rights." Interactive kiosks bring together historic documents, photographs, and music in a powerful and evocative way. There is also a service for anyone interested in tracing relatives who may have served with United States Colored Troops during the Civil War. At the center of a paved plaza is situated the "Spirit of Freedom," a sculpture by Ed Hamilton, which was unveiled on July 18, 1998. It is the first major art piece by a black sculptor on federal land in the District of Columbia. It stands 10 ft (3 m) tall and features uniformed black soldiers and a sailor poised to leave home.

Statue of President Roosevelt and granite tablets on Theodore Roosevelt Island

The elaborate fountain at the heart of the Dupont Circle intersection

### ❽ Iwo Jima Statue (US Marine Corps Memorial)

Meade St, between Arlington National Cemetery & Arlington Blvd. **Map** 1 B5. Ⓜ Rosslyn. ♿

The horrific battle of Iwo Jima that took place during World War II was captured by photographer Joe Rosenthal. His Pulitzer Prize-winning picture of five Marines and a Navy Corpsman raising the American flag on the tiny Pacific island came to symbolize in the American psyche the heroic struggle of the American forces in the war against Japan.

This image was magnificently translated into bronze by sculptor Felix DeWeldon and paid for by private donations. The three surviving soldiers from Rosenthal's photograph actually posed for DeWeldon; the other three men, however, were killed in further fighting on the islands. The Iwo Jima Memorial is dedicated to all members of the Marine Corps who have died defending their country.

A poignant memorial to the men who died in the battle of Iwo Jima

### ❾ Dupont Circle

**Map** 2 F2 & 3 A1. Ⓜ Dupont Circle.

This area to the north of the White House gets its name from the fountain and is at the intersection of Massachusetts, Connecticut, and New Hampshire Avenues, and 19th Street, NW. At the heart of this traffic island is the Francis Dupont Memorial Fountain, named for the first naval hero of the Civil War, Admiral Samuel Francis Dupont. Built by his family, the original memorial was a bronze statue that was moved eventually to Wilmington, Delaware. The present marble fountain, which was constructed in 1921, has four figures (which represent the sea, the wind, the stars,

Playing chess in Dupont Circle

and the navigational arts) supporting a marble basin.

The park area around the fountain draws a cross section of the community – chess players engrossed in their games, cyclists pausing at the fountain, picnickers, and tourists taking a break from sightseeing. Do not stray into the Circle after dark as it may not be safe at night.

In the early 20th century the Dupont Circle area was a place of grand mansions. Its fortunes then declined until the 1970s, when Washingtonians began to buy the decaying mansions. The district is now filled with art galleries, bars, restaurants, and bookstores. The old Victorian buildings have been divided into apartments, restored as single family homes, or converted into small office buildings. Dupont Circle is also the center of Washington's gay community. The bars and clubs on the section of P Street between Dupont Circle and Rock Creek Park are the most popular area for gay men and women to meet.

### ❿ National Geographic Museum

1145 17th St at M St, NW. **Map** 3 B2. **Tel** (202) 857-7700. Ⓜ Farragut North, Farragut West. **Open** 10am–6pm daily. **Closed** Dec 25. ♿ 📷 Ⓦ **nationalgeographic.com/museum**

This small museum is located in the National Geographic Society's headquarters, designed by Edward Durrell Stone, the architect behind the Kennedy Center. A series of permanent and temporary exhibitions documents the richness of nature and the diversity of human culture all over the world. Past exhibitions include the Terra-Cotta Warriors and an exploration of the Golden Age of the pharaohs.

Auguste Renoir's masterpiece, *The Luncheon of the Boating Party* (1881)

# ⓫ The Phillips Collection

1600 21st St at Q St, NW. **Map** 2 E2 & 3 A1. **Tel** (202) 387-2151. **M** Dupont Circle. **Open** 10am–5pm Tue–Sat (to 8:30pm Thu), 11am–6pm Sun. **Closed** Jan 1, Jul 4, Thanksgiving, Dec 25, Federal hols. 🚫 📷 11am Fri & Sat. ♿ 💻 📷
**W** phillipscollection.org

This is one of the finest collections of Impressionist works in the world and the first museum devoted to modern art in the United States. Duncan and Marjorie Phillips, who founded the collection, lived in the older of the museum's two adjacent buildings. Following the death of his father and brother in 1917, Duncan Phillips decided to open two of the mansion's rooms as The Phillips Memorial Gallery.

The couple spent their time traveling and adding to their already extensive collection. During the 1920s they acquired some of the most important modern European paintings, including *The Luncheon of the Boating Party* (1881) by Renoir, for which they paid $125,000 (one of the highest prices ever paid at the time).

In 1930 the Phillips family moved to a new home on Foxhall Road in northwest Washington and converted the rest of their former 1897

Georgian Revival residence into a private gallery. The Phillips Gallery was then reopened to the public in 1960 and renamed The Phillips Collection. The museum currently has over 3,000 pieces of 19th-, 20th-, and 21st-century American and European art.

The elegant Georgian Revival building that was the Phillips' home makes for a more intimate and personal gallery than the big Smithsonian art museums. The Phillips Collection is best known for its wonderful selection of Impressionist and Post-Impressionist paintings; *Dancers at the Barre* by Degas, *Self-Portrait* by Cézanne and *Entrance to the Public Gardens in Arles* by Van Gogh are just three examples. The museum also has one of the largest collections in the world of pieces by French artist Pierre

**Collector Duncan Phillips (1886–1966)**

Bonnard, including *The Open Window* (1921).

Other great paintings to be seen in the collection include El Greco's *The Repentant Saint Peter* (1600), *The Blue Room* (1901) by Pablo Picasso, and the huge *Ochre and Red on Red* (1954) by Mark Rothko. In addition to the permanent exhibits,

the museum supports traveling exhibitions, which start at The Phillips Collection before appearing in galleries around the country. The exhibitions often feature one artist (such as Georgia O'Keeffe) or one particular topic or period (such as the *Twentieth-Century Still-Life Paintings* exhibition).

The Phillips Collection encourages enthusiasts of modern art to visit the museum for a number of special events. On the first Thursday of each month the museum hosts "Phillips after 5." These evenings include gallery talks, live music, and light refreshments, and give people the opportunity to discuss the issues of the art world in a relaxed, social atmosphere. On Sunday afternoons from September through May, a series of concerts are staged in the gallery's Music Room. Running since 1941, these popular concerts are free to anyone who has purchased a ticket to the museum on that day. They range from piano recitals and string quartets to performances by established singers of world renown, such as the famous operatic soprano Jessye Norman.

The museum shop sells merchandise linked to permanent and temporary exhibitions. Books, posters, and prints can be found as well as ceramics, glassware, and other creations by contemporary artists. There are also hand-painted silks and artworks based on the major paintings in the collection.

*Entrance to the Public Gardens in Arles* (1888), by Vincent Van Gogh

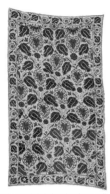

18th-century Turkish embroidery on silk in the Textile Museum

## ⑫ Textile Museum

2320 S St, NW. **Map** 2 E1. **Tel** (202) 667-0441. Ⓜ Dupont Circle. **Open** 10am–5pm Tue–Sat, 1–5pm Sun. **Closed** Dec 24 & 25, Federal hols. 🖼 donation. 🏷 "Highlights" tours 1:30pm Sat & Sun. Library: **Open** 11am–3pm Wed, noon–4pm Sat. 📷 ♿ call in advance. Ⓦ textilemuseum.org

George Hewitt Myers, the founder of the Textile Museum, began collecting oriental rugs while he was at college. In 1925 he opened a museum in his home to display his collection of 275 rugs and 60 textiles. It was a private museum, open only by appointment, until Myers' death in 1957.

Today the museum is still housed in Myers' home, which was designed by John Russell Pope, architect of the Jefferson Memorial *(see p81)*. The collection is also now in an adjacent building by Waddy B. Wood, architect of Woodrow Wilson's house.

There are around 17,000 objects in the collection from all over the world, including textiles from Peru, India, Indonesia, and Central America. Some pieces date from 3000 BC. The museum also hosts traveling exhibitions from other collections. During museum hours, the public can access the large formal gardens at the back of the building.

## ⑬ Woodrow Wilson House

2340 S St, NW. **Map** 2 E1. **Tel** (202) 387-4062. Ⓜ Dupont Circle. **Open** 10am–4pm Tue–Sun. **Closed** Federal hols. 🖼 🏷 ♿ Ⓦ woodrowwilsonhouse.org

Located in the Kalorama neighborhood, the former home of Woodrow Wilson (1856–1924), who served as president from 1913 to 1921, is the only presidential museum within the District of Columbia.

Wilson led the US through World War I and advocated the formation of the League of Nations, the precursor to the United Nations. Although exhausted by the war effort, Wilson campaigned tirelessly for the League.

In 1919 he collapsed from a stroke and became an invalid for the rest of his life. Many believe that Wilson's second wife, Edith Galt, assumed many of the presidential duties herself (she guided his hand when he signed documents). Unable to leave his sickbed, Wilson saw his dream, the League of Nations, defeated in the Senate. In 1920 he was awarded the Nobel Peace Prize – small consolation for the failure of the League.

Wilson and his wife moved to this townhouse, designed by Waddy B. Wood, at the end of his

Statue of Churchill, British Embassy

second term in 1921. Edith Galt Wilson arranged for the home to be bequeathed to the nation. Since then the building has been maintained as it was during the President's lifetime, containing artifacts from his life, such as his Rolls-Royce, and reflecting the style of an upper-middle-class home of the 1920s. The house today belongs to the National Trust for Historic Preservation.

## ⑭ Embassy Row

Massachusetts Avenue. **Map** 2 E1. Ⓜ Dupont Circle. *See also pp148–9.*

Embassy Row stretches along Massachusetts Avenue from Scott Circle toward Observatory Circle. It developed during the Depression when many of Washington's wealthy families were forced to sell their mansions to diplomats, who bought them for foreign missions. Since then, many new embassies have been built, often in the vernacular style of their native country, making Embassy Row architecturally fascinating.

At No. 2315 Massachusetts Avenue, the Embassy of Pakistan is an opulent mansion built in 1908, with a mansard roof (four steep sloping sides) and a rounded wall that hugs the corner.

Farther down the road, at No. 2349, is the Embassy of

An elaborately decorated room in the Georgian Revival Woodrow Wilson House

the Republic of Cameroon, one of the Avenue's great early 20th-century Beaux Arts masterpieces. This romantic, Norwegian chateau-style building was commissioned in 1905 to be the home of Christian Hauge, first Norwegian ambassador to the United States, before passing to Cameroon.

Situated opposite the Irish Embassy stands a bronze statue of the hanged Irish revolutionary Robert Emmet (1778–1803). The statue was commissioned by Irish Americans to commemorate Irish independence.

At No. 2536 is the India Supply Mission. Two carved elephants stand outside as symbols of Indian culture and mythology. In the park in front of the Indian Embassy is an impressive bronze sculpture of Mahatma Gandhi.

The British Embassy, at No. 3100, was designed by Sir Edwin Lutyens in 1928. The English-style gardens were planted by the American wife of the then British ambassador, Sir Ronald Lindsay. Outside the embassy is an arresting statue of Sir Winston Churchill by William M. McVey.

Façade of the Croatian Embassy on Massachusetts Avenue

## ⓯ Kalorama

**Map** 2 D1 & 2 E1.
Ⓜ Woodley Park or Duapont Circle.

The neighborhood of Kalorama, situated north of Dupont Circle, is an area of stately private homes and elegant apartment buildings. From its development at the turn of the 20th century as a suburb close to the city center, Kalorama (Greek for "beautiful view") has been home to the wealthy and upwardly mobile. Five presidents had homes here: Herbert Hoover,

The apartments at 2311 Connecticut Avenue, Kalorama

Franklin D. Roosevelt, Warren Harding, William Taft, and Woodrow Wilson. Only Wilson's home served as his permanent post-presidential residence.

Some of the most striking and ornate apartment buildings in Washington are found on Connecticut Avenue, south of the Taft Bridge that crosses Rock Creek Park. Most notable are the Georgian Revival-style Dresden apartments at No. 2126, the Beaux Arts-inspired Highlands building at number 1914, and the Spanish Colonial-style Woodward apartments at No. 2311 Connecticut Avenue. Also worth viewing is the Tudor-style building at No. 2221 Kalorama Road.

The best views of nearby Rock Creek Park (see p143) are from Kalorama Circle at the northern end of 24th Street.

## ⓰ Adams-Morgan

North of Dupont Circle, east of Rock Creek Park, and south of Mt. Pleasant. **Map** 2 E1 & 2 F1. Ⓜ Dupont Circle or Woodley Park.

Adams-Morgan was one of the first racially and ethnically diverse neighborhoods in the city. It was given its name in the 1950s when the Supreme Court ruled that Washington must desegregate its educational system, and forced the com-bination of two schools in the area – Adams (for white children) and Morgan (an all-black school). Packed with

cafés, bookstores, clubs, and galleries, the district is a vibrant and eclectic mix of African, Hispanic, and Caribbean immigrants, as well as white urban pioneers, both gay and straight. People are attracted by the neighborhood's lively streets and its beautiful, and relatively affordable, early 20th-century houses and apartments.

The area has a thriving music scene and, on any night, rap, reggae, salsa, and Washington's indigenous go-go can be heard in the clubs and bars. The cosmopolitan feel of Adams-Morgan is reflected in its wide variety of restaurants (see p189). Cajun, New Orleans, Ethiopian, French, Italian, Caribbean, Mexican, and Lebanese food can all be found along 18th Street and Columbia Road, the two main streets. Although the area is becoming increasingly modern and trendy, its 1950s Hispanic roots are still evident.

The area's cultural diversity is celebrated in September each year with food, music, and dance at the Adams-Morgan Day Festival (see p40).

It should be noted that this area can be dangerous after dark, so be wary if you are walking around at night. The area is not served by Metrorail and parking, especially on weekends, can be difficult.

Colorful mural on the wall of a parking lot in Adams-Morgan

# ❷ National Zoological Park

Established in 1889 as the Smithsonian's Department of Living Animals and sited on the Mall, Washington's National Zoo moved to its present location in 1891. The park, which covers 163 acres, was designed by Frederick Law Olmsted, the landscape architect responsible for New York's Central Park. Today, the zoo is home to more than 2,000 animals, many of which are endangered. The zoo also runs a number of breeding programs, one of the most successful of which is the Sumatran tiger program.

**Elephant Trails**
This exhibit gives an innovative home with diverse habitats to a small herd of Asian elephants, and is part of a campaign to save this endangered species.

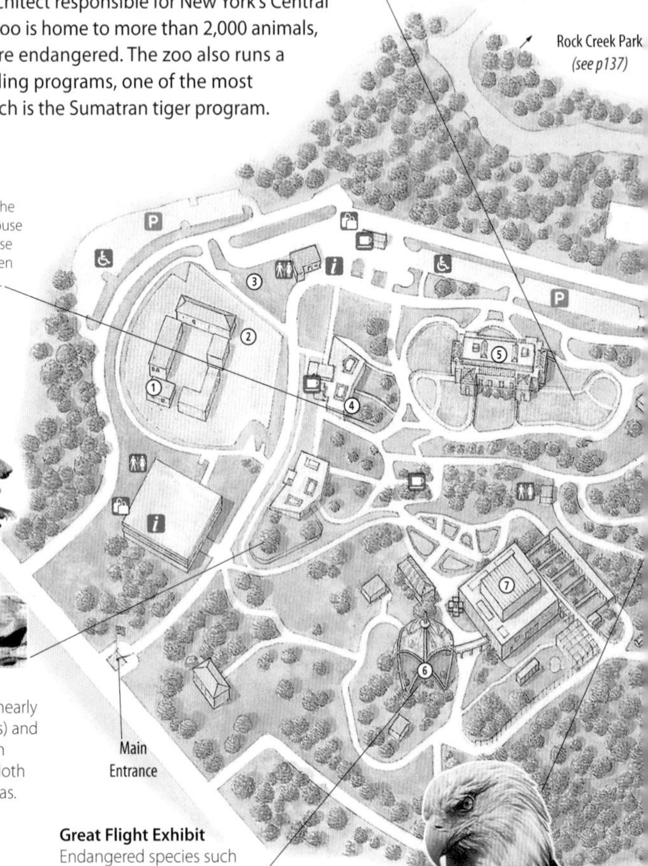

Rock Creek Park (see p137)

**Giant Panda Habitat**
The National Zoo was the first zoo in the US to house pandas. Since 1972 these beloved bears have been the zoo's top attraction.

**★ Asia Trail**
This exhibit covers nearly 6 acres (2.4 hectares) and features seven Asian species, including sloth bears and red pandas.

**Main Entrance**

**Great Flight Exhibit**
Endangered species such as the Guam rail and Bali Mynah can be seen here.

## Key to Animal Enclosures

① Cheetah Conservation Station
② Zebras
③ Wallabies
④ Giant Panda Habitat
⑤ Elephants
⑥ Great Flight Exhibit
⑦ Bird House
⑧ Golden Lion Tamarins
⑨ American Trail
⑩ Bald Eagles
⑪ Seals and Sea Lions
⑫ Andean Bears

⑬ Amazonia
⑭ Gibbon Ridge
⑮ Great Ape House
⑯ Small Mammal House
⑰ Invertebrates
⑱ Reptile Discovery Center
⑲ Lemur Island
⑳ Think Tank
㉑ Sumatran Tigers
㉒ Great Cats
㉓ Kids Farm

**Bald Eagle**
The only eagle unique to North America, the bald eagle is named for its white head, which appears to be "bald" against its dark body.

0 meters      100
0 yards      100

**Golden Lion Tamarins**
These endangered mammals are protected by an international conservation program, which includes breeding and conservation education.

## VISITORS' CHECKLIST

**Practical Information**
3001 Connecticut Ave, NW.
**Tel** (202) 673-4800.
w nationalzoo.si.edu
**Open** Apr–Oct: 10am–6pm daily (buildings), 6am–8pm daily (grounds); Nov–Apr: 10am–4:30pm daily (buildings), 6am–6pm daily (grounds).
**Closed** Dec 25.
call (202) 633-4888.

**Transport**
M Cleveland Park, Woodley Park-Zoo.

**★ Great Ape House**
Western Lowland Gorillas – whose males can weigh over 400 pounds (180 kg) – can be seen in the Great Ape House. Other occupants include tree-dwelling orangutans.

**★ Komodo Dragons**
These rare lizards can grow up to 10 ft (3 m) in length, and weigh up to 200 lbs (90 kg). They are the first to be born in captivity outside Indonesia.

**Sumatran Tigers**
Native to the Indonesian island of Sumatra, these are the smallest of all surviving tiger subspecies and are excellent swimmers.

**Amazonia**
This exhibit re-creates the Amazonian habitat. Visitors can see many creatures from poison-dart frogs to giant catfish.

## ⑰ Mary McLeod Bethune Council House National Historic Site

1318 Vermont Ave, NW. **Map** 3 B1. **Tel** (202) 673-2402. Ⓜ McPherson Square/U Street. **Open** 9am–5pm Mon–Sat. **Closed** Jan 1, Thanksgiving, Dec 25. ⓒ plus interactive tour for children. ⓖ Ⓦ nps.gov/mamc

Born in 1875 to two former-slaves, Mary McLeod Bethune was an educator and civil and women's rights activist. In 1904 she founded a college for impoverished black women in Florida, the Daytona Educational and Industrial School for Negro Girls. Renamed the Bethune-Cookman College, it is still going strong.

In the 1930s, President Franklin D. Roosevelt asked her to be his special advisor on racial affairs, and she later became director of the Division of Negro Affairs in the National Youth Administration. As part of Roosevelt's cabinet, Bethune was the first black woman to obtain a high position in the US government.

Bethune went on to found the National Council of Negro Women, which gives voice to the concerns of black women. The Council grew to have a membership of 10,000, and this

Mary McLeod Bethune

house on Vermont Avenue was bought by Bethune and the Council as its headquarters.

It was not until November 1979, 24 years after Bethune's death, that the original Council House was opened to the public, with photographs, manuscripts, and other artifacts from her life on display. In 1982 the house was declared a National Historic Site and was bought by the National Park Service.

Entrance to the Mary McLeod Bethune Council House

## ⑱ Hillwood Estate Museum and Gardens

4155 Linnean Ave, NW. **Tel** (202) 686-5807. Ⓜ Van Ness/ UDC. **Open** 10am–5pm Tue–Sat, 1–5pm Sun. **Closed** Jan, Federal hols. ⓖ ⓒ ⓠ ⓟ Ⓦ hillwoodmuseum.org

Hillwood was owned by Marjorie Merriweather Post, and it was opened to the public in 1977. The Museum contains the most comprehensive collection of 18th- and 19th-century Russian imperial art to be found outside of Russia, including Fabergé eggs and Russian Orthodox icons. It also has some renowned pieces of 18th-century French decorative art. The Gardens are set within a 25-acre estate, surrounded by woodlands in the heart of Washington, and have important collections of azaleas and orchids.

The stunning interior of the restored Lincoln Theatre

## ⑲ Lincoln Theatre

1215 U St, NW. **Map** 2 F1. **Tel** (202) 328-6000 (box office). Ⓜ U Street-Cardozo. **Open** 10am–6pm Mon–Fri. **Closed** Federal hols. ⓒ groups by appt. ⓖ Ⓦ thelincolntheatre.org

Built in 1922, the Lincoln Theatre was once the centerpiece of cultural life for Washington's downtown African American community. Like the Apollo Theater in New York, the Lincoln presented big-name entertainment, such as jazz singer and native Washingtonian Duke Ellington, Ella Fitzgerald, and Billie Holiday.

By the 1960s the area around the theater began to deteriorate; the 1968 riots turned U Street into a corridor of abandoned and burned-out buildings, and attendance at the theater dropped dramatically. By the 1970s the theater had closed down. Then, in the early 1980s fundraising began for the $10 million renovation. Even the original, highly elaborate plasterwork was carefully cleaned and repaired, and the theater reopened in 1994.

Today the Lincoln Theatre is a center for the performing arts, and one of the linchpins of U Street's renaissance. The magnificent auditorium hosts a program of concerts, stage shows, and events including the DC Film Festival (see p204).

## ⑳ National Zoological Park

*See pp140–41.*

# ㉑ Washington National Cathedral

*See pp144–5.*

# ㉒ Cleveland Park

Ⓜ Cleveland Park.

Cleveland Park is a beautiful residential neighborhood that resembles the picture on a postcard of small-town America. It was originally a summer community for those wanting to escape the less bucolic parts of the city. In 1885, President Grover Cleveland (1885–9) bought a stone farmhouse here as a summer home for his bride.

The town's Victorian summer houses are now much sought after by people wanting to be close to the city but live in a small-town environment. There are interesting shops and good restaurants, as well as a grand old Art Deco movie theater, called the Uptown.

# ㉓ Rock Creek Park

Ⓜ Cleveland Park. Rock Creek Park Nature Center: 5200 Glover Rd, NW. **Map** 2 D1–D3. **Tel** (202) 895-6070. Ⓜ Friendship Heights. 🚌 E2, E3, E4. **Open** 9am–5pm Wed–Sun. **Closed** Federal hols. 🗓 by appt. 🌐 **nps.gov/rocr**

Named for the creek that flows through it, Rock Creek Park bisects the city of Washington.

Pierce Mill, the 19th-century gristmill in Rock Creek Park

## The Shaw Neighborhood

This neighborhood is named for Union Colonel Robert Gould Shaw, the white commander of an all-black regiment from Massachusetts. He supported his men in their struggle to attain the same rights as white soldiers. Until the 1960s, U Street was the focus of black-dominated businesses and organizations. Thriving theaters, such as the Howard and the Lincoln, attracted top-name performers, and Howard University was the center of intellectual life for black students. The 1968 riots, sparked by the assassination of Dr. Martin Luther King, Jr., wiped out much of Shaw's business district, and many thought the area could never be revived. However, the restoration of the Lincoln Theatre, the renewal of the U Street business district, and an influx of homebuyers renovating historic houses, have all contributed to the rejuvenation. In the part of U Street closest to the U Street-Cardoza metro stop, many fashionable bars and clubs have opened.

Mural in the Shaw neighborhood depicting Duke Ellington

This 1,800-acre stretch of land runs from the Maryland border south to the Potomac River and constitutes nearly five percent of the city. Unlike the crowded lawns of Central Park, Rock Creek Park has a feeling of the wilderness. Although the elk, bison, and bears that used to roam the park have vanished, raccoons, foxes, and deer can still be found here in abundance.

The park was endowed in 1890 and is now run by the National Park Service. In addition to hiking and picnicking, the park has a riding stable and horse trails, tennis courts, and an 18-hole golf course. On Sundays, a portion of Beach Drive – one of the main roads running through the park – is closed to cars to allow cyclists and in-line skaters freedom of the road. The creek itself is inviting, with little eddies and waterfalls, but visitors are advised not to go into the water because it is polluted.

The **Rock Creek Park Nature Center** is a good place to begin an exploration of the park. It includes a small planetarium, and a 1-mile (1.6-km) nature trail, which is very manageable for children.

Pierce Mill near Tilden Street was an active gristmill, which was restored by the National Park Service in 1936. It was kept working as a visitor exhibit until 1993 when it was deemed unsafe to work any more. There is a barn next to the mill where works by local artists can be bought. The Carter Barron Amphitheater, near 16th Street and Colorado Avenue, stages free performances of Shakespeare's plays and summer jazz concerts.

# ㉑ Washington National Cathedral

The building of the Cathedral Church of Saint Peter and Saint Paul (its official name) began in 1907 and was completed in 1990. The world's sixth-largest cathedral, it dominates the city's skyline and measures 301 ft (94.8 m) from grade to the top of the central tower and 518 ft (158 m) in length – almost the length of two soccer fields. Built with Indiana limestone, the Washington National Cathedral boasts elements typical of Gothic religious architecture, such as soaring vaulting, stained glass windows, and intricate carvings. The exterior features fanciful gargoyles and dramatic sculpture. The cathedral has been the location of funeral and memorial services for several US presidents. Extensive renovations continue on some parts of the cathedral following an earthquake in 2011.

**Exterior**
A masterpiece of Gothic-style architecture, the towers of the cathedral dominate the skyline.

★ **Ex Nihilo** Above the center portal is *Ex Nihilo* by artist Frederick Hart. It depicts figures of men and women emerging from the swirling background.

**Main Entrance**
Three huge Gothic arches dominate the west façade, with pierced bronze gates depicting stories from the book of Genesis.

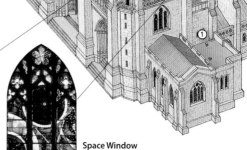

**KEY**

① George Washington Bay

② Pilgrim Observation Gallery

③ **The pinnacles** on the cathedral towers are decorated with leaf-shaped ornaments and topped by elaborately carved finials.

**Space Window**
Mankind's achievements in science and technology are commemorated in this window with the flight of Apollo 11 and a piece of moon rock.

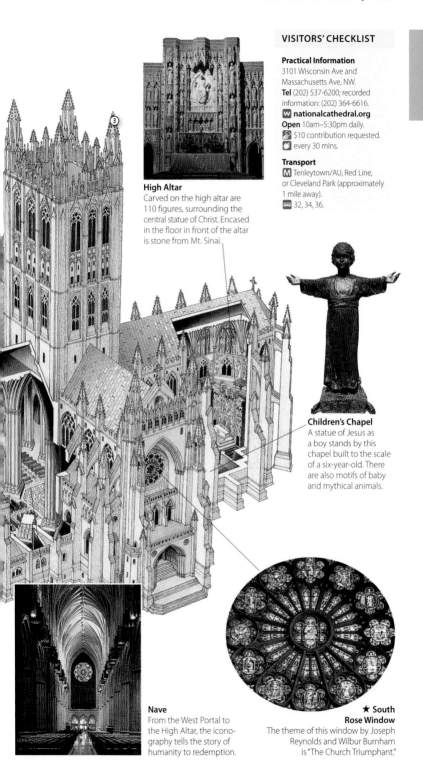

**High Altar**
Carved on the high altar are 110 figures, surrounding the central statue of Christ. Encased in the floor in front of the altar is stone from Mt. Sinai.

**VISITORS' CHECKLIST**

**Practical Information**
3101 Wisconsin Ave and Massachusetts Ave, NW.
**Tel** (202) 537-6200; recorded information: (202) 364-6616.
**W** nationalcathedral.org
**Open** 10am–5:30pm daily.
$10 contribution requested.
every 30 mins.

**Transport**
**M** Tenleytown/AU, Red Line, or Cleveland Park (approximately 1 mile away).
32, 34, 36.

**Children's Chapel**
A statue of Jesus as a boy stands by this chapel built to the scale of a six-year-old. There are also motifs of baby and mythical animals.

**Nave**
From the West Portal to the High Altar, the iconography tells the story of humanity to redemption.

**★ South Rose Window**
The theme of this window by Joseph Reynolds and Wilbur Burnham is "The Church Triumphant."

## ㉔ Basilica of the National Shrine of the Immaculate Conception

400 Michigan at 4th St, NE. **Tel** (202) 526-8300. Ⓜ Brookland-CUA. **Open** Apr 1–Oct 31: 7am–7pm daily; Nov 1–Mar 31: 7am–6pm daily. **nationalshrine.com**

Completed in 1959, this enormous Catholic Church is dedicated to the Virgin Mary. The church was designed in the shape of a crucifix and has many stained-glass windows. The building can seat a congregation of 2,500 people or more.

In the early 1900s, Bishop Thomas Shahan, rector of the Catholic University of America, proposed building a national shrine in Washington. Shahan gained the Pope's support in 1913, and in 1920 the cornerstone was laid. The Great Upper Church was dedicated on November 20, 1959. An unusual and striking combination of Romanesque and Byzantine styles, the shrine boasts classical towers as well as minarets in its design. The basilica's large interior includes a number of chapels, each with a distinctive design of its own.

Visitors can also enjoy the peaceful and extensive Prayer Garden, which covers almost an acre (4,050 sq m).

View down the nave to the Basilica's altar

Entrance to the Chinese Pavilion at the National Arboretum

## ㉕ National Arboretum

3501 New York Ave or 24th St & R St off Bladensburg Rd, NE. **Tel** (202) 245-2726. Ⓜ Stadium Armory, then Metrobus B-2. **Open** 8am–5pm daily. Museum: **Open** 10am–4pm daily. **Closed** Federal hols. by appt only. limited. **usna.usda.gov**

Tucked away in a corner of northeast Washington is the National Arboretum – a center for research, education, and the preservation of trees, shrubs, flowers, and other plants. The many collections here mean that the Arboretum is an ever-changing, year-round spectacle.

The Japanese Garden, which encompasses the National Bonsai and Penjing Museum, has bonsai that are from 20 to 380 years old. The herb garden has ten specialty gardens, where herbs are grouped according to use and historical significance. At the entrance to the garden is an elaborate 16th-century European-style "knot garden," with about 200 varieties of old roses. The National Grove of State Trees has trees representing every state.

## ㉖ Kenilworth Park and Aquatic Gardens

1550 Anacostia Ave, NE. **Tel** (202) 426-6905. Ⓜ Deanswood. **Open** 7am–4pm daily. **Closed** Jan 1, Thanksgiving, Dec 25. **nps.gov/keaq/index.htm**

Opened in the late 1800s, this tranquil park offers 12 acres (5 ha) of natural wetland areas and historic ponds filled with beautiful water lilies and other aquatic plants from around the world. In late summer, the lotus pond is covered with pink blossoms. Abundant wildlife can also be seen, including otters, turtles, frogs, salamanders, and water birds.

## ㉗ Howard University

2400 Sixth St, NW. **Tel** (202) 806-6100. Ⓜ Shaw-Howard. **howard.edu**

In 1866 the first Congregational Society of Washington considered establishing a seminary for the education of African-Americans – a school intended for "teachers and preachers." The concept expanded to include a multi-purpose university, and within two years the Colleges of Liberal Arts and Medicine of Howard University were founded, named for General Oliver O. Howard (1830–1909), an abolitionist and Civil War hero who later became a commissioner of the Freedman's Bureau. The impetus for establishing such a university was the arrival of newly-freed men from the South who were coming to the North seeking education to improve their lives. The university's charter was enacted by Congress and approved by President Andrew Jackson.

Famous graduates include Thurgood Marshall, who championed desegregation of public schools and was the first African-American Supreme Court Justice, Carter Woodson, Toni Morrison, Ralph Bunche, Stokely Carmichael, and Ossie Davis.

## Frederick Douglass (1817–95)

Born a slave around 1818, Frederick Douglass became the leading voice in the abolitionist movement that fought to end slavery in the United States. Douglass was taught to read and write by his white owners. At the age of 20 he fled to Europe. British friends in the anti-slavery movement purchased him from his former masters, and he was at last a free man. For most of his career he lived in New York, where he worked as a spokesman for the abolitionist movement. A brilliant speaker, he was sent by the American Anti-Slavery Society on a lecture tour and won added fame with the publication of his autobiography in 1845. In 1847 he became editor of the anti-slavery newspaper *The North Star*, named after the constellation point followed by escaping slaves on their way to freedom. During the Civil War *(see p23)*, Douglass was an advisor to President Lincoln and fought for the constitutional amendments that guaranteed equal rights to freed blacks.

Frederick Douglass

## ㉘ Frederick Douglass House

1411 W St, SE. **Tel** (202) 426-5961.
Ⓜ Anacostia. **Open** mid-Oct–mid-Apr: 9am–4:30pm daily; mid-Apr–mid-Oct: 9am–5pm daily. **Closed** Jan 1, Thanksgiving, Dec 25. 🅿 🅲
🅰 call ahead. 🆆 **nps.gov/frdo**

The abolitionist leader Frederick Douglass lived in Washington only toward the end of his illustrious career. After the Civil War he moved first to a townhouse on Capitol Hill, and then to Anacostia. In 1877 he bought this white-framed house, named it Cedar Hill, and lived here, with his family, until his death in 1895.

Douglass's widow opened Cedar Hill for public tours in 1903, and in 1962 the house was donated to the National Park Service. Most of the furnishings are original to the Douglass family and include gifts to Douglass from

"The Growlery" in the garden of the Frederick Douglass House

President Lincoln and the writer Harriet Beecher Stowe, author of *Uncle Tom's Cabin* (1852).

In the garden is a small stone building that Douglass used as an alternative study, and which he nicknamed "The Growlery." From the front steps of the house there is a magnificent view across the Anacostia River.

## ㉙ Anacostia Museum

1901 Fort Place, SE. **Tel** (202) 633-4820.
Ⓜ Anacostia. **Open** 10am–5pm daily for tours. **Closed** Dec 25.
🅲 by appointment only; call (202) 287-3369 or book online.
🅰 🆆 **anacostia.si.edu**

The full name of this museum is the Anacostia Museum and Center for African-American History and Culture. It is part of the Smithsonian Institution *(see p74)*, and is dedicated to increasing public understanding and awareness of the history and culture of people of African descent and heritage living in the Americas.

Basic needs such as housing, transportation, healthcare, and employment were long denied to members of the African-American community, and the Anacostia Museum sponsors exhibits addressing these concerns. Two of its major initiatives have been *Black Mosaic*, a research project on Washington's diverse Afro-Caribbean culture, and *Speak to MY Heart: African American Communities of Faith and Contemporary Life*.

The museum is as much a resource center as it is a space for art and history exhibitions; it has an extensive library and computers for visitors. Its collections include historical objects, documents, videos, and works of art. A nationally traveling exhibit, *Reflections in Black*, traces the history of African-American photography from 1840 to the present.

Façade of Cedar Hill, the Frederick Douglass House

# Three Guided Walks

The best way to discover Washington's historic neighborhoods, diverse architecture, parks and gardens is on foot. The first walk takes you up and down Massachusetts Avenue, past many of the city's larger embassies and grand, imposing mansions into Kalorama, a pretty area that's home to many of the smaller embassies. Afterwards, you may wish to spend more time exploring. You'll find at least one hidden gem; the Embassy area also houses the Phillips Collection (see p137) and several art galleries. On the walks through Georgetown and Old Town Alexandria you'll notice that many of the historic buildings you pass are open to the public.

**A Closer Look**

In Georgetown you could tour Dumbarton Oaks, Tudor Place, or Georgetown University (see pp122–9). In Alexandria you might look inside the churches, the Lyceum (the local history museum), the Lee-Fendall House, Gadsby's Tavern Museum, or the Carlyle House (see pp160–61).

Dumbarton Oaks, Georgetown (see p131)

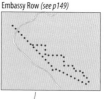

Embassy Row (see p149)

Georgetown (see pp150–51)

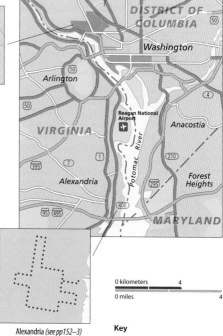

Carlyle House, a Georgian mansion on Fairfax Street, Alexandria (see p160)

Alexandria (see pp152–3)

0 kilometers    4
0 miles    4

**Key**

••• Walk route

# A Walk Around Embassy Row

For those fans of eclectic architecture this walk is a fascinating experience. Starting off west from Dupont Circle takes you along Massachusetts Avenue, past many of the larger embassies to the Italian Embassy and then back along Massachusetts Avenue to Kalorama, a quiet residential area where smaller embassies and museums are tucked away in its tree-lined streets.

⑦ Islamic Center's striking minaret

① Ornate Embassy of Indonesia

Walsh McLean (his daughter), who also owned the 44-carat Hope Diamond, which is at the Natural History Museum. Farther on, there's an Italianate palace, now home to the Society of Cincinnati ②, a charitable organization set up by officers who served George Washington. A statue of Civil War General Philip T. Sheridan on his horse greets you at Sheridan Circle ③. Walk around the circle to the left, passing the Irish and Romanian embassies. You'll see the former Turkish Embassy ④, an

garden behind the gate of the Japanese Embassy ⑤, a simple and graceful Georgian Revival building. After crossing the bridge over Rock Creek Park, you reach the Italian Embassy ⑥, a stunning contemporary structure that was designed by Piero Sartogo Architetti in Rome and Leo A. Daly in Washington. Its cantilevered copper eaves are reminiscent of a Renaissance palazzo. Cross Massachusetts Avenue and turn back toward Dupont Circle. Keep walking until you come to the the Islamic Center ⑦, a mosque with a 160-ft (48-m) minaret. Wander inside to see the exquisite tiles and carpets. (Head coverings for women are provided.) Turn left on California

**0 meters** 400
**0 yards** 400

At Dupont Circle Metro head northwest on the south side of Massachusetts Avenue. Look for the Indonesian Embassy ①. This Beaux Arts mansion was built at the turn of the century by an Irish immigrant from Tipperary who made his fortune in the gold mines. The house later became the property of Evalyn

### Tips for Walkers

**Starting point:** Dupont Circle Metro.
**Length:** 2.5 miles (4 km).
**Stopping off points:** Choose from one of several good restaurants near the Dupont Circle Metro stop.

ornate mansion that boasts a mixture of Romanesque and Turkish styles on the exterior, while inside there are Doric columns, marble floors, mosaic tiles, bronze statues, stained glass windows, and frescoes. It was built by Washington architect George Oakley Totten, who was inspired by palaces in Istanbul, for wealthy industrialist Edward Hamlin Everett. Known as the "bottle top king" (he obtained the patent for corrugated bottle tops), Everett staged elaborate musical evenings here. As you stroll along Massachusetts Avenue, take a look at the

Street, right onto 24th Street and left onto S Street past the Woodrow Wilson House ⑧ (the unpretentious home of the 28th president) and the Textile Museum ⑨. Go right onto 22nd Street, walking down the Spanish Steps to R Street. Turn left on R and right on 21st Street, passing the Phillips Collection ⑩, one of the country's most delightful modern art museums. Turn left on Q Street to make your way back to your start at the Dupont Circle Metro.

**Key**

• • • Walk route

# A 90-Minute Walk in Georgetown

Renowned for its beautiful and historic architecture, eclectic shops, and delightful restaurants, Georgetown has it all. Starting in upper Georgetown, this walk takes you along residential streets past grand homes and Federal-style rowhouses, past early churches and cemeteries, parks and river vistas, quiet lanes and crowded streets. The walk ends on M Street in the commercial heart of Georgetown at the oldest house built in the district. Details of many sights mentioned are in the section on Georgetown *(see pp122–3)*.

⑥ Dumbarton House, beautifully designed inside and out

and then left on 29th Street. Mt. Zion Church ⑧, on your right at 1334, was Washington's first African-American church, and has a tin ceiling that shows a West African influence *(see p128)*.

At the corner, turn right on Dumbarton Street, left on 30th Street, and right on N Street, which is full of elegant

Start at Wisconsin Avenue and S Street where you head east and then right on to 32nd Street. Dumbarton Oaks ① at 1703, a Federal-style mansion owned by Harvard University, contains a huge collection of pre-Columbian and Byzantine art, and may be worth returning to explore at length one afternoon *(see p129)*.

Turn left on R Street and right onto 31st Street. Admire Tudor Place ②, designed by the Capitol architect William Thornton on the right *(see p128)*. Turn left onto Avon Lane and left again on Avon Place. Walk across R Street to Montrose Park ③, which has a maze where you might like to meander for a bit, and then return to R Street. Head east and go into Oak Hill

Cemetery ④. James Renwick, architect of New York's St. Patrick's Cathedral, designed the chapel inside *(see p128)*.

Back on R Street, head east to 28th Street. Turn right past Evermay ⑤, a private Georgian manor, built by Scotsman Samuel Davidson in 1792. Turn left on Q Street. On your left, the Federal-style Dumbarton House ⑥, is noted for its beautiful 18th- and 19th-century furnishings. Make a left at the corner on 27th Street. Facing you is the Mt. Zion cemetery ⑦ where African-Americans were buried before the Civil War.

Turning around, walk back on 27th Street until you come to O Street. Turn right on O Street

## Tips for Walkers

**Starting point:** Wisconsin Ave & S Street. **Length:** 3 miles (5 km). **Getting there:** Metro Connection express bus from Foggy Bottom metro stop to Wisconsin Ave & R St, or Circulator bus from Union Station and points along K St NW.

⑪ Smith Row, American Federal-style architecture on N Street

③ Montrose Park, a tranquil space for city relaxation

18th-century architecture. On your right you pass 3017 N Street, the house where Jackie Kennedy once lived ⑨. At Wisconsin Avenue you can take a break at Martin's Tavern (est. 1933) or one of many cafés here. Turn right on Wisconsin and then left on O Street. Note the old streetcar tracks and St. John's Episcopal Church ⑩ at 3240, once attended by Thomas Jefferson. Turn left on Potomac Street, then right.

merchant and mayor. Farther along N Street is Georgetown University ⑭ (see p128). Turn left on 36th Street to find The Tombs bar, a favorite haunt of students. On Prospect Street ⑮ next to the Car Barn (once used to house trolleys and now part of the university), go down three flights of steep steps (where a scene from *The Exorcist* was filmed) to M Street, the city's busiest and most colorful street, and the Potomac River.

Cross M Street and turn left, passing the Key Bridge and the Francis Scott Key Park ⑯, named for the author of "The Star-Spangled Banner". Still on M Street, look for the sign to Cady's Alley at 3316, make a right, and go down the steps. Turn left on Cady's Alley ⑰, browse in the high-end home furnishing shops, left again on 33rd Street to return to M Street. Turn right and you may want to stop at Dean & DeLuca ⑱, a lively café and gourmet market built in 1866. Stroll past the Victorian-style Georgetown Park ⑲, a former tobacco warehouse that now houses a variety of shops. Cross Wisconsin Avenue and go along M Street to 31st Street. Turn right then left onto the towpath by the C & O Canal ⑳ for a block, turning right on Thomas Jefferson Street and head toward Washington Harbor ㉑ (see pp124–5). Walk through this large complex of shops to the waterfront. After admiring the magnificent river view, retrace your steps to M Street and visit the Old Stone House ㉒, which dates from pre-Revolutionary days.

⑭ Georgetown University

Walk along N Street for several blocks. You'll pass Smith Row ⑪ with its brick Federal-style houses at 3255-63, John and Jackie Kennedy's home ⑫ from 1957 to 1961 at 3307, and Cox's Row ⑬ at 3327-39, built by Colonel Cox, a former

### Key

• • • Walk route

0 meters 300
0 yards 300

⑳ Passenger barge on the C & O Canal, a reminder of 19th-century shippers

**For additional map symbols** see back flap

# A 90-Minute Walk in Alexandria

Stroll along cobblestone streets to see historic Alexandria, settled in the 18th century. This walk through the Old Town will take you by many historic homes, two of the oldest churches (George Washington attended both of them at one time or another), Gadsby's Tavern, and an old firehouse. The walk ends at the Torpedo Factory, now a thriving art center where over 200 artists exhibit their work. Afterward, go around to the back of the Torpedo Factory for a view of the Potomac River.

② Historic Farmer's Market in Market Square

Start at the Ramsay House Visitor Center ①, once the home of a Scottish merchant and city founder, William Ramsay. Built in 1724, it is the oldest house in Alexandria. Outside Ramsay House, you'll see Market Square ② where farmers have sold their produce for over 250 Years. At the corner of Fairfax and King Streets turn left onto South Fairfax Street. Walk past the Stabler-Leadbeater Apothecary Shop ③ (see p160), built in 1792. This was formerly run by Edward Stabler who worked with the "Society for the Relief of People Illegally Held in Bondage" to free enslaved African Americans. Turn left on Prince Street to find

211, which was the former home of Dr. Elisha Cullen Dick, the doctor who attended George Washington on his deathbed. At the corner is the Athenaeum ④, a Greek Revival building dating from 1851, once the Bank of the Old Dominion. Cross Lee Street and continue walking on Prince Street. This block, dubbed Captain's Row ⑤, is still paved with cobblestones and was once home to sea captains and shipbuilders. Turn right on Union Street. You'll pass several art galleries and

catch a glimpse of the river on your left. Turn right on Duke Street to see the Federal-style homes and pretty gardens. Turn left on South Fairfax Street. The Old Presbyterian Meeting House ⑥ (see p160), a brick church built by Scottish settlers in 1775 and rebuilt in 1837 after a fire, is on your right. On George Washington's death the bell of the Old Presbyterian tolled for four days. You'll find the Tomb of the Unknown Soldier of the American Revolution in the churchyard.

### Tips for Walkers

**Starting point:** The Ramsay House Visitor's Center.
**Length:** 2.5 m (4 km).
**Getting there:** Take the Dash bus from the King Street Metro stop to the Ramsay House Visitor's Center.
**Stopping Off Points:** The Friendship Firehouse is open Fri–Sun. For lunch try Gadsby's Tavern or one of the restaurants on King Street.

① Ramsay House, the oldest building in Alexandria

Go to the corner of South Fairfax Street and turn right onto Wolfe Street. This cuts through what was once a neighborhood called Hayti, home to many prominent African-American leaders in the early 1800s. Continue until you reach Royal Street. The house at 404 South Royal Street ⑦ is the home of George Seaton, a black master carpenter whose mother was freed by Martha Washington. Continue for three blocks. At 604 Wolfe Street is the Alexandria Academy ⑧, built with the support of George Washington and others. This free school was attended by white children before it became a school for African Americans in the first half of the 19th century.

Cross South Washington Street and turn right. After two blocks you'll come to the Lyceum ⑨, a building inspired by a Doric temple, which was originally a library, then a hospital for Union troops during the Civil War, and now a local history museum. A statue of a Confederate soldier, "Appomattox," stands in the center of the Prince and Washington Streets intersection, marking the spot where

⑯ Gadsby's Tavern, where President Jefferson's inaugural banquet was held

troops left Alexandria to join the Confederate army on May 24, 1861. Turn left on Prince Street and walk two blocks to South Alfred Street. Turn right to see the Friendship Firehouse ⑩ at 107. Turn right on King Street where you'll find colorful shops and restaurants. Turn left on Washington Street. Christ Church ⑪ will be on your left. Wander through the historic cemetery and into the church – this is where every year presidents have come to honor George Washington on his birthday. Continue on Washington Street past Lloyd House ⑫, a Georgian home built in 1796, once a station on the underground railroad. After two blocks turn right on Oronoco Street at the Lee-Fendall House ⑬ (see p161). The house, now a museum, was built by Philip Fendall who then married the sister of "Light Horse" Harry Lee (Robert E. Lee's father and a Revolutionary hero). Across the road at 607 Oronoco Street is Robert E. Lee's boyhood home ⑭ (see p160), which is now closed to the public. Alexandria loves

its dogs and they are all welcome at the Olde Towne School of Dogs on the corner of Oronoco and St. Asaph Streets. Turn right on St. Asaph and cross Princess Street with its cobblestones that were laid in the 1790s. Cross Cameron Street and turn left. A replica of the small house built by George Washington in 1769 is at 508 Cameron Steet ⑮.

Turning right on Royal Street, you'll find Gadsby's Tavern ⑯ (see p160), where Jefferson's inaugural banquet was held. Across the street is the City Hall ⑰. Continue on Cameron Street and cross Fairfax Street. The Bank of Alexandria, the city's oldest bank, established in 1792, stands on the corner. Next door is Carlyle House ⑱ (see p160), a Georgian mansion modeled after the Scottish estate Craigiehall. Go around to the rear to see the gardens. Back on Fairfax Street, continue on King Street and turn left. Enjoy the shop windows for two blocks to The Torpedo Factory on Union Street ⑲ (see p161), a dynamic arts center.

Portrait of Robert E. Lee ⑭

**Key**

• • • Walk route

0 meters 300

0 yards 300

⑲ The Torpedo Factory, with riverview studios, art galleries, and archaeology museum

Waterfalls at Great Falls Park, Virginia ▶

# EXCURSIONS BEYOND WASHINGTON, DC

# BEYOND WASHINGTON, DC

Within a half-day's drive of Washington lies enough history and natural beauty to satisfy the most insatiable sightseer. Alexandria and Williamsburg are a must for history buffs, while Chesapeake Bay and the islands of Chincoteague and Assateague offer a wealth of natural beauty. This area of Virginia and Maryland, along with parts of West Virginia and Pennsylvania, has been at the center of 400 years of turbulent American history.

Founded in 1623, Jamestown was the first permanent English settlement in America. In the 18th century, Williamsburg became the capital of Virginia and the first colony to declare independence from England. Today, Williamsburg is a living museum of the Colonial era.

The cultural influence of Europe is clearly seen in the architecture of this region. The two presidents largely responsible for crafting the character of the early republic lived in Virginia – George Washington at Mount Vernon, and Thomas Jefferson at Monticello. These homes reveal the lives their occupants led, at once imaginative, agrarian, inventive, comfortable – and, like many wealthy landowners, relying on slavery.

Cities and towns throughout the area have attractive historic districts that are a welcome contrast to the modern commercial strips on their outskirts.

Annapolis, for example, is a pleasant Colonial and naval port city. Baltimore also has a diverse charm, combining working-class neighborhoods and Old World character, and the town of Richmond blends the Old South's Victorian gentility with the luxuries of modern life.

Civil War battlefields are spread over the map as far as Gettysburg and tell the war's painful story with monuments, museums, cemeteries, and the very contours of the land itself.

The 105-mile (170-km) Skyline Drive through Shenandoah National Park, situated west of DC, makes the beautiful Blue Ridge Mountains accessible to hikers, cyclists, and drivers alike. To the east of the city, the Chesapeake Bay region attracts sailors and fishermen, as well as seafood lovers who can indulge in the delicious local specialty – blue crabs.

Mount Vernon Bike Trail

◀ Colorful clapboard house in Annapolis, Maryland

# Exploring Beyond Washington, DC

Just minutes outside the bustling center of Washington is a striking and varied area of mountains, plains, and historic towns. To the west are Virginia's Blue Ridge Mountains, the setting for Shenandoah National Park. To the south is the Piedmont, an area of gently rolling hills that supports the vineyards of Virginia's burgeoning wine industry. To the east, the Chesapeake Bay divides Maryland almost in two, and to the south it travels the length of the Virginia coastline. To the north is the big port city of Baltimore, with its pleasant waterfront promenade, shops, museums, and stunning National Aquarium.

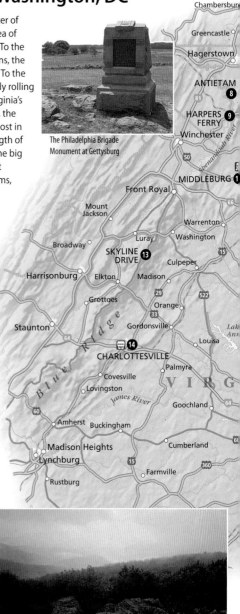

The Philadelphia Brigade Monument at Gettysburg

A re-created fort in Jamestown

## Sights at a Glance

For additional map symbols *see back flap*

The dramatic Bearfence Mountain, part of Shenandoah National Park

## Getting There

Four good interstate highways lace the area: I-95 runs south and north on the eastern side of Virginia; I-81 runs south and north in western Virginia; I-66 heads west from Washington; and I-270 goes toward Frederick. Trains depart from Union Station to most of the main towns, such as Baltimore, Alexandria, Richmond, Williamsburg, and Harpers Ferry, which is also served by the MARC *(see pp214–15)*. Virginia Railway Express goes from Union Station to Alexandria and Fredericksburg. Greyhound buses also travel to most towns.

Boats moored in the Chesapeake Bay area

# ❶ Old Town Alexandria

Old Town Alexandria has kept a special historical flavor, dating back to its incorporation in 1749. It is still a busy seaport and offers many historic sights, as well as shops selling everything from antique hat racks to banana splits. Restaurants are abundant, art thrives here, and the socializing goes on day and night, in and around Market Square.

### Exploring Alexandria

Alexandria's tree-lined streets are filled with elegant, historic buildings and make for a pleasant stroll *(see pp152–3)*. Alternatively, a boat tour offers an attractive prospect as does a leisurely lunch on the patio overlooking the waterfront. Nearby Founder's Park is the perfect place to bask on the grass by the river.

Façade of the elegant Carlyle House

### 🏠 Carlyle House

121 N Fairfax St. **Tel** (703) 549-2997.
**Open** 10am–4pm Tue–Sat, noon–4pm Sun; Last tour at 4pm. **Closed** Jan 1, Thanksgiving, Dec 25. 🖼 📷 ♿ (call in advance.) 📷
**W** nvrpa.org/park/carlyle_house

This elegant Georgian Palladian mansion was built by wealthy Scottish merchant John Carlyle in 1753. The house fell into disrepair in the 19th century but was bought in 1970 by the Northern Virginia Regional Park Authority; it has since been beautifully restored. A guided tour provides fascinating details about 18th-century daily life. One room, known as the "architecture room," has been deliberately left unfinished to show the original construction of the house. The back garden is planted with 18th-century plant species.

### 🏠 Stabler-Leadbeater Apothecary Museum

105 S Fairfax St. **Tel** (703) 746-3852.
**Open** Apr–Oct: 10am–5pm Tue–Sat, 1–5pm Mon, Sun; Nov–Mar: 11am–4pm Wed–Sat, 1–4pm Sun. **Closed** Jan 1, Thanksgiving, Dec 25. 🖼 📷 📷
**W** apothecarymuseum.org

Established in 1792, this family apothecary was in business for 141 years, until 1933. It is now a museum, and the shop's mahogany drawers still contain the potions noted on their labels. Jars containing herbal remedies line the shelves. Huge mortars and pestles and a collection of glass baby bottles are among 8,000 original objects. George Washington was a patron, as was Robert E. Lee, who bought the paint for his Arlington house here.

### 🏛 Gadsby's Tavern Museum

134 N Royal St. **Tel** (703) 838-4242.
**Open** Apr–Oct: 10am–5pm Tue–Sat, 1–5pm Sun, Mon; Nov–Mar: 11am–4pm Wed–Sat, 1–4pm Sun. **Closed** Federal hols. 🖼 📷 📷 📷
**W** alexandriava.gov/gadsbystavern

Dating from 1770, this tavern and the adjoining hotel, owned by John Gadsby, were the Waldorf-Astoria of their day. Now completely restored, they evoke the atmosphere of a hostelry in this busy port.

You can see the dining room with buffet and gaming tables, the bedrooms where travelers reserved not the room but a space in a bed, and the private dining room for the wealthy. The hotel's ballroom, where George and Martha Washington were fêted on his last birthday in 1799, can be rented out. This is also a working restaurant.

Interior of the Old Presbyterian Meeting House

### 🏠 Old Presbyterian Meeting House

323 S Fairfax St. **Tel** (703) 549-6670.
**Open** 8:15am–4:15pm Mon–Fri. 📷 ♿
**W** opmh.org

Memorial services for George Washington were held in this meeting house, founded in 1772. In the churchyard are buried Dr. John Craig, a close friend of Washington, merchant John Carlyle, the Reverend Muir, who officiated at Washington's funeral, and the American Revolution's unknown soldier.

### 🏠 Boyhood Home of Robert E. Lee

607 Oronoco St.
Unfortunately, the boyhood home of Robert E. Lee is currently a private residence and not open to the public. General Lee lived in this 1795 Federal townhouse from the age of 11 until he went to West Point Military Academy. The drawing room was the setting for the marriage of Mary Lee Fitzhugh to Martha Washington's grandson, George Washington Parke Custis.

Bedroom of Robert E. Lee

## Lee-Fendall House Museum

614 Oronoco St. **Tel** (703) 548-1789. **Open** 10am–3pm Wed–Sat, 1–3pm Sun. **Closed** Dec 25–Jan 31 (except 3rd Sun, Lee's birthday celebration). ⬛ once every hour, on the hour. ♿ 🌐 **leefendallhouse.org**

Philip Fendall built this stylish house in 1785, then married the sister of Revolutionary War hero "Light Horse" Harry Lee. Lee descendants lived here until 1904. The house is rich with artifacts from the Revolution to the 1930s Labor Movement.

Lee-Fendall House Museum

## Torpedo Factory Art Center

105 N Union St. **Tel** (703) 838-4565. **Open** 10am–6pm daily (to 9pm Thu). **Closed** Jan 1, Easter, July 4, Thanksgiving, Dec 25. ♿ 🌐 **torpedofactory.org**

Originally a real torpedo factory during World War II, it was converted into an arts center by a partnership between the town and a group of local artists in 1974. Today there is gallery and studio space for over 150 artists to create and exhibit their work. Visitors can watch a potter at his wheel, sculptors, printmakers, and jewelry-makers.

## Christ Church

Cameron & N Washington Sts. **Tel** (703) 549-1450. **Open** 9am–4pm Mon–Sat, 2–4:30pm Sun. **Closed** Jan 1, Thanksgiving, Dec 25. ♿ 🌐 **historicchristchurch.org**

The oldest church in continuous use in the town, this Georgian edifice was completed in 1773. George Washington's square pew is still preserved with his nameplate, as is that of Robert E. Lee.

On the other side of this Episcopalian church, a label reads "William E. Cazenove. Free pew for strangers." In the churchyard 18th-century gravestones wear away under the weather of the centuries.

## Farmers Market

Market Square, King & Fairfax Sts. **Tel** (703) 746-3200. **Open** 5:30–11am Sat.

This market dates back to the city's incorporation in 1749. George Washington, a trustee of the market, regularly sent produce to be sold at the market from his farm at Mount Vernon (see pp162–3). A very pleasant aspect of the market square today is its central fountain. Shoppers can find fresh fruits and vegetables, cut flowers, herbs, baked goods, meats, and crafts.

## VISITORS' CHECKLIST

**Practical Information**
Alexandria. 🗺 143,000.
ℹ Ramsay House Visitor Center, 221 King St (703-746-3300).
🌐 **visitalexandriava.com**

**Transport**
🚉 Union Station, 110 Callahan St.
Ⓜ King Street.

## Alexandria Old Town

**Museums and Galleries**
④ Gadsby's Tavern Museum
⑦ Stabler-Leadbeater Apothecary Museum

**Historic Buildings**
① Boyhood Home of Robert E. Lee
② Lee-Fendall House
⑥ Carlyle House

**Churches**
③ Christ Church
⑨ Old Presbyterian Meeting House

**Markets**
⑤ Farmers Market

**Art Centers**
⑧ Torpedo Factory Art Center

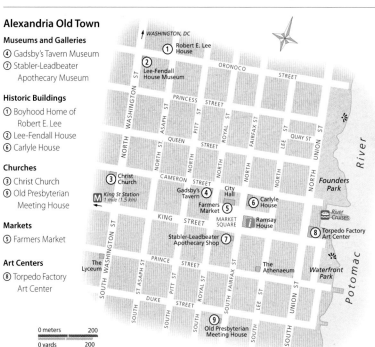

0 meters 200
0 yards 200

For keys to symbols see back flap

# ❷ George Washington's Mount Vernon Estate

This country estate on the Potomac River was George Washington's home for 45 years. Built as a farmhouse by his father, Augustine, Washington made many changes, including adding the cupola and curving colonnades. The house is furnished as it would have been during Washington's presidency (1789–97), and the 500-acre grounds still retain aspects of Washington's farm. The Ford Orientation Center and Donald W. Reynolds Museum offer exhibits about the life of the first US president, including his military and presidential career.

**Kitchen**
Set slightly apart from the main house, the kitchen has been completely restored.

**★ Mansion Tour**
Visitors can see the study and the large dining room, as well as Washington's bedroom and the bed in which he died.

**Slave Quarters**
Washington freed all his slaves in his will. Reconstructed quarters show their living conditions.

**KEY**

① Overseer's House

② Coach House

③ Stable

④ **The Lower Garden** was used for growing vegetables and berries. The boxwood bushes surrounding it were planted in Washington's time.

⑤ **The Bowling Green** was added to the estate by George Washington.

**★ Upper Garden**
The plants in this colorful flower garden are known to have grown here in Washington's time.

**Wharf**
Daytrip boats from central DC bring visitors to this wharf. Potomac cruise boats also stop off here.

**Pioneer Farm**

**VISITORS' CHECKLIST**

**Practical Information**
South end of George Washington Memorial Parkway, Fairfax County, VA. **Tel** (703) 780-2000.
W **mountvernon.org**
Distillery State Route 235 South: **Open** Apr–Oct: daily.
first floor.

**Transport**
M Yellow line to Huntington Station. Fairfax Connector bus 101 to Mount Vernon: call (703) 780-2000. Boat cruises: Apr–Aug: 8am–5pm; Mar, Sep, Oct: 9am–5pm; Nov–Feb: 9am–4pm.

★ **Pioneer Farm**
This exhibit demonstrates farming techniques that were pioneered by George Washington. There is also a replica of his unique 16-sided treading barn, which was created using authentic tools.

**Washington's Tomb**
In his will, Washington requested that a new brick tomb be built for his family at Mount Vernon. Washington died in 1799 but the tomb was not completed until 1831.

# ❸ Gunston Hall

10709 Gunston Road, Mason Neck, VA.
**Tel** (703) 550-9220. **Open** 9:30am–
5pm daily. **Closed** Jan 1, Thanksgiving,
Dec 25. 🅿 📷 🚻 ♿ 
W **gunstonhall.org**

This Georgian house, built in
1755, was the home of George
Mason, author of the 1776
Virginia Declaration of Rights.
Situated 20 miles (32 km) south
of Washington, DC, it is an
exquisite example of careful
historic restoration.

Of particular interest is the
finely carved woodwork in the
entrance hall, the chinoiserie
mantel and fireplace in the
formal dining room, and the
servants' staircase which was
used by the slaves so that they
wouldn't be seen by guests.
Outside are the beautiful
boxwood gardens.

# ❹ Annapolis

Anne Arundel County, MD.
🚇 36,000. 🛈 Annapolis and Anne
Arundel County Conference and
Visitors Bureau, 26 West St. (410)
280-0445. **Open** 9am–5pm.
W **visitannapolis.org**

The capital of Maryland,
Annapolis is the jewel of
Chesapeake Bay. It is defined
by the nautical character that
comes with 17 miles (27 km) of
shoreline and the longtime
presence of the US
Naval Academy.

A walk down Main
Street takes you past
the 200-year-old
Maryland Inn, and the
shops and restaurants,
to the City Dock lined
with boats. It is then a
short walk to the 150-
year- old **US Naval
Academy**. Inside the
visitor center is the
Freedom 7 space
capsule that
carried the first
American, Alan
Shepard, into space. The US
Naval Academy Museum in
Preble Hall is also worth visiting,
especially to see the gallery of
detailed ship models. The
**Maryland State House** is the

The beautiful formal gardens of the William Paca House, in Annapolis

oldest state capitol in
continuous use. Its Old Senate
Chamber is where the
Continental Congress
(delegates from each of the
American colonies) met when
Annapolis was briefly the capital
of the United States in 1783–4.

Annapolis teems with
Colonial-era buildings, most
still in everyday use. The
**William Paca House**, home of
Governor Paca, who signed
the Declaration of Independence, is a fine Georgian
house with an enchanting
garden, both of which have
been lovingly restored. The
**Hammond Harwood House**
has also been restored.
This masterpiece of
Georgian design was
named after the
Hammond and
Harwood families,
both prominent in the
area. Cornhill and
Duke of Gloucester
streets are beautiful
examples of the city's
historic residential
streets.

Many tours are
offered in
Annapolis,
including
walking, bus, and boat tours.
It is particularly enjoyable
to view the city from the
water, be it by sightseeing
boat, chartered schooner,
or even by kayak.

Tiffany window in the Naval
Academy, Annapolis

🏛 **US Naval Academy**
52 King George St. **Tel** (410) 293-8687.
**Open** 9am–5pm daily. Photo ID
needed. **Closed** Jan 1, Thanksgiving,
Dec 25. 📷 W **usna.edu**

🏛 **Maryland State House**
State Circle. **Tel** (410) 974-3400.
**Open** 9am–5pm (call ahead). Photo
ID needed. **Closed** Jan 1, Dec 25. 📷
11am & 3pm. ♿ W **msa.md.gov**

🏛 **William Paca House**
186 Prince George St. **Tel** (410) 990-
4543. **Open** 10am–5pm Mon–Sat,
noon–5pm Sun (weekends only in
winter). **Closed** Jan, Thanksgiving, Dec
24 & 25. 📷 🚻 W **annapolis.org**

🏛 **Hammond Harwood House**
19 Maryland Ave at King George St.
**Tel** (410) 263-4683. **Open** Apr–Oct:
noon–5pm Tue–Sun; Nov–Dec: noon–
4pm Tue–Sun. **Closed** Jan. 📷
W **hammondharwoodhouse.org**

# ❺ Baltimore

Chesapeake Bay, MD. 🚇 785,500.
🛈 Inner Harbor West Wall (410) 837-
4636. Visitor services (877) BALTIMORE.
🚉 🚌 W **baltimore.org**

There is much to do and see in
this pleasant city. A good place to
start is the Inner Harbor, the city's
redeveloped waterfront, with
the harborside complex of shops
and restaurants. The centerpiece
is the **National Aquarium**,
which has many exhibits,
including sharks, a seal pool, and
a dolphin show. The Harbor is
home to the **Maryland Science**

People walking along Baltimore's pleasant Inner Harbor promenade

**Center**, where "do touch" is the rule. The planetarium and an IMAX® theater thrill visitors with images of earth and space.

The **American Visionary Art Museum** has extraordinary works by self-taught artists whose materials range from matchsticks to faux pearls.

Uptown is the **Baltimore Museum of Art**, with its world-renowned collection of modern art, including works by Matisse, Picasso, Degas, and Van Gogh. There is also a large collection of Warhol pieces and two sculpture gardens featuring work by Rodin and Calder. Some galleries will be temporarily closed during a three-year renovation project.

The diversity of art at the **Walters Art Museum**, on Mount Vernon Square, includes pieces by Fabergé and Monet, among others; it is renowned for its ancient Egyptian art.

The Little Italy area is worth a visit for its knock-out Italian restaurants and also for the games of bocce ball (Italian lawn bowling) played around Pratt or Stiles Streets on warm evenings.

### National Aquarium

501 E Pratt St, Pier 3, N side of Inner Harbor. **Tel** (410) 576-3800. **Open** Hours vary. Call ahead or check website for details. **Closed** Thanksgiving, Dec 25. aqua.org

### Maryland Science Center

601 Light St. **Tel** (410) 685-5225. **Open** Hours vary. Call ahead or check website for details. **Closed** Thanksgiving, Dec 25. mdsci.org

### American Visionary Art Museum

800 Key Highway at Inner Harbor. **Tel** (410) 244-1900. **Open** 10am–6pm Tue–Sun. **Closed** Mon, Thanksgiving, Dec 25. avam.org

### Baltimore Museum of Art

N Charles St & 31st St. **Tel** (443) 573-1700. **Open** 10am–5pm Wed–Fri, 11am–6pm Sat & Sun. **Closed** Jan 1, Jul 4, Thanksgiving, Dec 25. artbma.org

### Walters Art Museum

600 N Charles St. **Tel** (410) 547-9000. **Open** 10am–5pm Wed–Sun (8pm 1st Fri of month). **Closed** Jan 1, Memorial Day, Jul 4, Thanksgiving, Dec 24, 25. weekends. thewalters.org

## ❻ Gettysburg National Military Park

1195 Baltimore Pike, Gettysburg, Adams County, PA. **Tel** (717) 334-1124. Park: **Open** 6am–7pm daily (to 10pm Apr–Oct). Visitor Center: **Open** 8am–5pm daily (to 6pm Apr–Oct). **Closed** Jan 1, Thanksgiving, Dec 25. nps.gov/gett

This 6,000-acre park, south of the town of Gettysburg, Pennsylvania, marks the site of the three-

### The Gettysburg Address

The main speaker at the dedication of the National Cemetery in Gettysburg on November 19, 1863 was the orator Edward Everett. President Lincoln had been asked to follow with "a few appropriate remarks." His two-minute, 272-word speech paid tribute to the fallen soldiers, restated his goals for the Civil War, and rephrased the meaning of democracy: "government of the people, by the people, for the people." The speech was inaudible to many, and Lincoln declared it a failure. However, once published, his speech revitalized the North's resolve to preserve the Union. Today it is known to every schoolchild in America.

Abraham Lincoln

day Civil War battle on July 1–3, 1863. It was the bloodiest event ever to take place on American soil, with 51,000 fatalities. A two- or three-hour driving tour begins at the visitor center. The National Cemetery, where Abraham Lincoln gave his Gettysburg Address, is opposite. Other sights include the Eternal Light Peace Memorial.

## ❼ Frederick

Frederick County, MD. 59,000. 19 E Church St (800) 999-3613, (301) 600-4046. **Open** 9am–5pm daily. **Closed** Jan 1, Easter, Thanksgiving, Dec 25. fredericktourism.org

Dating back to the mid-18th century, Frederick's historic center was renovated in the 1970s.

This charming town is a major antique center and home to hundreds of antique dealers. Its shops, galleries, and eateries are all in 18th- and 19th-century settings. Francis Scott Key, author of "The Star Spangled Banner," is buried in Mt. Olivet Cemetery.

The eye-catching architecture of the National Aquarium, Baltimore

## ❽ Antietam National Battlefield

Route 65, 10 miles (16 km) S of Hagerstown, Washington County, MD. **Tel** (301) 432-5124. **Open** Jun–Aug: 8:30am–6pm daily; Sep–May: 8:30am–5pm. **Closed** Jan 1, Thanksgiving, Dec 25. 🅿 🎥 ♿ **W** nps.gov/anti

One of the worst battles of the Civil War was waged here on September 17, 1862. There were 23,000 casualties but no decisive victory.

An observation tower offers a panoramic view of the battlefield. Antietam Creek runs peacefully under the costly Burnside Bridge. General Lee's defeat at Antietam inspired President Lincoln to issue the Emancipation Proclamation. The Visitors' Center movie recreating the battle is excellent.

John Brown's Fort in Harpers Ferry National Historic Park

## ❾ Harpers Ferry

171 Shoreline Dr, off Rte 340, Harpers Ferry, Jefferson County, WV. **Tel** (304) 535-6029. **Open** 8am–5pm daily. **Closed** Jan 1, Thanksgiving, Dec 25. 🅿 🎥 spring–fall. **W** nps.gov/hafe

Nestled at the confluence of the Shenandoah and Potomac rivers in the Blue Ridge Mountains is

Harpers Ferry National Historical Park. The town was named for Robert Harper, a builder from Philadelphia who established a ferry across the Potomac here in 1761. There are stunning views from Maryland Heights to the foot of Shenandoah Street, near abolitionist John Brown's fort. Brown's ill-fated raid in 1859 on the Federal arsenal, established by George Washington, became tinder in igniting the Civil War.

The great importance of the town led to the area being designated a national park in 1944. It has been restored by the National Park Service.

## ❿ Great Falls Park

Georgetown Pike, Great Falls, Fairfax County, VA. **Tel** (703) 285-2965. **Open** daily (closes at dusk). 🅿 🎥 ♿ **W** nps.gov/gwmp/grfa

The first view of the falls, near the visitor center, is breath-taking. The waters of the Poto-mac roar through a gorge of jagged rock over a 76-ft (23-m) drop at the point that divides Virginia's undulating Piedmont from the coastal plain. Only experienced kayakers are per-mitted to take to the turbulent whitewater below, which varies with rainfall upstream.

The park is crisscrossed by 15 miles (24 km) of hiking trails, some showing evidence of the commerce from the early 19th-century Patowmack, America's first canal. Guided nature walks are offered.

Situated just across the river, in Maryland, is the C&O Canal National Historical Park, entry to which is free for visitors to Great Falls Park.

The roaring waterfalls in Great Falls Park

The Red Fox Inn in Middleburg

## ⓫ Middleburg

Route 50, Loudoun County, VA. 🅟 600. 🛈 Visitors' Center, 12 N Madison St. **Tel** (540) 687-8888. **Open** 11am–3pm Mon–Fri, 11am–4pm Sat–Sun. **W** middleburgonline.com

Horse and fox are king in this little piece of England in the Virginia countryside. Middleburg's history began in 1728, with Joseph Chinn's fieldstone tavern on the Ashby's Gap Road, still operating today as the Red Fox Inn. Colonel John S. Mosby and General Jeb Stuart met here to plan Confederate strategy during the Civil War.

The exquisite countryside has thoroughbred horse farms, some opening during the Hunt Country Stable Tour in May.

Foxcroft Road, north of the town, winds past immaculate horse farms. East of Route 50 is **Chrysalis Vineyard and Winery**. On the Plains Road at the west end of town is **Piedmont Vineyards**, and a mile east of Middleburg is **Swedenburg Winery**. All three have tours and tastings.

🍇 **Chrysalis Vineyard**
23876 Champe Ford Rd. **Tel** (540) 687-8222. **Open** 10am–5:30pm daily. **Closed** Jan 1, Thanksgiving, Dec 25. **W** chrysaliswine.com

🍇 **Piedmont Vineyards**
Off Route 626. **Tel** (540) 687-5528. **Open** by appt Mon–Fri, 11am–5pm Sat, Sun. **Closed** Jan 1, Thanksgiving, Dec 24, 25, 31. **W** piedmontwines.com

🍇 **Swedenburg Winery**
23595 Winery Lane. **Tel** (540) 687-5219. **Open** by appt Mon–Thu, 11am–5pm Fri–Sun. **Closed** Jan 1, Thanksgiving, Dec 25. **W** swedenburgwines.com

## ⓬ Steven F. Udvar-Hazy Center

Near Dulles International Airport, intersection of Rtes 28 and 50, Chantilly, VA. **Tel** (703) 572-4118. 🚌 Bus from Dulles International Airport. **Open** 10am–5:30pm daily (to 6:30pm May 25–Sep 3). **Closed** Dec 25. 🚫 **W** nasm.si.edu/udvarhazycenter

This is a must for anyone who would like to view the Space Shuttles "Enterprise" and "Discovery," or who wants to find out about rockets and satellites, or see a rare Boeing B-29 Stratoliner. Opened in 2003 to coincide with the 100th anniversary of the Wright brothers' first powered flight, and named in honor of its major donor, this museum was built to display and also preserve historic aviation and space artifacts. The vast building of over 760,000 sq ft (7,000 sq m) houses exhibit hangars with more than 300 aircraft and spacecraft. Visitors can walk among exhibits and view hanging aircraft from elevated walkways. As well as an education center and Imax® theater, a Wall of Honor offers a permanent memorial to those men and women who contributed to America's space exploration and aviation heritage.

## ⓭ Skyline Drive

Skyline Drive runs along the backbone of the Shenandoah National Park's Blue Ridge Mountains. Originally farmland, the government designated the area a national park in 1926. Deer, wild turkey, bears, and bobcats inhabit the park, and wildflowers, azaleas, and mountain laurel are abundant. The park's many hiking trails and its 75 viewpoints offer stunning natural scenery.

① **Pinnacles Overlook**
The view of Old Rag Mountain with its outcroppings of granite is spectacular.

② **Whiteoak Canyon**
The Whiteoak Canyon Trail passes six waterfalls on its route.

North entrance station

④ **Camp Hoover**
At the end of Mill Prong Trail, this 160-acre resort was President Hoover's weekend retreat until 1933, when he donated it to the Park.

0 kilometers    10
0 miles    10

⑤ **Bearfence Mountain**
Although it is a bit of a climb up this mountain, partly on rock scramble, it is not too difficult, and the reward is a breathtaking 360-degree view of the surrounding landscape.

⑥ **Lewis Mountain**
This awe-inspiring view from Lewis Mountain shows Shenandoah Valley in spring, when the lush scenery is interspersed with beautiful wildflowers.

③ **Big Meadows**
Close to the Visitor Center, this meadow is kept in its centuries-old state. It was probably kept clear by fire from lightning or Indians. Deer can easily be seen here.

### Tips for Drivers

**Starting points:** north at Front Royal, central at Thornton Gap, south at Rockfish Gap.
**Length:** 105 miles (168 km), duration of 3–8 hrs depending on how many stops are taken.
**When to go:** Fall leaf colors draw crowds in mid-October. Wildflowers bloom through spring and summer.
**What it costs:** $15 per car, valid for 7 days ($10 Nov–Feb).

### Key

--- Walk route
▓▓▓▓ Road

For additional map symbols *see back flap*

# ⑭ Charlottesville

Virginia. 🏔 41,000. 🚗 🚌 ℹ️ Visitors Bureau, 610 E Main St; Monticello Visitors Center, Route 20 South. **Tel** (434) 293-6789, (877) 386-1103 (toll free). 🌐 **charlottesville.org**

Charlottesville was Thomas Jefferson's hometown. It is dominated by the University of Virginia, which he founded and designed, and also by his home, **Monticello**.

Jefferson was a Renaissance man: author of the Declaration of Independence, US president, farmer, architect, inventor, and vintner. It took him 40 years to complete Monticello, beginning in 1769. It is now one of the most celebrated houses in the country. The entrance hall doubled as a private museum, and the library held a collection of around 6,700 books.

The grounds include a large terraced vegetable garden where Jefferson grew and experimented with varieties.

The obelisk over Jefferson's grave in the family cemetery lauds him as "Father of the University of Virginia." Tours of the house are available year round.

Vineyards and wineries surround Charlottesville. Michie Tavern, joined to the Virginia Wine Museum, has been restored to its 18th-century appearance, and serves a buffet of typical Southern food.

Montpelier, on a 2,500 acre (1000 ha) site 25 miles (40 km) to the north, was the home of former US president James Madison.

### 🏛 Monticello

Route 53, 3 miles (5 km) SE of Charlottesville. **Tel** (434) 984-9822. **Open** Mar–Nov: 9am–6pm; Dec–Feb: 10am–4pm. **Closed** Dec 25. 🅿️ 📷 ♿ 🏠 🌐 **monticello.org**

# ⑮ Fredericksburg

Virginia. 🏔 22,600. 🚗 🚌 ℹ️ Fredericksburg Visitor Center, 706 Caroline St. **Tel** (800) 678-4748. **Open** 9am–5pm Mon–Sat (to 7pm May–Aug), 11am–5pm Sun. **Closed** Jan 1, Dec 25. 🌐 **visitfred.com**

Fredericksburg's attractions are its historic downtown district, and four Civil War battlefields, including The Wilderness. The Rising Sun Tavern and Hugh

The elegant dining room at Kenmore House

Mercer Apothecary Shop offer living history accounts of life in a town that began as a port on the Rappahannock River. **Kenmore Plantation**, home of George Washington's sister, is famous for its beautiful rooms.

The visitor center offers useful maps as well as horse-and-carriage or trolley tours.

### 🏛 Kenmore Plantation

1201 Washington Ave. **Tel** (540) 373-3381. **Open** Mar–Oct: 10am–5pm daily; Nov, Dec: 10am–4pm daily. **Closed** Jan, Feb, Thanksgiving, Dec 24, 25, 31. 🌐 **kenmore.org**

**George Washington's Ferry Farm**
268 Kings Hwy. **Tel** (540) 370-0732. **Open** as above.

## Monticello, Charlottesville

*Situated in the leafy foothills of the Blue Ridge Mountains, this Palladian masterpiece was built between 1769 and 1809 by Thomas Jefferson.*

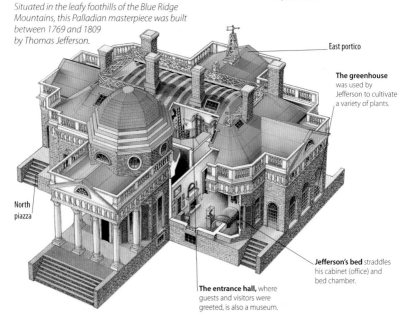

East portico

**The greenhouse** was used by Jefferson to cultivate a variety of plants.

North piazza

**Jefferson's bed** straddles his cabinet (office) and bed chamber.

**The entrance hall,** where guests and visitors were greeted, is also a museum.

# ⑯ Richmond

Virginia. 🚗 202,000. 🚌 🚆
ℹ️ Richmond Metropolitan
Convention and Visitors Bureau,
405 N Third St. **Tel** (804) 783-7450. Toll
free 888-RICHMOND. **Open** 9am–5pm
Mon–Fri. 🆆 visitrichmondva.com

Richmond, the old capital of
the Confederacy (see p21), still
retains an Old South aura.
Bronze images of Civil War
generals punctuate Monument
Avenue. Brownstones and
Victorian houses testify to
this area's postwar prosperity.
    The **Museum of the
Confederacy** contains Civil War
artifacts, including Robert E.
Lee's coat and sword. Another
popular museum is the
fascinating **Science Museum
of Virginia**.
    The Neo-Classical State
Capitol, inside which is the life-
sized Houdon sculpture of
George Washington,
was designed by
Charles Louis
Clérisseau.
    The **Virginia
Museum of Fine Arts**
has a fine collection
of world art and hosts
acclaimed special
exhibitions.

**Statue of Robert E. Lee
in Richmond**

🏛️ **Museum of the Confederacy**
1201 E Clay St. **Tel** (804) 649-1861.
**Open** 10am–5pm daily.
**Closed** Jan 1, Thanksgiving, Dec 25.
🎫 📷 🆆 moc.org

🏛️ **Science Museum of Virginia**
2500 W Broad St. **Tel** (804) 864-1400.
**Open** 9:30am–5pm Tue–Sat,
11:30am–5pm Sun.
**Closed** Thanksgiving, Dec 24 & 25.
🎫 ♿ 🖥️ 📷 🆆 smv.org

🏛️ **Virginia Museum of
Fine Arts**
200 N Boulevard. **Tel** (804) 340-1400.
**Open** 10am–5pm Sat–Wed, 10am–
9pm Thu & Fri. 🆆 vmfa.state.va.us

# ⑰ Chesapeake Bay

🆆 baydreaming.com
ℹ️ Tilghman Island: 🆆 tilghman
island.com

Known as "the land of pleasant
living," Chesapeake Bay offers
historic towns, fishing villages,
bed-and-breakfasts, seafood
restaurants, beaches, wildlife,
and farmland. The Chesapeake
Bay Maritime Museum, in the
town of St. Michael's, depicts
life on the bay, both past and
present. **Tilghman Island**, in
mid Chesapeake, has the last
commercial sailing fleet in
North America and hosts a
seafood festival every June.

# ⑱ Chincoteague and Assateague

Chincoteague, Accomack County, VA.
🚗 4,000. Assateague, Accomack
County, VA and MD (unpopulated).
🆆 nps.gov/asis ℹ️ Chincoteague
Chamber of Commerce, 6733 Maddox
Blvd. (757) 336-6161.
🆆 chincoteaguechamber.com

These sister islands offer
a wealth of natural beauty.
Chincoteague is a town
situated on the
Delmarva
(Delaware,
Maryland and
Virginia) Peninsula.
Assateague is an
unspoiled strip of
nature with an ocean
beach and hiking trails
that wind through
woods and marshes. It is
famously populated by wild
ponies, thought to be
descended from animals grazed
on the island by 17th-century
farmers. The woodlands and salt
marshes of Assateague attract
over 300 species of birds, and in
fall peregrine falcons and snow
geese fly in. Monarch butterflies
migrate here in October. There
are several campgrounds in the
area, and the ocean beach is
ideal for swimming and surf
fishing. **Toms Cove Visitor
Center** and **Chincoteague
Wildlife Refuge Center** can
provide extra information.

ℹ️ **Toms Cove Visitor Center**
**Tel** (757) 336-6577.

ℹ️ **Chincoteague
Wildlife Refuge Center**
**Tel** (757) 336-6122.

# ⑲ Yorktown and Jamestowne

York County, VA, and James City
County, VA. ℹ️ York County Public
Information Office (757) 890-3300.

Established in 1607, Jamestowne was the first permanent
English settlement in America.
It has 1,500 acres of marshland
and forest, threaded with tour
routes. There are ruins of the
original English settlement
and a museum. There is a
recreation of James Fort, full-
scale reproductions of the
ships that brought the first
colonists to America and a
traditional Indian village.
    Yorktown was the site of the
decisive battle of the American
Revolution in 1781. **Colonial
National Historical Park**'s
battlefield tours and exhibits
explain the siege at Yorktown.

🏛️ **Historic Jamestowne**
**Tel** (757) 856-1200.
**Open** 8:30am–4:30pm daily.
**Closed** Jan 1, Dec 25. 🎫 ♿ 📷
🆆 historicjamestowne.org

🌿 **Colonial National
Historical Park**
**Tel** (757) 898-2410. **Open** 9am–5pm
daily. **Closed** Jan 1, Thanksgiving,
Dec 25. 🎫 ♿ 🆆 nps.gov/colo

Historic Jamestowne, a re-creation of Colonial James Fort

# ⑳ Colonial Williamsburg

As Virginia's capital from 1699 to 1780, Williamsburg was the hub of the loyal British colony. After 1780 the town went into decline. Then in 1926, John D. Rockefeller embarked on a massive restoration project. Today, in the midst of the modern-day city, the 18th-century city has been re-created. People in colonial dress reenact the lifestyle of the original townspeople; blacksmiths, silversmiths, and cabinet makers show off their skills while horsedrawn carriages pass through the streets, providing visitors with a fascinating insight into America's past.

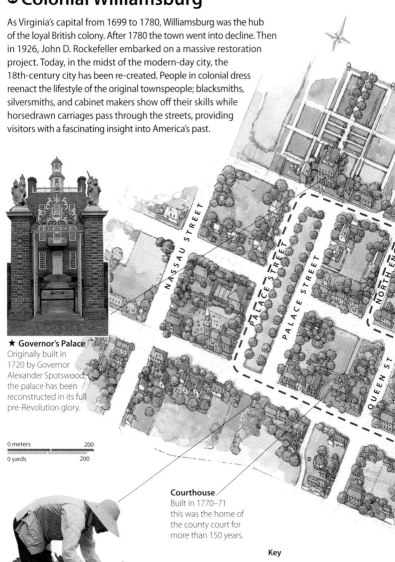

**★ Governor's Palace**
Originally built in 1720 by Governor Alexander Spotswood, the palace has been reconstructed in its full pre-Revolution glory.

0 meters 200
0 yards 200

**Courthouse**
Built in 1770–71 this was the home of the county court for more than 150 years.

**Key**
— Suggested route

**Nursery**
Costumed living-history interpreters work the land in Colonial Williamsburg using replica tools and the same techniques as the original settlers.

**Fifes and Drums Display**
Revolutionary field music is recreated in these colorful parades. Local school children begin learning these instruments aged ten.

### Print Office
This store stocks authentic 18th-century foods, including wine, Virginia ham, and peanuts.

**VISITORS' CHECKLIST**

**Practical Information**
101a Visitor Center Drive, Virginia
🌐 colonialwilliamsburg.com
ℹ️ Colonial Williamsburg:
1-800 447-8679. 🚌 🚙

**Transport**
🚌 🚉 🚐

### Milliner
Owned by Margaret Hunter, the milliner shop stocked a wide range of items. Imported clothes for women and children, jewelry, and toys could all be bought here.

### Raleigh Tavern
The Raleigh was once an important center for social, political and commercial gatherings. The original burned in 1859, but this reproduction has its genuine flavor.

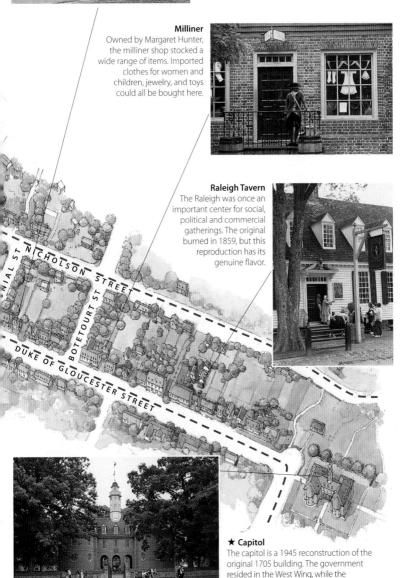

### ★ Capitol
The capitol is a 1945 reconstruction of the original 1705 building. The government resided in the West Wing, while the General Court was in the East Wing.

# TRAVELERS'
# NEEDS

# WHERE TO STAY

If you plan to be visiting the sights in Washington from dawn until midnight, you may simply need a roof over your head and a bed for your weary body. If you intend to take your time and relax, you may want to stay in a hotel with all the amenities: pool, health club, deluxe restaurant, and room service. Washington offers a wide range of accommodations. Generally, hotels that are closer to downtown and the Mall are more expensive, and those in the city suburbs are more affordable. Being a tourist destination as well as a business center, Washington's room rates are the second highest in the United States next to New York City. However, there are bargains to be had, especially during the off season and on weekends. A number of websites (see directory on p175) also offer special deals.

Lobby of the plush Capital Hilton *(see p178)*

## How to Reserve

Many hotels have toll-free numbers for making reservations. It is also often possible to preview the accommodation options on the hotel's website. Weekend rates are often much cheaper than week-day rates.

## Hotel Grading and Facilities

A five-star hotel will offer everything the visitor could wish for. Room service, health facilities, bathrooms with a Jacuzzi, valet parking, and 24-hour maid and butler service are just some of the luxury amenities provided, but at a price. At the opposite end of the spectrum, a one-star hotel will have a television and a telephone in the bedroom but may have shared bathrooms. Hotels of all price ranges are available in the city.

## Discounts

Washington has different "seasons" from other cities. When the cherry blossoms around the Tidal Basin bloom in April, it is impossible to find a

reasonably priced room in the city. Then in June the city is full of school groups taking end-of-the-year trips. Despite often broiling temperatures, families are lured to the capital in the summer. Labor Day in September is very big for tourists as is, of course, the Fourth of July.

However, you can find bargains during the winter months from November through March. Washington is a Monday-through-Friday convention town, so the best prices are on the weekend, often at a fraction of the vacation season, midweek rate.

## Hidden Extras

Beware the hefty 14.5% tax levied on hotels in Washington. Also note that most establishments will invariably charge you extra for parking in the hotel's parking lot. There is no way to escape the tax, but you can shop around for a hotel with free parking. If you have to park your car in a garage, you may have to pay close to $40 per day.

## Chains and Boutique Hotels

Staying at a **Hilton**, **Holiday Inn**, **Hyatt**, or **Marriott** hotel will guarantee a level of service and cleanliness mandated by the chain. An alternative to the large chain hotels are the increasingly popular boutique hotels. **Kimpton Hotels**, a national chain many of whose boutique hotels are housed in historic buildings, has several properties in Washington. These small, unique places all have their own character. The George Hotel on Capitol Hill *(see p176)*, for instance, is sleek and modern. It also houses Bistro Bis *(see p183)*, one of the city's most talked-about restaurants.

Other boutique hotels include the Henley Park *(see p177)*, which has the decor of a British aristocratic home and serves afternoon tea. The Morrison-Clark Inn *(see p177)* in Penn Quarter is a restored mansion filled with Victorian antiques. The Phoenix Park Hotel *(see p176)* on Capitol Hill has an Irish theme and staff – and a pub popular with Irish nationals and Irish-American politicians.

The George, a boutique hotel *(see p176)*

◀ Taking a break at a café, Union Station

## Business Travelers

Washington hotels accommodate the sophisticated communications needs of the business traveler. Wi-Fi is almost universally available in all rooms.

## Bed-and-Breakfasts

Although bed-and-breakfast accommodations are not as popular in the United States as they are in Europe, both American and foreign travelers are increasingly seeking them out as an alternative to the more sterile and expensive hotels.

**Bed-and-Breakfast Accommodations Ltd.** matches visitors with the perfect room in a bed-and-breakfast, an apartment or small hotel, or even a private home. They have 85 properties in the city and suburbs, and charge a one-time booking fee of $10. The online booking service **airbnb.com** offers a wide selection of unfurnished apartments and rooms in private homes at reasonable rates.

Entrance to the Hay-Adams *(see p179)*

## Budget Options

The best value accommodation option for young travelers in Washington is the welcoming **Hosteling International-Washington, DC**. It is located in the center of the city, in an area that is close to all major amenities and sights. Young travelers are advised to be cautious when returning after dark. The rate is around $40 per night for a bunk bed in a single-sex dormitory room.

## Disabled Travelers

Nearly all the large, modern hotels are wheelchair accessible, but the independent hotels and bed-and-breakfasts may not be. Call in advance to ask about stairs, elevators, and door widths if you have special needs.

## Children

Traveling with children may dictate your hotel reservations. There are many hotels, such as Sheraton Suites *(see p179)* and Georgetown Suites *(see p179)*, that have kitchens or kitchenettes or living rooms with sofabeds that provide space and privacy for parents. After walking around the Mall, children may crave a hotel with a pool or a game room. Consider a more expensive room in town rather than a less expensive room in the suburbs. The suburban rates may look appealing until you face a long drive to your hotel during Washington's rush hour.

Some hotels may ban children, but these are few and far between. More often than not hotels will be very accommodating toward young guests.

## Recommended Hotels

Washington has a wide variety of accomodations for every type of traveler. The hotels listed on pages 176–9 are grouped under five categories: Bed-and-Breakfast, Boutique, Business, Family, and Luxury. For those with limited funds, bed-and-breakfast hotels might be a good choice. While there are relatively few within the city, many can be found farther from the Mall and the city center. Accommodations recommended for families may have special children's programs, games rooms, a pool, or suite arrangements that include a kitchen. Business hotels have a full range of amenities, although they are not in the luxury category. Luxury hotels have spas, concierge services, and large restaurants – at a price of more than $400 a night. Finally, boutique hotels are smaller and often have a theme, but perhaps without the splendor of the luxury options.

The historic Jefferson hotel *(see p178)*

Throughout the listings, notable accommodations from each category are highlighted as DK Choice. These hotels offer a special experience, because of their superb amenities, beautiful interiors, excellent restaurant, or a combination of these.

# Where to Stay

## Bed-and-Breakfast

### Capitol Hill

**Maison Orleans** $
*414 5th St SE, 20003*
**Tel** *544-3694*    **Map** 4 F5
W bnblist.com
Housed in a beautiful 1902 Federal
row house, this hotel offers three
rooms furnished with antiques.

**The Carriage House on
Capitol Hill** $$
*3rd and South Carolina Ave SE, 20003*
**Tel** *(877) 893-3233*    **Map** 4 F5
W bedandbreakfastdc.com
This hotel has four rooms with
private bathrooms. A continental
breakfast is served in the lovely
courtyard, weather permitting.

### Penn Quarter

**Hosteling International** $
*1009 11th St NW, 20001*
**Tel** *737-2333*    **Map** 3 C2
W hiwashingtondc.org
Over 200 dorm-style beds are
on offer at this lodging in a
gentrified neighborhood. Most
rooms have shared bathrooms.

### Farther Afield

**Adams Inn** $
*1746 Lanier Place NW, Adams
Morgan, 20009*
**Tel** *745-3600*
W adamsinn.com
Good budget choice in an
upmarket neighborhood. Not all
rooms have their own bathroom.

### DK Choice

**Kalorama Guest House** $
*2700 Cathedral Ave NW,
Woodley Park, 20008*
**Tel** *588-8188*
W kaloramaguesthouse.com

One of the best deals in the city,
this homey, comfortable B&B
has a choice of rooms with or
without a private bathroom. A
delicious breakfast is served, and
home-made chocolate
chip cookies are on offer later in
the day. The beds are very
comfortable, but there are no
TVs in the guest rooms.

**The Swann House** $$
*1808 New Hampshire Ave NW,
Dupont Circle, 20009*
**Tel** *265-4414*    **Map** 2 F1
W swannhouse.com
The rooms in this stunning 19th-
century mansion all have private
bathrooms, some with a Jacuzzi,
and there is a swimming pool.

## Beyond Washington

**Atlantic Hotel** $$
*2 N Main St, Berlin, MD 21811*
**Tel** *(410) 641-3589*
W atlantichotel.com
A small, historic hotel offering
period charm, in a picture-
postcard town close to the
Maryland shore resorts. The
restaurant serves great seafood.

### DK Choice

**Colonial Houses** $$
*136 East Francis St,
Williamsburg, VA 23187*
**Tel** *(800) 447-8679*
W colonialwilliamsburg.com
These 18th-century houses,
right in the grounds of the
reconstructed colonial town
of Williamsburg, are furnished
with period reproductions.
Amenities include private
bathrooms and microwave
ovens, but do not expect the
spacious accommodations of a
modern hotel. Step out of the

**Price Guide**
Prices are based on one night's stay in
high season for a standard double room,
inclusive of service charges and taxes.

| | |
|---|---|
| $ | up to $200 |
| $$ | $200–$400 |
| $$$ | over $400 |

front door to see people in
18th-century costume re-
enacting the former colonial
lifestyle on the unpaved streets.

**Kenmore Inn** $$
*1200 Princess Anne St,
Fredericksburg, VA 22401*
**Tel** *(540) 371-7622*
W kenmoreinn.com
This nine-room establishment has
a gourmet restaurant that serves
an excellent Southern breakfast.

**The Red Fox Inn** $$$
*2 East Washington St,
Middleburg, VA 20117*
**Tel** *(540) 687-6301*
W redfox.com
Antique furnishings, a hearty
breakfast, and a great restaurant
are on offer at this inn set in
Virginia hunt and wine country.

## Boutique

### Capitol Hill

**Liaison** $$
*415 New Jersey Ave NW, 20001*
**Tel** *638-1616*    **Map** 4 E3
W affinia.com/laison
Part of the Affinia chain, Liaison
has an acclaimed restaurant,
rooftop pool, and attentive staff.

**Phoenix Park Hotel** $$
*520 North Capitol St NW, 20001*
**Tel** *(800) 824-5419*    **Map** 4 E3
W phoenixparkhotel.com
A comfortable, historic hotel
with an Irish theme, above the
Dubliner restaurant (see p183).

### DK Choice

**The George Hotel** $$$
*15 East St NW, 20001*
**Tel** *347-4200*    **Map** 4 E3
W hotelgeorge.com
This chic, modern Kimpton
hotel has state-of-the-art
rooms, an exemplary spa, the
excellent Bistro Bis restaurant,
and one of the city's best hotel
bars. With a hip political
theme, it is both eco-friendly
and pet-friendly, and hosts a
complimentary daily wine hour.

Luxurious bedroom in The Swann House, near Dupont Circle

Front entrance of the Hotel
Monaco in Alexandria

## Penn Quarter

**Henley Park Hotel** $$
*926 Massachusetts Ave NW, 20001*
**Tel** 638-5200 **Map** 4 C2
Ⓦ henleypark.com
This English-style hotel serves an
elegant high tea in front of the
lobby fireplace.

**Hotel Monaco** $$$
*700 F St NW, 20004*
**Tel** 628-7277 **Map** 3 C3
Ⓦ monaco-dc.com
A National Historic Landmark
retrofitted into a colorful hotel
with a chic bar and restaurant.

---

### DK Choice

**Morrison-Clark Inn** $$$
*1015 L St NW, 20001*
**Tel** 898-1200 **Map** 3 C2
Ⓦ morrisonclark.com
A well-appointed hotel, built in
1864 and filled with Victorian
antiques. Rooms vary from
standard doubles to two-room
parlor suites with marble
fireplaces and private balconies.
It has a lovely, wide veranda
and an excellent restaurant
serving Southern cuisine.

---

## The White House and Foggy Bottom

**Hotel Lombardy** $$
*2019 Pennsylvania Ave NW, 20002*
**Tel** 828-2600 **Map** 2 E3
Ⓦ hotellombardy.com
A historic hotel with 1920s decor,
but modern amenities. Spacious
rooms and attentive service.

## Georgetown

**The Georgetown Inn** $$
*1310 Wisconsin Ave NW, 20007*
**Tel** 333-8900 **Map** 1 C2
Ⓦ georgetowninn.com
An elegant hotel, but the rooms
overlooking the street can be
noisy. Good restaurant.

## Farther Afield

**The Churchill** $$
*1914 Connecticut Ave NW,
Dupont Circle, 20009*
**Tel** 797-2000 **Map** 2 E1
Ⓦ thechurchillhotel.com
In a Beaux-Arts building, this cozy
hotel has full amenities, including
24-hour room service and a spa.

**Palomar** $$
*2121 P St NW, Dupont Circle, 20037*
**Tel** 448-1801 **Map** 2 E2
Ⓦ hotelpalomar.com
Large rooms and modern
decor feature here. Enjoy
outstanding dining and fine
drinks at Urbana restaurant.

**Tabard Inn** $$
*1739 N St NW, Dupont Circle, 20036*
**Tel** 331-8528 **Map** 2 F2
Ⓦ tabardinn.com
A quaint, romantic inn tucked
into a side street. Meals are served
by a fire. A favorite for brunch.

**Topaz** $$
*1733 N St NW, Dupont Circle, 20036*
**Tel** (800) 775-1202 **Map** 2 F2
Ⓦ topazhotel.com
A Kimpton hotel with a wellness
theme, in-room spa treatments,
and a nightly wine reception.

**Dupont Circle Hotel** $$$
*1500 New Hampshire Ave, Dupont
Circle, 20009*
**Tel** 483-6000 **Map** 2 F2
Ⓦ doylecollection.com
This cosmopolitan hotel, part of
the Irish-owned Doyle Collection,
has a fitness center, attentive
service, and free Wi-Fi.

**Hotel Rouge** $$$
*1315 16th St NW, Dupont Circle, 20036*
**Tel** (800) 738-1202 **Map** 3 B1
Ⓦ rougehotel.com
A hip, Kimpton retreat, decorated
in red. The fashionable Bar Rouge
hosts the Red Hot Happy Hour.

## Beyond Washington

**The Bavarian Inn** $$
*164 Shepherd Grade Rd,
Shepherdstown, WV 25443*
**Tel** (304) 876-2551
Ⓦ bavarianinnwv.com
This romantic country chalet
overlooking the Potomac River has
gas fireplaces and whirlpool baths.

**Boar's Head Inn** $$
*200 Ednam Drive, Charlottesville,
VA 22903*
**Tel** 434-296-2181
Ⓦ boarsheadinn.com
Owned by the University of
Virginia, this lovely inn in a
historic college town has a
golf course and a spa.

**The Ashby Inn** $$$
*692 Federal St, Paris, VA 20130*
**Tel** 540-592-3900
Ⓦ ashbyinn.com
Every room is different at this
18th-century inn. It has a
Michelin-rated restaurant.

**Hotel Monaco** $$$
*480 King St, Alexandria, VA 22314*
**Tel** 703-549-6080
Ⓦ monaco-alexandria.com
A signature Kimpton hotel, with
colorful, lavish decor, located on
historic King Street. Amenities
include a fitness center and a
good restaurant.

**Lorien Hotel and Spa** $$$
*1600 King St, Alexandria, VA 22314*
**Tel** 877-959-7436
Ⓦ lorienhotelandspa.com
This luxury, eco-friendly hotel in
Old Town Alexandria has an
excellent spa.

**Maryland Inn** $$$
*58 State Circle, Annapolis, MD 21401*
**Tel** 410-263-2641
Ⓦ historicinnsofmaryland.com
Three historic houses, full of
antiques, make up this hotel,
which offers 18th-century charm
amid 21st-century comfort.

**Peabody Court Hotel** $$$
*612 Cathedral St, Baltimore, MD 21201*
**Tel** 410-727-7101
Ⓦ peabodycourthotel.com
Expect attentive service in this
old-world hotel. Good
promotional packages.

# Business

## Capitol Hill

**Washington Court Hotel** $$
*525 New Jersey Ave NW, 20001*
**Tel** 628-2100 **Map** 4 E3
Ⓦ washingtoncourthotel.com
This good-value hotel has
in-room Wi-Fi flatscreen TVs, a
restaurant, and offers special deals.

**Hyatt Regency** $$$
*400 New Jersey Ave NW, 20001*
**Tel** 737-1234 **Map** 4 E3
Ⓦ washingtonregency.hyatt.com
This 800-room hotel has full
amenities, including valet
parking and a large restaurant.

## The Mall

**L'Enfant Plaza Hotel** $$$
*480 L'Enfant Plaza SW, 20024*
**Tel** 484-1000 **Map** 4 C4
Ⓦ lenfantplazahotel.com
This pet-friendly hotel has several
dining venues and a pool. Perfect
for visiting the Smithsonian.

**For more information on types of hotels** *see p175*

The comfortable, modern Four Seasons hotel in Georgetown

### Mandarin Oriental $$$
*1330 Maryland Ave SW, 20024*
**Tel** *554-8588*          **Map** 4 C5
Ⓦ mandarinoriental.com
Luxury and convenience at a price. The CityZen restaurant is one of the best in the city.

## Penn Quarter

### Grand Hyatt $$$
*1000 H St NW, 20001*
**Tel** *582-1234*          **Map** 3 C3
Ⓦ grandwashington.hyatt.com
A huge convention hotel with an indoor pool, 32 meeting rooms, and a business center.

### Loews Madison Hotel $$$
*1177 15th St NW, 20005*
**Tel** *862-1600*          **Map** 3 B2
Ⓦ madisonhoteldc.com
This relatively small hotel offers a personal service. Each room has individual decor.

### Renaissance Marriott $$$
*999 9th St NW, 20001*
**Tel** *289-0947*          **Map** 3 C2
Ⓦ marriott.com
Popular for conferences, this hotel's amenities include a fitness center and several dining venues.

### The Westin $$$
*1400 M St NW, 20005*
**Tel** *429-1700*          **Map** 3 B2
Ⓦ westinwashingtondccitycenter.com
A large hotel with great weekend special deals, two full-service restaurants, plus a Starbucks.

## The White House and Foggy Bottom

### Capital Hilton $$$
*1001 16th St NW, 20036*
**Tel** *(885) 271-3621*          **Map** 2 B2
Ⓦ hilton.com
A stylish hotel with a health club and spa services.

**Key to prices** *see p176*

### The Fairmont $$$
*2401 M St NW, 20037*
**Tel** *429-2400*          **Map** 2 E2
Ⓦ fairmont.com
Amenities at The Fairmont include a state-of-the-art fitness center with an indoor pool and two restaurants.

### Renaissance Mayflower $$$
*1127 Connecticut Ave NW, 20036*
**Tel** *347-3000*          **Map** 2 F3
Ⓦ marriotthotels.com
Oozing historic charm, this hotel is a Washington landmark. Formal afternoon tea is served.

### The Westin $$$
*2350 M St NW, 20037*
**Tel** *429-0100*          **Map** 2 E2
Ⓦ westin.com
This hotel features modern decor and a full-service restaurant.

## Georgetown

### DK Choice

**Four Seasons** $$$
*2800 Pennsylvania Ave NW, 20007*
**Tel** *342-0444*          **Map** 2 D3
Ⓦ fourseasons.com
A highly acclaimed hotel overlooking parkland and the Potomac River, the Four Seasons offers large rooms, a great bar, three fitness centers and world-class restaurants, and impeccable service. The modern decor includes over 1,500 artworks scattered across the hotel.

## Farther Afield

### Marriott Wardman Park $$
*2660 Woodley Rd NW, Woodley Park, 20008*
**Tel** *328-2000*
Ⓦ marriott.com
A grand hotel with four dining venues, a pool, and a fitness center. Special packages on offer.

### Omni Shoreham $$
*2500 Calvert St NW, Woodley Park, 20008*
**Tel** *234-0700*
Ⓦ omnihotels.com
A luxurious hotel with 836 rooms, three dining venues, and a pool.

## Beyond Washington

### Hyatt Arlington $$
*1325 Wilson Blvd, Arlington, VA 22209*
**Tel** *703-525-1234*
Ⓦ arlington.hyatt.com
This comfortable hotel offers hypoallergenic rooms on request.

### The Jefferson $$
*101 West Franklin St, Richmond, VA 23220*
**Tel** *804-649-4750*
Ⓦ jeffersonhotel.com
This elegant historic hotel offers excellent Southern hospitality and modern amenities.

### Renaissance Harborplace $$$
*202 East Pratt St, Baltimore, MD 21202*
**Tel** *410-547-1200*
Ⓦ marriott.com
A luxurious hotel offering large rooms and great views of Baltimore harbor. There is an extra fee for parking and Wi-Fi.

### Ritz Carlton $$$
*1250 South Hayes St, Pentagon City, VA 22202*
**Tel** *703-415-5000*
Ⓦ ritzcarlton.com
Plush and convenient, this hotel is minutes from downtown DC and the National Airport, with covered access to the Fashion City mall.

# Family

## Capitol Hill

### Capitol Hill Hotel $$
*200 C St SE, 20003*
**Tel** *543-6000*          **Map** 4 F5
Ⓦ capitolhillhotel.com
This all-suite hotel is pet-friendly and has kitchenettes. Good for long stays.

### Courtyard Marriott $$
*140 L St SE, 20002*
**Tel** *479-0027*          **Map** 4 D2
Ⓦ marriott.com
A stylish hotel, housed in a former bank, with comfortable rooms and an indoor pool. Check the website for special deals.

## The Mall

### Holiday Inn $$
*550 C St SW, 20024*
**Tel** *877-859-5095*          **Map** 4 D5
Ⓦ holidayinn.com
Although a little worn, the Holiday Inn is in a good location and has a full restaurant service. All major attractions can be reached by foot.

## Penn Quarter

### Hotel Harrington $
*436 11th St NW, 20004*
**Tel** *628-8140*          **Map** 3 C3
Ⓦ hotel-harrington.com
This funky hotel offers simple, family rooms at a reasonable price. It has both a full-service and a fast-food restaurant.

## The White House and Foggy Bottom

**One Washington Circle**  $$
*1 Washington Circle NW, 20037*
**Tel** *872-1680*  **Map** 2 E3
W thecirclehotel.com
A modern hotel offering good-sized rooms with kitchenettes.

## Georgetown

**Holiday Inn**  $$
*2101 Wisconsin Ave NW, 20007*
**Tel** *338-4600*  **Map** 1 C1
W holidayinn.com
This standard Holiday Inn has a complimentary shuttle service to the Metro and an outdoor pool.

**Georgetown Suites**  $$$
*1111 30th St NW, 20007*
**Tel** *298-7800*  **Map** 2 D2
W georgetownsuites.com
A hotel with spacious, modern suites and fully equipped kitchens.

## Farther Afield

**Days Inn**  $
*4400 Connecticut Ave NW, Van Ness, 20008*
**Tel** *244-5600*
W daysinn.com
A basic motel with few amenities, but offering a good price.

## Beyond Washington

**Cacapon Resort State Park**  $
*818 Cacapon Lodge Dr, Berkeley Springs, WV 25411*
**Tel** *304-258-1022*
W cacaponresort.com
Cabins, cottages, and bungalows in a state park with nature trails, horseback riding, and swimming.

**Refuge Inn**  $
*7058 Maddox Blvd, Chincoteague, VA 23336*
**Tel** *757-336-5511*
W refugeinn.com
A resort near the Chincoteague Wildlife Refuge, with a pool, fitness center, plus rental bikes to explore the wild seashore.

**Wayside Inn**  $
*7783 Main St, Middletown, VA 22645*
**Tel** *540-869-1797*
W alongthewayside.com
A basic inn with a full-service restaurant nestled in a village in the Shenandoah Valley.

**Hyatt Regency Bethesda**  $$
*7400 Wisconsin Ave, Bethesda, MD 20814*
**Tel** *301-657-01234*
W bethesda.hyatt.com
This hotel has a restaurant, a pool, and hypoallergenic rooms.

**Sheraton Suites**  $$
*801 North Saint Asaph St, Alexandria, VA 22314*
**Tel** *1-703-836-4700*
W starwoodhotels.com
An all-suite hotel with sofa beds, refrigerators, and microwaves.

**Williamsburg Inn**  $$
*136 East Francis St, Wiliamsburg, VA 23187*
**Tel** *757-229-1000*
W colonialwilliamsburg.com
Comfortable, spacious rooms with Regency-style furnishings are on offer at this country inn.

# Luxury
## Penn Quarter

**Willard InterContinental**  $$$
*1401 Pennsylvania Ave NW, 20004*
**Tel** *628-9100*  **Map** 3 B2
W washington.intercontinental.com
This historic hotel has hosted almost every US president.

## The White House and Foggy Bottom

### DK Choice

**Hay-Adams**  $$$
*800 16th St NW, 20006*
**Tel** *638-6600*  **Map** 3 B2
W hayadams.com
A neighbor of the White House, this historic 1920s hotel is elegant and well appointed. The 145 rooms include 21 luxury suites, some with a view of the Washington Monument.

**The Jefferson**  $$$
*1200 16th St NW, 20036*
**Tel** *448-2300*  **Map** 2 F2
W jeffersondc.com
This hotel has a quiet, refined ambience and 96 elegantly appointed rooms.

**St. Regis**  $$$
*923 16th St and K St NW, 20006*
**Tel** *638-2626*  **Map** 3 B2
W starwoodhotels.com
Founded in 1926, this supremely elegant hotel has a sophisticated bar and restaurant.

**W Hotel**  $$$
*515 15th St NW, 20004*
**Tel** *661-2400*  **Map** 3 B3
W wwashingtondc.com
A hip hotel that attracts dance crowds on the weekends. The rooftop bar has stunning views.

## Georgetown

**The Graham Hotel**  $$$
*1075 Thomas Jefferson St NW, 20007*
**Tel** *202-337-0900*  **Map** 2 D3
W thegrahamgeorgetown.com
Luxury in the heart of Georgetown, with spacious, tranquil suites and a roof deck bar.

## Farther Afield

**The Fairfax**  $$$
*2100 Massachusetts Ave NW, Embassy Row, 20008*
**Tel** *293-2100*  **Map** 2 E2
W fairfaxhoteldc.come
This splendid hotel is a favorite among the city's political elite.

**Mansion on O Street**  $$$
*2020 O St NW, Dupont Circle, 20036*
**Tel** *496-2020*  **Map** 2 E2
W omansion.com
A 19th-century mansion with quirky decor. Features hidden rooms and secret passages.

## Beyond Washington

**Inn at Little Washington**  $$
*Middle St and Main St, Little Washington, VA 22747*
**Tel** *540-675-3800*
W theinnatlittlewashington.com
A sumptuous inn with extravagant decor, impeccable service, and a Michelin-starred restaurant.

The elegant dining room in The Jefferson hotel on 1200 16th St NW

**For more information on types of hotels** *see p175*

# WHERE TO EAT AND DRINK

Joseph Alsop, a renowned Washington host of the early 1960s, routinely gave lavish dinner parties in his Georgetown home. When asked why he gave so many parties, Alsop replied that it was because Washington had no good restaurants. Today the capital rivals New York, offering restaurants of every cuisine and price range.

Washington's cosmopolitan population enjoys a wide array of cuisines, from Ethiopian to Vietnamese, with many new styles of "fusion food" in between. The seafood is also superb, freshly caught from the nearby waters of Chesapeake Bay. Crab and shellfish feature regularly on menus, especially in coastal areas outside the city.

Graffiato restaurant *(see p185)*

## Places to Eat

Washington's restaurants are a reflection of its neighborhoods. Adams-Morgan has a mix of ethnic establishments, especially Salvadoran and Ethiopian, and cutting-edge cuisine. Perry's and Cashion's Eat Place *(see p190)* offer inventive fusion food with Asian and French influences, and the crowd is young and hip. An easy walk from the Mall, Washington's compact Chinatown in the Penn Quarter district has both expensive and moderately priced restaurants, such as the Spanish Jaleo *(see p184)*, Italian Graffiato, and Mexican Rosa Mexicana *(see p185)*. Few Asian restaurants have survived the gentrification of this area. Closer to the White House, a few of the old-guard stalwarts remain, including the historic Old Ebbitt Grill *(see p185)*, which specializes in superb regional seafood, and Georgia Brown's *(see p186)*, whose menu features Southern cuisine. Georgetown has a mix of expensive and inexpensive establishments. Good value can be found at Indian and

Vietnamese restaurants. More reasonable places, again mostly ethnic restaurants, are found closer to the Circle. The vortex of 14th Street and U Street has restaurants for a young crowd, including Eatonville, Busboys and Poets, and Marvin *(see p189)*.

All restaurants in Washington are air conditioned and most (except for a few located in historic buildings) are wheelchair accessible.

### Reservations

Reservations may be necessary for popular restaurants; the most fashionable can get booked up weeks in advance. Call ahead if there is somewhere you really want to go. However, walk-in diners are expected in most places. You may be placed on a waiting list and expected to return at the appointed time or wait in the adjacent bar.

### Prices and Paying

Restaurant prices range from the very cheap to the very expensive in Washington. Prices vary according to location, cuisine, and decor. All restaurants take major credit

cards, although street vendors and fast food places may only accept cash. Waiters rely on earnings from tips and a 15–20 percent tip is expected for good service in restaurants. The tip is not automatically added to the bill except in the case of large parties, which may incur an automatic 15 percent gratuity.

Unlike many European cities, the fixed-price meal is uncommon in Washington. Items are usually listed à la carte unless specified in the menu. Diners should expect to spend between $20 and $40 for dinner and a drink, including a tip, at a moderate restaurant. However, Indian, Ethiopian, Chinese, and Vietnamese restaurants are often considerably less expensive. You will generally be charged about 25 percent less for the same meal if you eat at lunchtime rather than in the evening, so visitors on a budget may choose to eat their main meal at lunchtime. Breakfasts are usually under $10 for bacon and eggs with coffee and juice, but some hotels include a free continental breakfast (rolls, coffee, and juice) in the cost of the room.

Chic interiors of Cashion's Eat Place in the Adams-Morgan neighborhood *(see p183)*

Mural on the side of Madam's Organ bar in Adams-Morgan *(see p189)*

## Opening Hours

It is unusual for a restaurant to be open 24 hours, except for those in very large hotels. Restaurants also rarely serve food continuously throughout the day; they usually have a break of several hours after lunch. Most restaurants are open all year (except Thanksgiving and Christmas Day) but a few may be closed on Sunday or Monday. It is best to call in advance. Restaurants often open for dinner between 5pm and 6pm, with the busiest period usually between 7pm and 8pm. The last seating is often at 9pm, and the last customers usually leave by 11pm. Bars are open until 2am. Remember that Metrorail trains stop running at 2am on Friday and Saturday, and at midnight the rest of the week.

## Alcohol

Restaurants are required by law to have a liquor license in order to sell alcohol, so you will notice that some do not offer it. Others may serve beer and wine only but not hard liquor or mixed drinks.

Bars rarely serve food other than perhaps some appetizers. Other restaurants may have a separate bar as well as a dining section. Patrons are not permitted to bring their own drinks to a restaurant. The drinking age in DC, in Maryland, and in Virginia is 21. Restaurateurs can and will ask for proof of age in the form of a driver's license or passport since the penalty for serving alcohol to underage drinkers is severe.

## Smoking

In the Districts of Columbia and Maryland smoking is not permitted in restaurants or any public buildings. The Smoke-free Workplace law came into effect in 2006 and extended to restaurants in 2007. If caught smoking, you could be fined several hundred dollars.

In the District of Virginia smoking is prohibited in many public buildings although some restaurants allow smoking but must have a designated no-smoking area.

## Dress Code

Dress varies from the very casual (shorts, t-shirt, and sneakers) to the very formal. In some restaurants men will not be admitted without a jacket and tie (the maître d' may have spares). But as a general guide, the more expensive the restaurant, the more formal the dress code will be. Some bars also have a very strict dress code, and customers may not be admitted in very casual dress. Respectable but casual attire is acceptable in the majority of establishments.

## What to Eat

Washington's cuisine is immensely multicultural, and you will find French, Chinese, Ethiopian, and Vietnamese restaurants, among others. The hot dog vendors along the Mall offer an alternative to a sit-down meal. Like in many cities in the US, Washington has a proliferation of reasonably priced food trucks that assemble at various places throughout the day, including tourist areas (track them on foodtruckfiesta.com).

## Children

The best indication as to whether children are welcome in a restaurant is the presence of a children's menu or the availability of high chairs. When dining in more formal places with children, it is best to reserve the earliest seating when the restaurant will not be too busy.

## Wheelchair Access

Restaurants are not required to be wheelchair accessible. In general, restaurants in older neighborhoods like Dupont Circle and Adams-Morgan are less likely to accommodate wheelchairs than modern establishments on K Street. The Smithsonian Museum restaurants are all accessible for the disabled.

## Recommended Restaurants

Washington has a broad spectrum of dining choices, ranging from food trucks to haute cuisine establishments. The restaurants listed on pages 183–91 include reasonably priced ethnic options, regional American cuisine, fine dining, and fast food establishments for busy families. From burgers and pizza to Ethiopian *wat* (stew), served on top of *injera* (flatbread), and Chesapeake Bay crab cakes, Washington has a plate for every palate.

Throughout the listings, DK Choice recommendations are highlighted in each area of the city. These offer the traveler a special experience and an insight into Washington, such as excellent local cuisine, dining in a historic building, superb ethnic food, a venue particularly popular with locals, or a fun and unusual setting such as a combination of restaurant, bookstore, and performance space.

Tony and Joe's Seafood Place on the side of Washington harbor *(see p189)*

# The Flavours of Washington, DC

Washington is a place where everyone has an opinion, and culinary preferences are no exception. For some it's a power dining town, where châteaubriand is the dish of choice and "two-martini lunches" are common. Others would point to nearby Chesapeake Bay, and its delectable seafood dishes that appear on many menus. Still others would see the city's vibrant ethnic communities as the key to current food trends. There's no disagreement, however, that DC's dining scene reflects the diversity of the city. As well as drawing on the bountiful harvest of the Atlantic, the city's chefs also make good use of seasonal, local produce from the farms of Maryland and Virginia.

Chef adding finishing touches to a dish at Founding Farmers *(see p186)*

## Power Dining

True to its reputation, the city boasts an impressive collection of "power dining" restaurants, where lobbyists, pundits, and lawyers gather for steaks and cocktails. Slip into a cozy booth at one of these reputed steakhouses and you're likely to spot at least a few members of the United States Congress.

## Global Flavours

As the capital of the United States, Washington has long served as a gathering place for leaders and dignitaries from across the country and around the world, who have brought their own recipes and culinary traditions to the city. Refugees from places such as El Salvador, Ethiopia, and Cambodia have settled in Washington, introducing its well-traveled, globally-minded citizens to unusual flavors and dishes. In such ethnically diverse neighborhoods as Adams-Morgan or Mount Pleasant, it's not unusual to find African, Asian, and South American restaurants standing side by side.

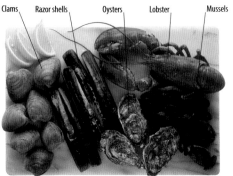

Clams   Razor shells   Oysters   Lobster   Mussels

Mouthwatering selection of Chesapeake Bay seafood

## Washington's Signature Dishes

Maryland crab cakes

The unique nature of the capital makes it difficult to pin down its specialty dishes. The *Washington Post* has made a case for the "half-smoke," a mildly spicy hybrid of hot dog and smoked sausage, smothered in chili and cheese and often sold in sidewalk kiosks. Ben's Chili Bowl *(see p189)*, is the best known purveyor, and a favorite of comedian Bill Cosby. Maryland Blue Crabs are also popular, often appearing as succulent crab cakes or tangy She-Crab Soup. The federal side of the city could be summed up with Senate Navy Bean Soup which has been served every day in the Senate Dining Room for more than 100 years. It's a humble, unassuming dish, and yet it is eaten on a regular basis by some of Washington's most influential residents.

**Senate Navy Bean Soup** uses navy (haricot) beans and ham hock to make a delicious, simple yet hearty soup fit for Senators.

# Where to Eat and Drink

## Capitol Hill

**Banana Café** $
Cuban **Map** 4 F5
500 8th St SE, 20003
**Tel** 543-5906
Enjoy a taste of the Carribean at reasonable prices. Occasional live music.

**Five Guys** $
American **Map** 4 E5
1100 New Jersey Ave SE, 20003
**Tel** 863-0570
This national chain started in Virginia. The burgers are often voted as the best in the country.

**Market Lunch** $
American **Map** F F4
Eastern Market, 225 7th St SE (at C St), 20003
**Tel** 547-8444
Crab cakes, local seafood, and excellent pancakes are served in a no-nonsense setting. Expect lines on weekends.

**Bullfeathers** $$
American **Map** F E5
410 1st St SE, 20003
**Tel** 488-2701
This restaurant-bar popular with local workers is known for its burgers and Trivia Night.

**Cava Mezze** $$
Mediterranean **Map** 4 F5
527 8th St SE, 20003
**Tel** 543-9090 **Closed** Mon
Incredible small plates and outstanding gyros are on offer here. The place is always packed.

**Dubliner** $$
Irish **Map** 4 E3
520 North Capitol St NW, 20001
**Tel** 737-3773
A favorite of Washington's Irish community, Dubliner serves generous helpings of pub food.

**Ethiopic** $$
Ethiopian **Map** 4 F3
401 H St NE, 20002
**Tel** 675-2066
A fresh, friendly addition to the city's Ethiopian culinary scene, with a pleasant dining room that overlooks the buzzing H Street.

**Good Stuff Eatery** $$
American **Map** 4 F5
303 Pennsylvania Ave SE, 20003
**Tel** 543-8222 **Closed** Sun
Great burgers and fries, including the Obama Burger. First Lady Michelle Obama is a patron.

**Sonoma** $$
Italian **Map** 4 F3
223 Pennsylvania Ave SE, 20003
**Tel** 544-8088
Great for sharing a big meal of locally sourced products. Elegant seating downstairs and casual dining upstairs.

**Tortilla Coast** $$
Mexican **Map** 4 F5
329 Pennsylvania Ave SE, 20003
**Tel** 542-6768
A friendly atmosphere and Tex-Mex food are the draw here. Kids will enjoy the burritos, and adults, the frozen margaritas.

### DK Choice

**Tunnicliff's** $$
American **Map** 4 F5
222 7th St, 20003
**Tel** 544-5680
Next to the Eastern Market, Tunnicliff's is a Washington institution – a popular, historic tavern that serves "stick-to-your-ribs" dishes, such as boar stew, and other hearty fare including burgers, quesadillas, and pizzas, as well as many beers on tap. Outdoor dining in summer and cozy indoor seating in winter.

**Price Guide**
Prices are based on a three-course meal per person, including tax, service, and half a bottle of house wine.

$ up to $20
$$ $20–$40
$$$ over $40

**We, the Pizza** $$
Italian **Map** 4 F5
305 Pennsylvania Ave SE, 20003
**Tel** 544-4008 **Closed** Sun
Known for their pizzas cooked in cast-iron pans, which some say are the best in the city. Also serves pasta, salads, and ice-cream.

**Acqua Al 2** $$$
Italian **Map** 4 F5
212 7th St SE, 20003
**Tel** 525-4375 **Closed** Mon
A duplicate of the flagship Acqua Al 2 in Florence, Italy. Pricey and crowded, but offers authentic fare.

**Belga Café** $$$
Belgian **Map** 4 F5
514 8th St SE, 20003
**Tel** 544-0100
A rare Belgian restaurant with a great selection of beer and, of course, mussels.

**Bistro Bis** $$$
French **Map** 4 E3
15 E St NW, 20001
**Tel** 661-2700
Upscale dining in the classy Hotel George Bistro Bis. Excellent duck and lamb dishes, and cream puffs.

**The Monocle** $$$
American **Map** 4 E3
107 D St NE, 20002
**Tel** 546-4488
A solid seafood and steak establishment near the Capitol. It gets crowded when Congress is in session.

**Montmartre** $$$
French **Map** 4 F5
327 7 St, SE 20003
**Tel** 544-1244 **Closed** Mon
A casual neighborhood restaurant right across from Eastern Market, Montmartre is a favorite for brunch.

**Toscana Café** $$$
Italian **Map** 4 F3
601 2nd St NE, 20002
**Tel** 525-2693
This is a small, hole-in-the wall eatery behind Union Station, but it serves authentic Tuscan cuisine. Reservations are needed as seating is limited in the tiny dining room.

Outdoor dining at the Bullfeathers restaurant-bar

**For more information on types of restaurants** see p181

# The Mall

### Atrium Café $
American      **Map** 3 C4
*400 Virginia Ave SW, 20560*
**Tel** 863-7590
Tucked away in L'Enfant Plaza, this tiny deli offers big, inexpensive sandwiches.

### Cascade Café $$
American      **Map** 4 D4
*4th & Constitution Ave NW, 20565*
**Tel** 712-7458
High-class cafeteria food in a stunning setting within the National Gallery of Art.

## DK Choice

### Mitsitam Café $$
American      **Map** 4 D4
*4th St & Independence Ave SW, 20565*
**Tel** 866-868-7774
Probably the most unusual, and one of the best restaurants in DC. Located in the National Museum of the American Indian, this café serves Native American cuisine from many tribes. The menu changes seasonally, but always includes bison and salmon. The Value Meal is a five-tribe sampler that is enough for two to share.

### Pavilion Café $$
American      **Map** 4 D4
*4th St & Constitution Ave NW, 20565*
**Tel** 289-3360
Enjoy sandwiches and salads in the National Gallery's Sculpture Garden. Wine is available too.

### CityZen $$$
American      **Map** 3 C5
*1330 Maryland Ave SW, 20024*
**Tel** 787-6006      **Closed** Sun & Mon
The 3-hour, 6-course tasting menu includes fish, lamb, and vegetarian options.

# Penn Quarter

### Chipotle $
Mexican      **Map** 3 C3
*601 F St NW, 20005*
**Tel** 347-4701
One of the few Mexican chains in the city. Stop here for fresh and cheap giant burritos.

### District of Pi $
Italian      **Map** 3 C3
*901 F St NW, 20004*
**Tel** 393-5484
Choose between the thick-crust "Chicago" or the thin-crust

Entrance of the popular Carmines on 7th Street NW

St. Louis pizza. District of Pi is big, noisy, and popular with families.

### Full Kee $
Chinese      **Map** 4 D3
*509 H St NW, 20001*
**Tel** 371-2233
Inexpensive, authentic Hong Kong-style food at one of the last Chinese restaurants in the area.

### Luke's Lobster $
Seafood      **Map** 3 C3
*624 E St NW, 20004*
**Tel** 347-3355
A tiny, shack-like restaurant serving unmatched lobster rolls.

### Merzi $
Indian      **Map** 3 C3
*415 7th St NW, 20004*
**Tel** 656-3794
Healthy Indian food that is ideal for a fast lunch or a reasonably priced dinner.

### Paul Bakery $
French      **Map** 3 C3
*801 Pennsylvania Ave NW, 20004*
**Tel** 524-4500
The DC branch of a famous French bakery offers takeouts as

well as sit-down brunches. Try the ham and cheese crepe.

### Austin Grill $$
Mexican      **Map** 3 C3
*750 E St NW, 20004*
**Tel** 393-3776
Better than a chain, but not as good, or as expensive, as some of its Penn Quarter competitors. Great for children.

### Carmines $$
Italian      **Map** 3 C3
*425 7th St NW, 20004*
**Tel** 737-7770
The DC branch of the Manhattan classic. Huge, family-style place serving large portions.

### District Chophouse & Brewery $$
American      **Map** 3 C3
*509 7th St 20002*
**Tel** 347-3434
Burgers, giant salads, and huge plates of seafood and beef are served here with handcrafted ales.

## DK Choice

### Jaleo $$
Spanish      **Map** 3 C3
*480 7th St, NW 20004*
**Tel** 628-7949
Owned by chef José Andrés, this restaurant offers some of the best tapas and sangria in the city. The menu changes often, keeping Jaleo fresh and witty, while retaining the old favorites such as spinach with pine nuts and chorizo.

### Oyamel $$
Mexican      **Map** 3 C3
*401 7th St NW, 20004*
**Tel** 628-1005
Enjoy a creative and modern menu at this popular Mexican

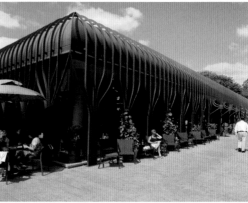

Eye-catching exterior of the Pavilion Café at the National Gallery

joint. The guacamole is made fresh to your taste. Great margaritas.

### Proof $$
American    Map 3 C3
*775 G St NW, 20001*
**Tel** *737-7663*
Chic, contemporary cuisine and an impressive wine list. The entrées are excellent.

### Rasika $$
Indian    Map 4 D3
*633 D St NW, 20004*
**Tel** *637-1222*    **Closed** *Sun*
High-end Indian cuisine served in a modern setting. Regional dishes plus traditional *tandoori* (cooked in a clay oven) and *sigri* (open barbecue).

### Rosa Mexicana $$
Mexican    Map 3 C3
*575 7th St NW, 20004*
**Tel** *783-5522*
Fresh Mexican food served outdoors. Very popular, so expect a wait without a reservation.

### Teaism $$
Japanese    Map 3 C3
*400 8th St NW, 20004*
**Tel** *638-6010*
Choose one of the many varieties of tea as an accompaniment to your delicate Japanese Bento box. The salty oat cookies are a winner.

### Zaytinya $$
Mediterranean    Map 3 C3
*701 9th St NW, 20001*
**Tel** *638-0800*
Another restaurant by renowned chef José Andrés. Stop here for Mediterranean tapas in a glamorous setting.

### Acadiana $$$
American    Map 3 C2
*901 New York Ave NW, 20004*
**Tel** *408-8848*
A classy evocation of New Orleans serving amazing gumbo, turtle soup, and oysters. The brunch is excellent.

### Brasserie Beck $$$
Belgian    Map 3 C2
*1101 K St NW, 20005*
**Tel** *408-1717*
Owned by local star chef, Robert Wiedmaier, Brasserie Beck serves *moules frites* and around 100 types of Belgian beer.

### Fogo de Chao $$$
Brazilian    Map 3 C3
*1101 Pennsylvania Ave NW, 20004*
**Tel** *347-4668*
This all-you-can-eat Brazilian eatery is a meat lover's dream. Just signal the attending

Elegant dining room at Acadiana

waiter to receive an unlimited supply of pork or beef.

### Graffiato $$$
Italian    Map 3 C3
*707 6th St NW, 20004*
**Tel** *289-3600*
Top chef Mike Isabella serves his Italian-American grandmother's recipes. Great pizza and pasta. Patrons rave about the pepperoni sauce.

### Oceanaire $$$
Seafood    Map 3 C3
*1201 F St NW, 20004*
**Tel** *347-2277*
This is a branch of the upscale national chain that specializes in excellent seafood including lobster and crab cakes.

### Old Ebbitt Grill $$$
American    Map 3 B3
*675 15th St NW, 20005*
**Tel** *347-4800*
Stop at Washington DC's oldest saloon for traditional American fare. Old Ebbitt Grill specializes in seafood, including outstanding crab cakes, and steak.

Diners in the Mediterranean-style Zaytinya restaurant

### Poste $$$
French    Map 3 C3
*555 8th St NW, 20004*
**Tel** *783-6060*
Enjoy great cocktails complemented by small plates such as sliders and fries at this bar in the stylish Hotel Monaco.

### The Source $$$
Asian    Map 3 D4
*575 Pennsylvania Ave NW, 20001*
**Tel** *637-6100*
Wolfgang Puck's pricey Asian fusion restaurant is located on the first floor of the Newseum.

## The White House and Foggy Bottom

### City Bites $
American    Map 2 E3
*1800 G St NW, 20006*
**Tel** *289-1820*
This tiny deli whips up delicious sandwiches and salads. Open for breakfast and lunch only.

### Cone E. Island $
American    Map 2 E3
*2000 Pennsylvania Ave NW, 20006*
**Tel** *822-8460*
A loud, tiny ice-cream shop on the campus of George Washington University.

### Johnny Rockets $
American    Map 2 E3
*2000 Pennsylvania Ave NW, 2006*
**Tel** *822-1260*
A franchise of great burger, fries, and shake joints that echo the 1950s.

### Potbelly Sandwich Shop $
American    Map 2 F4
*1701 Pennsylvania Ave, 20004*
**Tel** *775-1450*
Huge sandwiches, and a "skinny" menu with 30 percent fewer calories for the diet-conscious.

**For more information on types of restaurants** *see p181*

Façade of the sprawling Founding Farmers restaurant on Pennsylvania Avenue

### Aroma
Indian                    $$
                     **Map** 3 E3
*1919 I St NW, 20037*
**Tel** *833-4700*          **Closed** *Sun*
*Tandoori, biryani* (a rice-based
dish), and *vindaloo* (a spicy curried
dish) feature on the menu in this
traditional Indian restaurant.

### Bayou
American                  $$
                     **Map** 2 D3
*2519 Pennsylvania Ave NW, 20037*
**Tel** *223-6941*
A casual New Orleans restaurant
with an easy vibe, live music,
and Southern fare.

### Firefly
American                  $$
                     **Map** 3 A1
*1310 New Hampshire Ave NW, 20036*
**Tel** *861-1310*
Comfort food such as *matzoh*
(dumplings) soup and pot
roast can be enjoyed here.
Great brunch.

### McFadden's
Irish                     $$
                     **Map** 2 D3
*2401 Pennsylvania Ave NW, 20037*
**Tel** *223-2338*
One of a chain of Irish-themed
bars that cater to the college
crowd, serving beer and burgers.

Helpful waiting staff at Firefly, a restaurant
serving American comfort food

### One Fish, Two Fish
Asian                     $$
                     **Map** 2 D3
*2423 Pennsylvania Ave NW, 20037*
**Tel** *882-0977*
Reliably good sushi and other
Asian standards such as curries
and pan-fried noodles.

### The Public Bar
American                  $$
                     **Map** 3 F2
*1214 18th St, 20036*
**Tel** *223-2200*
A popular sports bar serving
wings, chips, and burgers. Large
crowds come to watch games.

### Ancora
Italian                   $$$
                     **Map** 2 D3
*600 New Hampshire Ave NW, 20037*
**Tel** *333-1600*
Tucked into the Watergate,
Ancora is chef Robert Kinkead's
take on contemporary Italian
cuisine. Pair it with a night at the
nearby Kennedy Center.

### Blue Duck Tavern
American                  $$$
                     **Map** 2 E3
*1201 24th St NW, 20037*
**Tel** *419-6755*
Consistently rated as one of the
best restaurants in DC, this trendy
spot has a wood-burning oven.
The duck, of course, is a specialty.

### The Bombay Club
Indian                    $$$
                     **Map** 2 F3
*815 Connecticut Ave NW, 20006*
**Tel** *659-3727*
Refined Indian cuisine by the
Rasika group. Fancy setting close
to the White House; one of Bill
Clinton's favorite eateries.

### DK Choice

### Founding Farmers
American                  $$$
                     **Map** 2 F3
*1924 Pennsylvania Ave NW, 20006*
**Tel** *822-8783*
Everything at Founding Farmers
is organic, sustainable, and
made from scratch. The
ingredients are high quality,
seasonal, and locally sourced.
The resolutely American menu
includes Yankee pot roast,
shrimp and grits, and chicken
pot pie. Vegetarians are well-
catered to as well. The delicous
apple pie and red velvet cake
are universal favorites.

### Georgia Brown's
American                  $$$
                     **Map** 3 B3
*950 15th St NW, 20005*
**Tel** *393-4499*
Located near the White House,
serving Lowcountry cuisine to a
clientele that includes high-
powered politicians.

### Marcel's
Belgian                   $$$
                     **Map** 2 D3
*2401 Pennsylvania Ave NW, 20037*
**Tel** *296-1166*
This restaurant has impeccable
service and a great menu. It
offers a free shuttle service to
the Kennedy Center for the
pre-theater crowd.

### Rasika West End
Indian                    $$$
                     **Map** 2 E3
*1190 New Hampshire Ave NW, 20037*
**Tel** *466-2500*
Modern Indian cuisine. The
highly rated menu is rivaled by
the dining room's elegant decor.

### Roof Terrace Restaurant $$$
American             **Map** 2 D3
*2700 F St NW, 20037*
**Tel** *416-8555*          **Closed** *Mon*
A casual eatery on the roof of the
Kennedy Center with skyline
views. Popular with theatergoers.

### Vidalia
American                  $$$
                     **Map** 3 A2
*1990 M St NW, 20036*
**Tel** *659-1990*
A high-end restaurant with
Southern roots. Sweetbreads,
shrimp and grits, duck, and the
Pie Plate are specialties.

**Westend Bistro** $$$
American     Map 2 E3
*1150 22nd St NW, 20037*
**Tel** *974-4900*
A popular restaurant located in the chic Ritz-Carlton hotel. The deceptively simple but sophisticated menu includes *tuna carpaccio* and flat iron steaks.

## Georgetown

**Booeymonger** $
American     Map 1 C2
*3265 Prospect St NW, 20007*
**Tel** *333-4810*
Consistently rated as the best in "cheap eats." Offers great sandwiches, sides, and soups.

**Café Divan** $
Turkish     Map 1 C2
*1834 Wisconsin Ave NW, 20007*
**Tel** *338-1747*
Well-priced Turkish food served in a stylish dining room, or as a takeout. Excellent doner kebabs and meze platter.

**Five Guys** $
American     Map 1 C2
*1335 Wisconsin Ave, 20007*
**Tel** *337-0400*
A franchise of the family-favorite burger chain. Unlimited peanuts, and excellent burgers and fries.

**Johnny Rockets** $
American     Map 2 D2
*3131 M St NW, 20007*
**Tel** *333-7994*
Part of a kitschy 1950s-themed chain that whips up great burgers, fries, and milkshakes.

**ShopHouse Southeast Asian Kitchen** $
Pan-Asian     Map 2 D2
*2805 M St NW, 20007*
**Tel** *627-1958*
Build yourself a satisfying budget meal from rice or noodles, meat or tofu, vegetables, and toppings.

**Sweetgreen** $
American     Map 1 C2
*3333 M St, 20007*
**Tel** *337-9339*
One of a small local chain that serves custom-made salads and superb frozen yogurt.

**Café Bonaparte** $$
French     Map 1 C2
*1522 Wisconsin Ave NW, 20007*
**Tel** *333-8830*
A tiny bistro-bar serving crepes, *croques monsieur* (grilled ham and cheese sandwiches), and classic coffees. Ample choice for brunch or dessert.

**Café La Ruche** $$
French     Map 2 D3
*1039 31st St NW, 20007*
**Tel** *965-2684*
A venerable café with classic bistro cuisine and delectable pastries. Sit on the patio with a coffee.

**Chadwick's** $$
American     Map 1 C3
*3025 K St NW, 20007*
**Tel** *333-2565*
Away from the tourist crowd, this homey restaurant-sports bar has burgers, beers, and sides such as artichoke dip and potato skins.

**Das Ethiopian Cuisine** $$
Ethiopian     Map 2 D2
*1201 28th St NW, 20007*
**Tel** *333-4710*
A range of meat, seafood, and vegetable entrées are on the menu here. Samplers are available for the uninitiated.

**El Centro D.F.** $$
Mexican     Map 2 D2
*1218 Wisconsin Ave NW, 20007*
**Tel** *333-4100*
Outstanding tacos, *carnitas*, and margaritas at the Georgetown branch of this Mexican favorite.

**Kafe Leopold** $$
Austrian     Map 1 C3
*3315 M St NW, 20007*
**Tel** *965-6005*
A beautiful café in a stunning setting near the canal. Artfully prepared small entrées, stellar desserts, and coffee.

### DK Choice

**Martin's Tavern** $$
American     Map 1 C2
*1264 Wisconsin Ave NW, 20007*
**Tel** *333-7370*
This Washington institution has been in the Martin family for four generations. Stop here for comfort food, including oyster stew, welsh rarebit, and burgers. For an

Colorful interior of the Italian restaurant Paolo's

intimate dinner sit in the "dugout" – a cozy space at the rear of the bar. This is where famous politicians have been known to eat and drink, and where JFK proposed to Jackie. Great atmosphere.

**Le Pain Quotidien** $$
French     Map 2 D2
*2815 M St NW, 20007*
**Tel** *315-5420*
A *boulangerie* (bakery) chain that has both takeout and dine-in at communal tables. Great brunch.

**Paolo's** $$
Italian     Map 1 C2
*1303 Wisconsin Ave NW, 20007*
**Tel** *333-7353*
Italian fare made California style. Great for people-watching, especially in the outdoor café.

**Patisserie Poupon** $$
French     Map 1 C2
*1645 Wisconsin Ave NW, 20007*
**Tel** *342-3248*    **Closed** *Mon*
A classic bistro-bakery with light fare including sandwiches, salads, and irresistible desserts. Possibly the best croissants outside of Paris.

Alfresco dining at Kafe Leopold, Georgetown

**For more information on types of restaurants** *see p181*

Patrons enjoying a meal on the patio of Café Milano, Georgetown

**Paul** $$
French    Map 1 C2
*1078 Wisconsin Ave NW, 20007*
**Tel** *524-4630*
An outstanding bakery with a small café serving croissants, sandwiches, and quiches.

**Pizzeria Paradiso** $$
Italian    Map 1 C2
*3282 M St NW, 20007*
**Tel** *337-1245*
Known for its artful thin-crust pizza and plethora of toppings, this pizzeria also has a large beer menu. Always crowded.

**Puro** $$
American    Map 1 C2
*1529 Wisconsin Ave NW, 20007*
**Tel** *787-1937*    **Closed** *Mon*
Nestled among the boutiques in Georgetown, Puro serves salads and tapas, plus Moroccan tea and special coffees.

**Serendipity 3** $$
American    Map 1 C2
*3150 M St NW, 20007*
**Tel** *333-5193*
The DC branch of the venerable New York Serendipity, known for comfort food in huge portions and generous ice-cream sundaes.

The elegant Middleburg Room at 1789, roofed with New England barn siding

**The Tombs** $$
American    Map 1 C2
*1226 36th St NW, 20007*
**Tel** *337-6668*
A hang-out for Georgetown University students, with a menu of sandwiches and salads.

**1789** $$$
American    Map 1 B2
*1226 36th St NW, 20007*
**Tel** *965-1789*
Traditional fine American food and impeccable service. A special-occasion restaurant with prices to match.

**Bandolero** $$$
Mexican    Map 1 C2
*3241 M St NW, 20007*
**Tel** *625-4488*
Chef Mike Isabella whips up modern Mexican cuisine and artisanal cocktails at this big, casual, and fun restaurant.

**Café Milano** $$$
Italian    Map 1 C2
*3251 Prospect St NW, 20007*
**Tel** *333-6183*
One of the best places for celebrity-watching. Fine Italian food as well as lighter fare, such as pizza.

**La Chaumiere** $$$
French    Map 2 D2
*2813 M St NW, 20007*
**Tel** *338-1784*
A charming eatery with a quaint atmosphere; great for a date. Duck, mussels, *escargot*, and rabbit are the specialties.

**Clyde's** $$$
American    Map 1 C2
*3236 M St NW, 20007*
**Tel** *333-9180*
A big, raucous pub with an excellent bar menu including ribs and crab cakes. Brunch lovers rave about the *challah* (yeast-leavened) French toast.

**Filomena** $$$
Italian    Map 1 C3
*1063 Wisconsin Ave NW, 20007*
**Tel** *338-8800*
This family-run restaurant serves food from Abruzzi, central Italy. Its dining room is decorated like a holiday fantasy during Christmas.

**Peacock Café** $$$
American    Map 1 C2
*3251 Prospect St NW, 20007*
**Tel** *625-2740*
A great place for brunch on the patio, especially on a sunny day. The menu includes gluten-free items and there's a juice bar.

**Sea Catch** $$$
American    Map 2 D2
*1054 31st St NW, 20007*
**Tel** *337-8855*    **Closed** *Sun*
Stop here for simple and tasty dishes of fresh, locally caught seafood, including huge lobsters and oysters.

**Sequoia** $$$
American    Map 2 D3
*3000 K St NW, 20007*
**Tel** *944-4200*    **Closed** *Mon*
The best restaurant on the riverfront and a favorite for brunch ($35 fixed price). It boasts a huge patio.

**Tony and Joe's Seafood Place** $$$
American    Map 2 D3
*3000 K St NW, 20007*
**Tel** *944-4545*
Enjoy seafood and salads on the riverfront patio here. Live jazz during the Sunday brunch.

**Unum** $$$
American    Map 2 D2
*2917 M St NW, 20007*
**Tel** *621-6959*
This highly rated restaurant has been dubbed a "small wonder" for its craft beers and seasonal menu of American fare with international influences.

# Farther Afield

### Ben's Chili Bowl $
American
*1213 U St NW, 20009*
**Tel** *667-0909*
Everyone, including Bill Cosby and President Obama, eats at Ben's. Famous for its renowned chili dog and half-smoke.

### BGR The Burger Joint $
American **Map** 2 E1
*1514 Connecticut Ave NW, Dupont Circle, 20036*
**Tel** *387-9338*
Sample fresh, seasonal burgers; the Greek burger with lamb is a favorite. The sweet potato fries are a must.

### Cactus Cantina $
Mexican
*3300 Wisconsin Ave NW, Cleveland Park, 20016*
**Tel** *686-7222*
Huge plates of Tex-Mex food make Cactus Cantina ideal for families. It has a big dining room and a large patio for eating alfresco.

### District 2 $
American
*3238 Wisconsin Ave NW, Cleveland Park, 20016*
**Tel** *362-0362*
A sports bar with great burgers and a half dozen TVs. There's an outdoor patio for alfresco beer.

### Madam's Organ $
American
*2461 18th St NW, Adams Morgan, 20009*
**Tel** *667-5370*
Live music every night, beer, and pub food. This mother-of-all dive bars is in Adams-Morgan – hence the pun.

Tony and Joe's Seafood Place, on the bank of the Potomac

### Pizza Mart $
Italian
*2445 18th St NW, Adams Morgan, 20009*
**Tel** *234-9700*
Known locally as "the big slice" for its mammoth, inexpensive pizza slices. Not the best pizza in town, but reasonable and quick.

### Sweetgreen $
American **Map** 2 E1
*1512 Connecticut Ave NW, Dupont Circle, 20036*
**Tel** *387-9338*
The Dupont Circle branch of a local chain that makes healthy salads. It has both standard and custom dishes for less than $10.

### 2Amys $$
Italian
*3715 Macomb St NW, Cleveland Park, 20016*
**Tel** *885-5700*
Stop here for genuine Italian pizza or unmatched small plates, including deviled eggs, *burrata* (Italian cheese), eggplant confit, and olives.

### Bistro La Bonne $$
French **Map** 3 B1
*1340 U St NW, 20009*
**Tel** *758-3413*
French staples include *steak-frites*, *escargot*, and lots of mussel choices. The bar on the third floor often has happy hour specials.

### DK Choice

### Busboys and Poets $$
American
*2021 14th St, 20009*
**Tel** *387-6138*
A restaurant, bookstore, and performance space that hosts poetry readings, author talks, and improv theater, frequented by a cross-section of locals. The food is excellent too. Popular for brunch, but get here before noon to avoid a packed house.

### Café Deluxe $$
American
*3228 Wisconsin Ave NW, Cleveland Park, 20008*
**Tel** *686-2233*
A bustling tavern and bistro serving comfort food. The service is attentive.

### Café Saint Ex $$
American **Map** 3 B1
*1847 14th St NW, 20009*
**Tel** *265-7839*
Named for the author of *The Little Prince*, this cozy aviation-themed bar/restaurant has impressive bar food and a good brunch menu.

The iconic Ben's Chili Bowl, a Washington institution

### Dino $$
Italian
*3435 Connecticut Ave NW, Cleveland Park, 20008*
**Tel** *686-2966*
Italian *enoteca* (wine shop) with a big heart. Owner Dean Gold makes trips to Italy to add recipes to his repertoire. Excellent wine list.

### Le Diplomate $$
French **Map** 3 B1
*1601 14th St NW, 20009*
**Tel** *332-3333*
A hotspot for the hip, with a retro Parisian decor and feel. Book ahead for dinner.

### Eatonville $$
American
*2121 14th St NW, 20009*
**Tel** *332-9672*
Southern food served with style and wit. The menu features catfish, fried green tomatoes, and po'boys (traditional Louisiana sandwiches). Ice tea is served out of a jar.

### Marvin $$
American
*2007 14th St NW, 20009*
**Tel** *797-7171*
Named after singer and songwriter Marvin Gaye, a DC native, this bistro has a rooftop beer garden and a casual vibe.

### Medium Rare $$
American
*3500 Connecticut Ave NW, Cleveland Park, 20008*
**Tel** *237-1432*
A great place for steak lovers, with a good-value fixed-price menu of steak, fries, salad, and bread. Amazing desserts.

**For more information on types of restaurants** see p181

Outdoor seating at Cashion's Eat Place in Adams Morgan

### One Lounge $$
American          **Map** 3 A1
*1606 20th St NW, 20009*
**Tel** 299-0909
A club-cum-restaurant with music and a happy hour. Serves pizza, tapas and small plates until 1am.

### Perry's Restaurant $$
American
*1811 Columbia Rd NW, Adams Morgan, 20009*
**Tel** 234-6218
The top-floor roof garden at this restaurant offers a fantastic view of Washington. It offers an eclectic menu, but is best known for its Sunday brunch.

### St. Arnold's Mussel Bar $$
Belgian
*3433 Connecticut Ave NW, Cleveland Park, 20008*
**Tel** 621-6434
Mussels of every description, as well as a great choice of Belgian beer, can be found at this bar. Reasonably priced happy hour.

### Ardeo + Bardeo $$$
American
*3311 Connecticut Ave NW, Cleveland Park, 20008*
**Tel** 244-6750
Two side-by-side eateries knocked into one, serving delicious modern American cuisine with Asian and Mediterranean influences. Dine on the romantic rooftop terrace in warm weather.

### BlackSalt $$$
American
*4883 MacArthur Blvd NW, Palisades, 20007*
**Tel** 342-9101
A restaurant specializing in inventive seafood; the corn-encrusted oysters and mussels are particular highlights of the menu.

### Cashion's Eat Place $$$
American
*1819 Columbia Rd NW, Adams Morgan, 20009*
**Tel** 797-1819
Seasonal American cuisine with Mediterranean influences. The menu changes daily and always includes a vegetarian entrée.

### Makoto $$$
Japanese
*4822 MacArthur Blvd NW, Palisades, 20016*
**Tel** 298-6866          **Closed** Mon
The best Japanese restaurant in DC, with a delicious fixed-price chef's menu. Take off your shoes at the threshold and enter Japan.

### Obelisk $$$
Italian          **Map** 3 A1
*2029 P St NW, 20036*
**Tel** 872-1180      **Closed** Sun & Mon
The fixed-price menu includes 10 courses served in a tiny dining room. High-end Italian cuisine.

### Palena $$$
American
*3529 Connecticut Ave NW, Cleveland Park, 20008*
**Tel** 537-9250
This award-winning restaurant serves fancy food, but the cheeseburger with vegetable *frites* is a hands-down favorite.

### Pearl Dive Oyster Palace $$$
Seafood          **Map** 3 B1
*1612 14th St NW, 20009*
**Tel** 986-8778
The waiters here explain the provenance of the oysters, most of which are served raw. Be sure to try the bourbon pecan pie. Trendy and expensive.

### Pulpo $$$
Spanish
*3407 Connecticut Ave NW, Cleveland Park, 20008*
**Tel** 450-6870
A new twist on tapas, including a mini burger trio and roasted squab. There's an all-you-can-eat-and-drink Sunday brunch.

### Restaurant Nora $$$
American          **Map** 2 E1
*2132 Florida Ave NW, Dupont Circle, 20008*
**Tel** 462-5143
America's first certified organic restaurant, supervised by organic food pioneer Nora Poullion. Seasonal dining at its best.

### Ripple $$$
American
*3417 Connecticut Ave NW, Cleveland Park, 20008*
**Tel** 244-7995
The intriguing menu here includes a charcuterie and grilled cheese bar, mushroom *agnolotti* (ravioli), and okra with ricotta.

## Beyond Washington

### The Crab Claw $
American
*304 Burns St, St. Michaels, MD 21663*
**Tel** (410) 745-2900
A popular crab eatery since 1965. The decor is simple, but the fresh seafood and cold beer are superb.

The cozy and inviting Restaurant Nora, America's original organic restaurant

**Key to prices** *see p183*

Michie Tavern, set amid sprawling gardens

### Michie Tavern $
American
*683 Thomas Jefferson Pkwy,*
*Charlottesville, VA 22902*
**Tel** *(434) 977-1234*
The Michie Tavern has been serving traditional American fare for over 200 years. Delicious fried chicken is the speciality.

### Yellow Brick Bank $
American
*201 East German St,*
*Shepherdstown, WV 25443*
**Tel** *(304) 876-2208*  **Closed** *Sun & Mon*
Set in a former bank building, Yellow Brick Bank serves locally sourced food and rich desserts.

### Christiana Campbells $$
American
*101 South Waller St,*
*Williamsburg, VA 23187*
**Tel** *(757) 229-2141*  **Closed** *Sun & Mon*
A colonial tavern that has been serving traditional cuisine since George Washington's time.

### Gadsby's $$
American
*134 North Royal St,*
*Alexandria, VA 22314*
**Tel** *(703) 746-4242*
Food from the Revolution era served in a genuine 18th-century tavern. Martha Washington's apple pie is a winner.

### Mama's on the Half Shell $$
Seafood
*2901 O'Donnell St,*
*Baltimore, MD 21224*
**Tel** *(410) 276-3160*
A neighborhood restaurant with excellent regional seafood. Oysters, crabs, and crab cakes are served in huge portions.

### Mon Ami Gabi $$
French
*7239 Woodmont Ave,*
*Bethesda, MD 20814*
**Tel** *(301) 654-1234*
A French bistro in suburban Maryland with traditional specialties: *steak-frites, bouillabaisse,* and crepes.

### Le Refuge $$
French
*127 North Washington St,*
*Alexandria, VA 22314*
**Tel** *(703) 548-4661*  **Closed** *Sun*
Sample the superb dover sole, frog legs, beef Wellington, and crème brulée at this family-run French restaurant.

### Vermilion $$
American
*1120 King St, Alexandria, VA 22314*
**Tel** *(703) 684-9669*
This restaurant is committed to supporting local farmers and regionally grown produce. Fixed-price "farm table" nights offer a chance to dine with chef Tony Chittum.

### DK Choice

**Inn at Little Washington** $$$
American
*309 Middle St,*
*Little Washington, VA 22747*
**Tel** *(540) 675-3800*
One of America's most famous restaurants. Chef Patrick O'Connell's culinary jewel offers flawless service, and has a refined, seasonal menu. The herbs come from O'Connell's kitchen garden. Do not miss the decadent chocolate Seven Deadly Sins dessert. Dining at this Michelin-starred organic restaurant is a once-in-a-lifetime experience.

### Old Angler's Inn $$$
American
*10801 MacArthur Blvd,*
*Potomac, MD 20854*
**Tel** *(301) 365-2425*  **Closed** *Wed*
This inn, dating from 1860, is next to the C&O Canal. Dine by the fire in winter and on the patio in summer. There's a formal menu for dinner and mussels or burgers for lunch.

### Ray's the Steaks $$$
American
*2300 Wilson Blvd,*
*Arlington, VA 22209*
**Tel** *(703) 841-7297*
Enjoy giant, perfectly cooked steaks in a no-frills setting. Fans also recommend the crab bisque.

### Restaurant Eve $$$
American
*110 South Pitt St,*
*Alexandria, VA 22314*
**Tel** *(703) 706-0450*  **Closed** *Sun*
A culinary showcase for chef Cathal Armstrong. The fixed-price menus in the tasting room are expensive, but the bistro and lounge are more reasonably priced alternatives.

### Willow $$$
American
*4301 North Fairfax Dr,*
*Arlington, VA 22203*
**Tel** *(703) 465-8800*  **Closed** *Sun*
This restaurant serves New American cuisine, including steak, lobster, chicken, and ricotta-stuffed squash blossoms. The desserts are outstanding.

The sunny patio with bay views at The Crab Claw

For more information on types of restaurants *see p181*

# SHOPPING IN WASHINGTON, DC

Washington's vast selection of stores makes shopping in the capital a pleasurable experience. Souvenirs can be found anywhere from fashion boutiques and specialist food stores to museum and gallery gift shops. The many museums on the Mall and around the city sell a wide variety of unusual gifts, reproduction prints, and replica artifacts selected from all over the world. Although the many smart shopping malls and department stores in the DC area can provide hours of shopping, Georgetown offers visitors a far more lively and authentic environment in which to browse. It is a neighborhood packed with fashionable clothing boutiques and endless interesting shops that sell everything from antiques to hair dye, from one-dollar bargains to priceless works of art.

East Hall of the Union Station shopping mall

## Opening Hours

Most department stores, shopping malls, and other centers are open from 10am until 8 or 9pm, Monday through Saturday, and from noon until 6pm on Sunday. Smaller shops and boutiques are generally open from noon until 6pm on Sundays, and from 10 until 6 or 7pm on all other days. Convenience stores such as supermarkets and local grocery stores may open for longer hours. Drugstores (pharmacies) are also often open for extended hours.

## How to Pay

Goods may be paid for in cash, in traveler's checks (in US dollars), or by credit card. VISA and MasterCard are the most popular credit cards in the United States, while American Express is often, but not always, accepted. A tax of 5.75% is added to all purchases at the cash register.

## Sales

Department stores, such as **Macy's** in the Penn Quarter area and **Nordstrom** farther out in Arlington, often hold sales during holiday weekends, including Memorial Day, the 4th of July, Labor Day, and Columbus Day. Check the newspapers for advertisements to find good prices on electronics, jewelry, kitchenwares, shoes, and clothing. White sales (towels and bedlinen) occur in January.

## Museum Shops

All the museums on the Mall have a wide selection of products on sale in their shops. The **National Gallery of Art** sells artwork reproductions, books, art-related games and children's toys, and the **Museum of African Art** offers a range of African textiles, ceramics, basketry, musical instruments, and books. In Penn Quarter, the **Smithsonian American Art Museum** shop has decorative items, books, and original handmade craft pieces.

The **National Museum of American History** shop carries a range of souvenirs such as American crafts, reproductions, and T-shirts, including merchandise inspired by the Star-Spangled Banner, as well as a range of books on American history. They also sell recordings from the 1940s to the 1970s, including Doo Wop, Motown, and Disco, from the Smithsonian Recordings and Smithsonian Folkways labels. Products can be purchased online too.

Also well worth a visit, near the White House, is the shop at the **Decatur House Museum**, home of Stephen Decatur, a naval hero from the War of 1812. It has a collection of items for sale related to Washington's history, art, and architecture.

For a selection of interesting books on architecture, contemporary design, and historic preservation, as well as a range of toys, ties, frames, and gifts, pay a visit to the **National Building Museum** shop at Judiciary Square.

Stalls selling an eclectic range of goods at Eastern Market

People walk past an Urban Outfitters store on M Street, Georgetown

## Malls and Department Stores

There are a few small-scale shopping malls in central Washington. **Union Station**, the beautifully renovated train station in the Capitol Hill area *(see p57)*, houses 130 shops and restaurants on three levels, in a very pleasant environment. There are name-brand stores as well as an extensive collection of specialty shops that sell clothing, gifts, jewelry, crafts, souvenirs, and more.

Two small shopping malls – **Mazza Gallerie** and **Chevy Chase Pavilion** – are located on upper Wisconsin Avenue in the Friendship Heights neighborhood. The metro is convenient, but there is also plenty of parking for cars. Visitors can shop at Bloomingdale's or Lord and Taylor department stores, or the specialty boutiques and name-brand stores.

The larger malls are located in the Maryland and Virginia suburbs. The **Fashion Center at Pentagon City** is easily reached by metro. Discount-hunters should head for the 230 outlets at **Potomac Mills**, situated 30 miles (48 km) south of the city on I-95.

## Galleries, Arts, and Crafts

Visitors will discover a cornucopia of art galleries and crafts shops in three of Washington's neighborhoods – Georgetown, Dupont Circle, and Adams-Morgan. Here visitors can spend a few hours feasting their eyes on the delightful objects on display.

Work by several local artists is on sale in the **Addison/ Ripley Fine Arts**, located in Georgetown. Some of the best pottery can be found in the **Appalachian Spring** shops in Georgetown and at Union Station. **Eastern Market** in Capitol Hill offers a vibrant mix of stalls from antiques to ethnic artifacts, and is best at weekends. Art lovers should browse along 7th Street, NW, between D Street and the Verizon Center. Among the highlights are pieces of sculpture and contemporary art at **Zenith Gallery** for sale from $50 to $50,000. Out of town, in Alexandria, the **Torpedo Factory Art Center** is excellent for lovers of all kinds of arts and crafts.

Torpedo Factory Art Center logo

## Souvenirs

Collectors' items and DC memorabilia are abundant at Political Americana and Made in America, two shops in **Union Station**. The **Old Post Office Pavilion** near Metro Center, is also worth a visit for DC souvenirs. The gift shops in the **Kennedy Center** sell gifts and books about the performing arts and Washington in general. People looking for religious items or unusual souvenirs should try the **Washington National Cathedral** museum and book shop in the basement of the cathedral or the Herb Cottage, a renovated octagonal baptistry in the Cathedral grounds.

## Clothes

Wisconsin Avenue and M Street in Georgetown are home to a wide range of clothing stores. National highstreet chains include **The Gap**, while those seeking something a little more out of the ordinary should visit **Urban Outfitters**, **Intermix**, and **Cusp**. **H & M**, the international discount store, sells clothing for men, women, and children at reasonable prices.

The space formerly known as Georgetown Park, situated on the intersection of Wisconsin Avenue and M Street, maintains street-facing modern shops while its Victorian-style interior is being redeveloped. There are high-end boutiques here as well as branded clothing stores. There is also a great variety of clothes shops to browse in the Friendship Heights neighborhood.

## Food and Wine

On Capitol Hill, you can shop for snacks and fresh produce or sit down for lunch in the bustling food hall of the Eastern Market, which also hosts an open-air farmers' market on Tuesdays.

For something more unusual, tasty, or exotic in the culinary field, there are several delicatessens worth visiting in Washington. In particular, try **Dean & Deluca** in Georgetown, which stocks an excellent selection of gourmet foods and also offers a fine range of American and European wines. While you are there, take the opportunity to sample the food and drinks available in the pleasant on-site café.

The Old Post Office Pavilion

One of many antique centers in Frederick

## Antiques

There are some wonderful hidden treasures to be discovered in the many antique stores scattered throughout Washington. Along Wisconsin Avenue, between P and S streets and also along M and O streets, there are around 20 antique shops. Some specialize in expensive antiques, others in prints, lamps, silverware, perfume bottles, or just interesting knick-knacks.

**Random Harvest** on Wisconsin Avenue carries both upholstered and wooden furniture from the ate 1800s through to the mid-20th century. It also stocks a carefully chosen selection of home accessories, including pillows, mirrors, and lamps.

Adams-Morgan and Dupont Circle are also good neighborhoods for antique hunting. **Brass Knob Architectural Antiques**, on 18th Street, is worth visiting for their range of salvaged curiosities, including clawfoot bathtubs and unusual antique light fixtures. Customers are bound to leave with just the perfect relic for their home, which could be anything from a chandelier to an iron gate.

There is also a number of centers for antiques outside central Washington. Kensington in Maryland and Old Town Alexandria in Virginia are areas rich in antiques. **Studio Antiques** in Alexandria sells all kinds of antiques, such as dolls, china, and silver, but specializes in books. In Frederick, Maryland, there is the enormous **Emporium Antiques**. This paradise for antiques lovers houses over 100 shops that sell everything from huge pieces of furniture through household wares to jewelry.

## Books and Music

Book lovers are spoiled for choice in Washington and will enjoy spending time browsing in the myriad bookstores that can be found in the city.

There are several excellent independent and second-hand bookstores, especially in the Dupont Circle area. In **Kramerbooks & Afterwords Café**, customers can sit with their new purchase while drinking a coffee. There is also a full-service restaurant. **Second Story Books** is DC's biggest second-hand store, which also offers CDs and vinyl, vintage prints and photographs, and other framed ephemera.

Farther north, on Connecticut Avenue, is the **Politics & Prose Bookstore**, a favorite among Washingtonians for its combination of books and coffee. Customers can chat with the knowledgeable staff, browse, or attend a reading. (The Sunday book review section of the *Washington Post* lists readings.) **Busboys and Poets** on 5th Street is a community hub for writers, activists, and thinkers. It combines a bookstore with a restaurant, bar, and performance space where author readings and open-mic poetry nights are held.

## Miscellaneous

The many department stores in and around Washington, such as **Macy's, Nordstrom**, and **Neiman-Marcus**, are well-stocked with good quality household wares from linens to cutlery and crockery. They are also prepared to order any out-of-stock items for their customers.

**Wake Up Little Suzie** sells unusual and unique gifts, such as handmade books, jewelry, and hanging mobiles. Similarly, **Chocolate Moose**, on L Street, is a treasure trove of the unusual and unconventional, including ceramics, chocolates, jewelry, and children's toys, among other things. **Tabletop DC** on 20th Street sells everything from utensils, toys, and jewelry, to placemats, picture frames, and calendars.

Everything in contemporary products for the home, from kitchenware to furniture, can be found at **Crate & Barrel** in Spring Valley. In Georgetown is **Restoration Hardware**, which offers everything from decorative door knobs through gardening supplies and lamps, to old-fashioned toys and the popular, heavy oak Mission furniture that originated in the Arts and Crafts Movement.

A bookstore and café are combined at Kramerbooks & Afterwords Café

# DIRECTORY

## Malls and Department Stores

### Bloomingdale's
5300 Western Ave,
Chevy Chase DC.
**Tel** (202) 774-3700.

### Chevy Chase Pavilion
5335 Wisconsin Ave, NW.
**Tel** (202) 686-5335.

### Fashion Center at Pentagon City
1100 South Hayes St,
Arlington, Virginia.
**Tel** (703) 415-2400.

### Lord & Taylor
5255 Western Ave,
Chevy Chase, MD.
**Tel** (202) 362-9600.

### Macy's Department Store
12th & G St, NW.
**Map** 3 C3.
**Tel** (202) 628-6661.

### Mazza Gallerie Mall
5300 Wisconsin Ave, NW.
**Tel** (202) 966-6114.

### Neiman-Marcus
Mazza Gallerie. **Map** 1 B1.
**Tel** (202) 966-9700.

### Nordstrom
Fashion Center at
Pentagon City.
**Tel** (703) 415-1121.

### Potomac Mills
Woodbridge, VA.
**Tel** (703) 496-9330.

### Union Station Shops
40 Massachusetts Ave,
NE. **Map** 4 E3.
**Tel** (202) 289-1908.

## Galleries, Arts, and Craft

### Addison/Ripley Fine Arts
1670 Wisconsin Ave, NW.
**Map** 1 C2.
**Tel** (202) 338-5180.

### Appalachian Spring
1415 Wisconsin Ave, NW.
**Map** 1 C2.
**Tel** (202) 337-5780.

### Eastern Market
225 7th St, SE.
**Map** 4 F4.
**Tel** (202) 698-5253.

### Torpedo Factory Art Center
105 N. Union St,
Alexandria, VA.
**Tel** (703) 838-4565.

## Antiques

### Brass Knob Architectural Antiques
2311 18th St, NW.
**Map** 3 A1.
**Tel** (202) 332-3370.

### Emporium Antiques
112 E. Patrick St, Frederick,
MD.
**Tel** (301) 662-7099.

### Georgetown Flea Market
Wisconsin Ave, between
S & T Sts, NW.
**Map** 1 C3.

### Random Harvest
1313 Wisconsin Ave, NW.
**Map** 1 C2.
**Tel** (202) 202-5569.

### Studio Antiques
524 N. Washington St,
Alexandria, VA.
**Tel** (703) 548-5188.

## Souvenirs

### Kennedy Center
New Hampshire Ave &
Rock Creek Parkway, NW.
**Map** 2 D4.
**Tel** (202) 467-4600.

### Old Post Office Pavilion
Pennsylvania Ave
& 12th St, NW.
**Map** 3 C3.
**Tel** (202) 289-4224.

### Washington National Cathedral
Massachusetts &
Wisconsin Ave, NW.
**Tel** (202) 537-6200.

## Books and Music

### Busboys and Poets
1025 5th St, NW.
**Map** 4 D3.
**Tel** (202) 789-2227.

### Kramerbooks & Afterwords Café
1517 Connecticut Ave,
NW. **Map** 2 E2.
**Tel** (202) 387-1462.

### Politics & Prose Bookstore
5015 Connecticut Ave,
NW. **Map** 2 E2.
**Tel** (202) 364-1919.

### Second Story Books
2000 P St, NW.
**Map** 1B1.
**Tel** (202) 659-8884.

## Museum Shops

### Decatur House Museum
1610 H St, NW.
**Map** 3 A3.
**Tel** (202) 842-0915.

### National Building Museum
401 F St, NW.
**Map** 4 D3.
*Tel* (202) 272-2448.

### National Gallery of Art
Constitution Ave at
6th St, NW.
**Map** 4 D4.
**Tel** (202) 842-4215.

### National Museum of African Art
950 Independence Ave,
SW. **Map** 3 C4.
**Tel** (202) 633-4600.

### National Museum of American History
The Mall between
12th and 14th Sts, NW.
**Map** 3 B4.
**Tel** (202) 357-1528.

## Clothes

### The Gap
1120 Connecticut Ave,
NW. **Map** 3 A2.
**Tel** (202) 429-0691.

### H & M
Georgetown Park
(Wisconsin Ave and
M St, NW).
**Map** 1 C2.
**Tel** (202) 298-6792.

### Urban Outfitters
3111 M St, NW.
**Map** 1 C2.
**Tel** (202) 342-1012.

## Food and Wine

### Dean & Deluca
3276 M St, NW.
**Map** 1 C2.
**Tel** (202) 342-2500.

## Miscellaneous

### Chocolate Moose
1743 L St, NW.
**Map** 2 F2.
**Tel** (202) 463-0992.

### Crate & Barrel
4820 Massachusetts Ave,
NW. **Tel** (202) 364-6100.

### Restoration Hardware
1222 Wisconsin Ave, NW.
**Map** 1 C2.
**Tel** (202) 625-2771.

### Tabletop DC
1608 20th St, NW.
**Map** 2 E2.
**Tel** (202) 387-7117.

### Wake-Up Little Suzie
3409 Connecticut
Ave, NW.
**Tel** (202) 244-0700.

# ENTERTAINMENT IN WASHINGTON, DC

Visitors to Washington will never be at a loss for entertainment, from flying a kite in the grounds of the Washington Monument to attending a concert at the Kennedy Center. The city's diverse, international community offers a rich array of choices. If you are looking for swing dancing you will find it; you will also hear different beats around town, including salsa, jazz, and rhythm and blues. Outdoor enthusiasts can choose from cycling on the Rock Creek bike path to canoeing on the Potomac River. If you are looking for something less active, take in a film at the Smithsonian. Theater-goers have a wide range of choices, from Shakespeare through highly respected repertory companies to Broadway musicals. No matter what your budget is, you will find something to do. There are more free activities in DC than in any other American city.

## Information Sources

The best places to find inform-ation on plays, movies, and concerts are the *Washington City Paper* and the Weekend section of Friday's edition of the *Washington Post*. Internet users can check out *Style Live*, the entertainment guide on the *Washington Post* website.

The "Where & When" section in the monthly *Washingtonian* magazine also lists events.

## Booking Tickets

Tickets may be bought in advance at box offices, or by phone and through the Internet. Tickets for all events at the **Kennedy Center** can be obtained through **Instant Charge**. Tickets for the Verizon Center, the Jiffy Lube Live, and the Warner Theater can be bought by phone through **Ticketmaster**. For Arena, Lisner Auditorium, Ford's Theatre, Merriweather Post Pavilion, and Woolly Mammoth tickets, contact www.tickets.com.

Auditorium of the Shakespeare Theatre on 7th Street

## Discount Tickets

Most theaters give group discounts, and several offer student and senior discounts for same-day performances. Half-price tickets for seats on the day of the performance may be obtained in person at **Ticketplace**, at 407 7th St, NW, or on their website.

In addition, theaters offer their own special discounts: The Arena sells a limited number of "Hottix," half-price seats, 30 to 90 minutes before the show. The Shakespeare Theatre offers 20 percent off for senior citizens Sunday through Thursday, 50 percent one hour before curtain rise for students, and discounts for all previews. The Kennedy Center has a limited number of half-price tickets available to students, senior citizens, and anyone with permanent disabilities. These go on sale at noon on the day of the performance (some are available before the first performance). Standing-room tickets may be available if a show is sold out.

## Free Events

The daily newspapers provide up-to-date listings of free lectures, concerts, gallery talks, films, book signings, poetry readings, and shows.

Local and international artists offer free performances on the Millennium Stage at the Kennedy Center every evening at 6pm.

The **National Symphony Orchestra** gives a free outdoor concert on the West Lawn of the Capitol on Labor Day and Memorial Day weekends, and on the Fourth of July. In summer, various military bands such as the **United States Marine Band**, the Navy, Air Force or the **US Army Band** give free concerts (contact them direct for details).

From October to June, the **National Gallery of Art** sponsors free Sunday evening concerts at

Façade of the John F. Kennedy Center for the Performing Arts

Courtyard concert in the National Gallery of Art

7pm in the West Garden Court, and also free summer jazz concerts on Friday evenings in the Sculpture Garden. Free lectures and gallery talks are held at the **Library of Congress** and at the National Gallery of Art.

## Open-Air Entertainment

During the summer months at **Wolf Trap Farm Park for the Performing Arts** world-famous performers can be seen on any night. Check their calendar of events and find your favorite form of entertain-ment – opera, jazz, Broadway musical, ballet, folk, or country music. You can bring a picnic to enjoy on the lawn.

On Thursday evenings in summer, the **National Zoo** hosts concerts on Lion Tiger Hill. They start at 6:30pm.

If you are in Washington in June try to catch the **Shakespeare Theatre Free for All** held at the Sidney Harman Hall in Penn Quarter.

The *Washington Post* lists the local fairs and festivals, held every weekend in warm weather. On the first weekend in May, the **Washington National Cathedral** sponsors the Flowermart, a festival featuring an old-fashioned carousel, children's games, crafts, and good food. The **Smithsonian Folklife Festival**, a two-week extravaganza held on the Mall at the end of June and early July, brings together folk artists from around the world. For details of other annual events in the city, see Washington, DC Through The Year *(pp38–41)*.

## Facilities for the Disabled

All the major theaters in Washington are wheelchair accessible. The Kennedy Center publishes a list of its upcoming sign-interpreted, audio-described, and captioned performances. For details of these and information on the venue's other accessibility services, check its website.

Many theaters, including the Kennedy Center, Ford's Theatre, the Shakespeare Theatre, and Arena Stage, have audio enhancement devices, as well as a limited number of signed performances. For the hearing impaired, TTY phone numbers are listed in the Weekend section of the *Washington Post*.

The National Gallery of Art provides assisted listening devices for lectures. Sign-language interpretation is available with three weeks' notice, and a telecommuni-cations device for the deaf (TDD) can be found near the Concourse Sales Shop. For those with limited sight, the theater Arena Stage offers audio description, touch tours of the set, and program books in large print and Braille.

## DIRECTORY

### Information Sources

**Washington City Paper**
w washingtoncitypaper.com

**Washington Post**
w washingtonpost.com

**Washingtonian**
w washingtonian.com

### Booking Tickets

**John F. Kennedy Center for the Performing Arts**
New Hampshire Ave at Rock Creek Parkway, NW.
**Map** 2 D4.
Tickets booked via Instant Charge **Tel** (202) 467-4600 or (800) 444-1324.
w kennedy-center.org

**Ticketmaster**
**Tel** (202) 397-7328.
w ticketmaster.com

**Tickets.com**
**Tel** (800) 955-5566.
w tickets.com

### Discount Tickets

**Ticketplace**
407 7th St, NW.
**Map** 3 D3.
w ticketplace.org

### Free Events

**Library of Congress**
1st St & Independence Ave, SE. **Map** 4 F4.
**Tel** (202) 707-5503.
w loc.gov/concerts

**National Gallery of Art**
Constitution Ave at 6th St, NW. **Map** 4 D4.
**Tel** (202) 737-4215.
w nga.gov

**National Symphony Orchestra**
**Tel** (202) 467-4600.

**US Army Band**
**Tel** (703) 696-3399.
w usarmyband.com

**US Marine Band**
**Tel** (202) 433-4011.
w marineband.usmc.mil

### Open-Air Entertainment

**National Zoo**
3001 Connecticut Ave, NW. **Tel** (202) 633-4800.
w nationalzoo.si.edu

**Shakespeare Theatre Free for All**
Sidney Harman Hall, 610 F St, NW. **Map** 4 D3.
w shakespearetheatre.org

**Smithsonian Folklife Festival**
**Tel** (202) 633-1000.
w festival.si.edu

**Washington National Cathedral**
Massachusetts and Wisconsin Aves, NW.
**Tel** (202) 537-6200.
w nationalcathedral.org

**Wolf Trap Farm Park for the Performing Arts**
1645 Trap Rd, Vienna, VA.
**Tel** (703) 255-1900 (info).
**Tel** (877) 965-3872 (tickets).
w wolftrap.org

# Cultural Events

For an evening out, Washington has much to offer. A seafood dinner on the waterfront followed by a play at Arena Stage, Washington's oldest repertory company; dancing at one of the clubs on U Street; jazz in Georgetown; a late-night coffee bar in Dupont Circle; or opening night at the opera at the Kennedy Center and a nightcap in the West End. Or if you are staying downtown and do not want to venture far from your hotel, see a show at the Warner or the National Theater, where the best of Broadway finds a home.

Dancing to live music at the Kennedy Center

Sign on the façade of the Warner Theatre on 13th Street

## Film and Theater

Independent and foreign-language films, as well as classic revivals, are screened at the state-of-the-art **Landmark's E Street Cinema**. Film festivals are held at the **Kennedy Center**. Museums such as **The National Gallery of Art** show films relating to current exhibitions. **The Library of Congress** offers a free film series of documentaries and films related to the exhibits in the museum, shown in the Mary Pickford Theater. The DC Film Festival is based at the Lincoln Theatre.

National touring theater companies bring shows to the **John F. Kennedy Center for the Performing Arts**, the **Warner**

**Theatre**, and the **National Theatre**. For a more intimate setting, try **Ford's Theatre**. **Arena Stage** has a well-established repertory company. **The Studio** and the **Woolly Mammoth Theatre** produce contemporary works.

**The Shakespeare Theatre** produces works in a modern, elegant setting. For plays performed in Spanish, seek out the **Gala Hispanic Theater**.

## Opera and Classical Music

Based at the Kennedy Center, the **Washington National Opera Company** is often considered one of the capital's crown jewels. Although many performances do sell out, standing room tickets are sometimes available. **The National Symphony Orchestra** performs classical and contemporary works.

A rich variety of chamber ensembles and choral groups perform regularly around the city. **The Washington Performing Arts Society** brings internationally renowned performers to DC.

## Dance

The Kennedy Center offers a magnificent ballet and dance season every year, with sell-out productions from the world's finest companies including the Bolshoi, the American Ballet Theater, the Royal Swedish Ballet, and the Dance Theater of Harlem.

**Dance Place** showcases its own professional modern dance companies, as well as international contemporary dance companies.

If you would prefer to take to the floor yourself, make your way to **Glen Echo Park** where people from ages 7 to 70 enjoy evenings of swing dancing, contra dancing (line dancing), Louisiana Cajun zydeco dancing, and waltzes. The Kennedy Center also occasionally has dancing to live bands.

## Rock, Jazz, and Blues

To see the "biggest names and the hottest newcomers" in jazz, head for the KC Jazz Club at the Kennedy Center. Oscar Brown, Jr., Phil Woods, Ernie Watts, and many more are featured here. You can hear international jazz stars at **Blues Alley** in Georgetown, or visit **Madam's Organ** in Adams-Morgan, home to some of the best R&B in Washington.

If you want to hear big-name rock stars or jazz artists, head to the **Verizon Center** *(see p104)*, the **Merriweather Post Pavilion** in Columbia, Maryland, or the **Jiffy Lube Live** in Manassas, Virginia.

Actors in a play at the highly respected Shakespeare Theatre

## Clubs, Bars, and Cafes

For late night dancing and clubbing, try the U Street neighborhood. Most highly recommended is the **930 Night Club**.

For salsa try the **Rumba Café** in Adams-Morgan. If you fancy a cigar and a martini, then check out **Ozio Martini and Cigar Lounge** downtown. **Black Cat**, with its schedule of both local and international bands, is the place for live independent and alternative music. Billiard parlors are also popular, as are the city's many coffee bars. **Cosi Dupont North** in Dupont Circle serves coffees and cocktails.

## Gay Clubs

Many of the gay bars in DC can be found in the Dupont Circle area. **JR's Bar and Grill** attracts young professionals. **The Fireplace** is popular and stays open late. If you're looking for a good meal, visit **Annie's Paramount Steak House** on 17th Street.

Interior of Rumba Café

# DIRECTORY

## Film and Theatre

**Arena Stage**
1101 6th St, SW.
**Map** 4 D5.
**Tel** (202) 554-9066.
W arenastage.org

**Ford's Theatre**
511 10th St, NW.
**Map** 3 C3.
**Tel** (202) 347-4833.
W fordstheatre.org

**Gala Hispanic Theater**
3333 14th St, NW.
**Tel** (202) 234-7174.

**Kennedy Center**
New Hampshire Ave &
Rock Creek Parkway, NW.
**Map** 2 D4.
**Tel** (202) 467-4600 or
(202) 467-4600.
W kennedy-center.org

**Landmark's
E Street Cinema**
Lincoln Square Building
at 555 11th St, NW.
**Map** 3 C3.
**Tel** (202) 783-9494.
W landmarktheatres.
com

**Library of Congress**
Mary Pickford Theater,
Madison Building,
101 Independence Ave, SE.
**Map** 4 E4.
**Tel** (202) 707-5677.
W loc.gov

**National
Gallery of Art**
Constitution Ave at
6th St, NW.
**Map** 4 D3.
**Tel** (202) 737-4215.
W nga.org

**National Theatre**
1321 Pennsylvania Ave,
NW. **Map** 3 B3.
**Tel** (202) 628-6161.
W nationaltheatre.org

**Shakespeare Theatre**
450 7th St, NW.
**Map** 3 C3.
**Tel** (202) 547-1122.
W shakespeare
theatre.org

**Signature Theatre**
4200 Campbell Ave,
Springfield, VA.
**Tel** (703) 820-9771.
W sig-online.com

**The Studio Theatre**
1501 14th St, NW.
**Map** 3 B1.
**Tel** (202) 332-3300.
W studiotheatre.org

**Warner Theatre**
13th St (between E and F
Sts), NW. **Map** 3 C3.
**Tel** (202) 783-4000.
W warnertheatre.com

**Woolly
Mammoth Theatre**
641 D St, NW.
**Map** 3 C3.
**Tel** (202) 393-3939.
W woollymammoth.net

## Opera and
Classical Music

**National Symphony
Orchestra**
**Tel** (202) 467-4600.

**Washington
Performing
Arts Society**
**Tel** (202) 785-9727.
W wpas.org

## Dance

**Dance Place**
3225 8th St, NE.
**Tel** (202) 269-1600.

**Glen Echo Park**
Spanish Ballroom,
7300 MacArthur Blvd,
Glen Echo, MD.
**Tel** (202) 634-2222.

## Rock, Jazz,
and Blues

**Blues Alley**
1069 Wisconsin Ave, NW.
**Map** 1 C3.
**Tel** (202) 337-4141.

**Jiffy Lube Live**
7800 Cellar Door Drive,
Bristow, VA.
**Tel** (703) 754-6400.
W nissanpavilion
online.com

**Madam's
Organ**
2461 18th St, NW.
**Map** 2 F1.
**Tel** (202) 667-5370.

**Merriweather
Post Pavilion**
Columbia, MD.
**Tel** (410) 715-5550.
W merriweather
music.com

## Clubs, Bars,
and Cafés

**9:30 Night Club**
815 V St, NW.
**Tel** (202) 265-0930.
W 930.com

**Black Cat**
1811 14th St, NW.
**Map** 3 B3.
**Tel** (202) 667-7960.

**Cosi Dupont
North**
1647 20th St, NW.
**Map** 3 A1.
**Tel** (202) 332-6364.

**Ozio Martini and
Cigar Lounge**
1813 M St, NW.
**Map** 3 A1.
**Tel** (202) 822-6000.

**Rumba Café**
2443 18th St, NW.
**Tel** (202) 588-5501.
W rumbacafe.com

## Gay Clubs

**Annie's
Paramount
Steak House**
1609 17th St, NW.
**Map** 2 F2.
**Tel** (202) 232-0395.

**The Fireplace**
2161 P St, NW.
**Map** 2 E2.
**Tel** (202) 293-1293.

**JR's Bar
and Grill**
1519 17th St, NW.
**Map** 2 F2.
**Tel** (202) 328-0090.

# Sports and Outdoor Activities

Washingtonians are known for putting in long hours – whether on the floor of the Senate, the office of a federal agency, or in a newsroom. They compensate, however, by taking their leisure hours very seriously by rooting for their favorite teams or spending as much time as possible outdoors. You can join in the fun at the Nationals Park Stadium or the Verizon Center, both of which attract hordes of fans. You can meet joggers, cyclists, and in-line skaters on the Mall and around the monuments.

## Spectator Sports

Fans of the NHL Capitals (National Hockey League), the NBA Wizards (National Basketball Association), and the WNBA Mystics (Women's National Basketball Association) should purchase tickets at the **Verizon Center**, an impressive sports arena that opened in 1997 and has helped revitalize the downtown area.

Depending on the season, you might also see Disney on Ice, the Harlem Globetrotters, or the Ringling Brothers Circus. Visit the Verizon's National Sports Gallery, which houses sports memorabilia and interactive sports games. There is plenty to eat at the Verizon Center, but you may prefer to slip out to one of the restaurants in Chinatown, which surrounds the center.

If you are not a season-pass holder, it is very difficult to get a ticket to a Washington Redskins game at the **FedEx Field** stadium, but you can always watch the game from one of Washington's popular sports

Redskins team member

bars. The DC United soccer team plays at the **RFK Stadium**. College sports are also very popular in DC – you will find Washingtonians cheering either for the **Georgetown Hoyas** or the **Maryland Terrapins**. Baseball fans lend their support to the Washington Nationals at **Nationals Park Stadium** in the southeast of the city.

## Fishing and Boating

From April to October, to fish or boat on the Potomac River, head to **Fletcher's Boat House** at Canal and Reservoir Roads. You will need to obtain a permit if you are between 16 and 64, which lasts for a year but does not cost much. You can fish from the riverbank or rent a row-boat, canoe or kayak, which are available by the hour or the day.

In Georgetown there are boats for rent at **Thompson's Boat Center** and **Jack's Boat House**. Fletcher's sells snacks; if you go to Thompson's or Jack's there are cafés and restaurants along the waterfront.

Cyclists enjoying the fine weather outdoors in DC

## Cycling

Rock Creek Park is one of Washington's greatest treasures and offers amazing respite from busy city life. Closed to traffic on weekends, it is a great place for cycling. Another popular trail is the Capital Crescent, which starts on the C&O Canal towpath in Georgetown and runs to Maryland.

One of the more beautiful bike trails in the area will take you 16 miles (26 km) to Mount Vernon. Bikes can be rented at Fletcher's Boat House, Thompson's Boat Center, **Bike and Roll**, or **Big Wheels** in Georgetown. For maps or trail information call or write to the **Washington Area Bicyclist Association**, or consult one of the bike rental shops in the city.

## Tennis, Golf, and Horseback Riding

Many neighborhood parks have outdoor tennis courts, available on a first-come, first-served basis. Two public clubs in the city accept reservations: **East Potomac Tennis Center** at Hains Point, and the **Washington Tennis Center**. Each has outdoor and indoor courts.

If you want to take in views of the monuments while walking the golf fairways, go to the **East Potomac Golf Course & Driving Range**. (There is an 18-hole miniature golf course here as well.) Two other courses are open to the public: **Langston Golf Course** on the Anacostia

RFK Stadium, a major sports and entertainment venue

River and **Rock Creek Golf Course**, tucked into Rock Creek Park. You will also find **Rock Creek Park Horse Center**, where you can make reservations for a guided trail ride.

## Exploring Nature

For an amazing array of trees and plants, visit the **National Arboretum** *(see p146)*, which covers 444 acres in northeast Washington. There is something interesting to see all year round in the arboretum. Special displays, such as the National Bonsai Collection of miniature plants, can be enjoyed at any time of year. To catch the best of the flowering shrubs, the beautiful camellias and magnolias flower in late March through early April, and the stunning, rich colors of the azaleas, rhododendron, and dogwood appear from late April through early May. There is a 1,600-ft (490-m) long "touch and see trail" at the garden for visually impaired visitors. An

The beautiful and tranquil grounds of the National Arboretum

alternative to the arboretum is **Kenilworth Park and Aquatic Gardens** *(see p146)*, which has ponds with more than 100,000 water lilies, lotuses, and other plants. It is a good idea to plan a trip early in the day when the blooms are open and before the sun gets too hot. Frogs and turtles can be seen regularly along the footpaths around the ponds. Park naturalists conduct

nature walks around the gardens on summer weekends.

One of the most enjoyable ways to spend time outdoors is with a picnic in the park. Visit **Dumbarton Oaks Park** in Georgetown when the wildflowers are in bloom, or visit **Montrose Park**, right next door to Dumbarton Oaks, where you can enjoy the variety of birds and the boxwood maze.

## DIRECTORY

### Spectator Sports

**FedEx Field**
Arena Drive,
Landover, MD.
**Tel** (301) 276-6000.
W redskins.com

**Georgetown Hoyas**
**Tel** (202) 687-4692.
W guhoyas.com

**Maryland Terrapins**
**Tel** (800) 462-8377.
W umterps.com

**Nationals Park Stadium**
1500 South Capitol St, SE.
**Tel** (202) 675-6287.

**RFK Stadium**
2400 East Capitol St, SE.
**Tel** (202) 587-5000.

**Verizon Center**
601 F St, NW.
**Map** 4 D3.
**Tel** (202) 628-3200.

### Fishing and Boating

**Fletcher's Boat House**
4940 Canal Rd, NW.
**Map** 1 A2.
**Tel** (202) 244-0461.

**Jack's Boat House**
3500 K St, NW.
**Map** 2 D2. **Tel** (202) 337-9642.

**Thompson Boat Center**
Rock Creek Parkway &
Virginia Ave, NW. **Map** 2
D3. **Tel** (202) 333-9543.
W thompsonboat
center.com

### Cycling

**Big Wheel Bikes**
1034 33rd St, NW. **Map** 1
C2. **Tel** (202) 337-0254.
W bigwheelbikes.com

**Bike and Roll**
1100 Pennsylvania Ave,
NW. **Map** 3 C3.
W bikethesites.com

**Washington Area Bicyclist Association**
2599 Ontario Rd, NW.
**Tel** (202) 518-0524.
W waba.org

### Tennis, Golf, and Riding

East Potomac Golf Course
972 Ohio Drive, SW at
Hains Point. **Map** 3 A5.
**Tel** (202) 554-7660.

**East Potomac Tennis Center**
1090 Ohio Drive, SW
at Hains Point.
**Map** 3 A5.
**Tel** (202) 554-5962.
W eastpotomac
tennis.com

**Langston Golf Course**
26th St & Benning Rd, NE.
**Tel** (202) 397-8638.

**Rock Creek Golf Course**
1600 Rittenhouse St, NW.
**Tel** (202) 882-7332.

**Rock Creek Park Horse Center**
Military & Glover Rds, NW.
**Tel** (202) 362-0117 (ext 0).
W rockcreekhorse
center.com

**Rock Creek Tennis Center**
16th & Kennedy Sts, NW.
**Tel** (202) 722-5949.
W rockcreektennis.com

### Exploring Nature

**Dumbarton Oaks Park**
Entrance on Lovers Lane,
off R & 31st Sts, NW.
**Map** 1 C1.

**Kenilworth Park and Aquatic Gardens**
1550 Anacostia Ave, NE.
**Tel** (202) 426-6905.

**Montrose Park**
R & 32nd Sts, NW.
**Map** 2 D1.

**National Arboretum**
24th & R Sts, NE.
**Tel** (202) 245-2726.

# Children's Washington, DC

Visiting the city's monuments can be one of the favorite and most memorable activities for children in DC. Book online in advance to arrange a tour with a park ranger, during which you take a trip in the elevator to the top of the Washington Monument, then walk down the steps. Young children will like feeding the ducks at the Reflecting Pool or Constitution Gardens. You can view the Jefferson Memorial from a paddleboat on the Tidal Basin, and before you leave Washington be sure to see the monuments lit up against the night-time sky.

Children in front of the National Museum of Natural History

## Practical Advice

A good source of information on specific events for children can be found in the "Going Out Guide" of *The Washington Post*. It also lists family-friendly museums and dining options. As you would expect in a major city, food is widely available in DC, whether it is hot dogs from a seller along the Mall or even strange space food (such as freeze-dried ice cream) from the **National Air and Space Museum** gift shop *(see pp64–7)*.

## Outdoor Fun

For a trip into the past, take a ride on a mule-drawn barge on the C&O Canal rom April to mid-October at Great Falls (contact the **C&O Canal Visitor Center** for details). Park Service rangers are dressed up in 19th-century costumes to add to the experience.

The beautiful wooded park of the **National Zoo** *(see pp140–41)* is a good place for a walk, and you can also enjoy watching elephant training, panda feeding, and sea lion demonstrations.

For a break from the Mall museums, take a ride on the **Carousel on the Mall** (open in summer only), in front of the Arts and Industries Building. Also worth a visit is the carousel in **Glen Echo Park** (open in summer only), built in 1921. From December to March, ice skaters can head for the **National Gallery of Art Sculpture Garden Ice Rink**. Skate rental equipment is available and visitors can also take part in group skating lessons.

Sea lion at the National Zoo

## Museums

The Discovery Center, a vast educational complex with an IMAX® theater, is housed in the **National Museum of Natural History** *(see pp72–3)*.

If you want to experience outer space, then see "To Fly!" and the Albert Einstein Planetarium at the **National Air and Space Museum**. A series of children's films and family programs are run by the **National Gallery of Art** *(see pp60–62)*. Children can discuss paintings and take part in a whole range of hands-on activities.

The **National Museum of the American Indian** *(see pp70–71)* has many events, workshops, films and demonstrations designed for the family. Similarly, the **National Museum of African Art** *(see p69)* hosts educative music and storytelling events. Children are always fascinated by the **National Postal Museum** *(see p55)*, with its many intriguing hands-on activities.

## Children's Theater

The Ripley Center of the Smithsonian houses the **Discovery Theater**, which stages puppet shows and plays. See a puppet show or fairytale production at the **Adventure Theatre** in Glen Echo Park. The theater company **Imagination Stage**, located north of Washington in Bethesda, Maryland, presents lively theater productions for children.

The **Kennedy Center** *(see pp120–21)* and **Wolf Trap Farm Park for the Performing Arts** also provide information on all sorts of children's events in the city.

Children's tour in Cedar Hill, the historic home of Frederick Douglass

## A Little Bit of History

Children studying American history will be fascinated by a visit to Cedar Hill, once the home of Frederick Douglass, in Anacostia. The video in the visitors' center helps to tell the amazing story of this American hero.

You can take a tour of **Ford's Theatre** *(see p98)* where President Lincoln was shot and the house across the street where he died.

The **Washington National Cathedral** *(see pp144–5)* provides a free brochure to take children on a self-guided scavenger hunt seeking carvings, specific images in stained-glass windows, and gargoyles. The National Building

Museum *(see p105)* runs special programs for children on Saturdays.

## Shopping

The **National Museum of Natural History** *(see pp72–3)* shops stock a wide variety of goods that will keep children enthralled. Favorites include books, natural history toys, games related to sea life, dinosaurs, and nature, as well as science kits which allow children to reproduce at home some of the wonders of the natural world on display in the museum.

Dinosaur Hall in the National Museum of Natural History

# DIRECTORY

### Practical Advice

**National Air and Space Museum**
6th St & Independence Ave, SW.
**Map** 4 D4.
**Tel** (202) 633-1000.

**National Museum of American History**
Constitution Ave between 12th & 14th Sts, NW. **Map** 3 B4.
**Tel** (202) 633-1000.

### Outdoor Fun

**C&O Canal Visitor Center**
1057 Thomas Jefferson St, NW. **Map** 2 D3.
**Tel** (202) 653-5190.

**Carousel on the Mall**
Arts and Industries Blg, 900 Jefferson Drive, SW.
**Map** 3 B4.
**Tel** (202) 633-1000.

**Glen Echo Park Carousel**
7300 MacArthur Blvd, Glen Echo, MD.
**Tel** (301) 320-1400 or (301) 634-2222.
W **glenechopark.org**

**National Gallery of Art Sculpture Garden Ice Rink**
7th St & Constitution Ave, NW. **Map** 4 D4.
**Tel** (202) 737-4215.

**National Zoo**
3001 Connecticut Ave.
Tel (202) 633-4888.

### Museums

**National Air and Space Museum**
6th St & Independence Ave, SW.
**Map** 4 D4.
**Tel** (202) 633-4629 (IMAX® film schedule).

**National Gallery of Art**
Constitution Ave between 3rd & 7th Sts, NW.
**Map** 4 D3.
**Tel** (202) 737-4215, (202) 789-3030 (children's film program).

**National Museum of African Art**
950 Independence Ave, SW.
**Map** 3 C4.
**Tel** (202) 633-4600.
W **nmafa.si.edu**

**National Museum of American History**
Constitution Ave between 12th & 14th Sts, NW.
**Map** 3 B4.
**Tel** (202) 633-1000.

**National Museum of the American Indian**
4th St & Independence Ave, SW. **Map** 4 D4.
**Tel** (202) 633-1000.
W **americanindian.si.edu**

**National Museum of Natural History**
10th St & Constitution Ave, NW. **Map** 3 C4.
**Tel** (202) 633-1000 (general information).
**Tel** (202) 633-4629 (IMAX® film schedule).

**National Postal Museum**
2 Massachusetts Ave, NE.
**Map** 4 E3.
**Tel** (202) 633-1000.

### Children's Theatre

**Adventure Theatre**
7300 MacArthur Blvd, Glen Echo Park, Md.
**Tel** (301) 634-2270.

**Discovery Theater**
1100 Jefferson Drive, SW.
**Map** 3 C4.
**Tel** (202) 633-8700.
W **discoverytheater.org**

**Imagination Stage**
4908 Auburn Ave, Bethesda, MD.
**Tel** (301) 280-1660.
W **imagination stage.org**

**Wolf Trap Farm Park for the Performing Arts**
1551 Trap Rd, Vienna, VA.
**Tel** (703) 255-1900.
W **wolftrap.org**

### A Little Bit of History

**Ford's Theatre**
511 10th St, NW.
**Map** 3 C3.
**Tel** (202) 347-4833.
W **fordstheatre.org**

**Frederick Douglass National Historic Site**
1411 W St, SE.
**Tel** (202) 426-5960.

**Washington National Cathedral**
Massachusetts & Wisconsin Aves, NW.
**Tel** (202) 537-6200 (Gargoyle tour).
W **cathedral.org**

### Shopping

**National Museum of Natural History Shops**
Constitution Ave between 12th and 14th Sts, NW.
**Map** 3 C4.
**Tel** (202) 633-2060.
W **mnh.si.edu**

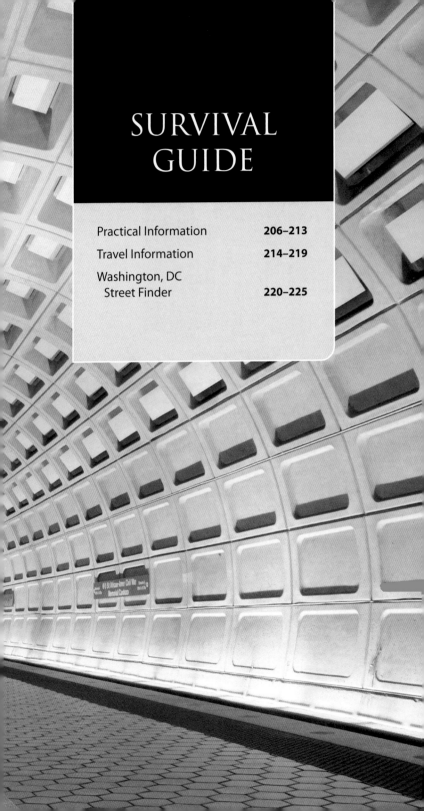

# SURVIVAL GUIDE

# PRACTICAL INFORMATION

Washington, DC is the heart of the American political world. It is a visitor-friendly place, especially for children and the disabled, since wheelchair accessibility is required almost everywhere, and most museums (including all under the Smithsonian umbrella *see pp100–103*) are free. The whole city shuts down on federal holidays, as well as anytime the government requires it to. With the US President and other world leaders coming and going, unexpected delays and closures can occur. Spring and fall are the best times to visit as the summers can be very hot and winters very cold.

Entrance to the White House Visitor Center

## Visas and Passports

Citizens of the UK, most western European countries, Canada, Japan, Australia, and New Zealand, need a valid passport and a return ticket to enter the US, and must register with the online Electronic System of Travel Authorization (ESTA) before departure. Visit https://esta.cbp.dhs.gov to obtain the ESTA; there is a small charge but it is valid for two years. Citizens of all other countries require a valid passport and a tourist visa. Entry requirements may change. Be sure to check with the US embassy in your country before you travel. Be aware that anyone entering the US on a visa will be photographed and have their fingerprints checked.

All visitors should carry photo identification at all times. Your possessions will be checked before entering museums and some places, like the Library of Congress, have metal detectors.

## Tourist Information

The Washington area is very welcoming to tourists. Visitor information desks at the airports will provide guides and maps, and staff will be able to answer questions. Major hotels usually have a knowledgeable guest services desk. Before you travel it may be worth contacting the **Destination DC** tourist office. The website provides information on special offers, local events, and free things to do.

## Opening Hours

Most banks and offices in DC are open from 9am to 5pm, Monday through Friday. Some banks are also open on a Saturday morning *(see p210)*. Malls or department stores Ware open daily and have extended hours on a certain day of the week. Stores rarely close for federal holidays; in fact, many federal holidays are big shopping days with special sales.

All Smithsonian Museums are open on federal holidays. Some private museums, like the Phillips Collection, are closed on Mondays. Many gas stations, convenience stores and select pharmacies *(see p209)* stay open 24 hours.

## Taxes and Tipping

Taxes will be added to hotel and restaurant charges, theater tickets, some grocery and store sales, and most other purchases. Be sure to ask whether the tax is included in the price displayed. Sales tax is 6 percent, hotel tax is 14.5 percent, with 10 percent tax on food and beverages.

Tipping is expected for most services: in restaurants tip 15–20 percent of the bill, give $2 per bag to airport and hotel porters, and $2 to valet parking attendants. Bartenders expect 50 cents to $1 per drink; if you visit a hair salon or barbershop, 15 to 20 percent of the bill should suffice.

## Alcohol and Cigarettes

The legal minimum age for drinking alcohol in Washington is 21, and you will need photo identification (I.D.) as proof of your age in order to purchase alcohol and be allowed into bars. It is illegal to drink alcohol in public parks or to carry an open container of alcohol in your car, and penalties for driving under the influence of alcohol are severe. Cigarettes can be purchased by those over 18 years old; proof of age will be required.

Smoking is prohibited in all public buildings, bars, restaurants, and stores.

## Electricity

Electricity flows at the standard US 110–120 volts, and a two-prong plug is required. For non-US appliances you will need a plug adapter and a voltage converter.

◄ Union Street Metrorail station

International Student Identity Card, accepted as I.D. in America

## Student Travelers

While students from abroad should purchase an International Student Identity Card (**ISIC**) before traveling to Washington, they may not use it often as many sights have free entry. Paying museums such as the Phillips Collection give a $2 discount on their regular admission. The ISIC handbook lists places and services in the US that offer discounts to card holders, including accommodations, museums, and theaters. The **Student Advantage Card** is available to all American college undergraduates and offers a range of discounts.

## Senior Travelers

Senior citizens are eligible for certain discounts with the appropriate proof of age. Amtrak gives a discount of 15 percent for persons over 62 on most trains (not valid for business or first class). Many movie theaters give reduced admission (usually $1 off the regular price) to those aged 60 or over. Most private museums offer a senior's discount similar to the student discount.

The **American Association of Retired Persons** is open to the over-50s. Members qualify for discounts of 5–30 percent on tours, hotels, and travel.

## Disabled Travelers

Washington is a model of accessibility and almost all public buildings, including most hotels and restaurants, are required to be wheelchair accessible. Streets have curb cuts and there are elevators at all Metro stations. The exceptions are historic areas like Georgetown, where 18th-century buildings and cobblestone streets make using a wheelchair problematic. For general advice, contact the **Society for Accessible Travel and Hospitality**.

## Gay and Lesbian Travelers

In 2009, Washington, DC passed a gay marriage act – one of the few places in the US to recognize same-sex union. The city's lively gay scene centers around Dupont Circle and the adjacent 17th, 14th, and P Streets. The **Human Rights Campaign**

**Headquarters** is home to the national organization for gay rights.

## Responsible Tourism

Like many places in the US, Washington, DC is increasingly aware of environmental issues. Visitors can be assured that most public organizations and many restaurants recycle their trash and, in 2009, the city enacted a law charging 5 cents for every plastic and paper bag given at grocery stores.

Local and organic produce are widely available, especially at weekend markets such as the Eastern Market (7am–6pm Sat, 9am–5pm Sun) and the Dupont Circle Farmers' Market (8:30am– 1pm; Jan–Mar: 10am– 1pm). The mother of the organic food movement in eastern USA is Restaurant Nora (*see p190*).

Many hotel chains touting their green credentials have representatives in DC, including Fairmont Hotels (*see p178*), cited as the best hotel chain by treehugger.com.

Local produce on sale at the Eastern Market

# DIRECTORY

## Embassies

**Australia**
1601 Massachusetts Ave, NW. **Map** 2 F2.
**Tel** (202) 797-3000.
w usa.embassy.gov.au

**Canada**
501 Pennsylvania Ave, NW.
**Map** 4 D3.
**Tel** (202) 682-1740.
w canadainternational.gc.ca/washington

**Ireland**
2234 Massachusetts Ave, NW. **Map** 3 A1.
**Tel** (202) 462-3939.
w irelandemb.org

**New Zealand**
37 Observatory Circle, NW. **Tel** (202) 328-4800.
w nzembassy.com/usa

**United Kingdom**
3100 Massachusetts Ave, NW.
**Tel** (202) 588-6500.
w britainusa.com

## Tourist Information

**Destination DC**
901 7th Street, NW.
**Map** 4 D2.
**Tel** (202) 289-7000.
w washington.org

## Student Travelers

**ISIC**
w isic.org

**Student Advantage Card**
w studentadvantage.com

## Senior Travelers

**American Association for Retired Persons**
601 E St, NW.
**Map** 4 D3.
**Tel** 888-687-2277.
w aarp.org

## Disabled Travelers

**Society for Accessible Travel and Hospitality**
**Tel** (212) 447-7284.
w sath.org

## Gay and Lesbian Travelers

**Human Rights Campaign Headquarters**
1640 Rhode Island Ave, NW.
**Tel** (202) 628-4160.
w hrc.org

# Personal Security and Health

Although as in any major city there is crime, Washington has made great efforts in reducing problems and cleaning up its streets, and with success. If you stick to the tourist areas, avoid straying into outlying districts, and take common sense precautions as in any big city, you should not run into any trouble. The main sights are located in safe areas where there are many people, and serious crime is rare. When visiting sights off the beaten track, take a taxi to and from the destination. Most importantly, pay attention to your surroundings, especially after dark.

## Law Enforcement

There are several different police forces in Washington, DC, including the Secret Service, the FBI (Federal Bureau of Investigation), and the more widespread M.P.D.C. (Metropolitan Police, Washington, DC) police. Many major sights also have their own police forces, such as the National Zoological Park Police and the United States Capitol Police.

At monuments, you will see green-uniformed Park Rangers. Their role is largely crowd control and as a source of information; many are trained historians.

Because the city is home to the President, whenever he travels, members of the law enforcement agencies follow. When foreign political leaders visit, the police are even more visible than usual: you will see them on horseback, on bicycles, in cars, and even on top of buildings.

As a visitor, should you encounter any trouble, approach any of the blue-uniformed M.P.D.C. officers that regularly patrol the city streets. All M.P.D.C officers carry weapons.

The DC police are well-known for their strict interpretation of the law. In other words: don't talk back, don't argue and never offer money in the form of a bribe; this could land you in jail.

M.P.D.C. officer

## What to be Aware of

Serious crime is rarely witnessed in the main sightseeing areas of Washington. However, avoid wandering into areas that you have no reason to visit, either during the day or at night. Pickpockets do operate in the city and will target anyone who looks like a tourist. Panhandlers (beggars) are also common, gathering near Metro stations and at shopping malls. It is best to keep walking, ignore their requests for money, and avoid engaging in conversation. Police officers regularly patrol the tourist areas, but it is still advisable to prepare the day's itinerary in advance, use common sense, and stay alert. Try not to advertise that you are a tourist; study your map before you set off, avoid wearing expensive jewellery, and carry your camera or camcorder securely. Carry small amounts of cash; credit cards are a more secure option. Keep these close to your body in a money belt or inside pocket. Before you leave home, make a photocopy of important documents, including your passport and visa, and keep them with you, though separate from the originals. Also make a note of your credit card numbers, in case of theft or loss. Keep an eye on your belongings at all times. It is a good idea to put any valuables in the hotel safe – do not carry them around with you. Most hotels will not guarantee the security of any belongings that you leave in your room.

## In an Emergency

Call 911 for police or fire assistance, or if you need an ambulance. If you are involved in a medical emergency, go to a hospital emergency room.

## Lost and Stolen Property

Although the chances of retrieving lost or stolen property are slim, you should report all stolen items to the police. Call the **Police Non-Emergency Line** for guidance. Make sure you keep a copy of the police report, which you will need when making your insurance claim.

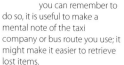

Hospital sign

In case of loss, it is useful to have a list of serial numbers or a photocopy of all documents; keep these separate as proof of possession. If you can remember to do so, it is useful to make a mental note of the taxi company or bus route you use; it might make it easier to retrieve lost items.

If your passport is lost or stolen, get in touch with your country's embassy or consulate (see p207). If you lose your credit card, most card companies have toll-free numbers for reporting a loss or theft (see p210).

## Hospitals and Pharmacies

It is possible to visit a doctor or dentist without being registered with them, but you will be asked to pay in advance. Keep all receipts for medical costs to make a claim on your insurance later. Depending on the limitations of your insurance, it is better to avoid the overcrowded city-owned hospitals and opt instead for one of the private hospitals. If

Police car

Ambulance

Fire engine

taken by ambulance, however, drivers are required to take you to the nearest hospital. If you require a dentist you can call the **District of Columbia Dental Society**, which provides a free referral service.

Pharmacists are usually able to offer basic medical advice, and there are some pharmacies with clinics attached to treat common illnesses and small injuries. Patients are seen by nurse practitioners or physician assistants. One such clinic is the **CVS Minute Clinic**, which has three locations in DC, and several in the Virginia and Maryland suburbs.

If you need a prescription, there are plenty of pharmacies in and around the city, some staying open 24 hours. CVS is the most common chain.

## Travel and Health Insurance

It is strongly recommended to obtain travel insurance before traveling to the United States. It is particularly important for visitors to have sufficient insurance for emergency medical and dental care, which can be very expensive in the States. Even with medical cover, you may have to pay for the services, then make a claim for reimbursement with your insurance company when you return home. Hospitals accept most credit cards, as do most doctors and dentists. Should you go to a hospital or seek medical assistance, be sure to take proof of your insurance with you. If you usually take medication, it is a good idea to bring a back-up supply with you and to ask your doctor to provide a copy of the prescription in case of loss or the need for more.

It is advisable to make sure your personal property is insured and to obtain cover for lost or stolen baggage and travel documents, as well as trip cancellation fees, legal advice, and accidental death or injury. Your insurance company or travel agent should be able to recommend a suitable policy.

## Legal Assistance

Non-US citizens requiring legal assistance should call their embassy *(see p207)*. Embassies will not lend you money but can help with advice on legal matters in emergencies. Should you be arrested for any reason, it is advisable to be cooperative, but you have the right to remain silent.

## Restrooms

Washington, DC does not have public restrooms. There are free bathrooms available in all visitor's centers, museums, and galleries, and all hotels and restaurants also have restrooms, but they may only be available to paying customers.

## DIRECTORY

### In an Emergency

**Police, Fire, Medical (all emergencies)**
**Tel** Call 911,
or dial 0 for the operator.

### Lost and Stolen Property

Police Non-Emergency Line
**Tel** 311.

### Hospitals and Pharmacies

**Area Hospitals**
**Tel** Call 411 for directory assistance.

**CVS 24-Hour Pharmacy**
1199 Vermont Ave, NW.
**Map** 3 B2.
**Tel** (202) 628-0720.
6 Dupont Circle, NW.
**Map** 2 F2.
**Tel** (202) 785-1466.
W cvs.com

**CVS Minute Clinic**
Several locations.
W minuteclinic.com

**DC Dental Society**
**Tel** (202) 547-7613.
W dcdental.org

**George Washington University Hospital**
(Private.) 900 23rd Street, NW.
**Map** 2 E3.
**Tel** (202) 715-4000.

**Georgetown University Hospital**
(Private.) 3800 Reservoir Road, NW.
**Map** 1 B2.
**Tel** (202) 444-2000.

**Medical Referral Services**
**Tel** (202) 342-2400.

**Washington Hospital Center**
(Private.) 110 Irving Street, NW.
**Tel** (202) 877-7000.

# CVS/pharmacy®
for all the ways you care℠

Logo for CVS pharmacies, a common pharmacy chain in Washington, DC

# Banking and Currency

Throughout Washington there are various places to access and exchange your money, from banks to cash machines to bureaux de change. The most important thing to remember is not to carry all your money and credit cards with you at once, and to be prepared to use ATM machines on Sunday when most banks and currency exchange offices are closed.

## Banks and Foreign Exchange

Generally, most banks are open Monday through Friday from 9am to 3pm, although some may close later, and Saturday mornings from 9am to noon or 1pm. Most banks are closed on Sundays and federal holidays (see p41). The exception is **TD Bank**, which has many branches with Sunday hours and is open on federal holidays.

Always ask if there are any special fees before you make your transaction. At most banks, traveler's checks in US dollars can be cashed with any photo identification, although passports are usually required to exchange foreign currency.

Foreign currency exchange is available at the main branches of large banks or at independent exchange offices. Among the best known are **American Express Travel Service** and **Thomas Cook/ Travelex**, both of which have branches in and around DC. Exchange offices are generally open weekdays from 9am to 5pm. Most exchange offices charge a fee or commission, so it is worth looking around to get the best value rates. Many major hotels can also change currency, but they often charge a higher rate of exchange or commission.

American Express
credit cards

## ATMs

Automated teller machines (ATMs) are found all over the Washington area, usually near the entrance to banks, or inside many convenience stores and supermarkets.

Widely accepted bank cards include Cirrus, Plus, Maestro, NYCE, and credit cards such as VISA or MasterCard. Note that a fee may be levied on your withdrawal (a pop-up screen should tell you the fee and ask if you want the transaction to continue). To minimize the risk of robbery, use ATMs in well-lit, populated areas only. Avoid withdrawing money at night or in isolated areas, and be aware of the people around you.

## Credit and Debit Cards

American Express, VISA, MasterCard/Maestro, and most international debit cards are widely accepted almost everywhere in Washington,

Customers withdrawing cash from Bank of America ATMs

from theaters and hotels to restaurants and shops. Indeed, it is advisable to carry a credit card when visiting Washington as it may be required to reserve a hotel or rental car and to pay for gasoline (petrol), especially at self-service stations.

If your credit card is lost or stolen, contact your card company immediately.

## Card Security

Because of the increasing problem of identity theft and card cloning, merchants may ask for photo identification when making a purchase.

If you are traveling overseas, alert your bank of your plans, or they may put a hold on your account if they see untoward charges.

## Emergency Funds (Wiring Money)

**MoneyGram** and **Western Union** both offer immediate money transfer for a fee. Both sender and recipient will need to locate an agent to set up the transfer and collect the funds (Western Union also has an online facility for sending funds.)

## Coins

*American coins come in 1-dollar, 50-, 25-, 10-, 5-, and 1-cent pieces. There are also goldtone $1 coins in circulation and State quarters, which feature an historical scene on one side. Each coin has a popular name: 25-cent pieces are called quarters, 10-cent pieces are called dimes, 5-cent pieces are called nickels, and 1-cent pieces called pennies.*

1-cent coin
(a penny)

5-cent coin
(a nickel)

10-cent coin
(a dime)

25-cent coin
(a quarter)

An American Eagle
on a $1 gold coin

## Bills (Bank Notes)

*The units of currency in the United States are dollars and cents. There are 100 cents to a dollar. Bank notes come in the following denominations: $1, $5, $10, $20, $50, and $100. Security features include subtle color hues and improved color-shifting ink in the lower right hand corner of the face of each note.*

1-dollar bill ($1)

5-dollar bill ($5)

10-dollar bill ($10)

20-dollar bill ($20)

50-dollar bill ($50)

100-dollar bill ($100)

# Communications and Media

The almost universal use of cell phones has caused the demise of coin-operated pay phones. It is now difficult to find a public pay phone in the street, although they are still available at main stations. Like most major cities, Washington, DC is thoroughly wired for Internet access. Free Wi-Fi is provided in many public places and there are several other ways to get online. Since Washington, DC is the political capital of the United States, news is readily available from newspapers, magazines, television, and radio.

## Cell Phones

Cell phone service in Washington is generally excellent. If you are coming from overseas and want to guarantee that your cell phone will work, make sure you have a quad-band phone. Tri-band phones from outside the US are also usually compatible but, because the US uses two frequency bands itself, it is recommended to contact your service provider for clarification before you travel; you may also need to activate the "roaming" facility.

Other options include buying a prepaid cell phone in the US or a SIM chip for a US carrier. Many car rental companies also rent cell phones for customers *(see p219)*.

## Public Telephones

In the last decade, the number of public pay phones in the United States has decreased by half and Washington is no exception. However, public pay phones are still available at Union Station, the Smithsonian Museums, and some Metro stations, and occasionally on the street. The area code for Washington is 202. When dialing within the district, omit the code. When dialing outside the district from within DC, you will need to use the appropriate area code. The area code for the Maryland suburbs is 301 and for the Virginia suburbs, 703.

Credit card calls can be made by calling 1-800-CALL-ATT. Directory Assistance is 411 and calls are charged at the local rate. Phone cards of various values can be purchased from most supermarkets, 24-hour stores, newspaper stands, and some branches of Western Union.

## Telephone Charges

Local calls cost around 50 cents for 3 minutes from pay phones. Calls made from hotel rooms will cost much more, so it is a good idea to locate a pay phone or use your cell. Operator assistance can also be used to help you connect your call, but again, this will cost more.

## Internet Access

Although Internet cafés are rare in Washington, many public places – such as bookstores, cafés, airports, and the Mall – have a free wireless service. Most hotels in the city have wireless Internet in their rooms, and many also have a dedicated business center (with computers) within the hotel. For those without their own laptops, computers (with Internet) are available for use in public libraries and in stores such as FedEx, DHL, and UPS.

Using the Internet in the reading room of a Washington public library

## Post Service

Post offices are open from 9am to 5pm, Mondays through Fridays, and have limited Saturday service, usually 9am to noon. Post offices are closed on all federal holidays. Stamps can also be bought from most major supermarkets, such as Giant and Safeway.

If the correct postage is affixed, you can send a letter by putting it in one of the blue mailboxes found on street corners all over Washington. Times of mail pickup are written inside the mailbox's lid; there are usually several collections a day. It is mandatory to use a five-digit zip code when sending mail. Be aware that small packages may not be posted in mailboxes for security reasons; they must be taken to a post office.

Depending on how far the mail needs to travel in the US, it can take from one to five days to

### Useful Dialing Codes

- To make a direct-dial call outside the local area code, but within the US and Canada, dial 1 before the area code. Useful area codes for DC and the surrounding area include: Washington, DC 202; Baltimore 410; MD 301, 240; Delaware 302; Northern Virginia 703; West Virginia 304.
- For international calls, dial 011 followed by the appropriate country code. Then dial the area code, omitting the first 0, and t he local number.
- To make an international call via the operator, dial 00; note that the call will be charged at a higher rate.
- For international operator assistance, dial 01.
- For local operator assistance, dial 0.
- For international directory inquiries, dial 00.
- For local directory inquiries, dial 411.
- For emergency police, fire, or ambulance services, dial 911.
- 1-800 and 888 indicate a toll-free number.

arrive at its destination. The most economical way to send international mail is First Class International at less than $1 per ounce, depending on the destination. Express and Priority mail are also available at the post office for a faster, though more expensive, service. If you are a visitor to the city and you wish to receive mail, poste restante, you can have it sent to you by addressing it care of "General Delivery" at the **Main Post Office**, or any other main post office, quoting the city name. They will hold the mail for 30 days for you to collect.

It is worth noting that USPS refers to the United States Postal Service, while UPS is a private courier company.

## Courier Services

Courier services are a popular, if more expensive, alternative to the postal service. Many hotels will arrange for your packages and letters to be shipped either by Federal Express (**FedEx**), **DHL**, a division of Deutsche Poste, or **UPS**. DHL only operates internationally while FedEx and UPS handle both national and international letters and packages. FedEx

Newspaper vendor

services are available at Fedex Office Centers (easily recognizable by the FedEx arrow logo); DHL is offered at independent office storefront locations like Parcel Plus. FedEx and UPS also have self-service kiosks throughout the city for letters and flat packages. Registration for self-service packages is completed online, and a label downloaded to attach to the package.

US mailbox

## Television and Radio

Televisions are everywhere in the United States, from bars and restaurants to hotels and stores. Most have cable hook-up, allowing access to more than 60 different channels. Some of the best to view are CBS, NBC, CNN, ABC, and Fox. For those interested in the political goings-on in the city, tune in to channels C-Span 1 and C-Span 2 to watch the proceedings in Congress as they are broadcast live. Radios can be found in most hotel rooms, as well as in rental cars, and offer a wide range of music, from country through classical and jazz to rock. Popular radio stations include National Public Radio (WAMU at 88.5), modern rock on WHFS (99.1), and soft rock on Easy 101 (101).

## Newspapers

The most widely read newspaper in the DC area is *The Washington Post*, which is also one of the best newspapers published in the country. The local *Washington Express* is widely available as are *USA Today*, *The Wall Street Journal*, and *The New York Times*. Newspapers can be bought from street dispensers (boxes on the sidewalk that dispense newspapers), newsstands, gas stations, convenience stores, hotel lobbies, and bookstores. They are also all available online. Newsstands and some bookstores carry newspapers from most large US cities and many foreign countries.

## DIRECTORY

### Postal Services

**Georgetown Station**
3050 K St, NW. **Map** 2 D2.

**Main Post Office**
Brentwood Station, 900 Brentwood Road, NE, Washington, DC 20066. **Tel** (202) 636-1581.

**Martin Luther King Jr. Station**
1400 L St, NW. **Map** 2 F3.
National Capitol Station
2 Massachusetts Ave, NE. **Map** 4 E3.

**Temple Heights Station**
1921 Florida Ave, NW. **Map** 2 E1.

### Courier Services

**DHL**
Branches all over the DC area. For customer services call: **Tel** (800) 225-5345.
 dhl.com

**FedEx**
Branches all over the DC area. For customer services call: Tel (800) 463-3339.
W fedex.com

**UPS**
Branches all over the DC area. For the nearest branch call: **Tel** (800) 275-8777.
W ups.com

## Washington Time

Washington is on Eastern Standard Time. Daylight Saving Time begins on the second Sunday in March, when clocks are set ahead 1 hour, and ends on the first Sunday in November, when clocks go back 1 hour.

| City and Country | Hours + or – EST | City and Country | Hours + or – EST |
|---|---|---|---|
| Chicago (US) | –1 | Moscow (Russia) | +8 |
| Dublin (Ireland) | +5 | Paris (France) | +6 |
| London (UK) | +5 | Sydney (Australia) | +15 |
| Los Angeles (US) | –3 | Tokyo (Japan) | +14 |
| Madrid (Spain) | +6 | Vancouver (Canada) | –3 |

# TRAVEL INFORMATION

Washington is easy to get to via any mode of transportation. Three airports serve the DC area; they are used by most major airlines for domestic and international flights. Two major bus lines also operate to the city, as do Amtrak trains, which arrive at and depart from Union Station, right in the center of Washington. Visitors often tend to travel first to DC, base themselves in the city, and then arrange day or weekend trips into Maryland and Virginia.

Glass-walled interior of Reagan National Airport

## Arriving by Air

There are three main airports in the Washington, DC area: **Dulles International Airport**, **Reagan National Airport**, and Baltimore-Washington International Thurgood Marshall Airport (known as **BWI**). Most of the major carriers, including American Airlines, British Airways, Air France, and United Airlines, fly to at least one of these airports. The majority of international and overseas flights land at Dulles International, 26 miles (42 km) west of Washington in Virginia. Dulles is not directly served by a Metro but there is a connecting shuttle service, the **Washington Flyer Coach Service**, to take new arrivals to West Falls Church

Metro. Between the coach service and the Metro, expect to spend up to an hour-and-a-half to reach the city center. Alternatively, the **SuperShuttle** share-ride bus service runs every hour and will drop passengers at their door. It is a cheaper option than a taxi but journey times depend on detours made to drop off the other passengers. Taxis are plentiful and are the quickest but most expensive option. Make sure the fare is negotiated before departure.

Located about 5 miles (8 km) outside the city in Arlington County, Virginia, the Reagan National Airport is the most convenient airport for central Washington. The city is easily accessible using the Metro, or by taking the SuperShuttle (every 30 minutes), or a taxi.

BWI Airport, which is situated 30 miles (48 km) northeast of DC, tends to be used by low-cost airlines. The Maryland Rail Commuter Service (**MARC**) is the cheapest way to get from the airport to the city, but it runs only on weekdays. Amtrak *(see p215)* offers the next-best train service for just a few dollars more. The SuperShuttle is also available

from BWI, but it is more costly and takes longer than a train ride. The taxi fare from BWI into central DC is rather expensive.

For security reasons, anyone arriving in the US on a visa is now photographed, and will have their fingerprints taken, before being allowed into the country *(see p206)*.

## Air Fares

The busiest season for travel to the US is March through June and September through early November. Christmas and Thanksgiving are also busy. Flights will be at their most expensive during these periods. Fwlights in June and July are usually the most expensive but there are many discounted accommodations at this time. Weekend flights are usually less expensive than weekdays, while Apex tickets are often the best deal. Apex tickets must be booked at least one week in advance, and your visit must include a Saturday night. Cheap air fares can be obtained by shopping around, so it is worth checking with the airlines and websites such as **Expedia**, **Kayak**, and **Priceline**.

The Washington Flyer, shuttling from Dulles to West Falls Church Metro

| Airport | Information | Distance/Time to Washington, DC | Taxi Fare | SuperShuttle |
|---------|-------------|----------------------------------|-----------|--------------|
| Dulles | (703) 572-2700 | 26 miles (42 km) 40 minutes | $50–5 | $26–35 |
| Reagan National | (703) 417-8000 | 5 miles (8 km) 15 minutes | $15–20 | $13–23 |
| BWI | (410) 859-7111 | 30 miles (48 km) 50 minutes | $62–5 | $32–42 |

Main concourse at Union Station

## Arriving by Train

**Amtrak** is one of the best ways to travel to the DC area. Trains from other cities arrive in Washington at Union Station. Trains are also available from Union Station to Baltimore, Philadelphia, Richmond, and Williamsburg. Amtrak offers a deluxe train service to New York City, called the Acela, which travels slightly faster and more comfortably than the regular train, but is more expensive. Trains (either the Acela or the slower Northeast Regional) to New York leave every hour. **MARC,** Maryland's commuter train, departs on weekdays to Baltimore.

## Arriving by Car

The center of Washington, DC is surrounded by Interstates I-95 and I-495, which together form the congested Capital Beltway. Driving on the Beltway, especially during rush hour, can be intimidating for the inexperienced driver. Interstate I-66 connects Washington to West Virginia, and Interstate I-50 heads east from DC to Annapolis, Maryland, and the surrounding areas. Beyond the Beltway, Interstate I-95 goes north toward Baltimore, Philadelphia, and New York. Interstate I-270 heads north to Frederick, Maryland.

## Arriving by Bus

Intercity buses are a great, economical way to get to Washington. As well as the traditional **Greyhound** buses, there are half a dozen bus companies serving DC, including **Megabus, Bolt Bus, Vamoose,** and the **Washington Deluxe**. Many are equipped with restrooms, free Wi-Fi, power outlets, and even DVD players. Tickets are sold on a scale – one-way to New York is generally about $25, but may be as little as $1 with advance purchase.

Greyhound buses depart from the bus terminal near Union Station, but many of the other bus companies leave from more central locations.

Greyhound bus, an inexpensive way to see the whole country

# DIRECTORY

## Arriving by Air

**BWI Airport**
Linthicam, MD.
**Tel** (410) 859-7111 or (800) I-FLY-BWI. Lost & Found
**Tel** (410) 859-7387.
Ⓦ bwiairport.com

**Dulles International Airport**
Chantilly, VA.
**Tel** (703) 572-2700. Lost & Found **Tel** (703) 572-8479.
Ⓦ metwashairports.com

**Reagan National Airport**
Arlington, VA.
**Tel** (703) 417-8000. Lost & Found **Tel** (703) 417-8560.
Ⓦ metwashairports.com

**SuperShuttle**
**Tel** (800) 258-3826 or (800) BLUE-VAN.
Ⓦ supershuttle.com

**Washington Flyer Coach Service**
**Tel** (888) 927-4359 or (888) WASH-FLY.
Ⓦ washfly.com

## Air Fares

**Expedia**
**Tel** 1-877-787-7186.
Ⓦ Expedia.com

**Kayak**
Ⓦ kayak.com

**Priceline**
Tel (800) 774-2354.
Ⓦ priceline.com

## Arriving by Train

**Amtrak**
Union Station, 50 Massachusetts Ave, NE.
**Tel** 1-800-872-7245.
Ⓦ amtrak.com

**MARC**
**Tel** (410) 539-5000 or 1-866-743-3682.
Ⓦ mtamaryland.com

## Arriving by Bus

**2000 New Century Travel**
Tel (215) 627-2666 or (917) 577-6781.
Ⓦ 2001bus.com

**Bolt Bus**
**Tel** 1-877-265-8287.
Ⓦ boltbus.com

**DC2NY**
**Tel** (202) 332-2691.
Ⓦ dc2ny.com

**Greyhound Busline**
**Tel** (800) 231-2222 or (800) 289-5160.
Ⓦ greyhound.com

**Megabus**
**Tel** 1-877-462-6342.
Ⓦ megabus.com

**Vamoose**
**Tel** (212) 695-6766 or (301) 718-0036.
Ⓦ vamoosebus.com

**Washington Deluxe**
**Tel** 1-866-287-6932 or 1-718-387-7523.
Ⓦ washny.com

# Getting Around Washington, DC

Washington has a very comprehensive public transportation system. Visitors and locals alike find that it is easier to get around by public transportation than by car, especially as they do not then have the aggravation of finding a much-coveted parking space. All the major tourist attractions in the capital are accessible on foot, by Metrorail, by Metrobus, or by taxi.

Busy night-time traffic in central Washington, DC

## Green Travel

With such an excellent public transportation system, it is easy to get around Washington, DC without causing undue harm to the environment. Almost every tourist sight is accessible via public transportation. Furthermore, Metrobus runs a fleet of buses powered by Compressed Natural Gas (CNG), a cleaner alternative to gasoline (petrol).

Cycling has become an increasingly popular way to travel in Washington, and there is an excellent network of cycle lanes throughout the center. Cycling has been further encouraged with the Capital Bikeshare self-hire scheme (see p217).

If it is necessary to use a taxi, visitors can encourage green practices by requesting a "hybrid" taxi, powered by a combination of battery and gasoline, although these cabs are not always available. If using a taxi in the Virginia suburbs, **Envirocab** runs an all-hybrid fleet. They are not licensed to operate in the District, however.

All car rental companies offer hybrid cars, but with limited availability. Book ahead to make sure your request is considered.

## Getting your Bearings

It is important to know that the city is made up of four quadrants: northeast (NE), northwest (NW), southeast (SE), and southwest (SW), with the US Capitol at the central point. Every address in DC includes the quadrant code (NE, and so on) and, with building numbers running into the thousands on the same street in each quadrant, its use is necessary to distinguish the location.

A useful tip for when you are first trying to find your way around the city is to remember that most numbered streets run North and South, and most lettered streets run East and West. However, be aware that there is no "J," "X," "Y," or "Z" Street, and that "I" Street is often written as "Eye" Street.

## Walking

Washington is a terrific city for walking, as long as you wear comfortable shoes and keep your wits about you. Many of the main sights are clustered around the Mall. In Georgetown, walking is the best way to soak up the atmosphere.

## Metrorail

A map of the Metrorail (see back endpaper and City Map) is one of the most important pieces of information visitors will need when trying to get around DC. The system takes some getting used to, and the instructions are in English only, so allow plenty of time when first using the Metrorail (or "Metro," as it is also called).

The cost of the fare depends on the time and distance you wish to travel, and ranges from $1.35 to $3.90. Tickets, or "farecards," for single or multiple trips can be bought from vending machines. Coins and bills (but no bills over $20) can be used to pay the exact fare; or add more money if you wish to use the farecard again. Passengers need to swipe their farecards through the turnstile at the beginning and end of the trip. If there is any unused fare left at the final destination the ticket will be returned to you; if not, the ticket will be retained. You can top up tickets for further trips. Metrorail passes are on offer for one day ($15) and seven days' ($40.50) travel. These can be used to transfer from Metro to bus. For convenience, it may be worth purchasing a SmarTrip card. This is a plastic rechargeable farecard which can also be used on other modes of public transportation in DC.

Five Metrorail lines operate in downtown DC, with frequent services: the Orange Line; Blue Line; Red Line; Yellow Line; and Green Line. Trains run from 5:30am to midnight Monday through Thursday, from 5:30am to 3am on Friday and 7am to 3am on Saturday, and from 7am to midnight on Sunday. Trains run frequently (less than 10 minutes' wait) and, on board, stops are announced at every station. The entire system is accessible for wheelchairs. One warning: eating, drinking, smoking or littering on the Metro is grounds for arrest.

Metro sign

Washington, DC Metrobus

## Metrobus

Metrobus is a fast, inexpensive way to get around. Fares can be paid either with exact change on boarding, with a SmarTrip card, or a Metrorail farecard pass (see Metrorail). The standard, off-peak fare is $1.45 (or $1.35 with SmarTrip). If paying with cash, there is a 25 cent charge for bus-to-bus transfers; if using SmarTrip, transfers are free within a 3-hour period. Up to two children under five can travel for free with a fare-paying passenger and there are discounts for disabled travelers and senior citizens. The **Circulator** bus links the main sights in the center and runs every 10 minutes. Fares are $1 for adults and 50 cents for kids.

Maps of all the bus routes are available in Metrorail stations, and maps of specific lines are posted at each bus stop.

Many Metrobuses are wheel-chair accessible with a "kneeling" feature that lowers the bus for the disabled rider.

## Taxis

Taxis can usually be hailed from the street corner of major arteries, but if you need to be somewhere at a specific time it is advisable to book. The **DC Taxi**

**Cab Commission** will provide names of cab companies. Taxi fares in DC are operated using time and distance meters. Passengers should expect to pay a starting "drop" rate of $3, and then $2.16 for every mile after this. Luggage, rush hour travel, and gas prices can all incur surcharges from 50 cents to $2, and each extra passenger costs $1.50. Be aware that drivers do not always know the way to addresses beyond the tourist center.

## Driving and Parking in the City

Driving in DC need not be stressful as long as you avoid the rush hour (between 6:30 and 9:30am, and 4 and 7pm on weekdays). During these times the direction of traffic flow can change, some roads become one way, and left turns may be forbidden to ease congestion. These changes are usually marked, but always pay close attention to the road. Curbside parking is hard to find at the more popular locations, and is illegal at rush hour in many areas. If using metered parking, it is important to keep within the

time limit; you could otherwise be fined, risk being clamped, or towed away. Parking restrictions on Sundays and public holidays are different from other days, so read the parking signs carefully.

## Cycling

There is a great network of cycle paths in DC. Bike shops rent out bikes, and will be able to suggest routes. They can usually provide route maps. **Better Bikes** will deliver a rental bike to you for a cost of $25–50 per day. **Capital Bikeshare** is a 24-hour, self-service hire scheme where bikes can be rented from more than 110 stations around the city. **Bike the Sites** offers bike rentals, as well as organized tours of the city.

Road sign

## Guided Tours

There are many city bus tours available in DC. **DC Tours** offers a hop-on-hop-off sightseeing service with numerous pick-up points. For something a bit different, **Old Town Trolley Tours** offers a ride around the main sites in an old-fashioned trolley bus. **DC Metro Food Tours** run culinary walking tours of several DC neighborhoods. **Bike and Roll** offers bike tours in and around the city, including a 1-hour Early Bird Fun Ride and a 10-mile (16-km) Capital Sites Ride. **DC Ducks** provides a tour of the city and a tour down the Potomac River.

## DIRECTORY

### Green Travel

**Envirocab**
Tel (703) 920-3333.
W envirotaxicab.com

### Metrorail and Metrobus

**Circulator**
Tel (202) 962-1423.
W dccirculator.com

**Metrorail and Metrobus**
600 5th St, NW,
Washington, DC 20001.

Tel (202) 637-7000.
Tel (202) 638-3780 TTY.
W wmata.com

### Taxis

**DC Taxi Cab Commission**
Tel (202) 645-6018.
W dctaxi.dc.gov

**Diamond Cab**
Tel (202) 387-6200.

**Yellow Cab**
Tel (202) 544-1212.

### Cycling

**Better Bikes**
W betterbikesinc.com

**Bike the Sites**
W bikethesites.com

**Capital Bikeshare**
W capitalbikeshare.com

### Guided Tours

**Bike and Roll**
Tel 866-736-8224.
W bikeandroll.com

**DC Ducks**
Tel 855-323-8257.
W dcducks.com

**DC Metro Food Tours**
Tel (202)-683-8847.
W dcmetrofoodtours.com

**DC Tours**
Tel 888-878-9870.
W dctours.us

**Old Town Trolley Tours**
Tel (202) 832-9800.
W trolleytours.com

# Exploring Beyond Washington, DC

There is much to see beyond Washington's city limits, and traveling by car is easy with a good map. Many of the sights are reachable by public transportation, but it is generally easier and quicker to drive. Car rental is widely available but often expensive. Buses and trains are a cheaper alternative, but your choice of destinations may be more limited.

Driving along the scenic Skyline Drive *(see p167)*, Virginia

## Car Rental

To rent a car in the US you must usually be at least 25 years old with a valid driving license and a clean driving record. All agencies require a major credit card. Damage and liability insurance is recommended just in case something unexpected should happen. It is advisable always to return the car with a full tank of gas; otherwise you will be required to pay the inflated fuel prices charged by the rental agencies. Check for any pre-existing damage to the car and note this on your contract.

It is often less expensive to rent a vehicle at an airport, as car rental taxes are $2 a day more in the city. Agencies with offices at the Washington airports include **Alamo**, **Avis**, **Budget**, and **Hertz**. You could also become a member of **Zip Car**, a car sharing scheme. These cars can be picked up from hundreds of locations across the city. Your car will come with fuel, insurance, and 180 miles (290 km) per day.

## Rules of the Road

The highway speed limit in the DC area is 55 mph (88 km/h) – much lower than in many European countries. In residential areas the speed limit ranges from 20 to 35 mph (32–48 km/h), and near schools it can be as low as 15 mph (24 km/h).

Roads are generally well-signed but it is still wise to plan your route ahead. It is important to obey the signs, especially "No U-turn" signs, or you risk getting a ticket. If you are pulled over by the police, be courteous or you risk facing an even greater fine.

In addition, all drivers are required to carry a valid drivers' license and be able to produce registration documents and insurance for their vehicle. Most foreign licenses are valid, but if your license is not in English, or does not have a photo ID, you must get an international driver's license. Many roads are surveyed by cameras that will issue a ticket even if you are going just a few miles per hour over the speed limit. This is not limited to major arteries.

Road sign

Interstate highways are abbreviated on signs with a capital "I" followed by a number. Avoid the Capital Beltway (I-495) at rush hour.

## Gasoline (Petrol)

Gas comes in three grades – regular, super, and premium. There is an extra charge if an attendant serves you, but patrons can fill their own tanks at self-service pumps without incurring an extra fee. Most stations are exclusively self-service and only accept credit cards. Gas is generally cheap in the US.

## Breakdowns

In the unlucky event of a break-down, the best course of action is to pull completely off the road and put on the hazard lights to alert other drivers that you are stationary. There are emergency phones along some of the major interstate highways, but in other situations breakdown services or even the police can be contacted from mobile phones. In case of breakdown, drivers of rental cars should contact their car rental company first.

Members of the American Automobile Association (AAA) can have their vehicle towed to the nearest service station to be fixed. For simple problems like a flat tire or a dead battery, the AAA will fix it or sell and install a new battery on site.

## Parking

Most of the major sights that lie beyond Washington have adequate parking for visitors, but there may be a charge to use the facility. In general it is good practice to read all parking notices carefully to avoid fines, being clamped, or being towed away. Do not park beside a fire hydrant, or you risk the car being towed.

Parking sign

## Tips and Safety Advice for Drivers

- Traffic drives on the right-hand side of the road.
- Seat belts are compulsory in front seats and suggested in the back; children under three must ride in a child seat in back.
- You can turn right at a red light as long as you first come to a complete stop, and if there are no signs that prohibit it. Be aware, however, that turning right on a red light is illegal in Virginia and will incur a fine.
- A flashing yellow light at an intersection means slow down, look for oncoming traffic, and proceed with caution.
- Passing (overtaking) is allowed on any multi-lane road, and you must pass on the left. On smaller roads safe passing places are indicated with a broken yellow line on your side of the double yellow line.
- Crossing a double-yellow line, either by U-turn or by passing the car in front, is illegal, and you will be charged a fine if caught.
- If a school bus stops, all traffic from both sides must stop completely and wait for the bus to drive off.

- Driving while intoxicated (DWI) is a punishable offense that incurs heavy fines or even a jail sentence. Do not drink if you plan to drive.
- Avoid driving at night if unfamiliar with the area. Washington's streets change from safe to dangerous in a single block, so it is better to take a taxi than your own car if you do not know where you are going.
- Single women should be especially careful driving in unfamiliar territory, day or night.
- Keep all doors locked when driving around.
- Do not stop in a rural area, or on an unlit block, if someone tries to get your attention. If a fellow driver points at your car, suggesting something is wrong, drive to the nearest gas station and get help. Do not get out of your car.
- Avoid sleeping in your car.
- Avoid short cuts and stay on well-traveled roads.
- Avoid looking at a map in a dark, unpopulated place. Drive to the nearest open store or gas station before pulling over.

## Bus Tours

Although Greyhound buses (see p215) do serve some towns beyond DC (such as Charlottesville and Richmond, with serveral departures daily), the easiest and most enjoyable way to see the sights by bus is on a private tour. Several companies offer bus tours of DC's historic surroundings. **Gray Line** takes you on the Black Heritage tour, to Gettysburg, Colonial Williamsburg, or Monticello; Tourmobile's (see p217) destinations include Mount Vernon, the Frederick Douglass House, and Arlington Cemetery; DC Tours (see p217) organizes combination day trips covering Gettysburg, Mount Vernon, Arlington Cemetery, Alexandria Old Town, and Charlottesville. Most bus tours depart from Union Station.

## Trains

Amtrak trains (see p215) travel from DC's central Union Station to New York City and most of the surrounding area, including Williamsburg, Richmond, and Baltimore. The MARC (see p215), Maryland's commuter rail, also runs from DC to Baltimore on weekdays for a few dollars less.

Tourists line the street to get on a red double decker tour bus

# Street Finder Index

## Key to the Street Finder

- Major sight
- Place of interest
- Other building
- 🚆 Railroad station
- Ⓜ Metrorail station
- 🚌 Bus station
- 🛈 Tourist information office
- ✚ Hospital with emergency room
- 🛡 Police station
- ✝ Church
- ☪ Mosque
- ✡ Synagogue
- ⋯ Pedestrian street
- 🚢 Ferry terminal
- ▬▪ State boundary
- —▪ DC quadrant boundary

## Key to Abbreviations used in the Street Finder

| | | | | | |
|---|---|---|---|---|---|
| Ave | Avenue | NE | Northeast | SE | Southeast |
| DC | District of Columbia | NW | Northwest | St | Street/Saint |
| | | Pkwy | Parkway | SW | Southwest |
| Dr | Drive | Pl | Place | VA | Virginia |

0 meters 300
0 yards 300
**1:19,100**

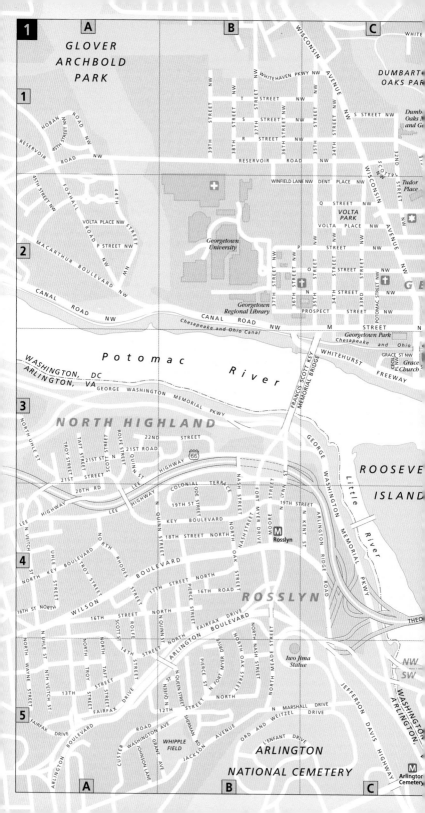

# Index

Page numbers in **bold** refer to main entries

# Acknowledgments

Dorling Kindersley would like to thank the following people whose contributions and assistance have made the preparation of this book possible.

## Main Contributors
Susan Burke lives in Virginia and works as an editor for the Air Line Pilots Association. She has taught creative writing for many years and has been a freelance editor of many books and journals primarily in the fields of sociology, economics, and politics.

Alice Powers is a freelance writer living in Washington, DC. She has written many articles for the Washington Post and other newspapers. She has also written several literary anthologies and teaches writing at the Corcoran College of Art and Design.

Jennifer Quasha lives in New York City but has a long association with Washington. She has written many articles on subjects ranging from travel to health, and has worked on other Dorling Kindersley books, including *Walking With Dinosaurs*.

Kem Sawyer has lived in Washington for over 20 years and has written children's books, feature articles and book reviews. She particularly enjoys writing about local history.

## Design and Editorial
*Managing Editor* Louise Lang
*Factchecker* Litta W. Sanderson
*Art Director* Gillian Allan
*Design and Editorial Assistance* Sue Megginson, Johnny Pau, Hugh Thompson.
*Proofreader* Stewart Wild
*Indexer* Hilary Bird
*Researcher* Sarah Miers

## Special Assistance
Particular thanks go to Kathleen Brooks at the National Air and Space Museum, Jessie Cohen and Leah Overstreet at the National Zoological Park, Julie Heizer at the Washington, DC Convention and Visitors' Association, Sarah Petty and Brennan Rash at the National Museum of American Art, Shannon Roberts at the National Gallery of Art and Morgan Zinsmeister at the National Museum of American Art. Thanks also to Dumbarton House, National Headquarters of The National Society of The Colonial Dames of America.

## Additional Photography
Max Alexander, Frank Greenaway, Paul Franklin, Dave King courtesy of Natural History Museum, Tim Mann, Ian O'Leary, Rough Guides/Angus Osborn, Jon Sawyer, Kim Sayer, Giles Stokoe, Clive Streeter, Scott Suchman, Matthew Ward, Stephen Whitehorn.

## Additional Illustration
Arun K. Pottirayil.

## Additional Cartography
Uma Bhattacharya

## Revisions Team
Louise Abbot, Namrata Adhwaryu, Ashwin Adimari, Emma Anacootee, Shruti Bahl, Tessa Bindloss, Vandana Bhagra, Subhashree Bharati, Divya Chowfin, Sherry Collins, Anne Coombes, Karen D'Souza, Anna Freiberger, Camilla Gersh, Lydia Halliday, Claudia Himmelreich, Sarah Holland, Rose Hudson, Bharti Karakoti, Zafar ul-Islam Khan, Esther Labi, Jude Ledger, Hayley Maher, Sam Merrell, Susan Millership, Rakesh Kumar Pal, Catherine Palmi, Sangita Patel, Pollyanna Poulter, Alice Powers, Khushboo Priya, Rada Radojicic, Pamposh Raina, Melanie Renzulli, Litta W. Sanderson, Sands Publishing Solutions, Kem Sawyer, Azeem Siddiqui, Susana Smith, Avantika Sukhia, Alka Thakur, Lauren Thomas, Conrad Van Dyk, Ajay Verma, Deepika Verma, Ros Walford, Dora Whitaker, Hugo Wilkinson.

## Additional Picture Research
Marta Bescos, Sumita Khatwani.

## Photography Permissions
Dorling Kindersley would like to thank the following for their assistance and kind permission to photograph at their establishments, as well as all the cathedrals, churches, museums, restaurants, hotels, shops, galleries and other sights too numerous to thank individually.

## Picture Credits
Key: a-above; b-below/bottom; c-centre; f-far; l-left; r-right; t-top.

Works of art have been reproduced with the permission of the following copyright holders:

©2006 Air Force Memorial Foundation 134bc; *John F. Kennedy Monument*, 1971 and *Albert Einstein Centennial Monument*, 1979 © Robert Berks Studios, Inc., All rights reserved – 33cra, 121cra, and 118bl respectively; United States Navy Memorial *Lone Sailor*, 1990 © Stanley Bleifeld 94bl; *Calder Mobile*, Alexander Calder © ARS, NY and DACS, London 2011 – 61bl; *Franklin D. Roosevelt and his dog Fala*, 1997 © Neil Estern 37br, 86tr; *Korean War Veterans Memorial* © KWVM Productions Inc., Memorial Designers: Cooper-Lecky Architects; Sculptor: Frank Gaylord 36tr and 85bl; *Hunger* George Segal © The George and Helen Segal Foundation/ DACS, London/VAGA, New York 2011 – 87tl; *Oscar S. Straus Memorial Fountain* © Adolph Alexander Weinman, 1947 – 95c; *Iwo Jima Memorial*, 1995 and *Seabees Memorial*, 1971 © Felix DeWeldon 36bl, 133cra; 1789 Restaurant: 188bl.

Acadiana/Simonsez.com: Chris Granger 185tl; Scott Suchman 5cra; AFP: Stephen Jaffe 27c; Joyce Naltchayan 38cr; Mario Tama 30br; Alamy Images: Jenny Andre 85c; David Coleman 68br; Rob Crandall 193tl; Ian Dagnall 218cla; John Foxx 11br; GhostWorx Images/Wm. Baker 84bl; William S. Kuta 84t; 134bc; LeighSmithImages 84cr; Dennis Macdonald 203tr; Nikreates 204-5; Kumar Sriskandan 172-3; Marmaduke St. John 13tr; Wiskerke 2-3; Allsport: Doug Pensinger 200c/b; Associated Press AP: Will Morris 135tl.

Dan Beigel: 121tc; Bridgeman Art Library, London & New York: Freer Gallery, Smithsonian Institution *Sheep and Goat* by Chao Meng Fu 58bc; National Gallery of Art, Washington D. C. *The Alba Madonna* (c. 1510) by Raphael (Raffaello Sanzio of Urbino, 1483–1520) 60cla; National Gallery of Art, Washington DC, East Building designed by I. M. Pei, 1978, suspended sculpture by Alexander Calder 61bl; The Phillips Collection, Washington DC *The Luncheon of the Boating Party* 1881 by Pierre Auguste Renoir (1841–1919) 137tl; The White House, Washington DC, *Portrait of Woodrow Wilson* by Sir William Orpen (1878–1931) 29tl; Bullfeather's/2themoonmedia.com:183bl.

Capitol Hilton Hotel: 174cl; Cashion's Eat Place: 180br, 190tl; Colonial Williamsburg Foundation: 170br; Corbis: 23clb, 24clb, 29cra, 30crb, 31tl/cr, 83tl; AFP: 27cb; Dave Bartruff: 33crb; Blend Images/Andersen Ross 212bc; Joseph Sohm; Chromosohm Inc. 37tr, 40br, 93bl; Corbis-Bettmann 25cb, 26tr, 26clb, 27tr, 29ca, 30clb, 31cla/cra/clb, 74br, 87c, 93cr, 98c, 153cl; James P. Blair 11t; Corcoran Gallery of Art 18; Philip James Corwin 85tr; EPA/ Michael Reynolds 210br; Hulton Deutsch Collection 25tl, 29br; Katherine Karnow 124br; Kelly-Mooney Photography 55t, 122, 148cl, 202bl; Brooks Kraft 12tl; Wally McNamee 119br; David Muench 158br; Richard T. Nowitz 1, 40cla, 41cr, 151c; Mark Peterson, 5cra; Moshe Shai 31bc; Sipa 27bc; Lee Snider/Photo Images 150tcl, 151br; Paul A. Souders 191br; Bequest of Mrs. Benjamin Ogle Tayloe, Collection of the Corcoran Gallery of Art 28cla; Mark Thiessen 41bl; Underwood & Underwood 80cra; UPI 94br; Oscar White 29clb; CVS/Pharmacy: 209bl.

Danita Delimont (Agent): David R. Frazier Photolibrary/NASM 67c; Karen Huntt Mason 39br; Carol Pratt 198tr; Scott Suchman 139clb, 214cla; Destination DC: 206, 207crb, 215tl;

Philippe Limet Dewez: 199tr; Dreamstime.com: Jiawangkun 56; Kropic 106; Luckydoor 219bl; Mesutdogan 88; Orhancam 44; Rabbit75 32, 42-3; Raodahead 154-5; Rosepeterson 156; Vanessagifford 130.

Firefly Restaurant/Kimpton Hotels and Restaurants: Scott Suchman 186bl; Founding Farmers: Greg Powers 186t; Renee Comet 182cl; Four Seasons Hotel Washington, DC: Tom McCavera 178tl; Michael Freeman: 52bc, 53cb, 64clb/br, 65tl, 67br; Freer Gallery of Art, Smithsonian Institution, Washington DC: 75tl.

Getty Images: AFP/Stephen Jaffe 209cla; Pablo Martinez Monsivais-Pool 29crb; Hotel George: 5c, 174br: Graffiato/Know Public Realtions: Greg Powers 180cla; Granger Collection, New York: 8-9, 19b, 20tr/cb, 21tr/clb/br, 22t/bc, 23tr/bc, 24bl, 25br, 28ca/clb/ bl/ bc/br, 29cla/bl, 49cra, 93ca, 93cl, 147tr.

Image Bank: Archive Photos 99br; Andrea Pistolesi 52cla, 80bl.

The Jefferson Hotel: 175tr, 179br.

Kiplinger Washington Collection: 80cla; Kramerbooks & Afterwords Cafe & Grill: 194br; Library of Congress: Carol M. Highsmith 48bc.

Matisse Restaurant: 180cl; Michie Tavern: 191tl; Courtesy Mount Vernon Ladies' Association: 162cla.

National Air and Space Museum © Smithsonian Institution: SI Neg. No. 99-15240-7–33cla; National Gallery of Art, Washington, DC: Samuel H. Kress Collection, Photo: Philip A. Charles Bust of Lorenzo de' Medici 59tl; Ailsa Mellon Bruce Fund, Photo: Bob Grove Ginevra de' Benci c. 1474 by Leonardo da Vinci 60tr; Samuel H. Kress Collection A Young Man With His Tutor by Nicolas de Largilliere, 1685–61tc; Samuel H. Kress Collection Christ Cleansing the Temple (d), pre-1570, by El Greco 62tr, Samuel H. Kress Collection Madonna and Child, 1320–1330 by Giotto 62cl; Collection of Mr. and Mrs. Paul Mellon Woman with a Parasol, 1875, by Claude Monet 6oclb; Harris Whittemore Collection Mother of Pearl and Silver: The Andalusian 1888-1900, by James McNeill Whistler 61br; Timken Collection Diana and Endymion, c. 1753, by Jean-Honore Fragonard 62br; Chester Dale Collection Miss Mary Ellison, 1880, by Mary Cassatt 63c; John Russell Pope (architect) 197tl; National Museum of American Art/© Smithsonian Institution: 58cl; 100tr, Gift of Mr. and Mrs. Joseph Harrison Old Bear, a Medicine Man, 1832, by George Catlin 101bl; Achelous and Hercules, 1947, © T. H. Benton and R. P. Benton Testamentary Trusts/VAGA, New York/DACS, London 2011 – 100–1c; Bequest of Helen Huntington Hull, granddaughter of William Brown Dinsmore who acquired the painting in 1873 for "The Locusts," the family estate in Dutchess County, New York Among the Sierra Nevada, California 1868 by Albert Bierstadt 100bl; Gift of John Gellatly In the Garden (Celia Thaxter in Her Garden), 1892, by Childe Hassam 101bc; © Untitled Press, Inc/VAGA, New York and DACS, London 2011 Reservoir, 1961, by Robert Raus-Chenberg 102cr; Gift of Anonymous Donors The Throne of the Third Heaven of the Nations Millenium General Assembly, c. 1950–1954, by James Hampton 102bl; Gift of the Georgia O'Keeffe Foundation Manhattan 1932 by Georgia O'keeffe 101blr; National Museum of American history/© Smithsonian Institution: 76cl/clb/bc, 77tl/cra, 78br, 79 all; National Museum of the American Indian: 70 -1 all; National Museum of Natural History/© Smithsonian Institution: 72bl, 73br; Dane Penland 73tl; National Park Service: J. Fenney 113t, 206cla; Richard Frear 167clb; Rick Latoff, courtesy www.Parkphotos. com 69br; Mary McLeod Bethune Council House NHS,

Washington D.C. 142c; National Portrait Gallery/© Smithsonian Institution: Gift of The Morris and Gwendolyn Cafritz Foundation and Smithsonian Institution Trust Fund Selfportrait, 1780–1784, by John Singleton Copley 101ca; Gift of Friends of President and Mrs. Reagan, Ronald Wilson Reagan, 1989, © Henry C. Casselli 103tr; Diana Ross and the Supremes, 1965, © Bruce Davidson/Magnum 103br; Transfer from the National Gallery of Art, Gift of Andrew W. Mellon, 1942, Pocahontas, Unidentified artist, English school, after the 1616 engraving by Simon van de Passe, after 1616 – 103c; Gift of the Morris and Gwendolyn Cafritz Foundation and the Regents' Major Acquisitions Fund, Smithsonian Institution Mary Cassatt, 1880–1884, by Edgar Degas 101tl; Courtesy National Portrait Gallery "Casey" Stengel, 1981 cast after 1965 plaster by © Rhoda Sherbell 101tr; National Postal Museum/© Smithsonian Institution: Jim O'Donnell 55c; National Zoological Park/© Smithsonian Institution: Jessie Cohen 140–1; Newseum: 95tl; Richard T. Nowitz: 64cla, 83crb; Abe Nowitz 39c.

Octagon Museum/American Architectural Foundation, Washington DC: 117bl.

Paolo's Ristorante/Capital Restaurant Concepts: 187tr; Phillips Collection: 137br/c; Popperfoto: Reuters 30cla/cr.

Restaurant Nora: 190br; Rex Features: 29tc; SIPA Press/Trippett 29cb.

Mae Scanlan: 33ca, 34tr, 38bl, 79t, 202tr; Shakespeare Theatre Company: 196cra, 198bl; Smithsonian National Air And Space Museum: 66br; Len Spoden Photography: 149tl/tr, 150br, 151tl, 153br/tr; Frank Spooner Pictures: Markel-Liaison 93br; Courtesy of The Spy Museum: 104tl/c; STA Travel Group: 207tl; SuperStock: age fotostock 12cr; Swann House Historic Dupont Inn: 176bl.

Textile Museum: Gift of Mrs. Charles Putnam 138tl; Topham Picturepoint: 127clb; TRH Pictures: National Air and Space Museum 65cr, 66cla.

University of Virginia: Library Special Collections Department, Manuscript Print Collection 129tl; United States Holocaust Memorial Museum: 83cr.

Courtesy of the Washington, DC Martin Luther King, Jr. National Memorial Project Foundation, Inc.: Gediyon Kifle 37tl; White House Collection, Courtesy White House Historical Association: 110cl/b, 111t/c/bl/br, 112bl, Peter Vitale 113bl; Bruce White 113cr. Zaytinya/Heather Freeman PR: Greg Powers and Audrey Crewe 185bc.

Front Endpaper: Corbis: Kelly-Mooney Photography Lclb; Dreamstime.com: Jiawangkun Rbc; Kropic Ltr; Mesutdogan Rtl; Orhancam Rtr; Rosepeterson Lbr; Vanessagifford Lbc.

Back Endpaper: © 2012 Washington Metropolitan Area Transit Authority.

Map Cover: Alamy Images: JLImages.

Jacket: Front Alamy Images: JLImages main; Spine: Alamy Images: JLImages t.

All other images © Dorling Kindersley. See www.dkimages.com for more information.

## Special Editions of DK Travel Guides

DK Travel Guides can be purchased in bulk quantities at discounted prices for use in promotions or as premiums. We are also able to offer special editions and personalized jackets, corporate imprints, and excerpts from all of our books, tailored specifically to meet your own needs.

To find out more, please contact:
in the United States SpecialSales@dk.com
in the UK travelspecialsales@uk.dk.com
in Canada DK Special Sales at general@tourmaline.ca
in Australia business.development@pearson.com.au

# M metro System Map

wmata.com
Customer Information Service: 202-637-7000
TTY Phone: 202-638-3780
Metro Transit Police: 202-962-2121

## Legend

**RD** Red Line • Glenmont / Shady Grove
**OR** Orange Line • New Carrollton / Vienna
**BL** Blue Line • Franconia-Springfield / Largo Town Center
**GR** Green Line • Branch Ave / Greenbelt
**YL** Yellow Line • Huntington / Fort Totten
**SV** Silver Line • Wiehle-Reston East / Largo Town Center

### Station Features
- ↪✈ Bus to Airport
- P Parking
- H Hospital
- ✈ Airport

### Connecting Rail Systems
ANTRAK  VRE  MARC

Transfer Station
Station in Service

Under Construction
Full-Time Service

Rush-Only Service: Monday-Friday
6:30am - 9:00am 3:30pm - 6:00pm

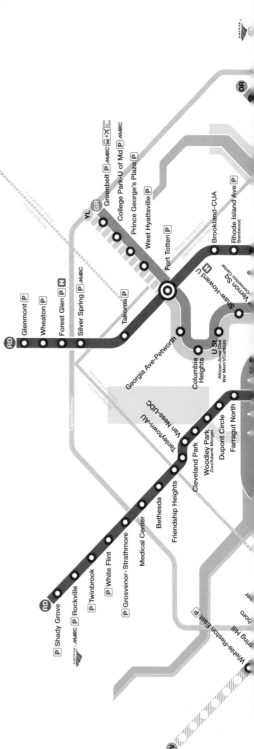